STREET ATLAS
Merseyside

Contents

III *Key to map symbols*

IV-V *Key to map pages*

VI *Administrative and post code boundaries*

1 *Street maps*

90 *Index of hospitals, railway stations, schools, shopping centres, street names and universities*

PHILIP'S

First colour edition published 1997 by

Ordnance Survey®
Romsey Road
Maybush
Southampton SO16 4GU

and

George Philip Ltd.
an imprint of Reed Books
Michelin House, 81 Fulham Road, London
SW3 6RB
and Auckland, Melbourne, Singapore and Toronto

ISBN 0-540-06482-3 (pocket edition)

© Crown copyright 1996

Printed and bound in Spain by Cayfosa

To the best of the Publishers' knowledge, the
information in this atlas was correct at the time of
going to press. No responsibility can be accepted
for any errors or their consequences.

The representation in this atlas of a road, track or
path is no evidence of the existence of a right of way.

**The mapping between pages 1 and 89 (inclusive)
in this atlas is derived from Ordnance Survey®
OSCAR® and Land-Line® data, and Landranger®
mapping.**

Ordnance Survey, OSCAR, Land-Line and
Landranger are registered trade marks of Ordnance
Survey, the National Mapping Agency of Great Britain

Key to map symbols

(22a)	**Motorway** (with junction number)
	Primary Routes (Dual carriageway and single)
	A Roads (Dual carriageway and single)
	B Roads (Dual carriageway and single)
	C Roads (Dual carriageway and single)
	Minor Roads
– – –	**Roads under construction**
•—•—•	**County boundaries**
	All Railways
	Miniature Railways
	Track or private road
⊥	**Gate or obstruction to traffic** (restrictions may not apply at all times or to all vehicles)
– – – –	**All paths, bridleways, BOATs, RUPPs, etc.**
	The representation in this atlas of a road, track or path is no evidence of the existence of a right of way
174	**Adjoining page indicator**

Acad	**Academy**	Mon	**Monument**
Cemy	**Cemetery**	Mus	**Museum**
C Ctr	**Civic Centre**	Obsy	**Observatory**
CH	**Club House**	Pal	**Royal Palace**
Coll	**College**	PH	**Public House**
Ex H	**Exhibition Hall**	Resr	**Reservoir**
Ind Est	**Industrial Estate**	Ret Pk	**Retail Park**
Inst	**Institute**	Sch	**School**
Ct	**Law Court**	Sh Ctr	**Shopping Centre**
L Ctr	**Leisure Centre**	Sta	**Station**
LC	**Level Crossing**	TH	**Town Hall/House**
Liby	**Library**	Trad Est	**Trading Estate**
Mkt	**Market**	Univ	**University**
Meml	**Memorial**	YH	**Youth Hostel**

⇄	**British Rail station**
🚂	**Private Railway station**
⬤	**Bus, coach station**
◆	**Ambulance station**
◆	**Coastguard station**
◆	**Fire station**
◆	**Police station**
✚	**Casualty entrance to hospital**
✝	**Churches, Place of worship**
H	**Hospital**
i	**Information Centre**
P	**Parking**
PO	**Post Office**
All Saints RC Jun Sch	**Important buildings, schools, colleges, universities and hospitals**
River Soar	**Water Name**
	Stream
	River or canal (minor and major)
	Water Fill
	Tidal Water
	Woods
	Houses

0	¼	½	¾	1 mile
0	250 m	500 m	750 m	1 Kilometre

The scale of the maps is 3.92 cm to 1 km (2½ inches to 1 mile)

The small numbers around the edges of the maps identify the 1 kilometre National Grid lines

IV

Key to map pages

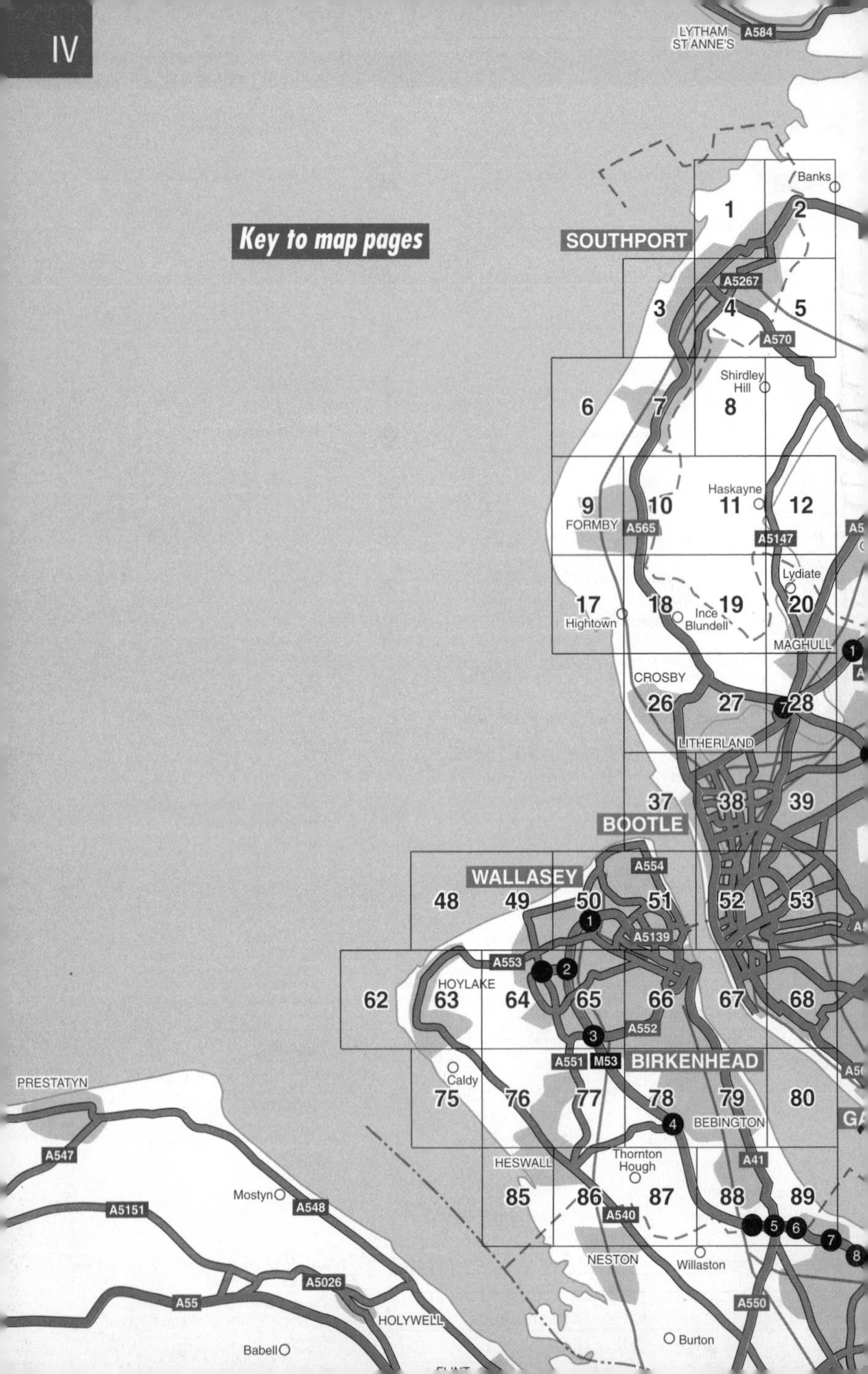

LYTHAM ST.ANNE'S A584

Banks

SOUTHPORT

1   **2**

A5267

3   **4**   **5**

A570

Shirdley Hill

6   **7**   **8**

Haskayne

9   **10**   **11**   **12**

FORMBY A565

A5147

A5

Lydiate

17   **18**   **19**   **20**

Hightown Ince Blundell

MAGHULL

CROSBY

26   **27**   **28**

LITHERLAND

37   **38**   **39**

BOOTLE

WALLASEY

48   **49**   **50**   **51**   **52**   **53**

A554

A5139

A553

62   **63**   **64**   **65**   **66**   **67**   **68**

HOYLAKE

A552

A551 M53 BIRKENHEAD

PRESTATYN

75   **76**   **77**   **78**   **79**   **80**

Caldy

BEBINGTON

GA

A547

HESWALL

Thornton Hough

A41

A5151

Mostyn A548

85   **86**   **87**   **88**   **89**

A540

A55

NESTON Willaston

A5026

A550

HOLYWELL

Babell

Burton

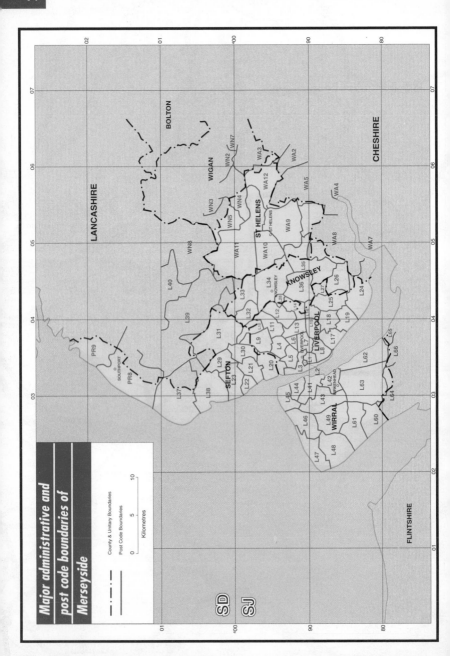

Major administrative and post code boundaries of Merseyside

County & Unitary Boundaries

Post Code Boundaries

Kilometres
0 5 10

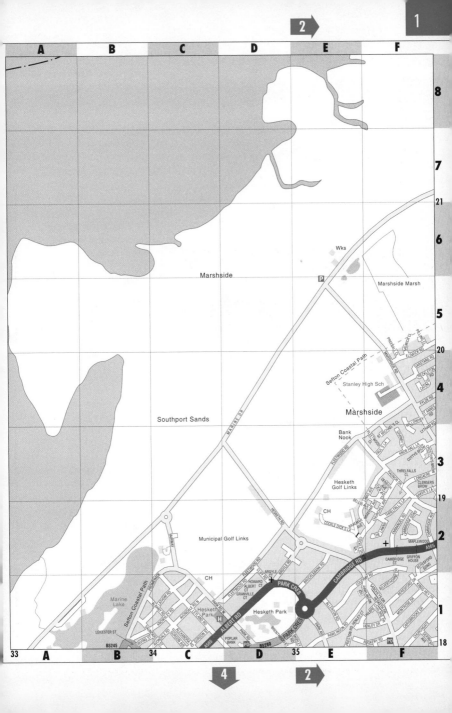

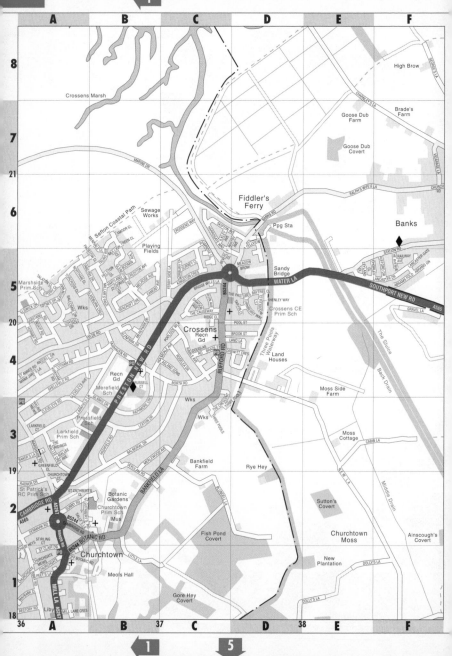

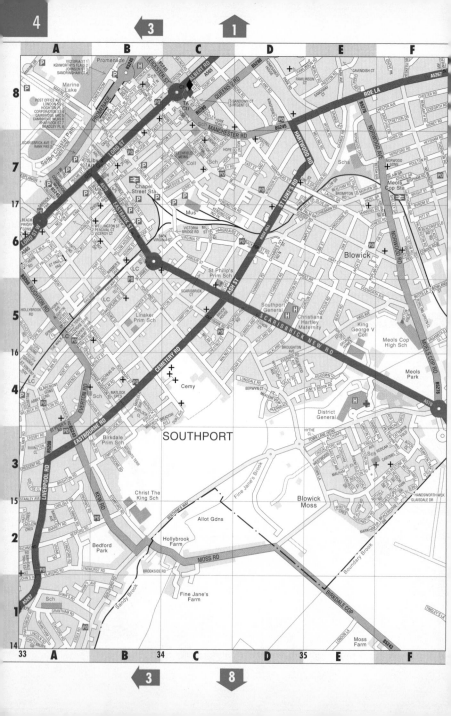

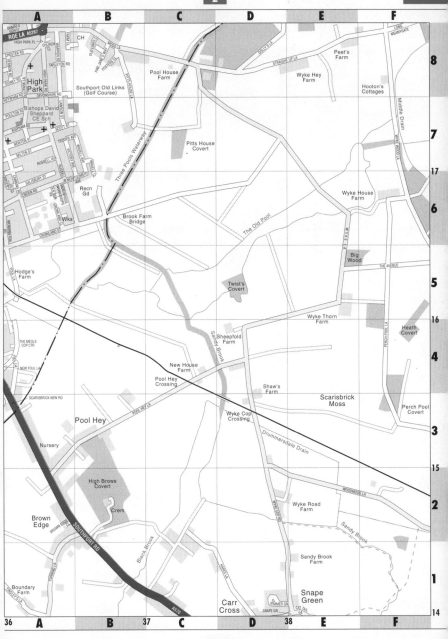

ROE LA A5267
HIGH PARK PL
CH
DOLL'S LA
LONG MEANYGATE
8
CHESTER RD
CHURCH RD
FIRE LANES CL
FOSTER CL
OLD LANE'S CL
MOSS LA
STRAIGHT UP LA
Peet's Farm
VERNON RD
WARREN RD
TAPLETON RD
Pool House Farm
Wyke Hey Farm
Hooton's Cottages
High Park
Southport Old Links (Golf Course)
DEVONSHIRE RD
Bishops David / Sheppard CE Sch
SCOTT ST
NEWTON ST
MILTON ST
Three Pools Waterway
Pitts House Covert
7
17
RUSSELL AV
Wyke House Farm
Recn Gd
Brook Farm Bridge
The Old Pool
6
Wks
WENNINGTON RD
CROWLAND ST
Hodge's Farm
WYKE LA
Big Wood
THE AVENUE
5
Twist's Covert
THE MEOLS COP CTR
NEW FOUL LA
Sandy Brook
Wyke Thorn Farm
PERCH POOL LA
Heath Covert
16
Sheepfold Farm
4
SCARISBRICK NEW RD
New House Farm
Pool Hey Crossing
POOL HEY LA
Shaw's Farm
Scarisbrick Moss
Perch Pool Covert
Pool Hey
Wyke Cop Crossing
Drummersdale Drain
3
Nursery
15
High Brows Covert
WOODMOSS LA
2
Brown Edge
Crem
BROWN EDGE
SOUTHPORT RD
Black Brook
WYKE COP RD
Wyke Road Farm
Sandy Brook
Boundary Farm
TURNING LA
THISTLE LA
A570
Sandy Brook Farm
SNAPE GN
CAT TAIL LA
Snape Green
1
14
Carr Cross
SNAPE GN

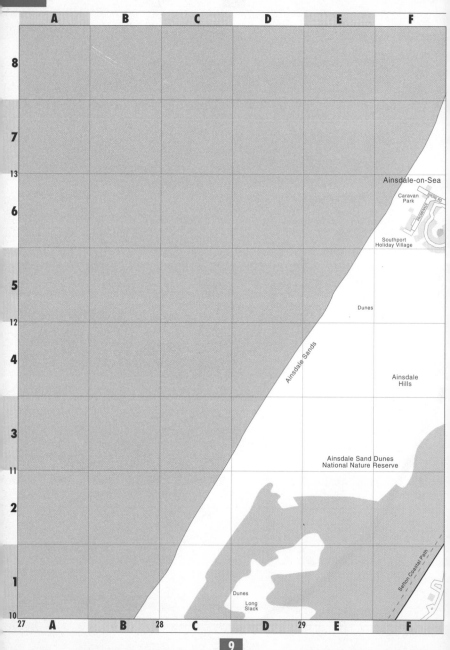

A **B** **C** **D** **E** **F**

8

7

13

6 Ainsdale-on-Sea

Caravan
Park

Southport
Holiday Village

5 Dunes

12

Ainsdale Sands

4 Ainsdale
Hills

3

Ainsdale Sand Dunes
National Nature Reserve

11

2

1

Sefton Coastal Path

Dunes

Long
Slack

10

27 **A** **B** 28 **C** **D** 29 **E** **F**

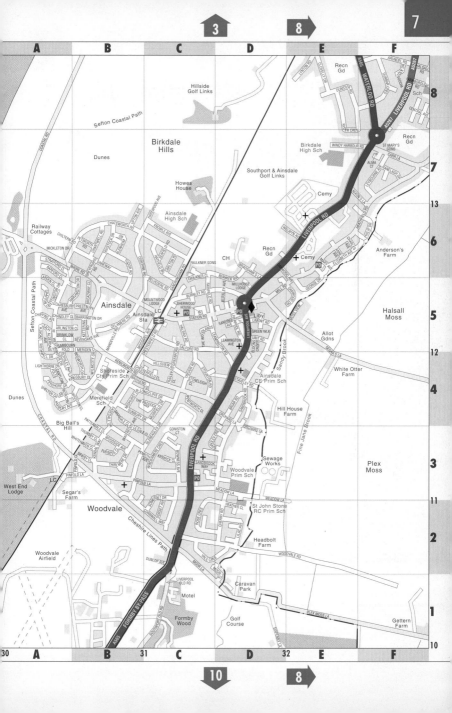

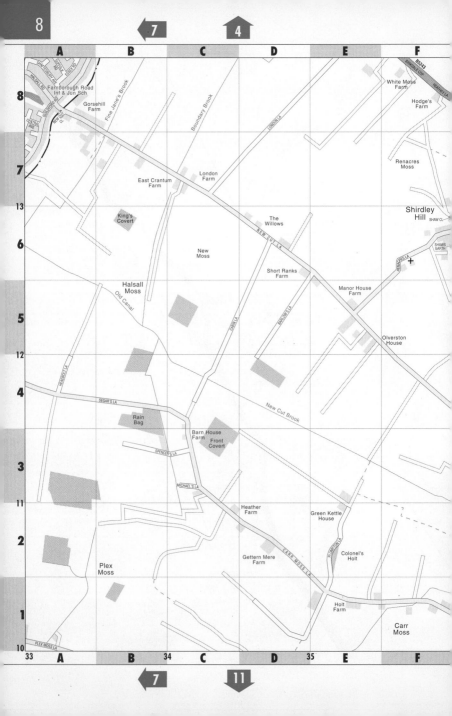

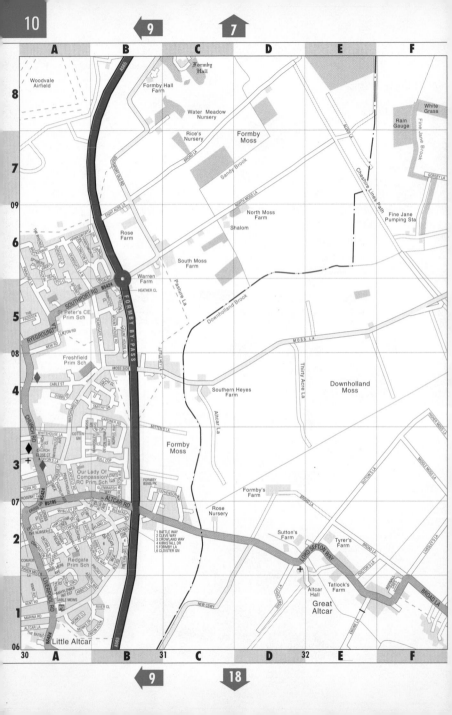

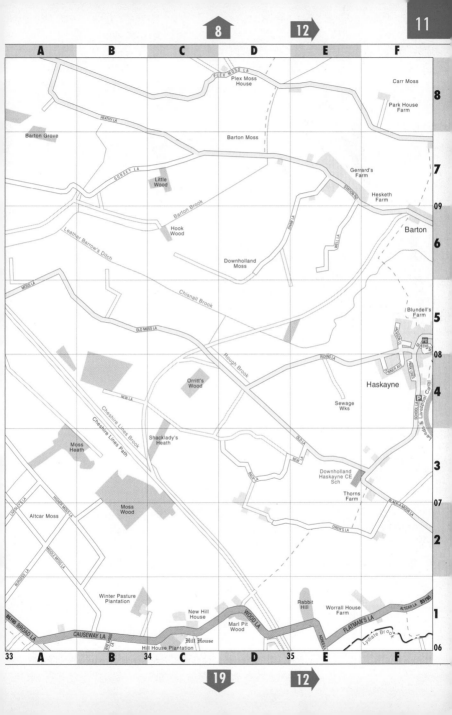

A   B   C   D   E   F

8
7
09
6
5
08
4
3
07
2
1
06

33   34   35

PLEX MOSS LA
Plex Moss House
Carr Moss
Park House Farm
HEATHY LA
Barton Grove
Barton Moss
Gerrard's Farm
GORSEY LA
Little Wood
Hesketh Farm
STATION RD
Barton Brook
Barton
Hook Wood
Leather Barrow's Ditch
Downholland Moss
SHAW LA
WILL LA
MOSS LA
Chisnall Brook
Blundell's Farm
OLD MOSS LA
JACKSON LA
PO
QUEENS
Rough Brook
RIDING LA
Haskayne
CARR'S RD
ABY CRES
Orritt's Wood
NEW LA
Sewage Wks
DICK LA
Cheshire Lines Brook
Cheshire Lines Path
Shacklady's Heath
DICK LA
BELM
Downholland Haskayne CE Sch
P
SCHOOL LA
Liverpool Canal
Leeds &
Moss Heath
BACK LA
Thorns Farm
BLACK-A-MOOR LA
Altcar Moss
LYDIATE LA
RIDGE MOSS LA
Moss Wood
OWEN'S LA
MOSS & MOSS LA
Winter Pasture Plantation
New Hill House
WOOD LA
Rabbit Hill
Worrall House Farm
ALTCAR LA
B5195
RUSHES LA
B5195 BROAD LA
CAUSEWAY LA
RYE CARR LA
Marl Pit Wood
FLATMAN'S LA
MOSS LA
Lydiate Brook
Hill House
Hill House Plantation

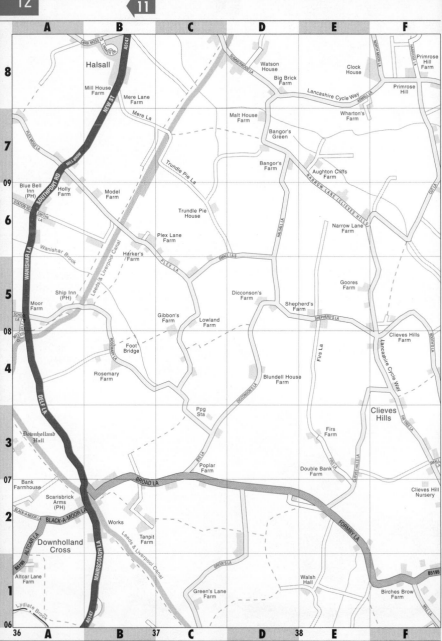

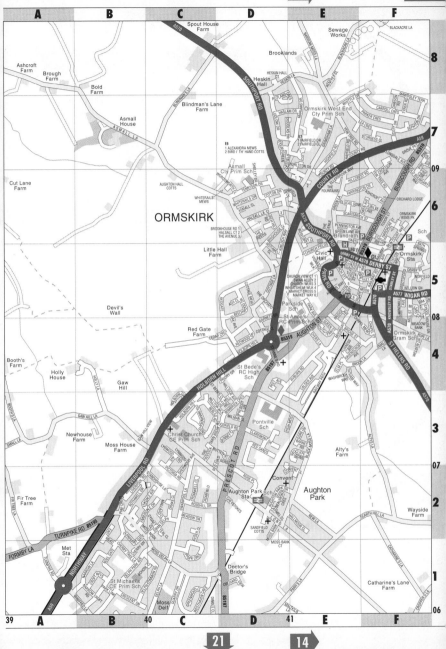

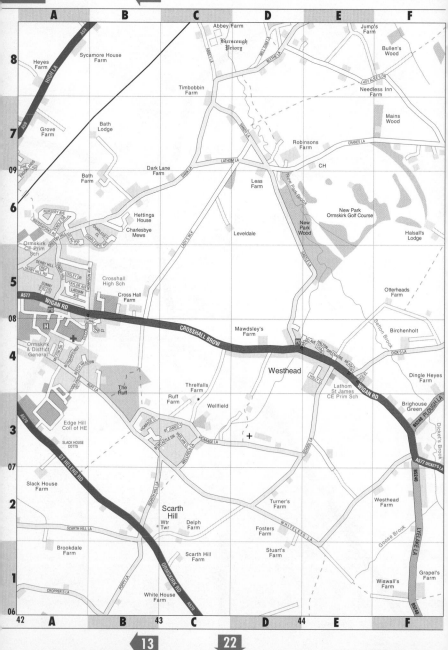

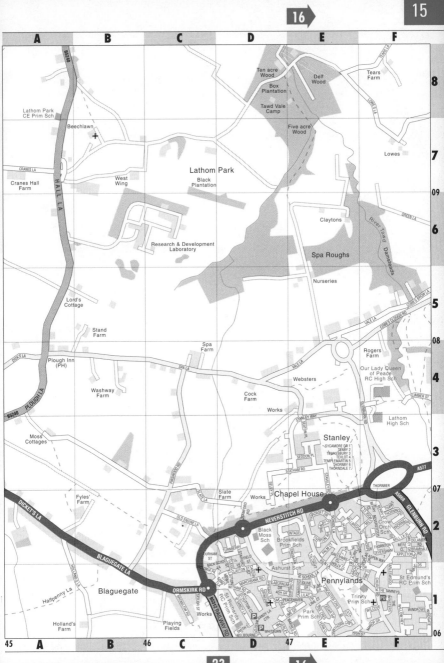

A   B   C   D   E   F

Ten acre Wood

Delf Wood

Tears Farm

Box Plantation

Tawd Vale Camp

Five acre Wood

Lathom Park CE Prim Sch

Beechlawn

Lowes

CRANES LA

West Wing

Lathom Park

Black Plantation

Cranes Hall Farm

HALL LA

Claytons

GREEN LA

River Tawd

Damsteads

Spa Roughs

Research & Development Laboratory

Nurseries

Lord's Cottage

VALE LA

COBBS CLOUGH RD

Stand Farm

Spa Farm

Rogers Farm

DICKS LA

Plough Inn (PH)

SPA LA

Websters

Our Lady Queen of Peace RC High Sch

SUMMER ST

PLOUGH LA

B5240

Washway Farm

Cock Farm

VALE LA

Lathom High Sch

GLENBURN RD

Works

STANLEY WAY

Moss Cottages

SEDDON PL

Stanley

SYCAMORE DR 1
JENBY 2
TRIMESBURY 3
TEVLOT 4
TEMPLEMARTIN 5
THORNEY 6
THORNDALE 7

A577

THORNBER

STATHAM RD

THORNLEY RD

Chapel House

GLENBURN RD

Fyles' Farm

Slate Farm

Works

NEVERSTITCH RD

DICKET'S LA

OLD ENGINE LA

Black Moss Sch

Brookfields Prim Sch

ST Ch Orch Sch

BLAGUEGATE LA

DURHAM ST

BACK SCHOOL LA

Ashurst Sch

THORNTON

Pennylands

St Edmund's RC Prim Sch

Halfpenny La

ORMSKIRK RD

MARCHBANK RD

CLAYTON

Trinity Prim Sch

WINDROWS

Blaguegate

St Richards RC Prim Sch

Park Prim Sch

Holland's Farm

Works

Playing Fields

WHITBURN

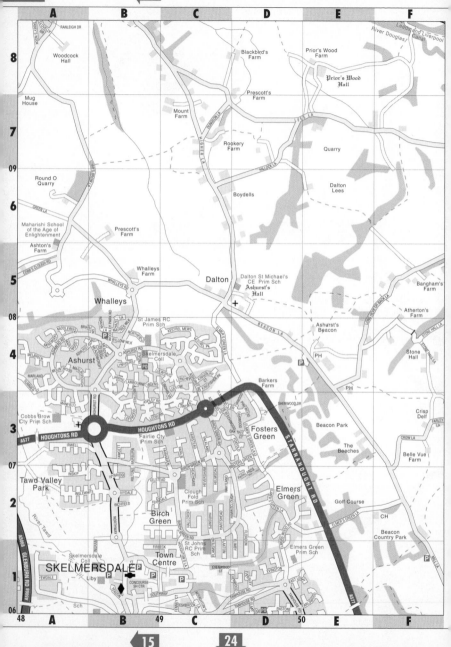

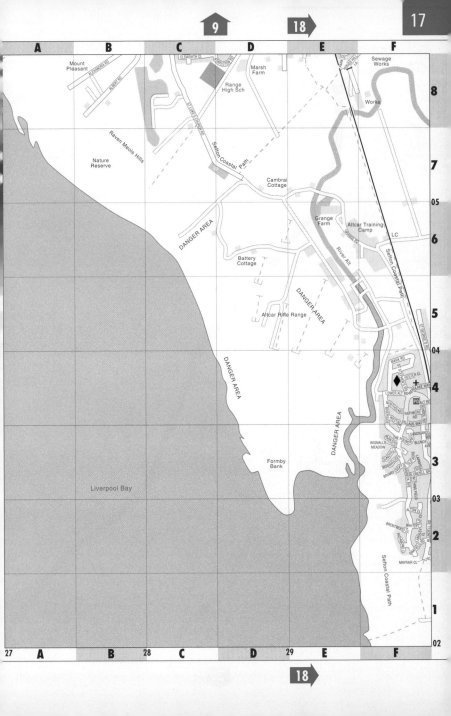

A   B   C   D   E   F

Mount
Pleasant

ALEXANDRA RD

ALBERT RD

ELSWORTH CL

ST LUKE'S CHURCH RD

PARK RD

RIDGE HILL

Sewage
Works

Marsh
Farm

Range
High Sch

Works

Raven Meols Hills

Sefton Coastal Path

Nature
Reserve

Cambrai
Cottage

DANGER AREA

Grange
Farm

Altcar Training
Camp

GRANGE RD

LC

River Alt

Sefton Coastal Path

ST GEORGE'S RD

Battery
Cottage

DANGER AREA

Altcar Rifle Range

DANGER AREA

DANGER AREA

MARK RD

CHESTER CL

LOWER ALT RD

ALT RD

RATHBONE RD

NORTHFIELD

WOODHOUSE

LAKE WAY

SCHOOL RD

ROSEMARY WAY

PO

THE ROCKS

GORSE WAY

WIGNALLS
MEADOW

BLUNDELL
AVE

ENDHANDS

MOORSIDE

SCHOOL

KIRKSTALL

BRIARY

BLUNDELL DR

KIRKSTALL

WATKINS FIELD

ALTON CL

BRENTWOOD CL

WHITE ST

ROCKS LANE

BRIER CL

MEADOW CL

MAYFAIR CL

GRANGE RD

BRUNSWICK

Formby
Bank

Liverpool Bay

Sefton Coastal Path

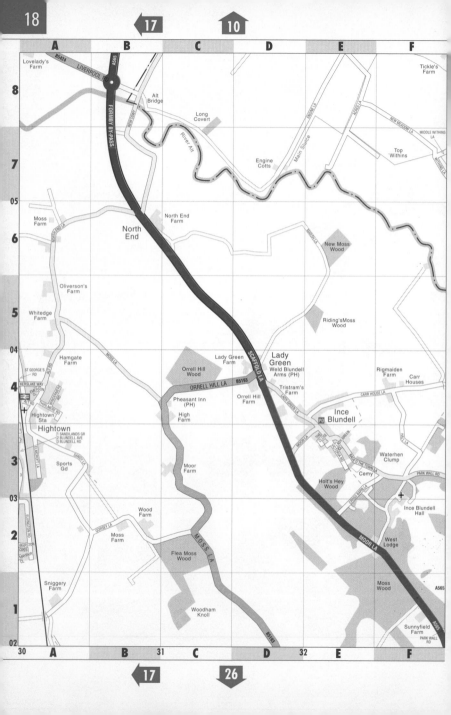

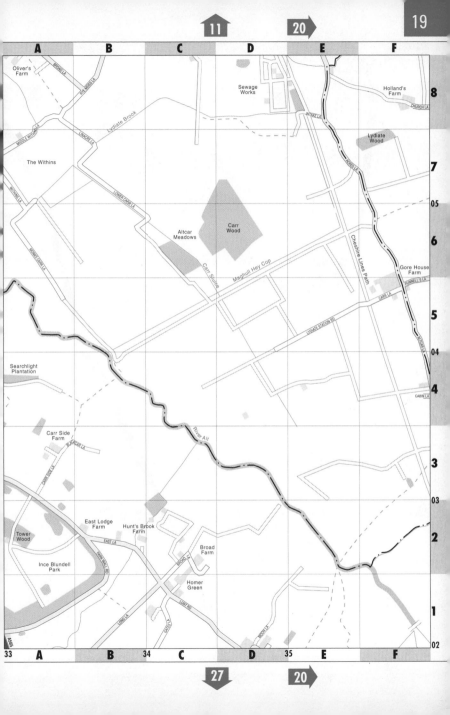

11
20
27
20

A   **B**   **C**   **D**   **E**   **F**

Oliver's Farm

Sewage Works

Holland's Farm

CHURCH LA.

8

BROAD LA.

RIVER ALT LA.

Lydiate Brook

MIDDLE WITHINS LA.

LINACRE LA.

Lydiate Wood

The Withins

MOSS LA.

7

WITHINS LA.

LOWER CARR LA.

Altcar Meadows

Carr Wood

05

MONKS CARR LA.

6

Cheshire Lines Path

Gore House Farm

DUNNELL'S LA.

Carr Slutch

Maghull Hey Cop

CARR LA.

5

Lydiate Station Rd

Searchlight Plantation

04

MILITARY LA.

4

CABIN LA.

River Alt

Carr Side Farm

BLANCAR LA.

3

CARR SIDE LA.

03

Tower Wood

East Lodge Farm

Hunt's Brook Farm

EAST LA.

Broad Farm

2

Ince Blundell Park

PARK WALL RD.

BROAD LA.

Homer Green

MOOR LA.

1

LONG LA.

GREEN LA.

LIGHT RD.

ALT LA.

02

33   **A**   **B**   34   **C**   **D**   35   **E**   **F**

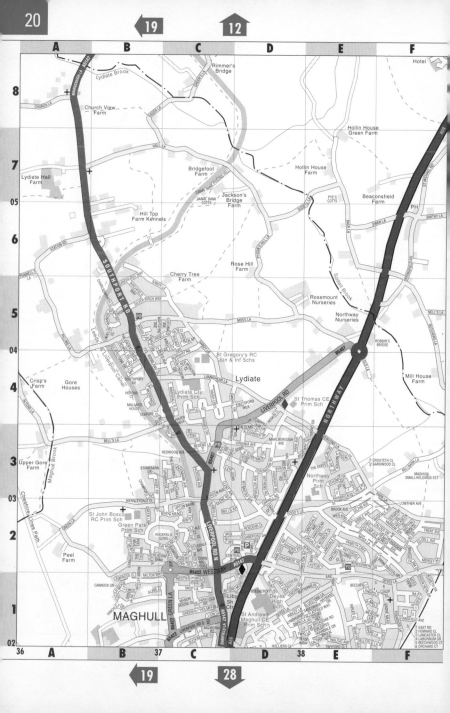

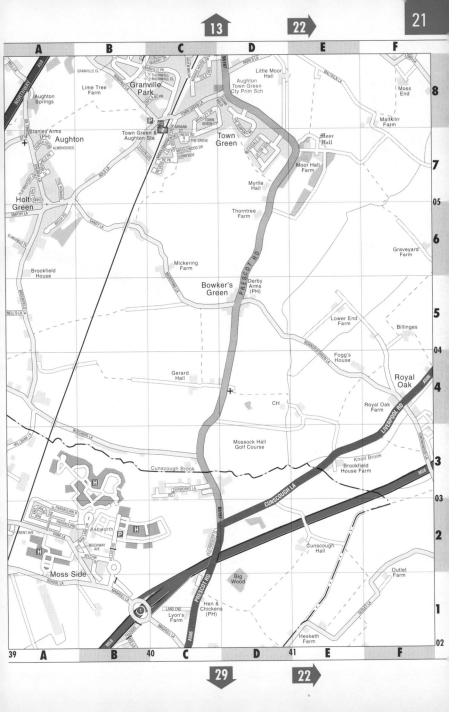

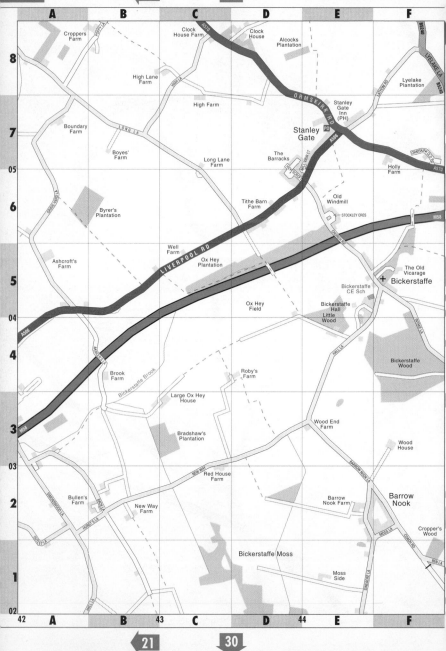

Croppers Farm
Clock House Farm
Clock House
Alcocks Plantation
High Lane Farm
ORMSKIRK RD
High Farm
Lyelake Plantation
LYELAKE LA
B5240
Boundary Farm
LONG LA
Stanley Gate Inn (PH)
Boyes' Farm
Stanley Gate
Long Lane Farm
The Barracks
A506
Holly Farm
ORMSKIRK OLD RD
A570
Byrer's Plantation
Tithe Barn Farm
Old Windmill
Well Farm
STOCKLEY CRES
M58
Ashcroft's Farm
LIVERPOOL RD
Ox Hey Plantation
The Old Vicarage
Bickerstaffe
Bickerstaffe CE Sch
Ox Hey Field
Bickerstaffe Hall Little Wood
HALL LA
Bickerstaffe Wood
M58
Brook Farm
Roby's Farm
Bickerstaffe Brook
Large Ox Hey House
Bradshaw's Plantation
Wood End Farm
Wood House
BARROW NOOK LA
NEW WAY
Red House Farm
Bullen's Farm
New Way Farm
HURST'S LA
Barrow Nook Farm
Barrow Nook
Cropper's Wood
MOSS LA
COPPY RD
Bickerstaffe Moss
Moss Side
STANLEY LA
BEN LA

A B C D E F

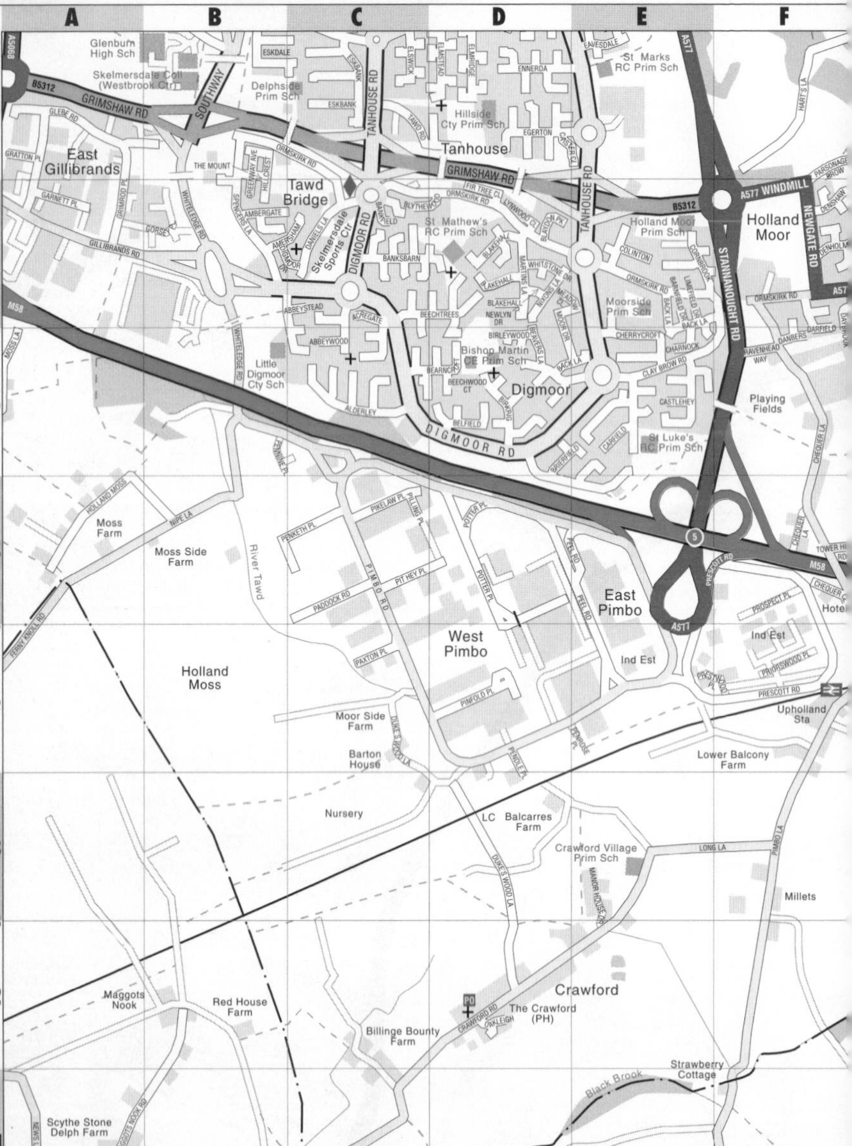

Glenburn High Sch
Skelmersdale Coll (Westbrook City)
Eskdale
Delphside Prim Sch
Eskbank
St Marks RC Prim Sch
Avesdale

8

GRIMSHAW RD
SOUTHWAY
TANHOUSE RD
ENNERDA
GRIFT
METAL
Hillside Cty Prim Sch
Tanhouse
Egerton

East Gillibrands
THE MOUNT
Tawd Bridge
GRIMSHAW RD
ELM TREE CT
St Mathew's RC Prim Sch
Holland Moor Prim Sch
Holland Moor

7

GILLIBRANDS RD
Skelmersdale Sports Ctr
DIGMOOR RD
BANKSBARN
BLYTHEWD
LIVINGSTON
TANHOUSE RD
COLINTON
Moorside Prim Sch
STANHAUGHT RD
NEWGATE RD
WINDMILL

05

MOSS LA
M58
ABBEYSTEAD
ACREGATE
BEECHTREES
BLAKEHAL NEWLYN
BIRLEYWOOD
CHERRYCROFT
CHARNOCK
DRINKSKIRK RD
BARNFIELD
RAVENHEAD WAY

Little Digmoor Cty Sch
ABBEYWOOD
BEARNCRO
Bishop Martin CE Prim Sch
BEECHWOOD CT
Digmoor
CLAY BROW RD
CASTLEHEY
Playing Fields

6

ALDERLEY
ALFRED
DIGMOOR RD
St Luke's RC Prim Sch
TOWER HL

Moss Farm
HOLLAND MOSS
WIPE LA
River Tawd
PENRETH PL
PRELOR PL
POTTERY R
PONTER PL
East Pimbo
PRESCOTT RD
M58
Hotel

5

Moss Side Farm
PADDOCK RD
PIT HEY PL
PITCH RD
FIELD RD
Ind Est
PROSPECT PL
Ind Est
CHEQUERS
04

Holland Moss
West Pimbo
Ind Est
A577
PRESCOTT RD
Upholland Sta

4

Moor Side Farm
PAXTURE PL
PIMBO RD PL
DUKES MOSS
PIMBO LA
Lower Balcony Farm

Barton House
Nursery
LC Balcarres Farm
Crawford Village Prim Sch
LONG LA

3

Crawford Village Prim Sch
MANOR HOUSE DR
Millets
03

Maggots Nook
Red House Farm
Crawford
BILLINGE RD
The Crawford (PH)
ALEIGH
Billinge Bounty Farm
Strawberry Cottage

2

Scythe Stone Delph Farm
BERRY LA
BLACK BROOK
CRAWFORD RD
Black Brook
Maddocks

1

Hay's House
02

48 A B 49 C D 50 E F

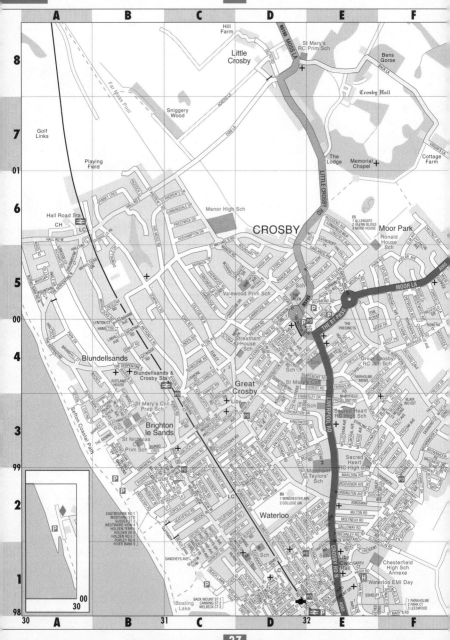

A B C D E F

8

Hill Farm

Little Crosby

St Mary's RC Prim Sch

Bens Gorse

BACK LA

MOSS LA

Crosby Hall

7

Golf Links

Far Moss Pool

Sniggery Wood

ACRES LA

DIBB LA

The Lodge

Memorial Chapel

Cottage Farm

01

Playing Field

6

Hall Road Sta

CH

LC

HALL RD W

Manor High Sch

CROSBY

LITTLE CROSBY RD

Moor Park

Ronald House Sch

E5
1 ALLENGATE
2 GLENN BLDGS
3 MOOR HOUSE

MOOR LA

5

Valewood Prim Sch

MOOR LA

5

Blundellsands

THE SERPENTINE

Sefton Coastal Path

Streatham House Sch

Blundellsands & Crosby Sta

Rutland House

The Green

THE PRECINCTS

00

4

St Mary's Coll Prep Sch

Great Crosby

St Mary's RC Sch

Liby

Great Crosby RC Jun Sch

Fairholme Mews

Maryfield Ind Est

Sacred Heart RC High Sch

LIVERPOOL RD

3

Brighton le Sands

St Nicholas CE Prim Sch

Merchant Taylors' Sch

Sacred Heart RC High Sch

99

D3
1 WINCHESTER AVE
2 COLLEGE GN

Waterloo

Chesterfield High Sch Annexe

2

EASTBOURNE RD 1
WORTHING ST 2
SUSSEX AVE 3
WESTWARD VIEW 4
HOLDEN TERR 5
HOLDEN GR 6
HOLDEN RD 7
PURLEY RD 8
RIVER BANK 9

LC

Civic Hall

GARTH

Waterloo EMI Day

P

SANDHEYS AVE

CROSBY RD N

1

Boating Lake

BACK MOUNT ST 1
CANNING ST 2
WELBECK CT 3

LC

ST MARY'S RD

98

00
30

A B C D E F

30 31 32

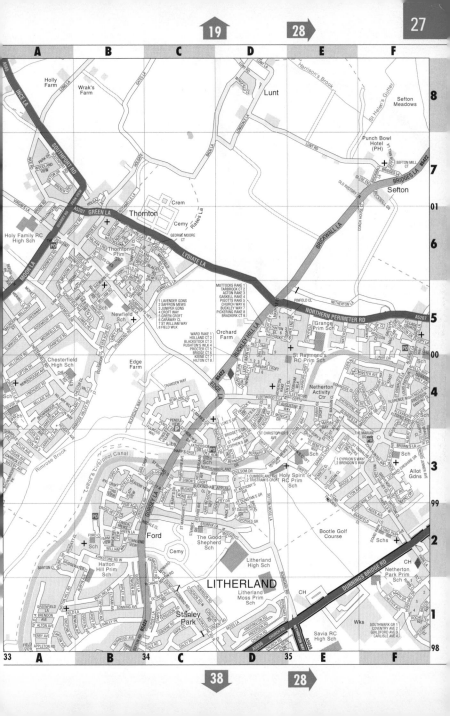

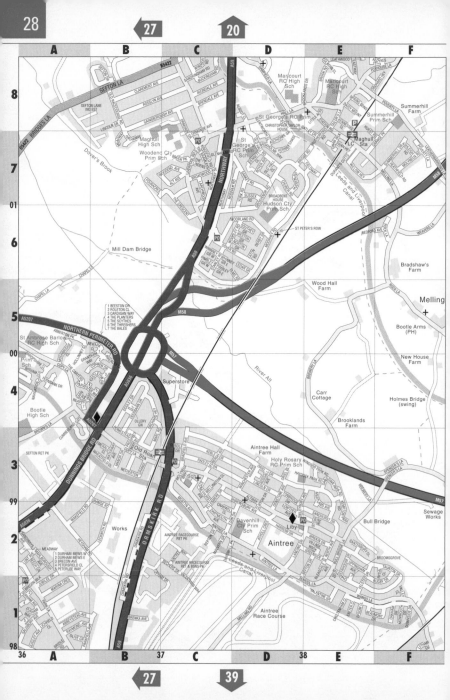

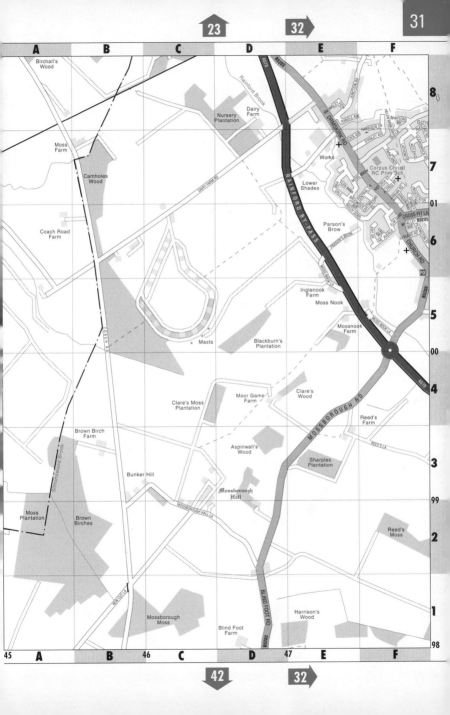

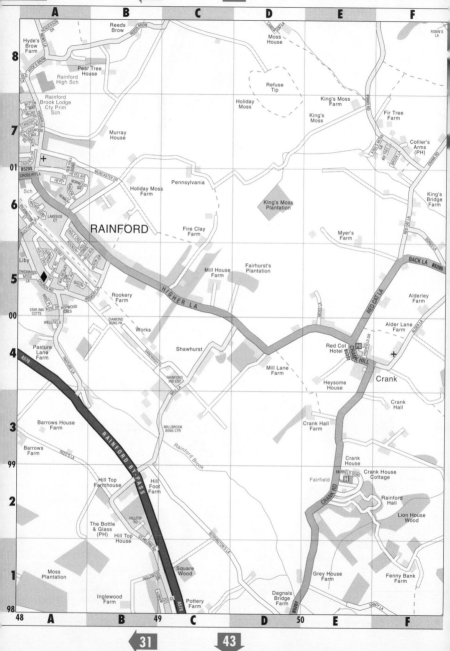

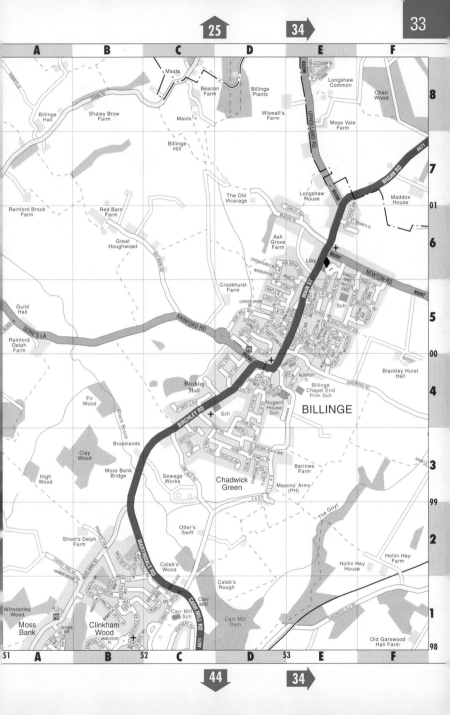

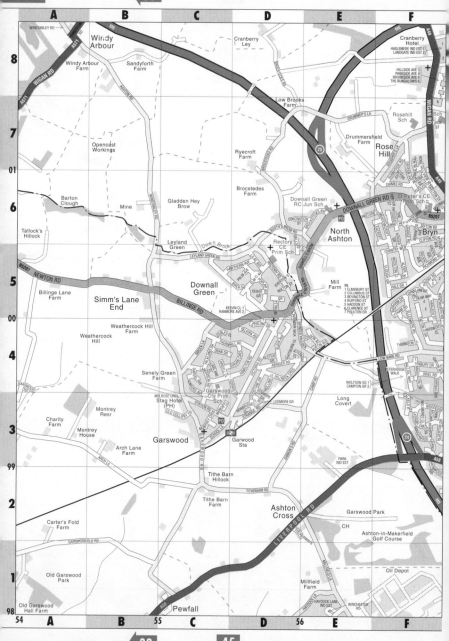

36

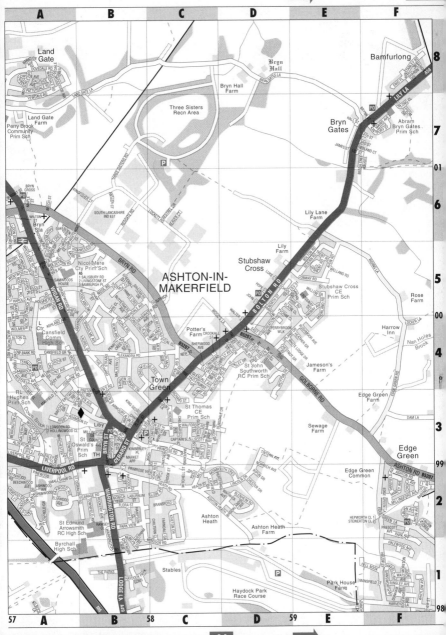

A   B   C   D   E   F

8

7

01

6

5

00

4

3

99

2

1

98

60   61   62

Abram

Abram Brow

Abram Hall Farm

Dover Lock Inn (PH)

Aye Bridge Farm

Nan Holes Brook

Balmer's Farm

Dam Lane Farm

Windy Bank Farm

Wigan Road Farm

ASHTON RD

Golbourne St Thomas's CE Jun & Inf Sch

Golbourne High Sch

Works

WARRINGTON RD

AYE BRIDGE RD

WIGAN RD

CHURCH ST

LOWTON RD

Hey Brook

A58

A573

LILY LA

Alexandra St

Verda St

CAMM ST

Morris's Farm

PARK LA

Lee Lane Farm

Chadwick's Farm

Leeds & Liverpool Canal

Crankwood

CRANKWOOD RD

Smith's Bridge

Works

Gerrard's Bridge

Lightshaw Hall

LIGHTSHAW LA

Critchley House

Pennington Flash Ctry Pk

Mossley Hall

Byrom Hall

BYROM LA

Laburnum Cottage

Bickershaw

Bickershaw CE Prim Sch

BICKERSHAW LA

ST JAMES CRES

FORRESTERS

B5237

Maypole Ind Est

MAYPOLE

B5207

DAM LA

B5207

Nan Holes Brook

LC

1 WHITECROFT AVE
2 HAGUE BUSH CL
3 MERCHANTS CRES
4 HOLLYBUSH SQ
5 THORNBUSH CL

1 THIRLMERE RD
2 TAYLOR ST
3 NORTHFIELD CT
4 WARRINGTON AVE
5 BOWLAND AVE
6 CHATBURN AVE

LAWRENCE CT 1
VICARAGE RD 2
MASON ST 3
STEPHENSON ST 4
ATKINSON ST 5
THIRLMERE AVE 6

| A | B | C | D | E | F |

Sefton Coastal Path

Marine Lake

ALBERT RD 1
DEACON CL 2

Radar Sta

P

E8
1 WATER ST
2 SANDRINGHAM AVE

BOSSOM CT

Seaforth

Port of Liverpool
Euro Rail Terminal

F7
1 BEDFORD PL
2 GLADSTONE AVE
3 RIVERSDALE RD
4 BELGRAVE RD

Royal Seaforth
Container Terminal

F6
1 LATHOM CL
2 LATHOM AVE
3 CLARENDON RD

Royal Seaforth Dock

Gladstone
Dock

Alexandra
Dock

Rock
Lighthouse

Perch
Rock

Marine Lake

1 MARINE PARK MANSIONS
2 BECKENHAM RD

KING'S PAR

Union
Terr

P

P

MARINE PROM

1 TIVOLI VILLA'S
2 VICTORIA RD
3 WATERS EDGE
APARTMENTS

A554

KING'S PAR

LB
Sta

WELLINGTON RD

30 A B 31 C D 32 E F

8
7
97
6
5
96
4
3
95
2
1
94

A5036 PRINCESS WAY

CROSBY RD S

SANDY RD

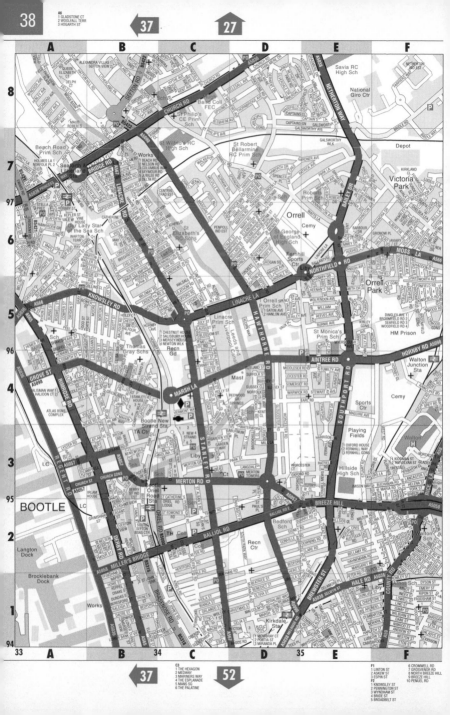

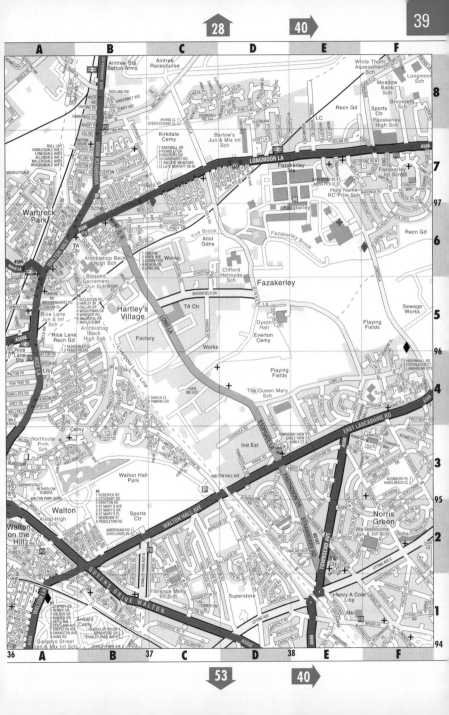

A B C D E F

8

Kirkby Municipal
Golf Course

CH

Sports
Ctr

VALLEY RD A506

LITTLE BROOK

Kirkby Brook

Brookfield
High Sch

Southdene

MORSTON WLK

Parkfield
Sch

Liby
PO

1 MOOR CT
2 COPPLE HOUSE LA

Burton's
Farm

Burton's
Bridge

VALLEY RD

Springfield
Sch

Cherryfield
Prim Sch

F8
1 THURSBY CRES
2 THURSBY CL
3 THURSBY WLK
4 GAYWOOD GN
5 GAYWOOD

A506 LONGMOOR LA

MOND RD

MORGAN
HTS

7

EAGLE
DENE

FALCON HEY

KESTRAL
DENE

Knowsley Brook

Gillmoss

The
Croft

RHOSESMOR CL 1
RHOSESMOR RD 2

MOORGATE RD

97

F Fazakerley Brook

GILLMOSS
IND EST

Shrog's
Farm

Knowsley
Bridge

Motel

A580

A5206

6

Sewage
Works

Works

EAST LANCASHIRE RD

WILLOW
HOUSE

WILLOWDENE

Knowsley
Wood

RANDLE
HTS

A580

B5194

M57

Sugar Brook

Our Lady &
St Swithin
RC Prim Sch

Randle's Bridge
Farm

5

Croxteth Brook

96

Ret
Pk

Croxteth
Community
Comp Sch

Croxteth

Liby

Craven
Wood

Stand
Lodge

1 TEWKESBURY CL
2 GOLDCREST CL

A580

River Alt

Croxteth
Cty Prim Sch

E4
1 ALDRIDGE CL
2 CHARMOUTH CL
3 ST CUTHBERT'S CL

SHOBDON CL

4

Cemy

St John Bosco
High Sch

C4
1 GRIFFIN WLK
2 DRAGON WLK
3 THRONE WLK
4 ORB WLK

Dam
Wood

1 HOLLINGBOURNE PL
2 COTTESBROOK PL
3 COTTESBROOK CL

Festival
Ct
MOLYNEUX
CT

REGAL
TOWER

Mull
Wood

DENHAM

HATFIELD

3

Dog & Gun

SCEPTRE
TOWER

CARTMEL
TERR

C3
1 SOVEREIGN HEY
2 DYMOKE RD
3 HEBDEN PAR
4 SWORD CL

F3
1 GREENFINCH CL
2 MISTLETHRUSH WAY
3 THORNBECK CT

95

De La Salle
Sch

OAKDALE CL

Croxteth
Country Park

Kennels

2

Monksdown
Sch

BARROW
Crox

Croxteth
Hall

Home Farm
House

STARLING GR

Old Kennels
House

1

City of Liverpool Community
Coll (Muirhead Ctr)

1 ROSEWOOD GDNS
2 MARCHAM WAY

P P
Lodge

P

Lodge

94

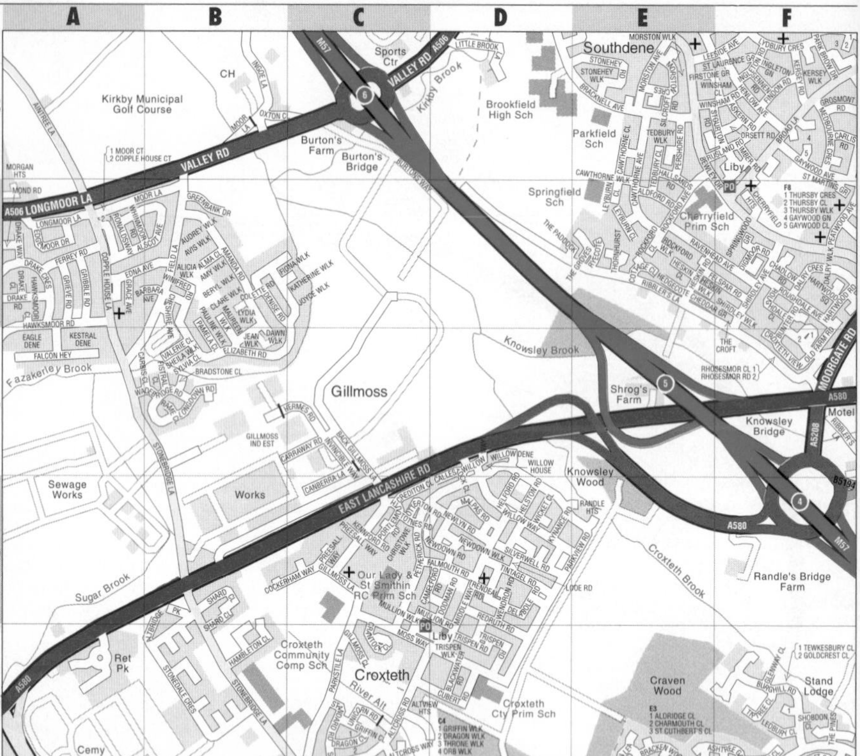

A1
1 BRANTHWAITE CL
2 HELMDON CL
3 GLASSONBY WAY
4 BRANTHWAITE GR
5 BLAISDON CL
6 NORRIS GREEN WAY

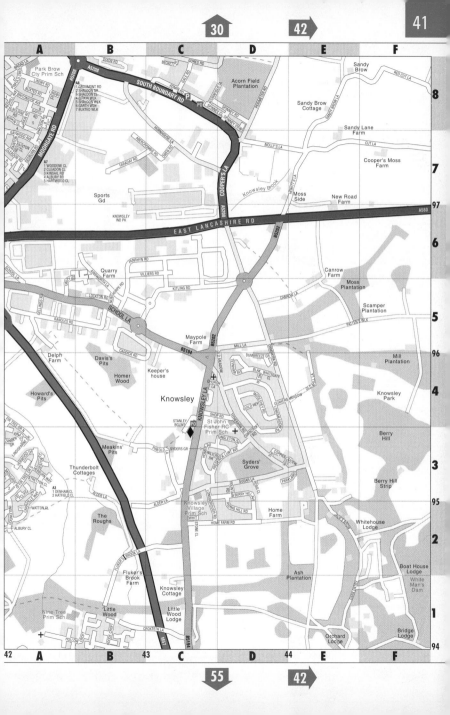

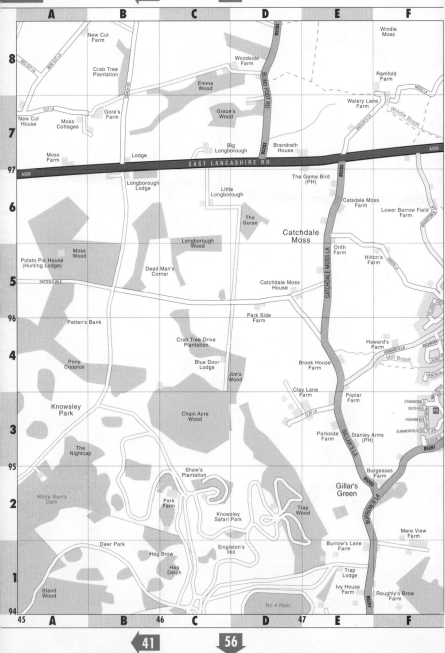

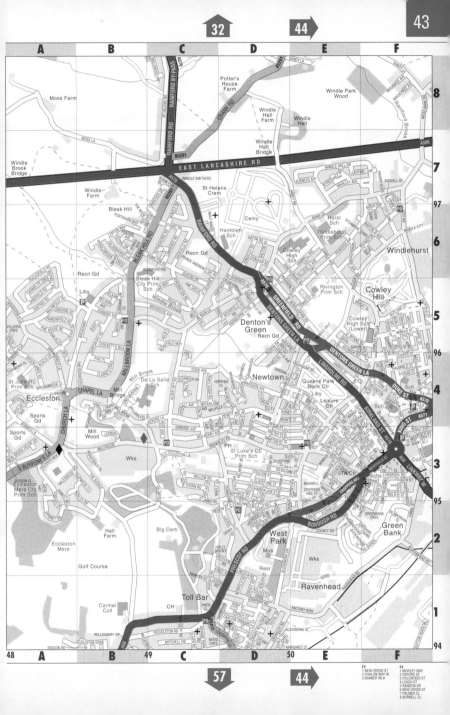

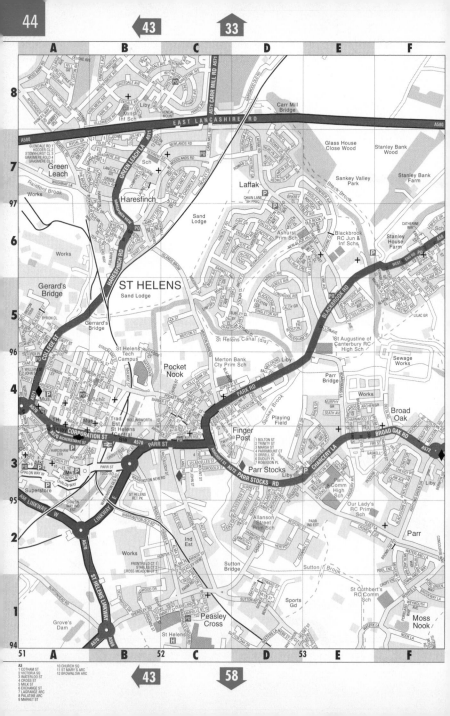

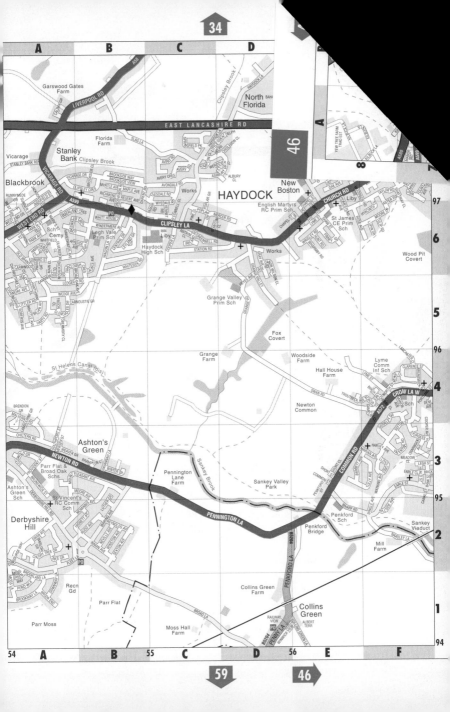

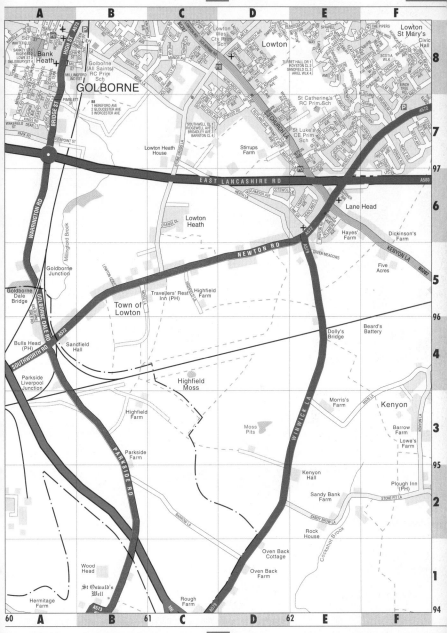

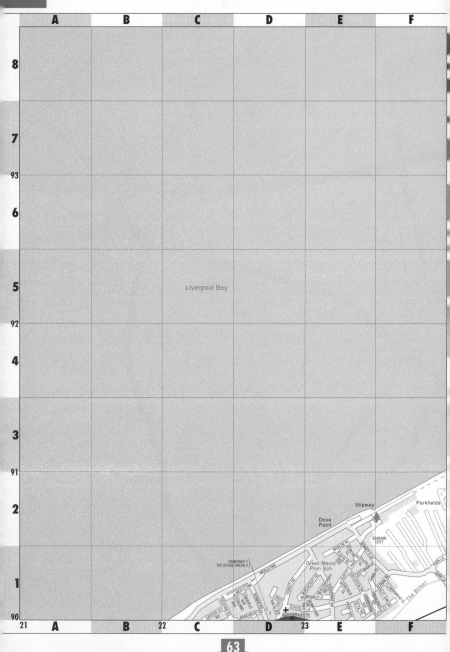

Liverpool Bay

Parkfields

Slipway

Dove
Point

SEABANK
COTT

Great Meols
Prim Sch

SANDIWAY 1
THE GOOSE GREEN 2

MEOLS PAR

The Birket

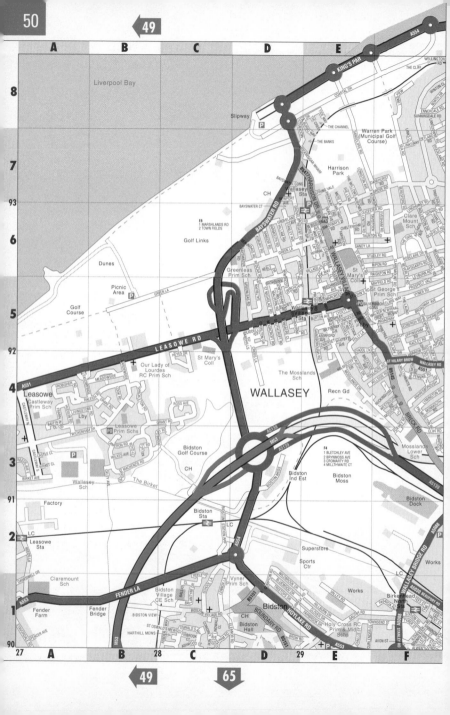

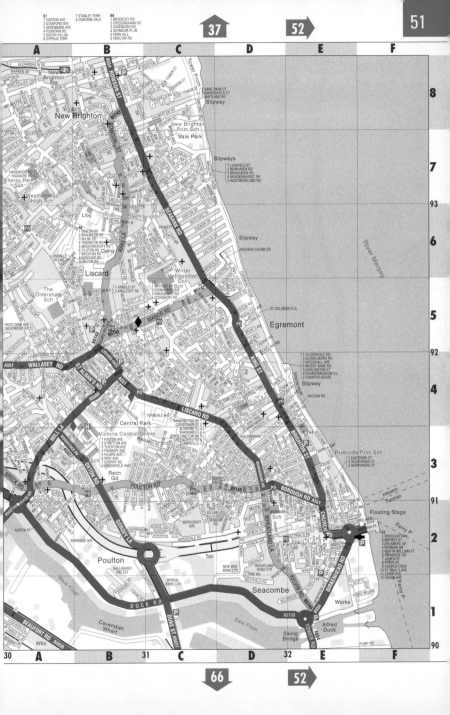

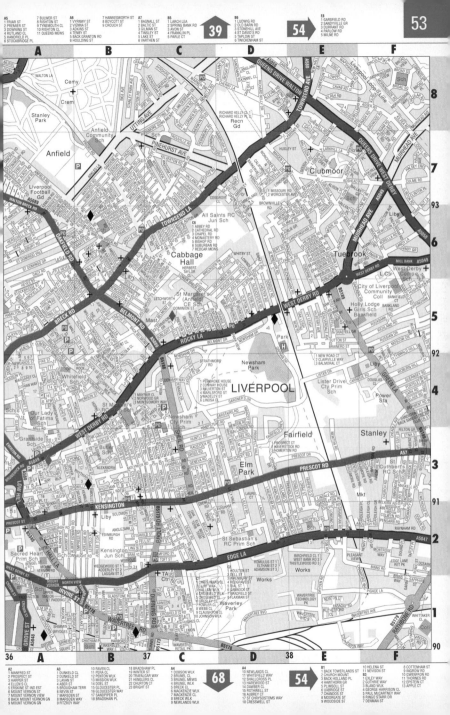

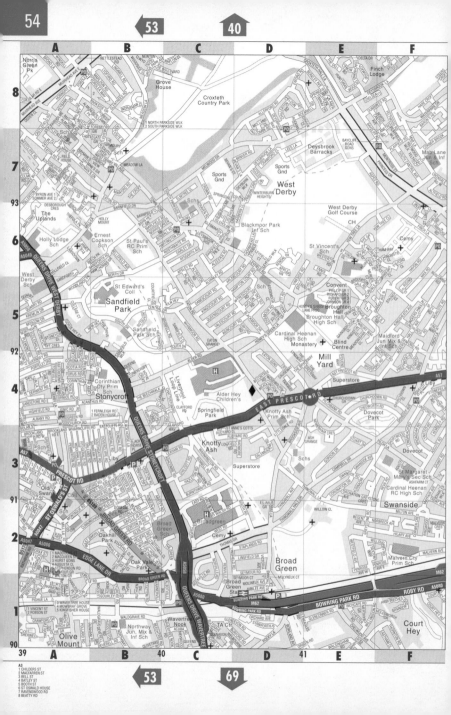

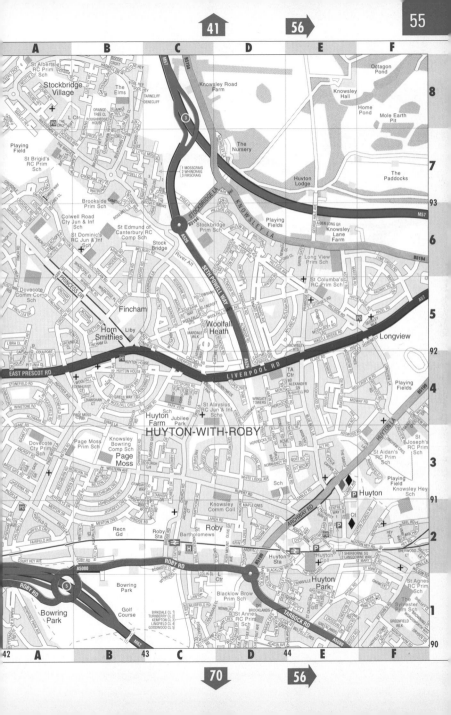

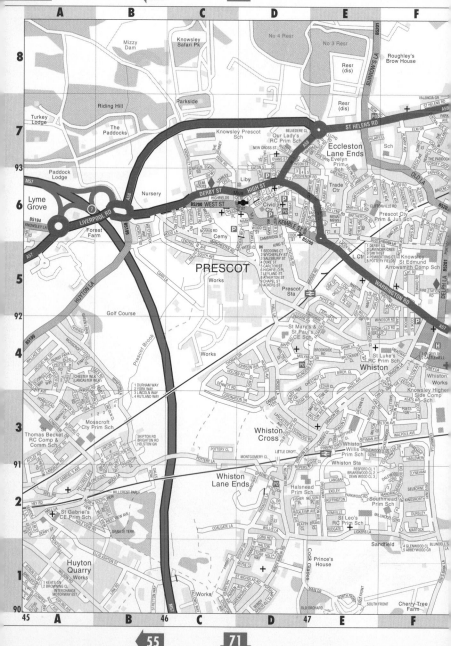

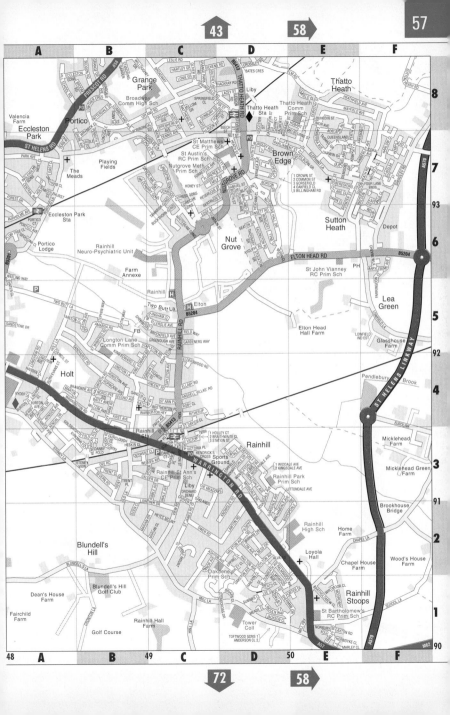

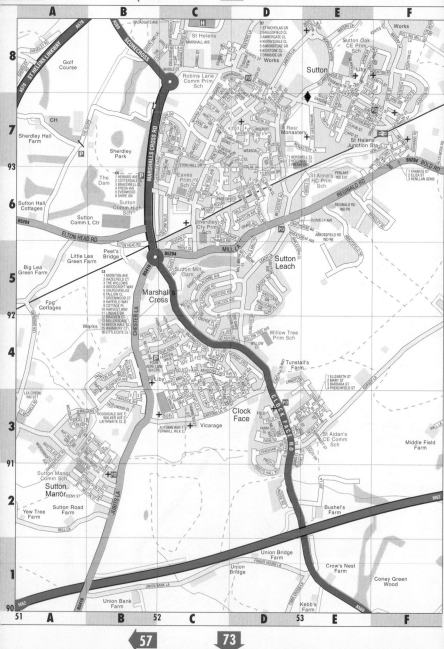

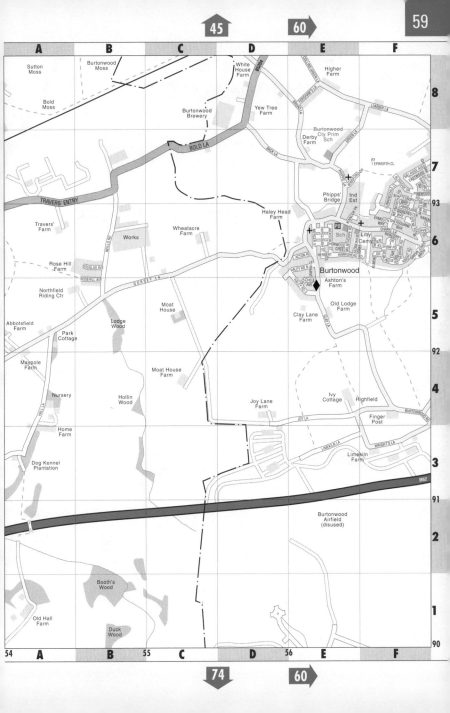

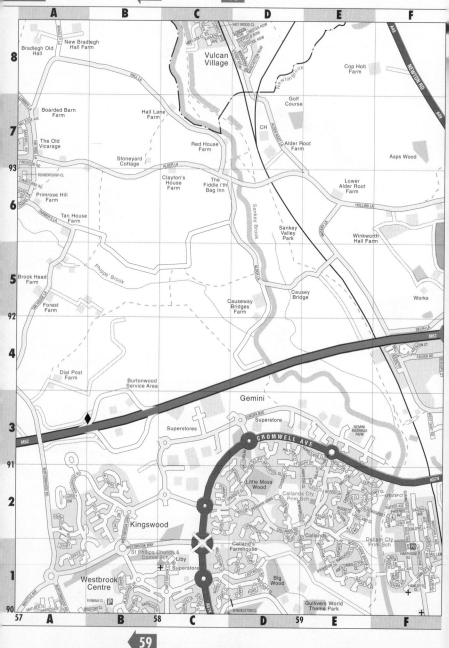

A B C D E F

8

Bradlegh Old Hall
New Bradlegh Hall Farm
Vulcan Village
HEY WOOD CL
LONDON ROW
CHESTER ROW
SHEFFIELD ROW
LIVERPOOL ROW
MANCHESTER ROW
HEYLOCK CL
KIRKACRES
Cop Holt Farm

Newton Brook
A49
NEWTON RD

Boarded Barn Farm
HALL LA
Hall Lane Farm
Golf Course
A49

7

The Old Vicarage
NEWLODGE AVE
TAY HELE
BRAWELL DR
Stoneyard Cottage
Red House Farm
ALDER LA
CH
Alder Root Farm
Asps Wood

93

PINEWOOD RD
ROXBOROUGH CL
CAMBORNE RD
Clayton's House Farm
The Fiddle i'th Bag Inn
Lower Alder Root Farm

6

KARETS
Primrose Hill Farm
Tan House Farm
PARKER'S LA
Sankey Brook
Sankey Valley Park
PARKER'S LA
HOLLINS LA
Winkworth Hall Farm

Phipps' Brook
ALDER LA

5

Brook Head Farm
Causey Bridge
Works

Forest Farm
Causeway Bridges Farm

92

Dial Post Farm
M62
DELPH LA

4

Burtonwood Service Area
FALCON CT
CALVER RD

Gemini

3

M62
BURTONWOOD RD
EUROPA BVD
Superstores
Superstore
Superstores
CROMWELL AVE
GEMINI BUSINESS PARK
WEST DR

91

PENKETH
OLIVER LANE
DRISCOLL CL
ST JOSEPH DR
Little Moss Wood
Callands Cty Prim Sch
BRANS LA
A574

2

TOURNEY GRN
LASKEY LA
WESTBROOK WAY
Kingswood
Callands
Dallam Cty Prim Sch

1

Westbrook Centre
St Philips Church & Comm Sch
Liby
Superstore
Calland's Farmhouse
Big Wood
Gullivers World Theme Park

90

FIRMAN CL
BRISTOW CL
SHACKLETON CL

57 A B 58 C D 59 E F

59

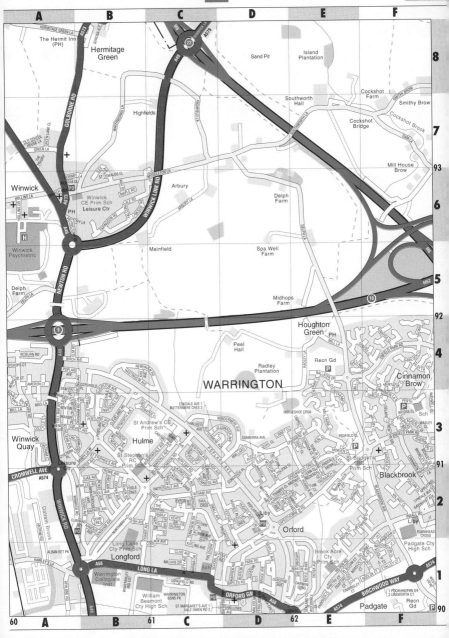

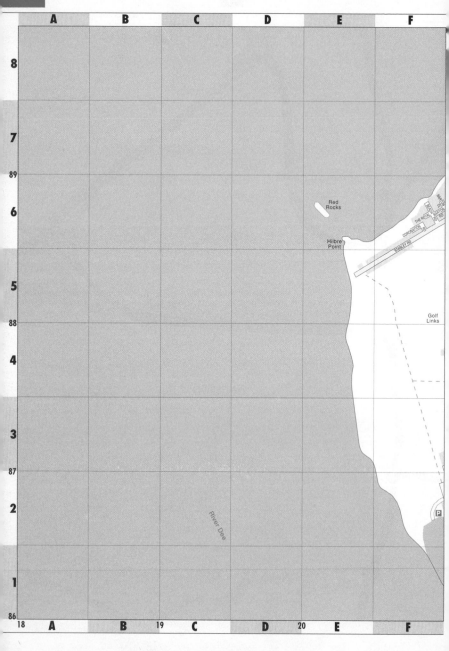

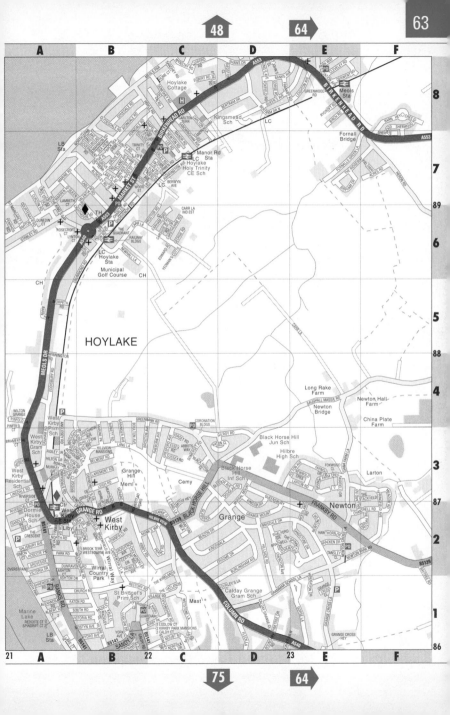

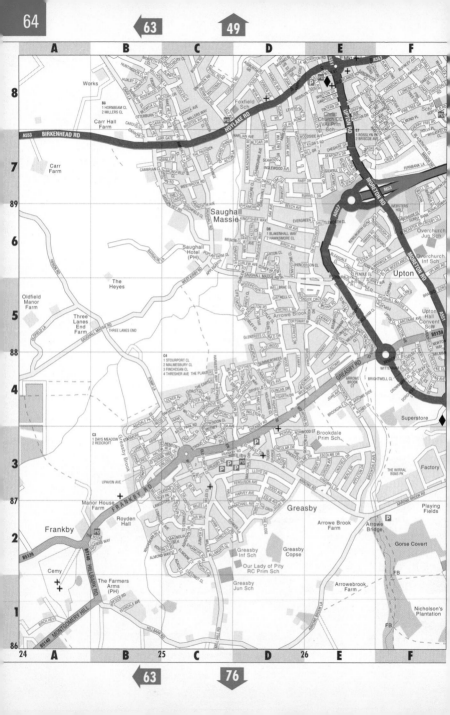

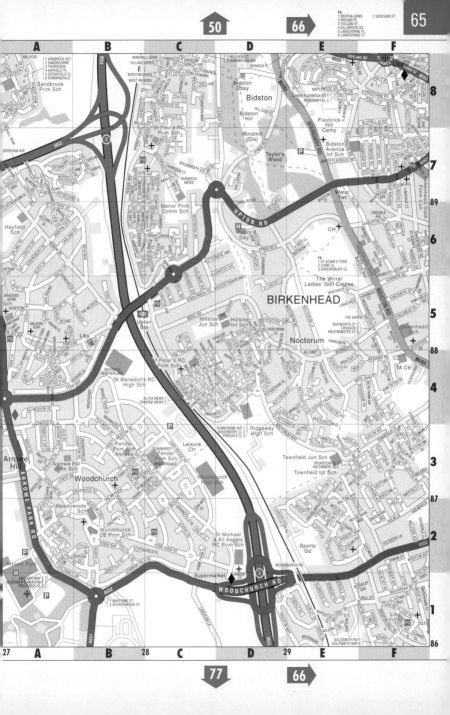

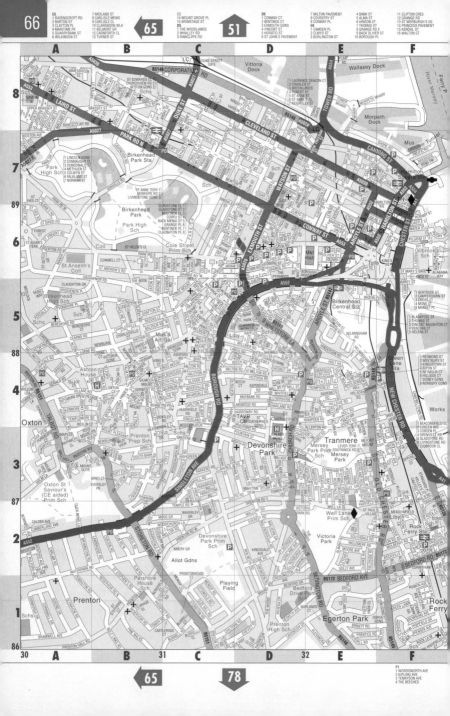

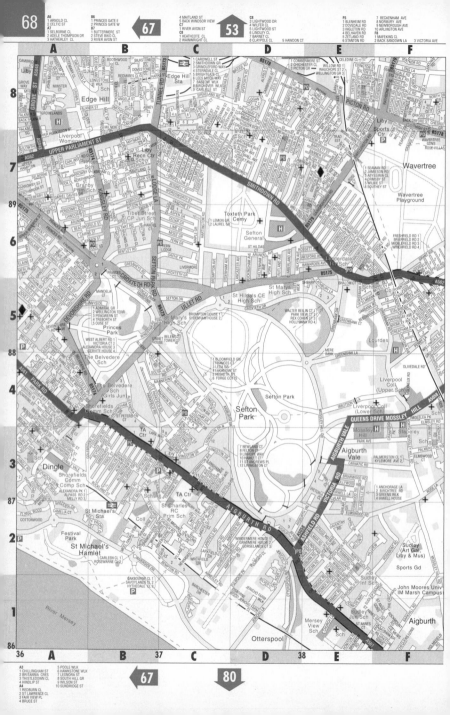

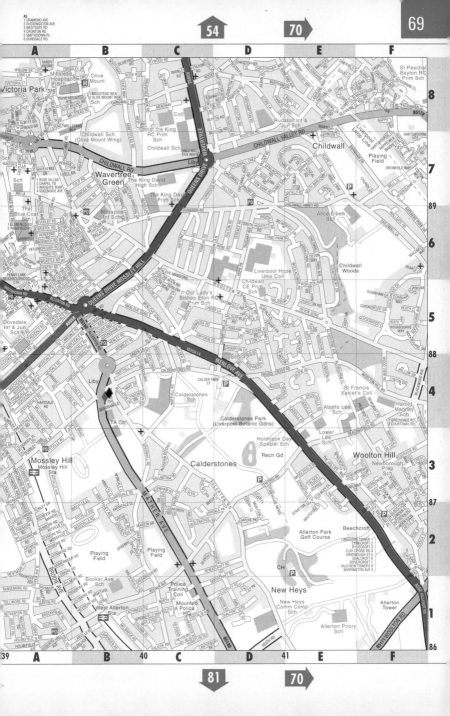

A1
1 CLAYTON CRES
2 HENDERSON RD
3 SQUIRES AVE
4 BRUNNER RD
5 MOND RD

C1
1 PARR ST
2 RUNNYMEDE CT
3 CLIFFE ST
4 HENRY ST
5 RUNNYMEDE GDNS

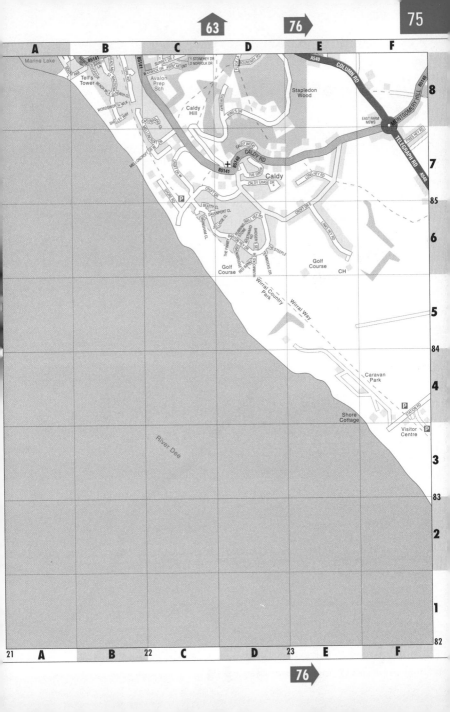

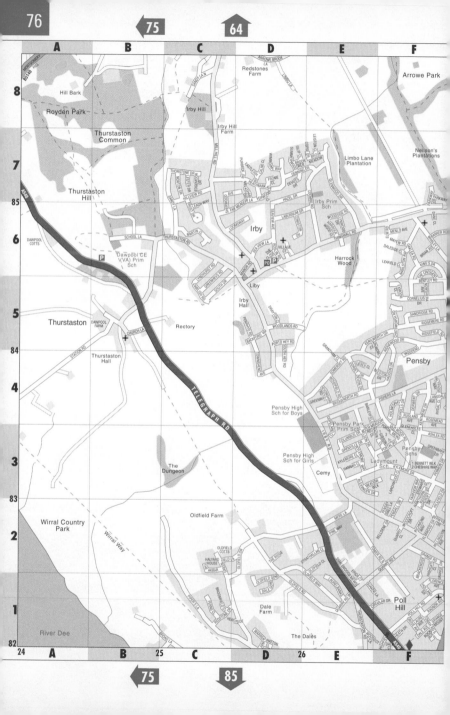

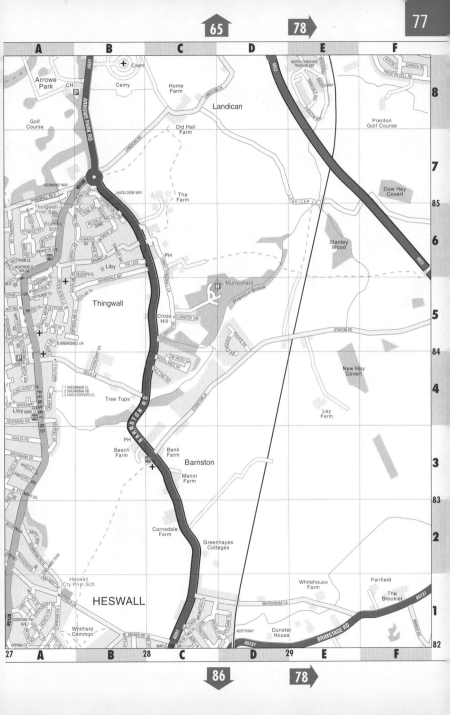

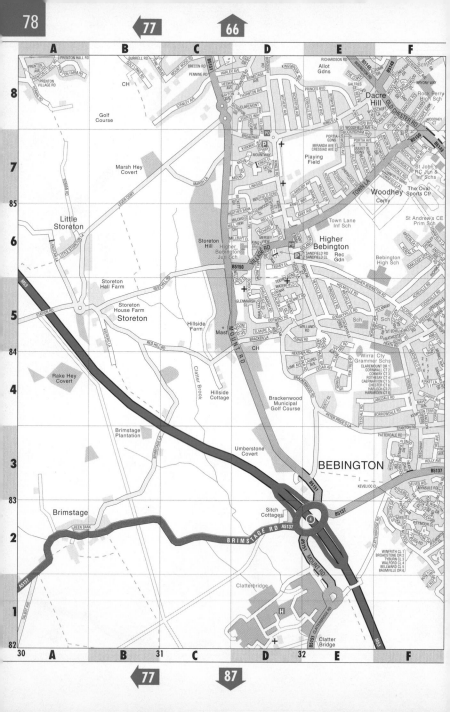

79
68

A B C D E F

8

7

85

6

5

84

4

3

83

2

1

82

Garston Channel

River Mersey

Eastham Channel

DULVERTON RD.

AIGBURTH RD

Aigburth Sta

City of Liverpool
Comm Coll
Riversdale Ctr

Greenways
Sch

RIVERVIEW HEIGHTS 1
LARCH CL 2
BURNT ASH CL 3
JACKSFIELD WAY 4

Oak
Wood

36 A B 37 C D 38 E F

79
89

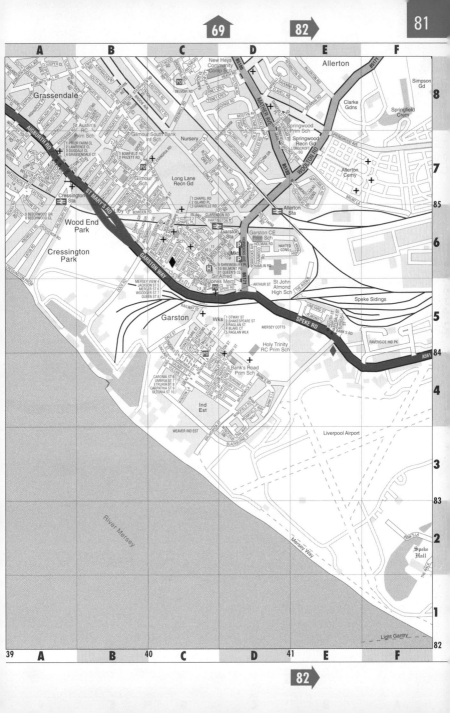

81
70

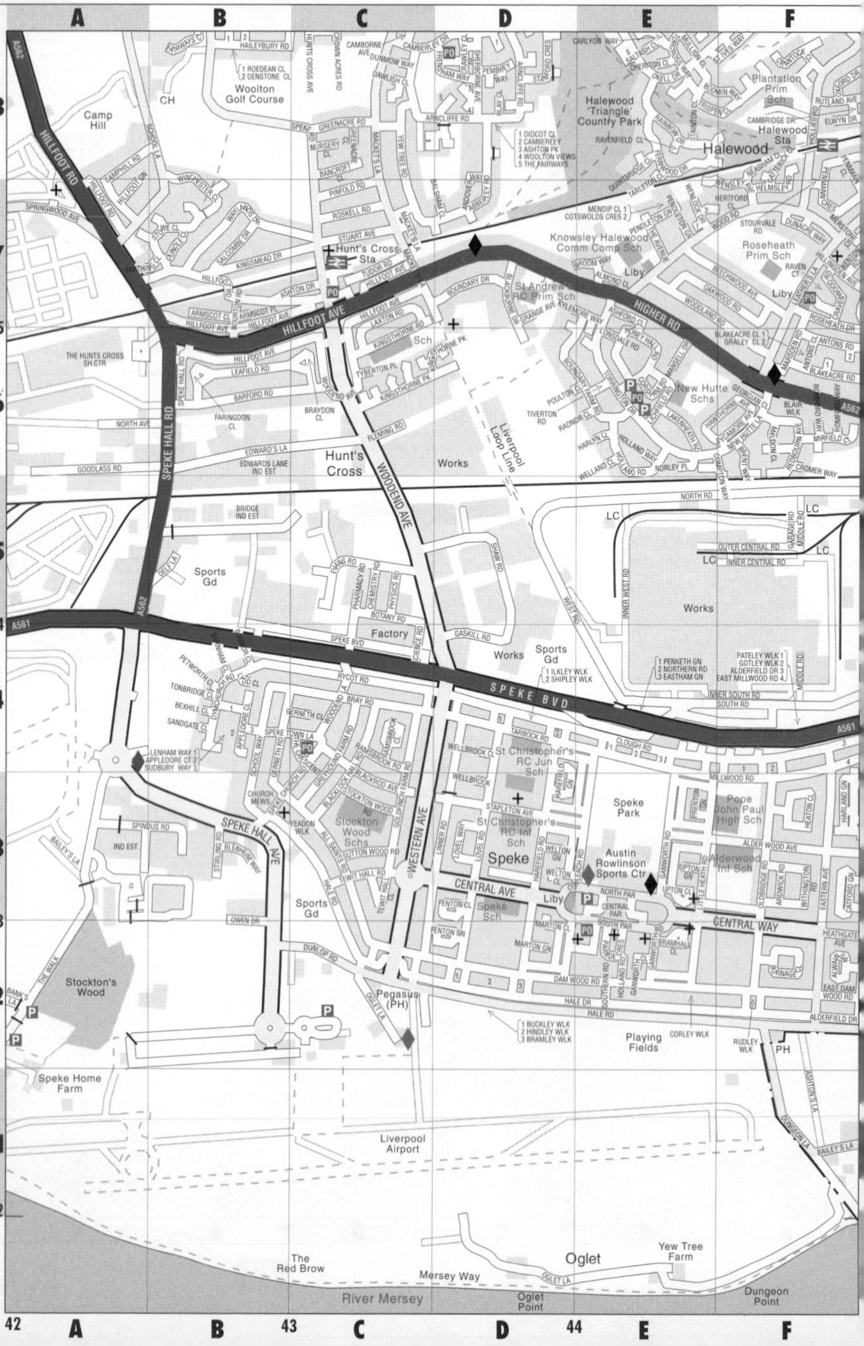
A
B
C
D
E
F
8
7
85
6
5
84
4
3
83
2
1
82
42
43
44
A562
A561
HILLFOOT RD
HILLFOOT AVE
HIGHER RD
SPEKE HALL RD
SPEKE HALL AVE
SPEKE BVD
WOODEND AVE
WESTERN AVE
CENTRAL AVE
CENTRAL WAY
Camp Hill
CH
Woolton Golf Course
HAILEYBURY RD
1 ROEDEAN CL
2 DENSTONE CL
SCHOOL LA
CAMPHILL RD
HILLFOOT GN
WINCHESTER CL
SPRINGWOOD AVE
KINGSMEAD DR
SALCOMBE DR
WAYLANDS DR
HUNTS CROSS AVE
CROWN ACRES RD
GREENACRE RD
NURSERY CL
BANCROFT CL
PINFOLD RD
ROSKELL RD
STUART AVE
MACKETS LA
YEW TREE RD
Hunt's Cross Sta
TUDOR RD
ASHTON DR
ARMSCOT CL
ARMSCOT PL
CAMBORNE AVE
DUNMOW WAY
DAWLISH CL
CAMBERLEY DR
FRENSHAM WAY
SHERBORNE AVE
PEMBREY WAY
ARNCLIFFE RD
ARNCLIFFE DR
1 DIDCOT CL
2 CAMBERLEY
3 ASHTON PK
4 WOOLTON VIEWS
5 THE FAIRWAYS
BALSHAM CL
ANDOVER WAY
ABBEYLEY RD
BOUNDARY DR
CARLYON WAY
SALTASH CL
CHERITON CL
OKELL DR
BODMIN WAY
TRISPEN CL
ST IVES WAY
Halewood 'Triangle' Country Park
RAVENFIELD CL
Plantation Prim Sch
Halewood
Halewood Sta
CAMBRIDGE DR
RUTLAND AVE
ELWYN DR
QUINTBRIDGE CL
TARLETON CL
FERNWOOD DR
MENDIP CL 1
COTSWOLDS CRES 2
PENDLETON GN
PENDLETON GN
WENLOCK DR
THE AVENUE
HERTFORD CL
WOOD RD
STOURVALE RD
DUNACRE WAY
Knowsley Halewood Comm Comp Sch
Roseheath Prim Sch
BROOM WAY
ALMOND CL
Liby
St Andrew's RC Prim Sch
GRANGE AVE
KYLEMORE WAY
BLACKBURNE DR
BEECHWOOD AVE
OAKWOOD RD
WOODLAND RD
ROSEHEATH DR
ASHFORD CL
HONEY HALL RD
LONSDALE RD
BLAKEACRE CL 1
GRALEY CL 2
ANTONS RD
BLAKEACRE RD
THE HUNTS CROSS SH CTR
LEAFIELD RD
BARFORD RD
FARINGDON CL
NORTH AVE
BRAYDON CL
LAXTON RD
KINGSTHORNE RD
KINGSTHORNE PK
TYBERTON PL
Sch
FLEMING RD
EDWARD'S LA
GOODLASS RD
EDWARDS LANE IND EST
Hunt's Cross
Works
Liverpool Loop Line
POULTON CL
TIVERTON RD
BOUNDARY FARM RD
TORRINGTON DR
RADNOR CL
HARLYN CL
HOLLAND WAY
WELLAND CL
NORLEY PL
New Hutte Schs
LAKENHEATH RD
GEORGIAN CL
HAWTHORNE AVE
SYCAMORE AVE
NEW HUTTE LA
BRENT WAY
COMPTON WAY
BLAIR WLK
MALDON CL
REDBOURN AVE
MIRFIELD CL
CROMER WAY
NORTH RD
BRIDGE IND EST
LC
OUTER CENTRAL RD
INNER CENTRAL RD
GARAGE RD
MIDDLE RD
INNER WEST RD
WEST RD
SHAW RD
DELF LA
Sports Gd
EVANS RD
PHARMACY RD
CHEMISTRY RD
PHYSICS RD
BOTANY RD
Factory
SCIENCE RD
GASKILL RD
SPEKE BVD
Works
Sports Gd
1 ILKLEY WLK
2 SHIPLEY WLK
1 PENKETH GN
2 NORTHERN RD
3 EASTHAM GN
PATELEY WLK 1
GOTLEY WLK 2
ALDERFIELD DR 3
EAST MILLWOOD RD 4
INNER SOUTH RD
SOUTH RD
BARNHAM CL
PETWORTH CL
TONBRIDGE CL
DYMCHURCH RD
BEXHILL CL
SANDGATE CL
APPLEDORE CT
RYCOT RD
BRAY RD
GERNETH CL
GERNETH RD
SPEKE TOWN LA
SCHOOL WAY
THE CRESCENT
GREYHOUND FARM RD
RAMSBROOK RD
RAMSBROOK CL
BLACKROD AVE
BLACKLOCK HALL RD
STOCKTON WOOD RD
GOLDFINCH FARM RD
Stockton Wood Schs
CHURCH MEWS
SPEKE CHURCH RD
YEADON WLK
ALL SAINTS RD
SUTTON WOOD RD
TEWIT HALL RD
HALE RD
LENHAM WAY 1
APPLEDORE CT 2
SUDBURY WAY 3
TARBOCK RD
CLOUGH RD
WELLBROOK CL
WELLBROOK
St Christopher's RC Jun Sch
St Christopher's RC Inf Sch
HAREFIELD GN
STAPLETON AVE
LINNER RD
LOVEL WAY
LOVEL RD
Speke
WELTON GN
WELTON CL
HAREFIELD RD
Speke Park
Austin Rowlinson Sports Ctr
MILLWOOD RD
Pope John Paul High Sch
PRENTON GN
HEATON CL
HARLAND GN
ALDER WOOD AVE
GANWORTH RD
UPTON GN
UPTON CL
LITTLE HEATH RD
Alderwood Inf Sch
OLDBRIDGE RD
ARDWICK RD
WITHINGTON RD
EASTERN AVE
CATFORD GN
NORTH PAR
CENTRAL PAR
SOUTH PAR
FENTON CL
FENTON GN
Speke Sch
MARTON CL
MARTON GN
PARADE CRES
BRAMHALL CL
HEATHGATE AVE
ALWAIN GN
ARNAGE CL
EAST DAM WOOD RD
DAM WOOD RD
SOUTHERN RD
HOLLAND RD
HALE DR
HALE RD
ALDERFIELD DR
1 BUCKLEY WLK
2 HINDLEY WLK
3 BRAMLEY WLK
Playing Fields
CORLEY WLK
RUDLEY WLK
PH
SPINDUS RD
IND EST
STIRLING RD
BLENHEIM WAY
BAILEY'S LA
OWEN DR
DUNLOP RD
OGLET LA
Pegasus (PH)
Sports Gd
THE WALK
Stockton's Wood
BANK'S LA
Speke Home Farm
Liverpool Airport
ASHTON'S LA
DUNGEON LA
BAILEY'S LA
The Red Brow
Mersey Way
Oglet
OGLET LA
Yew Tree Farm
River Mersey
Oglet Point
Dungeon Point

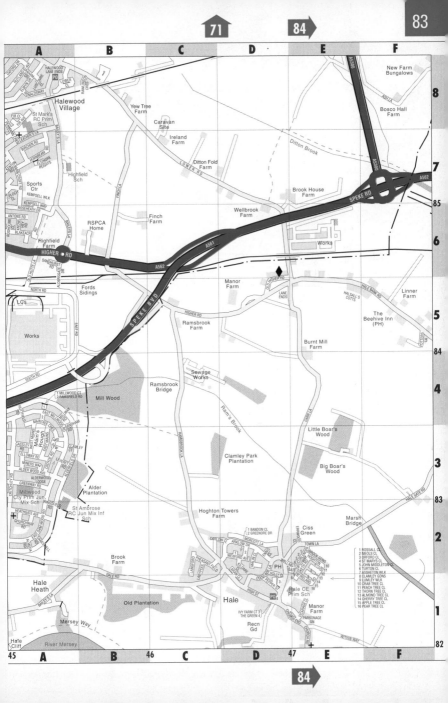

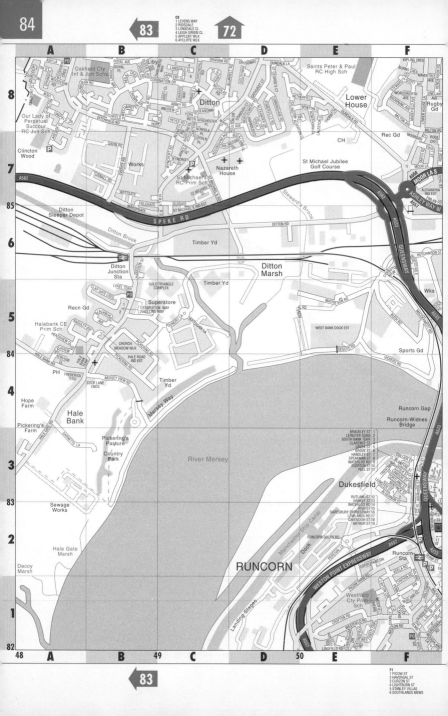

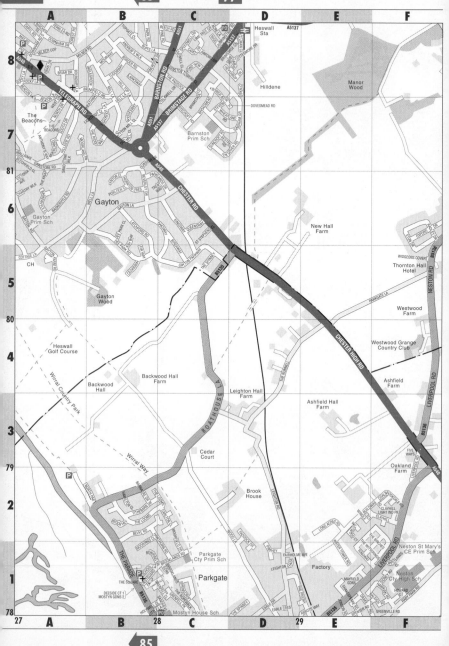

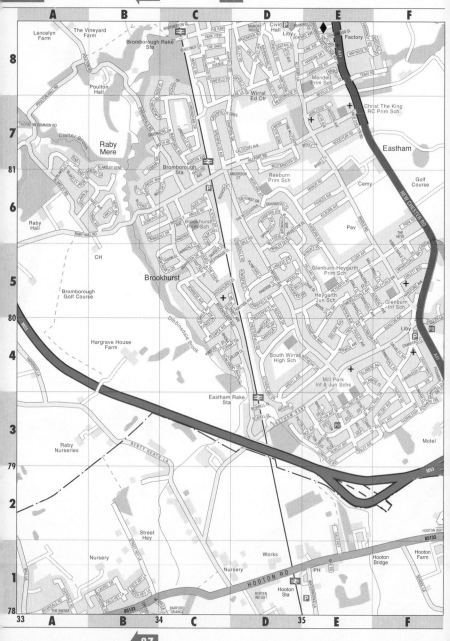

87
79

A B C D E F

8

Lancelyn
Farm

The Vineyard
Farm

Bromborough Rake
Sta

Brotherton Cl

The Raks
Park View
The Oaks
The Avenue

Manor
House

Bromborough Rd

Civic
Hall
Liby

Parkwood

Howard Ave

Factory

Bryn Road Cl

Poulton
Hall

Oakfield Rd

Wirral
Ed Ctr

Mendell
Prim Sch

Tebay Rd

7

Thornton Common Rd

Clatter Brook

Raby
Mere

Greendale Dr

Bromborough
Sta

Caldecott Ave

Allport Rd

Westminster Dr

Christ The King
RC Prim Sch

Eastham

81

Blakeley Dene

Anderson
Ct

Raeburn
Prim Sch

Manor Rd

Cemy

Golf
Course

6

Raby
Hall

Raby Hall Rd

Brookhurst
Prim Sch

The Scoops

Dearnford

Cranford Ave

Princes Ave

Auburn Rd

Pav

The Heys

Park Rd

New Chester Rd

5

Bromborough
Golf Course

CH

Brookhurst

Dibbinsdale Brook

Smokerise

Glenburn-Heygarth
Prim Sch

Heygarth
Jun Sch

Elgar Ave

Glenburn
Inf Sch

Liby

80

Hargrave House
Farm

M53

Eastham Rake
Sta

Bothwell Cl

Scarfell Cl

South Wirral
High Sch

Eastham Rake

Mill Park
Inf & Jun Schs

Cramford Rd

Motel

4

3

Raby
Nurseries

Benty Heath La

PO

M53

79

2

Street
Hey

Street La

Hooton Way

B5133

1

Nursery

Field Hey La

Nursery

Hooton Rd

Works

PH

Hooton
Sta

Hooton
Bridge

Hooton
Farm

78

Briarcake Rd

The Knowe

B5133

Barford
Grange

Rorten
Ind Est

PO

Waterwork La

Brook La

33 A 34 B C D 35 E F

87

Eastham
Ctry Pk
Visitor Ctr
Eastham Ferry

Eastham Ferry
Hotel

The Warrens
Farm

Wirral Metropolitan
Coll

Custom
House

Eastham Locks

CH

Queen
Elizabeth II
Dock

Golf Course

St DAVID RD

St JOHN'S RD

Tanks

Tanks

Tanks

Oil Storage
Depot

Tanks

Eastham
House

Tanks

Tanks

LC

David's
Rough

Hooton Park

LC

Booston
Wood

Kennel
Wood

REDVERS
AVE
VERNON AVE
HOOTON WAY

HOOTON RD
B5133

Hooton

Park
Farm

Motor Vehicle
Works

Rivacre
Wood

River Mersey

Manchester Ship Canal

RIVACRE RD

NEW CHESTER RD

WELSH RD A550

CHESTER RD A41

M53

B5132

8

7

81

6

5

80

4

3

79

2

78

1

36

37

38

A   B   C   D   E   F

Index

Street names are listed alphabetically and show the locality, the Postcode District, the page number and a reference to the square in which the name falls on the map page

Abbreviations used in the index

App **Approach**	Cl **Close**	Espl **Esplanade**	Orch **Orchard**	Sq **Square**
Arc **Arcade**	Comm **Common**	Est **Estate**	Par **Parade**	Strs **Stairs**
Ave **Avenue**	Cnr **Corner**	Gdns **Gardens**	Pk **Park**	Stps **Steps**
Bvd **Boulevard**	Cotts **Cottages**	Gn **Green**	Pas **Passage**	St **Street, Saint**
Bldgs **Buildings**	Ct **Court**	Gr **Grove**	Pl **Place**	Terr **Terrace**
Bsns Pk **Business Park**	Ctyd **Courtyard**	Hts **Heights**	Prec **Precinct**	Trad Est **Trading Estate**
Bsns Ctr **Business Centre**	Cres **Crescent**	Ind Est **Industrial Estate**	Prom **Promenade**	Wlk **Walk**
Bglws **Bungalows**	Dr **Drive**	Intc **Interchange**	Ret Pk **Retail Park**	W **West**
Cswy **Causeway**	Dro **Drove**	Junc **Junction**	Rd **Road**	Yd **Yard**
Ctr **Centre**	E **East**	La **Lane**	Rdbt **Roundabout**	
Cir **Circus**	Emb **Embankment**	N **North**	S **South**	

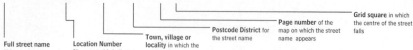

1st St. WN2 ..... 35 E7
3rd St. WN2 ..... 35 E7
4th St. WN2 ..... 35 F7
'a' Ct. WN4 ..... 35 B2
A K Bsns Pk. PR9 ..... 5 A6
Abacus Rd. L13 ..... 54 B4
Abberley Cl. WA10 ..... 43 F3
Abberley Rd. L25 ..... 82 D7
Abberton Pk. L30 ..... 28 A5
Abbey Cl. Birkenhead L41 ..... 66 F5
Abbey Cl. Ditton WA8 ..... 84 C8
Abbey Cl. Kirkby L31 ..... 29 F2
Abbey Cl. Little Altcar L37 ..... 10 B2
Abbey Cl. Orrell WN8 ..... 25 C7
Abbey Ct. L25 ..... 70 B2
Abbey Dr. WN5 ..... 25 E6
Abbey Gdns. PR8 ..... 4 A4
Abbey La. L40 ..... 14 C8
Abbey Rd. Ditton WA8 ..... 84 C8
Abbey Rd. Haydock WA11 ..... 45 E7
Abbey Rd. Liverpool L6 ..... 53 C6
Abbey Rd. St Helens WA10 ..... 43 F7
Abbey Rd. West Kirby L48 ..... 63 B2
Abbey St. L41 ..... 66 F5
Abbey View. L16 ..... 69 E7
Abbeyfield Dr. L11 & L12 ..... 40 D3
Abbeystead. WN8 ..... 24 C7
Abbeystead Ave. L30 ..... 28 A1
Abbeystead Rd. L15 ..... 69 B7
Abbeyway N. WA11 ..... 46 A7
Abbeyway S. WA11 ..... 46 A7
Abbeywood. WN8 ..... 24 C6
Abbeywood Gr. L35 ..... 56 F2
Abbot Cl. L43 ..... 65 C6
Abbots Cl. L37 ..... 10 A1
Abbots Dr. L63 ..... 78 F5
Abbots Hall Ave. WA9 ..... 58 D2
Abbots Way. Formby L37 ..... 10 B1
Abbots Way. West Kirby L48 ..... 63 C3
Abbotsbury Way. L12 ..... 40 E3
Abbotsfield Rd. WA9 ..... 58 E5
Abbotsfield Rd Ind Pk. WA9 ..... 58 E6
Abbotsford. L39 ..... 13 F5
Abbotsford Cl. WA3 ..... 36 D1
Abbotsford Gdns. L23 ..... 26 C3
Abbotsford Rd. Crosby L23 ..... 26 C2
Abbotsford Rd. Liverpool L11 ..... 39 F2
Abbotsford St. L44 ..... 53 F5
Abbott Dr. L20 ..... 38 E5
Abbotts Cl. L18 ..... 69 B3
Abbotts Way. WN5 ..... 33 D3
Abbottshey Ave. L18 ..... 69 B2

Abdale Rd. L11 ..... 39 F3
Aber St. **4** L6 ..... 53 A3
Abercrombie Rd. L33 ..... 41 C7
Abercromby Sq. L7 ..... 52 F1
Aberdale Rd. L13 ..... 54 B3
Aberdare Cl. WA5 ..... 60 E1
Aberdeen St. L41 ..... 66 C7
Aberford Ave. L45 ..... 50 E5
Abergele Rd. L13 ..... 53 F2
Abingdon Gr. L4 ..... 39 C2
Abingdon Rd.
  Birkenhead L49 ..... 64 B3
Abingdon Rd. Liverpool L4 ..... 39 C2
Abinger Rd. WN4 ..... 34 D4
Abney Cl. L7 ..... 68 B8
Abotts Lea Sch. L25 ..... 69 E4
Aboyne Cl. L9 ..... 53 C6
Abram Bryn Gates Prim Sch.
  WN2 ..... 35 F7
Abram St. L5 ..... 52 E5
Abrams Fold. PR9 ..... 2 F5
Abram Gn. PR9 ..... 2 F5
Abratio St. L41 ..... 66 D6
Abyssinia Cl. L15 ..... 68 E7
Acacia Ave. Huyton-w-R L36 ..... 55 D1
Acacia Ave. Widnes WA8 ..... 73 B3
Acacia Cl. L49 ..... 64 C2
Acacia Gr. Liverpool L9 ..... 39 B6
Acacia Gr. St Helens WA10 ..... 43 A4
Acacia Gr. Wallasey L44 ..... 51 E2
Acacia Gr. West Kirby L48 ..... 63 A2
Acacia St. WA12 ..... 45 F4
Acanthus Rd. L13 ..... 54 B4
Accacia Rd. L12 ..... 54 D7
Acer Leigh. L17 ..... 68 D2
Acheson Rd. L13 ..... 53 E6
Achilles Ave. WA2 ..... 61 B2
Ackerley Cl. WA2 ..... 61 F3
Ackers Hall Ave. L14 ..... 54 F5
Ackers Hall Cl. L14 ..... 54 F5
Ackers La. Crosby L23 & L38 ..... 26 C7
Ackers La. St Helens WA10 ..... 43 C4
Ackers Rd. L49 ..... 65 C2
Ackers St. **10** L34 ..... 56 D6
Acland Rd. L44 ..... 51 B4
Aconbury Cl. L11 ..... 39 F3
Aconbury Pl. L11 ..... 39 F3
Acorn Bsns Ctr. L33 ..... 30 B1
Acorn Cl. Bebington L63 ..... 78 D6
Acorn Cl. St Helens WA9 ..... 58 C4
Acorn Ct. L8 ..... 67 F6
Acorn St. WA12 ..... 46 D3
Acorn Way. L20 ..... 38 D5

Acornfield Cl. L33 ..... 41 C8
Acornfield Rd. L33 ..... 30 D2
Acre La. Bebington L62 ..... 88 D8
Acre La. Heswall L60 ..... 77 C1
Acrefield Ct. L42 ..... 66 B1
Acrefield Pk. L25 ..... 70 A3
Acrefield Rd. Birkenhead L42 ..... 66 C1
Acrefield Rd. Widnes WA8 ..... 72 B1
Acrefield Rd. Woolton L25 ..... 70 A3
Acregate. WN8 ..... 24 C7
Acres La. Great Altcar L38 ..... 18 E8
Acres La. Lydiate L31 & L39 ..... 19 E7
Acres Rd. Bebington L63 ..... 78 F6
Acres Rd. Hoylake L47 ..... 63 F7
Acresgate Ct. L25 ..... 70 A6
Acreville Rd. L63 ..... 78 F5
Acton Gr. L6 ..... 53 C6
Acton La. L46 ..... 64 C7
Acton Rake. L30 ..... 27 D5
Acton Rd. Birkenhead L42 ..... 67 A1
Acton Rd. Burtonwood WA5 ..... 59 E6
Acton Rd. Kirkby L32 ..... 29 C2
Acton Way. L7 ..... 68 C8
Acuba Gr. L41 ..... 66 E4
Acuba Rd. L15 ..... 54 C1
Ada St. WA9 ..... 44 C1
Adair Pl. L13 ..... 53 E7
Adair Rd. L13 ..... 53 E7
Adam St. L5 ..... 52 F6
Adams Cl. WA12 ..... 46 D2
Adamson St.
  Ashton-in-M WN4 ..... 35 A3
Adamson St. Liverpool L7 ..... 53 D2
Adaston Ave. L62 ..... 88 F4
Adcote Cl. L14 ..... 54 F3
Adcote Rd. L14 ..... 54 F3
Adderley St. L7 ..... 53 B2
Addingham Ave. WA8 ..... 84 A7
Addingham Rd. L18 ..... 69 B5
Addington St. L44 ..... 51 D3
Addison Sq. WA8 ..... 73 A1
Addison St. Bootle L20 ..... 38 A5
Addison St. Liverpool L20 ..... 52 D3
Addison Way. L3 ..... 52 D3
Adela Rd. WA7 ..... 84 F2
Adela Ave. L35 ..... 57 E7
Adelaide Pl. L5 ..... 52 E4
Adelaide Rd. Birkenhead L42 ..... 66 C4
Adelaide Rd. Bootle L21 ..... 37 F7
Adelaide Rd. Liverpool L7 ..... 53 B2
Adelaide St. Heswall L60 ..... 52 E6
Adelaide St. Wallasey L44 ..... 51 B3
Adelaide Terr. L22 ..... 26 C1

Adele Thompson Dr. **2** L8 ..... 68 A7
Adelphi St. L41 ..... 66 E6
Adkins St. **3** L5 ..... 53 A6
Adlam Cres. L9 ..... 39 E7
Adlam Rd. L10 & L9 ..... 39 E7
Adlington House. **8** L3 ..... 52 D3
Adlington St. **7** L3 ..... 52 D3
Admin Rd. L33 ..... 41 C8
Admiral Gr. L8 ..... 68 A5
Admiral St. L8 ..... 68 A5
Adrian's Way. L32 ..... 29 E2
Adshead Rd. L13 ..... 53 E7
Adstone Rd. L25 ..... 70 C5
Adswood Rd. L36 ..... 55 E3
Africander Rd. WA11 ..... 44 A8
Afton. WA8 ..... 72 A2
Agar Rd. L11 & L13 ..... 53 F7
Agate St. L6 ..... 53 A5
Agincourt Rd. L12 ..... 54 C5
Agnes Gr. L44 & L45 ..... 51 C5
Agnes Rd. L23 ..... 26 C3
Agnes Rd. L41 & L42 ..... 66 E3
Agnes St. WA9 ..... 58 C3
Agnes Way. L7 ..... 53 B1
Aiden Long Gr. L34 ..... 55 E6
Aigburth Dr. L17 ..... 68 C4
Aigburth Gr. L46 ..... 64 D8
Aigburth Hall Ave.
  L19 & L18 ..... 81 A8
Aigburth Hall Rd. L19 ..... 81 A8
Aigburth Rd. L17 & L19 & L18 ..... 68 D2
Aigburth St. L8 ..... 68 B8
Aigburth Sta. L17 ..... 80 E8
Aigburth Vale. Liverpool L17 ..... 68 D2
Aigburth Vale.
  Liverpool L17 & L18 ..... 68 E3
Aiken Cl. L8 ..... 67 F4
Ailsa Rd. L45 ..... 51 A5
Ainsdale CE Prim Sch. PR8 ..... 7 D4
Ainsdale Cl. Aintree L10 ..... 39 F8
Ainsdale Cl. Bebington L63 ..... 88 C5
Ainsdale Cl. Heswall L61 ..... 77 A5
Ainsdale Cl. Warrington WA5 ..... 74 F4
Ainsdale High Sch. PR8 ..... 7 C6
Ainsdale Rd. L20 ..... 38 D6
Ainsdale Sand Dunes Nat Res.
  PR8 ..... 6 E3
Ainsdale Sta. PR8 ..... 7 C5
Ainsworth Ave. L46 ..... 64 C6
Ainsworth La. L34 ..... 41 B6
Ainsworth Rd. WA10 ..... 43 D5
Ainsworth St. L3 ..... 52 E1
Aintree Cres. PR8 ..... 4 F4

Aintree La. Aintree L10 & L9 ..... 28 C2
Aintree La. Liverpool L10 ..... 40 A8
Aintree Race Course. L9 ..... 28 D1
Aintree Racecourse Ret & Bsns
  Pk. L10 ..... 28 C2
Aintree Racecourse Ret Pk.
  L10 ..... 28 C2
Aintree Rd. L20 ..... 38 E4
Aintree Sta Sefton Arms.
  L30 ..... 39 B8
Aintree Way. L9 ..... 28 C2
Airdale Cl. L43 ..... 65 C6
Airdale Rd. L15 ..... 68 F6
Airdrie Cl. L62 ..... 88 D3
Aire. WA8 ..... 72 B2
Airedale Cl. WA5 ..... 74 F7
Airegate. L31 ..... 20 B2
Airlie Gr. L13 ..... 53 D6
Airlie Rd. L47 ..... 63 B6
Aisthorpe Gr. L31 ..... 28 D7
Ajax Ave. WA2 ..... 61 B2
Akbar The. L61 ..... 76 C2
Akenside St. L20 & L21 ..... 38 A6
Alabama Way. L41 ..... 66 F6
Alamein Rd. L36 ..... 55 D4
Alastair Cres. L43 ..... 65 F1
Alban Rd. L16 ..... 69 D8
Alban Ret Pk. WA2 ..... 61 A1
Alban Ave. L34 ..... 56 F7
Albany Rd. Birkenhead L42 ..... 66 E2
Albany Rd. Liverpool L9 ..... 39 B7
Albany Rd. Liverpool L7 ..... 53 A2
Albany Rd. Liverpool L13 ..... 54 A4
Albany Rd. Prescot L34 ..... 56 E6
Albany Rd.
  Southport PR8 & PR9 ..... 1 C1
Albemarle Rd. L44 ..... 51 E3
Albert Ct. PR9 ..... 1 D1
Albert Dr. Bootle L20 & L9 ..... 38 F6
Albert Dr. Warrington WA5 ..... 74 D6
Albert Edward Rd. L7 ..... 53 A2
Albert Gr. Crosby L23 ..... 26 C4
Albert Gr. Liverpool L15 ..... 69 A8
Albert Pk. L17 ..... 68 B5
Albert Pl. PR8 ..... 4 B8
Albert Rd. Birkenhead L42 ..... 66 C4
Albert Rd. Formby L37 ..... 17 B8
Albert Rd. Hoylake L47 ..... 63 B6
Albert Rd. Litherland L22 ..... 37 D8
Albert Rd. Liverpool L13 ..... 53 D6
Albert Rd. Southport PR9 ..... 1 D1
Albert Rd. West Kirby L48 ..... 63 A1
Albert Rd. Widnes WA8 ..... 73 B1

Albert Schweitzer Ave. L30 27 F4
Albert Sq. WA8 73 B1
Albert St. Ashton-in-M WN4 . 35 B3
Albert St. Liverpool L7 53 A1
Albert St. St Helens WA10 44 A5
Albert St. Wallasey L45 37 C1
Albert Terr. Collins Green WA5 45 E1
Albert Terr. Southport PR8 4 A5
Albion Pl. L45 51 B8
Albion St. Birkenhead L41 66 F6
Albion St. Birkenhead L41 66 F7
Albion St. Liverpool L5 52 F6
Albion St. St Helens WA10 43 E4
Albion St. Wallasey L45 51 A8
Albourne Rd. L32 41 A8
Albury Cl. Haydock WA11 45 D7
Albury Cl. Liverpool L12 41 A2
Albury Rd. 4 L32 41 A7
Alcester Rd. L12 54 C6
Aldams Gr. L4 38 E1
Aldbourne Ave. L18 & L25 69 E5
Aldbourne Cl. L25 69 E4
Aldcliffe. WA3 47 F8
Alder Ave. Ashton-in-M WN4 34 F5
Alder Ave. Billinge WN5 33 D5
Alder Ave. Huyton-w-R L36 71 A8
Alder Ave. Widnes WA8 73 B3
Alder Cl. L34 & L35 56 F6
Alder Cres. L32 29 D3
Alder Gr. L22 26 D2
Alder Hey Children's Hosp. L14 54 C4
Alder Hey Rd. WA10 43 C4
Alder La. Burtonwood WA2 & WA5 60 C7
Alder La. Crank WA11 32 F4
Alder La. Cronton WA8 & L35 72 A5
Alder La. Formby L39 10 E7
Alder La. Knowsley L34 41 C2
Alder Rd. Bebington L63 78 E4
Alder Rd. Golborne WA3 47 F8
Alder Rd. Liverpool L12 & L13 & L14 54 C4
Alder Rd. Prescot L34 56 F6
Alder Root La. WA12 & WA2 & WA5 60 D7
Alder St. WA12 46 C3
Alder Wood Ave. L24 82 F3
Alderbank Rd. WA5 74 F6
Alderdale Ave. PR8 7 A5
Alderfield Dr. L24 83 A3
Alderley. WN8 24 C6
Alderley Ave. Birkenhead L41 65 F7
Alderley Ave. Golborne WA3 47 D7
Alderley Cl. WN5 33 E5
Alderley Rd. Hoylake L47 63 B7
Alderley Rd. Wallasey L44 51 B3
Aldersey St. L3 52 D3
Aldersgate. L42 66 F2
Aldersgate Dr. L26 83 A6
Alderson Cres. L37 9 F4
Alderson Rd. L15 68 D8
Alderville Rd. L4 39 C2
Alderwood Inf Sch. L24 82 F3
Alderwood Lodge. L24 83 A3
Aldford Cl. Bebington L63 88 B6
Aldford Cl. Birkenhead L43 65 E2
Aldford Rd. L32 40 E7
Aldridge Cl. 1 L12 40 E3
Aldridge Dr. WA5 59 F7
Aldrins La. L30 27 F5
Aldwark Rd. L14 55 A4
Aldwych Rd. L12 54 C5
Aldykes. L31 28 F8
Alexander Dr. Ditton WA8 84 D8
Alexander Dr. Heswall L61 76 E3
Alexander Dr. Maghull L31 20 D3
Alexander Fleming Ave. L30 27 F4
Alexander Gn. L36 55 E4
Alexander House. 7 L21 37 F7
Alexander Way. 5 L8 67 F4
Alexander Wlk. L4 52 F8
Alexandra Ct. Liverpool L6 53 B3
Alexandra Ct. 1 Wallasey L45 51 A8
Alexandra Dr. Birkenhead L42 66 E1
Alexandra Dr. Bootle L20 38 F6
Alexandra Dr. Liverpool L17 . 68 B4
Alexandra Dr. St Helens WA10 43 D2
Alexandra House. L17 68 B4
Alexandra Ind Est. WA8 84 F7
Alexandra Mews. 1 L39 13 E6
Alexandra Mount. L21 38 B8
Alexandra Pk. L17 68 B3
Alexandra Rd. Ashton-in-M WN4 35 B4
Alexandra Rd. Birkenhead L43 66 C5
Alexandra Rd. Bootle L22 37 E8
Alexandra Rd. Crosby L23 26 D4
Alexandra Rd. Formby L37 9 B1
Alexandra Rd. Liverpool L13 54 A2
Alexandra Rd. Liverpool L7 68 C8
Alexandra Rd. Southport PR9 4 D8
Alexandra Rd. Wallasey L45 51 A8
Alexandra Rd. West Kirby L48 63 A1
Alexandra St. Abram WN2 36 B8
Alexandra St. St Helens WA10 43 D1
Alexandra Terr. 9 L8 67 F7
Alexandra Villas. L21 38 B8
Alexandria Rd. L19 81 C7
Alfonso Rd. L4 52 D8
Alford Ave. WA9 58 B4
Alford St. L7 53 E2
Alfred Mews. 5 L1 67 E7
Alfred Rd. Birkenhead L43 66 C5
Alfred Rd. Haydock WA11 45 F7
Alfred Rd. Wallasey L44 51 E1
Alfred St. Liverpool L15 68 D8
Alfred St. Newton-le-W WA12 46 E3
Alfred St. Rainford WA11 31 F7
Alfred St. St Helens WA10 44 B4
Alfriston Rd. L12 54 C6
Algernon St. WA7 84 F3
Alice Elliott Sch. L16 69 E6
Alice St. WA9 58 E8
Alicia Wlk. L10 40 B7
Alison Ave. L42 66 F3
Alison Pl. L13 53 E7
Alison Rd. L13 53 E7
Alistair Dr. L63 88 C6
All Saints CE Jun Sch. WA8 72 B3
All Saints Cl. L30 27 E3
All Saints RC Inf Sch. L4 53 B6
All Saints RC Jun Sch. L6 53 C6
All Saints Rd. L24 82 C3
Allan Rd. WA11 44 C7
Allangate Cl. L49 64 C2
Allangate Rd. L19 81 B8
Allanson St. WA9 44 D3
Allanson Street Prim Sch. WA9 44 D2
Allcot Ave. L42 66 D2
Allenby Ave. L22 & L23 26 F2
Allenby Sq. L13 54 A2
Allendale Ave. Liverpool L9 39 B7
Allendale Ave. Rainhill L35 57 D3
Allengate. 1 L23 26 E5
Allerby Way. WA3 47 E8
Allerford Rd. L12 54 D8
Allerton Beeches. L18 69 C3
Allerton Dr. L18 69 B4
Allerton Gr. L42 66 E3
Allerton Park Golf Course. L25 69 E2
Allerton Priory Sch. L25 69 E1
Allerton Rd. Birkenhead L41 & L42 66 E3
Allerton Rd. Liverpool L18 69 A5
Allerton Rd. Liverpool L18 69 B5
Allerton Rd. Liverpool L18 & L25 69 D3
Allerton Rd. Liverpool L25 70 A2
Allerton Rd. Southport PR9 1 E1
Allerton Rd. Wallasey L45 51 A6
Allerton Rd. Widnes WA8 73 B1
Allerton Sta. L19 81 D6
Allesley Rd. L14 54 F5
Alleyne Rd. L4 53 D8
Allington St. L17 68 B3
Allonby Cl. L43 65 E4
Allport La. L62 88 D8
Allport Rd. L63 & L62 88 D7
Allports The. L62 88 D7
Allscott Way. WN4 35 C3
Alma Cl. Liverpool L10 40 B7
Alma Cl. Orrell WN8 25 C7
Alma Ct. Orrell WN8 25 C7
Alma Ct. Southport PR8 7 F7
Alma Hill. WN8 25 C7
Alma Par. WN8 25 C7
Alma Pl. WA9 44 C2
Alma Rd. Liverpool L17 80 E8
Alma Rd. Orrell WN8 25 C7
Alma Rd. Southport PR8 4 A4
Alma St. Bebington L62 79 A7
Alma St. 5 Birkenhead L41 . 66 E6
Alma St. Newton-le-W WA12 46 B3
Alma St. St Helens WA9 44 C2
Alma Vale Terr. L20 38 B3
Almacs Cl. L23 26 B3
Almeda Rd. L24 83 A2
Almond Ave. L30 27 C3
Almond Cl. Liverpool L26 82 E7
Almond Cl. St Helens WA11 . 44 F5
Almond Ct. L19 81 E5
Almond Dr. WA5 59 F6
Almond Pl. L46 64 F8
Almond Tree Cl. L24 83 E1
Almond Way. L49 64 C2
Almond's Gn. L11 & L12 54 A8
Almond's Gr. L12 54 A8
Almond's Turn. L30 27 D4
Almonds Pk. L12 54 A8
Almshouses. L39 21 A7
Alness Dr. L35 57 D2
Alnwick Dr. L46 64 C8
Alpass Rd. L17 68 B3
Alpha Dr. L42 67 A1
Alpha St. L20 & L21 38 B5
Alpine Cl. WA10 43 C4
Alpine St. WA12 46 A3
Alresford Rd. L19 80 F8
Alroy Rd. L4 53 A7
Alscot Ave. L10 40 B7
Alscot Cl. L31 28 D8
Alsop High Sch. L4 39 A2
Alston Cl. L62 79 C1
Alston Rd. L17 80 E8
Alstonfield Rd. L14 55 A4
Alt. WA8 72 B2
Alt Ave. L31 28 C7
Alt Rd. Bootle L20 38 C5
Alt Rd. Formby L37 10 B2
Alt Rd. Hightown L38 17 F4
Alt Rd. Huyton-w-R L36 55 E3
Alt St. L8 68 B7
Altbridge Pk. L11 40 B4
Altcar Ave. L15 68 D7
Altcar Dr. L46 64 D7
Altcar La. Formby L37 9 F1
Altcar La. Maghull L31 & L39 19 F5
Altcar Rd. Bootle L20 38 C5
Altcar Rd. Formby L37 10 B2
Altcross Rd. L11 40 C4
Altcross Way. L11 40 C4
Altfield Rd. L14 54 F7
Altfinch Cl. L14 55 A7
Altham Rd. Liverpool L11 53 F8
Altham Rd. Southport PR8 4 E2
Althorp St. L8 67 F3
Althorpe Dr. PR8 4 E3
Altmoor Rd. L36 55 D5
Alton Ave. L21 27 A1
Alton Cl. Ashton-in-M WN4 35 A4
Alton Cl. Hightown L38 17 F2
Alton Rd. Birkenhead L43 66 A5
Alton Rd. Liverpool L6 53 D5
Altview Hts. L11 40 C4
Altway. L10 28 D2
Altys La. L39 13 F3
Alundale Ct. 10 L20 38 C3
Alundale Rd. L14 54 E5
Alva Rd. L35 57 D2
Alvanley Pl. L43 66 C6
Alvanley Rd. Kirkby L32 29 C2
Alvanley Rd. Liverpool L12 54 C6
Alvega Cl. L62 79 C7
Alverstone Ave. L41 65 F7
Alverstone Rd. Liverpool L18 68 F5
Alverstone Rd. Wallasey L44 51 D3
Alverton Cl. WA8 84 D8
Alvina La. L4 52 E7
Alwain Gn. L24 82 F2
Alwen St. L41 50 F1
Alwyn Ave. L21 27 B1
Alwyn Gdns. L46 64 F8
Alwyn St. L17 68 B3
Amanda Rd. Liverpool L10 40 B7
Amanda Rd. Rainhill L35 57 B5
Amanda Way. L31 29 B4
Amaury Cl. L23 27 B5
Amaury Rd. L23 27 B5
Amber Way. L14 55 A7
Ambergate. WN8 24 B7
Ambergate Cl. 3 WA9 58 D7
Ambergate Rd. L19 81 B8
Amberley Ave. L46 64 C7
Amberley Cl. Birkenhead L46 64 C7
Amberley Cl. Liverpool L6 53 D7
Ambleside Ave. L46 64 D8
Ambleside Cl. Bebington L62 88 E7
Ambleside Cl. Heswall L61 77 A6
Ambleside Cres. WA2 61 C3
Ambleside Pl. WA11 33 B1
Ambleside Rd. Liverpool L18 69 D1
Ambleside Rd. Maghull L31 . 20 D2
Amelia Cl. Liverpool L6 52 F3
Amelia Cl. Widnes WA8 73 B4
Amersham. WN8 24 C7
Amersham Rd. L4 39 C2
Amery Gr. L42 66 C2
Amherst Rd. L17 68 C2
Amis Gr. WA3 47 E8
Amity St. L8 67 F5
Amos Ave. L21 38 C8
Ampleforth Cl. 3 L32 29 C1
Ampthill Rd. L17 68 D2
Ampulla Rd. L11 40 C3
Amy Wlk. L10 40 B7
Ancaster Rd. L17 68 D2
Anchor St. PR8 & PR9 4 B7
Anchorage La. L17 68 E3
Ancient Meadows. L9 39 B7
Ancroft Rd. L14 55 A3
Ancrum Rd. L33 29 D6
Anderson Ave. L20 38 A4
Anderson Cl. Heswall L61 77 A6
Anderson Cl. Rainhill L35 57 D1
Anderson Ct. L62 88 D6
Anderson Rd. L21 27 D1
Anderson St. L5 52 E6
Anderton Terr. L36 55 C2
Andover Cl. WA2 61 E1
Andover Way. L25 82 D8
Andreas Cl. PR8 4 B4
Andrew Ave. Billinge WN5 33 F5
Andrew Ave. Kirkby L31 29 B3
Andrew Carnegie Liby. L13 . 53 F4
Andrew Cl. WA8 84 C8
Andrew St. L4 38 F1
Andrew's Wlk. L60 86 B8
Andrews Cl. L37 9 E1
Andrews La. L37 9 E1
Andrews Yort. L37 9 E1
Anfield Community Sch. L4 53 B7
Anfield (Liverpool Football Club). L4 53 A7
Anfield Rd. L4 53 A7
Anfield Road Jun & Inf Schs. L4 53 B6
Angela St. L7 68 B8
Angers La. L31 29 B6
Anglesea Rd. L9 38 F3
Anglesea Way. L8 67 F4
Anglesey Rd. Wallasey L44 .. 51 B5
Anglesey Rd. West Kirby L48 63 A3
Anglezark Cl. L7 53 B2
Anglo Cl. L9 39 C8
Angus Rd. Bebington L63 88 C6
Angus Rd. Liverpool L11 53 F8
Ann St. WN8 23 E8
Annan Gr. WN4 35 E5
Annandale Cl. L33 29 D6
Annandale Gdns. WN8 25 A7
Anne Ave. PR8 7 E6
Anne Gr. WA9 58 C7
Anne St. WA9 58 D3
Annerley St. L7 68 C8
Annesley Rd. Liverpool L17 . 68 C1
Annesley Rd. Wallasey L44 . 51 C3
Annette Ave. WA12 46 A5
Annie Rd. L20 38 D6
Anscot Ave. L63 78 F6
Ansdell Dr. WA10 43 B5
Ansdell Gr. PR9 2 A4
Ansdell Rd. WA8 73 C2
Ansdell Villas' Rd. L35 57 C4
Anson Cl. WA2 61 E2
Anson Pl. L3 52 F2
Anson St. L3 52 F2
Anstey Cl. L46 49 B1
Anstey Rd. L13 54 B2
Ansty Cl. WA11 44 D6
Anthony's Way. L60 86 A7
Anthorn Cl. L43 65 D4
Antler Ct. WN4 35 B6
Antonio St. L20 38 E1
Antons Cl. L26 82 F6
Antons Rd. Heswall L61 77 A5
Antons Rd. Liverpool L26 82 F6
Antrim Cl. WA11 45 C6
Antrim Rd. WA2 61 A2
Antrim St. L13 53 E7
Anvil Cl. Bootle L20 38 B4
Anvil Cl. Orrell WN5 25 D5
Anzacs The. L62 79 C6
Anzio Rd. L36 55 D4
Apollo Cres. L33 29 E4
Apollo Way. Litherland L30 .. 27 F4
Apollo Way. Liverpool L6 53 B5
Apostles Way. L33 29 D5
Appin Rd. L41 66 E5
Apple Ct. 13 L6 53 B3
Apple Dell Ave. WA3 36 C1
Apple Tree Cl. Hale L24 83 E1
Apple Tree Cl. Huyton-w-R L28 55 B8
Appleby Cl. WA8 84 C8
Appleby Dr. L30 27 D3
Appleby Gn. L12 54 D6
Appleby Lawn. L27 71 A4
Appleby Rd. Hulme WA2 61 C3
Appleby Rd. Kirkby L33 29 E5
Appleby Rd. Liverpool L27 71 A4
Appleby Wlk. 5 Ditton WA8 84 C8
Appleby Wlk. Liverpool L27 . 71 A4
Applecorn Cl. WA9 58 D5
Appledore Cl. L24 82 B4
Appledore Ct. L24 82 B4
Appledore Gr. WA9 58 C5
Applegarth. L46 64 C6
Appleton Dr. L49 64 E3
Appleton Rd. Litherland L21 27 A1
Appleton Rd. Liverpool L4 39 A1
Appleton Rd. Skelmersdale WN8 15 F2
Appleton Rd. Widnes WA8 73 B1
Appleton St. WA9 44 C1
Appleton Village. WA8 73 B1
Appletree Cl. L18 69 C1
Appletree Gr. WA2 61 F2
April Gr. L6 53 D5
April Rise. L30 27 E3
Apsley Ave. L45 51 B6
Apsley Brow. L31 20 B1
Apsley Rd. Bebington L62 79 B8
Apsley Rd. Liverpool L12 54 C6
Aquarius Cl. L14 55 A4
Aragon Cl. L31 20 E3
Aran Cl. L24 83 D1
Arborn Dr. L49 65 A6
Arbour La. L32 & L33 30 B2
Arbour St. PR8 4 C6
Arbury Ave. WA11 44 D6
Arbury La. WA2 61 C6
Arcadia Ave. L31 20 D3
Arch Bishop Blanch High Sch. L7 53 A1
Arch La. WN4 34 B3
Archbishop Beck High Sch. L9 39 B4
Archbishop Beck High Sch. L9 39 B6
Archbishop Warlock Ct. L3 . 52 C4
Archer Cl. L4 52 E7
Archer Gr. WA9 44 E4
Archer St. L4 52 E7
Archerfield Rd. L18 69 B1
Archers Way. L49 65 A2
Archway Rd. L36 55 E2
Arctic Rd. L20 38 A3
Arden. WA8 72 A2
Arden Cl. PR8 7 A5
Ardennes Rd. L36 55 E3
Arderne Cl. L63 79 B2
Ardleigh Ave. PR8 4 E3
Ardleigh Cl. L13 53 F2
Ardleigh Gr. L13 53 F2
Ardleigh Pl. L13 53 F2
Ardleigh Rd. L13 53 F2
Ardmore Rd. L18 69 A2
Ardrossan Rd. L4 53 C8
Ardville Rd. L11 39 D3
Ardwick Rd. L24 82 F3
Ardwick St. WA9 44 C3
Argameols Cl. PR8 4 F5
Argarmeols Gr. L37 9 E5
Argarmeols Rd. L37 9 E6
Argo Rd. L22 26 D1
Argos Pl. L20 38 D1
Argos Rd. L20 38 D1
Argyle Ct. PR9 1 D1
Argyle Rd. Liverpool L4 53 B6
Argyle Rd. Liverpool L19 81 C6
Argyle Rd. Southport PR9 1 D2
Argyle St. Birkenhead L41 66 E5
Argyle St. Birkenhead L41 66 E6
Argyle St. Liverpool L1 & L72 67 D8
Argyle St. St Helens WA10 ... 43 F5
Argyle Street Hamilton Sq. L41 & L72 66 E7
Argyll Ave. L62 88 D4
Argyll Cl. WN4 34 C4
Ariel Wlk. WA3 47 E8
Arkenstone Cl. WA8 72 C2
Arkle Rd. L41 & L43 65 F8
Arkles La. L4 53 B7
Arkles Rd. L4 53 A6
Arklow Dr. L24 83 D2
Arkwood Cl. L62 79 C3
Arlescourt Rd. L12 54 D6
Arley Cl. L43 65 C6
Arley Dr. WA8 72 B2
Arley St. L3 52 C4
Arlington Ave. 10 L18 68 F5
Arlington Cl. PR8 7 A5
Arlington Ct. L43 65 F5
Arlington Dr. WA5 74 E4
Arlington Rd. L45 50 E6
Armill Rd. L11 40 C3
Armitage Gdns. L18 69 B1
Armley Rd. L4 53 B7

Armour Ave. WA2 ... 61 B2
Armour Gr. L13 ... 54 A2
Armoury Bank. WN4 ... 35 B3
Armoury The. L12 ... 54 B7
Armscot Cl. L25 ... 82 B7
Armscot Pl. L25 ... 82 B7
Arncliffe Dr. WA5 ... 59 F6
Arncliffe Rd. L25 ... 82 D8
Arnhem Rd. L36 ... 55 E3
Arnian Ct. L39 ... 21 C7
Arnian Rd. WA11 ... 31 F7
Arnian Way. WA11 ... 31 F7
Arno Ct. L43 ... 66 B3
Arno Rd. L42 & L43 ... 66 B3
Arnold Ave. WA10 ... 43 D5
Arnold Cl. 1 L8 ... 68 A6
Arnold Gr. L15 ... 69 A8
Arnold Pl. WA8 ... 84 C7
Arnold St. Liverpool L8 ... 67 F6
Arnold St. Wallasey L45 ... 51 B5
Arnot Cl. WA10 ... 43 F5
Arnot Cty Prim Jun & Inf Sch. L4 ... 38 F1
Arnot St. L4 ... 38 F1
Arnot Way. L63 ... 78 D7
Arnside. L21 ... 38 D8
Arnside Ave. Haydock WA11 45 B6
Arnside Ave. Rainhill L35 ... 57 A4
Arnside Rd. Birkenhead L43 . 66 A4
Arnside Rd. Huyton-w-R L36 55 B2
Arnside Rd. Liverpool L7 ... 53 C1
Arnside Rd. Southport PR9 ... 4 C7
Arnside Rd. Wallasey L45 ... 51 B5
Arnside Terr. PR9 ... 4 C7
Arrad St. L1 & L7 ... 67 F8
Arran Cl. WA11 ... 44 E6
Arranmore Rd. L18 ... 69 A2
Arrowe Ave. L46 ... 64 D7
Arrowe Brook Ct. L49 ... 64 E4
Arrowe Brook La. L49 ... 64 E1
Arrowe Brook Rd. L49 ... 64 F3
Arrowe Hill Prim Sch. L49 ... 65 A3
Arrowe Park Hospl. L49 ... 65 A2
Arrowe Park Rd. L49 & L61 .. 65 A2
Arrowe Rd. L49 ... 64 E3
Arrowe Side. L49 ... 64 E4
Arrowsmith Rd. WA11 ... 45 F7
Arthur St. Birkenhead L41 ... 66 C7
Arthur St. Birkenhead L41 ... 66 C8
Arthur St. Liverpool L19 ... 81 D5
Arthur St. Runcorn WA7 ... 84 F2
Arundel Ave. Liverpool L15 & L8 ... 68 D6
Arundel Ave. Wallasey L45 .. 50 F6
Arundel Cl. L61 ... 76 E5
Arundel Comp Sch. L18 ... 68 F5
Arundel Rd. PR8 ... 7 F8
Arundel St. Bootle L4 ... 38 F1
Arundel St. Liverpool L8 ... 68 A6
Arvon St. L20 ... 38 D6
Asbridge St. L8 ... 68 B7
Asbury Cl. L18 ... 69 D3
Asbury Rd. L45 ... 50 D6
Ascot Ave. L21 ... 38 A8
Ascot Cl. PR8 ... 3 E5
Ascot Dr. Bebington L63 ... 78 F5
Ascot Dr. Kirkby L33 ... 29 E5
Ascot Gr. L63 ... 78 F5
Ascot Pk. L23 ... 26 F4
Ascroft Rd. L9 ... 39 B8
Ash Ave. WA12 ... 46 C2
Ash Cl. Liverpool L15 ... 68 E8
Ash Cl. Ormskirk L39 ... 13 D5
Ash Cres. L36 ... 70 E8
Ash Gr. Bootle L21 ... 38 A6
Ash Gr. Formby L37 ... 9 C1
Ash Gr. Liverpool L15 ... 68 D8
Ash Gr. Orrell WN5 ... 25 F6
Ash Gr. Prescot L35 ... 56 E5
Ash Gr. Rainford WA11 ... 31 F6
Ash Gr. Skelmersdale WN8 ... 15 D1
Ash Gr. St Helens WA9 ... 58 C4
Ash Gr. Wallasey L45 ... 51 C7
Ash Grange. L14 ... 54 D3
Ash Grove Cres. WN5 ... 33 E6
Ash La. WA8 ... 84 A8
Ash Priors. WA8 ... 72 D3
Ash Rd. Bebington L63 ... 78 F7
Ash Rd. Birkenhead L42 ... 66 D4
Ash Rd. Bootle L21 ... 38 A7
Ash Rd. Haydock WA11 ... 45 E7
Ash Rd. Warrington WA5 ... 74 F4
Ash Rd. Winwick WA2 ... 61 B6
Ash St. Bootle L20 ... 38 C4
Ash St. Golborne WA3 ... 36 B2
Ash St. Southport PR8 ... 4 C5
Ash Tree Apartments. L44 .. 51 D3
Ash Vale. L15 ... 68 E8
Ash Villas. L44 ... 51 C2
Ash Way. L60 ... 86 B6
Ashbank Rd. L11 ... 40 B2
Ashbourne Ave. Crosby L23 26 C4
Ashbourne Ave. Litherland L30 ... 27 E2
Ashbourne Cres. L36 ... 55 B3
Ashbourne Rd. L17 ... 68 C2
Ashbrook Terr. L42 ... 79 A6
Ashburton Ave. L43 ... 65 F6
Ashburton Rd. Birkenhead L43 ... 65 F6
Ashburton Rd. Wallasey L44 51 B4
Ashburton Rd. West Kirby L48 ... 63 B2
Ashbury Dr. WA11 ... 45 D7
Ashbury Rd. L14 ... 55 B6
Ashby Cl. L46 ... 49 B1
Ashcombe Rd. L14 ... 54 C3
Ashcroft Ave. L39 ... 13 F6
Ashcroft Dr. L61 ... 76 F3
Ashcroft Rd. Formby L37 ... 9 F1
Ashcroft Rd. Kirkby L33 ... 30 C3
Ashcroft St. Bootle L20 ... 38 B3
Ashcroft St. St Helens WA9 . 44 C3
Ashdale. L36 ... 55 D2
Ashdale Cl. L37 ... 9 C2
Ashdale Pk. L49 ... 64 B4
Ashdale Rd. Crosby L22 ... 26 D2
Ashdale Rd. Liverpool L9 ... 39 A4
Ashdale Rd. Liverpool L18 ... 69 A5
Ashdown Cl. PR8 ... 4 E4
Ashdown Cres. WA9 ... 58 C4
Ashdown Dr. L49 ... 64 C2
Ashfarm Ct. L14 ... 54 F3
Ashfield. Liverpool L15 ... 68 D8
Ashfield. Rainhill L35 ... 57 D3
Ashfield Cres. Bebington L62 88 D8
Ashfield Cres. Billinge WN5 . 33 E4
Ashfield Rd. Bebington L62 .. 88 C8
Ashfield Rd. Liverpool L17 ... 68 E2
Ashfield Sch. L14 ... 54 D3
Ashfield St. L5 ... 52 C5
Ashford Cl. L26 ... 82 E7
Ashford Rd. Birkenhead L41 & L42 ... 66 C4
Ashford Rd. Hoylake L47 ... 63 C8
Ashford Way. WA8 ... 73 D1
Ashland Ave. WN4 ... 35 A4
Ashlar Gr. L17 ... 68 E3
Ashlar Rd. Crosby L22 ... 26 E2
Ashlar Rd. Liverpool L17 ... 68 E3
Ashlea Rd. L61 ... 77 A3
Ashleigh Rd. L31 ... 28 F7
Ashley Ave. L47 ... 48 F1
Ashley Cl. Kirkby L33 ... 29 E5
Ashley Cl. Rainhill L35 ... 57 D2
Ashley Rd. Skelmersdale WN8 ... 16 B3
Ashley Rd. Southport PR9 ... 4 C7
Ashley Sch. WA8 ... 72 D1
Ashley St. L42 ... 66 F2
Ashley Way W. WA8 ... 84 F7
Ashmead Rd. WN8 ... 16 A4
Ashmuir Hey. L32 ... 29 F1
Ashover Ave. L14 & L36 ... 55 A4
Ashridge St. WA7 ... 84 F3
Ashton Ave. L35 ... 57 C2
Ashton Cl. L62 ... 88 E3
Ashton Ct. L48 ... 63 A2
Ashton Dr. Liverpool L25 ... 82 C7
Ashton Dr. West Kirby L48 ... 63 A1
Ashton Heath. WN4 ... 35 D2
Ashton House Hospl. L43 ... 66 B4
Ashton Pk. L25 ... 82 D8
Ashton Rd. Golborne WA3 ... 36 A2
Ashton Rd. Newton-le-W WA12 ... 46 C5
Ashton Rd. Southport PR8 ... 3 F1
Ashton Rd. Windy Arbour WN4 &WN5 .. 34 B8
Ashton Sq. L25 ... 70 B1
Ashton St. Liverpool L3 ... 52 F1
Ashton St. Liverpool L13 ... 54 A3
Ashton's Green Sch. WA9 ... 45 A3
Ashton's La. L24 ... 82 F1
Ashtons Green Dr. WA9 ... 44 F3
Ashtree Ct. L14 ... 54 F3
Ashtree Gr. L12 ... 40 F4
Ashurst Cl. Liverpool L25 ... 70 B4
Ashurst Cl. St Helens WA11 . 44 E6
Ashurst Ct. L37 ... 9 E2
Ashurst Dr. WA11 ... 44 E6
Ashurst Gdns. WN8 ... 16 B4
Ashurst Prim Sch. WA11 ... 44 D6
Ashurst Rd. WN8 ... 16 B4
Ashurst Sch. WN8 ... 15 D1
Ashville Rd. Birkenhead L41 & L43 ... 66 B7
Ashville Rd. Wallasey L44 ... 51 D2
Ashwall St. WN8 ... 23 E8
Ashwater Rd. L11 & L12 ... 40 C2
Ashwell Ave. WA3 ... 36 D1
Ashwell St. L69 & L8 ... 67 E7
Ashwood. WN8 ... 16 C3
Ashwood Ave. Abram Brow WN2 ... 36 C7
Ashwood Ave. Ashton-in-M WN4 ... 35 A2
Ashwood Ave. Golborne WA3 ... 47 D8
Ashwood Cl. Kirkby L33 ... 29 E5
Ashwood Cl. Liverpool L27 ... 70 E5
Ashwood Ct. L43 ... 50 C1
Ashwood Dr. L12 ... 40 D3
Ashworth Hospl. L31 ... 21 B2
Askern Rd. L32 ... 40 F8
Askew Cl. L44 ... 51 D4
Askew St. 2 L4 ... 38 F1
Askham Cl. L8 ... 68 B7
Asland Gdns. PR9 ... 2 C4
Asmall Cl. L39 ... 13 D6
Asmall Cty Prim Sch. L39 ... 13 D6
Asmall La. L39 & L40 ... 13 B7
Aspen Cl. Heswall L60 ... 86 D8
Aspen Cl. Kirkby L33 ... 29 F6
Aspen Gr. Formby L37 ... 9 C1
Aspen Gr. Liverpool L8 ... 68 C6
Aspendale Rd. L42 ... 66 D4
Aspenwood. WN4 ... 35 A2
Aspes Rd. L12 ... 54 E7
Aspinal St. L34 ... 56 D6
Aspinall Cres. L37 ... 10 F1
Aspinall St. Birkenhead L41 . 66 C7
Asquith Ave. L41 ... 66 B7
Asser Rd. L11 & L13 ... 53 F8
Assheton Wlk. L24 ... 83 E2
Assissian Cres. L30 ... 27 E4
Aster Rd. WA11 ... 45 F7
Asterfield Ave. L63 ... 78 E7
Astley Cl. Rainford WA11 ... 31 F7
Astley Cl. Widnes WA8 ... 72 C3
Astley Rd. L36 ... 55 E5
Aston Cl. L43 ... 65 F3
Aston St. L19 ... 81 D5
Astonwood Rd. L42 ... 66 D3
Astor St. L4 ... 38 F2
Atheldene Rd. L4 ... 39 C1
Athelstan Cl. L62 ... 79 D1
Atherton Cl. L5 ... 52 E5
Atherton Dr. L49 ... 65 A3
Atherton Rake. L30 ... 27 D4
Atherton Rd. L9 ... 39 C6
Atherton St. Bickershaw WN2 ... 36 E8
Atherton St. 8 Prescot L34 56 D6
Atherton St. St Helens WA10 43 F4
Atherton St. Wallasey L45 ... 51 B8
Athlone Rd. WA2 ... 61 A1
Athol Cl. Bebington L62 ... 88 E5
Athol Cl. Newton-le-W WA12 45 F4
Athol Dr. L62 ... 88 E5
Athol St. Birkenhead L41 & L72 ... 66 E7
Athol St. Liverpool L5 ... 52 B5
Athol St. Liverpool L5 ... 52 C5
Athol St. Liverpool L5 ... 52 D5
Athole Gr. PR9 ... 4 F7
Atholl Cres. L10 ... 28 D2
Atkinson Art Gal. PR8 ... 4 B7
Atkinson Liby. PR8 ... 4 B7
Atkinson St. WN2 ... 36 B8
Atlantic Rd. L20 ... 38 B3
Atlantic Way. Bootle L30 ... 38 E8
Atlantic Way. Liverpool L3 ... 67 D4
Atlas Bsns Complex. L20 ... 38 A4
Atlas Ct. WA9 ... 44 B3
Atlas Rd. L20 ... 38 B4
Atlas St. WA9 ... 44 B4
Atterbury Cl. WA8 ... 72 C2
Atterbury St. L8 ... 67 E5
Attlee Rd. L36 ... 56 A3
Attwood St. 15 L4 ... 52 F7
Atwell St. L6 ... 53 A4
Aubourn Cl. WA8 ... 72 C3
Aubrey Ct. 16 L6 ... 53 A4
Auburn Rd. Liverpool L13 ... 53 E6
Auburn Rd. Wallasey L45 ... 51 A7
Aubynes The. L45 ... 50 E7
Audlem Ave. L43 ... 65 F3
Audley St. L3 ... 52 E2
Audre Cl. WA5 ... 74 D6
Audrey Wlk. L10 ... 40 B7
Aughton Cl. WN5 ... 33 E4
Aughton Hall Cotts. L39 ... 13 C6
Aughton Mews. PR8 ... 4 A5
Aughton Park Dr. L39 ... 13 D2
Aughton Rd. Bootle L20 ... 38 D5
Aughton Rd. Southport PR8 ... 4 A5
Aughton St. L39 ... 13 E4
Aughton St Michael's CE Prim Sch. L39 ... 13 B1
Aughton Town Green Cty Prim Sch. L39 ... 21 C8
August Rd. L6 ... 53 D5
August St. L20 ... 38 C5
Augusta Cl. L13 ... 54 A2
Aukland Gr. L35 ... 57 D6
Aukland Rd. L15 & L18 ... 69 A5
Austell Cl. WA11 ... 44 D7
Austin Ave. Downall Green WN4 ... 34 E4
Austin Ave. Grange Park L35 & WA10 ... 57 C8
Austin Rowlinson Sports Ctr. L24 ... 82 E3
Austin St. L44 ... 51 A2
Autumn Gr. L42 ... 78 E8
Autumn Way. WA9 ... 58 C3
Avalon Prep Sch. L48 ... 75 C8
Avebury Cl. Barrow's Green WA8 ... 73 F3
Avebury Cl. Golborne WA3 ... 47 E8
Avelon Cl. Birkenhead L43 ... 65 D5
Avelon Cl. Maghull L31 ... 20 B5
Avenue The. Banks PR9 ... 2 F5
Avenue The. Bebington L62 . 88 C8
Avenue The. Huyton-w-R L36 55 E3
Avenue The. Liverpool L19 ... 81 E5
Avenue The. Liverpool L26 ... 82 E7
Avenue The. Newton-le-W WA12 ... 46 D4
Avenue The. Ormskirk L39 ... 13 D6
Avenue The. Ormskirk L39 ... 13 E6
Avenue The. Orrell WN5 ... 25 D3
Avenue The. Rainford WA11 31 F6
Avenue The. Southport PR8 ... 5 F5
Avenue The. St Helens WA10 ... 43 B3
Averham Cl. WN4 ... 35 B2
Avery Cl. WA2 ... 61 E2
Avery Cres. WA11 ... 45 C7
Avery Rd. WA11 ... 45 C7
Avery Sq. WA11 ... 45 C7
Aviary Ct. L9 ... 38 F6
Aviemore Cl. WN4 ... 34 D4
Aviemore Rd. L13 ... 53 F3
Avis Wlk. L10 ... 40 B7
Avocet Cl. Hulme WA2 ... 61 D3
Avocet Cl. Newton-le-W WA12 ... 46 C4
Avolon Rd. L12 ... 54 D5
Avon. WA8 ... 72 A2
Avon Ave. WA5 ... 74 F4
Avon Cl. Kirkby L33 ... 29 F6
Avon Cl. Liverpool L4 ... 52 E8
Avon Ct. L23 ... 26 E5
Avon Rd. Ashton-in-M WN4 .. 35 E5
Avon Rd. Billinge WN5 ... 33 D3
Avon St. Birkenhead L41 ... 50 F1
Avon St. 3 Liverpool L6 ... 53 B5
Avondale Ave. Bebington L62 88 F5
Avondale Ave. Maghull L31 .. 28 C8
Avondale Ave. Wallasey L46 49 F1
Avondale Dr. WA8 ... 72 B1
Avondale Rd. Haydock WA11 45 C7
Avondale Rd. Hoylake L47 ... 63 B8
Avondale Rd. Liverpool L15 . 68 E6
Avondale Rd. Southport PR8 & PR9 ... 4 B8
Avondale Rd N. PR9 ... 1 C1
Avonmore Ave. L18 ... 69 A3
Awelon Cl. L12 ... 54 C8
Axbridge Ave. WA9 ... 58 D5
Axholme Cl. L61 ... 77 B5
Axholme Rd. L61 ... 77 A5
Ayala Cl. L9 ... 38 F7
Aycliffe Rd. L35 ... 57 D6
Aycliffe Wlk. 6 WA8 ... 84 C8
Aye Bridge Rd. WA3 ... 36 B5
Aylesbury Ave. L43 ... 65 E2
Aylesbury Rd. L45 ... 51 C7
Aylesford Rd. L13 ... 54 B3
Aylsham Cl. WA8 ... 72 C4
Aylsham Dr. L49 ... 65 A7
Aylton Rd. L36 ... 55 B4
Aylward Pl. L20 ... 38 B4
Ayr Cl. PR8 ... 4 F4
Ayrshire Gdns. WA10 ... 43 E2
Ayrshire Rd. L4 ... 53 C8
Aysgarth Ave. L12 ... 54 C6
Aysgarth Rd. L45 ... 50 F6
Azalea Gr. L26 ... 70 D2

Babbacombe Rd. Liverpool L16 ... 69 E6
Babbacombe Rd. Warrington WA5 ... 74 E4
Back Barlow La. L4 ... 52 E8
Back Bath St. PR8 ... 4 B8
Back Beau St. 8 L3 & L5 ... 52 E4
Back Bedford St. 2 L7 ... 67 F8
Back Belmont Rd. L6 ... 53 B5
Back Berry St. L1 ... 67 E8
Back Blackfield Terr. L4 & L5 ... 52 D7
Back Bold St. L1 ... 52 D1
Back Booth St. WA12 ... 46 A3
Back Boundary St. L5 ... 52 D6
Back Bridge St. WA12 ... 46 B3
Back Bridport St. L3 ... 52 E2
Back Brow. WN8 ... 25 C7
Back Canning St. L1 & L8 ... 67 F8
Back Catharine St. 9 L8 ... 67 F8
Back Chadwick Mount. L5 ... 52 E7
Back Chatham Pl. L7 ... 53 B1
Back Colquitt St. L1 ... 67 E8
Back Commutation Row. 2 L3 ... 52 E2
Back Egerton St N. 4 L8 ... 67 F7
Back Egerton St S. 5 L8 ... 67 F7
Back Falkner St S. L7 ... 68 A8
Back Forest Rd. PR8 ... 4 D6
Back Gibson St. 11 L8 ... 67 F7
Back Gillmoss La. L10 & L11 40 C6
Back Granton Rd. 5 L5 ... 53 A6
Back Guilford St. L6 ... 52 F3
Back Holland Pl. 3 L7 ... 53 B1
Back Hope Pl. L1 ... 67 E8
Back Huskisson St. 3 L8 ... 67 F7
Back Kelvin Gr. L8 ... 68 A6
Back Knight St. L1 ... 67 E8
Back La. Burtonwood WA5 ... 59 D7
Back La. Crank WA11 ... 32 F5
Back La. Cuerdley Cross WA5 74 A3
Back La. Haskayne L39 ... 11 D3
Back La. Holt Green L39 ... 20 E6
Back La. Little Crosby L23 ... 26 F8
Back La. Lunt L29 ... 27 C7
Back La. Royal Oak L39 ... 22 B2
Back La. Skelmersdale WN8 . 24 D6
Back La. Skelmersdale WN8 . 24 E7
Back Langham St. L4 ... 52 F8
Back Lawrence St. WA12 ... 46 A3
Back Leeds St. L3 ... 52 B2
Back Legh St. WA12 ... 46 A3
Back Lime St. L1 ... 52 D1
Back Little Canning St. 2 L8 ... 67 F7
Back Lord St. 26 L1 ... 52 D1
Back Luton Gr. L4 ... 52 F8
Back Market St. WA12 ... 46 A3
Back Maryland St. L1 & L69 . 67 E8
Back Menai St. L41 & L43 ... 66 C6
Back Mersey View. L22 ... 26 C2
Back Mount St. L22 ... 26 D1
Back Mount Vernon Gn. 8 L7 ... 53 A1
Back Mulberry St. L8 ... 67 F8
Back O The Town La. L38 ... 18 E3
Back Oliver St. 9 L41 ... 66 E6
Back Orford St. L15 ... 68 F8
Back Percy St. L8 ... 67 F7
Back Pickop St. 18 L3 ... 52 C2
Back Rathbone St. WA12 ... 46 A3
Back Renshaw St. 2 L1 ... 52 E1
Back Rockfield Rd. L4 ... 53 A7
Back Sandown La. 2 L15 ... 68 F8
Back Sandstone Rd. L13 ... 53 F4
Back School La. Orrell WN8 25 C7
Back School La. Skelmersdale WN8 ... 15 D2
Back Sea View. L47 ... 63 B7
Back Seel St. L1 & L72 ... 67 D8
Back Sir Howard St. L7 & L8 67 F8
Back South Rd. L22 ... 26 E1
Back St Bride St. 11 L8 ... 67 F8
Back Stanley Rd. L20 ... 38 C3
Back Towerlands St. 1 L7 . 53 B1
Back Virginia St. PR8 ... 4 B6
Back Wellesley Rd. L8 ... 68 A4
Back Westminster Rd. 3 L4 52 E8
Back Windsor View. 5 L8 .. 68 B7
Back Winstanley Rd. L22 ... 26 E2
Back York Terr. L5 ... 52 E6
Backford Cl. L43 ... 65 F3
Backford Rd. L61 ... 76 D5
Backford Way. L43 ... 65 F3
Badby Wood. L33 ... 29 F4
Baden House. L13 ... 54 B2
Baden Rd. L13 ... 54 B3
Bader Cl. L61 ... 76 E3
Badger Way. L43 ... 77 E8
Badger's Set. L48 ... 75 D6
Badgers Rake. L37 ... 9 C5
Badminton St. L8 ... 67 F3
Baffin Cl. L46 ... 50 A4
Bagnall St. 1 L4 ... 53 A7
Bagot Rd. L15 ... 68 D7
Baguley Ave. WA8 ... 84 A5
Bahama Cl. WA11 ... 45 D8
Bahama Rd. WA11 ... 45 D8
Bailey Dr. L20 ... 38 E7
Bailey St. L1 ... 67 E8

Bailey's La. Hale Heath L24 .. 83 A1
Bailey's La.
Halewood Village L26 .... 83 A7
Baileys Cl. WA8 .... 73 A5
Bainbridge Ave. WA3 .... 47 F8
Bainton Cl. L32 .... 41 A7
Bainton Rd. L32 .... 41 A7
Baird Ave. L20 .... 38 A4
Baker St. Liverpool L6 .... 53 A3
Baker St. St Helens WA9 .... 44 C3
Baker Way. L6 .... 53 A3
Baker's La. PR9 .... 2 A3
Bakers Green Rd. L36 .... 55 E4
Bakewell Gr. L9 .... 39 B7
Bakewell Rd. WA5 .... 60 A7
Bala Cl. WA5 .... 60 E2
Bala Gr. L44 .... 51 A3
Bala St. L4 .... 53 B6
Balcarres Ave. L18 .... 68 F5
Baldwin Ave. L16 .... 69 F8
Baldwin St. WA10 .... 44 A4
Bales The. L30 .... 28 A4
Balfe St. L21 .... 38 A6
Balfour Ave. L20 .... 38 B5
Balfour Rd. Birkenhead L43 .. 66 B5
Balfour Rd. Bootle L20 .... 38 B5
Balfour Rd. Southport PR8 .... 4 E5
Balfour Rd.
Wallasey L41 & L44 .... 51 A2
Balfour St. 10 Liverpool L4 ... 52 F7
Balfour St. Runcorn WA7 .... 84 F1
Balfour St. St Helens WA10 .. 43 D3
Balham Cl. WA8 .... 73 A4
Balker Dr. WA10 .... 43 F5
Ball Ave. L45 .... 51 A8
Ball St. WA9 .... 44 D4
Ball's Pl. PR8 .... 4 B7
Ball's Rd. L41 & L43 .... 66 B5
Ball's Rd E. L41 .... 66 C5
Ballantrae Rd. L18 .... 69 C3
Ballantyne Dr. L43 .... 50 C1
Ballantyne Gr. Bootle L20 .... 38 E6
Ballantyne Gr. Liverpool L13 53 F7
Ballantyne Pl. L13 .... 53 E6
Ballantyne Rd. L13 .... 53 F7
Ballard Rd. L48 .... 63 E3
Ballater Dr. WA2 .... 61 E4
Balliol Cl. L43 .... 50 C1
Balliol Gr. L22 & L23 .... 26 B2
Balliol Rd. L20 .... 38 C2
Balliol Rd E. L20 .... 38 D2
Balliol Way. WN4 .... 34 F4
Balm St. L7 .... 53 B2
Balmer St. WA9 .... 57 D8
Balmoral Ave. Crosby L23 .... 26 E3
Balmoral Ave.
Golborne WA3 .... 36 D1
Balmoral Ave.
St Helens WA9 .... 58 C7
Balmoral Cl. L33 .... 29 E5
Balmoral Ct. L13 .... 53 E5
Balmoral Dr. Formby L37 .... 9 E1
Balmoral Dr. Southport PR9 ... 2 B3
Balmoral Gdns. 6 L43 .... 65 F1
Balmoral Rd.
Ashton-in-M WN4 .... 35 A4
Balmoral Rd. Bootle L45 .... 37 C1
Balmoral Rd. 6 Liverpool L9 39 A6
Balmoral Rd.
Liverpool L6 & L7 .... 53 D3
Balmoral Rd. Maghull L31 .... 20 C1
Balmoral Rd. Widnes WA8 ... 73 A4
Balniel St. WA9 .... 58 E3
Balsham Cl. L25 .... 82 D7
Baltic Rd. L20 .... 38 B3
Baltic St. 2 L4 .... 53 A7
Baltimore St. 5 L1 .... 67 E8
Bamber Gdns. PR9 .... 5 A8
Bamburgh Pl. 3 WN4 .... 35 A5
Bampton Ave. WA11 .... 33 B1
Bampton Rd. L16 .... 69 D8
Banastre Dr. WA12 .... 46 F3
Banastre Rd. PR8 .... 4 B5
Banbury Ave. L25 .... 70 C2
Banbury Rd. WN5 .... 25 D2
Banbury Way. L43 .... 65 E2
Bancroft Cl. L25 .... 82 C8
Bancroft Rd. WA8 .... 73 D2
Bandon Cl. L24 .... 83 D2
Banff Ave. L63 .... 88 D5
Bangor Rd. L45 .... 50 D6
Bangor St. L5 .... 52 C5
Bank Ave. WN5 .... 25 D5
Bank Dene. L63 .... 79 A8
Bank Gdns. WA5 .... 74 E4
Bank La. L31 & L33 .... 29 D5
Bank Pas. Golborne WA3 .... 36 A1
Bank Pas. Southport PR8 .... 4 A7
Bank Rd. L20 .... 38 B3
Bank Sq. PR8 .... 4 B8
Bank St. 4 Birkenhead L41 . 66 E6
Bank St. Golborne WA3 .... 36 A1
Bank St. Newton-le-W WA12 45 F3
Bank St. St Helens WA10 .... 43 E3
Bank's La.
Liverpool L19 & L24 .... 81 D4
Bank's La. Liverpool L24 .... 81 F2
Bank's Rd.
Liverpool L19 & L24 .... 81 D4
Bank's Rd. Liverpool L19 .... 81 E5
Bank's Road Prim Sch. L19 . 81 D4
Bank's Way. L19 & L24 .... 81 D4
Bankburn Rd. L13 .... 53 E6
Bankfield. WN8 .... 24 C7
Bankfield Ct. L13 .... 53 F5
Bankfield La. PR9 .... 2 B2
Bankfield Rd. Liverpool L13 .. 53 F5
Bankfield Rd. Widnes WA8 .. 72 C1
Bankfield Sch The. WA8 .... 72 D1
Bankfield St. L20 .... 52 B8
Bankfields Dr. L62 .... 89 B5
Bankhall La. L20 & L5 .... 52 C7
Bankhall St. L20 .... 52 C8
Bankhall Sta. L20 .... 52 C8
Bankland Rd. L13 .... 53 F5
Banks Ave. L47 .... 63 D8
Banks Rd. Fiddler's Ferry PR9 2 D6
Banks Rd. Heswall L60 .... 85 D8
Banks Rd. West Kirby L48 .... 63 A1
Banks The. L45 .... 50 E7
Banksbarn. WN8 .... 24 C7
Bankside. L38 .... 17 F3
Bankside Ave. WN4 .... 35 A8
Bankside Rd. L63 & L42 .... 78 F8
Bankville Rd. L42 .... 66 E3
Banner Hey. L35 .... 56 D1
Banner St. Liverpool L15 .... 68 E7
Banner St. St Helens WA10 .. 43 F3
Banner Wlk. 3 WA10 .... 43 F3
Bannerman St. L7 .... 68 D8
Banning Cl. L41 .... 66 D7
Banstead Gr. L15 .... 69 B7
Barbara Ave. L10 .... 40 B7
Barbara St. WA9 .... 58 E3
Barber St. WA9 .... 44 C4
Barberry Cl. L46 .... 64 B8
Barbondale Cl. WA5 .... 74 F7
Barbour Dr. L20 .... 38 E6
Barbrook Way. L9 .... 39 B3
Barchester Dr. L17 .... 68 C1
Barclay St. L8 .... 67 F4
Barcombe Rd. L60 .... 77 D1
Bardale Gr. WN4 .... 35 A3
Bardley Cres. L36 .... 71 A7
Bardney Ave. WA3 .... 35 F2
Bardon Cl. L25 .... 70 C5
Bardsay Rd. L4 .... 39 A1
Bardsley Ave. WA5 .... 60 F1
Bardsley Cl. WN8 .... 25 A7
Barford Cl. Birkenhead L43 .. 65 B6
Barford Cl.
Skelmersdale WN8 .... 25 A7
Barford Cl. Southport PR8 .... 7 A6
Barford Cl. Warrington WA5 60 B1
Barford Grange. L64 .... 88 C1
Barford Rd. Huyton-w-R L36 . 55 F5
Barford Rd.
Liverpool L24 & L25 .... 82 B6
Bark Rd. L21 .... 27 C1
Barkbeth Rd. L36 .... 55 C5
Barkeley Dr. L21 .... 37 F6
Barker Cl. L36 .... 70 F8
Barker La. L49 .... 64 D2
Barker Rd. L61 .... 76 F6
Barker Way. L6 .... 53 B5
Barkerville Cl. L13 .... 53 D7
Barkfield Ave. L37 .... 9 E4
Barkfield La. L37 .... 9 D4
Barkhill Rd. L17 & L18 & L19 68 F1
Barkiss Cl. L8 .... 67 F5
Barleyfield. L61 .... 76 E4
Barlow Ave. L63 .... 79 A6
Barlow Gr. WA9 .... 45 A2
Barlow La. L4 .... 52 E8
Barlow St. L4 .... 52 E8
Barlow's Jun & Mix Inf Sch.
L9 .... 39 D7
Barlow's La. Liverpool L9 .... 39 D8
Barlow's La. Shirdley Hill L39 . 8 D5
Barlows Cl. L9 .... 39 D8
Barmouth Cl. WA5 .... 60 E2
Barmouth Rd. L45 .... 50 D6
Barmouth Way. L5 .... 52 C5
Barn Cl. L30 .... 28 A4
Barn Croft Rd. L26 .... 83 A7
Barn Hey. L47 .... 63 A5
Barn Hey Cres. L47 .... 63 F8
Barn Hey Gn. L12 .... 54 B6
Barn Hey Rd. L33 .... 30 A2
Barn La. WA12 & WA3 .... 46 F8
Barn Way. WA12 .... 46 B3
Barnacre Dr. L64 .... 86 B2
Barnacre La. L46 & L48 .... 64 B6
Barnard Rd. L43 .... 66 B5
Barncroft Pl. L23 .... 26 E6
Barndale Rd. L18 .... 69 A5
Barnes Cl. WA8 .... 73 D2
Barnes Dr. L31 .... 20 C3
Barnes Gn. L63 .... 79 A2
Barnes Rd. Ormskirk L39 .... 13 E3
Barnes Rd.
Skelmersdale WN8 .... 15 E1
Barnes Rd. Widnes WA8 .... 73 C2
Barnes St. L6 .... 53 A5
Barneston Rd. WA8 .... 73 E3
Barnet Cl. 7 L7 .... 68 C8
Barnett Ave. WA12 .... 45 E3
Barnfield Cl. Hoylake L47 .... 48 E1
Barnfield Cl. Litherland L30 ... 27 E2
Barnfield Cl. Liverpool L12 ... 54 B6
Barnfield Dr. Liverpool L12 ... 54 B6
Barnfield Dr.
Skelmersdale WN8 .... 24 E7
Barnham Cl. Golborne WA3 . 47 A8
Barnham Cl. Liverpool L24 ... 82 B4
Barnham Dr. L16 .... 69 F7
Barnhill Rd. L15 .... 69 A6
Barnhurst Cl. L16 .... 69 E7
Barnhurst Rd. L16 .... 69 E7
Barnmeadow Rd. L25 .... 70 A5
Barns The. L37 .... 10 A1
Barnsbury Rd. L4 .... 39 C2
Barnsdale Ave. L61 .... 77 B5
Barnside Ct. L16 .... 69 E7
Barnstaple Way. WA5 .... 74 E4
Barnston La. L46 .... 49 E1
Barnston Prim Sch. L60 .... 86 C7
Barnston Rd.
Heswall L60 & L61 .... 77 B4
Barnston Rd. Liverpool L9 .... 39 B7
Barnston Towers Cl. L60 .... 86 C8
Barnton Cl. WA3 .... 47 D7
Barnwell Ave. L44 & L45 .... 51 B5
Barnwood Rd. L36 .... 55 B4
Baron's Cl. WA8 .... 84 C8
Baron's Hey. L12 & L28 .... 54 F8
Baroncroft Rd. L25 .... 69 F3
Barren Gr. L43 .... 66 B4
Barrett Ave. PR8 .... 4 A2
Barrett Rd. PR8 .... 4 A2
Barrington Dr. PR8 .... 7 B5
Barrington Rd. Liverpool L15 68 E6
Barrington Rd. Wallasey L44 51 C3
Barrow Ave. WA2 .... 61 E2
Barrow Cl. L12 .... 40 C1
Barrow Hall La. WA5 .... 74 E7
Barrow Hall Lane Cty Prim Sch.
WA5 .... 74 E7
Barrow La. WA3 .... 47 C2
Barrow Nook La. L39 .... 22 E2
Barrow St. Ashton-in-M WN4 35 D5
Barrow St. St Helens WA10 .. 44 A3
Barrow's Green La. WA8 .... 73 E3
Barrow's Row. WA8 .... 73 B4
Barrowdale Rd. WA3 .... 47 B8
Barrowfield Rd. WA10 .... 43 A5
Barrymore Rd. L13 .... 53 F3
Barrymore Way. L63 .... 88 B6
Bartholomew Cl. L35 .... 57 E1
Bartlett St. L15 .... 68 E7
Barton Cl. Hoylake L47 .... 62 F6
Barton Cl. Litherland L21 .... 27 A2
Barton Cl. St Helens WA10 ... 43 F4
Barton Clough. WN5 .... 33 E5
Barton Hey Dr. L48 .... 75 D6
Barton Heys Rd. L37 .... 9 D1
Barton Rd. Bootle L9 .... 38 F4
Barton Rd. Hoylake L47 .... 63 A6
Barton St. 2 Birkenhead L41 66 C5
Barton St. Golborne WA3 .... 36 A1
Barwell Ave. WA11 .... 44 C6
Basil Cl. L16 .... 69 E8
Basil Rd. L16 .... 69 D8
Basildon Cl. WA9 .... 57 F7
Basing St. L19 .... 81 C7
Baskervyle Cl. L60 .... 86 A6
Baskervyle Rd. L60 .... 86 A6
Baslow Wlk. L7 .... 68 B8
Basnett St. L1 .... 52 D1
Bassendale Rd. L62 .... 79 E2
Bassenthwaite Ave.
Birkenhead L43 .... 65 D5
Bassenthwaite Ave.
Kirkby L33 .... 29 D4
Bassenthwaite Ave.
St Helens WA11 .... 44 A8
Basset Way. L25 & L27 .... 70 C6
Bates Cres. WA10 .... 57 D8
Batey Ave. L35 .... 57 B4
Bath Springs. L39 .... 13 F5
Bath St. Bebington L62 .... 79 B5
Bath St. Liverpool L3 .... 52 B2
Bath St. Seaforth L22 .... 37 D8
Bath St. Southport PR8 .... 4 B8
Bath St. St Helens WA10 .... 43 F3
Bath St N. PR8 & PR9 .... 4 B8
Bathgate Way. L33 .... 29 D6
Bathurst Rd. L19 .... 81 B7
Batley St. 4 L13 .... 54 A3
Battenberg St. L7 .... 53 A2
Battery Cl. L17 .... 68 C2
Battle Way. L37 .... 10 B2
Baucher Dr. L20 .... 38 E7
Baumville Dr. L63 .... 78 F2
Bawtry Ct. WA2 .... 61 E1
Baxters La. WA9 .... 58 D8
Baycliff Rd. L12 .... 54 F7
Baycliff Road Gdns. L12 .... 54 E7
Bayfield Rd. L19 .... 81 A7
Bayhorse La. L3 .... 52 F2
Bayswater Ct. L45 .... 50 D6
Bayswater Gdns. L45 .... 50 D7
Bayswater Rd. L45 .... 50 D6
Baythorne Rd. L4 .... 39 C2
Baytree Cl. PR9 .... 2 D5
Baytree Rd.
Birkenhead L42 .... 66 E
Baytree Rd. Frankby L48 .... 63 F2
Beach Bank. L22 .... 26 C2
Beach Gr. L45 .... 51 C7
Beach Lawn. L22 .... 26 C1
Beach Priory Gdns. PR8 .... 4 A6
Beach Rd. Bootle L21 .... 38 A7
Beach Rd. Hoylake L47 .... 62 F6
Beach Rd. Southport PR8 .... 3 F6
Beach Road Prim Sch. L21 .. 38 A7
Beach Wlk. L48 .... 75 B8
Beacham Rd. PR8 .... 4 E7
Beachcroft Rd. L47 .... 48 E1
Beachmews. PR8 .... 3 F6
Beacon Ct. L5 .... 52 F6
Beacon Ctry Pk. WN8 .... 16 E2
Beacon Dr. L48 .... 63 C2
Beacon Gr. WA11 .... 44 D6
Beacon La. Heswall L60 .... 86 A7
Beacon La. Liverpool L5 .... 52 F6
Beacon La.
Skelmersdale L40 & WN8 .... 16 D4
Beacon Rd. WN5 .... 33 E6
Beacon St. L5 .... 52 B5
Beacon View Dr. WN8 .... 25 B7
Beacons The. L60 .... 86 A7
Beaconsfield. L34 .... 56 D6
Beaconsfield Cl. L41 .... 66 F3
Beaconsfield Cres. WA8 .... 73 A4
Beaconsfield Gr. WA8 .... 73 B4
Beaconsfield Rd.
Bebington L62 .... 79 B7
Beaconsfield Rd.
Liverpool L18 & L25 .... 69 F3
Beaconsfield Rd.
Runcorn WA7 .... 84 E1
Beaconsfield Rd.
Seaforth L21 .... 37 F7
Beaconsfield Rd.
Southport PR9 .... 4 F6
Beaconsfield Rd.
St Helens WA10 .... 43 C5
Beaconsfield Rd.
Widnes WA8 .... 73 B4
Beaconsfield St. L8 .... 68 A6
Beadnell Dr. WA5 .... 74 F3
Beames Cl. L7 .... 53 C1
Beardsmore Dr. WA3 .... 36 E1
Bearncroft. WN8 .... 24 D6
Beatrice Ave. L63 .... 78 E7
Beatrice St. L20 .... 38 D1
Beattock Cl. L33 .... 29 D6
Beatty Ave. WA2 .... 61 C1
Beatty Cl. Prescot L35 .... 56 D2
Beatty Cl. West Kirby L48 .... 75 C6
Beatty Rd. 8 Liverpool L13 . 54 A3
Beatty Rd. Southport PR8 .... 4 E5
Beau St. L3 .... 52 E4
Beauclair Dr. L15 .... 69 C6
Beaufort. L37 .... 10 A2
Beaufort Cl. WA8 .... 84 A8
Beaufort Cty Prim Sch. L8 .. 67 E4
Beaufort Dr. L44 .... 50 E4
Beaufort Rd. L41 .... 51 A1
Beaufort St. Liverpool L8 .... 67 E5
Beaufort St. St Helens WA9 . 44 C1
Beaumaris Dr. L61 .... 77 B6
Beaumaris Rd. L45 .... 50 D6
Beaumaris St. L20 .... 52 C8
Beaumont Ave. WA10 .... 43 D4
Beaumont Cres. L39 .... 13 D2
Beaumont Dr. L10 .... 28 F1
Beaumont St. L8 .... 68 B7
Beauworth Ave. L49 .... 64 C3
Beaver Ct. WN4 .... 35 C6
Beaver Gr. L9 .... 39 A6
Beavers La. WN8 .... 24 D6
Bebington High Sch. L63 .... 78 F6
Bebington & New Ferry Sta.
L42 .... 79 A7
Bebington Rd.
Bebington L63 & L62 .... 79 A7
Bebington Rd.
Birkenhead L42 .... 66 E1
Bebles Rd. L39 .... 13 C3
Beccon House. L5 .... 52 E4
Bechers. WA8 .... 72 B3
Bechers Dr. L9 .... 28 C2
Bechers Row. L9 .... 38 F6
Beck Gr. WA11 .... 44 B8
Beck Rd. L20 .... 38 C5
Beckenham Ave. L18 .... 68 F5
Beckenham Rd. L45 .... 37 B1
Becket St. L4 .... 52 D7
Beckett Cl. L33 .... 41 C8
Beckett Gr. L63 .... 78 D7
Beckwith St. Birkenhead L41 66 C7
Beckwith St.
Liverpool L1 & L72 .... 67 D8
Beckwith St E. L41 .... 66 D7
Becky St. L6 .... 53 B5
Becontree Rd. L12 .... 54 D4
Bective St. L7 .... 68 C8
Bedale Wlk. L33 .... 29 F4
Bedburn Dr. L36 .... 55 B3
Bedford Ave. Birkenhead L42 66 E1
Bedford Ave. Maghull L31 .... 28 F6
Bedford Cl. Huyton-w-R L36 . 56 A3
Bedford Cl. 6 Liverpool L7 .. 67 F8
Bedford Cty Prim Sch. L20 .. 38 D2
Bedford Dr. L42 .... 66 D1
Bedford Drive Prim Sch.
L42 .... 66 D1
Bedford Pl.
Ashton-in-M WN4 .... 35 A5
Bedford Pl. Birkenhead L42 .. 67 A2
Bedford Pl. Bootle L20 .... 38 B1
Bedford Pl. 1 Seaforth L21 . 37 F7
Bedford Rd. Birkenhead L42 66 F2
Bedford Rd. Bootle L20 & L4 38 D2
Bedford Rd. Southport PR8 .... 4 A2
Bedford Rd. Wallasey L45 .... 51 B6
Bedford Rd E. L42 .... 67 A2
Bedford St. WA9 .... 44 D2
Bedford St N. L7 .... 52 F1
Bedford St S. L7 & L8 .... 67 F8
Bedford Wlk. 7 L8 .... 67 F8
Beech Ave. St Helens L49 .... 64 D6
Beech Ave. Crosby L23 .... 27 A6
Beech Ave. Golborne WA3 ... 47 F7
Beech Ave. Haydock WA11 .. 45 F7
Beech Ave. Heswall L61 .... 77 A4
Beech Ave. Kirkby L31 .... 29 B3
Beech Ave. Liverpool L17 .... 68 B2
Beech Ave. Prescot L34 .... 56 F7
Beech Ave. St Helens WA9 ... 58 C4
Beech Ave. Warrington WA5 74 C3
Beech Cl. Kirkby L32 .... 29 C3
Beech Cl. Liverpool L11 .... 40 D3
Beech Cl. Skelmersdale WN8 15 E1
Beech Ct. Birkenhead L42 .... 66 D4
Beech Ct. Liverpool L18 .... 69 D3
Beech Dr. L37 .... 9 D4
Beech Gdns. WA11 .... 31 E6
Beech Gn. L12 .... 54 A8
Beech Gr. Abram Brow WN2 36 C7
Beech Gr. Bootle L21 .... 37 F6
Beech Gr. Litherland L30 .... 28 A2
Beech Gr. Liverpool L9 .... 39 B6
Beech Gr. Southport PR9 .... 4 F7
Beech Hey La. L64 .... 88 B1
Beech La. L18 .... 69 C5
Beech Lawn. L19 .... 80 F7
Beech Meadow. L39 .... 14 A4
Beech Pk. Crosby L23 .... 27 A6
Beech Pk. Liverpool L12 .... 54 A6
Beech Rd. Bebington L63 .... 78 F7
Beech Rd. Birkenhead L42 .... 66 D4
Beech Rd. Golborne WA3 .... 36 A1
Beech Rd. Heswall L60 .... 86 C8
Beech Rd. Holt Green L39 ..... 21 A6
Beech Rd. Huyton-w-R L36 ... 55 E1
Beech Rd. Liverpool L4 .... 39 A2
Beech St. Ashton-in-M WN4 . 35 A6
Beech St. Bootle L20 .... 38 C4
Beech St. Liverpool L7 .... 53 C2
Beech St.
Thatto Heath WA10 .... 57 D8
Beech Terr. L7 .... 53 C2
Beech Tree Houses. WN2 ... 35 F7
Beecham Cl. L36 .... 55 D1
Beechbank Rd. L18 .... 68 F5
Beechburn Cres. L36 .... 55 B3
Beechburn Rd. L36 .... 55 A3
Beechcroft. L31 .... 20 D1
Beechcroft Rd. L44 .... 51 C2

Beechdale Rd. L18 69 A4
Beechdene Rd. L4 53 B7
Beechenhurst Prep Sch. L18 69 D4
Beeches The. 4 Birkenhead L42 66 F1
Beeches The. Liverpool L18 . 69 D4
Beeches The. Wallasey L46 . 49 E3
Beechfield. L31 20 E1
Beechfield Cl. L60 86 A7
Beechfield Gdns. PR8 3 F6
Beechfield Mews. PR9 4 C7
Beechfield Rd. L18 69 D4
Beechill Cl. L25 70 C4
Beechtree Rd. L15 54 B1
Beechtrees. WN8 24 D7
Beechurst Cl. L25 70 B5
Beechurst Rd. L25 70 B5
Beechwalk The. L12 & L13 & L14 54 B4
Beechway. Bebington L63 78 F3
Beechway. Maghull L31 21 B2
Beechway Ave. L31 21 B2
Beechwood. WN8 16 C3
Beechwood Ave. Ashton-in-M WN4 35 A2
Beechwood Ave. Liverpool L26 82 F7
Beechwood Ave. Newton-le-W WA12 46 D4
Beechwood Ave. Wallasey L45 50 E5
Beechwood Ave. Warrington WA5 74 F5
Beechwood Cl. Liverpool L19 81 A7
Beechwood Cl. Prescot L35 . 56 E4
Beechwood Cl. St Helens WA9 58 C4
Beechwood Cres. WN5 25 E6
Beechwood Ct. Maghull L31 20 F1
Beechwood Ct. Skelmersdale WN8 24 D6
Beechwood Dr. Birkenhead L43 65 C7
Beechwood Dr. Formby L37 9 C1
Beechwood Dr. Ormskirk L39 13 D5
Beechwood Gdns. L19 80 F7
Beechwood Gr. L19 81 A7
Beechwood Rd. Bebington L62 88 C8
Beechwood Rd. Bootle L21 38 B6
Beechwood Rd. Liverpool L18 69 D4
Beechwood Rd. Liverpool L19 80 F7
Beecroft Cl. WA5 60 D1
Beesley Rd. L34 56 C6
Beeston Cl. L43 65 C6
Beeston Dr. Heswall L61 76 F4
Beeston Dr. Maghull L30 28 B5
Beeston Gr. L19 81 A7
Beeston St. L4 52 F8
Beldale Pk. L32 29 C4
Beldon Cres. L36 55 B3
Belem Cl. L17 68 C5
Belem Tower. L17 68 C5
Belfast Rd. L13 54 B3
Belfield. WN8 24 D6
Belfield Cres. L36 55 E1
Belfield Dr. L43 66 B3
Belford Dr. L46 64 C8
Belfort Rd. L25 70 B4
Belfry Cl. Liverpool L14 54 E6
Belfry Cl. Wallasey L46 49 B1
Belgrave Ave. L44 51 C4
Belgrave Cl. WA8 73 E3
Belgrave Pl. PR8 3 F3
Belgrave Rd. Liverpool L17 68 B3
Belgrave Rd. 4 Seaforth L21 37 F7
Belgrave Rd. Southport PR8 3 F3
Belgrave St. L44 51 C4
Belhaven Rd. 4 L18 68 F5
Bell Cl. L36 70 F8
Bell House Rd. WA8 73 C1
Bell La. L35 58 A2
Bell Rd. L44 51 D3
Bell St. 3 L13 54 A3
Bell's Cl. L31 20 C4
Bell's La. L31 20 B3
Bellair Ave. L23 27 A4
Bellairs Rd. L11 53 E8
Bellamy Rd. L4 38 E2
Belldene Gr. L60 76 F2
Belle Vale Cty Jun Sch. L25 70 C5
Belle Vale Rd. L25 70 C5
Belle Vale Sh Ctr. L25 70 B6
Belle Vue Rd. Liverpool L25 . 70 B4
Belle Vue Rd. Wallasey L44 . 51 E2
Bellefield Ave. L12 54 B6
Bellew Rd. L11 53 F7
Bellfield Cres. L45 51 A8
Bellgreen Rd. L11 40 A2
Bellini Cl. L21 38 A6
Bellis Ave. PR9 1 F2
Bellmore St. L19 81 C7
Bellward Cl. L63 78 F2
Belmont. L41 66 C5
Belmont Ave. Bebington L62 79 C1
Belmont Ave. Golborne WA3 36 C1
Belmont Ave. Orrell WN5 25 D3
Belmont Cres. WA5 74 F6
Belmont Dr. Heswall L61 77 A3
Belmont Dr. Liverpool L6 53 D5
Belmont Gr. 11 Birkenhead L41 & L43 66 C5
Belmont Gr. Liverpool L6 53 C5
Belmont Pl. L19 81 C6
Belmont Rd. Liverpool L6 53 B5
Belmont Rd. Wallasey L45 37 B1
Belmont Rd. West Kirby L48 63 B3
Belmont Rd. Widnes WA8 73 E2
Belmont St. Southport PR8 4 A5
Belmont St. St Helens WA10 43 D3
Beloe St. L8 67 F4
Belper St. L19 81 B7
Belston Rd. L16 69 D8
Belton Rd. L36 55 D6
Belvedere Ave. WA9 58 D6
Belvedere Cl. L34 56 E7
Belvedere Dr. L37 9 F1
Belvedere Pk. L39 21 C7
Belvedere Rd. Ashton-in-M WN4 35 C4
Belvedere Rd. Newton-le-W WA12 46 B5
Belvedere Rd. Southport PR8 . 7 C5
Belvedere Sch (Girls Jun) The. L8 68 B4
Belvedere Sch The. L8 68 A4
Belvidere Pk. L23 26 E3
Belvidere Rd. Crosby L23 26 E3
Belvidere Rd. Liverpool L17 & L8 68 A4
Belvidere Rd. Wallasey L45 51 A5
Belvoir Rd. Liverpool L18 81 C8
Belvoir Rd. Widnes WA8 73 B1
Bembridge Cl. WA8 72 F4
Bempton Rd. L17 68 C2
Ben La. L39 23 A1
Ben Nevis Rd. L42 66 D2
Benbow St. L20 38 B2
Benedict St. L20 38 D1
Bengarth Rd. PR9 4 F8
Bengel St. L7 53 A2
Benledi St. L5 52 D5
Benmore Rd. L18 69 A2
Bennet's La. L47 48 E1
Bennett St. L19 81 C6
Bennett Wlk. L61 76 F3
Bennett's La. WA8 73 E1
Bennetts Hill. L43 66 B4
Bennison Dr. L19 81 A7
Benson Cl. L49 64 F4
Benson St. L1 52 E1
Bentfield. L17 & L19 80 F8
Bentfield Cl. L63 78 D7
Bentfield Gdns. L63 78 D7
Bentham Ave. WA2 61 C3
Bentham Cl. L43 65 E3
Bentham Dr. L16 69 D8
Bentham St. PR8 4 B5
Bentham's Way. PR8 4 C2
Bentinck Cl. L41 66 D6
Bentinck Ct. 2 L41 66 D6
Bentinck Pl. L41 & L43 66 C6
Bentinck St. Birkenhead L41 66 D6
Bentinck St. Liverpool L5 52 B5
Bentinck St. Runcorn WA7 84 F3
Bentinck St. St Helens WA9 . 44 D1
Bentley Rd. Birkenhead L43 . 66 B4
Bentley Rd. Heswall L61 76 F5
Bentley Rd. Liverpool L8 68 B6
Bentley St. WA9 58 C3
Benton Cl. L5 52 D6
Benty Cl. L63 78 E4
Benty Farm Gr. L61 77 A5
Benty Heath La. L63 & L64 & L66 88 B3
Benwick Rd. L32 29 B2
Berbice Rd. L15 & L18 69 A5
Beresford Ave. L63 79 A7
Beresford Cl. L43 66 A5
Beresford Ct. L43 66 A5
Beresford Dr. PR9 1 F1
Beresford Gdns. PR9 1 F2
Beresford Rd. Birkenhead L43 66 A5
Beresford Rd. Liverpool L8 67 F4
Beresford Rd. Wallasey L45 50 F7
Beresford St. Bootle L20 38 B1
Beresford St. 7 Liverpool L5 52 E4
Beresford St. St Helens WA9 57 E7
Bergen Cl. L20 38 E2
Berkeley Ave. L43 65 E1
Berkeley Dr. L45 51 C7
Berkeley Rd. L23 26 C5
Berkeswell Rd. L11 40 A1
Berkley Ave. L12 54 E8
Berkley St. L8 67 F7
Berkley Wlk. L8 67 F7
Bermuda Rd. L46 64 C8
Bernard Ave. L45 51 C7
Berner St. L41 66 D8
Berner's Rd. L19 81 B7
Berrington Ave. Liverpool L25 70 A2
Berrington Gr. WN4 35 A3
Berrington's La. WA11 32 C1
Berry Cl. WN8 15 F2
Berry Hill Ave. L34 41 D3
Berry Rd. WA8 72 D1
Berry St. Bootle L20 38 B2
Berry St. Liverpool L1 67 E8
Berry St. Skelmersdale WN8 15 F2
Berry St Ind Est. L20 38 B3
Berrylands Cl. L46 49 D1
Berrylands Rd. L46 49 D2
Berrys La. WA9 44 F1
Berrywood Dr. L35 56 F2
Bertha Gdns. 1 L41 65 F8
Bertha St. L41 65 F8
Bertram Dr. L47 63 D8
Bertram Dr N. L47 63 D8
Bertram Rd. L17 68 C4
Bertram St. WA12 46 A4
Berwick Ave. Bebington L62 . 88 E4
Berwick Ave. Southport PR8 .. 7 D5
Berwick Cl. Birkenhead L46 . 64 B8
Berwick Cl. Birkenhead L43 .. 65 C6
Berwick Cl. Liverpool L6 53 B4
Berwick Dr. L23 26 C5
Berwick St. L6 53 B4
Berwyn Ave. Heswall L61 77 A6
Berwyn Ave. Hoylake L47 63 C7
Berwyn Bvd. L63 78 E8
Berwyn Ct. PR8 4 D4
Berwyn Dr. L61 77 A2
Berwyn Gr. WA9 44 F3
Berwyn Rd. Liverpool L4 53 C8
Berwyn Rd. Wallasey L44 51 C5
Beryl Rd. L43 65 C5
Beryl St. L13 54 A1
Beryl Wlk. L10 40 B7
Besford House. L25 70 B5
Besford Rd. L25 70 B5
Bessborough Rd. L43 66 B4
Bessbrook Rd. L17 68 E2
Bessemer St. L8 67 F4
Beta Cl. L62 79 A7
Bethany Cres. L42 79 A5
Betjeman Gr. L16 69 E8
Betony Cl. L26 70 E1
Bettisfield Ave. L62 88 D6
Betula Cl. L9 39 C4
Beulah Ave. WN5 33 D4
Bevan Cl. WA9 57 D6
Bevan's Ct. L12 54 C7
Bevan's La. L12 54 D7
Beverley Ave. WN5 25 E1
Beverley Cl. PR9 2 C5
Beverley Dr. L60 86 B6
Beverley Gdns. L61 77 B6
Beverley Rd. Bebington L62 . 79 B8
Beverley Rd. Liverpool L15 ... 69 A6
Beverley Rd. Wallasey L45 ... 50 F6
Beversbrook Rd. L11 40 B2
Bevington Bush. L3 52 D3
Bevington Hill. 2 L3 52 D4
Bevington St. 3 Ashton-in-M WN4 34 F5
Bevington St. Liverpool L3 ... 52 D4
Bevyl Rd. L64 86 B2
Bewcastle Dr. L40 14 C3
Bewley Dr. Kirkby L32 & L33 40 F7
Bewsey St. WA10 43 D1
Bexhill Ave. WA2 61 B4
Bexhill Cl. L24 82 B4
Bianca St. L20 38 C1
Bibby Rd. PR9 2 A1
Bibby St. L13 53 F3
Bibby's La. L20 38 A5
Bickershaw CE Prim Sch. WN2 36 F8
Bickershaw La. WN2 36 F8
Bickerstaffe CE Sch. L39 22 E5
Bickerstaffe St. 1 Liverpool L3 52 E3
Bickerstaffe St. St Helens WA10 44 A3
Bickerton Ave. L63 78 D8
Bickerton Rd. PR8 3 F4
Bickerton St. L17 68 C3
Bickley Cl. WA2 61 F3
Bidder St. L3 52 E3
Bideford Ave. WA9 58 C5
Bideford Rd. WA5 74 E4
Bidston Ave. Birkenhead L41 & L43 65 F7
Bidston Ave. St Helens WA11 44 D5
Bidston Ave. Wallasey L45 ... 50 E6
Bidston Avenue Inf Sch. L43 65 E7
Bidston Ct. L43 65 E7
Bidston Green Ct. L43 65 C8
Bidston Green Dr. L43 65 C8
Bidston Ind Est. L45 50 D3
Bidston Moss. L45 50 D3
Bidston Obsy. L43 65 D8
Bidston Rd. Birkenhead L43 . 65 F5
Bidston Rd. Liverpool L4 53 B8
Bidston Sta. L43 50 C2
Bidston Station App. L43 50 C2
Bidston View. L43 50 C1
Bidston Village CE Sch. L43 50 C1
Bidston Village Rd. L41 & L43 50 C1
Bidstone Golf Course. L45 & L46 50 C3
Big Meadow Rd. L49 65 A4
Bigdale Dr. Kirkby L33 30 A3
Biggin Ct. WA2 61 E1
Bigham Rd. L6 53 C3
Biglands Dr. L36 70 F8
Billinge Chapel End Prim Sch. WN5 33 E4
Billinge Cres. WA11 44 D6
Billinge Rd. WN4 34 C5
Billinge St Aidan's CE Prim Sch. WN5 33 E5
Billinge & Winstanley St Mary's RC Prim Sch. WN5 33 D4
Billingham Rd. L35 57 D7
Billings Cl. L5 52 D6
Billings Hospl. WN5 25 D2
Billington Ave. WA12 46 C5
Billington Rd. WA8 72 B3
Bilston Rd. L17 80 E8
Bilton Cl. WA8 73 E2
Bingley Rd. L4 53 B7
Binns Rd. L13 & L7 53 F2
Binns Way. L13 53 F1
Binsey Cl. L49 64 D5
Birbeck Rd. L33 30 A3
Birbeck Wlk. L33 30 A3
Birch Ave. L9 39 B6
Birch Ave. Birkenhead L49 ... 64 D6
Birch Ave. St Helens WA10 .. 43 F6
Birch Ave. Warrington WA2 . 61 A4
Birch Cl. Birkenhead L43 66 B3
Birch Cl. Maghull L31 20 F1
Birch Cl. Prescot L35 56 E4
Birch Cres. WA12 45 F4
Birch Gdns. WA10 43 F6
Birch Gn. L37 9 D4
Birch Gr. Garswood WN4 34 D5
Birch Gr. Huyton-w-R L36 55 D2
Birch Gr. Liverpool L15 54 A1
Birch Gr. Prescot L35 56 E4
Birch Gr. Wallasey L45 51 C7
Birch Green Rd. WN8 16 C3
Birch Heys. L48 64 A1
Birch Rd. Abram WN2 36 B7
Birch Rd. Bebington L63 79 A4
Birch Rd. Birkenhead L43 66 B3
Birch Rd. Haydock WA11 45 E7
Birch Rd. Hoylake L47 63 E8
Birch Rd. Huyton-w-R L36 55 E1
Birch Rd. Widnes WA8 73 B3
Birch St. Liverpool L5 52 B5
Birch St. Skelmersdale WN8 . 23 E8
Birch St. Southport PR8 4 B4
Birch Tree Ave. WA11 43 F8
Birch Tree Ct. L12 54 A6
Birch Tree Rd. WA3 47 F8
Birchall St. L20 & L5 52 C7
Birchdale Cl. L49 64 D4
Birchdale Rd. Crosby L22 26 D1
Birchdale Rd. Liverpool L9 ... 39 B4
Birchen Rd. L26 83 A7
Birches Cl. L60 86 A8
Birches The. Formby L37 9 E5
Birches The. Huyton-w-R L28 55 A7
Birches The. Neston L64 86 F2
Birches The. Wallasey L44 ... 51 E2
Birchfield. L46 64 C7
Birchfield Ave. WA8 73 A2
Birchfield Cl. Birkenhead L46 64 C6
Birchfield Cl. Liverpool L7 53 E2
Birchfield Jun Mix & Inf Sch. L7 53 E2
Birchfield Rd. Liverpool L4 ... 39 A2
Birchfield Rd. Liverpool L7 ... 53 E2
Birchfield Rd. Widnes WA8 .. 73 A1
Birchfield Rd. Widnes WA8 .. 73 A3
Birchfield St. Liverpool L3 52 E3
Birchfield St. St Helens L35 . 57 D7
Birchfield Way. L31 20 B5
Birchill Rd. L33 30 C2
Birchley Ave. WN5 33 C3
Birchley Rd. WA11 & WN5 ... 33 C4
Birchley St. WA10 44 A4
Birchley View. WA11 33 B2
Birchmuir Hey. L32 29 F1
Birchover Wlk. L7 68 B8
Birchridge Cl. L62 79 C2
Birchtree Rd. L17 68 E3
Birchview Way. L43 65 D5
Birchway. L60 86 C5
Birchwood Ave. L41 & L72 ... 66 D7
Birchwood Cl. L41 & L72 66 E7
Birchwood Way. WA2 61 F1
Bird i' th' Hand Cotts. 2 L39 13 E6
Bird St. L15 & L7 68 C7
Birdwood Rd. L11 53 F8
Birkdale Ave. L63 88 C6
Birkdale Cl. Huyton-w-R L36 . 55 C1
Birkdale Cl. Liverpool L6 53 D6
Birkdale Cop. PR8 4 E1
Birkdale High Sch. PR8 7 E7
Birkdale Prim Sch. PR8 4 B3
Birkdale Rd. Warrington WA5 74 F4
Birkdale Rd. Widnes WA8 73 B5
Birkdale Sch for Hearing Impaired. PR8 3 E4
Birkdale Sta. PR8 3 F4
Birkdale Trad Est. PR8 4 A2
Birkenhead Central Sta. L41 66 E5
Birkenhead High Sch. L43 66 A5
Birkenhead North Sta. L41 .. 50 F1
Birkenhead Park Sta. L41 66 B7
Birkenhead Prep Sch. L43 66 A5
Birkenhead Rd. Hoylake L47 48 D1
Birkenhead Rd. Hoylake L47 & L46 63 E8
Birkenhead Rd. Raby L64 87 E1
Birkenhead Rd. Wallasey L41 & L44 51 E2
Birkenhead Sch. L43 65 F5
Birkenhead Sch (Boys). L43 66 A5
Birkenhead Sixth Form Coll. L43 65 F7
Birkenshaw Ave. L23 26 B4
Birket Ave. L46 50 A3
Birket Cl. L46 50 A3
Birket Sq. L46 49 F3
Birkett Rd. Birkenhead L42 ... 66 E1
Birkett Rd. West Kirby L48 ... 63 B3
Birkett St. L3 52 E3
Birkey La. L37 9 F2
Birkin Cl. L32 41 A8
Birkin Rd. L32 41 A8
Birkin Wlk. 4 L32 41 A8
Birkrig. WN8 24 D6
Birley Ct. 6 L8 67 F7
Birley St. WA12 46 D4
Birleywood. WN8 24 D6
Birnam Dr. L35 57 D2
Birnam Rd. L44 51 D3
Birstall Ave. WA11 44 C5
Birstall Rd. L6 53 B3
Birtles Rd. WA2 61 D1
Bishop Dr. L35 56 D1
Bishop Goss RC Jun Mix & Inf Sch. L3 52 D3
Bishop Martin CE Prim Sch. Liverpool L25 70 A2
Bishop Martin CE Prim Sch. Skelmersdale WN8 24 D6
Bishop Rd. 5 Liverpool L6 .. 53 C6
Bishop Rd. St Helens WA10 . 43 E5
Bishop Rd. Wallasey L44 51 B2
Bishop Reeves Rd. WA11 45 E7
Bishop Sheppard Ct. L3 52 C4
Bishopdale Cl. WA5 74 F7
Bishopdale Dr. L35 57 E2
Bishopgate St. L15 68 E8
Bishops Ct. Liverpool L25 70 B2
Bishops Ct. Warrington WA2 61 A4
Bishops David Sheppard CE Sch. PR9 5 A7
Bishops Way. WA8 73 D3
Bisley St. Liverpool L15 68 E7
Bisley St. Wallasey L45 51 B5
Bispham Dr. Ashton-in-M WN4 34 F5
Bispham Dr. Hoylake L47 63 E7
Bispham Hall Bsns Pk. WN5 25 C2
Bispham House. 6 L3 52 D3
Bispham Rd. PR9 4 F7

Bispham St. L3 52 D3
Bittern Cl. WA2 61 D3
Bixteth St. L2 & L3 52 C2
Black Denton's Pl. WA8 73 C1
Black Horse Cl. L48 63 C3
Black Horse Hill. L48 63 C3
Black Horse Hill Inf Sch. L48 63 D3
Black Horse Hill Jun Sch. L48 63 D3
Black Horse La. L13 54 B3
Black Horse Pl. L13 54 B3
Black Moss La. L39 13 E3
Black Moss Sch. WN8 15 D2
Black-A-Moor La. Haskayne L39 12 A1
Blackacre La. L39 & L40 13 E8
Blackberry Gr. L26 70 D2
Blackbrook Ave. WA2 61 F2
Blackbrook Cl. Liverpool L9 39 A3
Blackbrook Cl. Widnes WA8 72 C3
Blackbrook RC Inf Sch. WA11 44 E6
Blackbrook RC Jun Sch. WA11 44 E6
Blackbrook Rd. WA11 & WA9 44 E5
Blackburn Cl. WA3 47 E8
Blackburne Ave. WA8 84 B5
Blackburne Dr. L25 82 D7
Blackburne Pl. L1 & L8 67 F8
Blackburne St. L19 & L24 81 D3
Blackcar La. L29 19 B3
Blackdown Gr. WA9 44 F2
Blackfield St. L5 52 D6
Blackheath Dr. L46 49 F3
Blackhorse St. WA9 44 D4
Blackhurst Rd. L31 20 C5
Blackleyhurst Ave. WN5 33 E5
Blacklock Hall Rd. L24 82 C4
Blacklow Brow. L36 55 D2
Blacklow Brow Prim Sch. L36 55 D1
Blackmoor Dr. L12 & L14 54 D5
Blackmoor Park Inf Sch. L12 54 D6
Blackmoor Park Jun Sch. L14 54 D4
Blackpool St. L41 66 E5
Blackrod Ave. L24 82 C3
Blackshaw Dr. WA5 60 B1
Blackstock Ct. L30 27 D4
Blackstock St. L3 52 D3
Blackstone Ave. WA11 44 D5
Blackstone St. L5 52 B6
Blackthorn Cl. L46 64 F7
Blackthorne Cres. L28 55 B8
Blackthorne Rd. L4 & L9 39 C3
Blackwater Rd. L11 40 D4
Blackwood Ave. L25 69 F4
Blaguegate La. WN8 15 B2
Blair Dr. WA8 72 C3
Blair Gr. PR9 4 F7
Blair Ind Est. L23 26 F3
Blair Pk. L63 79 B3
Blair St. L8 67 E7
Blair Wlk. L26 82 F6
Blaisdon Cl. 5 L11 40 A1
Blake Ct. L19 81 C5
Blakeacre Cl. L26 82 F6
Blakeacre Rd. L26 83 A6
Blakefield Rd. L23 27 C6
Blakehall. WN8 24 D7
Blakeley Brow. L63 88 A6
Blakeley Ct. L63 88 A7
Blakeley Dene. L63 88 B7
Blakeley Rd. L63 88 A6
Blakeney Cl. L49 65 A7
Blakenhall Way. L49 64 D6
Blaking Dr. L34 41 D4
Bland Wlk. 3 L6 53 B3
Blandford Cl. PR8 3 F5
Blantyre Rd. L15 68 E6
Blantyre St. WA7 84 F3
Blay Cl. L25 82 D8
Blaydon Cl. L30 27 F1
Blaydon Gr. L35 57 D7
Blaydon Pk. WN8 24 D7
Blaydon Wlk. L43 65 F6
Bleak Hill Cl. WA10 43 C7
Bleak Hill Cty Prim Sch. WA10 43 C6
Bleak Hill Rd. WA10 43 B6
Bleasdale Ave. L10 28 E2
Bleasdale Cl. Birkenhead L49 64 E6
Bleasdale Cl. Ormskirk L39 21 D7
Bleasdale Rd. L18 69 B5
Bleasdale Way. L23 27 B4
Blenheim Ave. L21 38 C8
Blenheim Cl. WA2 61 E2
Blenheim Rd. Ashton-in-M WN4 35 D2
Blenheim Rd. 1 Liverpool L15 & L18 68 F5
Blenheim Rd. Southport PR8 7 B6
Blenheim Rd. Wallasey L44 51 D5
Blenheim St. L5 52 D5
Blenheim Way. Liverpool L24 82 B3
Blenheim Way. St Helens WA11 44 B6
Blessed Sacrement Jun Sch. L9 39 B6
Blessed Sacrement RC Inf Sch. L9 39 A6
Blessington Rd. L4 52 F7
Bletchley Ave. 1 L44 50 F4
Bligh St. L15 68 E7
Blind Foot Rd. WA11 42 D8
Blindman's La. L39 13 C7
Blisworth St. L21 38 B6
Blomfield Rd. L19 81 D8
Bloomfield Gn. L17 68 C4
Blossom St. L20 38 C5
Blucher St. L22 26 C1
Blue Bell La. L36 55 E4
Blue Coat Sch The. L15 69 A6
Bluebell Ave. Birkenhead L41 & L43 65 F8
Bluebell Ave. Haydock WA11 45 E7
Blueberry Fields. L10 & L9 39 F6
Bluefields St. L8 67 F6
Bluestone La. L31 20 E1
Bluewood Dr. L41 50 D1
Blundell Ave. Formby L37 9 B4
Blundell Ave. Hightown L38 17 F3
Blundell Ave. Southport PR8 3 F2
Blundell Cres. PR8 3 F2
Blundell Dr. PR8 3 F2
Blundell Gr. L38 17 F3
Blundell La. PR9 2 C2
Blundell Rd. Hightown L38 17 F3
Blundell Rd. Widnes WA8 84 D8
Blundell St. L1 & L72 67 D7
Blundell's Hill Golf Club. L35 57 B1
Blundell's La. L35 57 B2
Blundells Dr. L46 49 F1
Blundellsands & Crosby Sta. L23 26 C4
Blundellsands Rd E. L23 26 C4
Blundellsands Rd W. L23 26 B3
Blyth Hey. L30 27 D3
Blyth Rd. L63 88 C7
Blythe Ave. WA8 73 B5
Blythe La. L40 14 D8
Blythe Way. 6 L6 52 F4
Blythewood. WN8 24 D7
Blythswood St. L17 68 B3
Boaler St. L6 53 B3
Boardmans La. WA9 44 E4
Boathouse La. L64 86 C3
Bobbies La. WA10 43 A3
Bodden St. WA9 58 D4
Bodley St. L4 52 F7
Bodmin Ave. PR9 2 B5
Bodmin Gr. WA11 44 D7
Bodmin Rd. L4 39 A1
Bodmin Way. L26 82 F8
Bognor Cl. L24 82 B4
Bolan St. L13 54 A3
Bold La. Burtonwood WA5 & WA9 59 C7
Bold La. Maghull L39 21 B7
Bold Pl. L1 67 E8
Bold Rd. WA9 58 F7
Bold St. Liverpool L1 52 D1
Bold St. Southport PR8 & PR9 4 B8
Bold St. St Helens WA10 43 F3
Bolde Way. L62 79 A1
Boleyn The. L31 20 E3
Bollington Cl. L43 65 F3
Bolton Ave. L32 29 C2
Bolton Cl. Formby L37 10 A2
Bolton Cl. St Helens WA9 44 C4
Bolton House Rd. WN2 36 F8
Bolton Rd. Ashton-in-M WN2 & WN4 35 D5
Bolton Rd. Bebington L62 79 B5
Bolton Rd. Southport PR8 4 A4
Bolton Rd E. L62 79 C6
Bolton St. Garswood WN4 34 D5
Bolton St. Liverpool L1 & L3 52 E1
Bolton St. St Helens WA9 44 C4
Bolton Wlk. 3 L32 29 C2
Bond St. Liverpool L3 52 D4
Bond St. Prescot L34 56 D6
Bonnington Ave. L23 26 C5
Bonsall Rd. L12 54 C6
Boode Croft. L28 41 B1
Booker Ave. L18 & L19 69 C1
Booker Ave Sch. L18 69 B1
Booth St. 5 Liverpool L13 54 A3
Booth St. Newton-le-W WA12 46 A3
Booth St. Southport PR8 4 B8
Booth St. St Helens L35 57 D7
Booth's Brow Rd. WN4 34 D6
Booth's La. L39 12 F4
Boothwood Cl. Liverpool L7 68 B8
Bootle High Sch. L30 28 A4
Bootle New Strand Sta. L20 38 C4
Bootle Oriel Road Sta. L20 38 B2
Borax St. L13 54 A2
Border Rd. L60 86 B8
Borella Rd. L13 53 F6
Borough Pavement. L41 66 D6
Borough Pl. 10 L41 66 E6
Borough Rd. Bebington L42 78 D8
Borough Rd. Birkenhead L41 & L42 66 C4
Borough Rd. St Helens WA10 43 E2
Borough Rd. Wallasey L44 51 E3
Borough Rd E. Birkenhead L41 66 E6
Borough Rd E. Wallasey L44 51 E2
Borough Way. 1 L44 51 E2
Borron Rd. WA12 46 B5
Borrow Lane Cty Prim Sch. WA5 74 E7
Borrowdale. L37 9 F5
Borrowdale Ave. WA2 61 C3
Borrowdale Rd. Bebington L63 78 F4
Borrowdale Rd. Birkenhead L46 64 D7
Borrowdale Rd. Liverpool L15 68 E6
Borrowdale Rd. St Helens WA10 57 C8
Borrowdale Rd. Widnes WA8 84 C8
Boscow Cres. WA9 58 D7
Bosnia St. L8 68 A3
Bossom Ct. L22 37 E7
Bostock St. L5 52 E5
Boswell Rd. L43 65 F1
Boswell St. Bootle L20 38 A5
Boswell St. Liverpool L8 68 C7
Bosworth Cl. L63 78 F2
Bosworth Dr. PR8 7 B4
Bosworth Rd. WA11 44 D6
Botanic Gr. L7 53 C1
Botanic Pl. L7 53 C2
Botanic Rd. Liverpool L7 53 C1
Botanic Rd. Southport PR9 2 B2
Botany Rd. L24 82 C5
Botley Cl. L49 64 D5
Boulevard The. L12 54 B8
Boulting Ave. WA5 60 F1
Boulton Ave. Bebington L62 79 B8
Boulton Ave. West Kirby L48 63 B3
Boundary Dr. L23 26 D5
Boundary Dr. L25 82 D7
Boundary Farm Rd. L26 82 E6
Boundary La. Heswall L60 86 A8
Boundary La. Kirkby L33 30 F2
Boundary La. Liverpool L6 53 B4
Boundary Rd. Bebington L62 79 B7
Boundary Rd. Birkenhead L43 65 E7
Boundary Rd. Huyton-w-R L36 71 A8
Boundary Rd. Litherland L30 27 D1
Boundary Rd. Liverpool L36 70 F8
Boundary Rd. St Helens WA10 43 E3
Boundary Rd. Wallasey L43 50 D1
Boundary Rd. West Kirby L48 75 D8
Boundary St. Liverpool L5 52 B6
Boundary St. Liverpool L5 52 C6
Boundary St. Southport PR8 4 B4
Boundary St E. L5 52 E6
Boundary Wlk. L36 71 A8
Bourne Ave. WA3 47 D8
Bourne St. L6 53 B3
Bourton Rd. L25 82 B7
Bousfield St. L4 52 E7
Boverton Cl. WA5 60 E1
Bowden Cl. L12 40 E2
Bowden Rd. L19 81 B6
Bowden St. L21 38 B6
Bowdon Rd. L45 51 A6
Bowen Cl. WA8 72 D4
Bower Gr. L21 37 F7
Bower Rd. Heswall L60 86 C8
Bower Rd. Huyton-w-R L36 55 E4
Bower Rd. Liverpool L25 70 A4
Bower St. WA8 73 C1
Bowfell Cl. L63 88 D3
Bowfield Rd. L19 81 B7
Bowker's Green La. L39 21 E4
Bowland Ave. Ashton-in-M WN4 35 B4
Bowland Ave. Golborne WA3 36 C1
Bowland Ave. Liverpool L16 69 D8
Bowland Ave. St Helens WA9 58 B3
Bowland Cl. L62 79 D1
Bowland Dr. L21 27 C4
Bowles St. L20 38 A5
Bowley Rd. L13 53 F5
Bowling Green Cl. PR8 4 F5
Bowness Ave. Bebington L63 88 C5
Bowness Ave. Birkenhead L43 66 A2
Bowness Ave. Southport PR8 7 C3
Bowness Ave. St Helens WA11 44 B8
Bowness Ave. Warrington WA2 61 C2
Bowood Ct. WA2 61 A4
Bowood St. L8 67 F3
Bowring Cl. L8 68 A4
Bowring Dr. L64 86 B1
Bowring Park Ave. L14 & L16 55 A1
Bowring Park Golf Course. L36 70 B8
Bowring Park Rd. L13 & L14 & L16 54 E1
Bowring St. L8 68 A4
Bowscale Cl. L49 64 E5
Bowscale Rd. L11 40 A2
Boxdale Ct. L15 69 A4
Boxdale Rd. L18 69 A4
Boxmoor Rd. L18 69 A2
Boxtree Cl. L12 40 F4
Boxwood Cl. L36 55 C2
Boycott St. 8 L5 53 A6
Boyd Cl. L46 50 B3
Boydell Cl. L28 55 B7
Boyer Ave. L31 28 D7
Boyes Brow. L32 & L33 29 D4
Boyle Ave. WA2 61 E1
Boyton Ct. L7 68 C8
Brabant Rd. L17 68 E1
Braby Rd. L20 & L21 38 C6
Bracebridge Dr. PR8 4 F2
Bracewell Cl. 3 WA9 58 C6
Bracken Ct. 12 WA9 58 C4
Bracken Dr. L48 63 E2
Bracken La. L63 78 D5
Bracken Wood. L12 40 E4
Brackendale. L49 65 C3
Brackendale Ave. L9 39 B7
Brackenhurst Dr. L45 51 C7
Brackenhurst Gn. L32 & L33 29 E2
Brackenside. L60 76 F2
Brackenway. L37 10 A6
Brackenwood Gr. L35 56 F3
Brackenwood Inf Sch. L63 78 F5
Brackenwood Jun Sch. L63 78 E5
Brackenwood Municipal Golf Course. L63 78 D4
Brackenwood Rd. L63 78 E4
Brackley Cl. L44 51 A3
Brackley St. WA7 84 F3
Bracknell Ave. L32 40 E8
Bracknell Cl. L32 29 E1
Bradbourne Cl. L12 40 E3
Bradda Cl. L49 64 F7
Braddan Ave. L13 53 E5
Bradden Cl. L63 79 B2
Brade St. PR9 2 C4
Bradewell Cl. L4 52 E8
Bradewell St. 7 L4 52 E8
Bradfield Ave. L10 28 C3
Bradfield St. 7 L7 53 C2
Bradgate Cl. L46 49 B1
Bradkirk Ct. L30 27 D5
Bradlegh Rd. WA12 46 B1
Bradley Fold. L35 71 A8
Bradley La. WA5 & WA12 46 A1
Bradley Pl. PR8 4 B7
Bradley Rd. L21 38 C8
Bradley St. PR9 4 C8
Bradley Way. WA8 73 B1
Bradman Rd. Kirkby L33 30 D3
Bradman Rd. Wallasey L46 49 C1
Bradmoor Rd. L62 88 D8
Bradshaw Cl. WA10 43 D4
Bradshaw Pl. 18 L6 53 A3
Bradshaw St. WA8 73 A2
Bradshaw's La. PR8 7 D6
Bradstone Cl. L10 40 B6
Bradville Rd. L9 39 C7
Bradwell Cl. L48 63 D2
Bradwell Rd. WA3 47 E7
Brae St. L7 53 B2
Braehaven Rd. L45 51 C7
Braemar Ave. PR9 1 E2
Braemar Cl. L35 56 F3
Braemar St. L20 38 D1
Braemore Rd. L44 50 F4
Braeside Cres. WN5 33 D5
Braeside Gdns. Birkenhead L49 64 F5
Brahms Cl. L8 68 B6
Braid St. L41 66 D8
Brainerd St. L13 53 E5
Braithwaite Cl. L35 57 C3
Braithwaite Rd. WA3 47 D8
Bramberton Pl. L4 39 C1
Bramberton Rd. L4 39 C1
Bramble Ave. L41 65 F8
Bramble Cl. WA5 74 E3
Bramble Way. L46 49 D2
Brambling Pk. L26 70 E1
Bramcote Ave. WA11 44 D6
Bramcote Cl. L33 30 A4
Bramcote Rd. L33 30 A4
Bramcote Wlk. L33 29 F4
Bramerton Ct. L48 63 A3
Bramford Cl. L49 64 E5
Bramhall Cl. L24 82 E2
Bramhall Dr. L62 88 F4
Bramhall Rd. Seaforth L22 37 E8
Bramhall Rd. Skelmersdale WN8 15 F2
Bramley Ave. L63 78 E7
Bramley Cl. L27 70 E5
Bramley Wlk. L24 82 D2
Bramleys The. L31 28 C7
Brampton Ct. WA9 45 B3
Brampton Dr. L7 & L8 68 A8
Bramwell Ave. L43 66 A1
Bramwell St. WA9 44 E4
Brancker Ave. L35 57 B4
Brancote Ct. L43 65 F6
Brancote Gdns. L62 88 D7
Brancote Mount. L43 65 F6
Brancote Rd. L43 65 F6
Brandearth Hey. L28 55 B7
Brandon. WA8 72 B2
Brandon Cl. WN8 25 A7
Brandon St. L41 66 F6
Brandreth Cl. L35 57 C3
Brandreth Hospl. L39 13 E5
Brandwood Ave. WA2 61 B2
Branfield Cl. L12 40 E3
Bransford Cl. WN4 35 C2
Branstree Ave. L11 39 F2
Brantfield Ct. WA2 61 E2
Branthwaite Cl. 1 L11 40 A1
Branthwaite Cres. L11 40 A1
Branthwaite Gr. 4 L11 40 A1
Brasenose Rd. L20 38 C1
Brassey St. Birkenhead L41 66 B8
Brassey St. Liverpool L8 67 E6
Brattan Rd. L41 66 C4
Braunton Rd. Liverpool L17 68 E1
Braunton Rd. 2 Wallasey L45 51 A6
Bray Rd. L24 82 C4
Bray St. L41 66 B8
Braybrooke Rd. L11 40 A3
Braydon Cl. L25 82 C6
Brayfield Rd. L4 39 D1
Brechin Rd. L33 29 F2
Breck Cl. 5 L6 53 A4
Breck Pl. L44 51 A3
Breck Rd. Liverpool L6 53 A5
Breck Rd. Wallasey L44 50 F4
Breck Rd. Widnes WA8 73 B1
Breck Wlk. 8 L6 53 A4
Breckfield Comm Comp Sch. L5 52 F5
Breckfield Jun Mix Sch. L5 52 F6
Breckfield Pl. L5 52 F5
Breckfield Rd N. L5 & L6 53 A5
Breckfield Rd S. L6 53 A5
Breckside Ave. L44 50 E4
Breckside Pk. L6 53 C6
Brecon Ave. Litherland L30 27 F1
Brecon Ct. Formby L37 9 E4
Brecon Ct. Warrington WA5 60 E2
Brecon Rd. Bebington L42 78 C8
Brecon Rd. Birkenhead L42 66 C1
Brecon Wlk. L30 28 A1
Breeze Cl. L9 38 F3
Breeze Hill. Bootle L20 & L4 & L9 38 E2
Breeze Hill. 9 Bootle L4 38 F2
Breeze La. L9 38 F3
Breeze Rd. PR8 3 E2
Brelade Rd. L13 53 F4
Bremhill Rd. L11 39 F3
Bremner Cl. L7 53 C1
Brenda Cres. L23 27 A7
Brendale Ave. L31 28 C8

Brendon Ave. Litherland L21 27 A1
Brendon Ave. Warrington WA2 61 A3
Brendon Gr. WA9 45 A4
Brendon's Way. L30 27 E3
Brendor Rd. L25 70 B1
Brenig St. L41 50 F1
Brenka Ave. L9 28 B1
Brent Way. L24 & L26 82 F6
Brentfield. WA8 72 D2
Brentwood Ave. Crosby L23 26 F5
Brentwood Ave. Liverpool L17 68 C3
Brentwood Cl. Hightown L38 17 F2
Brentwood Cl. St Helens WA10 43 B3
Brentwood Ct. Southport PR9 1 D1
Brentwood St. L44 51 C3
Brereton Ave. Bebington L63 79 A6
Brereton Ave. Liverpool L15 69 A7
Bretherton Pl. L35 57 C4
Bretherton Rd. L34 56 E6
Bretlands Rd. L23 27 B6
Brett St. L41 66 B8
Bretton Fold. PR8 4 F5
Brewery La. Formby L37 9 F6
Brewery La. Litherland L31 28 E4
Brewster St. L20 & L4 38 E1
Brian Ave. L61 76 F6
Briar Cl. WN4 35 A4
Briar Dr. Heswall L60 86 A8
Briar Dr. Huyton-w-R L36 55 D2
Briar Rd. Golborne WA3 47 B8
Briar Rd. Southport PR8 7 D4
Briar St. L4 & L5 52 D7
Briardale Rd. Bebington L63 78 F7
Briardale Rd. Bebington L64 88 A1
Briardale Rd. Birkenhead L42 & L43 66 C4
Briardale Rd. Liverpool L18 69 A4
Briardale Rd. Wallasey L44 51 E2
Briarfield Ave. WA8 72 A1
Briarfield Rd. L60 86 B8
Briars Cl. L35 57 D1
Briars Gn. WN8 16 B4
Briars La. L31 20 E1
Briars The. PR8 3 F1
Briarswood Cl. Bebington L42 78 F8
Briarswood Cl. Prescot L35 56 F3
Briarwood Rd. L17 & L18 68 E3
Briary Croft. L38 17 F3
Brick St. Liverpool L1 & L72 67 D7
Brick St. Newton-le-W WA12 45 F3
Brickfields. L36 56 A1
Brickfields La. 1 L8 67 F4
Brickwall Gn. L29 27 F7
Brickwall La. L29 & L30 27 E6
Bride St. 4 L4 38 F2
Bridge Ave. L39 13 E5
Bridge Croft. L21 & L30 27 C3
Bridge Ct. Litherland L30 27 D4
Bridge Ct. West Kirby L48 63 A3
Bridge Farm Cl. L49 65 B4
Bridge Farm Dr. L31 20 F2
Bridge Gdns. L12 40 F1
Bridge Gr. PR8 4 B6
Bridge Ind Est. L24 82 B5
Bridge La. L30 27 E3
Bridge Rd. Bootle L21 38 B7
Bridge Rd. Crosby L22 & L23 26 C3
Bridge Rd. Huyton-w-R L36 55 C2
Bridge Rd. Liverpool L15 & L7 68 D8
Bridge Rd. Liverpool L18 69 A3
Bridge Rd. Maghull L31 28 D7
Bridge Rd. Prescot L34 & L35 56 E5
Bridge Rd. St Helens WA9 58 D2
Bridge Rd. West Kirby L48 63 A3
Bridge St. Bebington L62 79 B5
Bridge St. Birkenhead L41 & L72 66 E7
Bridge St. Bootle L20 38 B2
Bridge St. Golborne WA12 & WA3 47 A7
Bridge St. Newton-le-W WA12 46 B3
Bridge St. Ormskirk L39 13 E4
Bridge St. Southport PR8 4 B6
Bridge St. St Helens WA10 44 A3
Bridge Wills La. PR9 2 C5
Bridgecroft Rd. L45 51 B6
Bridgefield Cl. L25 70 B7
Bridgefield Forum (L Ctr). L26 71 A2
Bridgeford Ave. L12 54 A7
Bridgehall Dr. WN8 25 B7
Bridgeman St. WA10 43 D3
Bridgend Cl. WA8 72 D3
Bridgend Dr. PR8 7 C4
Bridgenorth Rd. L61 76 E4
Bridges La. Litherland L29 27 F7
Bridges La. Maghull L29 & L31 28 A8
Bridgeview Dr. L33 29 F4
Bridgewater Cl. L21 27 A2
Bridgewater St. L1 & L72 67 D7
Bridgewater Way. L35 & L36 71 A8
Bridgeway. L11 39 E1
Bridle Ave. L44 51 E2
Bridle Cl. Bebington L62 88 E7
Bridle Cl. Birkenhead L43 65 B6
Bridle Ct. WA9 58 C8
Bridle Pk. L62 88 E7
Bridle Rd. Bebington L62 88 E6
Bridle Rd. Bootle L30 38 F8
Bridle Rd. Maghull L30 28 A1
Bridle Rd. Wallasey L44 51 E2
Bridle Way. L20 & L30 38 F7
Bridport St. L3 52 E2
Brierfield. WN8 24 D6
Brierfield Rd. L15 68 F6
Brierley Cl. L30 28 B4
Briers Cl. WA2 61 F3
Briery Hey Ave. L33 29 F2
Brighouse Cl. L39 13 D6
Bright St. Birkenhead L41 66 C6
Bright St. 23 Liverpool L6 53 A3
Bright St. Southport PR9 4 F7
Brightgate Cl. L7 68 B8
Brighton Rd. Crosby L22 26 D1
Brighton Rd. Huyton-w-R L36 56 B3
Brighton Rd. Southport PR8 4 A3
Brighton St. L44 51 E3
Brighton Vale. L22 26 C2
Brightwell Cl. L49 64 F4
Brignall Gr. WA3 36 D1
Brill St. L41 66 B8
Brimelow Cres. WA5 74 E3
Brimstage Ave. L63 78 D8
Brimstage Cl. L60 86 C8
Brimstage Gn. L60 86 D8
Brimstage La. L63 78 B3
Brimstage Rd. Bebington L63 78 D2
Brimstage Rd. Bootle L4 38 E2
Brimstage Rd. Heswall L60 86 C7
Brimstage St. 15 L41 66 C5
Brindley Cl. L21 27 A2
Brindley Rd. Kirkby L32 29 C2
Brindley Rd. St Helens WA9 58 F6
Brindley St. Liverpool L8 67 D6
Brindley St. Runcorn WA7 84 F3
Brinklow Cl. PR8 7 A5
Brinley Cl. L62 88 D5
Brinton Cl. Liverpool L27 70 D6
Brinton Cl. Widnes WA8 84 E8
Brisbane Ave. L45 51 A8
Brisbane St. WA9 57 D8
Briscoe Ave. 2 L46 64 E7
Briscoe Dr. L46 64 E7
Bristol Ave. L44 51 C4
Bristol Rd. L15 69 A6
Bristow Cl. WA5 60 B1
Britannia Ave. L15 68 D7
Britannia Cres. 2 Liverpool L8 68 A3
Britannia Rd. L45 51 A4
Britonside Ave. L32 & L33 41 A8
Brittarge Brow. L27 70 E4
Britten Cl. L8 68 B6
Broad Green Comm Comp Sch. L13 54 B2
Broad Green Cty Prim Sch. L13 54 B2
Broad Green Rd. L13 54 B2
Broad Hey. L30 27 D3
Broad Hey Cl. L25 70 B3
Broad La. Burtonwood WA5 59 E8
Broad La. Formby L37 10 E2
Broad La. Haskayne L39 12 B2
Broad La. Haydock WA5 & WA9 45 C1
Broad La. Heswall L60 85 C8
Broad La. Kirkby L32 40 F8
Broad La. Liverpool L11 & L4 39 F1
Broad La. Liverpool L11 54 A8
Broad La. Maghull L37 & L38 19 A8
Broad La. Maghull L29 19 C2
Broad La. St Helens WA11 33 B1
Broad Oak Ave. Haydock WA11 45 A6
Broad Oak Ave. Warrington WA5 74 E4
Broad Oak Comm Prim Sch. WA9 45 A3
Broad Oak Rd. WA9 44 F3
Broad Pl. L11 53 F8
Broad Sq. L11 53 F8
Broad Square Cty Prim Sch. L11 53 F8
Broad View. L11 53 F8
Broadbelt St. 5 L4 38 F2
Broadbent House. L31 28 D7
Broadfield Ave. L43 65 C8
Broadfield Cl. L43 65 B8
Broadgate Ave. WA9 58 C8
Broadgreen. L15 54 B1
Broadheath Ave. L43 65 C7
Broadheath Terr. WA8 72 D1
Broadhurst St. L17 68 C3
Broadlands. PR8 3 E3
Broadley Ave. WA3 47 C7
Broadmead. Heswall L60 86 C7
Broadmead. Liverpool L19 81 E7
Broadoak Rd. Liverpool L14 54 F3
Broadoak Rd. Maghull L31 20 E1
Broadstone Dr. L63 78 F2
Broadway. Bebington L63 78 D7
Broadway. Birkenhead L49 64 E4
Broadway. Liverpool L11 39 E1
Broadway. St Helens WA10 43 B5
Broadway. St Helens WA10 57 C8
Broadway. Wallasey L45 50 F5
Broadway. Widnes WA8 72 A1
Broadway Ave. L45 50 F5
Broadway Cl. PR8 7 B5
Broadway Comm High Sch. WA10 57 C8
Broadwood Ave. L31 28 C7
Broadwood St. L15 68 E7
Brock Gdns. L24 83 E2
Brock Hall Cl. 14 WA9 58 C4
Brock St. L4 52 E8
Brockenhurst Rd. L9 39 A5
Brockholme Rd. L18 & L19 69 A1
Brocklebank La. L19 81 D8
Brocklebank Rd. PR9 1 E2
Brockley Rd. 1 L45 51 B8
Brockmoor Tower. L4 52 E8
Brockstedes Ave. WN4 34 E6
Brocstedes Rd. WN4 34 D7
Brodie Ave. L18 & L19 69 A1
Bromborough Golf Course. L63 88 A5
Bromborough Pool Prim Sch. L62 79 D5
Bromborough Rake Sta. L62 88 C8
Bromborough Rd. L63 & L62 79 B4
Bromborough Sta. L62 88 C7
Bromborough Village Rd. L62 79 E1
Brome Way. L63 79 B2
Bromilow Rd. Skelmersdale WN8 15 C1
Bromilow Rd. St Helens WA9 44 F2
Bromley Ave. Golborne WA3 47 D7
Bromley Ave. Liverpool L18 68 F5
Bromley Cl. Heswall L60 85 F7
Bromley Cl. Warrington WA2 61 F3
Bromley Rd. L45 51 A7
Brompton Ave. Crosby L23 26 C3
Brompton Ave. Liverpool L17 & L8 68 C6
Brompton Ave. Wallasey L44 51 C4
Brompton House. L17 68 C5
Brompton Rd. PR8 4 E7
Bromsgrove Rd. L49 64 C4
Bromyard Cl. L20 38 B4
Bronington Ave. L62 88 D6
Bronte Cl. L23 26 B4
Bronte St. Liverpool L3 52 E1
Bronte St. St Helens WA10 43 D4
Brook Acre Cty Prim Sch. WA2 61 E1
Brook Ave. L31 20 E2
Brook Cl. Cronton WA8 72 C6
Brook Cl. Wallasey L44 & L45 51 C5
Brook End. WA9 45 A1
Brook Hey. L64 86 B2
Brook Hey Dr. L33 30 A3
Brook Hey Wlk. L33 30 A3
Brook House. PR8 4 C5
Brook House Gr. WA10 43 A3
Brook La. Ormskirk L39 13 E4
Brook La. Rainford WA11 32 F7
Brook Lynn Ave. WA3 36 F1
Brook Meadow. L61 76 E7
Brook Pk. L31 28 C7
Brook Rd. Bootle L20 38 B3
Brook Rd. Litherland L23 27 A7
Brook Rd. Liverpool L9 39 A4
Brook Rd. Maghull L31 28 E8
Brook Side. L31 20 E1
Brook St. Ashton-in-M WN4 35 C2
Brook St. Bebington L62 79 A6
Brook St. Birkenhead L41 66 D8
Brook St. Golborne WA3 47 A8
Brook St. Liverpool L3 52 B2
Brook St. Prescot L35 56 F4
Brook St. Southport PR9 2 D4
Brook St. St Helens WA10 44 A3
Brook St. Widnes WA8 73 B1
Brook St E. L41 & L72 66 E7
Brook Terr. L48 63 B2
Brook Vale. L21 & L22 37 F8
Brook Wlk. L61 76 D7
Brookbridge Rd. L13 53 E6
Brookdale. WA8 72 A3
Brookdale Ave N. L49 64 E4
Brookdale Ave S. L49 64 E3
Brookdale Cl. L49 64 E4
Brookdale Prim Sch. L49 64 E3
Brookdale Rd. L15 68 E6
Brooke Rd E. L22 & L23 26 D2
Brooke Rd W. L22 26 C2
Brookfield Ave. Crosby L22 & L23 26 D3
Brookfield Ave. Rainhill L35 57 C5
Brookfield Ave. Seaforth L21 & L22 37 F8
Brookfield Dr. L9 39 C5
Brookfield Gdns. L48 63 B2
Brookfield High Sch. L32 40 D8
Brookfield La. L39 21 A5
Brookfield Rd. Skelmersdale WN8 25 B7
Brookfield Rd. West Kirby L48 63 B2
Brookfield St. WA12 46 B3
Brookfields Prim Sch. WN8 15 D2
Brookfields Sch. WA8 73 D2
Brookhill Cl. L20 38 D3
Brookhill Rd. L20 38 D4
Brookhouse Rd. L39 13 D6
Brookhurst Ave. L63 88 C5
Brookhurst Cl. L63 & L62 88 C5
Brookhurst Prim Sch. L63 88 C6
Brookhurst Rd. L63 88 C5
Brookland La. WA9 45 A1
Brookland Rd. L41 66 D5
Brookland Rd E. L13 54 A3
Brookland Rd W. L13 54 A3
Brooklands. Birkenhead L41 66 D7
Brooklands. Ormskirk L39 14 A6
Brooklands Ave. Ashton-in-M WN4 35 D2
Brooklands Ave. Seaforth L21 & L22 37 E8
Brooklands Dr. Maghull L31 28 D8
Brooklands Dr. Orrell WN5 25 D5
Brooklands Gdns. L64 86 C1
Brooklands Rd. Neston L64 86 C1
Brooklands Rd. Orrell WN8 25 C7
Brooklands Rd. St Helens WA10 43 A4
Brooklands The. L36 55 E1
Brooklet Rd. L60 77 C1
Brooks Alley. 4 L1 52 D1
Brooks Rd. L37 9 D2
Brooks The. WA11 44 A7
Brooks Way. L37 9 D2
Brookside Ave. Ashton-in-M WN4 34 F8
Brookside Ave. Liverpool L14 54 D4
Brookside Ave. Rainford WA11 31 E7
Brookside Ave. Seaforth L21 & L22 37 F8
Brookside Ave. St Helens WA10 43 C5
Brookside Cl. Billinge WN5 33 E5
Brookside Cl. Haydock WA11 45 B7
Brookside Cl. Liverpool L12 & L28 54 F8
Brookside Cl. Prescot L35 56 E4
Brookside Cres. L49 64 E5
Brookside Ct. L23 26 E4
Brookside Dr. L49 64 E5
Brookside Prim Sch. L28 55 B7
Brookside Rd. Prescot L35 56 E4
Brookside Rd. Southport PR8 4 C2
Brookside Sch. L10 39 F8
Brookside View. WA11 45 B7
Brookside Way. WA11 45 B7
Brookvale Cl. WA5 59 F6
Brookway. Birkenhead L49 64 E5
Brookway. Birkenhead L43 65 E1
Brookway. Heswall L43 77 E8
Brookway. Wallasey L45 51 A5
Brookway La. WA9 45 A1
Brookwood Rd. L36 55 E4
Broom Cl. L34 56 F6
Broom Hill. L43 65 F7
Broom Rd. WA10 57 B8
Broom Way. L26 82 E7
Broome Rd. PR8 4 B3
Broomfield Cl. L60 76 C1
Broomfield Gdns. L9 38 F5
Broomfield Rd. L9 38 F5
Broomlands. L60 85 E8
Broomleigh Cl. L63 78 D5
Broomsgrove. L10 28 E1
Broseley Ave. L62 79 C1
Broster Ave. L46 64 C8
Broster Cl. L46 64 C8
Brosters La. L47 48 D1
Brotherton Cl. L62 88 C8
Brougham Ave. L41 66 F3
Brougham Rd. L44 51 E3
Brougham Terr. 5 L6 53 A3
Broughton Ave. Golborne WA3 47 D7
Broughton Ave. Southport PR8 4 D4
Broughton Ave. West Kirby L48 63 A3
Broughton Dr. L19 81 A7
Broughton Hall High Sch. L14 54 E5
Broughton Hall Rd. L14 54 E5
Broughton Rd. L44 51 B3
Brow La. L60 85 F7
Brow Rd. L43 50 D1
Brow Side. L5 & L6 52 F4
Brown Edge Cl. PR8 5 A2
Brown Heath Ave. WN5 33 D3
Brown's La. L30 28 A3
Brownbill Bank. L27 70 E5
Browning Ave. Birkenhead L42 66 F1
Browning Ave. Widnes WA8 84 F8
Browning Cl. L36 56 A1
Browning House. L62 79 A7
Browning Rd. L22 26 D2
Browning Rd. L45 50 D5
Browning St. L20 38 A4
Brownlow Arc. 12 WA10 44 A3
Brownlow Hill. L1 & L3 & L7 52 F1
Brownlow La. WN5 25 C1
Brownlow Rd. L62 79 B7
Brownlow St. L3 52 F1
Brownmoor La. Crosby L23 26 F3
Brownmoor Pk. L23 26 F3
Brownville Rd. L13 53 E6
Brows Cl. L37 9 E3
Brows La. L37 9 E3
Broxholme Way. L31 28 D7
Broxton Ave. Birkenhead L43 65 F2
Broxton Ave. Orrell WN5 25 F7
Broxton Ave. West Kirby L48 63 B3
Broxton Cl. WA8 72 C3
Broxton Rd. 7 L45 51 A6
Broxton St. L15 68 E8
Bruce Ave. WA2 61 D1
Bruce Cres. L63 88 C6
Bruce St. 4 Liverpool L8 68 A4
Bruce St. St Helens WA10 43 E3
Brunel Cl. 2 L6 53 A4
Brunel Dr. L21 27 A2
Brunel Mews. 3 L6 53 A4
Brunel Wlk. 4 L6 53 A4
Brunner Rd. 4 WA8 73 A1
Brunsfield Cl. L46 64 C7
Brunstath Cl. L60 77 C1
Brunswick Bsns Pk. L8 67 D4
Brunswick Cl. 4 L4 52 E8
Brunswick Ct. L41 66 E7
Brunswick Enterprise Ctr. L8 67 D5
Brunswick Mews. L22 37 E7
Brunswick Par. L22 37 E8
Brunswick Pl. L20 52 B8
Brunswick Rd. Liverpool L3 & L6 52 F3
Brunswick Rd. Newton-le-W WA12 45 F4
Brunswick St. Liverpool L2 & L3 52 C1
Brunswick St. Liverpool L19 81 C3
Brunswick St. St Helens WA9 45 A3
Brunswick Way. L3 67 D5
Brunt La. L19 81 E7
Bruton Rd. L36 55 D6
Bryanston Rd. Birkenhead L42 66 A2
Bryanston Rd. Liverpool L17 68 B3
Bryant Rd. L21 38 B6
Bryceway The. L12 54 D4
Brydges St. L7 53 A1
Bryer Rd. L35 56 D4
Bryn Bank. L44 51 C4
Bryn Cross. WN4 35 A6
Bryn Gates La. WN2 & WN4 35 D8
Bryn Rd. WN4 35 B5
Bryn Rd S. WN4 35 C4
Bryn St. WN4 35 B3
Bryn Sta. WN4 35 A6
Brynford Hts. L5 52 E5
Brynmor Rd. L18 69 A1
Brynmoss Ave. 2 L44 50 F4

Brynn St. Ashton-in-M WN2 .. 35 F7
Brynn St. St Helens WA10 .... 44 A4
Bryony Cl. WN5 .... 25 D5
Bryony Way. L42 .... 78 F8
Brythen St. 22 L1 & L69 .... 52 D1
Buccleuch St. L41 .... 50 F1
Buchanan Rd. Bootle L4 & L9 38 F3
Buchanan Rd. Wallasey L44 . 51 D3
Buckfast Ave. WA11 .... 46 A7
Buckfast Cl. Litherland L30 ... 27 F4
Buckfast Cl. Warrington WA5 74 E3
Buckfast Dr. L37 .... 10 B2
Buckingham Ave. Bebington L63 .... 78 E7
Buckingham Ave. Birkenhead L43 .... 65 F7
Buckingham Ave. Liverpool L17 & L8 .... 68 D6
Buckingham Ave. Widnes WA8 .... 73 A4
Buckingham Cl. Litherland L30 .... 27 C3
Buckingham Cl. St Helens WA10 .... 43 F2
Buckingham Ct. L33 .... 29 F4
Buckingham Dr. WA11 .... 44 B6
Buckingham Gr. L37 .... 9 E1
Buckingham Rd. Liverpool L9 .... 39 A6
Buckingham Rd. Liverpool L13 .... 53 E5
Buckingham Rd. Maghull L31 .... 28 C8
Buckingham Rd. Wallasey L44 .... 50 F4
Buckingham St. L5 .... 52 E5
Buckland Cl. WA8 .... 84 D7
Buckland Dr. L63 .... 78 F2
Buckland St. L17 .... 68 B3
Buckley Hill La. L23 & L29 & L30 .... 27 D5
Buckley Way. L30 .... 27 D5
Buckley Wlk. L24 .... 82 D2
Buckthorn Cl. L28 .... 55 B7
Buckthorn Gdns. L35 .... 57 C6
Bude Cl. L43 .... 65 C6
Bude Rd. WA8 .... 72 E2
Budworth Ave. St Helens WA9 .... 58 B4
Budworth Ave. Widnes WA8 72 D2
Budworth Cl. L43 .... 65 E4
Budworth Ct. L43 .... 65 F5
Budworth Dr. L25 .... 70 D2
Budworth Rd. L43 .... 65 E5
Buerton Cl. L43 .... 65 E4
Buffs La. Heswall L60 .... 86 B8
Buildwas Rd. L64 .... 86 F2
Bulford Rd. L9 .... 39 E3
Bulkeley Rd. L44 .... 51 D3
Bull Bridge La. L10 .... 28 E2
Bull Cop. L37 .... 10 B3
Bull La. L9 .... 39 B7
Bullens Rd. Kirkby L32 .... 29 F1
Bullens Rd. Liverpool L4 .... 52 F8
Bullfinch Ct. L26 .... 70 E1
Bulrushes The. L8 .... 67 F3
Bulwer St. Birkenhead L42 ... 66 F2
Bulwer St. Bootle L20 .... 38 A5
Bulwer St. 7 Liverpool L5 & L6 .... 53 A5
Bundoran Rd. L17 .... 68 E2
Bungalow Rd. WA12 .... 46 E1
Bungalows The. Ashton-in-M WN4 .... 34 F7
Bungalows The. Raby L63 .... 87 B6
Bunter Rd. L32 .... 40 F7
Bunting Ct. L26 .... 70 D2
Burbo Bank Rd. L23 .... 26 B3
Burbo Bank Rd N. L23 .... 26 A5
Burbo Bank Rd S. L23 .... 26 B3
Burbo Cres. L23 .... 26 B3
Burbo Mansions. L23 .... 26 B3
Burbo Way. L45 .... 50 E8
Burden Rd. L46 .... 49 C1
Burdett Ave. L63 .... 79 A2
Burdett Cl. L63 .... 79 A2
Burdett Rd. L22 .... 26 D2
Burdett Rd. L45 .... 50 D5
Burdett St. L17 .... 68 C3
Burford Ave. Wallasey L44 ... 51 A3
Burford Rd. L16 .... 54 D1
Burgess Gdns. L31 .... 20 C2
Burgess' La. L37 .... 11 A1
Burgess St. L3 .... 52 E2
Burghill Rd. L12 .... 40 F4
Burkhardt Dr. WA12 .... 46 E3
Burland Cl. WA7 .... 84 F1
Burleigh Rd N. L4 & L5 .... 52 F7
Burleigh Rd S. L4 & L5 .... 52 F6
Burley Ave. WA3 .... 36 D1
Burley Cl. L32 .... 29 F1
Burlingham Ave. L48 .... 63 D2
Burlington Ave. L37 .... 10 B3
Burlington Rd. Southport PR8 3 F3
Burlington Rd. Wallasey L45 37 B1
Burlington St. 3 Birkenhead L41 .... 66 E6
Burlington St. Liverpool L3 .. 52 C4
Burman Cres. L19 .... 81 C7
Burman Rd. L19 .... 81 D7
Burnage Ave. WA9 .... 58 C4
Burnage Cl. L24 .... 82 F2
Burnand St. L4 .... 52 F7
Burnard Cl. L32 .... 29 F2
Burnard Cres. L32 & L33 .... 29 F2
Burnard Wlk. 2 L33 .... 29 F2
Burnell Cl. 8 WA10 .... 43 F4
Burnfell. WA3 .... 47 E7
Burnham Cl. Warrington WA5 .... 74 F5
Burnham Cl. Widnes WA8 .... 72 C3
Burnham Rd. L18 .... 69 C3
Burnie Ave. L20 .... 38 E5
Burnley Ave. Birkenhead L46 64 F8
Burnley Ave. Southport PR8 ... 7 D5
Burnley Cl. L6 .... 53 A4
Burnley Rd. PR8 .... 7 C5
Burnley Rd. L46 .... 64 F8
Burns Ave. L45 .... 51 A5
Burns Cl. Ashton-in-M WN4 .. 34 F6
Burns Cl. Liverpool L16 .... 69 F8
Burns Cl. Orrell WN5 .... 25 D1
Burns Cl. Prescot L35 .... 56 E3
Burns Cres. WA8 .... 84 F8
Burns Gr. Huyton-w-R L36 .... 56 A1
Burns Gr. Warrington WA2 ... 61 C2
Burns Rd. WA9 .... 58 A3
Burns St. L20 .... 38 A5
Burnsall Ave. WA3 .... 47 F8
Burnsall Dr. WA8 .... 72 C3
Burnsall St. L19 .... 81 E5
Burnside Ave. L44 .... 51 B2
Burnside Rd. L44 .... 51 B2
Burnt Ash Cl. L19 .... 80 F7
Burnthwaite Rd. L14 .... 54 C3
Burrell Cl. L42 .... 66 C1
Burrell Ct. L42 .... 66 C1
Burrell Dr. L46 .... 64 E7
Burrell Rd. Bebington L42 .... 78 C8
Burrell Rd. Birkenhead L42 ... 66 C1
Burrell St. L4 .... 52 F8
Burroughs Gdns. 1 L3 .... 52 D4
Burrow's La. L34 & WA10 .... 42 E2
Burrows Ave. WA11 .... 44 F5
Burrows Ct. Liverpool L3 & L5 .... 52 C4
Burrows Ct. St Helens WA9 .. 44 E3
Burrows St. WA11 .... 45 A6
Burscough Rd. L39 .... 13 F7
Burscough St. L39 .... 13 F6
Burton Ave. Rainhill L35 .... 57 A4
Burton Ave. Wallasey L45 .... 50 E5
Burton Cl. Liverpool L1 & L72 67 D8
Burton Cl. Rainhill L35 .... 57 A4
Burton Cl. Widnes WA8 .... 72 F3
Burton Rd. WA2 .... 61 D1
Burton St. L5 .... 52 C6
Burtonhead Rd. WA9 & WA10 .... 44 A1
Burtons Way. L11 & L32 .... 40 C8
Burtonwood Cty Prim Sch. WA5 .... 59 E7
Burtonwood Rd. WA5 .... 60 A2
Burtonwood Service Area. WA5 .... 60 B4
Burtree Rd. L14 .... 55 A6
Burwell Ave. L37 .... 9 D1
Burwell Cl. L33 .... 30 A3
Burwen Dr. L9 .... 38 F6
Bury Rd. PR8 .... 4 B3
Busby's Cotts. L45 .... 51 B8
Bush Rd. WA8 .... 84 F5
Bush Way. L60 .... 85 D8
Bushby's La. L37 .... 9 C2
Bushby's Pk. L37 .... 9 D2
Bushel's Dr. WA9 .... 58 E3
Bushey La. WA11 .... 23 E2
Bushey Rd. L4 .... 39 C1
Bushley Cl. L20 .... 38 B4
Butchers La. Ashton-in-M WN4 .... 35 B3
Butchers La. Maghull L31 & L39 .... 21 B3
Bute St. Liverpool L3 .... 52 E3
Bute St. Liverpool L3 & L5 .... 52 E4
Butleigh Rd. L36 .... 55 E5
Butler Cres. L6 .... 53 B3
Butler Jun Mix & Inf Sch. L6 .... 53 B3
Butler St. L6 .... 53 B3
Buttercup Way. L9 .... 39 B4
Butterfield Gdns. L39 .... 13 D3
Butterfield St. L4 .... 52 F7
Buttermere Ave. Ashton-in-M WN4 .... 35 B5
Buttermere Ave. Birkenhead L43 .... 65 C6
Buttermere Ave. St Helens WA11 .... 44 A8
Buttermere Ave. Warrington WA2 .... 61 C3
Buttermere Cl. Formby L37 .... 9 D3
Buttermere Cl. Kirkby L33 .... 29 D4
Buttermere Cl. Maghull L31 . 20 E1
Buttermere Cres. Rainford WA11 .... 23 F2
Buttermere Cres. Warrington WA2 .... 61 C3
Buttermere Gdns. L23 .... 26 F2
Buttermere Rd. L16 .... 70 A8
Buttermere St. 1 L8 .... 68 B7
Butterton Ave. L49 .... 64 D6
Butterwick Dr. L12 .... 40 E3
Button St. L1 .... 52 D1
Butts La. PR8 & PR9 .... 4 F5
Buxted Rd. L32 .... 41 A8
Buxted Wlk. 7 L32 .... 41 A8
Buxton Rd. L42 .... 67 A2
By-Pass The. L23 .... 26 E5
Bye La. L39 .... 12 C3
Byerley St. L44 .... 51 E3
Byland Cl. L37 .... 10 B2
Byles St. L8 .... 68 A4
Byng Pl. L4 .... 53 D8
Byng Rd. L13 & L4 .... 53 D8
Byng St. L20 .... 38 B2
Byrchall High Sch. WN4 .... 35 B1
Byrne Ave. L42 .... 66 F1
Byrom La. WA3 .... 36 F2
Byrom St. PR9 .... 4 F7
Byrom St. L1 & L3 .... 52 D2
Byrom Way. L3 .... 52 D3
Byron Ave. Liverpool L12 .... 54 A7
Byron Ave. Prescot L35 .... 56 F3
Byron Cl. Birkenhead L43 .... 77 F8
Byron Cl. Formby L37 .... 9 F4
Byron Cl. Huyton-w-R L36 .... 56 A1
Byron Cl. Orrell WN5 .... 25 F7
Byron Cl. St Helens WA10 .... 44 A5
Byron Ct. WA2 .... 61 C2
Byron House. L62 .... 79 A7
Byron Rd. Crosby L23 .... 26 C4
Byron Rd. Maghull L31 .... 20 D3
Byron St. Bootle L20 .... 38 A5
Byron St. Liverpool L19 .... 81 C5
Byton Wlk. L33 .... 30 A4
Byway The. L23 .... 26 E5

'c' Ct. WN4 .... 35 B2
Cabes Cl. L14 .... 55 A6
Cabin La. Maghull L31 .... 19 F4
Cabin La. Southport PR9 .... 2 F3
Cabin La. Southport L39 .... 8 C5
Cable Rd. Hoylake L47 .... 63 B7
Cable Rd. Prescot L35 .... 56 F4
Cable St. Formby L37 .... 10 A4
Cable St. Liverpool L1 .... 52 C1
Cable St. Southport PR8 .... 4 B7
Cabot Cl. WA5 .... 60 C1
Cabot Gn. L25 .... 69 E5
Caddick Rd. L34 .... 41 B5
Cadmus Wlk. 4 L6 .... 52 F4
Cadnam Rd. L25 & L27 .... 70 D5
Cadogan St. L15 & L7 .... 68 D8
Cadwell Rd. L31 .... 20 B5
Caernarvon Cl. L49 .... 65 A6
Caernarvon Ct. L63 .... 78 F4
Caerwys Gr. L42 .... 66 E4
Caird St. L6 .... 53 A3
Cairn Ct. WA9 .... 57 D8
Cairnmore Rd. L18 .... 69 A2
Cairns St. L8 .... 68 A6
Cairo St. Bootle L4 .... 38 E1
Cairo St. St Helens WA10 .... 43 D1
Caister Cl. WN8 .... 24 E8
Caithness Dr. Crosby L23 .... 26 F3
Caithness Dr. Wallasey L45 . 51 C6
Caithness Gdns. 4 L43 .... 65 F1
Caithness Rd. L18 .... 69 B1
Calday Gr. WA11 .... 45 A8
Calday Grange Cl. L48 .... 63 D1
Calday Grange Gram Sch. L48 .... 63 D1
Caldbeck Ave. WA2 .... 61 D2
Caldbeck Cl. WN4 .... 35 B4
Caldbeck Gr. WA11 .... 33 C1
Caldbeck Rd. L63 & L62 .... 79 E2
Calder Ave. Birkenhead L43 . 66 A2
Calder Ave. Ormskirk L39 .... 13 E4
Calder Cl. Kirkby L33 .... 30 A6
Calder Cl. Widnes WA8 .... 73 F3
Calder Dr. Liverpool L18 .... 69 C4
Calder Dr. Maghull L31 .... 20 F2
Calder Dr. Rainhill L35 .... 57 C3
Calder Grange. L25 .... 69 E3
Calder Park Ct. L18 .... 69 D4
Calder Rd. Bebington L63 .... 78 D5
Calder Rd. Liverpool L5 .... 52 F6
Calderfield Rd. L18 .... 69 D5
Calderhurst Dr. WA10 .... 43 B6
Calders The. L18 .... 69 C3
Calderstones Ave. L18 .... 69 C4
Calderstones Park (Liverpool Botanic Gdns). L18 .... 69 D4
Calderstones Rd. L18 .... 69 C4
Calderstones Sch. L18 .... 69 C4
Caldicott Ave. L62 .... 88 D7
Caldway Dr. L27 .... 70 E5
Caldwell Ave. WA5 .... 60 F2
Caldwell Cl. L33 .... 29 F5
Caldwell Dr. L49 .... 65 B2
Caldwell Rd. L19 .... 81 D6
Caldwell St. WA9 .... 44 D3
Caldy Chase Dr. L48 .... 75 D7
Caldy Ct. L48 .... 63 C1
Caldy Gr. WA11 .... 44 D5
Caldy Rd. Liverpool L9 .... 39 A7
Caldy Rd. Wallasey L45 .... 51 B5
Caldy Rd. West Kirby L48 .... 75 D7
Caldy Wood. L48 .... 75 D7
Caledonia St. L7 & L8 .... 67 F8
Calgarth Rd. L36 .... 55 C5
California Rd. L13 .... 53 D7
Callaghan Cl. L5 .... 52 D5
Callander Rd. L6 .... 53 D3
Callands Cty Prim Sch. WA5 60 E2
Callands Rd. WA5 .... 60 D2
Callestock Cl. L11 .... 40 D6
Callington Cl. L14 .... 55 A6
Callon Ave. WA11 .... 44 E5
Callow Rd. L15 .... 68 D7
Calne Cl. L61 .... 76 D7
Calstock Cl. WA5 .... 74 E3
Calthorpe St. L19 .... 81 B7
Calton Ave. L15 & L18 .... 69 A5
Calveley Ave. L62 .... 88 F4
Calveley Cl. L43 .... 65 E3
Calver Rd. Warrington WA2 . 61 A3
Calverhall Way. WN4 .... 35 A3
Cam St. L25 .... 69 F2
Camarthen Cres. L8 .... 67 D6
Camberley. L25 .... 82 D8
Camberley Cl. PR8 .... 3 E5
Camberley Dr. L25 .... 82 D8
Camborne Ave. L25 .... 70 C1
Cambourne Ave. WA11 .... 44 D7
Cambourne Rd. WA5 .... 59 F6
Cambria St. L6 .... 53 B3
Cambrian Cl. L46 .... 64 B7
Cambrian Rd. L46 .... 64 C7
Cambrian Way. L25 .... 70 B3
Cambridge Arc. PR8 .... 4 B7
Cambridge Ave. Bootle L21 . 38 B8
Cambridge Ave. Crosby L23 26 D5
Cambridge Ave. Southport PR9 .... 1 F2
Cambridge Ct. PR9 .... 1 F2
Cambridge Dr. Crosby L23 ... 26 C5
Cambridge Dr. Liverpool L26 82 F8
Cambridge Gdns. PR9 .... 1 F2
Cambridge Rd. Bebington L62 .... 88 E8
Cambridge Rd. Birkenhead L42 .... 66 B2
Cambridge Rd. Bootle L20 ... 38 D2
Cambridge Rd. Crosby L23 .. 26 C5
Cambridge Rd. Formby L37 .. 9 D1
Cambridge Rd. Liverpool L9 39 B8
Cambridge Rd. Orrell WN5 .. 25 F8
Cambridge Rd. Seaforth L21 & L22 .... 37 E8
Cambridge Rd. Skelmersdale WN8 .... 15 E1
Cambridge Rd. Southport PR9 1 E2
Cambridge Rd. St Helens WA10 .... 43 E4
Cambridge Rd. Wallasey L45 51 B7
Cambridge St. Liverpool L69 & L7 .... 67 F8
Cambridge St. Liverpool L69 & L7 .... 68 A8
Cambridge St. Liverpool L15 68 D8
Cambridge St. Prescot L34 .. 56 D6
Cambridge Wlks. PR8 .... 4 B7
Camdale Cl. L28 .... 55 B7
Camden Pl. 1 L41 .... 66 E6
Camden St. Birkenhead L41 & L72 .... 66 E7
Camden St. Liverpool L3 .... 52 E2
Camelford Rd. L11 .... 40 C5
Camelia Ct. L17 .... 68 A2
Camelot Cl. WA12 .... 45 F4
Cameron Ct. WA2 .... 61 A4
Cameron Rd. L46 .... 50 B3
Cameron St. L7 .... 53 C2
Camm St. WN2 .... 36 B8
Camp Rd. Garswood WN4 .... 34 E4
Camp Rd. Liverpool L25 .... 70 B1
Campania St. L19 .... 81 C4
Campbell Cres. WA5 .... 74 F6
Campbell Dr. L14 .... 54 E3
Campbell St. Bootle L20 .... 38 B3
Campbell St. Liverpool L1, L68, L72, L75 67 D8
Campbell St. St Helens WA10 .... 43 E4
Campbeltown Rd. L41 .... 66 F4
Camperdown St. L41 .... 66 F6
Camphill Rd. L25 .... 82 A8
Campion Cl. WA11 .... 44 B7
Campion Gr. WN4 .... 34 F4
Campion High Sch. L5 .... 52 E4
Campion Way. L36 .... 70 F7
Campsey Ash. WA8 .... 72 F4
Canal Bank Cotts. L31 .... 20 C7
Canal Bank Pygons Hill. L31 20 C7
Canal St. Bootle L20 .... 38 B2
Canal St. Newton-le-W WA12 45 F3
Canal St. St Helens WA10 .... 43 F2
Canal View. L31 .... 29 A3
Canalside Gr. L5 .... 52 C5
Canberra Ave. St Helens WA9 .... 57 E8
Canberra Ave. Warrington WA2 .... 61 D3
Canberra La. L10 .... 40 C5
Canberra Sq. WA2 .... 61 D2
Candia Tower. L5 .... 52 E6
Candleston Cl. WA5 .... 60 E1
Canning Pl. 5 L1 & L69 & L72 & L68 & L75 67 C8
Canning Rd. PR9 .... 5 A6
Canning St. Birkenhead L41 & L67 & L72 66 F7
Canning St. Crosby L22 .... 26 D1
Canning St. Liverpool L1 & L7 & L8 .... 67 F7
Canniswood Rd. WA11 .... 45 A6
Cannock Gn. L31 .... 20 B1
Cannon St. WA9 .... 58 C3
Canon Rd. L4 & L6 .... 53 C7
Canon Wilson Cl. WA11 .... 45 D6
Canrow La. L34 .... 41 E5
Cansfield Comm High Sch. WN4 .... 35 A4
Cansfield Gr. WN4 .... 35 A4
Cansfield St. WA10 .... 44 A4
Canterbury Ave. Crosby L22 26 D3
Canterbury Ave. Golborne WA3 .... 36 D1
Canterbury Cl. Formby L37 .... 9 F5
Canterbury Cl. Litherland L10 .... 28 E2
Canterbury Cl. Southport PR8 3 F4
Canterbury Pk. L18 .... 81 C8
Canterbury Rd. Birkenhead L42 .... 67 A1
Canterbury Rd. Wallasey L44 .... 51 C3
Canterbury Rd. Widnes WA8 84 C8
Canterbury St. Liverpool L3 . 52 E3
Canterbury St. Liverpool L19 81 D4
Canterbury St. St Helens WA10 .... 43 E5
Canterbury Way. Litherland L30 .... 27 F4
Canterbury Way. 1 Liverpool L3 .... 52 F3
Cantlow Fold. PR8 .... 7 A4
Cantsfield St. L7 .... 68 C7
Canvey Cl. L15 .... 69 B7
Cape Rd. L9 .... 39 C6
Capesthorne Rd. WA2 .... 61 D2
Capilano Pk. L39 .... 21 C8
Capper Gr. L36 .... 55 E3
Capricorn Cres. L14 .... 55 A5
Capricorn Way. L20 .... 38 B4
Capstick Cres. L25 .... 70 B6
Captain's La. Ashton-in-M WN4 .... 35 C3
Captain's La. Bootle L21 & L30 .... 38 E8
Captains Cl. L30 .... 38 D8
Captains Gn. L30 .... 38 D8
Caradoc Rd. L21 .... 38 A6
Caraway Cl. L23 .... 27 B5
Caraway Gr. WA10 .... 43 D4
Carbis Cl. L10 .... 40 B6
Carden Cl. L4 .... 52 E7
Cardiff St. WN8 .... 15 D1
Cardigan Ave. L41 .... 66 D6
Cardigan Cl. WA5 .... 60 D2

Cardigan Rd. Southport PR8 .. 3 F1
Cardigan Rd. Wallasey L45 .. 51 B7
Cardigan St. L15 .... 68 D8
Cardigan Way. Litherland L30 .... 28 B4
Cardigan Way. Liverpool L6 . 53 B4
Cardinal Heenan High Sch. L14 .... 54 D4
Cardinal Heenan RC High Sch. L14 .... 54 F3
Cardus Cl. L46 .... 64 B8
Cardwell St. L7 .... 68 B8
Carey Ave. L63 .... 78 D6
Carey St. WA8 .... 73 B1
Carfax Rd. L33 .... 30 A4
Carfield. WN8 .... 24 E6
Cargill Gr. L42 & L62 .... 79 B8
Carham Rd. L47 .... 63 C6
Carisbrooke Cl. L48 .... 75 C8
Carisbrooke Dr. PR9 .... 1 F1
Carisbrooke Pl. L4 .... 38 F1
Carisbrooke Rd. L20 & L4 .... 38 E1
Carkington Rd. L25 .... 70 C1
Carlaw Rd. L43 .... 66 A2
Carleen Cl. L17 .... 68 B2
Carleton House Prep Sch. L18 .... 68 F3
Carlett Bvd. L62 .... 88 F5
Carlingford Cl. L8 .... 68 A7
Carlis Rd. L32 .... 40 F8
Carlisle Ave. L30 .... 27 F1
Carlisle Cl. 9 Birkenhead L43 .... 66 C5
Carlisle Cl. Liverpool L4 .... 53 D8
Carlisle Mews. 8 L43 .... 66 C5
Carlisle Rd. PR8 .... 4 A2
Carlisle St. L7 .... 68 B8
Carlow Cl. L24 .... 83 D2
Carlow St. WA10 .... 43 D1
Carlton Ave. WN8 .... 25 A7
Carlton Cl. Ashton-in-M WN4 35 A5
Carlton Cl. Neston L64 .... 86 C2
Carlton La. Hoylake L47 .... 63 C8
Carlton La. Liverpool L13 .... 54 A4
Carlton Rd. Bebington L63 ... 79 B4
Carlton Rd. Birkenhead L42 & L43 .... 66 C4
Carlton Rd. Golborne WA3 ... 36 D1
Carlton Rd. Southport PR8 ..... 7 C6
Carlton Rd. Wallasey L45 ..... 51 B7
Carlton St. Liverpool L3 .... 52 B4
Carlton St. 5 Prescot L34 ... 56 D6
Carlton St. St Helens WA10 . 43 E3
Carlton Terr. L47 .... 63 C8
Carlyon Way. L26 .... 82 E8
Carmarthen Cl. WA5 .... 60 D2
Carmel Cl. Ormskirk L39 .... 13 D2
Carmel Cl. Wallasey L45 .... 51 B8
Carmel Coll. WA10 .... 43 A3
Carmel Ct. WA8 .... 73 B4
Carmelite Cres. WA10 .... 43 A5
Carmichael Ave. L49 .... 64 D2
Carnaby Cl. L36 .... 71 A8
Carnarvon Ct. L9 .... 39 A3
Carnarvon Rd. Liverpool L9 .. 39 A3
Carnarvon Rd. Southport PR8 3 F1
Carnarvon St. WA9 .... 57 D8
Carnatic Rd. L17 & L18 .... 68 E3
Carnation Rd. L9 .... 39 B3
Carnegie Ave. L23 .... 26 D3
Carnegie Cres. WA9 .... 58 E8
Carnegie Dr. WN4 .... 35 A5
Carnegie Rd. L13 .... 53 E4
Carnforth Ave. L32 .... 29 F1
Carnforth Cl. 12 Birkenhead L41 .... 66 C5
Carnforth Cl. Liverpool L12 .. 40 C1
Carnforth Rd. L18 .... 69 C2
Carno St. L15 .... 68 E8
Carnoustie Cl. Liverpool L14 54 F6
Carnoustie Cl. Wallasey L46 49 B1
Carnoustie Gr. WA11 .... 45 A5
Carnsdale Rd. L46 .... 64 F8
Carol Dr. L60 .... 86 C8
Carole Cl. WA9 .... 58 E6
Carolina St. L20 .... 38 C3
Caroline Pl. L43 .... 66 B5
Caronia St. L19 .... 81 C4
Carpathia St. L19 .... 81 C4
Carpenter's La. L48 .... 63 B2
Carpenters Row. 4 L1 & L72 .... 67 D8
Carr Bridge Rd. L49 .... 65 C3
Carr Cl. L11 .... 40 B2
Carr Croft. L21 .... 27 B3
Carr Gate. L46 .... 64 C7
Carr Hey. L46 .... 64 B7
Carr Hey Cl. L49 .... 65 C2
Carr House La. Birkenhead L46 .... 64 B8
Carr House La. Ince Blundell L38 .... 18 E4
Carr La. Hoylake L47 .... 63 B6
Carr La. Hoylake L48 .... 63 E5
Carr La. Huyton-w-R L36 .... 55 C1
Carr La. Liverpool L11 .... 40 A2
Carr La. Liverpool L24 & WA8 83 E4
Carr La. Maghull L31 .... 19 F5
Carr La. Prescot L34 .... 56 B5
Carr La. Southport PR8 .... 7 F7
Carr La. Wallasey L46 & L47 . 49 A1
Carr La E. L11 .... 40 B3
Carr La Ind Est. L47 .... 63 C6
Carr Meadow Hey. L30 .... 27 C3
Carr Mill Cres. WN5 .... 33 E4
Carr Mill Inf Sch. WA11 .... 44 B8
Carr Mill Jun Sch. WA11 .... 33 C1
Carr Mill Rd. Billinge WA11 & WN5 .... 33 D3
Carr Mill Rd. St Helens WA11 .... 44 C8
Carr Moss La. Haskayne L39 12 B8
Carr Moss La. Southport L39 .. 8 D2
Carr Rd. L20 .... 38 D7
Carr Side La. L29 & L38 .... 19 A3
Carr St. WA10 .... 43 D5
Carr's Cres. L37 .... 9 E1
Carr's Cres W. L37 .... 9 D1
Carraway Rd. L10 .... 40 C6
Carrfield Ave. L23 .... 27 A3
Carrick Ct. L23 .... 27 A3
Carrickmore Ave. L18 .... 69 A2
Carrington Rd. L45 .... 51 C6
Carrington St. L41 .... 66 A8
Carrock Rd. L63 & L62 .... 79 E2
Carroll Cres. L39 .... 13 F7
Carrow Cl. L46 .... 64 B7
Carrs Terr. L35 .... 56 D3
Carruthers St. L3 .... 52 C3
Carrville Way. L12 .... 41 A3
Carrwood Cl. WA11 .... 45 A6
Carsdale Rd. L18 .... 69 A5
Carsgoe Rd. L47 .... 63 C6
Carsington Rd. L11 .... 40 A2
Carstairs Rd. L6 .... 53 D4
Carsthorne Rd. L47 .... 63 C6
Cartbridge La. L26 & L35 .... 71 A2
Cartbridge Residential Sch. L26 .... 71 A1
Carter Ave. WA11 .... 32 A5
Carter St. L8 .... 67 F6
Carters The. Birkenhead L49 64 C4
Carters The. Litherland L30 .. 28 A4
Carterton Rd. L47 .... 63 C6
Cartier Cl. WA5 .... 60 C1
Cartmel Ave. Maghull L31 .... 20 E2
Cartmel Ave. St Helens WA10 .... 43 E7
Cartmel Ave. Warrington WA2 .... 61 C3
Cartmel Cl. Birkenhead L41 . 66 C5
Cartmel Cl. Huyton-w-R L36 . 55 D4
Cartmel Cl. Southport PR8 .... 4 F3
Cartmel Cl. Warrington WA5 60 E2
Cartmel Dr. Birkenhead L46 . 64 E7
Cartmel Dr. Formby L37 .... 10 B2
Cartmel Dr. Liverpool L12 .... 40 C1
Cartmel Dr. Rainhill L35 .... 57 A4
Cartmel Rd. L36 .... 55 C4
Cartmel Terr. L11 .... 40 C3
Cartmel Way. L36 .... 55 C4
Cartwright Cl. WA11 .... 31 F7
Carver St. L3 .... 52 F3
Caryl Gr. L8 .... 67 E4
Caryl St. Liverpool L8 .... 67 D5
Caryl St. Liverpool L72 & L8 .. 67 D6
Caryl St. Liverpool L8 .... 67 E4
Case Gr. L35 .... 56 E5
Case Rd. WA11 .... 45 D6
Cases St. 7 L1 .... 52 D1
Caspian Rd. L4 .... 39 D2
Cassia Cl. L9 .... 39 B4
Cassino Rd. L36 .... 55 E3
Cassio St. L20 .... 38 E2
Cassley Rd. L24 .... 83 A3
Cassville Rd. L15 & L18 .... 69 A6
Castell Gr. WA10 .... 43 F3
Casterton St. L7 .... 68 C8
Castle Ave. WA9 .... 44 E3
Castle Cl. L46 .... 50 A3
Castle Dr. Formby L37 .... 9 F1
Castle Dr. Heswall L60 .... 85 F8
Castle Fields Est. L46 .... 49 F4
Castle Gn. WA5 .... 60 B2
Castle Hill. Liverpool L2 .... 52 C1
Castle Hill. Newton-le-W WA12 .... 46 E4
Castle Keep. L12 .... 54 B7
Castle La. L40 .... 14 E5
Castle Rd. L45 .... 51 A6
Castle St. Birkenhead L41 .... 66 F6
Castle St. Liverpool L2 .... 52 C1
Castle St. Liverpool L25 .... 69 F2
Castle St. Southport PR9 .... 4 B8
Castle St. Widnes WA8 .... 73 D1
Castle Wlk. PR8 .... 4 A6
Castlefield Cl. L12 .... 54 A7
Castlefield Rd. L12 .... 54 A8
Castleford Rise. L46 .... 49 E3
Castleford St. L15 .... 69 A7
Castlegate Gr. L12 .... 54 B7
Castlegrange Cl. L46 .... 49 E4
Castleheath Cl. L46 .... 49 E3
Castlehey. WN8 .... 24 E6
Castlerigg Ct. L42 .... 66 C1
Castlesite Rd. L12 .... 54 B7
Castleton Dr. L30 .... 28 B4
Castletown Cl. L16 .... 69 E8
Castleview Rd. L12 .... 54 B7
Castleway N. L46 .... 50 A4
Castleway Prim Sch. L46 .... 50 A4
Castleway S. L46 .... 50 A3
Castlewell. L35 .... 56 F4
Castlewood Rd. L6 .... 53 B5
Castor St. L6 .... 53 B5
Cat Tail La. PR8 .... 5 E1
Catchdale Moss La. WA10 & WA11 .... 42 E5
Catford Cl. WA8 .... 72 C2
Catford Gn. L24 .... 82 F3
Catfoss Cl. WA2 .... 61 E1
Cath CE (Cathedral Church of Christ). L1 .... 67 E7
Cath RC (Metropolitan Cath of Christ The King). L3 .... 52 F1
Catharine St. L8 .... 67 F8
Catharine's La. L39 .... 13 F1
Cathcart St. L41 .... 66 D7
Cathcart Street Prim Sch. L41 .... 66 D7
Cathedral Cl. 3 L1 .... 67 E7
Cathedral Gate. L1 .... 67 E8
Cathedral Rd. 2 L6 .... 53 C6
Cathedral Wlk. L3 .... 52 F1
Catherine Ct. L21 .... 38 B6
Catherine St. Birkenhead L41 .... 66 D6
Catherine St. Bootle L21 .... 38 B6
Catherine Way. Newton-le-W WA12 .... 46 B2
Catherine Way. St Helens WA11 .... 44 F6
Catkin Rd. L26 .... 70 D2
Caton Cl. PR9 .... 1 F4
Catonfield Rd. L18 .... 69 D5
Catterall Ave. St Helens WA9 .... 58 D6
Catterall Ave. Warrington WA2 .... 61 D2
Catterick Cl. L26 .... 82 F8
Catterick Fold. PR8 .... 4 F3
Caulfield Dr. L49 .... 64 E3
Caunce Ave. Golborne WA3 . 47 A7
Caunce Ave. Haydock WA11 45 B6
Causeway Cl. L62 .... 79 B6
Causeway La. L37 .... 11 B1
Causeway The. Bebington L62 .... 79 B5
Causeway The. Liverpool L12 .... 54 D4
Causeway The. Southport PR9 2 C5
Cavan Rd. L11 .... 53 E8
Cavell Cl. L25 .... 70 A1
Cavendish Ct. PR9 .... 4 E8
Cavendish Dr. Birkenhead L42 .... 66 D1
Cavendish Dr. Liverpool L9 .. 39 A3
Cavendish Rd. Birkenhead L41 .... 66 B7
Cavendish Rd. Crosby L22 & L23 .... 26 C3
Cavendish Rd. Southport PR8 3 F3
Cavendish Rd. 3 Wallasey L45 .... 51 B8
Cavendish St. Birkenhead L41 .... 66 B8
Cavendish St. Runcorn WA7 84 F2
Cawdor St. Liverpool L8 .... 68 A6
Cawdor St. Runcorn WA7 .... 84 F3
Cawfield Ave. WA8 .... 72 D1
Cawthorne Ave. L32 .... 40 E8
Cawthorne Cl. L32 .... 40 E8
Cawthorne Wlk. L32 .... 40 E8
Caxton Cl. Birkenhead L43 .. 65 C6
Caxton Cl. Widnes WA8 .... 72 C3
Caxton Rd. L35 .... 57 E1
Cazneau St. L3 .... 52 D3
Cearns Rd. L43 .... 66 A5
Cecil Dr. WA10 .... 43 A4
Cecil Rd. Bebington L62 .... 79 B8
Cecil Rd. Birkenhead L42 .... 66 B2
Cecil Rd. Seaforth L21 .... 37 F6
Cecil Rd. Wallasey L44 .... 51 B4
Cecil St. Liverpool L15 .... 68 D8
Cecil St. St Helens WA9 .... 58 F7
Cedar Ave. Bebington L63 .... 78 E4
Cedar Ave. Golborne WA3 .... 47 F7
Cedar Ave. Widnes WA8 .... 73 B2
Cedar Cl. Liverpool L18 .... 69 D3
Cedar Cl. Prescot L35 .... 56 E4
Cedar Cres. Huyton-w-R L36 55 D1
Cedar Cres. Newton-le-W WA12 .... 46 D2
Cedar Cres. Ormskirk L39 .... 13 D4
Cedar Dr. Formby L37 .... 9 C1
Cedar Gr. Crosby L22 .... 26 D2
Cedar Gr. Garswood WN4 .... 34 D5
Cedar Gr. Haydock WA11 .... 45 E7
Cedar Gr. Liverpool L8 .... 68 C6
Cedar Gr. Maghull L31 .... 28 D6
Cedar Gr. Orrell WN5 .... 25 F6
Cedar Gr. Skelmersdale WN8 15 E1
Cedar Rd. Liverpool L9 .... 39 B6
Cedar Rd. Prescot L35 .... 56 D3
Cedar Rd. Warrington WA5 .. 74 F6
Cedar St. Birkenhead L41 .... 66 D5
Cedar St. Bootle L20 .... 38 C4
Cedar St. Newton-le-W WA12 .... 46 C2
Cedar St. Southport PR8 .... 4 D4
Cedar St. St Helens WA10 .... 43 D2
Cedar Towers. L33 .... 29 F3
Cedardale Rd. L9 .... 39 A4
Cedars The. Birkenhead L46 64 C7
Cedars The. Liverpool L12 .... 40 F3
Cedarway. L60 .... 86 B5
Cedarwood Cl. L49 .... 64 B4
Cedarwood Ct. L36 .... 70 E8
Celebration Dr. L6 .... 53 C5
Celedine Cl. L15 .... 68 E8
Celia St. L20 .... 38 D1
Celt St. L6 .... 53 C4
Celtic Rd. L47 .... 48 E1
Celtic St. 2 L8 .... 68 A6
Cemetery Rd. PR8 .... 4 C4
Central Ave. Bebington L62 .. 79 C1
Central Ave. Liverpool L24 ... 82 D3
Central Ave. Prescot L34 .... 56 C5
Central Ave. Southport PR8 ... 7 F8
Central Ave. St Helens L34 & L35 .... 57 A7
Central Dr. Haydock WA11 ... 45 B6
Central Dr. Liverpool L12 .... 54 B5
Central Dr. Rainford WA11 ... 31 F7
Central Par. L24 .... 82 E3
Central Park Ave. L44 .... 51 C4
Central Rd. Bebington L62 ... 79 B6
Central Rd. Bebington L62 ... 79 C4
Central Sq. L31 .... 20 D2
Central St. WA10 .... 44 A4
Central Sta. L1 .... 52 D1
Central Trad Est. L20 .... 38 C7
Central Way. Liverpool L24 .. 82 F2
Central Way. Newton-le-W WA12 .... 46 E2
Centre Way. Huyton-w-R L36 55 E2
Centreville Rd. L15 & L18 .... 69 A6
Centurion Cl. L47 .... 48 E1
Centurion Dr. L47 .... 48 E1
Century Rd. L23 .... 26 D4
Ceres St. L20 .... 38 C1
Cestrian Dr. L61 .... 77 A5
Chadlow Rd. L32 .... 40 F7
Chadwell Rd. L33 .... 29 F4
Chadwick Rd. WA11 .... 44 C7
Chadwick St. Birkenhead L46 64 E8
Chadwick St. Liverpool L3 .... 52 B3
Chaffinch Cl. L12 .... 40 F1
Chaffinch Glade. L26 .... 70 E1
Chain La. WA11 .... 44 E6
Chain Lane Sh Prec. WA11 . 44 D7
Chainhurst Cl. L27 .... 70 D5
Chalfont Rd. L18 .... 69 D1
Chalfont Way. L14 & L28 .... 55 B7
Chalgrave Cl. WA8 .... 73 F3
Chalkwell Dr. L60 .... 86 C7
Challis St. L41 & L43 .... 50 E1
Challoner Cl. L36 .... 70 F8
Chalon Way. WA10 & WA9 .. 44 A3
Chalon Way Ind Est. WA9 .. 44 A2
Chalon Way W. St Helens WA10 .... 44 A3
Chaloner Gr. L19 .... 80 F6
Chaloner St. L1 & L72 .... 67 D7
Chamberlain St. Birkenhead L41 .... 66 F4
Chamberlain St. St Helens WA10 .... 43 D3
Chamberlain St. Wallasey L44 .... 51 A2
Chambres Rd. PR8 .... 4 D5
Chambres Rd N. PR8 .... 4 D6
Chancel St. L4 .... 52 E7
Chancery La. WA9 .... 44 E3
Chandley Cl. PR8 .... 7 A5
Chandos St. 7 L7 .... 53 B1
Changford Gn. L33 .... 30 A3
Changford Rd. L33 .... 30 A3
Channel Rd. L23 .... 26 B3
Channel Reach. L23 .... 26 B3
Channel The. L45 .... 50 E8
Channell Rd. L6 .... 53 C3
Chantrell Rd. L48 .... 63 F2
Chantry Cl. L43 .... 65 C6
Chantry Wlk. Ashton-in-M WN4 .... 34 F5
Chantry Wlk. Heswall L60 .... 86 A6
Chapel Ave. L9 .... 39 A5
Chapel Gdns. L5 .... 52 D5
Chapel La. Burtonwood WA5 59 F6
Chapel La. Formby L37 .... 9 F3
Chapel La. Kirkby L31 .... 29 A4
Chapel La. Litherland L30 .... 27 F5
Chapel La. Litherland L30 ..... 28 A5
Chapel La. Rainhill L35 & WA9 .... 57 F2
Chapel La. St Helens WA10 .. 43 B4
Chapel La. Widnes WA8 .... 72 D4
Chapel Mews. L39 .... 13 F4
Chapel Pl. Ashton-in-M WN4 35 B3
Chapel Pl. Liverpool L19 .... 81 C6
Chapel Rd. Hoylake L47 .... 63 C8
Chapel Rd. 3 Liverpool L6 .. 53 C6
Chapel Rd. Liverpool L19 .... 81 C6
Chapel Rd. Warrington WA5 74 E3
Chapel St. Ashton-in-M WN4 35 B3
Chapel St. Haydock WA11 .... 45 E6
Chapel St. Liverpool L2 & L3 52 C2
Chapel St. Newton-le-W WA12 .... 46 B3
Chapel St. Ormskirk L39 .... 13 F4
Chapel St. 9 Prescot L34 .... 56 D6
Chapel St. Southport PR8 .... 4 B7
Chapel St. St Helens WA10 .. 43 F5
Chapel Street Sta. PR8 .... 4 B7
Chapel Terr. L20 .... 38 B3
Chapel Yd. L15 .... 69 A7
Chapelhill Rd. L46 .... 64 F8
Chapelhouse Wlk. L37 .... 10 A3
Chapman Cl. Liverpool L8 .... 67 E5
Chapman Cl. Widnes WA8 .... 72 D4
Chardstock Dr. L25 & L27 .... 70 C4
Charing Cross. L41 .... 66 D6
Charlecombe St. L42 .... 66 D4
Charlecote St. L8 .... 67 F3
Charles Ave. Southport PR8 ... 7 E6
Charles Ave. Warrington WA5 .... 74 F6
Charles Berrington Rd. L15 . 69 A6
Charles Rd. L47 .... 63 B6
Charles St. Birkenhead L41 .. 66 D7
Charles St. Golborne WA3 .... 36 A1
Charles St. St Helens WA10 . 44 A4
Charles Wlk. L14 .... 54 F3
Charlesbye Ave. L39 & L40 .. 14 B6
Charlesbye Cl. L40 .... 14 B6
Charlesville. L43 .... 66 B5
Charlesville Ct. L43 .... 66 B5
Charlesworth Cl. L31 .... 20 B5
Charley Wood Rd. L33 .... 30 C1
Charlotte Rd. L44 .... 51 D5
Charlotte Way. 14 L1 .... 52 D1
Charlotte's Meadow. L63 .... 79 A4
Charlton Ct. L43 .... 65 F6
Charlton Pl. L13 .... 54 A1
Charlton Rd. L13 .... 54 A1
Charlwood Ave. L36 .... 55 E1
Charlwood Cl. L43 .... 65 C6
Charmalue Ave. L23 .... 26 F4
Charmouth Cl. 2 L12 .... 40 E3
Charnley's La. PR9 .... 2 E7
Charnock Ave. WA12 .... 45 F3
Charnock Rd. L9 .... 39 D3
Charnwood Rd. L36 .... 55 B3
Charnwood St. WA9 .... 44 E4
Charter House. L44 .... 51 D4
Charterhouse Cl. L25 .... 70 B1
Charterhouse Dr. L10 .... 28 E2
Charterhouse Rd. L25 .... 70 B1
Chartmount Way. L25 .... 70 B4
Chartwell Rd. PR8 .... 7 B6
Chase Cl. PR8 .... 3 F4
Chase Heys. PR9 .... 2 A1
Chase The. Bebington L63 .... 88 C5
Chase The. Liverpool L36 .... 70 F8
Chase Way. L3 & L5 .... 52 E4
Chatburn Ave. WA3 .... 36 C1
Chatburn Wlk. 7 L8 .... 67 F4
Chater Cl. L35 .... 57 A5
Chatham Cl. L21 .... 37 F7
Chatham Pl. L7 .... 53 B1
Chatham Rd. L42 .... 67 A2

Cha – Cla 99

Chatham St. L69 & L7 ... 67 F8
Chatsworth Ave. Bootle L9 .. 38 F5
Chatsworth Ave. Wallasey L44 ... 51 C4
Chatsworth Cl. WN4 ... 34 F4
Chatsworth Cty Prim Mix & Inf Sch. L7 ... 68 B8
Chatsworth Dr. Liverpool L7 68 B8
Chatsworth Dr. Widnes WA8 72 C3
Chatsworth Rd. Birkenhead L42 ... 67 A2
Chatsworth Rd. Heswall L61 76 F5
Chatsworth Rd. Rainhill L35 57 B4
Chatsworth Rd. Southport PR8 ... 7 B6
Chatsworth St. L7 ... 53 B1
Chatterton Rd. L12 & L14 ... 54 C4
Chaucer Dr. L12 ... 40 F2
Chaucer Rd. WA10 ... 43 D6
Chaucer St. Bootle L20 ... 38 A4
Chaucer St. Liverpool L3 ... 52 D3
Cheadle Ave. L13 ... 53 F4
Cheapside. Formby L37 ... 10 A2
Cheapside. Liverpool L1 & L2 ... 52 C2
Cheapside Alley. 13 L2 ... 52 C2
Cheddar Cl. L25 ... 69 F2
Cheddar Gr. Burtonwood WA5 ... 59 F7
Cheddar Gr. Kirkby L32 ... 40 E7
Chedworth Dr. WA8 ... 72 C4
Chedworth Rd. L14 ... 54 E4
Cheldon Rd. L11 ... 40 C2
Chelford Ave. WA3 ... 47 D8
Chellowdene. L23 ... 27 A6
Chelmarsh Ave. WN4 ... 35 C3
Chelsea Ct. L12 ... 54 E8
Chelsea Lea. L9 ... 38 F6
Chelsea Rd. Bootle L21 ... 38 B6
Chelsea Rd. Liverpool L9 ... 39 A6
Cheltenham Ave. L17 & L8 .. 68 D6
Cheltenham Cl. L10 ... 28 E1
Cheltenham Cres. L36 ... 55 D1
Cheltenham Dr. Newton-le-W WA12 ... 46 C5
Cheltenham Dr. Orrell WN5 25 D2
Cheltenham Rd. L45 ... 50 E6
Cheltenham Way. PR8 ... 4 F3
Chelwood Ave. Liverpool L14 & L16 ... 54 E1
Chemical St. WA12 ... 46 B3
Chemistry Rd. L24 ... 82 C5
Chenotrie Gdns. L43 ... 65 D5
Chepstow Ave. L44 ... 51 C4
Chepstow Cl. WA5 ... 60 E2
Chepstow St. L4 ... 38 F1
Chequer Cl. WN8 ... 24 F5
Chequer La. WN8 ... 24 F6
Chequers Gdns. L19 ... 68 F1
Cheriton Ave. L48 ... 63 D2
Cheriton Cl. L26 ... 82 E8
Chermside Rd. L17 ... 68 E1
Cherry Ave. L4 ... 39 B1
Cherry Cl. Liverpool L4 ... 39 B1
Cherry Cl. Newton-le-W WA12 ... 45 F4
Cherry Gn. L39 ... 13 B1
Cherry La. Liverpool L4 ... 39 B1
Cherry La. Liverpool L13 & L4 53 D8
Cherry Rd. PR8 ... 7 D2
Cherry Sq. L44 ... 51 B4
Cherry Tree Ave. WA5 ... 74 F4
Cherry Tree Cl. Hale L24 ... 83 E1
Cherry Tree Cl. Haydock WA11 ... 45 A5
Cherry Tree Cl. Prescot L35 . 56 D3
Cherry Tree Dr. WA9 ... 45 A2
Cherry Tree La. Ormskirk L39 ... 13 B1
Cherry Tree La. St Helens WA11 ... 33 A2
Cherry Tree Rd. Birkenhead L46 ... 64 F8
Cherry Tree Rd. Golborne WA3 ... 47 F8
Cherry Tree Rd. Liverpool L36 ... 70 E8
Cherry Vale. L25 ... 70 B3
Cherrybank. L44 ... 51 B2
Cherrycroft. WN8 ... 24 E6
Cherrydale Rd. L18 ... 69 A4
Cherryfield Cres. L32 ... 29 E2
Cherryfield Dr. L32 ... 29 E2
Cherryfield Hts. L32 ... 40 F7
Cherryfield Prim Sch. L32 ... 40 E7
Cherrysutton. WA8 ... 72 B3
Cheryl Dr. WA8 ... 73 D1
Cheshire Acre. L49 ... 65 A2
Cheshire Ave. L10 ... 40 B7
Cheshire Cl. WA12 ... 46 E3
Cheshire Gdns. WA10 ... 43 E2
Cheshire Gr. L46 ... 64 E7
Cheshire Way. L61 ... 76 F3
Chesnut Gr. Birkenhead L41 & L42 ... 66 D4
Chesnut Gr. Bootle L20 ... 38 B4
Chesnut Gr. Liverpool L15 ... 69 A8
Chester Ave. Golborne WA3 47 D8
Chester Ave. Litherland L30 . 27 F1
Chester Ave. Southport PR9 .. 4 F8
Chester Cl. L23 ... 27 B4
Chester Ct. L63 ... 78 F4
Chester Dr. WN4 ... 35 D2
Chester High Rd. Heswall L64 ... 86 E4
Chester High Rd. Neston L64 ... 87 A1
Chester La. WA9 ... 58 B4
Chester Rd. Bebington L66 ... 89 A1
Chester Rd. Heswall L60 & L64 ... 86 C6
Chester Rd. Huyton-w-R L36 56 A4
Chester Rd. Liverpool L6 ... 53 D5
Chester Rd. Southport PR9 ... 4 F8
Chester Row. WA12 ... 60 D8
Chester St. Birkenhead L41 .. 66 F6
Chester St. Liverpool L8 ... 67 E7
Chester St. Prescot L34 ... 56 D6
Chester St. Wallasey L44 ... 51 A3
Chester St. Widnes WA8 ... 73 B1
Chester Wlk. L36 ... 56 A4
Chesterfield Cl. PR8 ... 7 C4
Chesterfield Dr. L33 ... 29 E5
Chesterfield High Sch. Crosby L23 ... 27 A4
Chesterfield High Sch (Annexe). Crosby L22 ... 26 F1
Chesterfield Rd. Bebington L62 ... 88 D4
Chesterfield Rd. Crosby L23 27 A4
Chesterfield Rd. Southport PR8 ... 7 C5
Chesterfield St. L8 ... 67 E7
Chesterton St. L19 ... 81 C4
Chestnut Ave. Crosby L23 ... 26 F6
Chestnut Ave. Liverpool L36 70 D8
Chestnut Ave. St Helens WA11 ... 44 F5
Chestnut Ave. Warrington WA5 ... 74 F6
Chestnut Ave. Widnes WA8 . 73 B2
Chestnut Cl. Birkenhead L49 64 C2
Chestnut Cl. Prescot L35 ... 56 E4
Chestnut Ct. WA8 ... 72 D1
Chestnut Gr. Ashton-in-M WN4 ... 35 D4
Chestnut Gr. Bebington L62 . 88 C8
Chestnut Gr. Bootle L20 ... 38 B5
Chestnut Gr. Golborne WA3 47 F8
Chestnut Gr. St Helens WA11 ... 44 D7
Chestnut House. L20 ... 38 B4
Chestnut Lodge Sch. WA8 .. 72 E1
Chestnut Rd. Liverpool L9 ... 39 C3
Chestnut Rd. Seaforth L21 ... 37 F8
Chestnut St. Liverpool L7 ... 52 F1
Chestnut St. Southport PR8 ... 4 C5
Chestnut Way. L37 ... 9 C1
Chetham Ct. WA2 ... 61 A3
Chetwode Ave. WN4 ... 35 B1
Chetwood Ave. L23 ... 26 F5
Chetwood Dr. WA8 ... 72 F4
Chetwynd Cl. L43 ... 65 F4
Chetwynd Rd. L43 ... 66 A5
Chetwynd St. L17 ... 68 B3
Chevasse Wlk. L25 ... 70 C3
Cheverton Cl. L49 ... 65 B3
Chevin Rd. L9 ... 39 A5
Cheviot Ave. St Helens WA9 44 F3
Cheviot Ave. Warrington WA2 ... 61 A3
Cheviot Cl. L42 ... 66 D1
Cheviot La. L33 ... 29 F6
Cheviot Rd. Birkenhead L42 . 66 D1
Cheviot Rd. Liverpool L7 ... 53 E2
Cheyne Cl. L23 ... 26 A3
Cheyne Gdns. L19 ... 80 F8
Cheyne Wlk. WA9 ... 57 F6
Chichester Cl. L15 ... 68 D8
Chidden Cl. L49 ... 64 C3
Chigwell Cl. L12 ... 40 E3
Chilcott Rd. L13 & L14 ... 54 C3
Child Wall Five Ways. L15 .. 69 C7
Childers St. 1 L13 ... 54 A3
Childwall Abbey Rd. L16 ... 69 E7
Childwall Ave. Birkenhead L46 & L49 ... 64 D7
Childwall Ave. Liverpool L15 68 D7
Childwall Bank Rd. L16 ... 69 D7
Childwall CE Prim Sch. L18 69 D5
Childwall Cl. L46 ... 64 D7
Childwall Cres. L16 ... 69 D7
Childwall Gn. L49 ... 65 A2
Childwall Golf Course. L27 . 70 E7
Childwall Hts. L25 ... 69 F7
Childwall La. Huyton-w-R L14 & L36 ... 55 A2
Childwall La. Liverpool L16 & L25 ... 69 F6
Childwall Mount Rd. L16 ... 69 D7
Childwall Park Ave. L16 & L18 ... 69 E6
Childwall Priory Rd. L15 & L16 ... 69 D7
Childwall Rd. L15 ... 69 B7
Childwall Sch. L15 ... 69 C7
Childwall Sch (Annexe). L15 69 B8
Childwall Sch (Olive Mount Wing). L15 ... 69 B8
Childwall Valley Rd. Liverpool L16 & L25 & L27 ... 70 C6
Chilington Ave. WA8 ... 84 D8
Chillerton Rd. L12 ... 54 D8
Chillingham St. 1 L8 ... 68 A3
Chiltern Ave. WA2 ... 61 A3
Chiltern Cl. Ashton-in-M WN4 ... 35 C2
Chiltern Cl. Kirkby L32 ... 29 C4
Chiltern Cl. Liverpool L12 ... 40 F2
Chiltern Cres. WA2 ... 61 A3
Chiltern Dr. L32 ... 29 C4
Chiltern Pl. WA2 ... 61 A3
Chiltern Rd. Birkenhead L42 66 C1
Chiltern Rd. Southport PR8 ... 7 B6
Chiltern Rd. St Helens WA9 . 45 A3
Chiltern Rd. Warrington WA2 ... 61 A3
Chilwell Cl. WA8 ... 72 D4
Chimes Rd. WN4 ... 34 F6
China Farm La. L48 ... 63 E3
Chindit Cl. L37 ... 9 D2
Chippenham Ave. L49 ... 64 C3
Chipping Ave. PR8 ... 7 A5
Chirk Way. L46 ... 64 F7
Chirkdale St. Bootle L4 ... 38 E1
Chirkdale St. 2 Liverpool L4 52 E8
Chisenhale St. L3 ... 52 C4
Chisledon Cl. WA11 ... 45 D7
Chislehurst Ave. L25 ... 70 B6
Chisnall Ave. WA10 ... 43 C4
Chiswell St. L7 ... 53 C2
Cholmondeley Rd. L48 ... 63 B2
Cholsey Cl. Birkenhead L49 .. 64 F4
Chorley Cl. Banks PR9 ... 2 F5
Chorley Rd. L34 ... 56 B6
Chorley St. WA10 ... 43 F4
Chorley Way. L63 ... 79 A1
Chorley's La. WA8 ... 73 E3
Chorlton Cl. L16 ... 69 F8
Chorlton Gr. L45 ... 50 D5
Chris Ward Cl. 1 L7 ... 53 C1
Christ Church CE Prim Sch. Birkenhead L41 ... 66 C5
Christ Church CE Prim Sch. Bootle L20 ... 38 D4
Christ Church CE Prim Sch. Ormskirk L39 ... 13 C3
Christ Church CE (VA) Prim Sch. L46 ... 64 E8
Christ The King RC Prim Sch. Bebington L62 ... 88 E7
Christ the King RC Prim Sch. Liverpool L15 ... 69 C8
Christ The King Sch. PR8 ... 4 B2
Christchurch Rd. L43 ... 66 B4
Christian St. L3 ... 52 E3
Christiana Hartley Maternity Hospl. PR8 ... 4 D5
Christie Cl. L66 ... 89 A2
Christie St. WA8 ... 73 D1
Christleton Cl. L43 ... 65 D2
Christmas St. L20 ... 38 D1
Christopher Cl. L16 ... 69 D8
Christopher Dr. L62 ... 89 A5
Christopher St. L4 ... 52 F8
Christopher Taylor House. L31 ... 28 D8
Christopher Way. L16 ... 69 D8
Christophers Cl. L61 ... 77 A4
Christowe Wlk. L11 ... 40 C5
Chudleigh Cl. L26 ... 70 E1
Chudleigh Rd. L13 ... 53 F3
Church Alley. L1 ... 52 D1
Church Ave. Bickershaw WN2 ... 36 F8
Church Ave. Liverpool L9 ... 39 B7
Church Cl. Formby L37 ... 10 A3
Church Cl. Southport PR9 ... 5 A8
Church Cl. Wallasey L44 ... 51 D4
Church Close Ct. L37 ... 10 A3
Church Cotts. L25 ... 70 C5
Church Cres. 9 L44 ... 51 E2
Church Dr. Bebington L62 ... 79 B6
Church Dr. Newton-le-W WA12 ... 46 C1
Church Dr. Orrell WN5 ... 25 D5
Church Dr Prim Sch. L62 ... 79 B6
Church End. L24 ... 83 D1
Church Farm Ct. L60 ... 85 F7
Church Fields. L39 ... 13 E5
Church Gdns. Bootle L20 ... 38 B3
Church Gdns. Wallasey L44 . 51 D4
Church Gn. Formby L37 ... 9 C2
Church Gn. Kirkby L32 ... 29 E3
Church Gn. Liverpool L16 ... 69 F7
Church Gr. L21 ... 37 F6
Church Gr. Seaforth L21 ... 37 F6
Church Hill. L44 ... 50 F5
Church Hill Rd. L39 ... 13 D6
Church La. Aughton L39 ... 21 A7
Church La. Bebington L62 ... 79 D1
Church La. Bebington L62 ... 89 A4
Church La. Birkenhead L49 .. 65 B2
Church La. Bootle L4 ... 38 F2
Church La. Golborne WA3 ... 47 D7
Church La. Kirkby L34 ... 41 C4
Church La. Liverpool L17 ... 68 E1
Church La. Maghull L39 ... 20 A8
Church La. St Helens WA10 . 43 A4
Church La. Thurstaston L61 . 76 B5
Church La. Wallasey L44 ... 51 D4
Church Meadow La. L60 ... 85 F7
Church Meadow Wlk. WA8 . 84 B5
Church Mews. L24 ... 82 B3
Church Mount. 2 L7 ... 53 B1
Church Rd. Bebington L63 ... 79 A4
Church Rd. Bickerstaffe L39 22 E6
Church Rd. Birkenhead L49 .. 65 A5
Church Rd. Birkenhead L42 .. 66 D3
Church Rd. Bootle L21 ... 38 C8
Church Rd. Bootle L20 ... 38 D6
Church Rd. Crosby L23 ... 26 E4
Church Rd. Formby L37 ... 10 A5
Church Rd. Hale L24 ... 83 E1
Church Rd. Haydock WA11 .. 45 E7
Church Rd. Huyton-w-R L36 . 55 C3
Church Rd. Litherland L21 & L30 & L22 .. 27 D1
Church Rd. Liverpool L4 ... 39 A1
Church Rd. Liverpool L13 ... 53 F3
Church Rd. Liverpool L15 & L18 ... 69 A6
Church Rd. Liverpool L25 ... 70 A3
Church Rd. Liverpool L26 ... 70 F1
Church Rd. Liverpool L19 ... 81 C5
Church Rd. Maghull L31 ... 28 D7
Church Rd. Raby L63 ... 87 B6
Church Rd. Rainford WA11 .. 32 A5
Church Rd. Seaforth L22 ... 37 E8
Church Rd. Skelmersdale WN8 ... 15 F1
Church Rd. Southport PR9 ... 2 F6
Church Rd. Wallasey L44 ... 51 E2
Church Rd. West Kirby L48 .. 63 B1
Church Rd N. L15 ... 69 A7
Church Rd S. L25 ... 70 A2
Church Rd W. L4 ... 38 F2
Church Sq. 10 WA10 ... 44 A3
Church St. Birkenhead L41 .. 66 F6
Church St. Bootle L20 ... 38 A3
Church St. Golborne WA3 ... 36 B1
Church St. Liverpool L1 ... 52 D1
Church St. Newton-le-W WA12 ... 46 E4
Church St. Ormskirk L39 ... 13 E5
Church St. Orrell WN8 ... 25 C7
Church St. Orrell WN5 ... 25 E5
Church St. Prescot L34 ... 56 D6
Church St. Southport PR9 ... 4 C7
Church St. St Helens WA10 .. 44 A3
Church St. Wallasey L44 .. 51 D4
Church Terr. L42 ... 66 D3
Church View. Aughton L39 ... 21 A7
Church View. Bootle L20 ... 38 B3
Church View. Liverpool L12 . 54 B7
Church View Ct. L39 ... 13 E5
Church Way. Formby L37 ... 9 C2
Church Way. Kirkby L32 ... 29 E3
Church Way. Litherland L30 . 27 D5
Church Wlk. Bootle L20 ... 38 B3
Church Wlk. Winwick WA2 .. 61 A6
Church Wlks. L39 ... 13 E5
Churchdown Cl. L14 ... 54 F4
Churchdown Gr. L14 ... 54 E4
Churchdown Rd. L14 ... 54 E4
Churchfield Rd. L25 ... 70 C5
Churchfields. Southport PR8 .. 3 F3
Churchfields. 5 St Helens WA9 ... 58 C4
Churchfields. Widnes WA8 .. 73 B5
Churchgate. Southport PR9 ... 1 F1
Churchgate Mews. PR9 ... 2 A1
Churchill Ave. PR9 ... 1 F2
Churchill Gr. L44 ... 51 C5
Churchill House. 6 L21 ... 37 F7
Churchill Ind Est. L9 ... 39 C8
Churchill Way. L1 & L3 ... 52 D2
Churchlands. 13 L44 ... 51 E2
Churchmeadow Cl. L44 ... 51 D4
Churchtown Ct. PR9 ... 2 A2
Churchtown Prim Sch. PR9 .. 2 B2
Churchview Rd. L41 ... 66 B8
Churchway Rd. L24 ... 83 A2
Churchwood Cl. L62 ... 79 D1
Churchwood Ct. L49 ... 65 B1
Churn Way. L49 ... 64 D4
Churnet St. L4 ... 52 E8
Churston Rd. L16 ... 69 E5
Churton Ave. L43 ... 65 F3
Churton Ct. 22 L6 ... 53 A3
Ciaran Cl. L12 ... 54 E8
Cicely St. L7 ... 53 B1
Cinder La. Bootle L20 ... 38 D7
Cinder La. Liverpool L18 ... 69 C5
Cinnamon Brow. WN8 ... 25 C6
Cinnamon Brow CE Prim Sch. WA2 ... 61 F3
Cinnamon La. WA2 ... 61 F2
Cinnamon La N. WA2 ... 61 F3
Circular Dr. Bebington L62 ... 79 B7
Circular Dr. Birkenhead L49 . 64 D3
Circular Dr. Heswall L60 ... 76 F1
Circular Rd. L41 ... 66 D5
Circular Rd E. Liverpool L11 . 53 F8
Circular Rd W. L11 ... 53 F8
Cirencester Ave. L49 ... 64 C4
Citrine Rd. L44 ... 51 D2
Citron Cl. L9 ... 39 B4
City Coll. L1 ... 52 C1
City Gdns. WA10 ... 43 F6
City of Liverpool Comm Coll. L13 ... 53 F5
City of Liverpool Comm Coll (Clarence St Centre). L3 ... 52 E1
City of Liverpool Comm Coll (Green Bank Ctr). L18 ... 68 F5
City of Liverpool Comm Coll (Muirhead Ctr). L12 ... 40 B1
City of Liverpool Comm Coll (Old Swan Ctr). L13 ... 54 A3
City of Liverpool Comm Coll (Riversdale Ctr). L19 ... 80 F7
City Rd. Bootle L4 ... 38 F1
City Rd. St Helens WA10 ... 43 F6
Civic Way. Bebington L63 ... 79 A5
Civic Way. Huyton-w-R L36 .. 55 E2
Clairville. PR8 ... 3 F5
Clairville Cl. L20 ... 38 C3
Clairville Way. L13 ... 53 E5
Clamley Ct. L24 ... 83 A3
Clamley Gdns. L24 ... 83 E2
Clandon Rd. L18 ... 69 D1
Clanfield Ave. WA8 ... 72 C3
Clanfield Rd. L11 ... 40 B1
Clap Gate Cres. WA8 ... 84 B5
Clapham Rd. L4 ... 53 B7
Clare Cl. WA9 ... 57 E7
Clare Cres. L44 ... 50 F4
Clare Rd. L20 ... 38 E2
Clare Terr. L5 ... 52 E6
Clare Way. L45 ... 50 F5
Clare Wlk. L10 ... 40 B7
Claremont Ave. Maghull L31 28 B8
Claremont Ave. Widnes WA8 ... 73 C4
Claremont Cl. L21 ... 37 F7
Claremont Dr. Ormskirk L39 13 D3
Claremont Dr. Widnes WA8 73 B4
Claremont Gdns. PR8 ... 4 A4
Claremont Rd. Billinge WN5 33 E5
Claremont Rd. Crosby L23 ... 26 E4
Claremont Rd. Liverpool L15 68 E6
Claremont Rd. Seaforth L21 37 F7
Claremont Rd. Southport PR8 4 A4
Claremont Rd. West Kirby L48 ... 63 B3
Claremont Way. L63 ... 78 D8
Claremount Dr. L63 ... 78 F4
Claremount Rd. L44 & L45 ... 50 F6
Claremount Sch. L46 ... 50 A1
Clarence Ave. WA8 ... 73 A4
Clarence House Sch. L37 ... 9 F6
Clarence Rd. Birkenhead L42 66 C3
Clarence Rd. Southport PR8 ... 4 A4
Clarence Rd. Wallasey L44 ... 51 D3
Clarence St. 6 Ashton-in-M WN4 ... 34 F5
Clarence St. Golborne WA3 . 36 A1
Clarence St. Liverpool L3 ... 52 E1
Clarence St. Newton-le-W WA12 ... 45 F4
Clarence St. Runcorn WA7 ... 84 F3

Clarendon Cl. L43 66 C5
Clarendon Ct. WA2 60 F4
Clarendon Gr. L31 20 C5
Clarendon Rd. Liverpool L6 53 C6
Clarendon Rd. Liverpool L19 81 C6
Clarendon Rd. 3 Seaforth L21 37 F6
Clarendon Rd. Wallasey L44 51 D4
Clarendon Wlk. 10 L41 & L43 66 C5
Claribel St. L8 68 A6
Clarke Ave. L42 66 E2
Clarke's Cres. WA10 43 B4
Classic Rd. L13 54 A4
Clatterbridge Hospl. L63 78 D1
Clatterbridge Rd. Bebington L63 78 E2
Clatterbridge Rd. Raby L63 87 D8
Claude Rd. L6 53 C6
Claughton Cl. 9 L7 53 C1
Claughton Dr. L44 51 B3
Claughton Firs. L43 66 B4
Claughton Gn. L43 66 B5
Claughton Pl. L41 & L43 66 C6
Claughton St. WA10 44 A3
Clavell Rd. L19 81 D8
Clay Brow Rd. WN8 24 E6
Clay Cross Rd. L25 69 F2
Clay La. Burtonwood WA5 59 E5
Clay La. St Helens WA10 42 E3
Clay St. L3 52 B4
Clayfield Cl. L20 38 D3
Clayford Cres. L13 & L14 54 C4
Clayford Pl. L14 54 B4
Clayford Rd. L14 54 C4
Clayford Way. L14 54 C4
Clayhill. L64 86 F2
Clayhill Light Ind Pk. L64 86 F2
Claypole Cl. 8 L7 68 C8
Clayton Ave. WA3 47 E8
Clayton Cres. Runcorn WA7 84 F1
Clayton Cres. Widnes WA8 72 F1
Clayton Ct. L44 51 A2
Clayton La. L44 51 A2
Clayton Mews. WN8 15 D1
Clayton Pl. 3 L41 & L43 66 C5
Clayton Sq. 8 L1 52 D1
Clayton St. Birkenhead L43 66 C5
Clayton St. Skelmersdale WN8 15 D1
Cleadon Cl. 2 L32 41 A7
Cleadon Rd. L32 41 A7
Cleary St. L20 38 B4
Clee Hill Rd. L42 66 C1
Clegg St. Liverpool L5 52 E4
Clegg St. Skelmersdale WN8 15 D1
Clement Gdns. L3 52 C4
Clementina Rd. L23 26 B4
Clemmey Dr. L20 38 E6
Clengers Brow. PR9 2 A3
Clent Ave. L31 20 C3
Clent Gdns. L31 20 C3
Clent Rd. L31 20 C3
Cleopas St. L8 67 F4
Cleve Way. L37 10 B2
Clevedon St. L8 68 A5
Cleveland Bldgs. 3 L1 & L72 67 D8
Cleveland Cl. L32 29 D4
Cleveland Dr. Ashton-in-M WN4 35 C4
Cleveland Dr. Golborne WA3 36 D1
Cleveland Rd. WA2 61 B3
Cleveland Sq. L1 & L72 67 D8
Cleveland St. Birkenhead L41 & L72 66 D8
Cleveland St. St Helens WA9 44 C1
Cleveley Pk. L18 69 D1
Cleveley Rd. Hoylake L47 63 E8
Cleveley Rd. Liverpool L18 69 D1
Cleveleys Ave. Southport PR9 2 A4
Cleveleys Ave. Widnes WA8 73 D2
Cleveleys Rd. PR9 2 A3
Cleves The. L31 20 E3
Clieves Hills La. L39 12 E3
Clieves Rd. L32 29 F1
Clifden Ct. L37 9 F3
Cliff Dr. L44 51 D5
Cliff Rd. Southport PR9 1 D1
Cliff Rd. Wallasey L44 51 A4
Cliff St. L7 53 C2
Cliff The. L45 50 F8
Cliffe St. 3 WA8 73 C1
Clifford Holroyde Sch. L9 39 D6
Clifford Rd. Southport PR8 4 A2
Clifford Rd. Wallasey L44 51 C3
Clifford Rd. Warrington WA5 74 F4
Clifford St. Birkenhead L41 66 A8
Clifford St. Liverpool L3 52 E2
Clifton Ave. Bebington L62 88 E3
Clifton Ave. Liverpool L26 70 E1
Clifton Cres. 11 L41 66 E6
Clifton Ct. L19 81 C8
Clifton Dr. L10 28 D2
Clifton Gr. 2 Liverpool L5 52 E4
Clifton Gr. Wallasey L44 51 D4
Clifton Rd. Ashton-in-M WN4 34 F6
Clifton Rd. Billinge WN5 33 D4
Clifton Rd. Birkenhead L41 66 D5
Clifton Rd. Formby L37 10 A5
Clifton Rd. Liverpool L6 53 D5
Clifton Rd. Southport PR8 4 F6
Clifton Rd E. L13 & L6 53 D6
Clifton St. Liverpool L19 81 C6
Clifton St. St Helens WA10 44 A4
Cliftonmill Meadows. WA3 46 F8
Cliftonville Rd. L34 56 E6
Clincton Cl. WA8 84 A8
Clincton View. WA8 84 A8
Clinning Rd. PR8 4 A2
Clint Rd. L7 53 C1
Clint Way. 2 L7 53 C1
Clinton Pl. L12 53 F7
Clinton Rd. L12 53 F7
Clipper View. L62 79 B8
Clipsley Cres. WA11 45 B7
Clipsley La. WA11 45 C6
Clive Ave. WA2 61 C1
Clive Lodge. PR8 3 F2
Clive Rd. Birkenhead L43 66 C4
Clive Rd. Southport PR8 3 F2
Clock Face Rd. WA8 & WA9 58 D3
Cloister Gn. L37 10 B2
Cloisters The. Crosby L23 26 D3
Cloisters The. Formby L37 9 F3
Cloisters The. St Helens WA10 43 B4
Clorain Cl. L33 30 A3
Clorain Rd. L33 30 A3
Close St. WA9 57 E7
Close The. Birkenhead L49 64 D2
Close The. Birkenhead L42 66 D1
Close The. Bootle L9 38 F4
Close The. Crosby L23 26 D3
Close The. Huyton-w-R L28 55 C7
Close The. Ince Blundell L38 18 E3
Close The. Irby L61 76 D6
Close The. St Helens WA10 43 A5
Close The. St Helens WA11 44 F5
Closeburn Ave. L60 85 E6
Clough Ave. WA2 61 B2
Clough Fold Prim Sch. WN8 16 C2
Clough Gr. WN4 34 F5
Clough Rd. L24 82 E4
Clovelly Ave. St Helens WA9 58 E6
Clovelly Ave. Warrington WA5 74 E7
Clovelly Ct. L49 64 D3
Clovelly Dr. Skelmersdale WN8 16 A8
Clovelly Dr. Southport PR8 7 E8
Clovelly Rd. L4 53 B6
Clover Ave. L26 70 D2
Clover Dr. L41 50 E1
Clover Hey. WA11 44 B7
Cloverdale Rd. L25 70 B7
Club St. WA11 33 A1
Clucas Gdns. L39 13 E6
Clwyd Gr. L12 54 B8
Clwyd St. Birkenhead L41 66 D6
Clwyd St. 2 Birkenhead L41 66 E6
Clwyd St. Wallasey L45 51 B7
Clyde Rd. L7 53 E2
Clyde St. Birkenhead L42 66 F2
Clyde St. Liverpool L20 52 C8
Clydesdale Rd. Hoylake L47 63 B8
Clydesdale Rd. Wallasey L44 51 D4
Coach House Ct. L29 27 F7
Coach Rd. L33 & L39 & WA11 & L34 31 B5
Coachmans Dr. L12 & L28 40 E1
Coal Pit La. L39 & WN8 23 D4
Coal St. L1 & L3 52 E2
Coalbrookdale Rd. L64 86 F2
Coalgate La. L35 56 C2
Coalville Rd. WA11 44 D6
Coastal Dr. L45 50 E8
Coastal Rd. Southport PR8 7 A4
Coastguard La. L64 86 B1
Cob Moor Ave. WN5 25 D1
Cob Moor Rd. WN5 25 D1
Cobb Ave. L21 38 B6
Cobb's Brow La. Skelmersdale WN8 16 A8
Cobb's Clough Rd. L40 15 F5
Cobbles The. L26 70 D2
Cobbs Brow Cty Prim Sch. WN8 16 A3
Cobden Ave. L41 66 F3
Cobden Ct. L41 66 F3
Cobden Pl. Birkenhead L42 66 F3
Cobden Pl. Liverpool L25 69 F2
Cobden Rd. PR9 5 A6
Cobden St. Liverpool L6 52 F3
Cobden St. Liverpool L25 69 F2
Cobden St. Newton-le-W WA12 46 D4
Cobden View. L25 69 F2
Coberg St. L41 66 D6
Cobham Ave. L9 38 F6
Cobham Rd. L46 64 D7
Cobham Wlk. L30 27 E4
Coburg Wharf. L3 67 C6
Cochrane St. L5 52 F5
Cock Lane Ends. WA8 84 B4
Cockburn St. L8 67 F3
Cockerell Cl. 3 L4 52 F7
Cockerham Way. L11 40 C5
Cocklade La. L24 83 D1
Cockle Dick's La. PR9 1 E2
Cockshead Rd. L25 70 B5
Cockshead Way. L25 70 B6
Cockspur St. L3 52 C2
Cockspur St W. L3 52 C2
Coerton Rd. L9 39 B7
Cokers The. L42 78 E8
Colbern Cl. L31 28 E8
Colby Cl. L16 69 E8
Colchester Rd. PR8 4 F3
Coldstone Dr. WN4 34 D4
Coldstream Cl. WA2 61 E3
Cole Ave. WA12 46 C4
Cole Cres. L39 21 C8
Cole St. L41 & L43 66 C6
Cole Street Prim Sch. L43 66 C6
Colebrooke Rd. L17 68 A3
Coleman Dr. L49 64 C3
Colemere Dr. L61 77 B6
Coleridge Ave. WA10 43 D4
Coleridge Rd. WN5 25 D1
Coleridge St. Bootle L20 38 A4
Coleridge St. Liverpool L6 & L7 53 B3
Coles Cres. L23 27 B6
Colesborne Rd. L11 40 B2
Coleshill Rd. L11 39 E3
Colette Rd. L10 40 B7
Coleus Cl. L9 39 B4
Colin Cl. L36 55 C2
Colindale Rd. L16 69 E7
Colinmander Gdns. L39 13 C3
Colinton. WN8 24 E7
Colinton St. L15 68 E8
College Ave. Crosby L23 26 D2
College Ave. Formby L37 9 E4
College Cl. Birkenhead L43 65 B6
College Cl. Formby L37 9 D4
College Cl. Southport PR8 4 A3
College Cl. Wallasey L45 50 E6
College Ct. L12 54 A5
College Dr. L63 79 A7
College Fields. L36 55 E1
College Green. 2 L23 26 D3
College La. 2 L1 52 D1
College Path. L37 9 D5
College Rd. Crosby L22 & L23 26 D3
College Rd. Orrell WN8 25 B8
College Rd N. L23 26 C5
College St. WA10 44 A5
College St N. L6 52 F3
College St S. L6 52 F3
College View. L20 38 C2
Collier St. WA7 84 F3
Collin Rd. L43 65 E8
Collingwood Rd. Bebington L63 79 B4
Collingwood Rd. Newton-le-W WA12 46 B3
Collins Cl. L20 38 A5
Collins Green La. WA5 45 E1
Collisdene Rd. WN5 25 E6
Colmore Ave. L63 79 A1
Colmore Rd. L11 39 E2
Colne Dr. WA9 58 D7
Colne Rd. WA5 59 F6
Colquitt St. L1 67 E8
Coltart Rd. L8 68 B6
Colton Rd. L25 70 A7
Colton Wlk. L25 69 F7
Columban Cl. L30 27 E3
Columbia Rd. Birkenhead L43 66 B4
Columbia Rd. Liverpool L4 39 A2
Columbia Rd. Prescot L34 56 E6
Columbine Cl. WA8 72 B4
Columbus Dr. L61 76 E3
Columbus Quay. L3 67 E3
Columbus St. 2 WN4 34 F5
Columbus Way. L21 38 B7
Column Rd. West Kirby L48 63 D1
Colville Ct. WA2 61 A3
Colville Rd. L44 51 A4
Colville St. L15 68 E8
Colwall Cl. L33 30 A2
Colwall Rd. L33 30 A2
Colwall Wlk. L33 30 A2
Colwell Cl. L14 55 A6
Colwell Rd. L14 55 A6
Colwell Road Cty Jun & Inf Sch. L14 55 A6
Colwyn Cl. WA5 60 E2
Colwyn Rd. L13 53 F2
Colwyn St. L41 66 A8
Colyton Ave. WA9 58 D5
Combermere St. Liverpool L8 67 F6
Combermere St. Liverpool L15 68 D8
Comely Ave. L44 51 D4
Comely Bank Rd. L44 51 D4
Comer Gdns. L31 20 C3
Comercial Rd. L5 52 C7
Comfrey Gr. L26 70 E2
Commell Ct. L43 66 B6
Commercial Rd. L62 79 E3
Common Field Rd. L49 65 B2
Common Rd. WA12 & WA5 45 E3
Common St. Newton-le-W WA12 45 E3
Common St. St Helens WA9 57 D7
Commutation Row. 1 L1 & L3 52 E2
Compton Cl. WA11 45 C7
Compton Rd. Liverpool L6 53 A4
Compton Rd. Southport PR8 4 B3
Compton Rd. Wallasey L41 50 D1
Compton Way. L24 & L26 82 F6
Compton Wlk. L20 38 B4
Comus St. L3 52 D3
Concert St. L1 52 D1
Concorde Pl. WA2 61 D2
Concordia Ave. L49 65 A5
Concourse Sh Ctr. WN8 16 B1
Concourse Way. WA9 45 A2
Condor Cl. L19 81 D6
Condron Rd. L21 27 C1
Condron Rd N. L21 27 C1
Coney Cres. L23 27 B5
Coney La. Huyton-w-R L36 71 A8
Coney La. Liverpool L35 & L36 70 F7
Coney Wlk. L49 64 D6
Conifer Cl. Kirkby L33 29 E5
Conifer Cl. Liverpool L9 39 B4
Conifer Ct. L37 10 A2
Conifer Gr. WA5 74 F7
Conifers The. L31 20 C3
Coningsby Dr. L45 51 A4
Coningsby Rd. L4 53 A7
Coniston Ave. Ashton-in-M WN4 35 B4
Coniston Ave. Bebington L63 88 C4
Coniston Ave. Birkenhead L43 65 C5
Coniston Ave. Orrell WN5 25 F7
Coniston Ave. Prescot L34 & L35 56 F6
Coniston Ave. Wallasey L45 50 E7
Coniston Ave. Warrington WA5 74 D4
Coniston Cl. Bebington L66 89 B2
Coniston Cl. Kirkby L33 29 D4
Coniston Cl. Liverpool L9 39 B7
Coniston Ct. PR8 7 C3
Coniston Dr. WN2 36 B8
Coniston Gr. WA11 44 A7
Coniston Rd. Formby L37 9 D2
Coniston Rd. Irby L61 76 D6
Coniston Rd. Maghull L31 20 E2
Coniston St. L5 & L6 53 A5
Coniston Way. WA11 23 F2
Conleach Rd. L24 82 E3
Connaught Cl. L41 66 A8
Connaught Dr. WA12 46 C2
Connaught Rd. L7 53 B2
Connaught Way. L41 66 A8
Connolly Ave. L20 38 E5
Conroy Way. WA12 60 C8
Consett Rd. L35 57 D6
Constance St. Liverpool L3 52 F2
Constance St. St Helens WA10 43 D2
Constantine Ave. L60 77 A1
Convent Cl. Birkenhead L41 & L42 66 D4
Convent Cl. Liverpool L19 81 A7
Convent Cl. Ormskirk L39 13 E2
Conville Bvd. L63 78 E8
Conway Ave. WA5 60 F2
Conway Cl. Bebington L63 78 D5
Conway Cl. Kirkby L33 29 D5
Conway Cl. Warrington WA5 74 F6
Conway Cres. WN5 33 E6
Conway Ct. Bebington L63 78 F4
Conway Ct. 1 Birkenhead L41 66 D6
Conway Dr. Billinge WN5 33 F5
Conway Dr. Newton-le-W WA12 46 E3
Conway Pl. 9 L41 66 D6
Conway Rd. WN4 35 E5
Conway St. Birkenhead L41 66 E6
Conway St. Liverpool L5 52 E5
Conway St. Wallasey L44 51 B4
Conwy Dr. L6 53 B4
Conyers Ave. PR8 3 F3
Coogee Ave. WA5 74 E7
Cook Ave. WA11 45 F7
Cook Rd. L46 50 B4
Cook St. Birkenhead L41 66 D5
Cook St. Liverpool L2 52 C1
Cook St. Prescot L34 56 D6
Cook St. Prescot L35 56 F4
Cooke St. WN4 34 F6
Cooks Rd. L23 26 D5
Cookson Rd. L21 38 A6
Cookson St. L1 67 E7
Coombe Rd. L61 76 E7
Cooper Ave. Newton-le-W WA12 45 F3
Cooper Ave. Warrington WA2 61 B2
Cooper Ave N. L18 69 A2
Cooper Ave S. L18 & L19 69 A1
Cooper Cl. L19 81 A8
Cooper La. WA11 45 C6
Cooper St. St Helens WA10 43 F4
Cooper St. Widnes WA8 73 B1
Cooper's La. L33 41 D7
Coopers Row. L22 37 E8
Copeland Cl. L61 76 E3
Copperas Hill. L1 & L3 52 E1
Copperas St. WA10 43 F3
Copperfield Cl. L8 67 F5
Copperwood Dr. L35 56 F3
Coppice Cl. Birkenhead L49 64 C2
Coppice Cl. Birkenhead L43 65 B6
Coppice Cres. L36 55 F4
Coppice Dr. WN5 25 D2
Coppice Gn. WA5 60 A1
Coppice Grange. L46 64 C7
Coppice La. L35 71 C7
Coppice Leys. L37 9 E3
Coppice The. Knowsley L34 41 D3
Coppice The. Liverpool L6 53 C6
Coppice The. Wallasey L45 51 A7
Coppins The. Warrington WA2 61 C2
Copple House Ct. L10 40 A7
Copple House La. L10 40 A7
Coppull Rd. L31 20 C4
Copse Gr. L61 76 E7
Copse The. Liverpool L16 & L18 69 D5
Copse The. Newton-le-W WA12 46 B4
Copthorne Rd. L32 29 B2
Copy Cl. L30 27 F5
Copy La. L30 & L9 28 B3
Copy Way. L30 27 F5
Coral Ave. Huyton-w-R L36 55 D3
Coral Ave. St Helens WA9 57 F7
Coral Ridge. L43 65 D6
Coral St. L13 54 A1
Coralin Way. WN4 34 F7
Corbet Cl. L32 29 C2
Corbet Wlk. 4 L32 29 C2
Corbridge Rd. L16 69 C7
Corbyn St. L44 51 E1
Corfu St. L41 66 C6
Corinth Tower. L5 52 E6
Corinthian Ave. L13 54 A4
Corinthian Cty Prim Sch. L13 54 B4
Corinthian St. Birkenhead L42 66 F2
Corinthian St. Seaforth L21 37 F7
Corinto St. L8 67 F6
Corley Wlk. L24 82 E2
Cormorant Dr. WA7 84 E2
Corn Mill Lodge. L31 20 C2
Corn St. L8 67 E5
Cornation Rd. L23 26 E4
Cornbrook. WN8 24 E7
Corncroft Rd. L34 41 D3
Corndale Rd. L18 69 A4
Corneghie Ct. PR8 3 F4
Cornel Way. L36 70 F8
Cornelian Gr. WN4 34 F5
Cornelius Dr. L61 76 F5
Corner Brook. L12 & L28 54 F7

Cornerhouse La. WA8 ... 72 D3
Cornett Rd. L9 ... 39 B7
Corney St. L7 ... 68 C7
Cornhill. L1 & L72 ... 67 D8
Cornice Rd. L13 ... 54 A4
Corniche Rd. L62 ... 79 B6
Cornwall Cl. L62 ... 79 B7
Cornwall Ct. L63 ... 78 F4
Cornwall Dr. L43 ... 66 A1
Cornwall Rd. WA8 ... 73 B3
Cornwall St. WA9 ... 44 E2
Cornwall Way. PR8 ... 7 C2
Cornwallis St. Liverpool L1 & L72 ... 67 D7
Cornwallis St. Liverpool L1 & L72 ... 67 E8
Corona Ave. L31 ... 20 C5
Corona Rd. Bebington L62 ... 79 C6
Corona Rd. Crosby L22 ... 26 D1
Corona Rd. Liverpool L13 ... 54 A4
Coronation Ave. Formby L37 10 A2
Coronation Ave. Liverpool L14 ... 54 E3
Coronation Ave. Wallasey L45 ... 51 B7
Coronation Bldgs. L48 ... 63 C4
Coronation Ct. L9 ... 39 F4
Coronation Dr. Bebington L62 ... 79 D3
Coronation Dr. Crosby L23 .. 26 D3
Coronation Dr. Haydock WA11 ... 46 A7
Coronation Dr. Liverpool L14 54 E3
Coronation Dr. Newton-le-W WA12 ... 46 E1
Coronation Dr. Prescot L35 . 56 C3
Coronation Dr. Warrington WA5 ... 74 F4
Coronation Dr. Widnes WA8 84 C8
Coronation Rd. Crosby L23 .. 26 D4
Coronation Rd. Hoylake L47 62 F6
Coronation Rd. Maghull L31 20 D3
Coronation Rd. St Helens WA10 ... 43 C5
Coronation St. WN4 ... 34 D6
Coronation Wlk. Billinge WN5 ... 33 D4
Coronation Wlk. Southport PR8 ... 4 A7
Coroner's La. WA8 ... 73 A4
Coronet Rd. L11 ... 40 C3
Coronet Way. WA8 ... 84 B8
Corporation Rd. L41 ... 66 C8
Corporation St. Southport PR8 ... 4 B7
Corporation St. St Helens WA10 & WA9 ... 44 A3
Corpus Christi RC Prim Sch. WA11 ... 31 F7
Corrie Dr. L63 ... 78 F4
Corsewall St. L7 ... 68 D8
Corsey Ave. L30 ... 27 C3
Corsham Rd. L26 ... 82 E6
Corsican Gdns. L35 ... 57 C7
Cortsway. L49 ... 64 E5
Cortsway W. L49 ... 64 D5
Corwen Cl. Birkenhead L46 .. 64 F7
Corwen Cl. Birkenhead L43 .. 65 B6
Corwen Cl. Warrington WA5 60 E1
Corwen Cres. L14 ... 54 F2
Corwen Dr. L30 ... 28 B4
Corwen Rd. Hoylake L47 ... 63 C7
Corwen Rd. Liverpool L4 ... 53 C8
Cosgrove Cl. L6 ... 53 D7
Cossack Ave. WA2 ... 61 C1
Costain St. L20 ... 52 C7
Cotham St. 1 WA10 ... 44 A3
Cotsford Cl. L36 ... 55 C4
Cotsford Pl. L36 ... 55 C4
Cotsford Rd. L36 ... 55 C4
Cotsford Way. L36 ... 55 C4
Cotswold Ave. WA3 ... 47 D6
Cotswold Gr. WA9 ... 45 A3
Cotswold Pl. WA2 ... 61 B4
Cotswold Rd. Birkenhead L42 ... 66 C1
Cotswold Rd. Warrington WA2 ... 61 B3
Cotswold St. L7 ... 53 B2
Cotswolds Cres. L26 ... 82 E7
Cottage Cl. Bebington L63 ... 88 C5
Cottage Cl. Kirkby L32 ... 40 E7
Cottage Cl. Ormskirk L39 ... 13 D4
Cottage Dr E. L60 ... 85 F5
Cottage Dr W. L60 ... 85 F5
Cottage La. Heswall L60 ... 85 F5
Cottage La. Ormskirk L39 ... 13 D5
Cottage Mews. L39 ... 13 D5
Cottage Pl. 9 WA9 ... 58 C4
Cottage St. L41 ... 66 D7
Cottenham St. 8 L7 ... 53 B3
Cotterdale Cl. 2 St Helens WA9 ... 58 C6
Cotterdale Cl. Warrington WA5 ... 74 F7
Cottesbrook Cl. L11 ... 40 A3
Cottesbrook Pl. L11 ... 40 A3
Cottesbrook Rd. L11 ... 40 A3
Cottesmore Dr. L60 ... 86 D8
Cottesmore Way. WA3 ... 36 B1
Cotton Dr. L39 ... 13 D6
Cotton Gn. L37 ... 10 B3
Cotton St. L3 ... 52 B4
Cottonwood. L8 ... 68 A2
Cottrell Cl. L19 ... 81 C4
Cottys Brow. PR9 ... 1 F3
Coudray Rd. PR9 ... 1 E1
Coulport Cl. L14 ... 55 A4
Coulsdon Pl. L8 ... 68 A4
Coulthard Rd. L42 ... 79 A8
Coulton Rd. WA8 ... 73 F3
Coultshead Ave. WN5 ... 33 E6
Counce Ave. WA12 ... 46 B1
Council Ave. WN4 ... 35 B3
Council St. L35 ... 57 A5
Countisbury Dr. L16 ... 69 E6
County Dr. WA10 ... 43 E2
County Rd. Bootle L4 ... 38 F1
County Rd. Kirkby L32 ... 29 E2
County Rd. Ormskirk L39 ... 13 E6
Court Ave. L26 ... 71 A1
Court Hey. L31 ... 20 E1
Court Hey Ave. L14 & L36 ... 55 A2
Court Hey Dr. L16 ... 54 F1
Court Hey Rd. L14 & L16 ... 54 F1
Court Rd. PR9 ... 4 C8
Court The. Bebington L63 ... 79 A4
Court The. Huyton-w-R L36 .. 55 C7
Courtenay Ave. L22 ... 26 C2
Courtenay Rd. Crosby L22 ... 26 C2
Courtenay Rd. Hoylake L47 . 63 A6
Courtenay Rd. Liverpool L25 70 A4
Courtfield. L39 ... 13 D7
Courtfields. Cl. L12 ... 54 B5
Courtgreen. L39 ... 13 D7
Courthope Rd. Liverpool L4 . 39 B1
Courtland Rd. Liverpool L18 69 B5
Courtney Ave. L44 ... 51 A3
Courtney Rd. L42 ... 79 A8
Courtyard Wks. L33 ... 30 C2
Covent Garden. L2 ... 52 C1
Coventry Ave. L30 ... 27 F1
Coventry Rd. L15 ... 69 A6
Coventry St. 8 L41 ... 66 D6
Coverdale Ave. L35 ... 57 D3
Coverdale Cl. WA5 ... 74 F7
Covertside. L48 ... 63 D2
Cowan Way. L6 ... 53 A4
Cowanway. WA8 ... 72 F5
Cowdrey Ave. L43 ... 50 C1
Cowley Cl. L49 ... 64 D5
Cowley High Sch. WA10 ... 43 E6
Cowley High Sch (Lower). WA10 ... 43 F5
Cowley Hill La. WA10 ... 43 E4
Cowley Rd. L4 ... 39 A1
Cowley St. WA10 ... 44 A5
Cowper Rd. L13 ... 54 B3
Cowper St. Bootle L20 ... 38 A5
Cowper St. St Helens WA9 ... 44 C1
Cowper Way. L36 ... 56 A1
Coyford Dr. PR9 ... 2 A4
Coylton Ave. L35 ... 57 D2
Crab St. WA10 ... 43 F4
Crab Tree Cl. L24 ... 83 E2
Crabtree Cl. L27 ... 70 E5
Cradley. WA8 ... 72 C2
Crag Gr. WA11 ... 33 B1
Craigburn Rd. L13 ... 53 E6
Craighurst Prim Sch. L25 ... 70 A7
Craighurst Rd. L25 ... 70 A7
Craigleigh Gr. L62 ... 88 F4
Craigmore Rd. L18 ... 69 A1
Craigs Rd. L13 ... 53 E6
Craigside Ave. L12 ... 54 A7
Craigwood Way. L36 ... 55 B3
Craine Cl. L4 ... 53 B8
Cramond Ave. 1 L15 & L18 69 A5
Cranberry Cl. WA10 ... 43 F5
Cranborne Ave. L47 ... 48 E1
Cranborne Rd. L15 ... 68 D7
Cranbourne Ave. Birkenhead L46 ... 64 D7
Cranbourne Ave. Birkenhead L41 ... 66 A7
Cranbrook Ave. WN4 ... 35 A4
Crane Ave. WA9 ... 58 D6
Cranehurst Rd. L4 ... 39 B2
Cranes La. L40 ... 14 E7
Cranfield Rd. L23 ... 27 A5
Cranford Cl. L62 ... 88 F4
Cranford Rd. L19 ... 81 B8
Cranford St. L44 ... 51 C2
Cranham Ave. WA3 ... 47 E7
Crank Hill. WA11 ... 32 E4
Crank Rd. Billinge WA11 & WN5 ... 33 B8
Crank Rd. Rainford WA11 ... 32 E2
Crank Rd. Rainford WA11 ... 32 F7
Crank Rd. St Helens WA11 ... 43 C7
Crankwood Rd. WN2 & WN7 36 D5
Cranleigh Pl. L25 ... 70 A6
Cranleigh Rd. L25 ... 70 A6
Cranmer St. Liverpool L5 ... 52 C5
Cranmer St. Liverpool L5 ... 52 D6
Cranmore Ave. L23 ... 26 F2
Cranshaw Ave. WA9 ... 58 D3
Cranshaw La. WA8 ... 73 B6
Cranston Rd. L33 ... 30 C2
Crantock Cl. Liverpool L11 ... 40 C4
Crantock Cl. Liverpool L26 ... 82 F8
Crantock Gr. WA10 ... 43 C7
Cranwell Cl. L10 ... 28 C2
Cranwell Rd. Birkenhead L49 64 B3
Cranwell Rd. Liverpool L25 .. 70 A7
Cranwell Wlk. L25 ... 70 A7
Crask Wlk. L33 ... 29 F4
Craven Ave. WA3 ... 47 E7
Craven Cl. L41 ... 66 D6
Craven Ct. WA2 ... 60 F4
Craven Lea. L12 ... 40 E4
Craven Rd. Liverpool L12 ... 54 C6
Craven Rd. Rainhill L35 ... 57 C3
Craven St. Birkenhead L41 ... 66 C6
Craven St. Liverpool L3 ... 52 E2
Cravenwood Rd. L26 ... 82 F7
Crawford Ave. Liverpool L15 & L18 ... 68 F5
Crawford Ave. Maghull L31 .. 20 B3
Crawford Ave. Widnes WA8 72 B1
Crawford Cl. Liverpool L12 ... 54 D7
Crawford Cl. St Helens WA9 58 D4
Crawford Dr. L15 ... 54 A1
Crawford Pk. L18 ... 68 F3
Crawford Rd. WA11 & WN8 . 24 D2
Crawford St. WA9 ... 58 E3
Crawford Village Prim Sch. WN8 ... 24 E3
Crawford Way. L13 & L7 ... 53 F1
Crawley Ave. WA2 ... 61 A3
Crawley Cl. L25 ... 82 D8
Crawshaw Ct. L36 ... 55 B4
Crediton Ave. PR9 ... 2 B5
Crediton Cl. L11 ... 40 C5
Creek The. L45 ... 50 E8
Cremorne Hey. L28 ... 55 B7
Crescent Ave. Ashton-in-M WN4 ... 35 A4
Crescent Ave. Formby L37 ... 9 E1
Crescent Ct. 6 L21 ... 38 A6
Crescent Gn. L39 ... 13 B1
Crescent Rd. Bootle L21 ... 38 A6
Crescent Rd. Crosby L23 ... 26 B5
Crescent Rd. Liverpool L9 ... 39 B4
Crescent Rd. Southport PR8 .. 3 F3
Crescent Rd. Wallasey L44 .. 51 C4
Crescent The. Bebington L63 78 E5
Crescent The. Birkenhead L49 ... 64 D3
Crescent The. Bootle L20 ... 38 E6
Crescent The. Crosby L22 ... 26 E1
Crescent The. Crosby L23 ... 27 A6
Crescent The. Huyton-w-R L36 ... 56 B2
Crescent The. Irby L61 ... 76 F6
Crescent The. Liverpool L24 82 C4
Crescent The. Maghull L31 .. 28 C6
Crescent The. Prescot L35 ... 56 F4
Crescent The. Southport PR9 . 2 C3
Crescent The. West Kirby L48 ... 63 A2
Cressida Ave. L63 ... 78 E7
Cressingham Rd. 2 L45 ... 51 B8
Cressington Ave. L42 ... 66 D1
Cressington Prom. L19 ... 81 A6
Cressington Sta. L19 ... 81 A7
Cresson. L43 ... 65 F5
Cresswell Cl. Litherland L30 . 27 F1
Cresswell Cl. Warrington WA5 ... 60 D2
Cresswell St. 18 Liverpool L6 ... 53 A4
Cresttor Rd. L25 ... 69 F3
Creswell St. WA10 ... 43 E3
Cretan Rd. L15 ... 68 D7
Crete Tower. L5 ... 52 E6
Crewe Gn. L49 ... 65 A2
Cricket Path. Formby L37 ... 9 F5
Cricket Path. Southport PR8 .. 3 F3
Cricklade Cl. L20 ... 38 B4
Cringles Dr. L35 ... 71 A7
Crispin Rd. L27 ... 70 E5
Crispin St. WA10 ... 43 E3
Critchley Rd. L24 ... 83 A3
Critchley Way. L33 ... 29 F5
Crockett's Wlk. WA10 ... 43 B5
Crockleford Ave. PR8 ... 4 E3
Crocus Ave. L43 ... 65 F7
Crocus St. L5 ... 52 D7
Croft Ave. Bebington L62 ... 79 D1
Croft Ave. Golborne WA3 ... 35 F2
Croft Ave. Orrell WN5 ... 25 D5
Croft Ave E. L62 ... 79 D2
Croft Bsns Pk. L62 ... 79 E2
Croft Cl. L43 ... 65 E4
Croft Dr. Birkenhead L46 ... 64 F7
Croft Dr. West Kirby L48 ... 75 C7
Croft Dr E. L48 ... 75 E6
Croft Dr W. L48 ... 75 C7
Croft Edge. L43 ... 66 B3
Croft End. WA9 ... 44 F1
Croft Field. L31 ... 20 E1
Croft Heys. L39 ... 13 B1
Croft La. Bebington L62 ... 79 D1
Croft La. Liverpool L9 ... 39 D7
Croft St. WA3 ... 47 A8
Croft The. Birkenhead L49 ... 64 D2
Croft The. Huyton-w-R L28 ... 55 A8
Croft The. Kirkby L32 ... 40 F7
Croft The. Liverpool L12 ... 54 B7
Croft The. Maghull L31 ... 20 B5
Croft The. Orrell WN5 ... 25 D3
Croft Way. L23 ... 27 B5
Crofters The. L49 ... 64 D4
Croftlands. WN5 ... 25 D4
Crofton Cres. L13 ... 54 B3
Crofton Rd. Birkenhead L42 . 66 E3
Crofton Rd. Liverpool L13 ... 54 B3
Crofton Rd. Runcorn WA7 ... 84 E1
Croftson Ave. L39 ... 13 F7
Croftsway. L60 ... 85 D8
Cromarty Rd. Liverpool L13 . 53 F2
Cromarty Rd. 3 Wallasey L44 ... 50 F4
Cromdale Gr. WA9 ... 44 E2
Cromdale Way. WA5 ... 74 E6
Cromer Dr. L45 ... 51 A5
Cromer Rd. Hoylake L47 ... 63 A7
Cromer Rd. Liverpool L17 ... 68 E1
Cromer Rd. Southport PR8 ... 3 E2
Cromer Way. L26 ... 82 F6
Cromfield. L39 ... 13 C2
Cromford Rd. L36 ... 55 E5
Crompton Ct. L18 ... 69 D5
Crompton Dr. L12 ... 40 E3
Crompton St. L5 ... 52 D5
Cromptons La. L16 & L18 ... 69 D5
Cromwell Ave. Warrington WA2 & WA5 ... 60 D3
Cromwell Cl. L39 ... 13 C2
Cromwell Rd. 6 L4 ... 38 F2
Crondall Gr. L15 ... 69 B7
Cronton Ave. L46 ... 49 F3
Cronton Ave. L35 ... 56 C1
Cronton CE Prim Sch. WA8 72 C6
Cronton La. Rainhill L35 & WA8 ... 57 B1
Cronton La. Widnes WA8 ... 72 F5
Cronton Park Ave. WA8 ... 72 C6
Cronton Park Cl. WA8 ... 72 C6
Cronton Rd. Cronton L35 & WA8 ... 72 C5
Cronton Rd. Huyton-w-R L35 & L36 ... 71 B7
Cronton Rd. 4 Liverpool L15 & L18 ... 69 A5
Cronulla Dr. WA5 ... 74 E7
Crookall St. WN4 ... 35 C4
Crookhurst Ave. WN5 ... 33 D6
Croome Dr. L48 ... 63 D2
Cropper St. L1 ... 52 E1
Cropper's La. L39 ... 14 A1
Croppers Hill. WA10 ... 43 E3
Croppers Hill Ct. WA10 ... 43 E3
Croppers Rd. WA2 ... 61 F3
Cropton Rd. L37 ... 9 F3
Crosby Cl. L49 ... 64 F6
Crosby Gn. L12 ... 54 A7
Crosby Gr. Bebington L64 ... 88 B1
Crosby Gr. St Helens WA10 .. 43 D1
Crosby Rd. PR8 ... 4 A3
Crosby Rd N. L22 ... 26 E1
Crosby Rd S. L21 & L22 ... 37 F7
Crosby Road North Prim Sch. L22 ... 26 E1
Crosender Rd. L22 & L23 ... 26 C3
Crosfield Cl. 5 L7 ... 53 C1
Crosfield Rd. Liverpool L7 ... 53 C1
Crosfield Rd. Prescot L35 ... 56 F4
Crosfield Rd. Wallasey L44 .. 51 C3
Crosfield Wlk. 4 L7 ... 53 C1
Crosgrove Rd. L4 ... 39 C1
Crosland Rd. L32 ... 30 A1
Cross Barn La. L38 ... 18 E3
Cross Farm Jun Mix & Inf Sch. L27 ... 70 F4
Cross Farm Rd. WA9 ... 44 C1
Cross Gn. L37 ... 10 A2
Cross Green Cl. L37 ... 10 A2
Cross Hey. L21 ... 27 B2
Cross Hey Ave. L43 ... 65 D5
Cross Hillocks La. L35 ... 71 E3
Cross La. Bebington L63 ... 78 F4
Cross La. Newton-le-W WA12 ... 46 B4
Cross La. Orrell WN5 ... 25 D3
Cross La. Wallasey L45 ... 50 D4
Cross Meadow Ct. WA9 ... 44 C2
Cross Pit La. WA11 ... 31 F6
Cross St. Bebington L62 ... 79 B5
Cross St. Birkenhead L41 ... 66 F6
Cross St. Crosby L22 ... 26 D1
Cross St. Golborne WA3 ... 47 A7
Cross St. Prescot L34 ... 56 E7
Cross St. Southport PR8 ... 4 B6
Cross St. 4 St Helens WA10 44 A3
Cross St. Widnes WA8 ... 73 C1
Cross The. L62 ... 79 D1
Crossacre Rd. L25 ... 70 B7
Crossdale Rd. Bebington L62 88 D5
Crossdale Rd. Crosby L22 & L23 ... 26 C3
Crossdale Way. WA11 ... 33 B1
Crossens CE Prim Sch. PR9 .. 2 C5
Crossens Way. PR9 ... 2 C6
Crossfield St. WA9 ... 44 B3
Crosshall Brow. L40 ... 14 C4
Crosshall High Sch. L40 ... 14 B5
Crosshall St. L1 ... 52 D2
Crossings The. WA12 ... 46 C3
Crossley Dr. Heswall L60 ... 85 D8
Crossley Dr. Liverpool L15 ... 69 B8
Crossley Rd. WA10 ... 43 D1
Crossvale Rd. L36 ... 55 E1
Crossway. Birkenhead L43 ... 65 E8
Crossway. Widnes WA8 ... 84 D8
Crossway Cl. WN4 ... 35 E5
Crossway The. L63 ... 87 C4
Crossways. L62 ... 79 D3
Crosswood Cres. L36 ... 55 C3
Crosthwaite Ave. L62 ... 88 F4
Croston Ave. L35 ... 57 B5
Croston Cl. WA8 ... 72 C3
Croston's Brow. PR9 ... 1 F3
Crouch St. 9 Liverpool L5 ... 53 A6
Crouch St. St Helens WA9 ... 58 D8
Crow La. WN8 ... 16 F3
Crow La E. WA12 ... 46 C4
Crow La W. WA12 ... 46 A4
Crow Orch Sch. WN8 ... 15 F2
Crow St. L8 ... 67 D6
Crow Wood La. WA8 ... 73 D2
Crow Wood Pl. WA8 ... 73 D3
Crow Wood Rd. WA3 ... 36 D1
Crowe Ave. WA2 ... 61 B2
Crowland Cl. PR9 ... 5 A6
Crowland St. PR9 ... 5 A6
Crowland Way. L37 ... 10 B2
Crowmarsh Cl. L49 ... 64 F4
Crown Acres Rd. L25 ... 82 C8
Crown Ave. WA8 ... 84 B8
Crown Cl. L37 ... 10 A2
Crown Fields Cl. WA12 ... 46 B5
Crown Gdns. WA12 ... 46 B4
Crown Park Dr. WA12 ... 46 B5
Crown Rd. L12 ... 54 C7
Crown St. Liverpool L7 ... 53 A1
Crown St. Liverpool L7 & L8 . 68 A8
Crown St. Newton-le-W WA12 ... 46 A3
Crown St. St Helens WA9 ... 57 D7
Crownway. L36 ... 55 D4
Crowther St. WA10 ... 43 E3
Croxdale Rd. Huyton-w-R L14 ... 55 A6
Croxdale Rd. Liverpool L14 .. 54 F7
Croxdale Rd W. L14 ... 55 A7
Croxteth Ave. Bootle L21 ... 38 B7
Croxteth Ave. Wallasey L44 ... 51 B4
Croxteth Cl. L31 ... 20 E3
Croxteth Comm Comp Sch. L11 ... 40 C5
Croxteth Ctry Pk. L12 ... 40 D2
Croxteth Cty Prim Sch. L11 40 D4
Croxteth Dr. Liverpool L17 ... 68 D5
Croxteth Dr. Rainford WA11 31 F7
Croxteth Gr. L17 & L8 ... 68 C6
Croxteth Hall La. Liverpool L11 & L12 ... 40 C2
Croxteth La. L28 & L34 ... 41 C1
Croxteth Rd. Bootle L20 ... 38 B5

Croxteth Rd. Liverpool L17 & L8 68 B5
Croxteth View. L32 40 F6
Croyde Cl. PR9 2 B5
Croyde Pl. WA9 58 C4
Croyde Rd. L24 83 A3
Croydon Ave. L18 68 F5
Croylands St. L4 52 E8
Crucian Way. L12 40 D3
Crump St. L1 67 E7
Crutchley Ave. L41 66 B8
Cubbin Cres. L5 52 D6
Cubert Rd. L11 40 D4
Cuckoo Cl. L25 70 A4
Cuckoo La. L25 70 A5
Cuckoo Way. L25 70 A4
Cuerdley Gn. WA5 74 A2
Cuerdley Rd. WA5 74 C3
Cullen Ave. L20 38 D5
Cullen Cl. L63 88 C4
Cullen St. L7 & L8 68 C7
Culme Rd. L12 & L13 53 F7
Culzean Cl. L12 40 E3
Cumber La. L35 56 F3
Cumberland Ave. Birkenhead L43 66 A2
Cumberland Ave. Litherland L30 27 C3
Cumberland Ave. Liverpool L15 & L17 68 D6
Cumberland Ave. St Helens WA10 57 B8
Cumberland Cl. L6 53 D7
Cumberland Cres. WA11 45 A6
Cumberland Gate. L30 28 A4
Cumberland Rd. Southport PR8 4 D5
Cumberland Rd. Wallasey L45 51 C7
Cumberland St. L1 52 C2
Cumbria Way. L12 40 C2
Cummings St. L1 67 E8
Cummins Ave. L37 9 E5
Cumpsty Rd. L21 27 C1
Cunard Cl. L43 65 C6
Cunard Rd. L21 38 B7
Cunliffe Ave. WA12 46 B5
Cunliffe St. 15 L2 52 C2
Cunningham Cl. Warrington WA5 74 F5
Cunningham Cl. West Kirby L48 75 C6
Cunningham Dr. Bebington L63 88 C7
Cunningham Dr. Runcorn WA7 84 E1
Cunningham Rd. Liverpool L13 54 A2
Cunningham Rd. Widnes WA8 84 D8
Cunscough La. L31 & L39 21 D3
Cuper Cres. L36 55 D4
Curate Rd. L4 & L6 53 C7
Curlender Cl. L41 50 E1
Curlender Way. L24 83 E2
Curlew Ave. L49 64 D6
Curlew Cl. L49 64 D6
Curlew Ct. L46 49 C1
Curlew Gr. L26 70 E1
Curlew Way. L46 49 C1
Currans Rd. WA2 61 B2
Curtana Cres. L11 40 C3
Curtis Rd. L4 39 C1
Curwell Cl. L63 79 B3
Curzon Ave. Birkenhead L41 66 B7
Curzon Ave. 1 Wallasey L45 51 B7
Curzon Rd. Birkenhead L42 66 B2
Curzon Rd. Crosby L22 26 E1
Curzon Rd. Hoylake L47 63 A7
Curzon Rd. Southport PR8 4 E5
Curzon St. 3 WA7 84 F1
Cusson Rd. L33 30 B1
Custley Hey. L28 55 B8
Custom House La. L1 52 C1
Cut La. Haskayne L39 & L40 12 F6
Cut La. Knowsley L33 41 F7
Cygnet Cl. L39 13 C2
Cygnet Ct. L33 30 A2
Cynthia Rd. WA7 84 F1
Cypress Ave. WA8 73 B2
Cypress Croft. L63 79 B3
Cypress Gdns. L35 57 C7
Cypress Rd. Liverpool L36 70 D8
Cypress Rd. Southport PR8 & PR9 4 F6
Cyprion's Way. L30 27 E3
Cyprus St. L34 56 D6
Cyprus Terr. 6 L45 51 B7
Cyril Gr. L17 68 E2
D'Arcy Cotts. L63 87 B6
Dacre St. Birkenhead L41 66 E6
Dacre St. Bootle L20 38 B1
Dacre's Bridge La. L35 71 D6
Dacy Rd. L4 & L5 53 A6
Daffodil Cl. WA8 73 E4
Daffodil Rd. Birkenhead L41 65 F7
Daffodil Rd. Liverpool L15 69 B7
Dagnall Ave. WA5 60 F2
Dagnall Rd. L32 29 D1
Dahlia Cl. L9 39 B4
Dailton Rd. WN8 25 A7
Dairy Farm Rd. WA11 31 C7
Daisy Ave. WA12 46 C2
Daisy Bank Rd. WA5 74 F4
Daisy Mount. L31 28 E8
Daisy St. L5 52 D7
Dakin Wlk. L33 29 F2
Dalby Cl. WA11 44 C5
Dale acre Cty Prim Sch. L21 27 C3
Dale Acre Dr. L21 & L30 27 C3
Dale Ave. Bebington L62 88 D8
Dale Ave. Heswall L60 76 F1
Dale Cl. Maghull L31 20 C2
Dale Cl. Widnes WA8 84 A8
Dale Cres. WA9 58 D6
Dale Ct. L60 76 F1
Dale End Rd. L61 77 C4
Dale Gdns. L60 76 D1
Dale Hey. Bebington L66 88 E2
Dale Hey. Wallasey L44 51 B3
Dale La. L33 30 B4
Dale Mews. L25 70 B4
Dale Rd. Bebington L62 88 D6
Dale Rd. Golborne WA3 47 A7
Dale St. Liverpool L1 & L2 52 C2
Dale St. Liverpool L19 81 C5
Dale The. WA5 74 F5
Dale View. WA12 46 E4
Dale View Cl. L61 77 A5
Dalecrest. WN5 25 D1
Dalegarth Ave. L12 40 F1
Dalehead Pl. WA11 33 B1
Dalehurst Cl. L44 51 D4
Dalemeadow Rd. L14 54 D3
Dales Row. L36 56 B2
Daleside Ave. WN4 35 A8
Daleside Cl. L61 76 F6
Daleside Rd. L33 29 F3
Daleside Wlk. L33 29 F3
Dalesway. L60 85 E8
Dalewood. L12 40 E3
Dalewood Gdns. L35 56 F2
Daley Pl. L20 38 E7
Daley Rd. L21 27 C1
Dallam Cty Prim Sch. WA5 60 F1
Dallas Gr. 3 L9 39 A6
Dallington Ct. L13 54 B2
Dalmeny St. L17 68 B3
Dalmorton Rd. L45 51 C8
Dalry Cres. L32 40 F7
Dalry Wlk. L32 40 F7
Dalrymple St. L5 52 D5
Dalston Dr. WA11 33 B1
Dalton Cl. L12 40 C2
Dalton Gr. WN4 35 A4
Dalton Rd. L45 51 C7
Dalton St Michael's CE Prim Sch. WN8 16 D5
Daltry Cl. L12 54 A7
Dam La. Ashton-in-M WA3 35 F3
Dam La. Winwick WA3 61 F7
Dam Wood Rd. L24 82 E2
Damerham Croft. L25 70 A7
Damerham Mews. L25 70 A7
Damfield La. Maghull L31 20 C1
Damfield La. Maghull L31 28 D8
Damian Dr. WA12 46 A5
Dan's Rd. WA8 73 E2
Danbers. WN8 24 F6
Danby Cl. L5 52 F5
Danby Fold. L35 57 B3
Dane Cl. Heswall L49 76 F6
Dane Ct. Rainhill L35 57 C3
Dane St. L4 38 F1
Danefield Pl. L19 81 D8
Danefield Rd. Birkenhead L49 64 C2
Danefield Rd. Liverpool L19 81 D8
Danefield Terr. L19 81 D7
Danehurst Rd. Liverpool L9 39 B7
Danehurst Rd. Wallasey L45 50 F7
Danesbury Cl. WN5 33 E4
Danescourt Rd. Birkenhead L41 66 A8
Danescourt Rd. Liverpool L12 54 C5
Danescroft. WA8 72 B3
Daneswell Dr. L46 49 F1
Daneswell Rd. L24 83 A2
Daneville Rd. L11 & L4 39 D2
Daneway. PR8 7 B6
Danger La. L46 49 F1
Daniel Cl. L20 38 A6
Daniel Davies Dr. L8 68 A7
Daniels La. WN8 24 C7
Dannette Hey. L28 55 C7
Dansie St. L3 52 F1
Dante Cl. L9 39 C8
Danube St. L7 & L8 68 C7
Darby Gr. L19 81 B6
Darby Rd. L19 81 A8
Darent Rd. WA11 45 B7
Daresbury Ave. PR8 7 A5
Daresbury Ct. WA8 73 E3
Daresbury Expressway. WA7 84 F2
Daresbury Rd. St Helens WA10 43 B5
Daresbury Rd. Wallasey L44 51 A4
Darfield. WN8 24 F7
Dark Entry. L34 41 E1
Dark La. Maghull L31 20 E1
Dark La. Ormskirk L40 14 C6
Darley Cl. WA8 72 B3
Darley Dr. L12 54 C6
Darleydale Dr. L62 88 F5
Darlington Cl. L44 51 D4
Darlington St. L44 51 D4
Darmond Rd. L33 30 A3
Darmond's Gn. L48 63 B3
Darmonds Green Ave. L6 53 D7
Darnley St. L8 67 E5
Darrel Dr. L7 68 C7
Darrel St. L7 68 C7
Darsefield Rd. L16 69 E7
Dartington Rd. L16 69 D8
Dartmouth Ave. L10 28 C2
Dartmouth Dr. L30 27 C3
Darvel Ave. WN4 34 C4
Darwall Rd. L19 81 D8
Darwen Gdns. WA2 61 E1
Darwen St. L5 52 B5
Darwick Dr. L36 71 A8
Darwin Gr. WA9 57 E7
Daryl Rd. L60 86 A8
Daulby St. L3 52 F2
Dauntsey Brow. L25 70 B7
Dauntsey Mews. L25 70 B7
Davenham Ave. L43 65 F3
Davenham Cl. L43 65 F2
Davenham Rd. L37 9 F3
Davenhill Cty Prim Sch. L10 28 D2
Davenhill Pk. L10 28 C2
Davenport Cl. L48 75 C6
Davenport Rd. L60 85 E7
Daventree Rd. L45 51 B5
Daventry Rd. L17 68 E2
David St. L8 67 F4
Davids Wlk. L25 70 C3
Davidson Rd. L13 54 A3
Davies Ave. WA12 46 C4
Davies St. Bootle L20 38 D4
Davies St. Liverpool L1 & L2 52 C2
Davies St. St Helens WA9 44 C4
Davis Rd. L46 50 B3
Davy Cl. WA10 43 B5
Davy St. L5 53 A6
Dawber Cl. 14 L6 53 A4
Dawber St. WN4 35 D4
Dawley Cl. WN4 35 A3
Dawlish Cl. L25 82 C8
Dawlish Dr. PR9 2 A5
Dawlish Rd. Irby L61 76 C5
Dawlish Rd. Wallasey L44 51 A4
Dawn Cl. WA9 57 E7
Dawn Wlk. L10 40 B6
Dawpool CE (VA) Prim Sch. L61 76 B6
Dawpool Cotts. L61 76 A6
Dawpool Dr. Bebington L62 88 C7
Dawpool Dr. Birkenhead L46 64 E8
Dawpool Farm. L61 76 B5
Dawson Ave. Birkenhead L41 66 B8
Dawson Ave. Southport PR9 2 C5
Dawson Ave. St Helens WA9 58 D7
Dawson Gdns. L31 20 C2
Dawson Rd. L39 13 F7
Dawson St. L1 52 D1
Dawson Way. 21 L1 52 D1
Dawstone Rd. L60 86 A7
Dawstone Rise. L60 85 F7
Day St. L13 54 A3
Daybrook. WN8 24 F7
Dayfield. WN8 25 B7
Days Meadow. 1 L49 64 C3
De Grouchy St. L48 63 B3
De La Salle Sch. Liverpool L11 40 B2
De La Salle Sch. St Helens WA10 43 B4
De Villiers Ave. L23 26 E5
Deacon Cl. L22 37 D8
Deacon Ct. Liverpool L25 70 B2
Deacon Ct. Seaforth L22 37 D8
Deacon Rd. WA8 73 B1
Deacon Trad Est. WA12 46 A2
Deakin St. L41 65 F8
Dealcroft. L25 69 F2
Dean Ave. L45 50 E6
Dean Cl. Billinge WN5 33 D3
Dean Cl. Orrell WN8 25 C7
Dean Cres. WA2 61 B2
Dean Ct. WA3 47 A7
Dean Dillistone Ct. 4 L1 67 E7
Dean Meadow. WA12 46 C4
Dean Patey Ct. 2 L1 67 E7
Dean Rd. WA3 47 A7
Dean St. L22 37 D8
Dean Way. WA9 58 B2
Dean Wood. L35 56 F2
Dean Wood Ave. WN5 25 E8
Dean Wood Golf Course. WN8 25 D8
Deane Rd. L7 53 C2
Deans Ct. L37 9 F5
Deans Way. L41 & L43 65 F8
Deansburn Rd. L13 53 E6
Deanscales Rd. L11 40 A2
Deansgate La. L37 10 B5
Deansgate La N. L37 10 A6
Deansway. WA8 84 C8
Dearham Ave. WA11 44 B7
Dearne Cl. L14 54 E5
Dearnford Ave. L62 88 D6
Dearnford Cl. L62 88 D6
Dearnley Ave. WA11 44 E5
Deauville Rd. L9 39 C7
Debra Cl. L31 29 B4
Dee Cl. L33 29 F6
Dee Ct. L25 70 C3
Dee House. L25 70 C3
Dee La. L48 63 A2
Dee Park Cl. L60 86 B6
Dee Park Rd. L60 86 B5
Dee Rd. L35 57 B3
Dee Side. L60 85 C8
Dee View Rd. L60 85 F8
Deeley Cl. L7 53 C1
Deep Dale. WA5 74 F6
Deepdale. WA8 72 C3
Deepdale Ave. Bootle L20 38 A5
Deepdale Ave. St Helens WA11 33 C1
Deepdale Cl. L43 65 C6
Deepdale Dr. L35 57 D3
Deepdale Rd. L25 70 A7
Deepfield Dr. L36 70 F8
Deepfield Rd. L15 68 F6
Deerbarn Dr. L30 28 B4
Deerbolt Cl. L32 29 C3
Deerbolt Cres. L32 29 C3
Deerbolt Way. L32 29 C3
Deeside Cl. L43 65 B6
Deeside Ct. L64 86 B1
Deirdre Ave. WA8 73 A1
Delabole Rd. L11 40 D5
Delafield Cl. WA2 61 F3
Delagoa Rd. L10 & L9 39 F6
Delamain Rd. L13 53 E6
Delamere Ave. Bebington L62 88 E4
Delamere Ave. Golborne WA3 47 E6
Delamere Ave. St Helens WA9 58 A3
Delamere Ave. Widnes WA8 72 C1
Delamere Cl. Bebington L62 88 E4
Delamere Cl. Birkenhead L43 65 B6
Delamere Cl. Liverpool L11 40 D3
Delamere Gr. 3 L44 51 E2
Delamere Rd. Skelmersdale WN8 15 F2
Delamere Rd. Southport PR8 7 B5
Delamere Way. WN8 25 A7
Delamore Pl. L4 38 E1
Delamore St. Bootle L4 38 E1
Delamore St. 1 Liverpool L4 52 E8
Delavor Cl. L60 85 E8
Delavor Rd. L60 85 E8
Delaware Cres. L32 29 C3
Delf La. Haskayne L39 12 A5
Delf La. Liverpool L4 39 A2
Delf La. Liverpool L24 82 B5
Delfby Cres. L32 30 A1
Dell Cl. Bebington L63 88 B6
Dell Ct. Birkenhead L43 65 F1
Dell Gr. L42 79 B8
Dell La. L60 86 B7
Dell Prim Sch The. L8 67 B1
Dell St. 2 L7 53 C2
Dell The. Birkenhead L42 67 B1
Dell The. Liverpool L12 54 E8
Dell The. Orrell WN8 25 B7
Dellfield La. L31 20 E1
Dellside Cl. WN4 34 D5
Dellside Gr. WA9 58 C8
Delph Common Rd. L39 13 C1
Delph Ct. L21 38 A8
Delph La. Formby L37 9 C3
Delph La. Ormskirk L39 13 C1
Delph La. Prescot L35 56 F5
Delph La. Warrington WA2 60 F4
Delph La. Winwick WA2 61 E6
Delph Park Ave. L39 13 B1
Delph Rd. Crosby L23 & L38 26 D8
Delph Top. L39 14 A6
Delphside Cl. WN5 25 D5
Delphside Prim Sch. WN8 24 C8
Delphside Rd. WN5 25 D5
Delphwood Dr. WA9 44 B1
Delta Dr. L12 54 E8
Delta Rd. Bootle L21 38 B7
Delta Rd. St Helens WA9 44 F4
Delta Rd E. L42 67 B1
Delta Rd W. L42 67 B1
Deltic Way. L30 39 A8
Delves Ave. L63 78 F3
Delyn Cl. L42 66 E1
Demesne St. L44 51 E3
Denbigh Ave. Southport PR9 1 F3
Denbigh Ave. St Helens WA9 58 C7
Denbigh Rd. Bootle L9 38 F3
Denbigh Rd. Wallasey L44 51 D3
Denbigh St. L5 52 B5
Dencourt Rd. L11 40 B1
Dene Ave. WA12 45 F4
Denebank Rd. L4 53 B7
Denecliff. L36 55 B8
Denehurst Cl. WA5 74 F4
Denes Way. L28 55 A7
Deneshey Rd. L47 63 C8
Denford Rd. L14 54 F5
Denham Cl. L12 41 A3
Denholme. Orrell WN8 25 A7
Denholme. Skelmersdale WN8 24 F7
Denise Ave. WA5 74 E5
Denise Rd. L10 40 B7
Denison Gr. WA9 57 E7
Denman Dr. L6 53 C4
Denman Gr. 4 L44 51 E2
Denman St. 7 L7 53 B3
Denman Way. L6 53 C4
Denmark Rd. PR9 2 A2
Denmark St. L22 26 D1
Dennett Cl. L31 28 D7
Dennett Rd. L35 56 C4
Denning Dr. L61 76 D7
Dennis Ave. WA10 57 C7
Denny Cl. L49 64 F4
Densham Ave. WA2 61 B2
Denshaw. WN8 24 F7
Denston Cl. L43 65 B7
Denstone Ave. L10 28 D3
Denstone Cl. L25 82 B8
Denstone Cres. L14 55 B5
Dentdale Dr. L5 52 E4
Denton Dr. L45 51 C6
Denton Gr. L6 53 C5
Denton St. Liverpool L8 67 F4
Denton St. Widnes WA8 73 C1
Dentons Green La. WA10 43 E5
Dentwood St. L8 68 A4
Denver Rd. L32 29 C1
Depot Rd. L33 30 D4
Deptford Cl. L25 70 C6
Derby Cl. WA12 46 B3
Derby Dr. WA11 32 A5
Derby Gr. L31 28 D6
Derby Hill Cres. L39 14 A5
Derby Hill Rd. L39 14 A5
Derby La. L13 54 A4
Derby Rd. Birkenhead L41 & L42 66 D4
Derby Rd. Bootle L20 38 B2
Derby Rd. Formby L37 9 E5
Derby Rd. Golborne WA3 47 C8
Derby Rd. Huyton-w-R L36 55 E2
Derby Rd. Liverpool L20 & L5 52 C7
Derby Rd. Skelmersdale WN8 23 C8
Derby Rd. Southport PR8 & PR9 4 C7
Derby Rd. Wallasey L45 51 A6
Derby Rd. Widnes WA8 73 B4
Derby Rd. Widnes WA8 73 D4
Derby Row. WA12 60 D8
Derby Sq. Birkenhead L43 66 C5
Derby Sq. Liverpool L1 52 C1
Derby Sq. Prescot L34 56 E6

Derby St. Birkenhead L41 & L43 66 C5
Derby St. Huyton-w-R L36 56 A2
Derby St. Liverpool L13 53 F3
Derby St. Newton-le-W WA12 46 B3
Derby St. Ormskirk L39 13 F5
Derby St. Prescot L34 56 C6
Derby St W. L39 13 E5
Derbyshire Hill Rd. WA9 45 A2
Dereham Ave. L49 65 A7
Dereham Cres. L10 39 F7
Derek Ave. WA2 61 E1
Derna Rd. L36 55 D3
Derwent Ave. Formby L37 9 D2
Derwent Ave. Golborne WA3 36 C1
Derwent Ave. Prescot L34 56 F6
Derwent Ave. Southport PR9 1 F1
Derwent Cl. Bebington L63 78 D5
Derwent Cl. Kirkby L33 29 D4
Derwent Cl. Maghull L31 20 F2
Derwent Cl. Rainhill L35 57 B3
Derwent Dr. Bebington L66 89 B2
Derwent Dr. Bootle L21 & L30 38 D8
Derwent Dr. Heswall L61 76 F4
Derwent Dr. Wallasey L45 51 A6
Derwent Rd. Ashton-in-M WN4 35 E5
Derwent Rd. Bebington L63 78 D5
Derwent Rd. Birkenhead L43 66 B4
Derwent Rd. Crosby L23 26 F2
Derwent Rd. Hoylake L47 63 E8
Derwent Rd. Orrell WN5 25 F8
Derwent Rd. St Helens WA11 44 B7
Derwent Rd. Widnes WA8 72 C1
Derwent Rd E. L13 54 A4
Derwent Rd W. L13 53 F4
Derwent Sq. L13 54 A4
Desborough Cres. L12 54 A7
Desford Ave. WA11 44 D6
Desford Cl. L46 49 B1
Desford Rd. L19 80 F8
Desilva St. L36 56 A2
Desmond Cl. L43 65 C6
Desmond Gr. L23 26 F3
Desoto Rd. WA8 84 E5
Desoto Rd E. WA8 84 F6
Desoto Rd W. WA8 84 F6
Deva Cl. L33 29 E7
Deva Rd. L48 63 A2
Deveraux Dr. L44 51 C3
Deveraux Rd. L44 51 C3
Deverell Gr. L15 54 B1
Deverell Rd. L15 54 B1
Deverill Rd. L42 66 E1
Devizes Dr. L61 76 D7
Devizes Mews. L25 70 B7
Devoke Ave. WA11 33 A1
Devon Ave. L44 & L45 51 C5
Devon Cl. L23 26 A3
Devon Dr. L61 76 E4
Devon Farm Way. L37 10 B3
Devon Gdns. Birkenhead L42 66 F1
Devon Gdns. Liverpool L16 69 E5
Devon Pl. WA8 73 B3
Devon St. Liverpool L3 & L6 52 F2
Devon St. St Helens WA10 43 D4
Devon Way. Huyton-w-R L36 56 A4
Devon Way. Liverpool L16 69 E6
Devondale Rd. L18 69 A5
Devonfield Rd. L9 38 F5
Devonport St. L8 67 F5
Devonshire Cl. L43 66 B5
Devonshire Gdns. WA12 46 C2
Devonshire Park Prim Sch. L42 66 C2
Devonshire Pl. Birkenhead L43 66 A5
Devonshire Pl. Liverpool L5 52 E6
Devonshire Rd. Birkenhead L49 64 E5
Devonshire Rd. Birkenhead L43 66 B5
Devonshire Rd. Crosby L22 & L23 26 C3
Devonshire Rd. Heswall L61 76 E4
Devonshire Rd. Liverpool L8 68 A5
Devonshire Rd. Southport PR9 5 A8
Devonshire Rd. St Helens WA10 43 D5
Devonshire Rd. Wallasey L44 51 B4
Devonshire Rd. West Kirby L48 63 C1
Devonshire Rd W. L8 68 A5
Dewey Ave. L9 39 B8
Dewlands Rd. L21 37 F8
Dewsbury Rd. L4 53 C7
Dexter St. L8 67 E6
Deyburn Wlk. L12 54 D7
Deycroft Ave. L33 30 A4
Deycroft Wlk. L33 30 A4
Deyes End. L31 20 E1
Deyes High Sch. L31 20 D1
Deyes La. Maghull L31 20 D1
Deyes La. Maghull L31 20 F1
Deysbrook La. L12 & L28 54 E8
Deysbrook Side. L12 54 D7
Deysbrook Way. L12 54 D8
Dial Rd. L42 66 D3
Dial St. 5 L7 53 C2
Diamond Bsns Pk. WA11 32 B4
Diamond St. L3 & L5 52 D4
Diana Rd. L20 38 D7
Diana St. L4 53 A8
Diane Rd. WN4 35 E5
Dibb La. L23 26 C7
Dibbins Gn. L63 88 B7
Dibbins Hey. L63 79 B2
Dibbinsdale Rd. L63 88 B7
Dibbinview Gr. L63 79 B2
Dicconson St. WA10 44 A4
Dicconson Way. L39 14 A5
Dicconson's La. L39 12 D4
Dick's La. L40 14 F4
Dickens Ave. L43 65 F1
Dickens Cl. L43 65 F1
Dickens Dr. WN2 36 C8
Dickens Rd. WA10 57 C8
Dickens St. L8 67 F6
Dickenson St. 8 L1 & L72 67 D8
Dicket's La. WN8 & L40 15 A2
Dickinson Cl. Formby L37 9 F2
Dickinson Cl. Haydock WA11 45 A6
Dickinson Rd. L37 9 F2
Dickson St. L3 52 B4
Didcot Cl. L25 82 D8
Didsbury Cl. L32 29 F2
Digg La. L46 49 D1
Digmoor Dr. WN8 24 C7
Digmoor Rd. Kirkby L32 40 F7
Digmoor Rd. Skelmersdale WN8 24 D6
Dignum Mead. L27 70 E5
Dilloway St. WA10 43 E4
Dinas La. L14 & L36 55 B4
Dinesen Rd. L19 81 C7
Dingle Ave. Newton-le-W WA12 45 F2
Dingle Ave. Orrell WN8 25 C8
Dingle Brow. L8 68 A3
Dingle Cl. L39 13 C1
Dingle Gr. L8 68 A4
Dingle Grange. 5 L8 68 A3
Dingle La. L17 & L8 68 A3
Dingle Mount. L8 68 A3
Dingle Rd. Birkenhead L42 66 C4
Dingle Rd. Liverpool L8 68 A3
Dingle Rd. Orrell WN8 25 B7
Dingle Vale. L17 & L8 68 A3
Dingley Ave. L9 38 F6
Dingwall Dr. L49 64 E3
Dinmore Rd. L44 51 B4
Dinorwic Rd. Liverpool L4 53 A6
Dinorwic Rd. Southport PR8 4 A2
Dinsdale Rd. L62 79 E2
District General Hospl. PR8 4 E4
District (VC) Prim Sch The. WA12 46 A4
Ditchfield. L37 10 A2
Ditchfield Pl. WA8 84 B8
Ditchfield Rd. Warrington WA5 74 E3
Ditchfield Rd. Widnes WA8 84 B8
Ditton CE Prim Sch. WA8 72 A1
Ditton Cty Prim Sch. WA8 72 D1
Ditton Junction Sta. WA8 84 B6
Ditton La. L46 49 E3
Ditton Rd. WA8 84 D6
Dixon Ave. WA12 46 C5
Dixon Cl. WA11 46 A8
Dixon Rd. L33 41 B8
Dobbs Dr. L37 10 A4
Dobson St. L6 53 A4
Dobson Wlk. 1 L6 53 A4
Dock Rd. Liverpool L19 81 B5
Dock Rd. Wallasey L41 & L44 51 C1
Dock Rd. Widnes WA8 84 F5
Dock Rd N. L62 79 C6
Dock Rd S. L62 79 D4
Doctor's La. L37 10 E2
Dodd Ave. Birkenhead L49 64 D3
Dodd Ave. St Helens WA10 43 C4
Dodd's La. L31 20 D2
Doddridge Rd. L8 67 D5
Dodleston Cl. L43 65 D4
Dodman Rd. L11 40 D5
Dodworth Ave. PR8 4 E5
Doe's Meadow Rd. L63 88 B7
Doel St. 14 L6 53 A3
Dolly's La. Southport PR9 5 D8
Domar Cl. L32 29 F1
Dombey St. L8 67 F6
Domingo Dr. L33 29 D5
Dominic Cl. L16 69 E8
Dominic Rd. L16 69 E8
Dominion St. L6 53 C5
Domville. L35 56 E2
Domville Dr. L49 65 A3
Domville Rd. L13 54 A1
Donalds Way. L17 68 E1
Donaldson St. L4 & L5 53 A6
Doncaster Dr. L49 64 F6
Donegal Rd. L13 54 B2
Donhead Mews. L25 70 B7
Donne Ave. L63 79 A3
Donne Cl. L63 79 A3
Donnington Cl. L36 70 D8
Donnington Lodge. PR8 3 F6
Donsby Rd. L9 39 B6
Dooley Dr. L30 28 B4
Doon Cl. L4 52 E8
Dorbett Dr. L23 26 F2
Dorchester Cl. L49 64 F4
Dorchester Pk. L25 70 B6
Dorchester Rd. WN8 25 A7
Dorchester Way. WA5 59 F6
Doreen Ave. L46 64 D8
Dorgan Cl. L35 57 C4
Doric Gn. WN5 25 D3
Doric Rd. L13 54 A4
Doric St. Birkenhead L42 66 F2
Doric St. Seaforth L21 37 F7
Dorien Rd. L13 53 F2
Dorincourt. L43 66 A4
Dorking Gr. L15 69 B6
Dormie House Sch. L48 63 A2
Dorothy St. Liverpool L7 53 B1
Dorothy St. St Helens WA9 57 E8
Dorrit St. L8 67 F6
Dorset Ave. Liverpool L15 68 D7
Dorset Ave. Southport PR8 7 C2
Dorset Cl. L20 38 D3
Dorset Dr. L61 76 E4
Dorset Gdns. L42 66 F1
Dorset Rd. Huyton-w-R L36 56 A3
Dorset Rd. Liverpool L6 53 D5
Dorset Rd. St Helens WA10 43 D1
Dorset Rd. Wallasey L45 51 A7
Dorset Rd. West Kirby L48 63 C3
Dosen Brow. L27 70 E6
Douglas Ave. Billinge WN5 33 D3
Douglas Ave. Burtonwood WA9 59 B6
Douglas Ave. Orrell WN8 25 B7
Douglas Cl. Liverpool L13 53 F4
Douglas Cl. Widnes WA8 73 F3
Douglas Dr. Birkenhead L46 64 D8
Douglas Dr. Maghull L31 20 F2
Douglas Dr. Ormskirk L39 13 D7
Douglas Dr. Orrell WN5 25 F7
Douglas Pl. L20 38 B1
Douglas Rd. Liverpool L4 53 B6
Douglas Rd. Southport PR9 2 C4
Douglas Rd. West Kirby L48 63 D3
Douglas St. Birkenhead L41 66 E6
Douglas St. St Helens WA10 43 D3
Douglas Way. L33 29 F6
Doulton Cl. L43 65 B7
Doulton St. WA10 43 D3
Douro Pl. L13 53 F2
Douro St. L3 52 E4
Dove Ct. L25 70 B3
Dove St. Golborne WA3 36 A2
Dove St. Liverpool L8 68 B7
Dove Street Inf Sch. L8 68 B7
Dovecot Ave. L14 54 F4
Dovecot Pl. L14 54 F3
Dovecote Comm Comp Sch. L14 55 A5
Dovecote Cty Prim Sch. L14 55 A3
Dovecote Gn. WA5 60 A1
Dovedale Ave. Bebington L62 88 E5
Dovedale Ave. Maghull L31 20 C2
Dovedale Cl. L43 65 F2
Dovedale Cres. WN4 35 A8
Dovedale Ct. WA8 72 B3
Dovedale Inf & Jun Sch. L15 69 A5
Dovedale Rd. Ashton-in-M WN4 35 A8
Dovedale Rd. Hoylake L47 63 B8
Dovedale Rd. Liverpool L18 69 A4
Dovedale Rd. Wallasey L45 51 A7
Dovepoint Rd. L47 48 E1
Dover Cl. L41 66 D7
Dover Rd. Bootle L9 38 F6
Dover Rd. Maghull L31 28 C6
Dover Rd. Southport PR8 3 F2
Dovercliffe Rd. L13 54 B3
Dovercroft. L25 69 F2
Dovesmead Rd. L60 86 C7
Dovestone Cl. L7 68 B8
Dovey St. L8 68 A5
Doward St. WA8 73 C2
Dowhills Dr. L23 26 B5
Dowhills Pk. L23 26 B6
Dowhills Rd. L23 26 B5
Downall Green RC Jun Sch. WN4 34 E6
Downall Green Rd. WN4 34 E6
Downes Gn. L63 79 A1
Downham Cl. L25 69 F5
Downham Dr. L60 86 A8
Downham Gn. L25 69 F5
Downham Rd. L42 66 E3
Downham Rd N. L60 & L61 77 A2
Downham Rd S. L60 77 A1
Downham Way. L25 69 F5
Downham Wlk. WN5 25 D1
Downholland Haskayne CE Sch. L39 11 E3
Downing Cl. L43 66 B3
Downing Rd. L20 38 E2
Downing St. 3 L5 53 A5
Downland Way. WA9 44 F2
Downs Rd. WA10 43 D2
Downs The. L23 26 B3
Downside. WA8 72 B3
Downside Cl. L30 27 E4
Downside Dr. L10 28 F1
Downway La. WA9 45 A1
Dowsefield La. L18 & L25 69 E3
Dragon Cl. L11 40 C4
Dragon Cres. L35 56 F4
Dragon Dr. L35 56 E3
Dragon La. L35 56 E3
Dragon Wlk. 2 L11 40 C4
Dragon Yd. WA8 73 B4
Drake Cl. Liverpool L10 40 A7
Drake Cl. Ormskirk L39 13 C2
Drake Cl. Prescot L35 56 E2
Drake Cl. Warrington WA5 60 D1
Drake Cres. Liverpool L10 40 A7
Drake Pl. L10 39 F7
Drake Rd. Liverpool L10 40 A7
Drake Rd. Neston L64 86 E1
Drake Rd. Wallasey L46 50 B4
Drake St. Bootle L20 38 B1
Drake St. St Helens WA10 43 D4
Drake Way. L10 40 A7
Drakefield Rd. L11 39 E3
Draw Well Rd. L33 30 D2
Draycott St. L8 67 F3
Drayton Cl. Irby L61 76 D5
Drayton Cl. Runcorn WA7 84 F1
Drayton Cres. WA11 44 D6
Drayton Rd. 3 Liverpool L4 39 A2
Drayton Rd. Wallasey L44 51 D3
Drennan Rd. Liverpool L18 & L19 & L25 81 E8
Drewell Rd. L18 68 F3
Drewitt Cres. PR9 2 D4
Driffield Rd. L34 56 C6
Drinkwater Gdns. 2 L3 52 E3
Drive The. L12 54 B5
Driveway. Prescot L35 56 E2
Driveway. Prescot L35 56 F2
Droitwich Ave. L49 64 C4
Dromore Ave. L18 69 A3
Dronfield Way. Liverpool L25 69 F7
Druid St. WN4 35 C2
Druids' Cross Gdns. L18 69 D4
Druids' Cross Rd. L18 69 D4
Druids Pk. L18 69 E4
Druids Way. L49 65 A2
Druidsville Rd. L18 & L25 69 E4
Drummer's La. WN4 34 E7
Drummond Ct. WA8 73 D2
Drummond Rd. Crosby L23 27 B5
Drummond Rd. Hoylake L47 63 B6
Drummond Rd. Liverpool L4 39 C1
Drummoyne Ct. L23 26 A5
Druridge Dr. WA5 74 F4
Drury La. L2 52 C1
Dryburgh Way. 5 L4 52 E8
Dryden Ave. WN4 34 F6
Dryden Cl. Birkenhead L43 65 C7
Dryden Cl. Prescot L35 56 E3
Dryden Gr. L36 55 F1
Dryden Pl. WA2 61 C2
Dryden Rd. L15 & L7 53 E1
Dryden St. Bootle L20 38 A5
Dryden St. Liverpool L5 52 D4
Dryebeck Gr. WA9 58 D6
Dryfield Cl. L49 64 D4
Drysdale St. L8 68 A4
Dublin St. L3 52 B4
Ducie St. L8 68 B6
Duck Pond La. L42 66 A2
Duckinfield St. L3 52 F1
Duddingston Ave. Crosby L23 26 E2
Duddingston Ave. 2 Liverpool L15 & L18 69 A5
Duddon Ave. L31 20 F2
Duddon Cl. L43 65 F3
Dudley Cl. L43 66 B4
Dudley Cres. L62 89 B3
Dudley Gr. L23 26 E2
Dudley Pl. WA9 44 D3
Dudley Rd. Liverpool L15 & L18 68 F5
Dudley Rd. Wallasey L45 51 A8
Dudley St. WN4 35 A5
Dudlow Ct. L18 69 C5
Dudlow Dr. L18 69 C5
Dudlow Gdns. L18 69 C6
Dudlow La. L18 69 C5
Dudlow Nook Rd. L18 69 C6
Dugdale Cl. L19 81 A7
Duke Ave. PR8 4 C4
Duke Of York Cotts. L62 79 A6
Duke St. Ashton-in-M WN4 35 C3
Duke St. Birkenhead L41 66 C8
Duke St. Formby L37 9 F2
Duke St. Golborne WA3 36 A1
Duke St. Liverpool L1 & L68 & L72 & L75 67 D8
Duke St. Liverpool L19 81 C6
Duke St. Newton-le-W WA12 46 B3
Duke St. 4 Prescot L34 56 D6
Duke St. Seaforth L22 37 D8
Duke St. Southport PR8 4 B5
Duke St. St Helens WA10 43 F4
Duke St. Wallasey L45 51 B8
Duke Street Gate. L41 66 C8
Duke Street La. L1 & L72 67 D8
Duke's Wood La. WN8 24 D3
Dukes Rd. L5 52 E6
Dukes Way. L37 9 F2
Dulas Gn. L32 30 A1
Dulas Rd. Kirkby L32 30 A1
Dulas Rd. Liverpool L15 69 B6
Dulverton Rd. L17 80 E8
Dumbarton St. L4 38 F1
Dumbrees Rd. L12 54 F8
Dumbreeze Gr. L34 41 D4
Dumfries Way. L33 29 D6
Dunacre Way. L26 82 F7
Dunbabin Rd. L15 & L16 69 C6
Dunbar Cres. PR8 7 F8
Dunbar Rd. PR8 3 F1
Dunbar St. L4 38 F2
Dunbeath Ave. L35 57 D2
Dunbeath Cl. L35 57 D1
Dunblane Cl. WN4 34 C4
Duncan Ave. WA12 46 C5
Duncan Cl. WA10 43 F2
Duncan Dr. L49 64 D4
Duncan St. WA10 43 E3
Duncan St. Birkenhead L41 66 F6
Duncan St. Liverpool L1 67 E7
Duncansby Cres. WA5 74 E6
Duncansby Dr. L63 88 C4
Dunchurch Rd. L14 54 F5
Duncombe Rd N. L19 81 B7
Duncombe Rd S. L19 81 B7
Dundale Rd. L13 54 B3
Dundalk La. WA8 84 D8
Dundalk Rd. WA8 84 E8
Dundas St. L20 38 B1
Dundee Cl. WA2 61 F4
Dundee Gr. L44 51 A3
Dundonald Rd. L17 68 E1
Dundonald St. L41 66 A8
Dunedin Ct. L47 63 A6
Dunedin St. WA9 57 E8
Dunes Dr. L37 9 C4
Dunfold Cl. L32 29 F1
Dungeon La. Liverpool L24 82 F1
Dungeon La. Skelmersdale WN8 16 C7
Dunham Ave. WA3 35 F1
Dunham Cl. L62 88 F3
Dunham Rd. L15 54 B1
Dunkeld Cl. 1 L6 53 A3
Dunkeld St. 2 L6 53 A3
Dunkirk Rd. PR8 3 F2
Dunlin Ave. WA12 46 C4
Dunlin Cl. Liverpool L27 70 E4
Dunlin Cl. Warrington WA2 61 E3
Dunlop Ave. PR8 7 C2
Dunlop Dr. L31 29 B4
Dunlop Rd. L24 82 C2
Dunluce St. L4 38 E1
Dunmail Ave. WA11 33 C1
Dunmore Rd. L13 53 F3
Dunmow Way. L25 82 C8

Dunnerdale Rd. L11 .... 40 A2
Dunnett St. L20 .... 38 B1
Dunning Cl. L49 .... 64 E5
Dunnings Bridge Rd. Litherland L30 & L31 .... 28 B4
Dunnock Cl. Liverpool L25 .... 70 A5
Dunnock Cl. Warrington WA2 .... 61 E3
Dunraven Rd. L48 .... 63 A2
Dunriding La. WA10 .... 43 D3
Dunscroft. WA9 .... 58 D7
Dunsdale Dr. WN4 .... 35 C3
Dunsdon Cl. L18 & L25 .... 69 E4
Dunsdon Rd. L18 .... 69 E5
Dunsford. WA8 .... 72 B3
Dunsop Ave. WA9 .... 58 D4
Dunstan La. L7 .... 68 C8
Dunstan St. L15 .... 68 E8
Dunster Gr. Heswall L60 .... 86 B7
Dunster Gr. St Helens WA9 .. 58 D4
Dunster Rd. PR8 .... 7 E8
Durant's Cotts. L31 .... 28 E7
Durban Ave. L23 .... 26 E5
Durban Rd. Liverpool L13 .... 54 B3
Durban Rd. Wallasey L45 .... 51 C6
Durban St. Golborne WN2 & WN7 .... 36 E4
Durden St. Liverpool L7 .... 68 C7
Durham Ave. L30 .... 28 A1
Durham Mews E. L30 .... 28 A1
Durham Mews W. L30 .... 28 A1
Durham Rd. Seaforth L21 .... 37 F7
Durham Rd. Widnes WA8 .... 73 B3
Durham St. Liverpool L19 .... 81 D4
Durham St. Skelmersdale WN8 .... 15 D2
Durham Way. Litherland L30 28 A1
Durham Way. Prescot L36 ... 56 A3
Durley Dr. L43 .... 65 E1
Durley Rd. L9 .... 39 B6
Durlston Cl. WA8 .... 72 C2
Durnford Hey. L25 .... 70 C6
Durning Rd. L7 .... 53 C1
Durrant Rd. 3 L11 .... 53 E8
Durrell Way. WA3 .... 47 E8
Durrington Bank. L25 .... 70 C6
Dursley. L35 .... 56 F2
Dursley Dr. WN4 .... 35 D4
Durston Rd. L16 .... 69 D8
Durweston Wlk. L25 .... 70 C6
Dutton Dr. L63 .... 78 F2
Duxbury Cl. Maghull L31 .... 20 E3
Duxbury Cl. Rainford WA11 . 32 A7
Duxford Ct. WA2 .... 61 E1
Dwerryhouse La. L11 & L12 . 40 B2
Dwerryhouse St. L72 & L8 ... 67 D6
Dyer St. WA3 .... 35 F1
Dyers La. L39 .... 13 E4
Dyke St. L6 .... 53 A4
Dykin Cl. WA8 .... 73 E3
Dykin Rd. WA8 .... 73 E3
Dymchurch Rd. L24 .... 82 B4
Dymoke Rd. 2 L11 .... 40 C3
Dyson Hall. L9 .... 39 D5
Dyson Hall Dr. L9 .... 39 D5
Dyson St. Bootle L4 .... 38 F1
Dyson St. St Helens WA9 .... 44 B1

Eager La. L31 .... 20 B8
Eagle Cres. WA11 .... 32 A6
Eagle Dene. L10 .... 40 A6
Eaglehall Rd. L11 & L9 .... 39 F4
Eaglehurst Rd. L25 .... 70 B4
Eagles Ct. L32 .... 29 E2
Eaglesfield Cl. 2 WA9 .... 58 D7
Ealing Rd. L9 .... 39 B7
Eamont Ave. PR9 .... 2 B5
Eardisley Rd. L15 & L18 .... 69 B6
Earl Rd. L20 .... 38 E4
Earl St. Bebington L62 .... 79 B8
Earl St. St Helens WA9 .... 44 C4
Earl's Cl. L23 .... 26 D3
Earle Cl. WA12 .... 45 F3
Earle Cres. L64 .... 86 D1
Earle Dr. L64 .... 86 D1
Earle House. L62 .... 79 B8
Earle Jun Mix & Inf Sch. L7 68 C7
Earle Jun Mix & Inf Sch. L7 68 D8
Earle Rd. L15 & L7 & L8 .... 68 C8
Earle St. 1 Liverpool L3 .... 52 C2
Earle St. Newton-le-W WA12 46 A3
Earlestown Dist CE Jun Sch. WA12 .... 46 A3
Earlestown Sta. WA12 .... 46 B3
Earlsfield Rd. L15 .... 68 F6
Earlston Rd. L45 .... 51 B6
Earlswood. WN8 .... 16 E1
Earp St. L19 .... 81 C6
Easby Cl. L37 .... 10 A2
Easby Rd. L4 & L5 .... 52 D7
Easby Wlk. L4 .... 52 D7
Easedale Dr. PR8 .... 7 B4
Easedale Wlk. L33 .... 29 D5
Easenhall Cl. WA8 .... 73 C5
Easington Rd. L35 & WA9 .... 57 D6
East Albert Rd. L17 .... 68 B4
East Ave. WA3 .... 36 C1
East Cl. L34 .... 57 A7
East Dam Wood Rd. L24 .... 83 A2
East Farm Mews. L48 .... 75 F8
East Front. L35 .... 56 E1
East La. L29 & L38 .... 19 B2
East Lancashire Rd. Haydock WA11 .... 45 C8
East Lancashire Rd. Knowsley L33 & L34 .... 41 C6
East Lancashire Rd. Liverpool L11 .... 40 C5
East Lancashire Rd. Newton-le-W WA11 & WA12 & WA3 .... 46 C7
East Lancashire Rd. St Helens WA10 & WA11 .... 43 C7
East Lancashire Rd. St Helens WA11 .... 44 C8
East Leigh. WN8 .... 16 D1
East Mains. L24 .... 83 A3
East Mead. L39 .... 13 B2
East Meade. L31 .... 20 C2
East Millwood Rd. L24 .... 83 A4
East Mount. WN5 .... 25 F6
East Orchard La. L9 .... 39 E7
East Prescot Rd. L13 & L14 . 54 D4
East Rd. Liverpool L14 .... 54 C2
East Rd. Liverpool L24 .... 83 A5
East Rd. Maghull L31 .... 20 F1
East Side. WA9 .... 44 C2
East St. Ashton-in-M WN4 .... 35 D4
East St. Crosby L22 .... 26 D1
East St. Liverpool L3 .... 52 C2
East St. Prescot L34 .... 56 E6
East St. Southport PR9 .... 4 D7
East St. Wallasey L41 & L44 . 51 E1
East St. Widnes WA8 .... 73 D1
East Way. L46 .... 49 F1
Eastbank St. PR8 .... 4 B6
Eastbourne Rd. Birkenhead L41 & L43 .... 66 C6
Eastbourne Rd. Crosby L22 . 26 B2
Eastbourne Rd. Liverpool L9 39 B7
Eastbourne Rd. Southport PR8 .... 4 A3
Eastbourne Way. L6 .... 52 F3
Eastbury Cl. WA8 .... 73 C5
Eastcliffe Rd. L13 .... 54 B3
Eastcote Rd. L19 .... 81 C8
Eastcott Cl. L49 .... 64 C3
Eastcroft. L33 .... 29 F5
Eastcroft Park Prim Sch. L33 .... 29 F5
Eastcroft Rd. L44 .... 51 C2
Eastdale Rd. L15 .... 68 F8
Eastern Ave. Bebington L62 . 79 D3
Eastern Ave. Liverpool L24 ... 82 F3
Eastern Dr. L19 .... 81 A7
Eastfield Dr. L17 .... 68 C3
Eastfield Wlk. L32 .... 29 C1
Eastham Cl. L16 .... 54 F1
Eastham Cres. WA9 .... 58 C4
Eastham Ctry Pk. L62 .... 89 A8
Eastham Gn. L24 .... 82 E4
Eastham Mews. L62 .... 89 A4
Eastham Rake. L63 & L62 & L66 .... 88 D3
Eastham Rake Sta. L62 .... 88 D3
Eastham Village Rd. L62 .... 89 A5
Eastlake Ave. L5 .... 52 F5
Eastleigh Dr. L61 .... 76 D7
Eastman Rd. L13 .... 53 E7
Easton Rd. Bebington L62 .... 79 B8
Easton Rd. Huyton-w-R L36 .. 55 A3
Eastpark Ct. L44 .... 51 E3
Eastview Cl. L43 .... 65 D4
Eastway. Birkenhead L49 .... 64 E4
Eastway. Maghull L31 .... 20 E1
Eastway. Widnes WA8 .... 72 D1
Eastway Prim Sch. L46 .... 49 F1
Eastwell Rd. WN4 .... 35 A3
Eastwood. L8 .... 68 A3
Eastwood Ave. WA12 .... 46 F3
Eastwood Rd. WA5 .... 59 F7
Eaton Ave. Bootle L21 .... 38 B7
Eaton Ave. Bootle L20 .... 38 D5
Eaton Ave. Wallasey L44 .... 51 C4
Eaton Cl. Huyton-w-R L36 .... 55 D2
Eaton Cl. Liverpool L12 .... 54 A7
Eaton Gdns. L12 .... 54 D4
Eaton Grange. L12 .... 54 C5
Eaton Rd. Birkenhead L43 .... 66 B5
Eaton Rd. Liverpool L12 & L14 .... 54 C5
Eaton Rd. Liverpool L19 .... 81 A6
Eaton Rd. Maghull L31 .... 28 D6
Eaton Rd. St Helens WA10 ... 43 D6
Eaton Rd. West Kirby L48 .... 63 B1
Eaton Rd N. L12 .... 54 A7
Eaton St. Liverpool L3 .... 52 C3
Eaton St. Prescot L34 .... 56 D7
Eaton St. Wallasey L44 .... 51 B5
Eaves La. WA9 .... 58 C6
Eaves Prim Sch. WA9 .... 58 C6
Eavesdale. WN8 .... 24 E8
Ebenezer Howard Rd. L21 .. 27 C1
Ebenezer Rd. L7 .... 53 C3
Ebenezer St. Birkenhead L42 67 A2
Ebenezer St. St Helens WA11 .... 44 F6
Eberle St. L2 .... 52 C2
Ebony Cl. L46 .... 64 B8
Ebony Way. L33 .... 29 E5
Ebor La. L5 .... 52 E4
Ebrington St. L19 .... 81 C7
Eccles Gr. WA9 .... 58 E3
Eccles Rd. L37 .... 9 D1
Ecclesall Ave. L21 .... 38 D8
Ecclesfield Rd. WA10 .... 43 A6
Eccleshall Rd. L62 .... 79 C6
Eccleshill Rd. L13 .... 54 A5
Eccleston Ave. L62 .... 79 C1
Eccleston Cl. L43 .... 65 F3
Eccleston Gdns. St Helens WA10 .... 43 B1
Eccleston Gdns. St Helens WA10 .... 57 A8
Eccleston Lane Ends Prim Sch. L34 .... 56 F7
Eccleston Mere Cty Prim Sch. WA10 .... 43 A3
Eccleston Park Sta. L35 .... 57 A6
Eccleston Rd. 1 L9 .... 39 A6
Eccleston St. Prescot L34 .... 56 D6
Eccleston St. St Helens WA10 .... 43 E3
Edale Cl. L62 .... 88 E5
Edale Rd. L18 .... 69 B4
Eddisbury Rd. 4 Wallasey L44 .... 51 C5
Eddisbury Rd. West Kirby L48 .... 63 A4
Eddisbury Way. L12 .... 54 A7
Eddleston St. WN4 .... 34 F6
Eden Ave. Rainford WA11 .... 31 E7
Eden Ave. Southport PR9 .... 1 F2
Eden Cl. Kirkby L33 .... 29 F6
Eden Cl. Rainhill L35 .... 57 B2
Eden Dr N. L23 .... 27 A3
Eden Dr S. L23 .... 27 A3
Edendale. WA8 .... 72 B2
Edenfield Cl. PR8 .... 4 E3
Edenfield Cres. L36 .... 55 F4
Edenfield Rd. L15 .... 69 A6
Edenhall Dr. L25 .... 70 C2
Edenhurst Ave. Liverpool L16 & L36 .... 70 A8
Edenhurst Ave. 2 Wallasey L44 .... 51 C5
Edenhurst Cl. Formby L37 .... 9 C2
Edenhurst Ct. Huyton-w-R L36 .... 55 B4
Edenhurst Dr. L37 .... 9 C2
Edenpark Rd. L42 .... 66 C3
Edgar Ct. L41 .... 66 D7
Edgar St. Liverpool L3 .... 52 D3
Edgar St. St Helens WA9 .... 44 B1
Edgbaston Cl. L36 .... 55 C1
Edgbaston Way. L43 .... 65 C8
Edge Gr. L7 .... 53 E2
Edge Green La. WA3 .... 35 F2
Edge Green Rd. WA3 & WN4 35 F4
Edge Green St. WN4 .... 35 D4
Edge Hall Rd. WN5 .... 25 E5
Edge Hill Coll of HE. L39 .... 14 A3
Edge Hill Sta. L7 .... 68 C8
Edge La. Crosby L23 .... 27 B5
Edge La. Liverpool L13 & L7 . 53 D2
Edge Lane Dr. L13 .... 54 B2
Edge Lane Ret Pk. L13 .... 53 F2
Edge St. L35 .... 57 C6
Edgefield Cl. L43 .... 65 D4
Edgefold Rd. L32 .... 29 F1
Edgehill Rd. L46 .... 64 D8
Edgeley Gdns. L9 .... 38 F6
Edgemoor Cl. Birkenhead L43 .... 65 B7
Edgemoor Cl. Crosby L23 .... 27 B5
Edgemoor Cl. Liverpool L12 . 54 D5
Edgemoor Dr. Crosby L23 .... 27 A5
Edgemoor Dr. Irby L61 .... 76 C7
Edgemoor Dr. Liverpool L10 40 A7
Edgemoor Rd. L12 .... 54 D5
Edgerley Pl. WN4 .... 35 A3
Edgerton Rd. Birkenhead L43 .... 66 A6
Edgerton Rd. Golborne WA3 47 F8
Edgewood Dr. L62 .... 88 D5
Edgewood Rd. Birkenhead L49 .... 64 F6
Edgewood Rd. Hoylake L47 . 48 D1
Edgeworth Cl. WA9 .... 58 E8
Edgeworth Rd. WA3 .... 35 F1
Edgeworth St. WA9 .... 58 E7
Edgley Dr. L39 .... 14 A5
Edgworth Rd. L4 .... 53 B6
Edinburgh Cl. L30 .... 39 A8
Edinburgh Dr. Birkenhead L43 .... 66 A1
Edinburgh Dr. Huyton-w-R L36 .... 71 A8
Edinburgh Rd. Formby L37 .... 9 E1
Edinburgh Rd. Liverpool L7 .. 53 A2
Edinburgh Rd. Wallasey L45 51 B5
Edinburgh Rd. Widnes WA8 84 A8
Edinburgh Tower. L5 .... 52 E5
Edington St. L15 .... 68 E8
Edith Rd. Bootle L20 .... 38 D6
Edith Rd. Liverpool L4 .... 53 A6
Edith Rd. Wallasey L44 .... 51 E3
Edith St. WA9 .... 58 F7
Edith St. Runcorn WA7 .... 84 F3
Edmondson St. WA9 .... 44 F3
Edmonton Cl. L5 .... 52 D6
Edmund St. L3 .... 52 C2
Edna Ave. L10 .... 40 A7
Edrich Ave. L43 .... 65 C8
Edward Dr. WN4 .... 35 B4
Edward Jenner Ave. L30 .... 27 F3
Edward Rd. Hoylake L47 .... 63 C6
Edward Rd. Prescot L35 .... 56 F5
Edward Rd. Warrington WA5 74 D6
Edward St. Haydock WA11 .... 45 A6
Edward St. 4 Liverpool L3 .. 52 E1
Edward St. St Helens WA9 .. 44 D1
Edward St. Widnes WA8 .... 73 D1
Edward's La. L24 .... 82 B6
Edwards Lane Ind Est. L24 . 82 B6
Edwards Way. WA8 .... 84 C8
Edwin St. WA8 .... 73 C1
Effingham St. L20 .... 38 B1
Egan Rd. L43 .... 65 E8
Egbert Rd. L47 .... 63 C8
Egdon Cl. WA8 .... 73 E2
Egerton. WN8 .... 24 D8
Egerton Dr. L48 .... 63 B2
Egerton Gr. L45 .... 51 B5
Egerton Park Cl. L42 .... 66 E1
Egerton Rd. Bebington L62 .. 79 B7
Egerton Rd. Liverpool L15 .... 68 D7
Egerton Rd. Prescot L34 .... 56 C6
Egerton St. Abram WN2 .... 36 B7
Egerton St. Liverpool L7 & L8 67 F7
Egerton St. Runcorn WA7 .... 84 F3
Egerton St. St Helens WA9 .. 44 D1
Egerton St. Wallasey L45 .... 51 C8
Egerton Wharf. L41 & L72 ... 66 E8
Eglington Ave. L35 .... 56 D2
Egremont Cl. L27 .... 71 A4
Egremont Lawn. L27 .... 71 A4
Egremont Prim Sch. L44 .... 51 D4
Egremont Prom. L44 & L45 . 51 D5
Egremont Rd. L27 .... 71 A4
Egypt St. WA8 .... 84 F7
Eight Acre La. L37 .... 10 B6
Eileen Craven Jun Mix Sch. L4 .... 52 F8
Eilian Gr. L14 .... 54 D2
Elaine Cl. Ashton-in-M WN4 . 35 D5
Elaine Cl. Widnes WA8 .... 73 C1
Elaine St. L8 .... 67 F6
Elbow La. L37 .... 9 F3
Elcombe Ave. WA3 .... 47 E7
Elder Gdns. L19 .... 81 B8
Elder Gr. L48 .... 63 B2
Elderdale Rd. L4 .... 53 B7
Eldersfield Rd. L11 .... 40 B2
Elderswood Rd. L35 .... 57 C4
Elderwood Rd. L42 .... 66 E3
Eldon Cl. WA10 .... 43 E2
Eldon Gdns. WN4 .... 35 A6
Eldon Gr. L3 .... 52 D4
Eldon Pl. Birkenhead L41 .... 66 D6
Eldon Pl. Liverpool L3 .... 52 D4
Eldon Rd. Birkenhead L42 .... 66 F2
Eldon Rd. Wallasey L44 .... 51 B4
Eldon St. Liverpool L3 .... 52 C4
Eldon St. St Helens WA10 .... 43 E2
Eldonian Way. L3 & L5 .... 52 C4
Eldons Croft. PR8 .... 7 D5
Eldred Rd. L16 .... 69 C6
Eleanor Rd. Birkenhead L43 . 65 D8
Eleanor Rd. Bootle L20 .... 38 D6
Eleanor Rd. Wallasey L46 .... 49 D1
Eleanor St. L20 .... 38 B1
Elephant La. L35 & WA9 .... 57 E7
Elfet St. L41 .... 65 F8
Elgar Ave. L62 .... 88 E5
Elgin Ave. WN4 .... 34 D4
Elgin Dr. L45 .... 51 C6
Elgin Way. L41 & L72 .... 66 E7
Eliot St. L20 .... 38 B5
Eliza St. WA9 .... 58 F7
Elizabeth Ave. PR8 .... 7 E6
Elizabeth Rd. Bootle L20 .... 38 D6
Elizabeth Rd. Haydock WA11 45 E7
Elizabeth Rd. Huyton-w-R L36 .... 71 A8
Elizabeth Rd. Liverpool L10 & L11 .... 40 B6
Elizabeth St. Liverpool L3 & L7 .... 52 F2
Elizabeth St. St Helens WA9 58 E3
Elizabeth St. St Helens WA9 58 E8
Elkan Cl. WA8 .... 73 E2
Elkan Rd. WA8 .... 73 E2
Elkstone Rd. L11 .... 40 B1
Ellaby Rd. L35 .... 57 C4
Ellamsbridge Rd. WA9 .... 58 E8
Ellel Gr. L6 .... 53 C5
Ellen Garden. WA9 .... 58 E7
Ellen St. WA9 .... 58 E7
Ellen's Cl. 4 L6 & L7 .... 53 A2
Ellen's La. L63 & L62 .... 79 B5
Elleray Park Rd. L45 .... 51 A7
Elleray Park Sch. L45 .... 51 A7
Ellerbrook Way. L39 .... 13 E6
Ellergreen Rd. L11 .... 40 A2
Ellerman Rd. L3 & L8 .... 67 F3
Ellerslie Ave. L35 .... 57 C5
Ellerslie Rd. L13 .... 53 E6
Ellerton Cl. WA8 .... 72 D3
Ellerton Way. L12 .... 40 E3
Ellesmere Dr. L10 .... 28 C3
Ellesmere Gr. L45 .... 51 B7
Ellesmere Rd. WN4 .... 34 F4
Elliot St. Liverpool L1 .... 52 D1
Elliot St. St Helens WA10 .... 43 E3
Elliott Ave. WA3 .... 36 B1
Elliott-Clark Sch. L1 .... 67 E8
Ellis Ashton St. L35 & L36 .... 56 B1
Ellis Pl. L8 .... 67 F5
Ellis Rd. WN5 .... 33 D4
Ellison Dr. WA10 .... 43 C4
Ellison St. L13 .... 53 F4
Ellison Tower. L5 .... 52 E5
Ellon Ave. L35 .... 57 D2
Elloway Rd. L24 .... 83 A3
Elm Ave. Birkenhead L49 .... 64 D6
Elm Ave. Crosby L23 .... 26 F6
Elm Ave. Garswood WN4 .... 34 D5
Elm Ave. Golborne WA3 .... 36 A1
Elm Ave. Newton-le-W WA12 46 C2
Elm Ave. Widnes WA8 .... 73 B2
Elm Bank. 7 L5 .... 52 F7
Elm Cl. Heswall L61 .... 77 A4
Elm Cl. Liverpool L12 .... 40 F3
Elm Ct. L23 .... 26 C4
Elm Dr. Billinge WN5 .... 33 D5
Elm Dr. Birkenhead L49 .... 64 C3
Elm Dr. Formby L37 .... 9 D1
Elm Dr. Seaforth L21 .... 37 F6
Elm Gdns. WA11 .... 31 F6
Elm Gr. Birkenhead L41 & L42 .... 66 D4
Elm Gr. Hoylake L47 .... 63 C7
Elm Gr. Liverpool L7 .... 53 A1
Elm Gr. Prescot L34 .... 56 F7
Elm Gr. Skelmersdale WN8 .. 15 E1
Elm Gr. Widnes WA8 .... 73 B1
Elm Hall Dr. L15 & L18 .... 69 A5
Elm House. Crosby L22 .... 26 D1
Elm House. Prescot L34 .... 56 C6
Elm House Mews. L25 .... 70 B4
Elm Park Rd. L45 .... 51 A7
Elm Pl. L39 .... 13 E4
Elm Rd. Abram WN2 .... 36 C7
Elm Rd. Bebington L63 .... 78 F7
Elm Rd. Birkenhead L42 .... 66 B2
Elm Rd. Birkenhead L42 .... 66 D3
Elm Rd. Haydock WA11 .... 45 E7
Elm Rd. Heswall L61 .... 76 F6
Elm Rd. Kirkby L32 .... 29 D3
Elm Rd. Liverpool L4 .... 39 A2
Elm Rd. Seaforth L21 .... 37 F6
Elm Rd. Southport PR8 .... 4 B4
Elm Rd. St. Helens WA10 & WA9 .... 57 E8
Elm Rd. Warrington WA2 .... 61 A4
Elm Rd. Warrington WA5 .... 74 F4
Elm Rd N. L42 .... 66 B2
Elm St. Birkenhead L41 .... 66 D6
Elm St. Huyton-w-R L36 .... 56 A2
Elm Terr. Hoylake L47 .... 63 C7
Elm Terr. Liverpool L7 .... 53 C2

Elm Tree Rd. WA3 47 F8
Elm Vale. L6 & L7 53 D3
Elmar Rd. L17 68 E2
Elmbank Rd. Bebington L62 79 B6
Elmbank Rd. Liverpool L18 68 E5
Elmbank St. L44 51 C3
Elmcroft La. L38 18 A3
Elmdale Cl. L37 9 D2
Elmdale Rd. L9 39 A4
Elmdene Ct. L49 64 C2
Elmer's Green La. Skelmersdale WN8 16 C4
Elmer's Green La. Skelmersdale WN8 16 D2
Elmers Green Prim Sch. WN8 16 D1
Elmers Wood Rd. WN8 16 D2
Elmfield Cl. WA9 57 E8
Elmfield Rd. L9 39 A5
Elmham Cres. L10 39 F7
Elmhurst Rd. L25 70 B7
Elmore Cl. L5 52 F5
Elmridge. Skelmersdale WN8 24 D8
Elms House Rd. L13 53 F2
Elms Rd. L31 28 D6
Elms The. Golborne WA3 47 F7
Elms The. Huyton-w-R L28 55 B8
Elms The. Liverpool L17 & L18 68 A4
Elms The. Maghull L31 20 D3
Elms The. Runcorn WA7 84 F1
Elms The. Southport PR8 3 F6
Elms The. Southport PR8 4 C5
Elmsbury St. 1 WN4 34 F5
Elmsdale Rd. L18 69 A5
Elmsfield Cl. L25 70 A5
Elmsfield Pk. L39 21 A6
Elmsfield Rd. L23 27 B6
Elmsley Ct. L18 69 A3
Elmsley Rd. L18 68 F4
Elmstead. WN8 24 D8
Elmswood Ave. L35 57 D1
Elmswood Ct. L18 68 F3
Elmswood Gr. L36 55 C3
Elmswood Rd. Birkenhead L42 66 D4
Elmswood Rd. Liverpool L17 & L18 68 E2
Elmswood Rd. Wallasey L44 51 D4
Elmtree Cl. L12 54 C7
Elmtree Gr. L43 65 E8
Elmure Ave. L63 78 D5
Elmwood. WN8 16 C3
Elmwood Ave. Ashton-in-M WN4 35 A2
Elmwood Ave. Crosby L23 27 A5
Elmwood Dr. L60 & L61 76 F2
Elphin Gr. L4 39 A1
Elric Wlk. L33 29 F3
Elsbeck Gr. WA9 58 D6
Elsie Rd. L4 53 B6
Elsinore Ct. L23 26 C3
Elsinore Heights. L26 83 A7
Elsmere Ave. L17 68 C3
Elson Rd. L37 9 D1
Elstead Gr. WN4 34 D4
Elstead Rd. Kirkby L32 29 C1
Elstead Rd. Liverpool L9 39 E4
Elston Ave. WA12 46 C5
Elstow St. L5 52 D7
Elstree Rd. L6 53 D3
Elswick. WN8 24 C8
Elswick Gn. PR9 2 A5
Elswick Rd. PR9 1 F4
Elswick St. L8 67 F3
Eltham Ave. L21 27 B1
Eltham Cl. Birkenhead L49 65 B2
Eltham Cl. Widnes WA8 73 E3
Eltham Gn. L49 65 B2
Eltham St. L7 53 D2
Eltham Wlk. WA8 73 E3
Elton Ave. Crosby L23 26 C4
Elton Ave. Litherland L30 27 E3
Elton Cl. Bebington L62 88 E3
Elton Cl. Golborne WA3 47 E7
Elton Day Hospl. L35 57 C5
Elton Dr. L63 79 A3
Elton Head Rd. St Helens L35 & WA9 57 E6
Elton St. L4 38 F2
Elvington Rd. L38 18 A2
Elway Rd. WN4 35 C4
Elworth Ave. WA8 73 A5
Elworthy Ave. L26 70 F1
Elwy St. L8 68 A5
Elwyn Dr. L26 83 A8
Elwyn Rd. L47 48 E1
Ely Ave. L46 64 C8
Ely Cl. L30 27 F1
Embledon St. L8 68 B7
Emerald Cl. L30 28 B3
Emerald St. L8 67 F3
Emerson Cl. L38 18 A4
Emerson St. L8 67 F7
Emery St. L4 38 F1
Emily St. L35 57 C7
Emlyn St. WA9 44 D1
Emmanuel Rd. PR9 1 F2
Emmett St. WA9 44 C1
Empire Rd. L21 38 B6
Empress Cl. L31 20 B1
Empress Rd. Liverpool L7 53 B2
Empress Rd. Liverpool L6 53 C6
Empress Rd. Wallasey L44 51 C4
Emstrey Wlk. 1 L32 29 C2
Endborne Rd. L9 39 A6
Endbutt La. L23 26 E3
Enderby Ave. WA11 44 D6
Endfield Pk. L19 81 B8
Endmoor Rd. L36 55 D5
Endsleigh Rd. Crosby L22 26 B2
Endsleigh Rd. Liverpool L13 53 E3
Enerby Cl. L43 65 C7
Enfield Ave. L23 26 E4
Enfield Park Rd. WA2 61 F4
Enfield Rd. L13 54 B2
Enfield St. WA10 43 E2
Enfield Terr. L43 66 B5
Enford Dr. WA9 58 D7
Engine La. L37 18 E8
English Martyrs RC Prim Sch. Bootle L21 38 C8
English Martyrs RC Prim Sch. Haydock WA11 45 E7
English Martyrs RC Prim Sch. Kirkby L33 29 D4
Enid Pl. WN2 35 F8
Enid St. L8 67 F6
Ennerdale. WN8 24 D8
Ennerdale Ave. Ashton-in-M WN4 35 B5
Ennerdale Ave. Bebington L62 88 F4
Ennerdale Ave. Maghull L31 20 E2
Ennerdale Ave. St Helens WA11 33 B1
Ennerdale Ave. Warrington WA2 61 B3
Ennerdale Cl. Formby L37 9 D3
Ennerdale Cl. Kirkby L33 29 D5
Ennerdale Dr. Bootle L21 & L30 38 D8
Ennerdale Dr. Ormskirk L39 13 B2
Ennerdale Rd. Birkenhead L43 65 E1
Ennerdale Rd. Formby L37 9 E3
Ennerdale Rd. Wallasey L45 50 F8
Ennerdale St. 3 L3 52 D4
Ennis Cl. L24 83 D2
Ennis Rd. L12 54 E6
Ennisdale Dr. L48 63 D2
Ennismore Rd. Crosby L23 26 C5
Ennismore Rd. Liverpool L13 53 F3
Ensor St. L20 38 B1
Enstone. WN8 16 D1
Enstone Ave. L21 27 A1
Enstone Rd. L25 82 B6
Ensworth Rd. L18 69 B5
Enterprise Workshops. PR9 5 A6
Epping Ave. WA9 58 B3
Epping Cl. L35 57 D2
Epping Ct. L60 77 A1
Epping Gr. L15 69 B6
Epsom Cl. L10 28 E1
Epsom Dr. WN2 35 F7
Epsom St. WA9 44 F4
Epsom Way. L5 52 D5
Epstein Ct. 12 L6 53 B3
Epworth Cl. 1 WA5 59 F7
Epworth St. L6 & L7 52 F2
Eremon Cl. L9 39 D8
Erfurt Ave. L63 79 A4
Eric Gr. L44 51 A4
Eric Rd. L44 51 A4
Eric St. WA8 73 C2
Erica Ct. L60 76 E1
Eridge St. L8 68 A3
Erl St. L9 39 A6
Ermine Cres. L5 52 F5
Ernest Cookson Sch. L12 54 A6
Errington Ct. L17 80 F8
Errington St. L20 & L5 52 C6
Errol St. L17 68 B3
Errwood Cl. L24 83 E2
Erskine Cl. WA11 44 E6
Erskine Ind Est. 5 L6 52 F3
Erskine Rd. L44 51 C3
Erskine St. L6 52 F2
Erskine St Ind Est. 5 L7 53 A2
Erylmore Rd. L18 69 A1
Escolme Dr. L49 64 E3
Escor Rd. L25 70 A6
Eshe Rd. L23 26 C4
Eshe Rd N. L23 26 C4
Eshelby Cl. L22 26 F1
Esher Cl. L43 65 C7
Esher Rd. Bebington L62 79 B8
Esher Rd. Liverpool L6 & L7 53 C3
Esk St. L20 52 B8
Eskbank. WN8 24 C8
Eskbrook. WN8 16 C1
Eskburn Rd. L13 53 E6
Eskdale. WN8 24 B8
Eskdale Ave. Bebington L62 88 E5
Eskdale Ave. Ormskirk L39 13 C2
Eskdale Ave. St Helens WA11 44 B8
Eskdale Ave. Wallasey L46 49 C1
Eskdale Ave. Warrington WA2 61 C3
Eskdale Cl. L37 9 D2
Eskdale Dr. Formby L37 9 D2
Eskdale Dr. Maghull L31 20 E2
Eskdale Rd. Ashton-in-M WN4 35 B4
Eskdale Rd. Liverpool L9 39 A6
Eslington St. L19 81 A7
Esmond St. L6 53 B5
Esonwood Rd. L35 56 D3
Espin St. 3 L4 38 F1
Esplanade. Birkenhead L8 67 A2
Esplanade. Southport PR8 3 F7
Esplanade The. 4 Bootle L20 38 C3
Esplanade The. Liverpool L8 67 C1
Esplen Ave. L23 26 F5
Essex Rd. Huyton-w-R L36 56 B4
Essex Rd. Southport PR8 8 A8
Essex Rd. West Kirby L48 63 C3
Essex St. L8 67 F5
Essex Way. L20 38 D4
Esther St. WA8 73 C1
Esthwaite Ave. WA11 44 C8
Ethel Rd. L44 51 D3
Ethelbert Rd. L47 63 C8
Etna St. Birkenhead L42 66 F2
Etna St. Liverpool L13 53 F3
Eton Ct. L18 69 D5
Eton Dr. Heswall L63 86 F6
Eton Dr. Litherland L10 28 D2
Eton Hall Dr. WA9 58 C7
Eton St. L4 38 F1
Eton Way. WN5 25 F8
Etruria St. L19 81 C4
Etruscan Rd. L13 54 A4
Ettington Dr. PR8 7 A5
Ettington Rd. L4 53 B7
Ettrick Cl. L33 29 D6
Eurolink. WA9 57 F4
Europa Bvd. Birkenhead L41 & L72 66 E6
Europa Bvd. Warrington WA5 60 D3
Euston Gr. L43 66 C5
Euston St. L4 38 F2
Evans Cl. WA11 45 F7
Evans Rd. Hoylake L47 63 B7
Evans Rd. Liverpool L24 82 C5
Evans St. L34 56 D7
Evelyn Ave. Prescot L34 56 E6
Evelyn Ave. St Helens WA9 44 E3
Evelyn Prim Sch. L34 56 E7
Evelyn Rd. L44 51 C3
Evelyn St. WA9 44 E3
Evenwood. Skelmersdale WN8 16 D1
Evenwood. 5 St Helens WA9 58 C6
Evenwood Ct. WN8 16 C1
Everard Rd. PR8 4 D4
Everdon Wood. L33 29 F3
Evered Ave. L9 39 A4
Everest Rd. Birkenhead L42 66 D2
Everest Rd. Crosby L23 26 E4
Evergreen Cl. L49 64 E6
Everite Rd. WA8 84 B7
Everleigh Cl. L43 65 B7
Eversleigh Dr. L63 79 A4
Eversley. Skelmersdale WN8 16 D1
Eversley. Widnes WA8 72 B2
Eversley Pk. L43 66 B3
Eversley St. Liverpool L8 68 A6
Eversley St. Liverpool L8 68 A7
Everton Brow. L3 & L6 52 E4
Everton Gr. WA11 44 D5
Everton Park Prim Sch. L6 53 A4
Everton Rd. Liverpool L6 52 F4
Everton Rd. Southport PR8 4 A4
Everton St. Garswood WN4 34 D5
Everton St. Liverpool L6 52 F4
Everton Terr. L5 & L6 52 F4
Everton Valley. L4 & L5 52 E7
Everton View. L20 38 B2
Every St. L6 53 B4
Evesham Cl. L25 69 F2
Evesham Rd. Liverpool L4 39 D1
Evesham Rd. Wallasey L45 50 F6
Evington. WN8 16 D1
Ewanville. L36 55 E1
Ewart Rd. Bootle L21 38 A7
Ewart Rd. Liverpool L16 70 A8
Ewart Rd. St Helens WA11 44 B6
Ewden Cl. L16 69 E7
Exchange Pas E. 6 L2 52 C2
Exchange Pas W. 5 L2 52 C2
Exchange Pl. L35 57 C3
Exchange St. 6 WA10 44 A3
Exchange St E. L2 52 C2
Exchange St W. L2 52 C1
Exeley. L35 56 E2
Exeter Cl. L10 28 E1
Exeter Rd. Bootle L20 38 C2
Exeter Rd. Wallasey L44 51 C5
Exeter St. WA10 43 D3
Exford Rd. L12 54 D8
Exley Way. 1 L6 53 B3
Exmoor Cl. Heswall L61 76 F5
Exmoor Cl. Southport PR9 2 B6
Exmouth Gdns. 3 L41 66 D6
Exmouth St. L41 66 D6
Exmouth Way. Birkenhead L41 66 D6
Exmouth Way. Burtonwood WA5 59 F6
Extension View. WA9 58 D8

Factory La. WA8 73 C3
Factory Row. WA10 43 E1
Fair View. WN5 33 D5
Fair View Ave. WN5 33 D5
Fair View Pl. 3 L8 68 A4
Fair Way. WA10 43 C5
Fairacre Rd. L19 81 A8
Fairacres Rd. L63 79 A4
Fairbairn Rd. L22 26 E1
Fairbank St. L15 68 E7
Fairbeech Ct. L43 65 C7
Fairbeech Mews. L43 65 C7
Fairbourne Cl. WA5 60 E3
Fairbrook Dr. L41 50 E1
Fairbrother Cres. WA2 61 D2
Fairburn. WN8 16 B3
Fairburn Cl. WA8 73 E3
Fairburn Rd. L13 53 E6
Fairclough Cl. L35 57 B3
Fairclough Cres. WA11 45 A6
Fairclough La. L43 66 B4
Fairclough Rd. Huyton-w-R L36 55 C5
Fairclough Rd. Rainhill L35 57 B3
Fairclough Rd. St Helens WA10 43 C4
Fairclough St. Burtonwood WA5 59 E6
Fairclough St. 6 Liverpool L1 52 D1
Fairclough St. Newton-le-W WA12 46 B3
Fairfax Pl. L11 39 D2
Fairfax Rd. Birkenhead L41 & L42 66 E4
Fairfax Rd. Liverpool L11 39 E2
Fairfield. L23 26 E4
Fairfield Ave. L14 & L36 55 A2
Fairfield Cl. Huyton-w-R L36 55 A2
Fairfield Cl. 2 Ormskirk L39 13 E7
Fairfield Cres. Birkenhead L46 64 D8
Fairfield Cres. Huyton-w-R L36 55 A2
Fairfield Cres. Liverpool L6 53 D4
Fairfield Cty High Sch. WA8 73 B3
Fairfield Dr. 1 Ormskirk L39 13 E7
Fairfield Dr. West Kirby L48 63 E3
Fairfield Gdns. WA11 32 E2
Fairfield Hospl. WA11 32 E2
Fairfield Rd. Birkenhead L42 66 E2
Fairfield Rd. Southport PR8 7 C5
Fairfield Rd. St Helens WA10 43 D5
Fairfield Rd. Widnes WA8 73 B2
Fairfield St. L7 53 E3
Fairfields Cty Inf Sch. WA8 73 B2
Fairford Cres. L14 54 B4
Fairford Rd. L14 54 B4
Fairhaven. Kirkby L33 29 E5
Fairhaven. Skelmersdale WN8 16 C3
Fairhaven Cl. L42 66 F2
Fairhaven Dr. L63 88 C5
Fairhaven Rd. Southport PR9 2 B4
Fairhaven Rd. Widnes WA8 73 C2
Fairholme Ave. Ashton-in-M WN4 35 B4
Fairholme Ave. Neston L64 86 D1
Fairholme Ave. St Helens L34 & L35 57 A6
Fairholme Cl. L12 54 A8
Fairholme Mews. L23 26 E4
Fairholme Rd. L23 26 E4
Fairhurst Terr. L34 56 E6
Fairlawn Cl. L63 88 A6
Fairlawn Ct. L43 65 F5
Fairlawne Cl. L33 29 E5
Fairlie. WN8 16 C3
Fairlie Cres. L20 38 D7
Fairlie Cty Prim Sch. WN8 16 C3
Fairlie Dr. L35 57 D2
Fairmead Rd. Liverpool L11 39 E2
Fairmead Rd. Wallasey L46 49 F1
Fairoak Cl. L43 65 C7
Fairoak Mews. L43 65 C7
Fairstead. WN8 16 C3
Fairthorn Wlk. L33 30 A3
Fairview Ave. L45 51 B5
Fairview Cl. Ashton-in-M WN4 35 B4
Fairview Cl. Birkenhead L43 66 B3
Fairview Rd. L43 66 B3
Fairview Way. L61 76 F3
Fairway. Huyton-w-R L36 56 A4
Fairway. Southport PR9 1 C2
Fairway Cres. L62 79 D4
Fairway N. L62 79 D3
Fairway S. L62 79 D3
Fairway The. L14 54 D4
Fairways. L25 26 D5
Fairways Cl. L25 82 B8
Fairways Ct. L37 9 C5
Fairways The. Garswood WN4 34 D2
Fairways The. Liverpool L25 82 D8
Falcon Cres. L27 70 F4
Falcon Hey. L10 40 A6
Falcon Rd. L41 & L42 & L43 66 C4
Falcondale Rd. WA2 61 B6
Falconer St. L20 38 A6
Falconhall Rd. L9 39 F4
Falkland. WN8 16 C3
Falkland Dr. WN4 34 C4
Falkland Rd. Southport PR8 4 D5
Falkland Rd. Wallasey L44 51 D4
Falkland St. Birkenhead L41 66 A8
Falkland St. Liverpool L3 52 F2
Falklands App. L11 39 E2
Falkner Sq. L7 & L8 68 F7
Falkner St. Liverpool L1 & L7 & L8 67 F8
Fallow Cl. 6 WA9 58 C4
Fallowfield. L33 29 E4
Fallowfield Rd. L15 69 A6
Fallows Way. L35 71 C8
Falmouth Dr. WA5 74 E3
Falmouth Rd. L11 40 D5
Falstaff St. L20 52 C8
Falstone Rd. L33 30 A4
Far Meadow La. L61 76 D7
Far Moss Rd. L23 26 B6
Faraday Rd. Knowsley L33 41 B7
Faraday Rd. Liverpool L13 & L7 53 E1
Faraday St. L5 & L6 53 A5
Farefield Ave. WA3 35 F2
Fareham Rd. L7 53 D2
Faringdon Cl. L25 82 B6
Faringdon Rd. WA2 61 B6
Farley Ave. L62 79 C1
Farley La. WN8 16 F3
Farlow Rd. L42 66 F1
Farm Cl. Birkenhead L49 64 C4
Farm Cl. Southport PR9 5 A8
Farm Cl. St Helens WA9 58 D3
Farm Meadow Rd. WN5 25 E5
Farm Rd. WA9 58 D3
Farm View. L21 27 B2
Farm Way. WA12 46 E1
Farmbrook Rd. L25 70 B7
Farmdale Cl. L18 69 B2
Farmdale Dr. L31 20 E1
Farmer Pl. L20 38 E7
Farmer's La. WA5 60 A6
Farmfield Dr. L43 65 C7
Farmside. L46 49 F3
Farnborough Rd. PR8 7 F8
Farnborough Road Inf & Jun Sch. PR8 8 A8
Farndale. WA8 73 A5
Farndale Gr. WN4 35 C2
Farndon Ave. St Helens WA9 58 B4
Farndon Ave. Wallasey L45 50 E6
Farndon Dr. L48 63 E3
Farndon Way. L43 65 F4
Farnworth Ave. L46 49 F4

Farnworth CE Prim Sch. WA8 73 A4
Farnworth Cl. WA8 73 B4
Farnworth Rd. WA5 74 C4
Farnworth St. Liverpool L6 & L7 53 B3
Farnworth St. St Helens WA9 44 C4
Farnworth St. Widnes WA8 73 B4
Farr Hall Dr. L60 85 E7
Farr Hall Rd. L60 85 F8
Farrar St. L13 53 E7
Farrell Cl. L31 29 B4
Farrier Rd. L33 30 A2
Farrier Wlk. WA9 58 C4
Farriers Way. Birkenhead L48 64 B2
Farriers Way. Bootle L30 38 F8
Farringdon Cl. WA9 57 F6
Farrington Dr. L39 13 E6
Farthing Cl. L25 82 B7
Fatherside Dr. L30 27 C3
Faulkner Cl. PR8 7 C6
Faulkner Gdns. PR8 7 C6
Faversham Rd. L11 39 E3
Fawcett. WN8 16 B3
Fawcett Rd. L31 20 D3
Fawley Rd. Liverpool L18 69 C2
Fawley Rd. Rainhill L35 57 E1
Fazakerley Cl. L9 39 A4
Fazakerley High Sch. L10 39 F7
Fazakerley Hospl. L9 39 E6
Fazakerley Inf Sch. L10 39 F7
Fazakerley Rd. Liverpool L9 39 A4
Fazakerley Rd. Prescot L35 56 E4
Fazakerley St. L3 52 B2
Fazakerley Sta. L9 39 D7
Fearnhead Cross. WA2 61 F2
Fearnley Rd. L41 66 D5
Fearnley Way. WA12 46 B1
Fearnside St. L7 68 C8
Feather La. L60 85 E8
Feeny St. WA9 58 B2
Feilden Rd. L63 79 A4
Felicity Gr. L46 49 D1
Fell Gr. WA11 44 A8
Fell St. Liverpool L7 53 B5
Fell St. Wallasey L44 51 E2
Felltor Cl. L25 69 F3
Fellview. PR9 2 D6
Felmersham Gn. L11 39 F3
Felspar Rd. L32 40 F7
Felstead. WN8 16 B2
Felsted Ave. L25 70 C2
Felsted Dr. L10 28 E1
Felthorpe Cl. L49 65 B7
Felton Cl. L46 64 C8
Felton Ct. L17 68 C3
Felton Gr. L13 53 F3
Feltons. WN8 16 B2
Feltwell Rd. L4 53 B6
Feltwood Cl. L12 54 F7
Feltwood Rd. L12 54 F8
Feltwood Wlk. L12 54 E7
Fender Ct. L49 65 D1
Fender La. L43 & L46 50 B1
Fender Prim Sch. L49 65 C3
Fender Prim Sch Annexe. L49 65 B3
Fender View Rd. L46 65 A8
Fender Way. Birkenhead L43 & L49 65 B7
Fender Way. Heswall L61 77 A4
Fenderside Rd. L43 65 C8
Fenham Dr. WA5 74 F4
Fenney Ct. WN8 16 C1
Fenton Cl. Liverpool L24 82 D3
Fenton Cl. St Helens WA10 43 F4
Fenton Cl. Widnes WA8 72 C3
Fenton Gn. L24 82 D2
Fenwick St. L2 52 C1
Ferguson Ave. L49 64 D3
Ferguson Dr. WA2 61 D1
Ferguson Rd. Litherland L21 27 C1
Ferguson Rd. Liverpool L11 & L13 53 E8
Fern Ave. WA12 46 D2
Fern Bank. Maghull L31 20 E1
Fern Bank. Rainford WA11 31 E7
Fern Cl. Liverpool L27 70 E4
Fern Cl. Skelmersdale WN8 15 E1
Fern Gr. Birkenhead L43 65 D4
Fern Gr. Bootle L20 38 C4
Fern Gr. Liverpool L8 68 C6
Fern Hey. L23 27 B5
Fern Hill. 5 L45 51 B8
Fern Lodge. L8 68 B6
Fernbank Ave. L36 55 D2
Fernbank Dr. L30 28 A4
Fernbank La. L49 64 F7
Ferndale. WN8 16 C2
Ferndale Ave. Birkenhead L48 64 B1
Ferndale Ave. Wallasey L44 51 C4
Ferndale Cl. WA8 73 E7
Ferndale Rd. Crosby L22 26 E2
Ferndale Rd. Hoylake L47 63 B8
Ferndale Rd. Liverpool L15 68 E6
Fernhill Ave. L20 38 E3
Fernhill Cl. L20 38 E3
Fernhill Dr. L8 68 A6
Fernhill Gdns. L20 38 E3
Fernhill Mews E. L20 38 E3
Fernhill Mews W. L20 38 E3
Fernhill Rd. L20 38 E4
Fernhill Sports Ctr. L20 38 D6
Fernhill Way. L20 38 E3
Fernhill Wlk. WA9 58 C3
Fernhurst Gate. L39 13 B1
Fernhurst Rd. L32 29 C1
Fernie Cres. L8 67 F5
Fernlea Ave. L35 57 D7
Fernlea Gr. WN4 34 D5
Fernlea Mews. L43 65 C8
Fernlea Rd. L60 86 A8
Fernleigh Rd. L13 54 B3
Fernley Rd. PR8 4 A5
Ferns Cl. L60 76 C1
Ferns Rd. L63 78 D5
Fernwood Dr. L26 82 E8
Fernwood Rd. L17 68 E3
Ferny Brow Rd. L49 65 B3
Ferny Knoll Rd. Bickerstaffe WA11 23 F4
Ferny Knoll Rd. Skelmersdale WA11 & WN8 24 A4
Ferrer St. WN4 34 F6
Ferrey Rd. L10 40 A7
Ferries Cl. L62 79 B8
Ferry Rd. L62 89 A6
Ferry Side La. PR9 2 C5
Ferry View Rd. L44 51 E2
Festival Ave. WA2 61 D2
Festival Cres. WA2 61 D2
Festival Ct. L11 40 B3
Festival Rd. WA11 32 A5
Ffrancon Dr. L63 78 F7
Fiddler's Ferry Rd. WA8 73 D1
Fidler St. WA10 43 D1
Field Ave. L21 38 A8
Field Cl. Bebington L62 79 C8
Field Cl. St Helens WA9 58 D3
Field Hey La. L64 88 B1
Field House. L12 54 A7
Field La. Bootle L21 38 A8
Field La. Litherland L21 27 B1
Field La. Liverpool L10 40 B7
Field Rd. St Helens WA9 58 D3
Field Rd. Wallasey L45 51 B7
Field St. Liverpool L3 52 E3
Field St. Skelmersdale WN8 15 D2
Field View. L21 27 A1
Field Way. L35 & WA9 57 C5
Field Wlk. L23 27 B5
Field's End. L36 70 E8
Fieldfare Cl. L25 70 A5
Fieldgate. WA8 84 B6
Fielding St. L6 & L7 53 A3
Fieldsend Cl. L27 70 E4
Fieldside Rd. L42 66 E2
Fieldton Rd. L11 40 B3
Fieldview Dr. WA2 61 C1
Fieldway. Bebington L63 78 D8
Fieldway. Heswall L60 77 C1
Fieldway. Hoylake L47 63 F7
Fieldway. Liverpool L15 69 C8
Fieldway. Liverpool L36 70 F8
Fieldway. Maghull L31 28 E7
Fieldway. Wallasey L45 51 A5
Fieldway. Widnes WA8 73 E2
Fieldway Ct. L41 66 C8
Fifth Ave. Birkenhead L43 65 B7
Fifth Ave. Liverpool L9 39 D7
Filbert Cl. L33 29 F6
Filton Rd. L14 55 B6
Finborough Rd. L4 39 C1
Finch Ave. WA11 32 A5
Finch Cl. Huyton-w-R L14 55 A6
Finch Cl. St Helens WA9 58 D3
Finch Ct. L41 66 D7
Finch Dene. L14 54 F6
Finch La. Huyton-w-R L14 & L12 55 A6
Finch La. Liverpool L14 54 F5
Finch La. Liverpool L26 83 B7
Finch Lea Dr. L14 55 A5
Finch Meadow Cl. L9 39 F4
Finch Pl. L3 52 F2
Finch Rd. L14 55 A6
Finch Way. L14 54 F5
Fincham Cl. L14 & L36 55 B5
Fincham Gn. L14 55 B5
Fincham Rd. L14 & L36 55 A5
Fincham Sq. L14 55 A5
Finchdean Cl. 3 L49 64 C4
Finchley Dr. WA11 44 C7
Finchley Rd. L4 53 B7
Finchley Special Sch. L13 54 A2
Findlay Cl. WA12 46 C2
Findley Dr. L46 49 F3
Findon Rd. L32 40 F8
Fine Jane's Way. PR9 5 B8
Fingall Rd. L15 69 B6
Finger House La. WA8 58 D1
Fingland Rd. L15 68 E7
Finlan Rd. WA8 84 F7
Finlay St. L6 & L7 53 C3
Finney Gr. WA11 45 E6
Finney The. L48 75 D6
Finningley Ct. WA2 61 E1
Finsbury Pk. WA8 73 C5
Finstall Rd. L63 79 A2
Finvoy Rd. L13 53 E7
Fiona Wlk. L10 40 B7
Fir Ave. L26 83 A8
Fir Cl. L26 83 A8
Fir Cotes. L31 20 E1
Fir Gr. L9 39 C8
Fir La. L15 69 A7
Fir Rd. L22 26 E2
Fir St. Southport PR8 4 F6
Fir St. St Helens WA10 & WA9 57 D8
Fir St. Widnes WA8 73 C2
Fir Tree Ave. WA3 47 F8
Fir Tree Cl. Rainford WA11 32 F7
Fir Tree Cl. Skelmersdale WN8 24 D7
Fir Tree Dr N. L12 40 E4
Fir Tree Dr S. L12 40 E3
Fir Tree La. Burtonwood WA5 60 A7
Fir Tree La. Haskayne L39 12 F3
Fir Tree La. Ormskirk L39 13 A2
Fir Tree Wlk. WA3 47 F8
Fir Way. L60 86 B5
Firbeck. WN8 16 C1
Firbrook Ct. L43 50 C1
Firdale Rd. L9 39 A4
Firdene Cres. L43 65 E4
Fire Station Rd. L35 56 F5
Firethorne Rd. L26 70 D2
Firman Cl. WA5 60 B1
Firs Ave. L63 78 F3
Firs Cl. L37 9 D5
Firs Cres. L37 9 D5
Firs La. L39 12 E3
Firs Link. L37 9 D4
Firscraig. L36 55 C7
Firshaw Rd. L47 48 C1
First Ave. Birkenhead L43 65 C6
First Ave. Crosby L23 26 D4
First Ave. Liverpool L9 39 C7
First Ave. Rainhill L35 57 B4
Firstone Gr. L32 40 F8
Firswood Rd. L40 & WN8 15 C3
Firthland Way. WA9 44 F2
Firwood. WN8 16 D3
Firwood Gr. WN4 35 A2
Fisher Ave. Abram WN2 36 C7
Fisher Ave. Prescot L35 56 D2
Fisher Ave. Warrington WA2 61 B2
Fisher Cl. L62 79 B8
Fisher Dr. Orrell WN5 25 E7
Fisher Dr. Southport PR9 4 F7
Fisher Pl. L35 56 D2
Fisher St. Liverpool L8 67 D6
Fisher St. St Helens WA9 58 E8
Fishermans Cl. L37 9 E6
Fishers La. L61 76 F4
Fishguard Cl. 5 L6 52 F4
Fistral Cl. L10 40 B6
Fistral Dr. WA10 43 B6
Fitzclarence Way. L6 52 F4
Fitzgerald Rd. L13 54 A3
Fitzpatrick Ct. L3 52 C4
Fitzroy Way. 9 L6 53 A3
Five Ways. L64 86 F3
Fiveways. WA10 43 A4
Flail Cl. L49 64 C4
Flambards. L49 65 B3
Flamstead. WN8 16 C1
Flander Cl. WA8 72 C2
Flatfield Way. L31 20 E1
Flatman's La. L39 11 E1
Flatt La. L43 65 F3
Flawn Rd. L11 53 E8
Flaxfield Rd. L37 10 A3
Flaxhill. L46 49 D1
Flaxman St. 8 L7 53 C2
Flaxton. WN8 16 C1
Flaybrick Cl. L43 65 E8
Fleck La. L48 63 D1
Fleet Croft Rd. L49 65 A2
Fleet La. WA9 44 E2
Fleet St. L1 52 D1
Fleetwood Cl. PR9 1 F3
Fleetwood Cotts. L30 27 E4
Fleetwood Rd. PR9 1 E3
Fleetwood's La. L30 27 D4
Fleming Ct. L3 52 C4
Fleming Rd. L24 82 C6
Flemington Ave. L4 39 D1
Fletcher Ave. L42 66 E2
Fletcher Dr. L19 81 A7
Flimby. WN8 16 D1
Flinders St. L5 52 D6
Flint St. L1 & L72 & L8 67 D7
Flora St. WN4 35 B2
Floral Wood. Liverpool L8 68 A2
Flordon. WN8 16 D2
Florence Ave. L60 76 F1
Florence Cl. L9 38 F3
Florence Melly Inf Sch. L4 39 C1
Florence Nightingale Cl. L30 27 F4
Florence Rd. L44 51 E3
Florence St. Birkenhead L41 66 D6
Florence St. Liverpool L4 52 F8
Florence St. St Helens L35 57 C7
Florentine Rd. L13 54 A4
Florida Ct. L19 81 B8
Flowermead Cl. L47 48 F1
Fluker's Brook La. L28 & L34 41 B2
Foinavon Cl. L9 38 F7
Fold St. WA3 36 A1
Folds La. WA11 44 B7
Folds Rd. WA11 44 F5
Folds The. L63 87 A6
Foley Cl. L4 52 E7
Foley St. L4 52 E7
Folkestone Rd. PR8 4 F3
Folly La. L44 & L45 50 E5
Fontenoy St. L3 52 D2
Fonthill Cl. L4 52 D7
Fonthill Rd. L4 52 D8
Ford Cl. Birkenhead L49 65 B4
Ford Cl. Bootle L20 38 E7
Ford Cl. Litherland L21 27 B2
Ford Dr. L49 65 B5
Ford La. L21 & L30 27 B3
Ford La. Birkenhead L49 65 B5
Ford Rd. Birkenhead L49 65 A5
Ford Rd. Prescot L35 56 F6
Ford St. L3 52 C3
Ford View. L21 27 B3
Ford Way. L49 65 B4
Fordcombe Rd. L25 70 C4
Fordham Cl. PR8 4 E3
Fordham St. L4 52 E8
Fordhill View. L46 65 A8
Fordland Cl. WA3 36 E1
Fordlea Rd. L12 54 A8
Fordlea Way. L12 54 A8
Fordton Leisure Ctr. WA2 61 A3
Forefield Cty Inf Sch. L23 27 A4
Forefield Junior Sch. L23 27 A4
Forefield La. Crosby L23 27 A4
Forest Cl. Hoylake L47 48 D1
Forest Cl. Prescot L34 56 F7
Forest Ct. L43 66 A6
Forest Dr. Huyton-w-R L36 55 C3
Forest Dr. Skelmersdale WN8 16 C3
Forest Gn. L12 54 B8
Forest Gr. L34 & L35 56 F7
Forest Lawn. L12 54 B8
Forest Mead. WA10 43 A3
Forest Rd. Birkenhead L41 & L43 66 A6
Forest Rd. Heswall L60 86 A8
Forest Rd. Hoylake L47 48 D1
Forest Rd. Southport PR8 4 D6
Forest Rd. St Helens WA9 58 A2
Forfar Rd. L13 53 D6
Forge Cl. Cronton WA8 72 C5
Forge Cl. Westhead L40 14 E4
Forge Cotts. L17 68 C4
Forge Rd. WA5 74 F5
Forge St. L20 52 C8
Formby Bridge. L37 9 E2
Formby Bsns Pk. L37 10 B3
Formby By-Pass. Formby L37 10 B5
Formby By-Pass. Hightown L37 18 B8
Formby Cl. WA5 74 F4
Formby Fields. L37 10 A2
Formby Gdns. L37 9 F4
Formby High Sch. L37 9 E4
Formby La. Formby L37 10 B2
Formby La. Haskayne L39 12 E2
Formby Point Caravan Pk. L37 9 B1
Formby Rd. WA10 43 D1
Formby St. L37 9 E2
Formby Sta. L37 9 E2
Formosa Dr. L10 39 F7
Formosa Rd. L10 39 F6
Formosa Way. L10 39 F7
Fornalls Green La. L47 63 E7
Forres Gr. WN4 34 D4
Forrest St. L1 & L72 67 D8
Forrester Ave. L35 57 C7
Forresters Cl. WN2 36 E8
Forshaw Ave. WA10 57 C8
Forshaw's La. WA5 59 E8
Forster St. WA3 36 A1
Forsythia Cl. L9 39 C3
Fort St. L45 51 C7
Forth St. L20 52 C8
Forthlin Rd. L18 69 C1
Forton Lodge. 3 L23 26 C4
Forwood Rd. L62 88 D8
Foscote Rd. L33 30 A4
Foster Rd. L37 9 D2
Foster St. Liverpool L20 & L5 52 C7
Foster St. Widnes WA8 73 B1
Fosters Cl. PR9 5 B8
Fosters Gr. WA11 44 F5
Fosters Green Rd. WN8 16 D3
Fosters Rd. WA11 44 F6
Foul La. PR8 & PR9 5 A5
Foundry La. WA8 84 C5
Foundry St. Newton-le-W WA12 46 B3
Foundry St. St Helens WA10 & WA9 44 A3
Fountain Ct. L23 26 A5
Fountain Rd. Knowsley L34 41 D3
Fountain Rd. 4 Wallasey L45 51 B7
Fountain St. Birkenhead L42 66 D3
Fountain St. St Helens L35 57 C6
Fountains Ave. WA11 45 F7
Fountains Cl. L4 52 F7
Fountains Ct. L4 52 D7
Fountains Rd. L4 & L5 52 D7
Fountains The. L39 13 E6
Fountains Way. L37 10 B2
Four Acre Dr. L21 27 B2
Four Acre La. WA9 58 C4
Four Acre Lane Sh Ctr. WA9 58 B4
Four Lane Ends. St Helens WA9 57 F7
Four Lanes End. Raby L63 87 D5
Fouracres. L31 28 C7
Fourth Ave. Birkenhead L43 65 B6
Fourth Ave. Liverpool L9 39 D7
Fourways Cl. L27 70 D7
Fowell Rd. L45 51 B8
Fowler Cl. 7 L7 53 C1
Fox Cover Rd. L60 86 D7
Fox Hey Rd. L44 50 F4
Fox Pl. WA10 44 A4
Fox St. Birkenhead L41 66 C6
Fox St. Liverpool L3 52 E4
Fox's Bank La. L35 71 F7
Foxcote. WA8 72 B2
Foxcovers Rd. L63 79 A3
Foxdale Cl. Birkenhead L43 66 A5
Foxdale Cl. Southport PR8 4 E3
Foxdale Rd. L15 68 F6
Foxfield Rd. L47 63 D8
Foxfield Sch. L46 64 D8
Foxfold. WN8 16 D3
Foxglove Ave. L26 70 E1
Foxglove Cl. L11 & L9 39 F4
Foxglove Rd. L41 65 F7
Foxhill Cl. Formby L37 9 C3
Foxhill Cl. Liverpool L8 68 A6
Foxhill La. L26 70 F2
Foxhouse La. L31 20 F1
Foxhunter Dr. L9 39 C8
Foxleigh. L26 70 E1
Foxshaw Cl. L35 56 D1
Foxton Cl. St Helens WA11 44 D5
Foxton Cl. Wallasey L46 49 B1
Foxwood. Liverpool L12 54 E8
Foxwood. St Helens L35 57 C7
Foxwood Cl. L48 63 E3
Foy St. WN4 35 B3
Frailey Cl. PR8 7 C4
Frampton Rd. L4 39 D2
Frances Ct. L17 68 C4
Franceys St. L3 52 E1
Francis Ave. Birkenhead L46 64 D8
Francis Ave. Birkenhead L43 66 B6
Francis Cl. Rainhill L35 57 C4
Francis Cl. Widnes WA8 84 C8
Francis St. WA9 58 F7
Francis Way. L16 69 E8

- Frank St. 3 Liverpool L8 67 E5
- Frank St. Widnes WA8 73 C1
- Frankby Ave. L44 51 A4
- Frankby Cl. L49 64 B3
- Frankby Gr. L49 64 F5
- Frankby Rd. Birkenhead L48 & L49 64 B3
- Frankby Rd. Hoylake L47 63 D8
- Frankby Rd. Liverpool L4 53 C8
- Frankby Rd. West Kirby L48 63 E2
- Franklin Pl. 4 L6 53 B5
- Franklin Rd. L46 50 A4
- Franton Wlk. 2 L32 29 C2
- Fraser Rd. WA5 74 D6
- Fraser St. L3 52 E2
- Frawley Ave. WA12 46 C5
- Freckleton Rd. Southport PR9 1 F4
- Freckleton Rd. St Helens WA10 43 C1
- Freda Ave. 4 WA9 58 C6
- Frederick Banting Cl. L30 27 F4
- Frederick Gr. L15 69 A8
- Frederick Lunt Ave. L34 41 D3
- Frederick St. Ashton-in-M WN4 35 A5
- Frederick St. Liverpool L1 & L72 67 C8
- Frederick St. St Helens WA9 58 F8
- Frederick St. Widnes WA8 73 B1
- Frederick Terr. WA8 84 A4
- Freedom Cl. L7 68 A8
- Freehold St. L7 53 E3
- Freeland St. L4 52 E7
- Freeman St. Birkenhead L41 & L72 66 E7
- Freeman St. Liverpool L7 68 C8
- Freemantle Ave. WA9 57 F7
- Freemasons' Row. L3 52 D3
- Freemont Rd. L12 54 A7
- Freeport Gr. L9 39 B7
- Freesia Ave. L9 39 B4
- Freme Cl. L11 40 B3
- French St. St Helens WA10 43 D1
- French St. Widnes WA8 73 D1
- Frenchfield St. WA9 58 D3
- Frensham Cl. L63 78 F2
- Frensham Way. L25 82 D8
- Freshfield Caravan Pk. L37 9 B6
- Freshfield Cl. L36 55 C3
- Freshfield Ct. L37 9 E4
- Freshfield Prim Sch. L37 10 A4
- Freshfield Rd. Formby L37 9 E4
- Freshfield Rd. Liverpool L15 68 F6
- Freshfield Sta. L37 9 E5
- Freshford. WA9 58 D6
- Freshwater Cl. WA5 74 D7
- Friar St. 1 Liverpool L5 53 A5
- Friar St. St Helens WA10 43 F6
- Friars Ave. WA5 74 E5
- Friars Cl. L63 78 F5
- Friars Wlk. L37 10 B2
- Friary RC Prim Sch. L3 52 E4
- Friends La. WA5 74 D6
- Frinsted Rd. L11 40 A1
- Frobisher Rd. L46 50 A4
- Frodsham Dr. WA11 44 D5
- Frodsham St. Birkenhead L41 & L42 66 E4
- Frodsham St. Bootle L4 38 F1
- Frogmore Rd. L13 53 E3
- Frome Cl. L61 76 D7
- Frome Way. L25 70 D1
- Frontfield Ct. WA9 44 C2
- Frost Dr. L61 76 C6
- Frost St. L7 53 C2
- Fry St. WA9 44 F3
- Fuchsia Wlk. L49 64 C2
- Fulbeck. WA8 72 C2
- Fulbrook Cl. L63 78 F2
- Fulbrook Rd. L63 78 F2
- Fulford Cl. L14 54 F6
- Fulmar Cl. Liverpool L27 70 E5
- Fulmar Cl. St Helens WA11 44 B6
- Fulmar Gr. L12 40 E3
- Fulshaw Cl. L27 70 D6
- Fulton Ave. L48 63 E3
- Fulton St. L5 52 B6
- Fulwood Ave. PR8 4 D4
- Fulwood Cl. L17 68 D2
- Fulwood Dr. L17 68 C2
- Fulwood Pk. L17 68 D1
- Fulwood Rd. Golborne WA3 47 E7
- Fulwood Rd. Liverpool L17 68 C2
- Fulwood Way. L21 27 C4
- Funchal Ave. L37 9 D1
- Furlong Cl. Ashton-in-M WN2 35 F7
- Furlong Cl. Liverpool L9 39 D8
- Furness Ave. Formby L37 9 F3
- Furness Ave. Liverpool L12 40 C1
- Furness Ave. Ormskirk L39 13 E4
- Furness Ave. St Helens WA10 43 E7
- Furness Cl. PR8 7 B3
- Furness St. L4 52 E7
- Furze Way. L46 49 E1
- Fylde Rd. PR9 2 B4
- Gable Ct. L11 39 E3
- Gable Mews. L37 10 A1
- Gable St. WA12 46 B3
- Gable View. L11 39 E3
- Gables Cl. WA2 61 F3
- Gabriel Cl. L46 64 F8
- Gainford Cl. WA8 72 C3
- Gainford Rd. L14 55 A6
- Gainsborough Ave. L31 28 B8
- Gainsborough Cl. L14 54 E5
- Gainsborough Ct. WA8 72 B1
- Gainsborough Rd. Birkenhead L49 64 F6
- Gainsborough Rd. Liverpool L15 68 E6
- Gainsborough Rd. Southport PR8 3 E3
- Gainsborough Rd. Wallasey L45 50 E5
- Gairloch Cl. WA2 61 F4
- Gaisgill Ct. WA8 72 C1
- Gale Ave. WA5 60 F1
- Gale Rd. Kirkby L33 41 C8
- Gale Rd. Litherland L21 27 C1
- Galemeade. L11 40 B3
- Gales Croft. L27 70 E6
- Galion Way. WA8 72 F3
- Gallagher Ind Est. L44 51 B2
- Gallery The. L37 9 F3
- Galloway Rd. L22 26 E2
- Galloway St. L15 & L7 68 D8
- Galston Ave. L35 57 D2
- Galston Cl. L33 29 D6
- Galsworthy Ave. L30 38 E7
- Galsworthy Pl. L30 38 E8
- Galsworthy Wlk. L30 38 E7
- Galton St. L3 52 B3
- Galtres Ct. L42 78 E8
- Galtres Pk. L63 & L42 78 E8
- Gamble Ave. WA10 43 E6
- Gamble Inst (Liby & Coll). WA10 44 A3
- Gambler Terr. L8 67 F7
- Gamlin St. L41 66 A8
- Gamstom Wood. L32 29 C1
- Ganney's Meadow Rd. L49 65 C2
- Gannock St. 6 L7 53 C2
- Gantley Ave. WN5 25 D3
- Gantley Cres. WN5 25 D3
- Gantley Rd. WN5 25 D4
- Ganton Cl. Southport PR8 4 E3
- Ganton Cl. Widnes WA8 73 B4
- Ganworth Cl. L24 82 E2
- Ganworth Rd. Liverpool L24 82 E2
- Ganworth Rd. Liverpool L24 82 E3
- Garage Rd. L24 82 F5
- Garden Hey Rd. Birkenhead L46 64 C6
- Garden Hey Rd. Hoylake L47 48 C1
- Garden La. Liverpool L9 39 D7
- Garden La. Liverpool L3 52 F4
- Garden La. 1 Wallasey L46 49 E1
- Garden Lodge Gr. L27 70 D5
- Garden Pl. L20 38 C3
- Garden St. L25 70 A2
- Garden View. L20 38 C3
- Garden Way. L20 38 C3
- Garden Wlk. L34 56 D6
- Gardeners Way. L35 & WA9 57 C5
- Gardenia Gr. L17 & L8 68 A2
- Gardens Rd. L63 79 B5
- Gardenside. L46 50 B4
- Gardenside St. L6 52 F3
- Gardiners Pl. WN8 23 E8
- Gardner Ave. L20 38 E7
- Gardner Rd. Formby L37 10 B4
- Gardner Rd. Liverpool L13 53 E5
- Gardner's Dr. L6 53 D4
- Gardner's Row. L3 52 D3
- Gareth Ave. WA11 44 B6
- Garfield Terr. L49 65 A5
- Garfourth Cl. L19 81 D7
- Garfourth Rd. L19 81 D7
- Garmoyle Rd. L15 68 E6
- Garnet St. Liverpool L13 53 F1
- Garnet St. St Helens WA9 58 D7
- Garnett Ave. L4 52 E8
- Garnett Gn. L39 13 D4
- Garnett Pl. WN8 24 A7
- Garnetts La. Tarbock Green L35 71 D1
- Garnetts La. Widnes WA8 84 A3
- Garrick Ave. L46 64 C8
- Garrick Par. PR8 4 A6
- Garrick Rd. L43 77 F8
- Garrick St. L15 & L7 68 C7
- Garrigill Cl. WA8 73 C5
- Garrowby Dr. L36 55 C3
- Garsdale Ave. L35 57 D2
- Garsdale Cl. 2 WA5 74 F7
- Garsfield Rd. 1 L4 53 E8
- Garside Ave. WA3 47 D7
- Garstang Rd. PR9 2 A5
- Garston CE Prim Sch. L19 81 D6
- Garston Old Rd. L19 81 C7
- Garston RC Prim Sch. L19 81 C6
- Garston Sta. L19 81 D6
- Garston Way. L19 81 D5
- Garswood Ave. WA11 32 A7
- Garswood Cl. Maghull L31 20 E3
- Garswood Cl. Wallasey L46 49 E4
- Garswood Cres. WN5 33 E4
- Garswood Cty Prim Sch. WN4 34 C4
- Garswood Old Rd. WA11 & WN4 33 E1
- Garswood Rd. Billinge WN5 33 F4
- Garswood Rd. Garswood WA11 34 C3
- Garswood St. Ashton-in-M WN4 35 B3
- Garswood St. Liverpool L8 67 F3
- Garswood St. St Helens WA10 44 A4
- Garter Cl. L11 40 C3
- Garth Bvd. L63 78 E8
- Garth Ct. L22 26 E1
- Garth Dr. L18 69 C4
- Garth Rd. L32 41 A8
- Garth The. Birkenhead L43 65 F5
- Garth The. Huyton-w-R L36 55 E3
- Garth Wlk. 6 L32 41 A8
- Garthdale Rd. L18 69 B4
- Garthowen Rd. L7 53 D2
- Garton Dr. WA3 36 E1
- Gartons La. WA9 58 C3
- Garway. L25 70 C3
- Garwood Cl. Warrington WA5 60 B1
- Garwood Cl. Warrington WA5 60 C1
- Garwood Sta. WN4 34 D3
- Gascoyne St. L3 52 C3
- Gaskell Ct. WA9 44 F3
- Gaskell Rake. L30 27 D5
- Gaskell St. WA9 44 D2
- Gaskell's Brow. WN4 34 E5
- Gaskill Rd. L24 82 D4
- Gatcliff Rd. L13 53 E7
- Gateacre Brow. L25 70 B4
- Gateacre Park Dr. L16 & L25 69 F6
- Gateacre Rise. L25 70 B4
- Gateacre Sch. L25 70 A5
- Gateacre Vale Rd. L25 70 B3
- Gategill Gr. WN5 25 D3
- Gates La. L29 19 C1
- Gathurst Ct. WA8 84 D8
- Gathurst Rd. WN5 25 E8
- Gatley Dr. L31 28 E7
- Gautby Rd. L41 & L43 50 E1
- Gavin Rd. WA8 84 B7
- Gaw Hill La. L39 13 B3
- Gaw Hill View. L39 13 B3
- Gawsworth Cl. L43 65 F3
- Gawsworth Rd. WA3 35 F1
- Gaybeech Cl. L43 65 B8
- Gayhurst Ave. WA2 61 F2
- Gayhurst Cres. L11 40 A2
- Gaynor Ave. WA11 45 F7
- Gayton Ave. Bebington L63 78 C8
- Gayton Ave. Wallasey L45 51 B8
- Gayton Farm Rd. L60 86 A5
- Gayton La. L60 86 B6
- Gayton Mill Cl. L60 86 B7
- Gayton Parkway. L60 & L64 86 C5
- Gayton Prim Sch. L60 86 A6
- Gayton Rd. Heswall L60 86 A6
- Gaywood Ave. L32 40 F8
- Gaywood Cl. Birkenhead L43 65 C7
- Gaywood Cl. 5 Kirkby L32 40 F8
- Gaywood Ct. L23 26 B3
- Gaywood Gn. 4 L32 40 F8
- Gelling St. L8 67 F5
- Gellings Rd. L34 41 A5
- Gemini Bsns Park. WA5 60 E3
- Gemini Cl. L20 38 B4
- Geneva Rd. Liverpool L6 53 C3
- Geneva Rd. Wallasey L44 51 D2
- Genista Cl. L9 39 A3
- Gentwood Rd. L36 55 D3
- George Dr. PR8 7 E5
- George Hale Ave. L34 & L36 55 E6
- George Harrison Cl. 4 L6 53 B3
- George Moore Ct. L23 27 C6
- George Rd. L47 63 C6
- George St. Ashton-in-M WN4 35 C4
- George St. Birkenhead L41 & L72 66 E7
- George St. Liverpool L3 52 C2
- George St. Newton-le-W WA12 46 A4
- George St. St Helens WA10 44 A3
- George's Dock Gates. L2 & L3 52 B1
- George's La. PR9 2 F8
- George's Precinct. WA5 74 D6
- George's Terr. WN5 25 D5
- Georges Dockway. L3 52 B1
- Georges Par. L3 52 B1
- Georges Pierhead. L3 52 B1
- Georgia Ave. L63 & L62 79 E3
- Georgian Cl. Liverpool L26 82 F6
- Georgian Cl. St Helens L35 57 A6
- Georgian Pl. L37 9 E1
- Geraint St. L8 67 F6
- Gerald Rd. L43 66 A4
- Gerard Ave. L45 51 A7
- Gerard Rd. Wallasey L45 50 F6
- Gerard Rd. West Kirby L48 63 B3
- Gerard St. Ashton-in-M WN4 35 B3
- Gerard St. Liverpool L3 52 E2
- Gerards La. WA9 58 D7
- Germander Cl. L26 70 E1
- Gerneth Cl. L24 82 C4
- Gerneth Rd. L24 82 B4
- Gerosa Ave. WA12 & WA2 61 B8
- Gerrard Pl. WN8 23 F7
- Gerrard Rd. WN5 33 E5
- Gerrard's La. L26 & L27 70 F3
- Gertrude Rd. L4 53 B6
- Gertrude St. Birkenhead L41 66 F6
- Gertrude St. St Helens L35 57 D7
- Geves Gdns. L22 26 E1
- Ghyll Gr. WA11 33 B1
- Gibbon's Rd. WN4 34 D3
- Gibbons Ave. WA10 43 C3
- Gibraltar Row. L3 52 B2
- Gibson Cl. L61 76 F3
- Gibson St. 13 L8 67 F7
- Giddygate La. L31 29 B7
- Gidlow Rd. L13 53 F3
- Gidlow Rd S. L13 53 F2
- Gilbert Cl. L63 78 F2
- Gilbert Rd. L35 56 F5
- Gilbert St. L1 & L72 67 D8
- Gilbrook Sch. L41 66 F6
- Gildart St. L3 52 F2
- Gildarts Gdns. L3 52 D4
- Gilead St. L7 53 B2
- Gill St. L3 52 F2
- Gillar's La. WA10 42 E3
- Gillars Green Dr. WA10 43 A3
- Gillbrook Sq. 4 L41 65 F8
- Gillibrands Rd. WN8 24 A7
- Gillmoss Cl. L11 40 C4
- Gillmoss Ind Est. L10 40 B6
- Gillmoss La. L11 40 C5
- Gills La. L61 77 B4
- Gilman St. 3 L4 53 A7
- Gilmour Mount. L43 66 B4
- Gilmour Sch. L19 81 B7
- Gilmour South Bank Inf Sch. L19 81 B7
- Gilpin Ave. L31 20 E2
- Gilroy Rd. Liverpool L6 53 B3
- Gilroy Rd. West Kirby L48 63 D3
- Gilsecroft Ave. L33 30 A4
- Giltbrook Cl. WA8 72 F3
- Gilwell Ave. L46 & L49 64 E7
- Gilwell Cl. L46 64 E7
- Ginnel The. L62 79 B5
- Gipsy Gr. L18 69 E5
- Gipsy La. L16 & L18 69 E5
- Girton Ave. Ashton-in-M WN4 34 F4
- Girton Ave. Bootle L20 38 E2
- Girtrell Cl. L49 64 D5
- Girtrell Rd. L49 64 D5
- Girvan Cres. WN4 34 D4
- Gisburn Ave. WA3 35 F2
- Givenchy Cl. L16 69 E8
- Gladden Pl. WN8 23 E8
- Glade Rd. L36 55 E4
- Glade The. L47 48 D1
- Gladeville Rd. L17 & L18 68 E3
- Gladstone Ave. Liverpool L16 70 A8
- Gladstone Ave. 2 Seaforth L21 37 F7
- Gladstone Cl. L41 66 C6
- Gladstone Ct. 1 Bootle L21 38 A6
- Gladstone Ct. 4 Seaforth L21 37 F6
- Gladstone Hall Rd. L62 79 B4
- Gladstone Rd. Birkenhead L42 66 F3
- Gladstone Rd. Liverpool L9 39 A3
- Gladstone Rd. Liverpool L7 53 B1
- Gladstone Rd. Liverpool L19 81 C6
- Gladstone Rd. Seaforth L21 37 F7
- Gladstone Rd. Southport PR9 4 F6
- Gladstone Rd. Wallasey L44 51 D3
- Gladstone St. Birkenhead L41 66 C6
- Gladstone St. 1 Liverpool L3 52 C3
- Gladstone St. Liverpool L25 69 F2
- Gladstone St. St Helens WA10 43 D3
- Glaisdale Cl. WN4 35 C3
- Glaisdale Dr. PR8 4 F3
- Glaisher St. L5 53 A6
- Glamis Dr. PR9 2 B3
- Glamis Gr. WA9 58 C7
- Glamis Rd. L13 53 E6
- Glamorgan Cl. WA10 43 F2
- Glan Aber Pk. L12 54 E8
- Glasier Rd. L46 49 C1
- Glaslyn Way. L9 39 A3
- Glassonby Cres. L11 40 A1
- Glassonby Way. 3 L11 40 A1
- Glastonbury Cl. L6 53 D7
- Glasven Rd. L33 29 F3
- Gleadmere. WA8 72 C2
- Gleaston Cl. L62 79 D1
- Gleave Rd. WA5 59 F6
- Gleave Sq. Liverpool L6 53 A4
- Gleave St. WA10 44 A5
- Glebe Ave. WN4 35 C2
- Glebe Cl. L31 20 B1
- Glebe End. L29 27 F7
- Glebe Hey. L27 70 E5
- Glebe Hey Rd. L49 65 A3
- Glebe La. WA8 73 B5
- Glebe Pl. PR8 4 B7
- Glebe Rd. Skelmersdale WN8 24 A8
- Glebe Rd. Wallasey L45 51 A6
- Glebelands Rd. L46 64 E8
- Glegg St. L3 52 B4
- Gleggside. L48 63 C2
- Glegside Rd. L33 30 A2
- Glen Park Rd. L45 51 A7
- Glen Rd. L13 54 B2
- Glen Ronald Dr. L49 64 D5
- Glen The. Bebington L62 79 C3
- Glen The. Liverpool L18 69 C3
- Glen Vine Cl. L16 69 F8
- Glenacres. L25 70 A3
- Glenalmond Rd. L44 51 D4
- Glenathol Rd. L18 69 C2
- Glenavon Rd. Birkenhead L43 66 A1
- Glenavon Rd. Liverpool L16 54 C1
- Glenbank. L22 26 C2
- Glenbank Cl. L9 39 A5
- Glenburn Ave. L62 88 E4
- Glenburn High Sch. WN8 24 B8
- Glenburn Inf Sch. L62 88 F5
- Glenburn Rd. Skelmersdale WN8 16 A1
- Glenburn Rd. Skelmersdale WN8 23 F8
- Glenburn Rd. Wallasey L44 51 D3
- Glenburn-Heygarth Prim Sch. L62 88 E5
- Glenby Ave. L23 26 F2
- Glencairn Rd. L13 53 F3
- Glencoe Rd. L45 51 C6
- Glenconner Rd. L16 54 E1
- Glencourse Rd. WA8 73 A5
- Glencoyne Dr. PR9 2 B5
- Glencroft Cl. L36 55 C5
- Glendale Ave. WN4 35 C4
- Glendale Cl. L8 67 F3
- Glendale Gr. L63 79 B2
- Glendale Rd. WA11 44 A7
- Glendale Way. L37 9 F2
- Glendevon Rd. Huyton-w-R L36 55 E1
- Glendevon Rd. Liverpool L15 & L16 54 D1
- Glendower Rd. L22 26 E1
- Glendower St. L20 38 C1
- Glendyke Rd. L18 69 C2
- Gleneagles Cl. L61 76 F3
- Gleneagles Dr. Haydock WA11 45 A5
- Gleneagles Dr. Southport PR8 7 C3
- Gleneagles Dr. Widnes WA8 73 B5
- Gleneagles Rd. L14 & L16 54 D1
- Glenfield Cl. Birkenhead L43 65 C8
- Glenfield Cl. Wallasey L46 49 B1
- Glenfield Rd. L15 69 A6

Glengariff St. L13 53 E7
Glenhead Rd. L19 81 B8
Glenholm Rd. L31 28 C7
Glenluce Rd. L19 69 B1
Glenlyon Rd. L15 & L16 69 C8
Glenmarsh Cl. Bebington L63 78 D5
Glenmarsh Cl. Liverpool L12 54 C6
Glenmarsh Way. L37 10 B3
Glenmaye Cl. L12 40 E2
Glenmore Ave. L18 69 A3
Glenmore Rd. L43 66 A4
Glenn Bldgs. 2 L23 26 E5
Glenn Pl. WA8 72 E1
Glenpark Dr. PR9 2 B4
Glenrose Rd. L25 70 A3
Glenrose Terr. PR8 4 A5
Glenside. L18 69 C2
Glentrees Cl. L49 64 D5
Glentrees Rd. L12 54 B8
Glentworth Cl. L31 28 D7
Glenvale Wlk. 7 L6 52 F4
Glenville Cl. L25 70 B4
Glenway. L33 29 F6
Glenway Cl. L12 40 F4
Glenwood Cl. L35 56 F2
Glenwood Dr. L61 76 E7
Glenwyllin Rd. L22 26 F1
Globe Rd. L20 38 B4
Globe St. L4 52 E7
Gloucester Ave. 2 WA3 47 B8
Gloucester Pl. 15 L6 53 A3
Gloucester Rd. Bootle L20 38 D4
Gloucester Rd. Huyton-w-R L36 56 A3
Gloucester Rd. Liverpool L6 53 D5
Gloucester Rd. Southport PR8 3 F5
Gloucester Rd. Wallasey L45 50 E6
Gloucester Rd. Widnes WA8 73 B3
Gloucester Rd N. L6 53 D6
Gloucester St. WA9 44 D2
Gloucester Way. 16 L6 53 A3
Glover Pl. L20 38 B4
Glover St. Birkenhead L42 & L43 66 C4
Glover St. Newton-le-W WA12 46 C3
Glover St. St Helens WA10 43 F3
Glover's Brow. L32 29 C4
Glover's La. L30 27 E4
Glyn Ave. L62 88 E7
Glyn Rd. L44 51 B5
Glynn St. L15 68 F8
Glynne Gr. L16 70 A8
Glynne St. L20 38 D6
Golborne (All Saints) RC Prim Sch. WA3 47 B8
Golborne Cty Prim Sch. WA3 47 A8
Golborne Dale Rd. WA12 47 A5
Golborne Enterprise Pk. WA3 36 A1
Golborne Rd. Ashton-in-M WA3 & WN4 35 E4
Golborne Rd. Golborne WA3 47 C8
Golborne Rd. Winwick WA12 & WA2 61 A7
Golborne St. WA12 46 E4
Golbourne High Sch. WA3 36 C1
Golbourne St Thomas' CE Jun & Inf Sch. WA3 36 B1
Gold Triangle Complex. WA8 84 C5
Goldcliffe Cl. WA5 60 D3
Goldcrest Cl. L12 40 F4
Goldcrest Mews. L26 70 E1
Golden Gr. 3 L4 39 A1
Goldfinch Cl. L26 70 E1
Goldfinch Farm Rd. L24 82 C3
Goldie St. L4 52 F7
Goldsmith Rd. 1 L43 65 F1
Goldsmith St. Bootle L20 38 A4
Goldsmith St. Liverpool L6 53 B3
Goldsmith Way. 2 L43 65 F1
Goldsworth Fold. L35 57 B3
Golf Links Rd. L42 78 B8
Golf Rd. L37 9 E5
Gondover Ave. L9 38 F6
Gonville Rd. L20 38 D2
Gooch Dr. WA12 46 D2
Good Shepherd Sch The. L21 27 C2
Goodacre Rd. L9 39 B7
Goodaker's Meadow. L49 65 A2
Goodall Pl. L4 52 E8
Goodall St. L4 38 E1
Goodban St. WA9 58 E8
Goodison Ave. L4 52 F8
Goodison Park (Everton Football Club). L4 52 F8
Goodison Pl. L4 38 F1
Goodison Rd. Bootle L4 38 F1
Goodison Rd. Liverpool L4 52 F8
Goodlass Rd. L24 82 A6
Goodleigh Pl. WA9 58 C5
Goodwood Cl. L36 55 D1
Goodwood St. L5 52 D5
Goose Green The. L47 48 D1
Goostrey Cl. L63 79 B1
Gordale Cl. WA5 74 F7
Gordon Ave. Bebington L62 88 E7
Gordon Ave. Birkenhead L49 64 E3
Gordon Ave. Crosby L22 26 C2
Gordon Ave. Garswood WN4 34 E4
Gordon Ave. Haydock WA11 45 F7
Gordon Ave. Maghull L31 20 C3
Gordon Ave. Southport PR9 1 C1
Gordon Ct. L49 64 E3
Gordon Dr. Liverpool L14 54 E3
Gordon Dr. Liverpool L19 81 A7
Gordon Pl. L18 69 A3
Gordon Rd. Seaforth L21 37 F6
Gordon Rd. Wallasey L45 51 C7
Gordon St. Birkenhead L41 66 C6
Gordon St. Liverpool L15 68 E7
Gordon St. Southport PR9 4 C8
Gordonstoun Cres. WN5 25 F7
Gore Dr. L39 13 E3
Gore St. Liverpool L2 52 C1
Gore St. Liverpool L8 67 E6
Gore's La. WA11 33 A5
Gores La. Formby L37 9 F5
Gores La. Rainford WA11 32 F6
Gores Rd. L33 30 C1
Gorse Ave. L12 40 B1
Gorse Cres. L44 51 C2
Gorse Hey Ct. L12 & L13 54 A5
Gorse La. L48 63 E1
Gorse Rd. L47 63 D8
Gorse Way. L37 9 C4
Gorsebank Rd. L18 68 E5
Gorsebank St. L44 51 C3
Gorseburn Rd. L13 53 E6
Gorsedale Pk. L44 51 D2
Gorsedale Rd. Liverpool L18 69 A4
Gorsedale Rd. Wallasey L44 51 C2
Gorsefield. Formby L37 10 A6
Gorsefield. St Helens L35 57 D7
Gorsefield Ave. L62 88 D5
Gorsefield Cl. L62 88 D5
Gorsefield Rd. Birkenhead L42 66 C3
Gorsefield Rd. Crosby L23 27 A5
Gorsehill Rd. Heswall L60 77 A1
Gorsehill Rd. Wallasey L45 51 A8
Gorselands Ct. L17 68 D2
Gorsewood Cl. L25 70 C5
Gorsewood Gr. L25 70 C5
Gorsewood Rd. L25 70 B5
Gorsey Brow. WN5 33 E5
Gorsey Brow Cl. WN5 33 D5
Gorsey Cop Way. L25 70 A6
Gorsey Croft. L34 & L35 56 F7
Gorsey La. Burtonwood WA5 & WA9 59 C5
Gorsey La. Haskayne L39 11 B7
Gorsey La. Hightown L38 18 B2
Gorsey La. Litherland L21 27 C2
Gorsey La. Wallasey L41 & L44 51 B2
Gorsey La. Widnes WA8 73 E1
Gorsey Pl. WN8 24 B7
Gorseyville Cres. L63 78 E5
Gorseyville Rd. L63 78 E5
Gorst St. 11 L4 52 F7
Gort Rd. L36 55 E3
Gorton Rd. L13 54 B2
Goschen St. 7 Birkenhead L43 65 F8
Goschen St. 6 Liverpool L5 52 F7
Goschen St. Liverpool L13 53 F3
Gosford St. L8 67 F4
Gosforth Rd. PR9 4 F8
Gosport Cl. WA2 61 F1
Goswell St. L15 68 E8
Gotham Rd. L63 79 B3
Gothic St. L42 66 F2
Gotley Wlk. L24 82 F4
Gough Ave. WA2 61 B2
Gough Rd. L13 53 E7
Gourley Rd. L13 54 B1
Gourley's La. L48 63 D1
Government Rd. L47 63 B7
Govett Rd. L35 57 D7
Gower St. Bootle L20 38 B5
Gower St. Liverpool L1,L3,L69 & L72 67 C8
Gower St. St Helens WA9 44 D1
Goyt Hey Ave. WN5 33 E5
Graburn Rd. L37 9 F4
Grace Ave. L10 40 A7
Grace Rd. L9 39 A6
Grace St. Liverpool L8 67 F4
Grace St. St Helens WA9 58 C8
Gradwell St. 1 L1 52 D1
Grafton Cres. L8 67 E6
Grafton Dr. Birkenhead L49 65 B4
Grafton Dr. Southport PR8 7 A5
Grafton Gr. L8 67 E4
Grafton Rd. L45 51 B7
Grafton St. Birkenhead L43 66 B5
Grafton St. Liverpool L72 & L8 67 D6
Grafton St. Liverpool L8 67 E4
Grafton St. Liverpool L8 67 E5
Grafton St. Liverpool L8 67 E6
Grafton St. Liverpool L8 67 F3
Grafton St. Newton-le-W WA12 46 B3
Grafton St. St Helens WA10 43 D3
Grafton Wlk. L48 63 C2
Graham Cl. WA8 72 C1
Graham Dr. L26 83 A8
Graham Rd. West Kirby L47 & L48 63 A3
Graham Rd. Widnes WA8 84 C8
Graham St. WA9 44 C4
Graham's Rd. L36 55 F2
Grain Ind Est. L8 67 E4
Grainger Ave. Birkenhead L43 65 F1
Grainger Ave. Bootle L20 38 E5
Grainger Ave. West Kirby L48 63 B3
Graley Cl. L26 82 F6
Grammar School La. L48 63 D1
Grampian Ave. L46 64 E8
Grampian Rd. L7 53 E2
Grampian Way. Bebington L62 88 E4
Grampian Way. Birkenhead L46 64 E8
Grampian Way. Golborne WA3 36 D1
Granams Croft. L30 27 D4
Granard Rd. L15 69 A6
Granborne Chase. L32 29 B3
Granby Cl. PR9 1 F3
Granby Cres. L63 79 A2
Granby Prim Sch. L8 68 A7
Granby St. L8 68 A6
Grandison Rd. L4 39 C1
Grange Ave. Liverpool L12 & L14 54 E5
Grange Ave. Liverpool L25 82 D7
Grange Ave. Southport PR9 4 E8
Grange Ave. Wallasey L45 51 B6
Grange Ave N. L14 54 F5
Grange Cl. WA3 47 C6
Grange Cres. L66 89 A2
Grange Cross Cl. L48 63 E1
Grange Cross Hey. L48 63 E1
Grange Cross La. L48 63 E1
Grange Dr. Heswall L60 76 F2
Grange Dr. Raby L63 87 A7
Grange Dr. St Helens WA10 57 B8
Grange Dr. Widnes WA8 72 D1
Grange Farm Cres. L48 63 E3
Grange La. Formby L37 9 E5
Grange La. Liverpool L25 70 A5
Grange Mount. Birkenhead L43 66 C5
Grange Mount. Heswall L60 76 F1
Grange Mount. West Kirby L48 63 D2
Grange Old Rd. L48 63 C2
Grange Park Rd. WA10 57 C8
Grange Pk. L31 28 F7
Grange Pl. L43 66 C6
Grange Prim Sch. L30 27 E5
Grange Rd. Ashton-in-M WN4 34 F6
Grange Rd. Birkenhead L41 66 D6
Grange Rd. 12 Birkenhead L41 66 E6
Grange Rd. Haydock WA11 & WA12 45 D5
Grange Rd. Heswall L60 76 F2
Grange Rd. Hightown L38 17 E6
Grange Rd. Litherland L30 28 B2
Grange Rd. Southport PR9 4 E7
Grange Rd. West Kirby L48 63 B2
Grange Rd E. 8 L41 66 E6
Grange Rd W. L41 & L43 66 C6
Grange St. L6 53 D5
Grange Terr. L15 68 F7
Grange The. L44 51 C4
Grange Vale. L42 67 A1
Grange Valley. WA11 45 D6
Grange Valley Prim Sch. WA11 45 D5
Grange Way. L25 70 A5
Grange Weint. L25 70 B4
Grangehurst Ct. L25 70 B4
Grangemeadow Rd. L25 70 A5
Grangeside. L25 70 A5
Grangewood. L14 & L16 54 F1
Granite Terr. L36 56 A2
Granston Cl. WA5 60 E2
Grant Ave. L15 68 F6
Grant Cl. Huyton-w-R L14 55 A3
Grant Cl. St Helens WA10 43 E4
Grant Cl. Warrington WA5 60 D1
Grant Ct. 9 L20 38 C3
Grant Rd. Huyton-w-R L14 55 A4
Grant Rd. Wallasey L46 50 C4
Grant St. WA12 46 A3
Grantham Cl. Heswall L61 76 E4
Grantham Cl. Southport PR8 4 A1
Grantham Cres. WA11 44 D5
Grantham Rd. Kirkby L33 29 E5
Grantham Rd. Southport PR8 4 A1
Grantham St. L6 & L7 53 B3
Grantham Way. L30 28 B4
Grantley Rd. L15 69 B6
Grantley St. WN4 35 A5
Granton Cl. L37 9 E3
Granton Rd. L5 53 A6
Grantside Sch. L6 53 A3
Grantwood. WN4 35 A5
Granville Ave. L31 20 C2
Granville Cl. Ormskirk L39 21 B8
Granville Cl. Wallasey L45 50 E6
Granville Ct. PR9 1 D1
Granville Pk. L39 21 C8
Granville Rd. Liverpool L15 68 D7
Granville Rd. Liverpool L19 81 C6
Granville Rd. Southport PR8 3 D4
Granville St. WA9 44 D3
Grasmere Ave. Birkenhead L43 65 C5
Grasmere Ave. Orrell WN8 25 B7
Grasmere Ave. Orrell WN5 25 F8
Grasmere Ave. Prescot L34 56 F6
Grasmere Ave. St Helens WA11 44 B7
Grasmere Ave. Warrington WA2 61 E3
Grasmere Cl. Kirkby L33 29 D4
Grasmere Cl. St Helens WA11 44 B7
Grasmere Ct. WA11 44 B7
Grasmere Dr. Ashton-in-M WN4 35 B5
Grasmere Dr. Bootle L21 38 E8
Grasmere Dr. Wallasey L45 51 A6
Grasmere Fold. WA11 44 B7
Grasmere Gdns. L23 26 F3
Grasmere House. L17 68 D2
Grasmera Rd. Formby L37 9 D3
Grasmere Rd. Maghull L31 20 D2
Grasmere St. L5 & L6 53 B5
Grasmere Terr. WN2 36 B8
Grass Wood Rd. L49 65 C3
Grassendale Ct. L19 81 A7
Grassendale La. L19 81 A7
Grassendale Prom. L19 80 F6
Grassendale Rd. L19 81 A7
Grassington Cres. L25 70 C2
Grassmoor Cl. L62 88 E8
Grasville Rd. L42 66 E3
Gratrix Rd. L62 88 D8
Gratton Pl. WN8 24 A8
Grave-Yard La. L39 22 A6
Gravel La. PR9 2 F5
Gray Ave. WA11 45 D6
Gray Gr. L36 70 F8
Gray St. L20 38 A5
Graylands Pl. L4 39 C1
Graylands Rd. Bebington L62 79 C6
Graylands Rd. Liverpool L4 39 C2
Grayling Dr. L12 40 D3
Grays Ave. L35 56 F6
Grayson St. L1 & L72 67 D8
Graysons Rd. WA11 31 F8
Grayston Ave. WA9 58 D6
Greasby Inf Sch. L49 64 D2
Greasby Jun Sch. L49 64 D1
Greasby Rd. Birkenhead L49 64 E4
Greasby Rd. Wallasey L44 51 A4
Great Ashfield. WA8 72 D3
Great Charlotte St. 20 L1 52 D1
Great Crosby RC Jun Sch. L23 26 E4
Great Crosshall St. L3 52 D2
Great Delph. WA11 45 D7
Great George Pl. L1 & L69 67 E7
Great George St. L1 & L69 67 E7
Great George's Rd. L22 37 E8
Great Hey. L29 & L30 27 D5
Great Homer St. L3 & L5 52 E5
Great Howard St. L3 & L5 52 B4
Great Meols Prim Sch. L47 48 E1
Great Mersey St. L5 52 D6
Great Newton St. L3 52 F1
Great Orford St. L3 52 F1
Great Richmond St. L3 52 E3
Great Sankey Cty High Sch. WA5 74 E7
Great Sankey L Ctr. WA5 74 D8
Greaves St. L8 67 F5
Grebe Ave. WA10 57 B7
Grecian St. L21 37 F8
Grecian Terr. L5 52 F6
Gredington St. L8 68 A4
Greek St. Liverpool L3 52 E2
Greek St. Runcorn WA7 84 F3
Green Bank. L63 78 A2
Green Croft. L23 27 B5
Green End La. WA9 58 C8
Green End Pk. L12 54 A7
Green Gates. L36 55 E6
Green Hey Dr. L30 27 D3
Green Heys Dr. L31 20 F1
Green Jones Brow. WA5 59 F6
Green La. Bebington L63 79 A5
Green La. Birkenhead L41 66 E4
Green La. Bootle L21 38 A7
Green La. Burtonwood WA5 59 E7
Green La. Crosby L22 26 C2
Green La. Crosby L23 27 B6
Green La. Formby L37 9 F5
Green La. Litherland L21 27 B2
Green La. Liverpool L3 52 E1
Green La. Liverpool L13 53 F4
Green La. Liverpool L18 69 B5
Green La. Liverpool L16 & L18 69 C5
Green La. Maghull L31 20 A2
Green La. Maghull L31 20 C1
Green La. Ormskirk L39 13 E6
Green La. Orrell WN5 25 D3
Green La. Rainford WA11 32 A5
Green La. Skelmersdale L40 16 A6
Green La. St Helens WA10 42 F5
Green La. Wallasey L45 & L46 50 C5
Green La. Wallasey L45 50 D6
Green La. Widnes WA8 72 E1
Green La. Winwick WA2 61 A7
Green La N. L16 69 D6
Green Lane Ave. L39 13 E6
Green Lane Cl. WA2 61 A7
Green Lane Sta. L41 66 E4
Green Lawn. Birkenhead L42 66 F1
Green Lawn. Huyton-w-R L36 56 A4
Green Lawn Gr. L42 66 F1
Green Leach Ave. WA11 44 B7
Green Leach Ct. WA11 44 B7
Green Leach La. WA11 44 B7
Green Link. L31 20 B2
Green Meadows. WA3 47 E5
Green Mount. L49 65 A5
Green Oaks Path. WA8 73 C1
Green Oaks Way. WA8 73 C1
Green Park Dr. L31 20 B1
Green Park Prim Sch. L31 20 B2
Green Pk. L30 27 F5
Green Rd. L34 56 C7
Green St. L3 & L5 52 C4
Green The. Bebington L62 79 D5
Green The. Crosby L23 26 D5
Green The. Hale L24 83 D1
Green The. Liverpool L13 54 C2
Green The. Raby L63 87 C4
Green The. West Kirby L48 75 D7
Green Way. Huyton-w-R L36 55 B4
Green Way Cl. L36 55 B4
Green Wlk. PR8 7 D5
Green's La. L31 & L39 12 C1
Greenacre. L40 14 E4
Greenacre Cl. L25 82 C8
Greenacre Dr. L63 88 C7
Greenacre Rd. L25 82 C8
Greenacres Cl. L43 65 C8
Greenall Ave. WA5 74 D4
Greenall Ct. 11 L34 56 D6
Greenall St. Ashton-in-M WN4 35 B5
Greenall St. St Helens WA10 43 E4
Greenbank. Abram WN2 36 B7
Greenbank. Seaforth L22 37 E8
Greenbank Ave. Maghull L31 20 C3
Greenbank Ave. Orrell WN5 25 D3
Greenbank Ave. 3 Wallasey L45 51 B7
Greenbank Cres. WA10 43 F3
Greenbank Ct. L17 68 E5
Greenbank Dr. L10 40 B7
Greenbank Dr. Heswall L61 77 A3

Greenbank Dr. Liverpool L15 & L17 .... 68 E5
Greenbank Dr. Southport PR8 3 E2
Greenbank High Sch. PR8 ..... 3 E1
Greenbank La. L17 & L18 ..... 68 E5
Greenbank Rd. Birkenhead L42 .... 66 C3
Greenbank Rd. Liverpool L17 & L18 .... 68 F5
Greenbank Rd. West Kirby L48 .... 63 C4
Greenburn Ave. WA11 .... 33 C1
Greencroft Rd. L44 .... 51 C3
Greendale Rd. Bebington L62 .... 79 B5
Greendale Rd. Liverpool L25 69 F4
Greene's Rd. L35 .... 56 D2
Greenfield Cl. Newton-le-W WA12 .... 46 C4
Greenfield Cl. Southport PR9 . 2 A3
Greenfield Dr. L36 .... 70 F8
Greenfield Gr. L36 .... 70 F8
Greenfield La. Heswall L60 & L61 .... 76 C2
Greenfield La. Litherland L21 27 A1
Greenfield Rd. Liverpool L13 54 A3
Greenfield Rd. St Helens WA10 .... 43 E5
Greenfield View. WN5 .... 33 D4
Greenfield Way. Liverpool L18 .... 69 C1
Greenfield Way. Wallasey L44 .... 51 B4
Greenfield Wlk. L36 .... 55 F1
Greenfields Ave. L62 .... 88 C7
Greenfields Cres. Ashton-in-M WN4 .... 35 B4
Greenfields Cres. Bebington L62 .... 88 C7
Greenfinch Cl. 1 Liverpool L12 .... 40 F3
Greenfinch Cl. Liverpool L26 70 E1
Greenford Cl. WN5 .... 25 D6
Greenford Rd. PR8 .... 7 C4
Greenhaven. WN8 .... 25 B7
Greenheath Way. L46 .... 49 F3
Greenhey Pl. WN8 .... 23 F8
Greenheys Gdns. 5 L8 .... 68 B6
Greenheys Rd. Irby L61 .... 76 C5
Greenheys Rd. Liverpool L8 . 68 B6
Greenheys Rd. Wallasey L44 51 B4
Greenhill Ave. L18 .... 69 C4
Greenhill Cl. L18 .... 69 B2
Greenhill Cres. WN5 .... 33 F5
Greenhill Pl. L36 .... 55 E1
Greenhill Rd. Billinge WN5 .. 33 F5
Greenhill Rd. Liverpool L18 .. 69 B2
Greenhill Rd. Liverpool L19 .. 81 C8
Greenholme Cl. L11 .... 40 A3
Greenhow Ave. L48 .... 63 B3
Greenlake Rd. L18 .... 69 B2
Greenland St. L1 & L69 & L72 .... 67 D7
Greenlands. L36 .... 55 E1
Greenlea Cl. Bebington L63 .. 78 F6
Greenlea Cl. Orrell WN5 ...... 25 D5
Greenleaf St. L7 & L8 .... 68 C7
Greenleas Prim Sch. L45 ..... 50 D6
Greenleas Rd. L45 .... 50 D5
Greenleigh Rd. L18 .... 69 B2
Greenloon's Dr. L37 .... 9 C3
Greenloon's Wlk. L37 .... 9 C2
Greenock St. L3 .... 52 B3
Greenodd Ave. L12 .... 40 C1
Greenore Dr. L24 .... 83 D2
Greenough Ave. L35 .... 57 C5
Greenough St. L25 .... 69 F2
Greens Wlk. L17 .... 68 E3
Greensbridge La. L26 & L35 71 B2
Greenshank Cl. WA12 .... 46 C4
Greenside. L6 .... 52 F3
Greenside Ave. Litherland L10 .... 28 E2
Greenside Ave. Liverpool L15 .... 69 A7
Greenslate Ct. WN5 .... 25 E3
Greenslate Rd. WN5 .... 25 E3
Greenville Cl. L63 .... 78 F5
Greenville Dr. L31 .... 20 C1
Greenville Rd. Bebington L63 78 F5
Greenville Rd. Neston L64 .... 86 F1
Greenway. Ashton-in-M WN4 35 A4
Greenway. Bebington L62 ..... 79 D3
Greenway. Birkenhead L49 .. 64 E5
Greenway. Crosby L23 .... 27 A5
Greenway. Heswall L61 .... 76 E4
Greenway. Warrington WA5 74 E7
Greenway Ave. WN8 .... 24 B8
Greenway Cl. WN8 .... 15 E2
Greenway Rd. Birkenhead L42 .... 66 D3
Greenway Rd. Liverpool L24 83 A3
Greenway Rd. Runcorn WA7 84 F1
Greenway Rd. Widnes WA8 . 73 B1
Greenway The. L12 & L14 .... 54 E4
Greenways. WN5 .... 25 D3
Greenways Sch. L19 .... 80 F7
Greenwell Rd. WA11 .... 45 C6
Greenwich Ct. L9 .... 39 B8
Greenwich Rd. L9 .... 39 B7
Greenwood Cl. Ormskirk L39 13 C1
Greenwood Cl. Prescot L34 . 56 E6
Greenwood Cres. WA2 .... 61 E2
Greenwood Ct. 7 WA9 .... 58 C4
Greenwood Dr. WA12 .... 46 D2
Greenwood La. L44 .... 51 C5
Greenwood Rd. Birkenhead L49 .... 65 B3
Greenwood Rd. Hoylake L47 63 E8
Greenwood Rd. Liverpool L18 .... 69 B1
Greetby Hill. L39 & L40 .... 14 A6
Greetham St. L1 & L72 .... 67 D8
Gregory Cl. L16 .... 69 E8
Gregory Way. L16 .... 69 E8
Gregson Ct. L45 .... 51 C8
Gregson Rd. Liverpool L14 ... 54 C2
Gregson Rd. Prescot L35 ...... 56 D5
Gregson Rd. Widnes WA8 .... 73 C1
Gregson St. L6 .... 52 F3
Gregson's Ave. L37 .... 9 E5
Greig Way. L8 .... 67 F5
Grenfell Cl. L64 .... 86 C1
Grenfell Pk. L64 .... 86 C1
Grenfell Rd. L13 .... 53 E8
Grenloe Cl. L27 .... 70 F5
Grenville Cres. L63 .... 88 C7
Grenville Dr. L61 .... 76 E3
Grenville Rd. L42 .... 66 F3
Grenville St S. L1 & L72 .... 67 E8
Grenville Way. L42 .... 66 F3
Gresford Ave. L15 & L17 ...... 68 E6
Gresford Ave. Birkenhead L43 .... 66 A2
Gresford Ave. West Kirby L48 .... 63 C3
Gresford Cl. Prescot L35 ...... 56 F3
Gresford Cl. Warrington WA5 .... 60 E1
Gresham St. L7 .... 53 E2
Gresley Cl. 6 L7 .... 53 C1
Gressingham Rd. L18 .... 69 C2
Greta St. L8 .... 68 A5
Gretton Rd. L14 .... 55 B5
Grey Rd. Ashton-in-M WN4 .. 35 A4
Grey Rd. Liverpool L9 .... 39 A4
Grey Rock Wlk. L6 .... 53 B4
Grey St. Liverpool L8 .... 67 F6
Grey St. Liverpool L8 .... 67 F7
Greyfriars. WN4 .... 34 F4
Greyfriars Rd. PR8 .... 7 B6
Greyhound Farm Rd. L24 .... 82 C4
Greystoke Cl. L49 .... 64 F4
Greystokes. L39 .... 13 D2
Greystone Cres. L14 .... 54 E3
Greystone Pl. L10 .... 39 F7
Greystone Rd. Liverpool L10 39 F7
Greystone Rd. Liverpool L14 54 E2
Greystone Rd. Warrington WA5 .... 74 F4
Gribble Rd. L10 .... 40 A7
Grierson St. L8 .... 68 B7
Grieve Rd. L10 .... 40 A7
Griffin Ave. L46 .... 64 E8
Griffin Cl. Burtonwood WA5 . 59 E5
Griffin Cl. Liverpool L11 .... 40 C4
Griffin Cl. St Helens WA10 ... 42 F4
Griffin Mews. WA8 .... 73 B3
Griffin St. WA9 .... 58 E7
Griffin Wlk. 1 L11 .... 40 C4
Griffith's Rd. L36 .... 55 E2
Griffiths Cl. L49 .... 64 C3
Griffiths Dr. PR9 .... 4 F8
Griffiths St. 6 L1 .... 67 E8
Griffon House. PR9 .... 1 F2
Grimley Ave. L20 .... 38 A4
Grimrod Pl. WN8 .... 24 A7
Grimshaw La. L39 .... 13 E7
Grimshaw Rd. WN8 .... 24 D8
Grimshaw St. Bootle L20 ...... 38 B2
Grimshaw St. Golborne WA3 36 A1
Grimshaw St. St Helens WA9 58 C6
Grindleford Way. L7 .... 68 B8
Grinfield St. L7 .... 53 A1
Grinshill Cl. L8 .... 68 A6
Grinstead Cl. PR8 .... 3 F1
Grinton Cres. L36 .... 55 D2
Grisedale Ave. WA2 .... 61 B3
Grisedale Cl. L37 .... 9 E3
Grisedale Rd. L62 .... 88 F8
Grizedale. WA8 .... 72 B2
Grizedale Ave. WA11 .... 44 B8
Grizedale Rd. L5 .... 52 F6
Groarke Dr. WA5 .... 74 D5
Groes Rd. L19 .... 81 B7
Grogan Sq. L20 .... 38 D6
Gronow Pl. L20 .... 38 E6
Grosmont Rd. Kirkby L32 ..... 40 F8
Grosvenor Ave. Crosby L23 . 26 E2
Grosvenor Ave. Golborne WA3 .... 47 D8
Grosvenor Ave. West Kirby L48 .... 63 B2
Grosvenor Cl. PR8 .... 3 E3
Grosvenor Dr. L45 .... 51 B8
Grosvenor Gdns. Newton-le-W WA12 .... 46 C2
Grosvenor Gdns. Southport PR8 .... 3 F3
Grosvenor Pl. Birkenhead L43 .... 66 A5
Grosvenor Pl. Southport PR8 . 3 F3
Grosvenor Rd. Birkenhead L43 .... 66 B5
Grosvenor Rd. 7 Bootle L4 38 F2
Grosvenor Rd. Haydock WA11 .... 45 B7
Grosvenor Rd. Hoylake L47 . 63 B6
Grosvenor Rd. Liverpool L15 68 E7
Grosvenor Rd. Liverpool L19 81 A6
Grosvenor Rd. Maghull L31 .. 28 D6
Grosvenor Rd. Prescot L34 .. 56 D6
Grosvenor Rd. Southport PR8 3 E4
Grosvenor Rd. St Helens WA10 .... 43 D2
Grosvenor Rd. Wallasey L45 51 B8
Grosvenor Rd. Widnes WA8 73 B5
Grosvenor St. Liverpool L3 ... 52 D3
Grosvenor St. Wallasey L44 . 51 B4
Grove Ave. L60 .... 76 F1
Grove Mead. L31 .... 20 F1
Grove Park Ave. L12 .... 54 B8
Grove Pk. Liverpool L8 .... 68 C6
Grove Pk. Ormskirk L39 .... 13 F7
Grove Pk. Southport PR9 .... 4 F8
Grove Pl. Hoylake L47 .... 63 B7
Grove Pl. Liverpool L4 .... 52 E7
Grove Rd. Birkenhead L42 .... 66 F2
Grove Rd. Hoylake L47 .... 63 B7
Grove Rd. Liverpool L6 & L7 . 53 D3
Grove Rd. Orrell WN8 .... 25 C8
Grove Rd. Wallasey L45 .... 50 E6
Grove Rd. Wallasey L45 .... 50 F7
Grove Side. L7 .... 68 A8
Grove Sq. L62 .... 79 A7
Grove St. Ashton-in-M WN4 . 35 A4
Grove St. Bebington L62 .... 79 B7
Grove St. Bootle L20 .... 38 C4
Grove St. Liverpool L7 & L8 .. 68 A8
Grove St. Liverpool L15 .... 68 F8
Grove St. Runcorn WA7 .... 84 F3
Grove St. Southport PR8 .... 4 A4
Grove St Prim Sch. L42 .... 79 B7
Grove Terr. Hoylake L47 .... 63 B7
Grove Terr. Southport PR8 ..... 4 A5
Grove The. Bebington L63 .... 79 A5
Grove The. Birkenhead L43 .. 66 B3
Grove The. Golborne WA3 .... 36 D1
Grove The. Huyton-w-R L28 . 55 C7
Grove The. Liverpool L13 ..... 53 F5
Grove The. Ormskirk L39 ...... 21 C7
Grove The. St Helens WA10 . 43 C5
Grove The. Wallasey L44 ...... 51 C3
Grove The. Warrington WA5 74 F4
Grove Way. L7 .... 68 A8
Grovedale Rd. L18 .... 68 F5
Grovehurst Ave. L14 .... 54 F4
Groveland Ave. Hoylake L47 63 B7
Groveland Ave. Wallasey L45 .... 50 D6
Groveland Rd. L45 .... 50 D6
Grovelands. L7 .... 68 A8
Grovenor Cl. L30 .... 27 F3
Groves The. L32 .... 40 E7
Groveside. L48 .... 63 A2
Grovewood. Prescot L35 ...... 56 F3
Grovewood. Southport PR8 ... 3 E5
Grovewood Ct. L43 .... 66 B3
Grundy Cl. Southport PR8 ...... 4 E5
Grundy Cl. Widnes WA8 .... 72 F3
Grundy Homes. PR8 .... 4 E5
Grundy St. Golborne WA3 .... 47 A7
Grundy St. Liverpool L20 & L5 .... 52 C6
Guardian Ct. L48 .... 63 B1
Guelph St. L7 .... 53 A2
Guernsey Rd. Liverpool L13 . 54 A4
Guernsey Rd. Widnes WA8 .. 73 E3
Guffitt's Rake. L47 .... 48 E1
Guffitts Cl. L47 .... 48 E1
Guild Hey. L34 .... 41 D4
Guildford Avenue. L30 .... 27 F1
Guildford Rd. Southport PR8 . 4 B2
Guildford St. L44 .... 51 D4
Guildhall Rd. L9 .... 39 A6
Guillemot Way. L26 .... 70 E1
Guilsted Rd. L11 .... 40 A2
Guinea Gap. L44 .... 51 E3
Guion Rd. L21 .... 38 B7
Guion St. L6 .... 53 B4
Gullivers World Theme Park. WA5 .... 60 E1
Gulls Way. L60 .... 85 E7
Gunning Ave. WA10 .... 43 B5
Gunning Cl. WA10 .... 43 B5
Gurnall St. 13 L4 .... 52 F7
Guthrie Way. 2 L6 .... 53 B3
Gutticar Rd. WA8 .... 72 B1
Gwendoline Cl. L61 .... 77 A5
Gwendoline St. L8 .... 67 F6
Gwenfron Rd. 10 L6 & L7 ..... 53 B3
Gwent Cl. L6 .... 53 B5
Gwent St. L8 .... 68 A6
Gwladys St. L4 .... 38 F1
Gwladys Street Jun & Mix Inf Sch. L4 .... 39 A1
Gwydir St. L8 .... 68 A5
Gwydrin Rd. L18 .... 69 C5

Hackett Ave. L20 .... 38 D6
Hackthorpe St. L5 .... 52 E7
Hadassah Gr. L17 .... 68 C4
Hadden Cl. L35 .... 57 A4
Haddock St. L20 .... 38 B1
Haddon Ave. L9 .... 38 F6
Haddon Dr. Heswall L61 .... 76 F4
Haddon Dr. Widnes WA8 ..... 72 C3
Haddon Rd. Birkenhead L42 . 67 A2
Haddon Rd. Golborne WA3 .. 36 D2
Haddon St. 5 WN4 .... 34 F5
Haddon Wlk. L12 .... 40 E3
Hadfield Ave. L47 .... 63 B7
Hadfield Cl. WA8 .... 73 E2
Hadfield Gr. L25 .... 70 C3
Hadleigh Rd. L32 .... 29 F1
Hadley Ave. L62 .... 79 C1
Hadlow Gdns. L41 .... 66 E4
Hadstock Ave. L37 .... 9 D1
Hadwens Bldgs. 20 L3 .... 52 C2
Haggerston Rd. L4 .... 39 A2
Hague Bush Cl. WA3 .... 36 E1
Hahnemann Rd. L4 .... 38 E2
Haig Ave. Birkenhead L46 ..... 64 F8
Haig Ave. Southport PR8 .... 4 E5
Haig Rd. WA8 .... 73 A1
Haigh Cres. L31 .... 20 C4
Haigh Ct. PR8 .... 4 F6
Haigh Rd. L22 .... 26 E1
Haigh St. L3 & L6 .... 52 F3
Haileybury Ave. L10 .... 28 D2
Haileybury Rd. L25 .... 82 B8
Hailsham Rd. L19 .... 80 F8
Halby Rd. L9 .... 39 B6
Halcombe Rd. L12 .... 54 D7
Halcyon Rd. L41 & L42 & L43 66 C4
Haldane Ave. L41 .... 65 F7
Haldane Rd. L4 .... 39 A2
Hale Bank Rd. WA8 .... 83 F5
Hale Bank Terr. WA8 .... 84 A4
Hale CE Prim Sch. L24 .... 83 E1
Hale Dr. L24 .... 82 E2
Hale Gate Rd. Liverpool L24 & WA8 .... 83 F3
Hale Gate Rd. Widnes WA8 . 84 A3
Hale Gr. WN4 .... 34 F5
Hale Rd. Bootle L4 .... 38 E1
Hale Rd. Liverpool L24 .... 82 C3
Hale Rd. Liverpool L24 .... 82 E2
Hale Rd. Wallasey L45 .... 51 C6
Hale Rd. Widnes WA8 .... 84 C7
Hale Road Ind Est. WA8 .... 84 B4
Hale St. L2 .... 52 C2
Hale View Rd. L36 .... 56 A2
Halebank CE Prim Sch. WA8 .... 84 A5
Halefield St. WA10 .... 43 F4
Halewood Ave. WA3 .... 35 F1
Halewood CE Prim Sch. L26 71 A1
Halewood Cl. L25 .... 70 B4
Halewood Dr. Liverpool L25 . 70 B2
Halewood Dr. Liverpool L25 . 70 C2
Halewood Lane Ends. L26 ... 83 A8
Halewood Pl. L25 .... 70 C3
Halewood Rd. L25 .... 70 C3
Halewood Sta. L26 .... 82 F8
Halewood 'Triangle' Ctry Pk. L26 .... 82 E8
Halewood Way. L25 .... 70 C2
Haley Rd N. WA5 .... 59 E6
Haley Rd S. WA5 .... 59 E5
Halidon Ct. L20 .... 38 A4
Halifax Cl. WA2 .... 61 D2
Halifax Cres. L23 .... 27 B6
Halifax Rd. PR8 .... 7 C5
Halkirk Rd. L18 .... 69 C1
Halkyn Ave. L15 & L17 .... 68 D6
Halkyn Dr. L5 & L6 .... 53 A5
Hall Ave. WA8 .... 72 A1
Hall Brow Cl. L39 & L40 .... 14 B4
Hall Dr. Birkenhead L49 .... 64 C2
Hall Dr. Kirkby L32 .... 29 E2
Hall Gn. WN8 .... 25 B7
Hall Green Cl. WN8 .... 25 B7
Hall La. Bickerstaffe L39 .... 22 E4
Hall La. Burtonwood WA9 ..... 59 A4
Hall La. Cronton WA8 .... 72 C8
Hall La. Huyton-w-R L36 .... 56 A2
Hall La. Ince Blundell L38 ..... 18 F3
Hall La. Kirkby L32 .... 29 E2
Hall La. Kirkby L33 & L39 ...... 30 A8
Hall La. Liverpool L9 .... 39 B6
Hall La. Liverpool L7 .... 53 A2
Hall La. Maghull L31 .... 20 B7
Hall La. Maghull L31 .... 28 D8
Hall La. Newton-le-W WA5 ... 60 B8
Hall La. Orrell WN3 & WN5 .. 25 F4
Hall La. Prescot L34 & L35 .... 56 D5
Hall La. Skelmersdale L40 ..... 15 A6
Hall Nook. WA5 .... 74 F3
Hall Rd. WA11 .... 45 E7
Hall Rd E. L23 .... 26 B6
Hall Rd W. L23 .... 26 A6
Hall Road Sta. L23 .... 26 A6
Hall St. Ashton-in-M WN2 ..... 35 E7
Hall St. Southport PR9 .... 4 C7
Hall St. St Helens WA10 & WA9 ...... 44 B4
Hall St. St Helens WA9 .... 58 E3
Hall Terr. WA5 .... 74 E7
Hallam Wlk. 3 L7 .... 53 C1
Hallbridge Gdns. WN8 .... 25 B8
Hallcroft. WN8 .... 16 C2
Hallfields Rd. WA2 .... 61 D1
Hallmoor Cl. L39 .... 13 E2
Hallows Ave. WA2 .... 61 D1
Hallsands Rd. L32 .... 40 E8
Hallside Cl. L19 .... 81 A8
Halltine Cl. L23 .... 26 A6
Hallville Rd. L18 .... 69 B5
Halsall Cl. L23 .... 26 E5
Halsall Ct. L39 .... 13 D6
Halsall Gn. L63 .... 79 B1
Halsall La. Formby L37 .... 9 F3
Halsall La. Haskayne L39 ...... 12 D6
Halsall La. Ormskirk L39 .... 13 D6
Halsall Rd. Bootle L20 .... 38 C5
Halsall Rd. Southport PR8 ...... 8 A8
Halsall St. L34 .... 56 D7
Halsall's Cotts. WA8 .... 83 E5
Halsbury Rd. Liverpool L6 & L7 .... 53 C3
Halsbury Rd. Wallasey L45 .. 51 B6
Halsey Ave. L12 .... 53 F7
Halsey Cres. L12 .... 53 F7
Halsnead Ave. L35 .... 56 C1
Halsnead Prim Sch. L35 .... 56 D2
Halstead Cl. 4 L32 .... 29 C1
Halstead Rd. Bootle L20 & L9 38 F6
Halstead Rd. Wallasey L44 .. 51 C3
Halstead Wlk. L32 .... 29 C1
Halton Chase. L40 .... 14 E4
Halton Cres. L49 .... 64 B3
Halton Hey. L35 .... 56 D1
Halton Rd. Maghull L31 .... 20 D3
Halton Rd. 9 Wallasey L45 51 A6
Halton Rd. Warrington WA5 74 F6
Halton St. WA11 .... 45 E6
Halton View Rd. WA8 .... 73 C1
Halton Wlk. L25 .... 70 C6
Halton Wood. L31 .... 29 B3
Halville Rd. L44 .... 51 C3
Halyard House. L61 .... 76 C2
Hamble Dr. 2 WA5 .... 74 F3
Hambledon Dr. L49 .... 64 D4
Hambleton Cl. Liverpool L11 40 B4
Hambleton Cl. Widnes WA8 72 C3
Hamblett Cres. WA11 .... 44 B6
Hamblett Sch. WA10 .... 43 D6
Hamer St. WA10 .... 43 F4
Hamil Cl. L47 .... 48 E1
Hamilton Cl. L64 .... 86 B2
Hamilton Ct. L23 .... 26 B4
Hamilton La. L41 & L72 .... 66 E7
Hamilton Rd. Garswood WN4 .... 34 D4
Hamilton Rd. Liverpool L5 .... 52 F5
Hamilton Rd. St Helens WA10 .... 43 C6
Hamilton Rd. Wallasey L45 .. 51 A8
Hamilton Sq. L41 .... 66 F7
Hamilton Square Sta. L41 .... 66 F7
Hamilton St. L41 .... 66 F6

Hamlet Ct. L17 ... 68 C3
Hamlet Rd. L45 ... 50 F6
Hamlin Rd. L19 ... 81 D6
Hammersley Ave. WA9 ... 58 C3
Hammersley St. WA9 ... 58 C3
Hammill Ave. WA10 ... 43 E6
Hammill St. WA10 ... 43 D5
Hammond Rd. L33 ... 30 C3
Hammond St. WA9 ... 44 D2
Hampden Gr. L42 ... 66 E4
Hampden Rd. L42 ... 66 E4
Hampden St. L4 ... 38 F2
Hampshire Ave. L30 ... 27 C3
Hampson Cl. WN4 ... 35 B2
Hampson St. L6 ... 53 C5
Hampstead Rd. Liverpool L6 53 C4
Hampstead Rd. Wallasey L44 ... 51 C3
Hampton Cl. WA8 ... 73 E3
Hampton Court Rd. L12 ... 54 D5
Hampton Dr. WA8 ... 72 C5
Hampton Pl. WA11 ... 44 B6
Hampton Rd. Formby L37 ... 9 E1
Hampton Rd. Southport PR8 .. 4 C5
Hampton St. L8 ... 67 F7
Hanbury Rd. L4 ... 53 D8
Handel Ct. L8 ... 68 B6
Handfield Pl. 5 L5 ... 53 A5
Handfield Rd. L22 ... 26 E1
Handfield St. L5 ... 53 A5
Handford Ave. L62 ... 88 F5
Handley Ct. L19 ... 80 F8
Handley St. WA7 ... 84 F3
Hands St. L21 ... 38 B6
Handsworth Wlk. PR8 ... 4 F3
Hanford Ave. L9 ... 38 F6
Hankey Dr. L20 ... 38 E5
Hankey St. WA7 ... 84 F2
Hankin St. L5 ... 52 D5
Hankinson St. L13 ... 54 A1
Hanley Cl. WA8 ... 72 C1
Hanley Rd. WA8 ... 72 C1
Hanlon Ave. L20 ... 38 D6
Hanmer Rd. L32 ... 29 B2
Hannah Cl. L61 ... 76 E3
Hannan Rd. L6 & L7 ... 53 C3
Hanns Hall Rd. L64 ... 87 D8
Hanover Cl. L43 ... 65 F6
Hanover St. Liverpool L1 ... 52 D1
Hanover St. Liverpool L1 & L72 ... 67 C8
Hans Rd. 9 L4 ... 39 A1
Hanson Pk. L43 ... 65 E5
Hanson Rd. L9 ... 39 C5
Hants La. L39 ... 13 E6
Hanwell St. L6 ... 53 B6
Hanworth Cl. L12 ... 40 E3
Hapsford Rd. L21 ... 38 B6
Hapton St. L5 ... 52 E6
Harbern Cl. L12 ... 54 D6
Harbord Rd. L22 ... 26 C1
Harbord St. L7 ... 53 B1
Harborne Dr. L63 ... 78 F2
Harbury Ave. PR8 ... 7 A4
Harcourt Ave. L44 ... 51 E3
Harcourt St. Birkenhead L41 66 C7
Harcourt St. Liverpool L4 ... 52 D7
Hard La. WA10 ... 43 E6
Hardacre St. L39 ... 13 F6
Hardie Ave. L46 ... 49 C1
Hardie Cl. WA9 ... 58 A3
Hardie Rd. L36 ... 56 A3
Harding Ave. Bebington L63 79 A4
Harding Ave. Warrington WA2 ... 61 E1
Harding Cl. L5 ... 53 A5
Harding St. L8 ... 68 B7
Hardinge Rd. L19 ... 81 D8
Hardknott Rd. Bebington L62 88 E8
Hardman St. L1 & L69 ... 67 E8
Hardshaw Ctr. WA10 ... 44 A3
Hardshaw St. St Helens WA10 ... 44 A3
Hardshaw St. St Helens WA10 ... 44 A4
Hardwick Rd. WN4 ... 35 A5
Hardy St. Liverpool L1 & L72 67 D7
Hardy St. Liverpool L1 ... 67 E8
Hardy St. Liverpool L19 ... 81 D4
Hare Croft. L28 ... 54 F8
Harebell Cl. L37 ... 9 F1
Harebell St. L5 ... 52 D7
Harefield Gn. L24 ... 82 D3
Harefield Rd. L24 ... 82 D3
Hares La. PR8 ... 5 D1
Haresfinch Rd. WA10 & WA11 ... 44 B6
Haresfinch View. WA11 ... 44 B6
Harewell Rd. L11 ... 40 A1
Harewood Ave. PR8 ... 7 C6
Harewood Rd. L45 ... 51 A7
Harewood St. 13 L6 ... 53 A4
Hargate Rd. L33 ... 29 F2
Hargate Wlk. 3 L33 ... 29 F2
Hargrave Ave. L43 ... 65 E3
Hargrave Cl. L43 ... 65 E3
Hargrave La. Bebington L63 & L64 ... 88 A4
Hargrave La. Raby L63 ... 87 F5
Hargreaves Ct. WA8 ... 73 D1
Hargreaves Rd. L17 ... 68 C3
Hargreaves St. Southport PR8 4 C6
Hargreaves St. St Helens WA9 ... 44 E3
Harington Cl. L37 ... 9 D3
Harington Gn. L37 ... 9 D3
Harington Rd. L37 ... 9 D4
Harke St. L7 ... 68 B8
Harker St. L3 ... 52 E3
Harland Dr. WN4 ... 35 C3
Harland Gn. Liverpool L24 ... 82 F3
Harland Rd. L42 ... 66 D4
Harlech Cl. WA5 ... 60 E2
Harlech Ct. L63 ... 78 F4
Harlech Rd. L23 ... 26 C3
Harlech St. L44 ... 51 E2
Harlech St. Ashton-in-M WN4 34 F5
Harlech St. Bootle L4 ... 38 F1
Harleston Rd. L33 ... 30 A3
Harleston Wlk. L33 ... 30 A3
Harley Ave. L42 ... 78 C8
Harley St. 2 L9 ... 39 A6
Harlian Ave. L46 ... 64 D7
Harlow Cl. WA9 ... 57 F7
Harlow St. L8 ... 67 F4
Harlyn Cl. L26 ... 82 E6
Harmony Way. L13 ... 54 A1
Harold Ave. WN4 ... 35 A5
Harold Magnay Sch. L25 ... 69 F4
Harold Rd. WA11 ... 45 F7
Harp's Croft. L30 ... 27 C3
Harper Rd. L9 ... 39 A4
Harper St. 3 L6 & L7 ... 53 A2
Harptree Cl. L35 ... 56 E3
Harradon Rd. L9 ... 39 B7
Harridge La. L40 ... 12 F8
Harrier Dr. L26 ... 70 E1
Harringay Ave. L18 ... 68 F5
Harrington Ave. L47 ... 63 C7
Harrington Rd. Crosby L23 .. 26 D4
Harrington Rd. Litherland L21 ... 27 D1
Harrington Rd. Liverpool L3 . 67 E4
Harrington St. L2 ... 52 C1
Harris Cl. L63 ... 79 A2
Harris Dr. L20 & L30 ... 38 D7
Harris St. St Helens WA10 ... 43 E4
Harris St. Widnes WA8 ... 73 C1
Harrismith Rd. L10 ... 39 F6
Harrison Dr. Bootle L20 ... 38 E3
Harrison Dr. Haydock WA11 45 A6
Harrison Dr. Rainford WA11 31 F8
Harrison Dr. Wallasey L45 ... 50 E7
Harrison Hey. L36 ... 55 E1
Harrison Sq. WA5 ... 60 F1
Harrison St. WA8 ... 84 B6
Harrison Way. Liverpool L3 .. 67 E4
Harrison Way. Newton-le-W WA12 ... 46 C4
Harrock Wood Cl. L61 ... 76 E6
Harrocks Cl. L30 ... 27 D5
Harrod Dr. PR8 ... 3 E3
Harrogate Cl. Bebington L62 88 D4
Harrogate Cl. Warrington WA5 ... 60 A1
Harrogate Dr. L5 ... 52 F5
Harrogate Rd. Bebington L42 79 A8
Harrogate Rd. Bebington L62 ... 88 D4
Harrogate Way. PR9 ... 2 C6
Harrogate Wlk. L42 ... 79 A8
Harrops Croft. L30 ... 27 E4
Harrow Cl. Litherland L30 ... 27 F2
Harrow Cl. Orrell WN5 ... 25 F8
Harrow Cl. Wallasey L44 ... 50 F5
Harrow Dr. L10 ... 28 D2
Harrow Gr. L62 ... 88 E8
Harrow Rd. Liverpool L4 ... 53 B6
Harrow Rd. Wallasey L44 ... 50 F5
Harrowby Cl. L8 ... 68 A7
Harrowby Rd. L42 ... 66 D4
Harrowby Rd. Seaforth L21 . 37 F7
Harrowby Rd. Wallasey L44 . 51 E4
Harrowby Rd S. L42 ... 66 C4
Harrowby St. L8 ... 68 A7
Harsnips. WN8 ... 16 C2
Hart St. Liverpool L3 ... 52 E2
Hart St. Southport PR8 & PR9 4 E6
Hart's La. WN8 ... 24 F8
Hartdale Rd. Crosby L23 ... 27 B6
Hartdale Rd. Liverpool L18 ... 69 A4
Hartford Cl. L43 ... 65 F3
Harthill Ave. L18 ... 69 B4
Harthill Mews. L43 ... 50 C1
Harthill Rd. L18 ... 69 C4
Hartington Ave. L41 ... 66 B7
Hartington Rd. Liverpool L12 54 C6
Hartington Rd. Liverpool L17 & L7 & L8 ... 68 C6
Hartington Rd. Liverpool L19 81 D6
Hartington Rd. St Helens WA10 ... 43 D5
Hartington Rd. Wallasey L44 51 B4
Hartismere Rd. L44 ... 51 D3
Hartland. WN8 ... 16 C2
Hartland Ave. PR9 ... 2 B5
Hartland Cl. WA8 ... 73 A5
Hartland Rd. L11 ... 39 E2
Hartley Ave. L9 ... 39 B5
Hartley Cl. 4 L4 ... 52 F7
Hartley Cres. Southport PR8 .. 3 F2
Hartley Gr. Kirkby L33 ... 29 F5
Hartley Gr. St Helens WA10 . 57 C8
Hartley Quay. L3 & L69 & L72 ... 67 C8
Hartley Rd. PR8 ... 3 F2
Hartnup St. Liverpool L5 ... 52 F6
Hartnup St. Liverpool L4 & L5 ... 53 A6
Hartopp Rd. L25 ... 70 A6
Hartopp Wlk. L25 ... 70 A7
Hartsbourne Ave. L25 & L16 70 A6
Hartsbourne Cl. L25 ... 69 F7
Hartsbourne Hts. L25 ... 69 F7
Hartsbourne Wlk. L25 ... 70 A7
Hartshead. WN8 ... 16 C2
Hartswell Cl. WA3 ... 36 A2
Hartwell St. L21 ... 38 B6
Hartwood Cl. 5 L32 ... 41 A7
Hartwood Rd. Kirkby L32 ... 40 F7
Hartwood Rd. Southport PR9 . 4 D7
Hartwood Sq. L32 ... 40 F7
Harty Rd. WA11 ... 45 A5
Harvard Ct. WA2 ... 61 A3
Harvard Gr. L34 ... 56 E7
Harvest La. L46 ... 49 D1
Harvest Way. 10 WA9 ... 58 C4
Harvester Way. Birkenhead L49 ... 64 C4
Harvester Way. Litherland L30 ... 28 A4
Harvey Ave. Birkenhead L49 64 D3
Harvey Ave. Newton-le-W WA12 ... 45 F3
Harvey La. WA3 ... 35 F1
Harvey Rd. L45 ... 51 A6
Harvington Dr. PR8 ... 7 B5
Harwich Gr. L16 ... 69 F8
Harwood Rd. L19 ... 81 D6
Haselbeech Cl. L11 ... 39 F3
Haselbeech Cres. L11 ... 39 F3
Haseldine St. WN4 ... 34 F6
Hasfield Rd. L11 ... 40 B2
Haslam Dr. L39 ... 13 D7
Haslemere. L35 ... 56 F3
Haslemere Dr. WA5 ... 74 D4
Haslemere Ind Est. WN4 ... 34 F8
Haslemere Rd. L25 ... 70 B6
Haslemere Way. L25 ... 70 B6
Haslingden Cl. L13 ... 54 B2
Hassal Rd. L42 ... 79 A8
Hastie Cl. L27 ... 70 E6
Hastings Ave. WA2 ... 61 B4
Hastings Dr. L36 ... 71 A8
Hastings Rd. Crosby L22 ... 26 B2
Hastings Rd. Southport PR8 ... 3 E1
Haswell Dr. L28 ... 55 B8
Hatchmere Cl. L43 ... 65 F3
Hatfield Cl. Liverpool L12 ... 41 A3
Hatfield Cl. St Helens WA9 .. 57 F7
Hatfield Gdns. L36 ... 55 F1
Hatfield Rd. Bootle L20 ... 38 E3
Hatfield Rd. Southport PR8 ... 7 C6
Hathaway. L31 ... 28 B7
Hathaway Cl. L25 ... 70 A6
Hathaway Rd. L25 ... 70 A6
Hatherley Ave. L22 & L23 ... 26 E2
Hatherley Cl. 3 L8 ... 68 A7
Hatherley St. Liverpool L8 ... 68 A7
Hatherley St. Wallasey L44 .. 51 E2
Hathersage Rd. L36 ... 55 F5
Hatton Ave. L62 ... 88 E3
Hatton Cl. L60 ... 76 D1
Hatton Garden. L1 & L2 & L3 52 D2
Hatton Hill Prim Sch. L21 ... 27 B2
Hatton Hill Rd. L21 ... 27 A1
Hattons La. L16 ... 69 C6
Hauxwell Gr. WA11 ... 44 B6
Havannah La. WA9 ... 45 B3
Havelock Cl. WA10 ... 43 F3
Haven Brow. L39 ... 21 C8
Haven Rd. L10 ... 39 F8
Haven Wlk. L31 ... 20 C4
Havergal St. 2 WA7 ... 84 F1
Haverstock Rd. L6 ... 53 D3
Haverton Wlk. L12 ... 40 E3
Hawarden Ave. Birkenhead L43 ... 66 C6
Hawarden Ave. Liverpool L15 & L17 ... 68 E6
Hawarden Ave. Wallasey L44 ... 51 C4
Hawarden Ct. L63 ... 78 F4
Hawarden Gr. L21 ... 38 A6
Hawdon Ct. 9 L7 ... 68 C8
Hawes Ave. WA11 ... 44 C8
Hawes Cres. WN4 ... 35 B5
Hawesside St. PR8 & PR9 ... 4 C7
Haweswater Ave. WA11 ... 45 A6
Haweswater Cl. L33 ... 29 D5
Haweswater Gr. L31 ... 20 F2
Hawgreen Rd. L32 ... 29 B1
Hawick Cl. L33 ... 29 D6
Hawke Gn. L36 ... 71 A7
Hawke St. L3 ... 52 E1
Hawkesworth St. 7 L4 ... 53 A6
Hawkins Rd. L64 ... 86 F1
Hawkins St. L6 & L7 ... 53 C3
Hawks Way. L60 ... 85 E8
Hawksclough. WN8 ... 16 D2
Hawkshead Ave. L12 ... 40 C1
Hawkshead Cl. L31 ... 20 E2
Hawkshead Dr. L21 & L30 ... 38 D8
Hawkshead Rd. WA5 ... 59 E6
Hawkshead St. PR8 & PR9 ... 4 D7
Hawksmoor Cl. L10 ... 40 A7
Hawksmoor Rd. L10 ... 40 A7
Hawksmore Cl. L49 ... 64 D6
Hawkstone St. Liverpool L8 . 68 A4
Hawkstone St. Liverpool L8 . 68 A5
Hawkstone Wlk. 6 L8 ... 68 A4
Hawksworth Cl. L37 ... 10 A6
Hawksworth Dr. L37 ... 10 A6
Hawley's Cl. WA5 ... 60 F1
Hawley's La. WA2 & WA5 ... 61 A1
Haworth Dr. L20 ... 38 D7
Hawthorn Ave. Garswood WN4 ... 34 D5
Hawthorn Ave. Newton-le-W WA12 ... 46 D3
Hawthorn Ave. v WN5 ... 25 F6
Hawthorn Ave. Widnes WA8 ... 73 B2
Hawthorn Cl. WN5 ... 33 D5
Hawthorn Cres. WN8 ... 15 E1
Hawthorn Dr. Heswall L61 ... 76 F2
Hawthorn Dr. St Helens WA10 ... 43 B4
Hawthorn Dr. West Kirby L48 ... 63 E2
Hawthorn Gr. 4 L7 ... 53 B1
Hawthorn La. L62 ... 88 D8
Hawthorn Rd. Huyton-w-R L36 ... 55 C2
Hawthorn Rd. Neston L64 ... 86 C1
Hawthorn Rd. Prescot L34 ... 56 E6
Hawthorne Ave. Liverpool L26 ... 82 F6
Hawthorne Ave. Warrington WA5 ... 74 F6
Hawthorne Cl. WA11 ... 45 A5
Hawthorne Cres. L37 ... 10 A2
Hawthorne Dr. L64 ... 88 B1
Hawthorne Gr. Southport PR9 4 F7
Hawthorne Gr. Wallasey L44 51 E2
Hawthorne Rd. Birkenhead L42 ... 66 D3
Hawthorne Rd. Bootle L20 & L21 & L70 ... 38 D5
Hawthorne Rd. St Helens WA9 ... 58 D6
Hawthornes The. L25 & L27 70 C6
Hawthorns Gr. L12 ... 54 B6
Haxted Gdns. L19 ... 81 D6
Haycastle Cl. WA5 ... 60 E1
Haydn Rd. L14 ... 54 F6
Haydock High Sch. WA11 ... 45 B6
Haydock La. Garswood WA11 ... 34 E1
Haydock La. Haydock WA11 45 C7
Haydock La Ind Est. WA11 . 45 E8
Haydock Park Gdns. WA12 . 35 B1
Haydock Park Golf Course. WA12 ... 46 F6
Haydock Park Race Course. WA12 ... 35 D1
Haydock Park Rd. L10 ... 28 E3
Haydock Rd. L45 ... 51 C7
Haydock St. Ashton-in-M WN4 ... 35 B2
Haydock St. Newton-le-W WA12 ... 46 A3
Haydock St. St Helens WA10 44 A3
Hayes Ave. L35 ... 56 E5
Hayes Dr. L31 ... 29 B3
Hayes St. L35 & WA10 & WA9 ... 57 C8
Hayes The. L25 ... 70 B2
Hayfield Rd. L39 ... 13 E7
Hayfield Sch. L49 ... 65 A6
Hayfield St. 14 L4 ... 52 F7
Hayfield Way. 8 WA9 ... 58 C4
Hayles Cl. L25 ... 70 A6
Hayles Gr. L25 ... 70 A6
Hayles Way. L25 ... 70 A6
Haylock Cl. L8 ... 67 F4
Hayman's Cl. L12 ... 54 A7
Hayman's Gn. L12 ... 54 A7
Hayman's Gr. L12 ... 54 A7
Haymans Gn. L31 ... 20 E1
Haywood Cl. WA3 ... 36 E1
Haywood Gdns. WA10 ... 43 D2
Hazekbank Gdns. L37 ... 9 E5
Hazel Ave. Kirkby L32 ... 29 C3
Hazel Ave. Prescot L35 ... 56 E4
Hazel Gr. Bebington L63 ... 78 E4
Hazel Gr. Crosby L23 ... 26 F3
Hazel Gr. Golborne WA3 ... 47 B8
Hazel Gr. Irby L61 ... 76 D7
Hazel Gr. Liverpool L9 ... 39 B6
Hazel Gr. Southport PR8 & PR9 ... 4 E7
Hazel Gr. St Helens WA10 ... 43 C3
Hazel La. WN8 ... 16 B4
Hazel Mews. L31 ... 29 B3
Hazel Rd. Birkenhead L41 ... 66 D5
Hazel Rd. Hoylake L47 ... 63 B7
Hazel Rd. Huyton-w-R L36 ... 55 F5
Hazeldale Rd. L9 ... 39 A4
Hazeldene Ave. Heswall L61 77 B6
Hazeldene Ave. Wallasey L45 ... 51 A5
Hazeldene Way. L61 ... 77 B7
Hazelfield Ct. 2 WA9 ... 58 C4
Hazelhurst Rd. L4 ... 53 B7
Hazelslack Rd. L11 ... 40 A2
Hazelwood. L49 ... 64 D5
Hazelwood Cl. WA9 ... 58 B3
Hazelwood Gr. L26 ... 70 D2
Hazlehurst Cl. L37 ... 9 C2
Hazlehurst Gr. WN4 ... 35 C4
Hazleton Rd. L14 ... 54 C3
Head St. L8 ... 67 E6
Headbolt La. Kirkby L33 ... 29 F4
Headbolt La. Southport PR8 ... 8 A4
Headbourne Cl. L25 ... 69 F7
Headingley Cl. Liverpool L36 70 C8
Headingley Cl. St Helens WA9 ... 58 C6
Headington Rd. L49 ... 64 D5
Headland Cl. Golborne WA3 47 E6
Headland Cl. West Kirby L48 75 B8
Headley Cl. WA10 ... 43 F3
Heald St. WA12 ... 45 F3
Healy Cl. L27 ... 71 A4
Heanor Dr. PR8 ... 4 F3
Hearne Rd. WA10 ... 43 D4
Heath Cl. Liverpool L25 ... 69 F5
Heath Cl. Prescot L34 ... 56 F7
Heath Cl. West Kirby L48 ... 75 B8
Heath Dale. L63 ... 78 F3
Heath Dr. Birkenhead L49 ... 65 A6
Heath Dr. Heswall L60 ... 76 F1
Heath Hey. L25 ... 69 F5
Heath La. L64 ... 88 C1
Heath Rd. Ashton-in-M WN4 35 C2
Heath Rd. Bebington L63 ... 78 F5
Heath Rd. Huyton-w-R L36 ... 55 B5
Heath Rd. Liverpool L19 & L18 ... 81 D8
Heath Rd. Warrington WA5 .. 74 F5
Heath Rd. Widnes WA8 ... 72 D2
Heath St. Ashton-in-M WN4 . 35 C2
Heath St. Golborne WA3 ... 47 A8
Heath St. St Helens L35 ... 57 D7
Heath View. L21 ... 27 B3
Heathbank Ave. Irby L61 ... 76 D7
Heathbank Ave. Wallasey L44 ... 51 A3
Heathbank Rd. L42 ... 66 D3
Heathcliff House. L4 ... 39 B1
Heathcote Cl. 1 L7 ... 68 C8
Heathcote Gdns. L63 ... 78 F5
Heathcote Rd. L4 ... 38 F2
Heather Bank. L63 ... 78 D6
Heather Brae. WA12 ... 46 A4
Heather Brow. L41 & L43 ... 65 F7
Heather Cl. Formby L37 ... 10 B5
Heather Cl. Kirkby L33 ... 29 E4
Heather Cl. Liverpool L4 ... 52 F8
Heather Cl. Southport PR8 ... 7 D2

Heather Ct. L4 52 F8
Heather Dene. L62 79 D2
Heather Gr. WN4 35 E4
Heather Rd. Bebington L63 78 D4
Heather Rd. Heswall L60 77 A1
Heather Way. L23 27 C6
Heatherdale Cl. L43 66 C4
Heatherdale Rd. L18 69 A4
Heatherdene Rd. L48 63 B3
Heatherland. L49 65 B4
Heatherlea Cl. WN8 25 C7
Heathers Croft. L30 27 E3
Heatherways. L37 10 A6
Heathey La. PR8 8 F8
Heathfield. L33 29 E4
Heathfield Ave. WA9 57 E8
Heathfield Cl. Bootle L21 38 C6
Heathfield Cl. Formby L37 10 A6
Heathfield Dr. L33 29 E4
Heathfield House. L61 77 A6
Heathfield Rd. Bebington L63 78 F4
Heathfield Rd. Birkenhead L43 66 C4
Heathfield Rd. Crosby L22 26 C2
Heathfield Rd. Liverpool L15 & L18 69 B6
Heathfield Rd. Maghull L31 28 F7
Heathfield Rd. Southport PR8 7 F6
Heathfield St. L1 52 E1
Heathgate. WN8 16 C2
Heathgate Ave. L24 83 A2
Heathland Rd. WA9 58 C4
Heathlands The. L46 49 E3
Heathmoor Ave. WA3 47 D6
Heathmoor Rd. L46 49 D1
Heathside. L60 76 D1
Heathview Cl. WA8 84 A5
Heathview Rd. WA8 84 A5
Heathwaite Cres. L11 40 A1
Heathway. L60 86 B7
Heathwood. L12 54 B5
Heathy La. L39 & PR8 11 B8
Heaton Cl. Liverpool L24 82 F3
Heaton Cl. Orrell WN8 25 A7
Hebburn Way. L12 41 A3
Hebden Par. 3 L11 40 C3
Hebden Rd. L11 40 B3
Hebdon Cl. WN4 35 A5
Hector Pl. L20 38 D1
Hedgebank Cl. L9 39 D8
Hedgecote. L32 40 E7
Hedgecroft. L23 27 C6
Hedgefield Rd. L25 70 B6
Hedges Cres. L13 53 E7
Helen Bank Dr. WA11 31 F7
Helen St. Ashton-in-M WN4 35 A4
Helen St. Golborne WA3 35 F1
Helena Rd. WA9 58 F7
Helena St. Birkenhead L41 66 E5
Helena St. Bootle L9 38 F3
Helena St. 10 Liverpool L7 53 B1
Helford Rd. L11 40 D5
Heliers Rd. L13 54 B2
Hell Nook. WA3 35 F1
Helmdon Cl. 2 L11 40 A1
Helmingham Gr. L41 66 E4
Helmingham Rd. L41 66 E4
Helmsdale. WN8 16 C2
Helmsley Rd. L26 82 F7
Helsby Ave. L62 88 F3
Helsby Rd. L9 39 B7
Helsby St. Liverpool L7 53 A1
Helsby St. St Helens WA9 44 E1
Helston Ave. Liverpool L26 70 F1
Helston Ave. St Helens WA11 44 D7
Helston Cl. Southport PR9 2 B5
Helston Cl. Warrington WA5 74 E5
Helston Gn. L36 56 B3
Helston Rd. L11 40 D5
Helton Cl. L43 65 E3
Hemans St. L20 38 A4
Hemer Terr. L20 38 A5
Hemingford St. L41 66 D6
Hemlock Cl. L12 40 D3
Hempstead Cl. WA9 57 F7
Henderson Cl. Birkenhead L49 64 E6
Henderson Cl. Warrington WA5 74 D6
Henderson Dr. WA11 32 A8
Henderson Rd. Huyton-w-R L36 56 A3
Henderson Rd. 2 Widnes WA8 73 A1
Henderson Rd. Widnes WA8 84 F8
Hendon Rd. L6 53 D4
Hendon Wlk. L49 64 C3
Henglers Cl. 21 L6 53 A3
Henley Ave. L21 38 A8
Henley Cl. L63 79 A2
Henley Ct. Southport PR9 1 E1
Henley Ct. St Helens WA10 43 D1
Henley Dr. PR9 1 F1
Henley Rd. L18 69 B5
Henllan Gdns. WA9 58 F7
Henlow Ave. L32 40 F8
Henry Edward St. L3 52 D3
Henry St. Birkenhead L41 66 E6
Henry St. Liverpool L13 & L7 53 F2
Henry St. Liverpool L1 & L72 67 D8
Henry St. St Helens WA10 43 F4
Henry St. 4 Widnes WA8 73 C1
Henthorne Rd. L62 79 B8
Henthorne St. L43 66 C5
Hepworth Cl. WN3 35 E2
Herald Cl. L11 40 C3
Herald St. L19 81 C6
Heralds Cl. WA8 84 C8
Heralds Gn. WA5 60 A2
Herbarth Cl. L9 38 F3
Herbert St. Burtonwood WA5 59 E6
Herbert St. St Helens WA9 58 F7
Herbert Taylor Cl. L6 53 C5
Herculaneum Ct. L8 67 F3
Herculaneum Rd. L8 67 E4
Herdman Cl. L25 70 B5
Hereford Ave. 1 WA3 47 B8
Hereford Ave. L49 64 E6
Hereford Cl. WN4 35 C2
Hereford Dr. L30 27 F1
Hereford Rd. Liverpool L15 69 A6
Hereford Rd. Seaforth L21 37 F7
Hereford Rd. Southport PR9 4 F7
Heriot St. L5 52 D6
Heriot Wlk. L5 52 D6
Hermes Cl. L30 38 E8
Hermes Rd. L10 40 C6
Hermitage Gr. L20 38 D6
Hermitage Green La. WA2 & WA12 61 A8
Hero St. L20 38 D2
Heron Ct. L26 70 E1
Heron Gr. WA11 32 B5
Heron Rd. L47 & L48 64 A6
Herondale Rd. L18 69 A5
Heronhall Rd. L9 39 F4
Heronpark Way. L63 79 B2
Herons Ct. L31 20 B4
Herrick St. L13 53 F3
Herschell St. L5 53 A6
Hertford Dr. L45 51 C6
Hertford Rd. L20 38 C2
Hertford St. WA9 44 D2
Hesketh Ave. L42 66 D1
Hesketh Cl. WA5 74 F4
Hesketh Dr. PR9 1 F1
Hesketh Dr. Heswall L60 77 A1
Hesketh Dr. Maghull L31 20 F1
Hesketh Golf Links. PR9 1 E3
Hesketh Meadow La. WA3 47 F8
Hesketh Rd. Hale L24 83 E2
Hesketh Rd. Southport PR9 1 D2
Hesketh St. L17 68 C4
Heskin Cl. Kirkby L32 40 E7
Heskin Cl. Maghull L31 20 D4
Heskin Cl. Rainhill L35 57 B3
Heskin Hall Ct. L39 13 D8
Heskin La. L39 13 D8
Heskin Rd. L32 40 E7
Heskin Wlk. L32 40 E7
Hessle Dr. L60 85 F7
Hester Cl. L38 17 F4
Heswall Ave. Bebington L63 78 C8
Heswall Ave. St Helens WA9 58 B4
Heswall Cty Prim Sch. L60 77 A1
Heswall Golf Course. L60 86 A4
Heswall Mount. L61 77 A5
Heswall Rd. L9 39 B7
Heswall Sta. L60 86 D8
Hetherlow Towers. L9 39 A3
Heversham. WN8 16 C2
Heward Ave. 1 WA9 58 C6
Hewitson Ave. L13 53 F6
Hewitson Rd. L13 53 F6
Hewitt Ave. WA10 43 D4
Hewitt's La. L33 & L34 41 E7
Hewitts Pl. 14 L2 52 C2
Hexagon The. 1 L20 38 C3
Hexham Cl. L35 57 D6
Hey Green Rd. L15 68 E8
Hey Green Road Jun Mix & Inf Sch. L15 68 E8
Hey Lock Cl. WA12 60 C8
Hey Pk. L36 55 F2
Hey Rd. L36 55 F2
Hey Wood Cl. WA12 60 C8
Heyburn Rd. L13 53 E6
Heydale Rd. L18 69 A4
Heydean Rd. L18 69 C1
Heydean Wlk. L18 69 C1
Heydon Cl. L37 9 D1
Heyes Ave. Haydock WA11 45 D5
Heyes Ave. Rainford WA11 32 A6
Heyes Dr. L45 50 C4
Heyes Gr. WA11 32 A6
Heyes Mount. L35 57 C2
Heyes Rd. Orrell WN5 25 E6
Heyes Rd. Widnes WA8 84 C8
Heyes St. L5 53 A5
Heyescroft. L39 22 D6
Heygarth Dr. L49 64 D4
Heygarth Jun Sch. L62 88 E5
Heygarth Rd. L62 88 E5
Heys Ave. L62 88 D8
Heys The. Bebington L62 88 F5
Heys The. Southport PR8 3 D4
Heyscroft Rd. L25 70 B2
Heysham Lawn. L27 71 A4
Heysham Rd. Litherland L30 & L70 & L9 28 A2
Heysham Rd. Liverpool L27 & L35 71 A3
Heysham Rd. Southport PR9 4 F7
Heysmoor Heights. 4 L8 68 B6
Heythrop Dr. L60 86 D8
Heyville Rd. L63 78 E5
Heywood Ave. WA3 36 B1
Heywood Bvd. L61 77 A6
Heywood Cl. Formby L37 9 E3
Heywood Cl. Heswall L61 77 A6
Heywood Ct. L15 54 C1
Heywood Gdns. WA3 36 B1
Heywood Rd. L15 69 C8
Heyworth St. L5 & L6 52 F5
Hickmans Rd. L41 & L44 51 B1
Hicks Rd. Bootle L21 38 A7
Hicks Rd. Crosby L22 26 E1
Hickson Ave. L31 20 C3
High Bank Cl. L43 65 D5
High Banks. L31 20 C3
High Beeches. L16 54 F1
High Beeches Cres. WN4 35 A6
High Clere Cres. L36 55 E5
High La. Bickerstaffe L39 22 C8
High La. Ormskirk L39 & L40 14 A8
High Moss. L39 13 E3
High Mount. L60 85 F8
High Park Pl. PR9 5 A8
High Park Rd. PR9 5 A8
High Park St. L8 68 A5
High St. Bebington L62 79 E1
High St. Golborne WA3 47 A8
High St. Hale L24 83 D1
High St. Liverpool L2 52 C2
High St. Liverpool L15 68 F7
High St. Liverpool L25 70 A2
High St. Newton-le-W WA12 46 D4
High St. Prescot L34 56 D6
High St. Runcorn WA7 84 F2
High St. Skelmersdale WN8 15 E1
Highacre Rd. L45 51 A7
Higham Ave. St Helens WA10 42 F3
Higham Ave. Warrington WA5 60 F1
Higham Sq. 4 L5 52 E4
Highbank Dr. L19 81 E6
Highcroft Ave. L63 79 A5
Highcroft The. L63 78 F5
Higher Ashton. WA8 72 F3
Higher Bebington Jun Sch. L63 78 D6
Higher Bebington Rd. L63 78 E5
Higher End Pk. L30 27 E5
Higher La. Liverpool L9 39 D5
Higher La. Orrell WN8 25 C7
Higher La. Rainford WA11 32 C5
Higher La. Skelmersdale WN8 16 C7
Higher Moss La. L37 11 A2
Higher Parr St. WA9 44 C3
Higher Rd. Liverpool L25 & L26 82 E7
Higher Rd. Liverpool L26 83 B6
Higher Rd. Liverpool L24 & L26 & WA8 83 C5
Highfield. L33 29 F5
Highfield Ave. WA3 46 F8
Highfield Cl. L44 51 A4
Highfield Cres. Birkenhead L42 66 F1
Highfield Cres. Widnes WA8 73 A2
Highfield Ct. L42 66 F1
Highfield Dr. Birkenhead L49 64 D4
Highfield Dr. Rainford WA11 32 E4
Highfield Gr. Birkenhead L42 66 F1
Highfield Gr. Crosby L23 26 F5
Highfield La. Golborne WA3 47 C5
Highfield La. Winwick WA2 61 C7
Highfield Pk. L31 20 F1
Highfield Pl. 6 L34 56 D6
Highfield RC Prim Sch. L42 78 F8
Highfield Rd. Birkenhead L42 66 F1
Highfield Rd. Bootle L21 38 A8
Highfield Rd. Bootle L9 38 F4
Highfield Rd. Liverpool L13 54 A4
Highfield Rd. Ormskirk L39 13 E7
Highfield Rd. Southport PR9 2 B3
Highfield Rd. Widnes WA8 73 A2
Highfield S. L63 & L42 79 A8
Highfield Sch. Birkenhead L43 65 F6
Highfield Sch. Liverpool L26 83 A7
Highfield St. Liverpool L2 & L3 52 C2
Highfield St. St Helens WA9 58 D8
Highfield View. L13 54 A4
Highfields. Heswall L60 76 F1
Highfields. Prescot L34 56 C6
Highgate Cl. L60 76 F2
Highgate Rd. Maghull L31 20 D3
Highgate Rd. Orrell WN8 25 B7
Highgate St. L7 53 A1
Highgreen Rd. L42 66 C3
Highgrove Pk. L19 81 A8
Highlands Rd. WA7 84 F1
Highoaks Rd. L25 70 B1
Highpark Rd. L42 66 C3
Highsted Gr. L33 29 F5
Hightor Rd. L25 69 F3
Hightown Sta. L38 18 A4
Highville Rd. L16 69 D6
Highwood Ct. L33 29 F4
Highwoods Cl. WN4 35 B5
Hignett Ave. WA9 45 B2
Higson Ct. L8 68 A3
Hilary Ave. Golborne WA3 36 D1
Hilary Ave. Liverpool L14 54 F2
Hilary Cl. Liverpool L4 53 C8
Hilary Cl. Prescot L34 56 E7
Hilary Cl. Warrington WA5 74 D6
Hilary Cl. Widnes WA8 73 E3
Hilary Dr. L49 65 A6
Hilary Mansions. 10 L44 51 A4
Hilary Rd. L4 53 C8
Hilberry Ave. L13 53 E5
Hilbre Ave. Heswall L60 85 E6
Hilbre Ave. Wallasey L44 51 A4
Hilbre Cl. PR9 1 F1
Hilbre Ct. L48 63 A1
Hilbre Dr. PR9 1 F1
Hilbre High Sch. L48 63 D3
Hilbre Rd. L48 63 B1
Hilbre St. Birkenhead L41 66 D8
Hilbre St. Liverpool L3 52 E1
Hilbre View. L48 63 C2
Hilcrest Rd. L4 39 D1
Hilda Rd. L12 54 E5
Hildebrand Cl. L4 53 C8
Hildebrand Rd. L4 53 C8
Hilden Pl. WA2 61 E1
Hilden Rd. WA2 61 E1
Hill Crest. L20 & L4 38 E2
Hill Gr. L46 64 E7
Hill Rd. L43 65 E6
Hill Ridge. L43 65 D5
Hill School Rd. WA10 57 A8
Hill St. Crosby L23 26 F3
Hill St. Liverpool L3 & L8 67 D6
Hill St. Liverpool L8 67 E6
Hill St. Southport PR9 4 B7
Hill St. St Helens WA10 44 A5
Hill Top La. L60 86 B8
Hill View. WA8 72 F5
Hill View Dr. L49 65 A6
Hillam Rd. L45 50 D6
Hillary Cres. L31 20 D1
Hillary Dr. L23 27 A4
Hillary Rd. L62 88 E5
Hillary Wlk. L23 27 A4
Hillbark Rd. L48 & L49 64 B1
Hillbeck Cres. WN4 34 D4
Hillbrae Ave. WA11 33 A1
Hillburn Dr. L41 50 E1
Hillcrest. Maghull L31 20 F1
Hillcrest. Skelmersdale WN8 24 B8
Hillcrest Ave. L36 56 A2
Hillcrest Dr. L49 64 C3
Hillcrest Par. L36 56 A2
Hillcrest Rd. Crosby L23 27 A4
Hillcrest Rd. Ormskirk L39 13 E6
Hillcroft Rd. Liverpool L25 69 F4
Hillcroft Rd. Wallasey L44 51 C2
Hilldean. WN8 25 C8
Hillfield Dr. L61 76 F3
Hillfoot Ave. L25 82 C7
Hillfoot Cl. L43 65 C8
Hillfoot Gn. L25 82 A7
Hillfoot Rd. L25 82 A8
Hillhead Rd. L20 38 E2
Hillingden Ave. Liverpool L26 82 F7
Hillingdon Ave. Heswall L60 & L61 76 F2
Hillingdon Rd. L15 69 B6
Hillock La. WN8 16 D7
Hills Moss Rd. WA9 58 F7
Hills Pl. L15 69 A7
Hillside Ave. Ashton-in-M WN4 34 F8
Hillside Ave. Huyton-w-R L36 55 D6
Hillside Ave. Newton-le-W WA12 45 F2
Hillside Ave. Ormskirk L39 13 D3
Hillside Ave. St Helens WA10 43 E6
Hillside Cl. Billinge WN5 33 D5
Hillside Cl. Bootle L20 & L4 38 E2
Hillside Cres. L36 55 D6
Hillside Ct. Birkenhead L41 66 E4
Hillside Ct. Liverpool L25 70 B3
Hillside Cty Prim Sch. WN8 24 D8
Hillside Dr. L25 70 B3
Hillside Golf Links. PR8 7 C8
Hillside Gr. WA5 74 F4
Hillside High Sch. L20 38 E3
Hillside Inf Sch. L43 65 D5
Hillside Jun Sch. L43 65 D5
Hillside Rd. Birkenhead L43 65 D8
Hillside Rd. Birkenhead L41 & L42 66 E4
Hillside Rd. Heswall L60 86 A7
Hillside Rd. Huyton-w-R L36 55 E5
Hillside Rd. Liverpool L18 69 B5
Hillside Rd. Southport PR8 3 E1
Hillside Rd. Wallasey L44 50 F4
Hillside Rd. West Kirby L48 63 D2
Hillside St. L6 52 F3
Hillside Sta. PR8 3 E1
Hillside View. L43 66 A3
Hillsview Rd. PR8 7 C4
Hilltop Rd. Liverpool L16 69 D7
Hilltop Rd. Rainford WA11 32 B2
Hilltop Wlk. L39 13 C3
Hillview. L17 68 E2
Hillview Ave. L48 63 B3
Hillview Ct. L43 65 C8
Hillview Gdns. L25 69 F3
Hillview Mansions. L48 63 B3
Hillview Rd. L61 76 C7
Hillwood Cl. L63 79 A1
Hilton Cl. L41 66 D6
Hilton Ct. L30 27 D4
Hilton Gr. L48 63 A3
Hilton St. WN4 35 C3
Hinchley Gn. L31 20 B1
Hinckley Rd. WA11 44 C6
Hind St. L41 66 E5
Hindburn Ave. L31 20 F2
Hinderton Dr. Heswall L60 85 F6
Hinderton Dr. West Kirby L48 63 E1
Hinderton La. L64 87 A1
Hinderton Rd. Birkenhead L41 & L42 66 E5
Hinderton Rd. Raby L64 87 B1
Hindle Ave. WA5 60 F1
Hindley Beech. L31 20 C2
Hindley Wlk. L24 82 D2
Hindlip St. 4 L8 68 A3
Hinson St. 6 Birkenhead L41 66 E6
Hinton St. Bootle L21 38 B6
Hinton St. Liverpool L6 & L7 53 C3
Hobart St. Liverpool L5 52 E6
Hobart St. St Helens WA9 57 E8
Hoblyn Rd. L43 65 E8
Hockenhall Alley. 12 L1 & L2 52 C2
Hockenhull Cl. L63 79 A2
Hodder Ave. L31 20 F2
Hodder Cl. WA11 44 B7
Hodder Pl. L5 52 F6
Hodder Rd. L5 52 F6
Hodder St. L5 52 F6
Hodge St. PR8 4 B7
Hodgkinson Ave. WA5 60 F1
Hodnet Dr. WN4 35 C3
Hodson Pl. L6 53 A4
Hodson St. PR8 4 C6
Hogarth St. 3 L21 38 A6
Hogarth Wlk. L4 52 D8
Hoggs Hill La. L37 9 F1
Hoghton Cl. WA9 58 F8
Hoghton Gr. PR9 4 C8
Hoghton Pl. PR9 4 B7
Hoghton Rd. Hale L24 83 E2
Hoghton Rd. St Helens WA9 58 F7
Hoghton St. PR8 & PR9 4 C7
Holbeck St. L4 53 C7
Holborn Dr. L39 13 C3

Holborn Hill. Birkenhead L41 66 E4
Holborn Hill. Ormskirk L39 13 C4
Holborn Sq. L41 66 E4
Holborn St. L7 53 A2
Holbrook Cl. WA9 58 C6
Holcombe Ave. WA3 47 C8
Holcombe Cl. L49 64 D4
Holden Gr. L22 26 C2
Holden Rd. Crosby L22 26 C2
Holden Rd. Prescot L35 56 C4
Holden Rd E. L22 26 C2
Holden St. L7 68 A8
Holden Terr. L22 26 C2
Holdsworth St. L7 53 B2
Holford Way. WA12 46 F3
Holgate. L23 & L29 27 B7
Holgate Dr. WN5 25 E6
Holgate Pk. L23 27 B7
Holland Ct. L30 27 D4
Holland Gr. L60 76 F1
Holland Moor Prim Sch. WN8 24 E7
Holland Moss. WA11 & WN8 24 A5
Holland Rd. Liverpool L24 82 E2
Holland Rd. Liverpool L26 82 E6
Holland Rd. Wallasey L45 51 C7
Holland St. L7 53 D3
Holland Way. L26 82 E6
Holland's La. WN8 15 A1
Holley Ct. L35 57 C3
Holliers Cl. L31 20 E1
Hollies Rd. L26 82 F8
Hollies The. Liverpool L25 69 E3
Hollies The. Southport PR8 3 F6
Hollin Hey Cl. WN5 33 D3
Hollingbourne Pl. L11 40 A3
Hollingbourne Rd. L11 40 A3
Hollingwood Cl. Ashton-in-M WN4 35 A3
Hollingworth Cl. Liverpool L9 39 B3
Hollinhey Cl. L30 28 A5
Hollins Cl. WN4 34 D4
Hollins Dr. WA2 61 A6
Hollins La. WA2 60 F6
Hollins Way. WA8 84 B5
Hollow Croft. L28 41 B1
Holloway. WA7 84 F1
Holly Ave. Bebington L63 78 F3
Holly Ave. Newton-le-W WA12 46 D3
Holly Bank Gr. WA9 44 C4
Holly Cl. Hale L24 83 D2
Holly Cl. Skelmersdale WN8 15 E1
Holly Cl. St Helens WA10 43 B4
Holly Cl. Westhead L40 14 E4
Holly Cres. WA11 32 A5
Holly Ct. L20 38 B5
Holly Farm Rd. L19 81 D6
Holly Fold La. WA11 23 E3
Holly Gr. Birkenhead L41 66 E4
Holly Gr. Huyton-w-R L36 55 B2
Holly Gr. Seaforth L21 37 F6
Holly Hey. L35 56 D1
Holly La. Ormskirk L39 13 B4
Holly La. Rainford WA11 & WN8 23 E4
Holly Lodge Girls Sch Bankfield. L13 53 F5
Holly Lodge Sch. L12 54 A6
Holly Mount. WA10 43 D2
Holly Mount. L12 54 A6
Holly Pl. L46 64 F7
Holly Rd. Golborne WA3 47 C8
Holly Rd. Haydock WA11 45 A6
Holly Rd. Liverpool L7 53 D2
Holly Rd. Warrington WA5 74 E5
Holly St. L20 38 C4
Holly Terr. WA5 74 F5
Hollybank Ct. 5 L41 66 D5
Hollybank Rd. Birkenhead L41 66 D5
Hollybank Rd. Liverpool L18 68 E5
Hollybrook Rd. PR8 4 A5
Hollybush Sq. WA3 36 E1
Hollycourt. 10 L5 53 A6
Hollydale Rd. L18 69 A5
Hollyfield Rd. L9 38 F5
Hollymead Cl. L25 70 B4
Hollytree Rd. L25 70 B3
Hollywood Rd. L17 68 E3
Holm Hey Rd. L43 65 F1
Holm La. L43 65 F2
Holm View Cl. L43 66 A3
Holman Rd. L19 81 D6
Holmdale Ave. PR9 2 C4
Holme Cl. L34 57 A7
Holme Rd. WA10 43 C3
Holme St. L20 & L5 52 C6
Holmefield Ave. L19 69 A1
Holmefield Gr. L31 20 C1
Holmefield Rd. L18 & L19 69 A1
Holmes La. L21 38 A7
Holmes St. L7 & L8 68 C7
Holmesway. L61 76 F4
Holmfield. L43 65 F2
Holmfield Gr. L36 70 F8
Holmlands Cres. L43 65 E2
Holmlands Dr. L43 65 E2
Holmlands Way. L43 65 E2
Holmleigh Rd. L25 70 A6
Holmrook Day Special Sch. L25 69 E3
Holmrook Rd. L11 40 A3
Holmside Cl. L46 64 F8
Holmside La. L43 65 F2
Holmville Rd. L63 78 E5
Holmway. L63 78 F5
Holmwood Ave. L61 77 C5
Holmwood Cl. Ashton-in-M WN4 35 A5
Holmwood Cl. Formby L37 9 D3
Holmwood Dr. L37 9 D4
Holmwood Dr. L61 77 C5
Holt Ave. Billinge WN5 33 D4
Holt Ave. Birkenhead L46 64 E8
Holt Coppice. L39 21 A7
Holt Cres. WN5 33 D4
Holt Hill. L41 & L42 66 E4
Holt Hill Terr. L41 & L42 66 E5
Holt La. Liverpool L27 70 E6
Holt La. Liverpool L27 70 E7
Holt La. Rainhill L35 57 A5
Holt Rd. Birkenhead L41 & L42 66 E4
Holt Rd. Liverpool L7 53 C2
Holt St. WN5 25 D5
Holtswell Cl. WA3 36 E1
Holwood Gdns. L37 9 D4
Holy Angel's Prim Schs. L32 29 D3
Holy Cross Cl. 5 L3 52 D3
Holy Cross RC Mid Sch. L41 50 E1
Holy Cross RC Prim Sch. WA10 44 B4
Holy Cross RC Prim Sch. L41 50 E1
Holy Cross & St Mary's Mix Inf Sch. L3 52 D3
Holy Family High Sch. L23 27 A6
Holy Family RC Prim Sch. Cronton WA8 72 D5
Holy Family RC Prim Sch. Liverpool L25 70 D1
Holy Family RC Prim Sch. Southport PR9 4 E7
Holy Name RC Prim Sch. L10 39 E7
Holy Rosary RC Prim Sch. Litherland L10 28 C3
Holy Rosary RC Prim Sch. Litherland L10 28 D3
Holy Trinity CE Prim Sch. Formby L37 9 F3
Holy Trinity CE Prim Sch. Southport PR9 4 C7
Holy Trinity RC Prim Sch. L19 81 D5
Holyhead Cl. WA5 60 D3
Holyrood. L23 26 A4
Holyrood Ave. WA8 73 A4
Holywell Cl. Neston L64 86 B1
Holywell Cl. St Helens WA9 58 D6
Home Farm Cl. L49 65 C2
Home Farm Rd. Birkenhead L49 65 C2
Home Farm Rd. Knowsley L34 41 D2
Homechase Hse. PR8 3 F4
Homedove House. 1 L23 26 C4
Homer Rd. L34 41 C3
Homerton Rd. L6 53 D3
Homesands House. PR9 4 D8
Homestall Rd. L11 40 A2
Homestead Ave. Haydock WA11 45 E6
Homestead Ave. Litherland L30 28 B3
Homestead Cl. L36 56 A3
Homestead Mews. L48 63 B2
Honey Hall Rd. L26 82 E6
Honey St. L35 57 C7
Honey's Green La. L12 54 D5
Honey's Green Lane Prec. L14 54 D4
Honeys Green Cl. L12 54 D5
Honeysuckle Cl. Liverpool L26 70 D2
Honeysuckle Cl. Widnes WA8 73 B4
Honeysuckle Dr. L9 39 B3
Honister Ave. St Helens WA11 44 C8
Honister Ave. Warrington WA2 61 C2
Honister Cl. L27 71 A3
Honister Wlk. L27 71 A3
Honiston Ave. L35 57 B4
Honiton Rd. L17 68 E1
Honiton Way. WA5 74 E4
Hood Rd. WA8 72 F1
Hood St. Bootle L20 38 A5
Hood St. Liverpool L1 52 D2
Hood St. Wallasey L44 51 D3
Hoole Rd. L49 65 B3
Hoose Ct. L47 63 C7
Hooton Gn. L66 89 B2
Hooton La. L65 & L66 89 B1
Hooton Rd. Bebington L64 & L66 88 D1
Hooton Rd. Liverpool L9 39 B7
Hooton Sta. L66 88 D1
Hooton Way. L66 89 A2
Hope Pk. L16 69 D6
Hope Pl. L1 & L7 67 E8
Hope Sq. PR9 4 D7
Hope St.Ashton-in-M WN4 35 D5
Hope St. Birkenhead L41 66 D7
Hope St. Liverpool L1 ,L3,L69, L7 & L8 67 F8
Hope St. Newton-le-W WA12 46 B3
Hope St. Prescot L34 56 D6
Hope St. Southport PR9 4 C7
Hope St. Wallasey L45 51 B8
Hope Way. 8 L8 67 F8
Hopfield Rd. Birkenhead L46 64 F8
Hopfield Rd. Birkenhead L46 65 A8
Hopkins Cl. WA10 43 D4
Hopwood Cres. WA11 32 A5
Hopwood St. Liverpool L5 52 C5
Hopwood St. Liverpool L5 52 D5
Horace St. WA10 43 E4
Horatio St. 5 L41 66 D6
Hornbeam Cl. Birkenhead L46 64 B8
Hornbeam Cl. St Helens WA11 44 F5
Hornbeam Rd. Liverpool L9 39 C3
Hornbeam Rd. Liverpool L26 83 A7
Hornby Ave. Bebington L62 79 D1
Hornby Ave. Bootle L20 38 B5
Hornby Bvd. L20 & L21 38 B6
Hornby Chase. L31 28 D7
Hornby Cl. L9 38 F4
Hornby Cres. WA9 58 D4
Hornby Ct. L62 79 D1
Hornby Flats. L21 38 B6
Hornby La. Liverpool L16 & L18 69 D5
Hornby La. Winwick WA2 61 A6
Hornby Pk. L18 69 D5
Hornby Pl. L9 39 A5
Hornby Rd. Bebington L62 79 C1
Hornby Rd. Bootle L20 38 B5
Hornby Rd. Bootle L20 38 C4
Hornby Rd. Bootle L9 38 F5
Hornby Rd. Southport PR9 2 A4
Hornby St. Birkenhead L41 66 F6
Hornby St. Bootle L21 38 A6
Hornby St. Crosby L23 26 E4
Hornby Wlk. L5 52 C4
Horncastle Cl. WA3 47 F8
Horne St. L6 53 B4
Hornhouse La. L33 41 C7
Hornsey Rd. L4 53 B7
Hornspit La. L11 & L12 54 A8
Horridge Ave. WA12 46 C5
Horringford Rd. L19 80 F8
Horrocks Ave. L19 81 D6
Horrocks Cl. L36 55 D4
Horrocks Rd. L36 55 D3
Horseman Pl. L44 51 E2
Horseshoe Cres. WA2 61 E3
Horsfall Gr. L8 67 E4
Horsfall St. L8 67 E4
Horwood Ave. L35 57 B4
Hoscote Pk. L48 63 A2
Hose Side Rd. L45 51 A7
Hospital St. WA10 44 B4
Hostock Cl. L35 56 D2
Hotel St. WA12 46 B3
Hotham St. L3 52 E2
Hothfield Rd. L44 51 D3
Hotspur St. L20 52 C8
Hough Green Rd. WA8 72 B3
Hough Green Sta. WA8 72 A2
Houghton Cl. WA12 46 B3
Houghton Croft. WA8 72 C5
Houghton Ct. L49 65 B3
Houghton La. 12 L1 52 D1
Houghton Rd. L49 65 B3
Houghton St. Liverpool L1 52 D1
Houghton St. Newton-le-W WA12 46 B3
Houghton St. Prescot L34 56 D6
Houghton St. Rainhill L35 57 C3
Houghton St. Widnes WA8 73 D2
Houghton Way. 15 L1 52 D1
Houghton's La. Knowsley WA10 & WA11 42 F6
Houghton's La. Skelmersdale WN8 16 C1
Houghtons Rd. WN8 16 B3
Houghwood Grange. WN4 34 F3
Hougoumont Ave. L22 26 E1
Hougoumont Gr. L22 26 E1
Houlding St. 6 L4 53 A6
Houlston Rd. L32 29 B2
Houlston Wlk. L32 29 B2
Houlton St. 1 L7 53 C2
Hoverty Prec. WA12 46 B1
Howard Ave. L62 88 D8
Howard Cl. Litherland L21 27 C2
Howard Cl. Maghull L31 20 F1
Howard Ct. Neston L64 86 F1
Howard Ct. Southport PR9 1 D1
Howard Dr. L19 81 A7
Howard Florey Ave. L30 27 F4
Howard St. WA10 & WA9 57 D8
Howard's La. WA10 42 F4
Howards La. WN5 25 F7
Howards Rd. L61 77 B6
Howbeck Cl. L43 65 F6
Howbeck Ct. L43 65 F5
Howbeck Dr. L43 65 F6
Howbeck Rd. L43 65 F5
Howden Dr. L36 55 A3
Howe St. L20 38 B1
Howell Dr. L49 64 D2
Howell Rd. L62 79 A7
Howells Cl. L31 20 D2
Howson Rd. WA2 61 C3
Howson St. Birkenhead L42 66 F2
Hoylake Cottage Hospl. L47 63 C8
Hoylake Gr. WA9 58 C4
Hoylake Holy Trinity CE Sch. L47 63 C7
Hoylake Rd. Birkenhead L46 64 D8
Hoylake Rd. Wallasey L46 49 F1
Hoylake Rd. Wallasey L41 & L43 50 D2
Hoylake Sta. L47 63 B6
Hoyle Rd. L47 63 C8
Huddleston Rd. L15 54 B1
Huddlestone Cl. L49 65 C3
Hudson Cty Prim Sch. L31 28 D6
Hudson Rd. Maghull L31 28 D7
Hudson Rd. Wallasey L46 50 A4
Hugh Baird Coll F Ed. Bootle L20 38 C2
Hugh Baird Coll F Ed. Bootle L21 38 C8
Hughenden Rd. L13 53 F5
Hughes Ave. Prescot L35 56 D4
Hughes Ave. Warrington WA2 61 D2
Hughes Cl. L7 53 C1
Hughes Dr. L20 38 E6
Hughes La. L43 66 B3
Hughes Pl. WA2 61 D2
Hughes St. Liverpool L6 53 A4
Hughes St. Liverpool L19 81 C5
Hughes St. St Helens WA9 58 D8
Hughestead Gr. L19 81 B6
Hughson St. L8 67 E5
Hulme St. PR8 4 A7
Hulmewood. L63 79 A7
Hulton Ave. L35 56 F4
Humber Cl. Liverpool L4 52 E8
Humber Cl. Widnes WA8 73 F3
Humber Cres. WA9 58 C6
Humber Rd. WA2 61 E2
Humber St. L41 50 F1
Hume Ct. L47 63 C8
Hummocks Dr. L48 75 D6
Humphrey St. L20 38 D6
Humphreys Hey. L23 27 B5
Huncote Ave. WA11 44 D6
Hunslett Rd. L9 39 B6
Hunstanton Cl. L49 65 A7
Hunt Rd. Haydock WA11 45 E6
Hunt Rd. Maghull L31 20 D1
Hunt's Cross Sta. L25 82 C7
Hunter Ave. WA2 61 B3
Hunter St. Liverpool L3 52 D2
Hunter St. St Helens WA9 44 C2
Hunter's La. L15 69 A7
Huntingdon Cl. L46 64 B8
Huntingdon Gr. L31 20 C4
Huntley Ave. WA9 58 C7
Huntley Gr. WA9 58 C7
Huntly Rd. L6 53 C3
Hunts Cross Ave. Liverpool L25 70 B3
Hunts Cross Ave. Liverpool L25 70 C2
Hunts Cross Jun Mix & Inf Sch. L25 82 C6
Hunts Cross Sh Ctr The. L24 82 A6
Huntsman Wood. L12 54 E8
Hurlingham Rd. L4 39 C2
Hurlston Dr. L39 13 E7
Hurrell Rd. L41 50 D1
Hursley Rd. L9 39 E4
Hurst Bank. L63 78 F8
Hurst Gdns. L13 54 A2
Hurst Park Cl. L36 56 A4
Hurst Park Dr. L36 56 A4
Hurst Rd. L31 28 E7
Hurst Sch. WA10 43 E6
Hurst St. Liverpool L13 54 A2
Hurst St. Liverpool L1 & L72 67 C8
Hurst's La. L39 22 B2
Hurstlyn Rd. L18 69 C1
Huskisson St. L1 & L7 & L8 67 F7
Hutchinson St. Liverpool L6 53 A3
Hutchinson St. Widnes WA8 84 F6
Hutchinson Wlk. L6 53 A3
Huttfield Rd. L24 83 A4
Hutton Ct. WN8 15 D1
Hutton Rd. WN8 15 D1
Hutton Way. L39 13 E5
Huxley Cl. L46 64 B8
Huxley St. L13 53 D7
Huyton Ave. WA10 43 E6
Huyton Church Rd. L36 55 F2
Huyton Coll. L36 55 E2
Huyton Hey Rd. L36 55 F2
Huyton House Cl. L36 55 B4
Huyton House Rd. L36 55 B4
Huyton La. Huyton-w-R L36 55 F3
Huyton La. Huyton-w-R L34 & L36 56 A5
Huyton Sta. L36 55 E2
Huyton with Roby CE (VA) Sch. L36 55 D3
Hyacinth Cl. WA11 45 F6
Hyde Rd. L22 26 D1
Hyde's Brow. WA11 32 A8
Hydro Ave. L48 63 B1
Hygeia St. L6 53 B4
Hylton Ave. L44 51 A4
Hylton Rd. L19 81 D8
Hyslop St. L8 67 E6
Hythe Ave. L21 38 C8
Hythe Cl. PR8 4 E3
Hythedale Cl. L17 68 C2

Ibbotson's La. L17 & L18 68 E4
Ibstock Rd. L20 38 B5
Iffley Cl. L49 64 D5
Ikin Cl. L43 50 C1
Ilchester Rd. Liverpool L16 54 E1
Ilchester Rd. Wallasey L41 50 F1
Ilchester Rd. Wallasey L44 51 D3
Ilex Ave. WA2 61 B7
Ilford Ave. Crosby L23 26 D5
Ilford Ave. Wallasey L44 51 B3
Ilford St. L3 52 F2
Ilfracombe Rd. WA9 58 C5
Iliad St. L5 52 E4
Ilkley Ave. PR9 2 C6
Ilkley Wlk. L24 82 D4
Ilsley Cl. L49 64 F4
Imber Rd. L32 40 F8
Imison St. L4 38 F3
Imison Way. L4 38 E3
Imperial Ave. L45 51 C6
Imrie St. L4 38 F2
Ince Ave. Bebington L62 88 E3
Ince Ave. Bootle L21 38 B7
Ince Ave. Crosby L23 26 D5
Ince Ave. Liverpool L4 53 B8
Ince Cl. L43 65 F4
Ince Cres. L37 9 D3
Ince Gr. L43 65 F4
Ince La. L23 & L38 27 A8
Ince Rd. L23 27 A7
Incemore Rd. L18 & L19 69 B1
Inchcape Rd. Liverpool L16 54 E1
Inchcape Rd. Wallasey L45 50 D5
Inchfield. WN8 16 B2
Index St. L4 38 F1
Ingestre Ct. L43 66 A3
Ingestre Rd. L43 66 A3
Ingham Ave. WA12 46 B1
Ingham Rd. WA8 72 F4
Ingle Gn. L23 26 A5
Ingleborough Rd. L42 66 D2
Ingleby Rd. Bebington L62 79 B8
Ingleby Rd. Wallasey L44 51 A3
Ingledene Rd. L18 69 D5

Inglegreen. L60 86 B8
Ingleholme Gdns. L34 57 A7
Ingleholme Rd. L18 & L19 69 A1
Inglemere Rd. L42 66 E2
Inglemoss Dr. WA11 32 C1
Inglenook Rd. WA5 74 F4
Ingleton Cl. L49 64 D4
Ingleton Dr. WA11 33 B1
Ingleton Gn. L32 40 F8
Ingleton Rd. Kirkby L32 40 F8
Ingleton Rd. 3 Liverpool L18 68 F5
Ingleton Rd. Southport PR8 4 E3
Inglewhite. WN8 16 A2
Inglewood. L12 41 A2
Inglewood Ave. L46 64 D7
Inglewood Rd. WA11 43 C8
Inglis Rd. L9 39 B7
Ingoe Cl. L32 29 B1
Ingoe La. L32 40 B8
Ingram. WN8 16 B1
Ingrave Rd. L4 39 C2
Ingrow Rd. 9 L6 & L7 53 B3
Inigo Rd. L13 54 B4
Inley Cl. L63 79 A2
Inley Rd. L63 79 A2
Inman Ave. WA9 45 B2
Inman Rd. Birkenhead L49 64 E6
Inman Rd. Bootle L21 38 B7
Inner Central Rd. L24 82 F5
Inner Forum. L11 39 E2
Inner South Rd. L24 82 F4
Inner West Rd. L24 82 E5
Insall Rd. Liverpool L13 54 B1
Insall Rd. Warrington WA2 61 F2
Inskip. WN8 16 A2
Inskip Rd. PR9 2 A4
Intake La. Bickerstaffe L39 & WA11 23 B2
Intake La. Maghull L39 19 E8
Interchange Motorway Est. L36 56 A1
Inveresk Ct. L43 65 E6
Invincible Cl. L30 38 E8
Invincible Way. L10 40 C6
Inwood Rd. L19 81 D7
Iona Cl. L12 41 A3
Ionic Rd. L13 54 A4
Ionic St. Birkenhead L42 66 F2
Ionic St. Seaforth L21 37 F7
Irby Ave. L44 51 A4
Irby Prim Sch. L61 76 E7
Irby Rd. Heswall L60 & L61 76 E3
Irby Rd. Liverpool L4 53 C8
Irbyside Rd. L48 64 B1
Ireland Rd. Hale L24 83 E1
Ireland Rd. Haydock WA11 45 C6
Ireland St. WA8 73 D2
Irene Ave. WA11 44 C7
Irene Rd. L16 69 C6
Ireton St. L4 38 F2
Iris Ave. L41 65 F7
Iris Cl. WA8 72 C2
Irlam Dr. L32 29 E2
Irlam House. L20 38 B3
Irlam Pl. L20 38 B4
Irlam Rd. L20 38 B4
Ironside Rd. L36 55 D3
Irton Rd. PR9 4 E8
Irvin Ave. PR9 2 C5
Irvine Rd. L42 66 D2
Irvine St. L7 53 A1
Irving Cl. L9 39 C8
Irving St. PR8 1 B1
Irwell. WN8 16 A3
Irwell Cl. L17 68 E3
Irwell House. L17 68 E3
Irwell La. L17 68 E3
Irwell Rd. WN5 25 F7
Irwell St. L3 52 C1
Irwin Rd. WA9 58 C7
Isaac St. L8 67 F4
Isabel Gr. L13 53 E7
Isherwood Cl. WA2 61 F3
Island Pl. L19 81 C6
Island Rd. L19 81 C6
Island Rd S. L19 81 D6
Islands Brow. WA11 44 C6
Islington. Crosby L23 26 D4
Islington. Liverpool L3 52 E2
Islington Sq. L3 52 F2
Islip Cl. L61 76 D7
Ismay Dr. L44 51 D5
Ismay Rd. L21 38 B7
Ismay St. L4 38 F1
Ivanhoe Ave. WA3 36 D1
Ivanhoe Rd. Crosby L23 26 C4
Ivanhoe Rd. Liverpool L17 68 C4
Ivatt Way. L7 53 C1
Iver Cl. WA8 72 C6
Ivernia Rd. L4 39 B2
Ivor Rd. L44 51 C5
Ivory Dr. L33 29 E5
Ivy Ave. Bebington L63 78 E5
Ivy Ave. Liverpool L19 81 B7
Ivy Ave. Newton-le-W WA12 46 C2
Ivy Ct. WA9 44 C3
Ivy Farm Ct. L24 83 D1
Ivy Farm Rd. L35 57 B4
Ivy House Rd. WA3 36 D1
Ivy La. L46 49 E1
Ivy Leigh. L13 53 E5
Ivy Rd. WA3 47 B8
Ivy St. Ashton-in-M WN4 35 B3
Ivy St. Birkenhead L41 66 F6
Ivy St. Southport PR8 4 D6
Ivybridge. WN8 16 B2
Ivydale. WN8 16 B2
Ivydale Rd. Birkenhead L42 66 E3
Ivydale Rd. Liverpool L9 39 B4
Ivydale Rd. Liverpool L18 69 A4
Ivyhurst Cl. L19 80 F8

Jack McBain Ct. L3 52 C4
Jack's Brow. L34 41 E2
Jacksfield Way. L19 80 F7
Jackson Cl. Bebington L63 78 F8
Jackson Cl. Haskayne L39 11 F5
Jackson Cl. Rainhill L35 57 D1
Jackson St. Birkenhead L41 66 E5
Jackson St. Burtonwood WA5 59 E6
Jackson St. Haydock WA11 45 A7
Jackson St. Liverpool L19 81 C6
Jackson St. St Helens WA9 44 C2
Jacob St. L8 67 F4
Jacqueline Ct. L36 55 C2
Jacqueline Dr. L36 56 A4
Jade Cl. Kirkby L33 30 A3
Jamaica St. L1 & L72 & L8 67 D7
James Clarke St. L5 52 C4
James Ct. L25 70 B2
James Ct Apartments. L25 70 B2
James Gr. WA10 43 E2
James Holt Ave. L32 29 D2
James Hopkins Way. L4 52 D7
James Larkin Way. L4 & L5 52 D7
James Rd. Haydock WA11 45 F7
James Rd. Liverpool L25 70 B2
James St. Ashton-in-M WN2 35 E7
James St. Birkenhead L43 66 C4
James St. Liverpool L1 & L2 & L3 52 C1
James St. Liverpool L19 81 C6
James St. St Helens WA9 58 D3
James St. 7 Wallasey L44 51 E2
James Street Sta. L2 52 C1
Jamesbrook Cl. L41 66 A8
Jamieson Ave. L23 27 A4
Jamieson Rd. L15 68 E7
Jane St. WA9 58 F7
Jane's Brook Rd. PR8 4 E4
Janet St. L7 53 B1
Jarrett Rd. L33 30 A4
Jarrett Wlk. L33 30 A4
Jarrow Cl. L43 66 B4
Jasmine Cl. Birkenhead L46 & L49 64 D7
Jasmine Cl. Liverpool L5 52 F4
Jasmine Ct. L36 55 F5
Jasmine Mews. L8 68 A3
Jason St. L5 52 E6
Jason Wlk. L5 52 E6
Java Rd. L4 39 D1
Jean Wlk. L10 40 B6
Jedburgh Dr. L33 29 D6
Jeffereys Cres. L36 55 B2
Jeffereys Dr. L36 55 A2
Jeffreys Dr. L49 64 D5
Jellicoe Cl. L48 75 D6
Jenkinson St. L3 52 E3
Jennet Hey. WN4 34 F6
Jericho Cl. L17 68 D2
Jericho Farm Cl. L17 68 D1
Jericho Farm Wlk. L17 68 D1
Jericho La. L17 68 D1
Jermyn St. L8 68 B6
Jerningham Rd. L11 39 D3
Jersey Ave. L21 27 B1
Jersey Cl. L20 38 C3
Jersey St. Bootle L20 38 C3
Jersey St. St Helens WA9 58 C3
Jesmond St. L15 68 D8
Jessamine Rd. L42 66 E3
Jeudwine Cl. L25 70 B1
Joan Ave. Birkenhead L46 64 D8
Joan Ave. Birkenhead L49 64 E4
Jocelyn Cl. L63 79 A3
John Bagot Cl. L5 52 E5
John F Kennedy Hts. L3 52 E4
John Hunter Way. L30 27 F3
John Lennon Dr. L6 53 B3
John Middleton Cl. L24 83 E2
John Moores Cl. L7 68 A8
John Moores Univ. Liverpool L3 52 C2
John Moores Univ. Liverpool L3 52 D2
John Moores Univ. Liverpool L3 52 D3
John Moores Univ. Liverpool L3 52 E1
John St. Ashton-in-M WN4 35 D5
John St. Birkenhead L41 & L72 66 F7
John St. Golborne WA3 47 A8
John St. Liverpool L3 52 F3
John St. St Helens WA10 44 A4
Johns Ave. WA11 45 E7
Johnson Ave. Newton-le-W WA12 46 B5
Johnson Ave. Prescot L35 56 D4
Johnson Gr. L14 54 E5
Johnson Rd. L43 65 F1
Johnson St. Liverpool L1 & L2 & L3 52 D2
Johnson St. Southport PR8 & PR9 4 B8
Johnson St. St Helens WA9 44 C4
Johnson Wlk. 10 L7 53 C1
Johnson's La. WA8 73 E1
Johnston Ave. L20 38 E6
Jones Farm Rd. L25 70 C4
Jones St. L3 52 E1
Jonson Rd. L64 86 E1
Jonville Rd. L9 39 C7
Jordan St. L1 & L72 67 D7
Joseph Lister Cl. L30 27 F3
Joseph St. St Helens WA9 58 E7
Joseph St. Widnes WA8 73 C2
Joseph Williams Prim Sch. L25 70 C6
Joy La. Burtonwood WA5 59 E4
Joy La. St Helens WA9 58 E2
Joyce Wlk. L10 40 C7
Jubilee Ave. Liverpool L14 54 D1
Jubilee Ave. Ormskirk L39 13 F6
Jubilee Ave. Orrell WN5 25 D4
Jubilee Ave. Warrington WA5 74 E4
Jubilee Cres. Bebington L62 79 B5
Jubilee Cres. Haydock WA11 45 F7
Jubilee Dr. Litherland L30 28 A1
Jubilee Dr. Liverpool L7 53 B2
Jubilee Dr. Prescot L35 56 D2
Jubilee Dr. Skelmersdale WN8 23 E8
Jubilee Dr. West Kirby L48 63 B3
Jubilee Gr. L44 51 D3
Jubilee Rd. Bootle L21 38 B7
Jubilee Rd. Crosby L22 & L23 26 C3
Jubilee Rd. Formby L37 9 D1
Jubilee Way. WA8 72 E1
Jubits La. WA8 & WA9 & L35 58 B2
Juddfield St. WA11 45 A7
Judges Dr. L6 53 C4
Judges Way. L6 53 C4
Julian Way. WA8 72 F4
Julie Gr. L14 54 F5
Juliet Ave. L63 78 E7
Juliet Gdns. L63 78 E7
July Rd. L6 53 D5
July St. L20 38 C5
Junction La. Newton-le-W WA12 46 B3
Junction La. St Helens WA9 58 F7
Junction Rd. WA11 31 E8
June Ave. L62 88 E8
June Rd. L6 53 D5
June St. L20 38 C4
Juniper Cl. Birkenhead L49 64 C2
Juniper Cl. Huyton-w-R L28 55 B8
Juniper Cl. St Helens WA10 43 D4
Juniper Gdns. L23 27 B6
Juniper St. L20 52 C8
Jupiter Cl. L6 53 B5
Jurby Ct. WA2 61 F1
Justin Way. L35 57 B5
Juvenal Pl. L3 52 E4
Juvenal St. L3 52 D4

Kaigh Ave. L23 26 D5
Kale Cl. L48 63 B1
Karan Way. L31 29 B3
Karen Cl. WA5 60 A6
Karonga Rd. L10 & L9 39 F7
Karonga Way. L10 39 F7
Karslake Rd. Liverpool L18 68 F5
Karslake Rd. Wallasey L44 51 D3
Katherine Wlk. L10 40 C7
Kearsley Cl. L4 52 E7
Kearsley St. L4 52 E7
Keates St. WA9 58 F8
Keats Ave. Orrell WN5 25 D1
Keats Ave. Prescot L35 56 F3
Keats Gn. L36 56 A1
Keats Gr. WA2 61 C2
Keats House. L62 79 A7
Keats St. L20 38 B5
Keble Dr. Litherland L10 28 C3
Keble Dr. Wallasey L45 50 D6
Keble Rd. L20 38 C2
Keble St. L6 & L7 53 A3
Kedleston St. L8 68 A4
Keegan Dr. L44 51 E2
Keele Cl. L43 50 C2
Keenan Dr. L20 38 E5
Keene Ct. L30 27 D4
Keepers La. L63 78 B5
Keighley Ave. L45 50 E5
Keightley St. L41 66 D7
Keir Hardie Ave. L20 38 E5
Keith Ave. 5 Liverpool L4 39 A1
Keith Ave. Warrington WA5 74 E6
Keith Ct. 4 L4 38 F1
Keith Dr. L63 88 D5
Kelbrook Cl. WA9 58 D6
Kelday Cl. L32 & L33 29 E2
Kelkbeck Cl. L31 20 F2
Kellet's Pl. L42 66 F3
Kellett Rd. L46 50 B3
Kellitt Rd. L15 68 E7
Kelly Dr. L20 38 E5
Kelly St. L34 56 E6
Kelmscott Dr. L44 50 E4
Kelsall Ave. Bebington L62 88 F3
Kelsall Ave. St Helens WA9 58 B4
Kelsall Cl. Bebington L62 88 E3
Kelsall Cl. Birkenhead L43 65 F3
Kelsall Cl. Widnes WA8 72 D1
Kelso Cl. L33 29 D6
Kelso Rd. L6 & L7 53 C3
Kelton Gr. L17 68 E2
Kelvin Cl. WN4 34 D4
Kelvin Gr. L8 68 A6
Kelvin Rd. Birkenhead L41 66 E4
Kelvin Rd. Wallasey L41 & L44 51 E1
Kelvinside. Crosby L23 26 F3
Kelvinside. Wallasey L44 51 E1
Kemberton Dr. WA8 73 A5
Kemble St. Liverpool L7 53 B2
Kemble St. Prescot L34 56 D6
Kemlyn Rd. L4 & L5 53 A7
Kempsell Way. L26 83 A7
Kempsell Wlk. L26 83 A7
Kempsey Gr. WA9 57 E7
Kempson Terr. L63 78 F4
Kempston St. L3 52 E2
Kempton Cl. Huyton-w-R L36 55 D1
Kempton Cl. Newton-le-W WA12 46 D5
Kempton Park Fold. PR8 4 F3
Kempton Park Rd. L10 28 E2
Kempton Rd. Bebington L62 79 B8
Kempton Rd. Liverpool L15 68 D8
Kemsley Rd. L14 54 F4
Kenbury Cl. L33 30 A4
Kenbury Rd. L33 30 A4
Kendal Ave. WA2 61 C2
Kendal Cl. Bebington L63 78 F6
Kendal Cl. Rainford WA11 23 F2
Kendal Dr. Maghull L31 20 E2
Kendal Dr. Rainford WA11 23 F2
Kendal Dr. Rainhill L35 57 A4
Kendal Dr. St Helens WA11 44 B8
Kendal Gr. WN4 35 B4
Kendal Mount. WA11 44 C8
Kendal Pk. L12 54 D6
Kendal Rd. Liverpool L16 69 E7
Kendal Rd. Wallasey L44 51 A2
Kendal Rd. Widnes WA8 72 C1
Kendal St. 15 L41 66 E6
Kendal Way. PR8 7 B3
Kendrick's Cross. L35 57 C3
Kendricks Fold. L35 57 B3
Kenilworth Cl. L25 69 E3
Kenilworth Dr. L61 76 F5
Kenilworth Gdns. Birkenhead L49 64 E6
Kenilworth Gdns. Newton-le-W WA12 46 C1
Kenilworth Rd. Crosby L23 26 C3
Kenilworth Rd. Golborne WA3 47 E7
Kenilworth Rd. Liverpool L16 69 D7
Kenilworth Rd. Southport PR8 7 B4
Kenilworth Rd. Wallasey L44 51 E3
Kenilworth St. L20 38 B3
Kenilworth Way. L25 69 E3
Kenley Ave. WA8 72 D5
Kenley Cl. L6 53 C4
Kenmare Rd. L15 68 E6
Kenmay Way. L33 30 A3
Kenmore Gr. WN4 34 D4
Kenmore Rd. L43 65 E1
Kennelwood Ave. L33 29 F3
Kennessee Cl. L31 28 E8
Kennet Rd. Bebington L63 78 D5
Kennet Rd. Haydock WA11 45 C6
Kenneth Cl. L30 27 E3
Kenneth Rd. WA8 84 C8
Kennford Rd. L11 40 C5
Kensington. L6 & L7 53 B2
Kensington Ave. WA9 58 C7
Kensington Gdns. L46 64 E8
Kensington Ind Pk. PR9 4 C6
Kensington Jun Sch. L7 53 B2
Kensington Rd. Formby L37 9 E1
Kensington Rd. Southport PR9 4 C6
Kensington St. L6 & L7 53 A2
Kent Ave. Bootle L21 38 C8
Kent Ave. Formby L37 10 A1
Kent Cl. Bebington L63 88 B8
Kent Cl. Bootle L20 38 D4
Kent Rd. Formby L37 10 A1
Kent Rd. Southport PR8 4 A4
Kent Rd. St Helens WA9 58 D7
Kent Rd. Wallasey L44 51 A3
Kent St. Birkenhead L43 66 B4
Kent St. Liverpool L1 & L72 67 D8
Kent St. Widnes WA8 73 B1
Kent Way. WA12 46 B1
Kentmere Ave. WA11 33 C1
Kentmere Dr. L61 76 F4
Kentmere Pl. WA2 61 A3
Kenton Cl. L37 9 F6
Kenton Rd. L26 83 A7
Kents Bank. L12 40 C1
Kenview Cl. WA8 84 A4
Kenway. WA11 32 A6
Kenworthys Flats. PR8 4 B8
Kenwright Cres. WA9 58 D8
Kenwyn Rd. L45 51 B5
Kenyon Ave. WA5 74 E5
Kenyon La. Golborne WA3 47 F3
Kenyon La. Golborne WA3 47 F5
Kenyon Rd. L15 69 A5
Kenyon's La. Formby L37 10 A3
Kenyon's La. Haydock WA11 45 F8
Kenyons La. L31 20 E3
Kepler St. Bootle L21 38 A6
Kepler St. Liverpool L5 52 F4
Keppel St. L20 38 B1
Kerfoot's La. WN8 23 C8
Kerr Gr. WA9 44 E3
Kerris Cl. L17 68 C2
Kerrysdale Cl. 4 WA9 58 D7
Kersey Rd. L32 40 F8
Kersey Wlk. L32 40 F8
Kershaw Ave. L23 & L70 26 F3
Kershaw St. WA8 72 D1
Kershaw Way. WA12 46 C5
Kerslake Way. L38 18 A4
Kerswell Cl. WA9 58 D6
Kestral Dene. L10 40 A6
Kestral Gr. L26 70 D2
Kestrel Ave. L49 64 D6
Kestrel Cl. Birkenhead L49 64 D6
Kestrel Cl. St Helens WA11 44 B6
Kestrel Ct. PR9 4 D7
Kestrel Dr. WN4 35 C6
Kestrel Mews. WN8 16 C4
Kestrel Pk. WN8 16 C4
Kestrel Rd. Birkenhead L46 64 C8
Kestrel Rd. Heswall L60 86 C7
Keswick Ave. Bebington L63 88 C4
Keswick Ave. Warrington WA2 61 C2
Keswick Cl. Maghull L31 20 E2
Keswick Cl. Southport PR8 7 C3
Keswick Cl. Widnes WA8 72 C1
Keswick Cres. WA2 61 C2
Keswick Dr. L21 & L30 38 E8
Keswick Pl. L43 65 D8
Keswick Rd. Liverpool L18 69 D2
Keswick Rd. St Helens WA10 43 E5
Keswick Rd. Wallasey L45 50 E7
Keswick Villas. L16 70 A8
Keswick Way. Liverpool L16 70 A8
Keswick Way. Rainford WA11 23 F2
Kettering Rd. PR8 7 B5
Kevelioc Cl. L63 78 F3
Kew Rd. Formby L37 9 D1
Kew Rd. Southport PR8 4 B3
Kew St. L5 52 D5
Kew Woods Cty Prim Sch. PR8 4 F3
Keybank Rd. L12 54 A8
Kiddman St. L4 38 F3
Kidstone Cl. 6 WA9 58 D7

Kilbuck La. WA11 46 A8
Kilburn Ave. Ashton-in-M WN4 35 D4
Kilburn Ave. Bebington L62 88 E6
Kilburn Gr. WA9 57 E7
Kilburn Rd. WN5 & WN8 25 C5
Kilburn St. L21 38 B6
Kildale Cl. L31 20 C2
Kildare Cl. L24 83 D2
Kildonan Rd. L17 68 E2
Kilford Cl. WA5 60 E2
Kilgarth Sch. L41 66 B8
Kilgraston Gdns. L17 & L19 68 F1
Killarney Gr. L44 51 A3
Killarney Rd. L13 54 B3
Killester Rd. L25 70 B4
Killington Way. L4 52 E8
Kilmalcolm Cl. L43 65 F4
Kilmore Cl. L9 39 C8
Kilmory Ave. L25 70 C2
Kiln Cl. WA10 43 C5
Kiln Hey. L12 54 C5
Kiln La. Skelmersdale WN8 15 E1
Kiln La. St Helens WA10 43 C5
Kiln Rd. L49 65 A3
Kilnyard Rd. L23 26 D4
Kilrea Cl. L11 53 F8
Kilrea Cl. Liverpool L11 & L13 53 F8
Kilrea Rd. Liverpool L11 & L13 53 E8
Kilrea Rd. Liverpool L11 & L13 53 F8
Kilsail Rd. 3 L32 41 A7
Kilsby Dr. WA8 73 E2
Kilshaw Rd. WA5 59 F6
Kilshaw St. L6 53 A4
Kilsyth Cl. WA2 61 F4
Kimberley Ave. Crosby L23 26 D3
Kimberley Ave. St Helens WA9 57 F7
Kimberley Cl. L8 68 A7
Kimberley Dr. L23 26 D3
Kimberley Pl. WN4 35 B3
Kimberley Rd. L45 51 B6
Kimberley St. L43 65 F8
Kindale Rd. L43 65 E1
Kinder Gr. WN4 34 F6
Kinder St. L6 52 F3
King Ave. L20 38 E5
King David High Sch The. L15 69 C7
King David Prim Sch The. L15 69 C7
King Edward Cl. L35 57 B4
King Edward Rd. Rainhill L35 57 B4
King Edward Rd. St Helens WA10 43 E6
King Edward St. L3 52 B2
King Edward's Dr. L62 79 B6
King George Cl. WN4 35 B3
King George Dr. L44 & L45 51 D6
King George Rd. WA11 46 A7
King George V Coll. PR8 4 E5
King George's Dr. L62 79 B6
King St. Birkenhead L42 67 A1
King St. Crosby L22 26 D1
King St. Liverpool L19 81 C4
King St. Newton-le-W WA12 46 B3
King St. Prescot L34 56 D6
King St. Southport PR8 4 A6
King St. St Helens WA10 43 F4
King St. Wallasey L44 51 D4
King's Ave. Golborne WA3 47 F7
King's Ave. Hoylake L47 63 D8
King's Brow. L63 78 D6
King's Ct. Bebington L63 78 D6
King's Ct. Birkenhead L43 66 B4
King's Dr. Heswall L61 76 F6
King's Dr. West Kirby L48 75 D8
King's Gap The. L47 63 A6
King's La. L63 & L42 78 E8
King's Moss La. WA11 32 F7
King's Par. Wallasey L45 37 A1
King's Par. Wallasey L45 50 E8
King's Rd. Ashton-in-M WN4 35 A5
King's Rd. Bebington L63 & L42 78 D7
King's Rd. Bootle L20 38 C1
King's Sq. L41 66 F6
Kingfield Rd. L9 38 F5
Kingfisher Cl. Kirkby L33 29 E6
Kingfisher Cl. Liverpool L27 70 F5
Kingfisher Ct. WN4 35 B6
Kingfisher Ct. Southport PR9 4 D8
Kingfisher Dr. WA11 44 B6
Kingfisher Gr. L12 40 F1
Kingfisher House. L13 54 A1
Kingfisher Pk. WN8 16 C4
Kingfisher Way. L49 64 D6
Kingham Cl. Liverpool L25 70 C2
Kingham Cl. Widnes WA8 73 D1
Kinglake Rd. L44 51 D5
Kinglake St. L7 53 B1
Kinglass Rd. L62 79 B3
Kings Cl. Bebington L63 78 D7
Kings Cl. Formby L37 9 E2
Kings Cl. Liverpool L17 68 C2
Kings Ct. Hoylake L47 63 A7
Kings Ct. Seaforth L21 37 F7
Kings Dock St. L1 & L72 67 D7
Kings Dr. Liverpool L25 70 B2
Kings Dr. Liverpool L27 70 D5
Kings Hey Dr. PR9 1 F1
Kings Mount. L41 & L43 66 C4
Kings Parade. L3 67 C7
Kings Pk. L21 37 F7
Kings Rd. Crosby L23 26 D4
Kings Rd. Formby L37 9 E2
Kings Rd. Golborne WA3 47 A7
Kings Rd. St Helens WA10 43 D2
Kings Wharf. L44 51 F1
Kings Wlk. L8 67 A1
Kingsbrook Way. L42 78 D8
Kingsbury. L48 63 D2
Kingsbury Cl. PR8 7 B4
Kingsbury Ct. WN8 16 C4
Kingscourt Rd. L12 54 C5
Kingsdale Ave. Birkenhead L42 66 D2
Kingsdale Ave. Rainhill L35 57 D3
Kingsdale Rd. Liverpool L18 69 A5
Kingsdale Rd. Warrington WA5 74 F7
Kingsdown Rd. Abram WN2 36 B7
Kingsdown Rd. Liverpool L11 40 B1
Kingsdown St. L41 66 E4
Kingsfield Rd. L31 28 C7
Kingsheath Ave. L14 54 F5
Kingsland Cres. L11 39 E3
Kingsland Rd. Birkenhead L42 & L43 66 C4
Kingsland Rd. Liverpool L11 39 E3
Kingsley Ave. L62 88 E3
Kingsley Cl. Heswall L61 77 A3
Kingsley Cl. Maghull L31 20 C5
Kingsley Rd. Liverpool L8 68 B7
Kingsley Rd. St Helens WA10 43 D6
Kingsley Rd. Wallasey L44 51 B3
Kingsley St. L41 66 A8
Kingsmead Dr. L25 82 B7
Kingsmead Gr. L43 65 F5
Kingsmead Rd. Birkenhead L43 65 F5
Kingsmead Rd. Wallasey L46 49 F2
Kingsmead Rd N. L43 65 F5
Kingsmead Rd S. L43 65 F5
Kingsmead Sch. L47 63 D8
Kingsnorth. L35 56 F2
Kingsthorne Pk. L24 & L25 82 C6
Kingsthorne Rd. L25 82 C6
Kingston Ave. WA5 74 E6
Kingston Cl. Birkenhead L46 64 E8
Kingston Cl. Liverpool L14 54 E5
Kingston Cres. PR9 2 C5
Kingsville Rd. L63 78 E5
Kingswalk. L48 63 C2
Kingsway. Bebington L63 78 D7
Kingsway. Crosby L22 & L23 26 E2
Kingsway. Heswall L60 86 C6
Kingsway. Huyton-w-R L36 55 D4
Kingsway. Newton-le-W WA12 46 C2
Kingsway. Prescot L34 & L35 56 E5
Kingsway. Southport PR8 4 A7
Kingsway. St Helens WA11 44 A8
Kingsway. Wallasey L45 51 A6
Kingsway. Widnes WA8 73 A1
Kingsway Entrance. L1 52 D2
Kingsway Ind Pk. L3 52 D4
Kingsway Par. L36 55 C4
Kingsway Prim Sch. L44 51 D2
Kingsway (Tunnel). L3 & L44 52 B3
Kingswell Cl. L7 68 B8
Kingswood Ave. Crosby L22 26 F2
Kingswood Ave. Liverpool L9 39 B7
Kingswood Bvd. L63 78 E8
Kingswood Ct. L33 29 F4
Kingswood Dr. L23 26 D3
Kingswood Rd. 3 Wallasey L44 51 C5
Kingswood Rd. Warrington WA5 60 A2
Kingswood Schs. PR8 3 F5
Kington Rd. L48 63 A3
Kinley Gdns. L20 38 E5
Kinloch Cl. L26 83 A7
Kinloch Way. L39 13 D6
Kinloss Rd. L49 64 C3
Kinmel Cl. Birkenhead L41 66 D7
Kinmel Cl. Liverpool L4 53 D8
Kinmel St. Liverpool L8 68 A5
Kinmel St. St Helens WA9 58 C8
Kinnaird Rd. L45 51 A6
Kinnaird St. L8 68 A3
Kinnerton Cl. L46 64 B8
Kinnock Pk. WA5 59 E6
Kinross Ave. WN4 34 C4
Kinross Cl. WA2 61 F4
Kinross Rd. Liverpool L10 39 F7
Kinross Rd. Seaforth L22 37 E8
Kinross Rd. Wallasey L45 50 D6
Kintbury St. WN2 35 F7
Kintore Cl. L63 88 C4
Kintore Dr. WA5 74 D6
Kintore Rd. L19 81 B7
Kipling Ave. 2 Birkenhead L42 66 F1
Kipling Ave. Huyton-w-R L36 71 A8
Kipling Ave. Warrington WA2 61 C1
Kipling Cres. WA8 84 F8
Kipling Gr. WA9 58 A3
Kipling St. L20 38 A5
Kirby Cl. L48 63 C1
Kirby Mount. L48 75 C8
Kirby Pk. L48 63 C1
Kirby Rd. L20 38 D6
Kirk Rd. L20 38 C6
Kirk St. L5 52 E6
Kirkacre Ave. WA12 60 C8
Kirkbridge Cl. L27 71 A4
Kirkbridge Lawn. L27 71 A4
Kirkbridge Wlk. L27 71 A4
Kirkby Bank Rd. L33 30 C2
Kirkby CE Prim Sch. L32 29 E2
Kirkby Municipal Golf Course. L10 40 A8
Kirkby Park Mansions. L48 63 C1
Kirkby Row. L32 29 D3
Kirkby Sta. L32 29 C3
Kirkcaldy Ave. WA5 74 D6
Kirkdale Gdns. WN8 25 A7
Kirkdale Prim Sch. L4 52 D8
Kirkdale Rd. L4 & L5 52 E6
Kirkdale Sta. L20 38 D1
Kirkdale Vale. L4 & L5 52 E7
Kirket Cl. L63 79 A4
Kirket La. L63 79 A4
Kirkfield Gr. L42 67 A1
Kirkham Ave. WA3 47 E6
Kirkham Rd. Southport PR9 2 A4
Kirkham Rd. Widnes WA8 73 C2
Kirkham St. WN2 36 B8
Kirklake Bank. L37 9 C2
Kirklake Rd. L37 9 D2
Kirkland Ave. L42 66 D2
Kirkland Cl. L9 38 F7
Kirkland Rd. L45 51 C8
Kirkland St. WA10 43 F4
Kirklands The. L48 63 C2
Kirklees Rd. PR8 3 F1
Kirkmaiden Rd. L19 81 B8
Kirkman Fold. L35 57 B3
Kirkmore Rd. L18 69 A2
Kirkmount. L49 65 A5
Kirkside Cl. L11 & L12 40 D3
Kirkstall Dr. L37 10 B2
Kirkstall Rd. PR8 3 F2
Kirkstone Ave. St Helens WA11 44 C8
Kirkstone Ave. Warrington WA2 61 C2
Kirkstone Rd N. L21 27 C1
Kirkstone Rd S. L21 & L30 38 D8
Kirkstone Rd W. L21 27 B2
Kirkway. Bebington L63 78 D7
Kirkway. Birkenhead L49 64 E4
Kirkway. Birkenhead L49 64 F5
Kirkway. Wallasey L45 51 B7
Kitchen St. L1 & L72 67 D7
Kitchener Dr. L9 38 F6
Kitchener St. WA10 43 E4
Kitling Rd. L34 41 C5
Kiverley Cl. L25 69 E3
Kiveton Dr. WN4 35 C2
Knap The. L60 86 A6
Knaresborough Rd. L44 50 F4
Knight Rd. WA5 59 F6
Knight St. L1 67 E8
Knighton Rd. L4 39 D1
Knightsway. L22 26 F2
Knob Hall La. PR9 1 F3
Knoclaid Rd. L13 53 E7
Knoll The. L43 66 A3
Knotty Ash Prim Sch. L12 54 D4
Knotty Mews. L25 70 C3
Knowe The. L64 88 A1
Knowl Hey Rd. L26 83 A6
Knowle Ave. PR8 7 C6
Knowles House Ave. WA10 42 F3
Knowles St. Birkenhead L41 66 C7
Knowles St. Widnes WA8 73 C2
Knowsley All Saints RC High Sch. L32 29 E1
Knowsley Ave. WA3 36 B1
Knowsley Bowring Comp Sch. L36 55 B3
Knowsley Cl. L42 67 A1
Knowsley Comm Coll. Huyton-w-R L36 55 D3
Knowsley Comm Coll Bracknell Ctr. Kirkby L32 29 D1
Knowsley Comm Coll Kirkby Ctr. Kirkby L32 29 D2
Knowsley Ct. L8 67 A1
Knowsley Halewood Comm Comp Sch. L26 82 E7
Knowsley Hey Sch. L36 55 F2
Knowsley Higher Side Comp Sch. L35 56 F3
Knowsley Hts. L36 55 E5
Knowsley Ind Pk. L33 30 C2
Knowsley La. Huyton-w-R L34 & L36 55 D6
Knowsley La. Knowsley L34 41 C4
Knowsley Park La. L34 56 C7
Knowsley Prescot Sch. L34 56 C7
Knowsley Rd. Birkenhead L42 67 A1
Knowsley Rd. Bootle L20 38 B5
Knowsley Rd. Liverpool L19 81 A6
Knowsley Rd. Ormskirk L39 13 F5
Knowsley Rd. Rainhill L35 57 D2
Knowsley Rd. Southport PR8 & PR9 1 C1
Knowsley Rd. St Helens WA10 43 D3
Knowsley Rd. Wallasey L45 51 A6
Knowsley Road Prim Sch. WA10 43 E3
Knowsley Ruffwood Comp Sch. L33 29 F3
Knowsley Saf Pk. L34 42 C2
Knowsley Safari Pk. L34 56 C8
Knowsley St. 1 L4 38 F2
Knowsley St Edmund Arrowsmith Comp Sch. L35 56 F5
Knowsley View. WA11 31 E8
Knowsley Village Prim Sch. L34 41 C3
Knox Cl. L62 79 B6
Knox St. L41 66 F6
Knutsford Gn. L46 49 E1
Knutsford Rd. L46 49 E1
Knutsford Wlk. L31 20 D4
Kramar Wlk. 1 L33 29 F2
Kremlin Dr. L13 54 A5
Kylemore Ave. Liverpool L18 69 A2
Kylemore Cl. L61 76 E3
Kylemore Dr. L61 76 F3
Kylemore Rd. L43 66 A4
Kylemore Way. L61 76 E3
Kylemore Way. Liverpool L26 82 E7
Kynance Rd. L11 40 D5

Laburnum Ave. Liverpool L36 70 E8
Laburnum Ave. St Helens WA11 44 D7
Laburnum Cres. L32 29 D3
Laburnum Dr. WN8 15 D1
Laburnum Gr. Irby L61 76 D6
Laburnum Gr. Liverpool L15 69 A8
Laburnum Gr. Maghull L31 20 F1
Laburnum Gr. Southport PR8 & PR9 4 F7
Laburnum La. WA5 & WA8 74 C5
Laburnum Pl. L20 38 D3
Laburnum Rd. Birkenhead L43 66 C4
Laburnum Rd. Golborne WA3 47 F7
Laburnum Rd. Liverpool L7 53 D3
Laburnum Rd. Wallasey L45 51 B7
Laburnum St. WN4 35 B2
Lace St. L3 52 D2
Lacey Rd. L34 & L35 56 E5
Lacey St. WA10 57 D8
Lad La. L3 52 B2
Lady Alice's Dr. L40 14 E8
Lady Green Cl. L38 18 E3
Lady Green La. L38 18 D4
Lady Lever Art Gallery The. L62 79 B6
Lady's Wlk. L40 14 C6
Ladybarn Ave. WA3 46 F7
Ladybower Cl. L7 68 B8
Ladyewood Rd. L44 51 C3
Ladyfield. L43 65 C7
Ladyfields. L12 54 B5
Ladymount RC Prim Sch. L61 76 F3
Ladypool. L24 83 C2
Ladysmith Ave. WN4 35 C3
Ladysmith Rd. L10 39 F6
Ladywood Rd. WA5 60 D1
Laffak Rd. WA11 44 D7
Lafford La. WN8 25 C8
Laggan St. L7 53 B2
Lagrange Arc. 7 WA10 44 A3
Laird Cl. L41 & L43 65 F8
Laird St. L41 66 A8
Lairds Pl. L3 52 D4
Laithwaite Cl. WA9 58 B3
Lake Pl. L47 63 B7
Lake Rd. Hoylake L47 63 B7
Lake Rd. Liverpool L15 69 A7
Lake St. 5 L4 53 A7
Lake View. L35 71 E8
Lakeland Ave. WN4 35 C4
Lakeland Cl. 7 L1 & L72 67 D8
Lakemoor Cl. WA9 58 D7
Lakenheath Rd. L26 82 E6
Lakes Dr. WN5 25 E6
Lakeside Ave. WN5 25 E3
Lakeside Cl. WA8 84 A8
Lakeside Ct. Rainford WA11 32 A6
Lakeside Ct. Wallasey L45 51 C8
Lakeside Gdns. WA11 32 A6
Lakeside Lawn. L27 71 A3
Laleston Cl. WA8 84 E8
Lambert St. L3 52 E2
Lambert Way. 3 L3 52 E2
Lambeth Ct. L47 63 A7
Lambeth Rd. L4 & L5 52 D7
Lambeth Wlk. L4 52 D7
Lambourn Ave. WA8 72 C5
Lambourne. WN8 16 B4
Lambourne Gr. WA9 45 A4
Lambourne Rd. L4 39 D1
Lambshear La. L31 20 C4
Lambton Rd. L17 68 B3
Lammermoor Rd. L18 69 A2
Lampeter Cl. WA5 60 E2
Lampeter Rd. L6 53 C6
Lamport Cl. WA8 73 E3
Lamport St. 2 L8 67 E5
Lancaster Ave. Crosby L23 26 D3
Lancaster Ave. Golborne WA3 47 C8
Lancaster Ave. Liverpool L17 & L8 68 D6
Lancaster Ave. Prescot L35 56 D3
Lancaster Ave. Wallasey L45 51 C5
Lancaster Ave. Widnes WA8 72 A2
Lancaster Cl. Bebington L62 79 B6
Lancaster Cl. Liverpool L5 52 D6
Lancaster Cl. Maghull L31 20 F1
Lancaster Cl. Newton-le-W WA12 45 F4
Lancaster Cl. Southport PR8 3 E4
Lancaster Cres. WN8 15 E1
Lancaster Dr. PR9 2 F5
Lancaster Gate. PR9 2 F5
Lancaster Gdns. PR8 3 E4
Lancaster Rd. Formby L37 9 E1
Lancaster Rd. Huyton-w-R L36 56 A4
Lancaster Rd. Southport PR8 3 E4
Lancaster Rd. Widnes WA8 73 B3
Lancaster St. L9 38 F3
Lancaster St. Liverpool L5 52 D6
Lancaster Wlk. Huyton-w-R L36 56 A4
Lancaster Wlk. Liverpool L5 52 D6
Lance Cl. L5 & L6 52 F5
Lance Gr. L15 69 A7
Lance La. L15 & L18 69 A7
Lancelyn Ct. L63 79 A3
Lancelyn Terr. L63 78 F4
Lancing Ave. WA2 61 A4
Lancing Cl. L25 70 D1
Lancing Dr. L10 28 D2
Lancing Rd. L25 70 D1
Lancing Way. L25 70 D1
Lancots La. WA9 58 D8
Land End. L31 21 C1
Land Gate La. WN4 35 B8
Land La. PR9 2 D4
Lander Rd. L21 38 C6
Lander Road Prim Sch. L21 38 C6
Landford Ave. L11 & L9 39 E4
Landford Pl. L9 39 E4
Landgate Ind Est. WN4 34 F8
Landican La. L49 & L61 77 E7
Landican Rd. L49 & L61 77 B7
Landor Cl. WA3 47 E8
Landseer Rd. L5 & L6 52 F5
Lane Ends. WA8 83 D5
Lane Head Ave. WA3 47 F8
Lanfranc Cl. L16 69 E8

Lanfranc Way. L16 69 E8
Lang La. L48 63 B3
Lang La S. L48 63 C2
Langbar. L35 56 E2
Langdale Ave. Formby L37 9 D2
Langdale Ave. Golborne WA3 36 C1
Langdale Ave. Heswall L61 76 F4
Langdale Cl. Formby L37 9 D2
Langdale Cl. L32 29 F1
Langdale Cl. Warrington WA2 61 E2
Langdale Cl. Widnes WA8 84 C8
Langdale Cres. WN2 36 B8
Langdale Dr. L31 20 E2
Langdale Gdns. PR8 3 F1
Langdale Gr. WA11 44 B7
Langdale Rd. Bebington L63 78 F4
Langdale Rd. Liverpool L15 68 E6
Langdale Rd. Wallasey L45 51 A7
Langdale St. L20 38 D3
Langfield. WA3 47 E7
Langfield Gr. L62 88 D5
Langford. L24 83 C2
Langford Rd. L19 80 F8
Langham Ave. L17 68 C3
Langham Ct. L4 52 F8
Langham St. L4 52 F8
Langholm Rd. WN4 34 C4
Langholme Hts. L11 39 F4
Langland Cl. Liverpool L4 53 D8
Langland Cl. Warrington WA5 60 E2
Langley Ave. WA12 46 B1
Langley Cl. Bebington L63 79 A2
Langley Cl. Golborne WA3 36 C1
Langley Cl. Hightown L38 17 F2
Langley Cl. Liverpool L12 40 F3
Langley Rd. L63 79 A2
Langley St. L8 67 E6
Langrove St. L5 52 E5
Langsdale St. Liverpool L3 52 E3
Langsdale St. Liverpool L3 & L6 52 F3
Langstone Ave. L49 64 C3
Langton Cl. WA8 72 B3
Langton Rd. L33 29 F5
Langton Rd. Liverpool L15 68 D7
Langtree. WN8 16 B3
Langtree St. WA9 44 C3
Langtry Cl. L4 52 D8
Langtry Rd. L4 52 D8
Lansbury Ave. WA9 44 E3
Lansbury Rd. L36 56 A2
Lansdown. L12 54 A6
Lansdowne Cl. L41 66 A8
Lansdowne Ct. 6 L41 65 F8
Lansdowne Pl. 5 Birkenhead L43 65 F8
Lansdowne Pl. Liverpool L5 52 F6
Lansdowne Rd. Birkenhead L41 & L43 65 F8
Lansdowne Rd. Southport PR8 4 E6
Lansdowne Rd. Wallasey L45 50 F7
Lanville Rd. L19 69 B1
Lanyork Rd. L3 52 B3
Lapford Cres. L33 30 A4
Lapford Wlk. L33 30 A4
Lapwing Cl. L12 40 F1
Lapwing Ct. L26 70 E1
Lapworth St. L5 52 D6
Larch Ave. Newton-le-W WA12 46 C2
Larch Ave. Warrington WA5 74 E5
Larch Ave. Widnes WA8 73 B2
Larch Cl. Billinge WN5 33 D5
Larch Cl. Golborne WA3 47 F6
Larch Cl. Liverpool L19 80 F7
Larch Cl. Skelmersdale WN8 15 E1
Larch Gr. L15 54 A1
Larch Lea. 1 L6 53 B5
Larch Rd. Birkenhead L41 & L42 66 D5
Larch Rd. Haydock WA11 45 E7
Larch Rd. Huyton-w-R L36 55 D2
Larch St. PR8 4 E6
Larch Towers. L33 29 F3
Larch Way. L37 9 D4
Larchdale Gr. L9 39 B4
Larchfield Rd. L23 27 B5
Larchwood Ave. L31 28 C7
Larchwood Cl. Heswall L61 76 F3
Larchwood Cl. Liverpool L25 70 B5
Larchwood Dr. L63 78 F7
Larcombe Ave. L49 64 F5
Lark La. L17 68 C4
Lark Way. L17 68 C3
Larkfield Cl. L17 68 C2
Larkfield Ct. PR9 2 A3
Larkfield Gr. L17 68 C2
Larkfield La. PR9 2 A3
Larkfield Prim Sch. PR9 2 A3
Larkfield Rd. L17 68 C2
Larkfield View. L15 68 E8
Larkhill. WN8 16 B4
Larkhill Ave. L49 65 A7
Larkhill Cl. L13 53 E7
Larkhill Gr. L38 17 F3
Larkhill La. Formby L37 9 C4
Larkhill La. Liverpool L13 53 E7
Larkhill Pl. L13 53 F7
Larkhill View. L13 53 F7
Larkhill Way. L49 65 A7
Larksway. L60 86 B8
Larton Rd. L48 63 E3
Lascelles Rd. L19 81 D7
Lascelles St. WA9 44 C3
Latchford Rd. L60 86 B6
Late Moffatt Rd W. L9 39 B7
Latham Ave. Newton-le-W WA12 46 C4
Latham Ave. Ormskirk L39 14 A5
Latham St. L5 52 D6
Latham Way. L63 79 B2
Lathbury La. L17 68 E5
Lathom Ave. 2 Seaforth L21 37 F6
Lathom Ave. Wallasey L44 51 B4
Lathom Cl. 1 L21 37 F6
Lathom Dr. Maghull L31 20 E3
Lathom Dr. Rainford WA11 31 F7
Lathom High Sch. WN8 15 F3
Lathom La. L40 14 C7
Lathom Park CE Prim Sch. L40 15 A8
Lathom Rd. Bickerstaffe L39 22 F8
Lathom Rd. L20 38 C5
Lathom Rd. Huyton-w-R L36 55 E2
Lathom Rd. Southport PR8 & PR9 1 C1
Lathom St James CE Prim Sch. L39 14 E4
Lathum Cl. L35 56 E5
Latimer Cl. WN5 25 F7
Latimer St. L5 52 D5
Latrigg Rd. L17 68 E2
Lauder Cl. L33 29 D6
Launceston Dr. WA5 74 E3
Laund The. L45 50 F5
Laurel Ave. Bebington L63 78 E4
Laurel Ave. Heswall L60 76 F1
Laurel Ave. Newton-le-W WA12 46 D3
Laurel Bank. WA8 73 A3
Laurel Ct. Liverpool L7 53 D3
Laurel Ct. St Helens WA11 44 B7
Laurel Dr. Bebington L64 88 B1
Laurel Dr. Knowsley WA10 42 F4
Laurel Dr. Skelmersdale WN8 15 E2
Laurel Gr. Ashton-in-M WN4 35 B4
Laurel Gr. Crosby L22 26 D2
Laurel Gr. Golborne WA3 47 D8
Laurel Gr. Liverpool L8 68 C6
Laurel Gr. Liverpool L36 70 E8
Laurel Gr. Southport PR8 & PR9 4 E7
Laurel Rd. Birkenhead L42 66 D4
Laurel Rd. Liverpool L7 53 D2
Laurel Rd. Prescot L34 56 E6
Laurel Rd. St Helens WA10 43 D2
Laurel Rd. St Helens WA11 44 F5
Laurelbanks. L60 76 E1
Laurelhurst Ave. L61 77 A4
Laurels The. L46 49 E3
Laurence Deacon Ct. L41 66 D7
Lauriston Rd. L4 39 C1
Lavan Cl. L6 53 A3
Lavan St. 3 L6 53 A3
Lavender Cres. L34 56 E6
Lavender Gdns. L23 27 B5
Lavender Way. L9 39 B4
Lavender Wlk. WN4 34 D5
Lavrock Bank. L8 67 E4
Lawford Dr. L60 86 C8
Lawler St. L21 38 B6
Lawns Ave. Bebington L63 88 B6
Lawns Ave. Orrell WN5 & WN8 25 C5
Lawns The. Birkenhead L43 65 D7
Lawns The. Southport PR9 1 F2
Lawrence Cl. L19 81 A7
Lawrence Ct. WN2 36 B8
Lawrence Cty Prim Inf Sch. L15 68 D7
Lawrence Gr. L15 68 E7
Lawrence Jun Mix Sch. L15 68 D7
Lawrence Rd. Liverpool L15 68 E7
Lawrence Rd. St Helens WA10 43 C6
Lawrence St. WA12 46 A3
Lawrenson St. WA10 43 E3
Lawson St. PR9 5 A7
Lawson Wlk. L12 40 D3
Lawton Ave. L20 38 E5
Lawton Rd. Crosby L22 & L23 26 D2
Lawton Rd. Huyton-w-R L36 55 C1
Lawton Rd. Rainhill L35 57 D2
Lawton St. 1 L1 52 E1
Laxey St. L8 67 E6
Laxton Rd. L25 82 C7
Layford Cl. L36 55 D6
Layford Rd. L36 55 D5
Layton Ave. L43 65 F1
Layton Cl. L25 70 C2
Layton Rd. L25 70 C2
Lazenby Cres. WN4 34 F3
Lea Cl. L43 65 E4
Lea Cres. L39 13 F7
Lea Cross Gr. WA8 72 C3
Lea Green Ind Est. WA9 58 A3
Lea Green Rd. L35 & WA9 58 A4
Lea Rd. L44 51 D5
Leach Croft. L28 55 A7
Leach La. WA9 58 D5
Leach St. 4 WA10 43 F4
Leach Way. L61 76 C6
Leacroft. WN4 34 F6
Leadenhall Cl. L5 52 F6
Leafield Cl. L61 76 F6
Leafield Rd. L24 & L25 82 B6
Leamington Ave. Newton-le-W WA12 46 C1
Leamington Ave. Southport PR8 7 D5
Leamington Jun & Inf Schs. L11 39 D2
Leamington Rd. Liverpool L11 39 D2
Leamington Rd. Southport PR8 7 D5
Leander Rd. L45 51 A5
Leas The. Heswall L61 77 B6
Leas The. Wallasey L45 50 E7
Leasowe Ave. L45 50 E6
Leasowe Gdns. L46 49 E4
Leasowe Prim Lower Sch. L46 50 B4
Leasowe Prim Sch. L46 50 B4
Leasowe Rd. Liverpool L9 39 B7
Leasowe Rd. Wallasey L45 & L46 50 C5
Leasowe Sta. L46 50 A2
Leasoweside. L46 50 A4
Leather La. 7 L2 52 C2
Leather's La. L26 82 F7
Leatherbarrows La. L31 29 A6
Leatherbarrows La. Maghull L31 28 F7
Leathwood. L31 28 E8
Leaway. L49 64 D4
Leawood Gr. L46 64 F8
Leckwith Rd. L30 28 B2
Leda Gr. L17 68 C4
Ledburn. WN8 16 B3
Ledbury Cl. Birkenhead L43 65 E2
Ledbury Cl. Liverpool L12 40 F4
Ledbury Cl. St Helens WA10 43 B3
Ledger Rd. WA11 45 A5
Ledmore Gr. WN4 34 D3
Ledsham Cl. L43 65 E4
Ledsham Rd. L32 29 C2
Ledsham Wlk. L32 29 C2
Ledson Gr. L39 21 B7
Lee Cl. L35 57 D1
Lee Hall Rd. L25 & L27 70 C5
Lee La. WN2 36 B8
Lee Manor High Sch. L27 70 D5
Lee Park Ave. L25 70 C5
Lee Park Golf Course. L27 70 D4
Lee Rd. L47 63 C7
Lee St. WA9 58 E8
Lee Vale Rd. L25 & L27 70 C4
Leece St. 4 L1 67 E8
Leecourt Cl. L12 54 D5
Leeds St. L3 52 C3
Leeming Cl. L19 81 C5
Lees Ave. L42 66 F2
Lees La. Liverpool L12 54 D7
Lees La. Skelmersdale WN8 16 E7
Lees Moor Way. L7 68 B8
Lees Rd. L33 & L32 30 B2
Leeside Ave. L32 29 F1
Leeside Cl. L32 29 F1
Leeswood. Crosby L22 26 E1
Leeswood. Skelmersdale WN8 16 B3
Leeswood Rd. L49 65 A4
Legh Rd. Bebington L62 79 B7
Legh Rd. Haydock WA11 45 B6
Legh St. Ashton-in-M WN4 35 B2
Legh St. Golborne WA3 47 A8
Legh St. Newton-le-W WA12 46 A3
Legh Vale Prim Sch. WA11 45 B6
Legion La. L62 79 D1
Legion Rd. WA10 57 D8
Leicester Ave. L22 26 D2
Leicester Rd. L20 38 D4
Leicester St. Southport PR8 & PR9 4 B8
Leicester St. St Helens WA9 57 D8
Leigh Ave. WA8 73 A1
Leigh Green Cl. 4 WA8 84 C8
Leigh Pl. 9 L1 52 D1
Leigh Rd. L48 63 B3
Leigh St. 10 L1 52 D1
Leighs Hey Cres. L32 29 F2
Leighton Ave. Hoylake L47 63 E8
Leighton Ave. Maghull L31 20 D2
Leighton Chase. L64 86 D1
Leighton Rd. Birkenhead L41 66 E4
Leighton Rd. Neston L64 86 D2
Leighton St. L4 38 E1
Leinster Gdns. WA7 84 F3
Leinster Rd. L13 54 B3
Leinster St. WA7 84 F3
Leison St. L5 52 D7
Leiston Cl. L61 76 E7
Lemon Cl. L7 53 C1
Lemon Gr. L8 68 C6
Lemon St. L5 52 D6
Lemon Tree Wlk. WA10 43 D1
Lendel Cl. L37 9 E3
Lenfield Dr. WA11 44 F6
Lenham Way. L24 82 B4
Lennox Ave. L45 51 B7
Lennox La. L43 50 C1
Lenthall St. L4 38 F2
Lenton Ave. L37 9 D4
Lenton Rd. L25 70 C5
Leominster Rd. L44 51 B4
Leon Cl. WA5 74 D7
Leonard Cheshire Dr. L30 27 F3
Leonard St. WA9 58 F7
Leonards Cl. L36 55 D6
Leonora St. 7 L8 68 A4
Leopold Gr. WA9 58 C5
Leopold Rd. Crosby L22 26 C2
Leopold Rd. Liverpool L7 53 B2
Leopold St. L44 51 E3
Lesley Rd. PR8 & PR9 4 E7
Leslie Ave. L49 64 D3
Leslie Rd. WA10 57 C8
Lesseps Rd. L8 68 C7
Lessingham Rd. WA8 72 F3
Lester Cl. L4 52 E7
Lester Dr. Irby L61 76 C7
Lester Dr. St Helens WA10 43 A5
Lestock St. L8 67 E7
Leta St. Birkenhead L41 66 E6
Leta St. L4 38 F1
Leta St. Liverpool L4 39 A1
Letchworth St. L6 53 C5
Lethbridge Cl. L5 52 D6
Lethbridge Rd. PR8 4 D5
Letitia St. L8 67 F5
Letterstone Cl. 3 L6 52 F4
Letterstone Wlk. 2 L6 52 F4
Leven St. L4 52 E8
Levens Hey. L46 64 D8
Levens Way. 1 WA8 84 C8
Lever Ave. 11 L44 51 E2
Lever Cswy. L63 78 B7
Lever St. WA9 58 D3
Lever Terr. L42 66 E3
Leveret Rd. L24 83 A3
Leveson Rd. L13 54 B1
Lewis Ave. WA5 60 F2
Lewis Gr. WA8 72 D1
Lewis St. WA10 43 E3
Lewisham Rd. Bebington L62 79 C6
Lewisham Rd. Liverpool L11 40 A1
Lexham Rd. L13 & L14 54 C3
Lexton Dr. PR9 2 B3
Ley Cl. WA9 58 C4
Leybourne Ave. PR8 7 F7
Leybourne Cl. L25 70 A6
Leybourne Gn. L25 70 A6
Leybourne Gr. L25 70 A5
Leybourne Rd. L25 70 A6
Leyburn Cl. L32 40 E7
Leyburn Rd. L45 50 F6
Leyfield Cl. L12 54 D6
Leyfield Ct. L12 54 D6
Leyfield Rd. L12 54 D6
Leyfield Wlk. L12 54 D6
Leyland Cl. PR9 2 E5
Leyland Gr. WA11 45 B6
Leyland Green Rd. WN4 34 C5
Leyland Rd. Rainford WA11 31 F6
Leyland Rd. Southport PR8 & PR9 1 C1
Leyland St. 7 L34 56 D6
Leyland Way. L39 13 F5
Liberton Ct. L5 52 F6
Liberty St. L15 68 E7
Libra Cl. L14 55 A5
Lichfield Ave. Crosby L22 26 D3
Lichfield Ave. Golborne WA3 47 D8
Lichfield Cl. L30 28 A1
Lichfield Gr. WN4 35 C2
Lichfield Rd. Liverpool L15 69 A6
Lichfield Rd. Liverpool L26 82 E6
Lichfield St. L45 51 C7
Lickers La. L35 56 E2
Liddell Ave. L31 29 B4
Liddell Ct. L45 50 D5
Liddell Rd. L12 & L13 53 F7
Lidderdale Inf Sch. L15 68 E6
Lidderdale Rd. L15 68 E6
Lidgate Cl. L33 29 F5
Lifeboat Rd. L37 9 B1
Liffey St. L8 68 B7
Lifton Rd. L33 30 A2
Lightbody St. L5 52 C5
Lightburn St. 4 WA7 84 F1
Lightfoot Cl. L60 86 B7
Lightfoot La. L60 86 B7
Lighthorne Dr. PR8 7 A4
Lighthouse Rd. L47 63 B6
Lightshaw La. WA3 36 B4
Lightwood Dr. 3 L7 68 C8
Lightwood St. 5 L7 68 C8
Lilac Ave. Garswood WN4 34 D5
Lilac Ave. Southport PR8 7 D2
Lilac Ave. Widnes WA8 73 B2
Lilac Gr. Billinge WN5 33 D4
Lilac Gr. Liverpool L36 70 D8
Lilac Gr. Skelmersdale WN8 15 E1
Lilac Gr. St Helens WA11 44 F5
Lilac Rd. WA3 36 A1
Lilford Ave. L9 38 F6
Lilford Dr. WA5 74 F6
Lilley Rd. L7 53 D2
Lillian Rd. L4 53 B6
Lillie Cl. L43 65 C8
Lilly Gn. L4 39 B1
Lilly Gr. L4 39 B1
Lilly Vale. L7 53 D3
Lillyfield. L60 85 F6
Lily Ave. WA12 46 D2
Lily La. WN2 35 F7
Lily Pl. WN4 35 C2
Lily Rd. L21 38 B6
Lily St. WN4 35 E5
Limbo La. L49 76 D8
Lime Ave. Bebington L63 78 D4
Lime Ave. Widnes WA8 73 B2
Lime Cl. Abram WN2 36 C7
Lime Cl. Liverpool L13 54 A4
Lime Ct. WN8 15 E1
Lime Gr. L21 38 A6
Lime Gr. Golborne WA3 47 E6
Lime Gr. Liverpool L8 68 C6
Lime Gr. Rainford WA11 31 F6
Lime Gr. Skelmersdale WN8 15 E1
Lime St. Liverpool L1 52 D2
Lime St. Southport PR8 4 E6
Lime Street Sta. L3 & L1 52 E2
Lime Tree Cl. L9 39 B4
Lime Tree Gr. L60 86 C8
Lime Tree Way. L37 9 C2
Lime Vale Rd. WA11 & WN5 33 C3
Limedale Rd. L18 69 B5
Limefield Dr. WN8 24 E7
Limehurst Gr. L62 88 D6
Limekiln Ct. L5 52 D4
Limekiln La. Burtonwood WA5 59 E3
Limekiln La. 1 Liverpool L3 52 D3
Limekiln La. Liverpool L3 & L5 52 D4
Limekiln La. Wallasey L41 & L44 51 A2
Limes The. L49 64 F5
Limont Rd. PR8 7 D5
Linacre La. L20 & L70 38 D5
Linacre La. Maghull L37 & L38 19 B7
Linacre Prim Sch. L20 38 C5
Linacre Rd. L20 & L21 38 B6
Linaker Dr. L39 12 B8
Linaker Prim Sch. PR8 4 B5
Linaker St. PR8 4 B5
Linbeck Gr. WA3 36 E1
Linbridge Rd. L14 54 F6
Lincoln Ave. WA3 36 D1
Lincoln Cl. Huyton-w-R L36 56 B3
Lincoln Cl. Liverpool L6 53 B4
Lincoln Cres. WA11 44 B6
Lincoln Dr. Ashton-in-M WN4 35 D2

Lincoln Dr. Litherland L10 ... 28 D3
Lincoln Dr. Wallasey L45 ... 51 C6
Lincoln Gdns. L41 ... 66 A8
Lincoln Gn. L31 ... 28 B8
Lincoln House Mus. WA10 ... 44 A4
Lincoln Rd. Southport PR8 ... 4 A1
Lincoln Rd. St Helens WA10 43 D2
Lincoln Sq. WA8 ... 73 B2
Lincoln St. Birkenhead L41 ... 51 A1
Lincoln St. Liverpool L19 ... 81 D4
Lincoln Way.
Huyton-w-R L36 ... 56 B3
Lincoln Way. Rainhill L35 ... 57 D1
Lincombe Rd. L36 ... 55 C4
Lind St. L4 ... 38 F1
Lindale Dr. 11 WA9 ... 58 C4
Lindale Rd. L7 ... 53 E3
Lindale Rd N. L41 ... 65 F7
Lindby Cl. L32 ... 41 A8
Lindby Rd. L32 ... 41 A8
Linden Ave.
Ashton-in-M WN4 ... 34 F5
Linden Ave. Crosby L23 ... 26 C4
Linden Ave. Litherland L30 ... 27 F2
Linden Ave. Orrell WN5 ... 25 E6
Linden Ct. Orrell WN5 ... 25 E6
Linden Ct. Widnes WA8 ... 72 F4
Linden Dr. Birkenhead L43 ... 65 E1
Linden Dr. Liverpool L36 ... 70 E8
Linden Gr.
Billinge WA11 & WN5 ... 33 C3
Linden Gr. Orrell WN5 ... 25 E6
Linden Gr. Wallasey L45 ... 51 B7
Linden Rd. L27 ... 70 E5
Linden Way.
St Helens WA10 ... 43 B4
Linden Way. Widnes WA8 ... 72 F4
Linden Wlk. WN5 ... 25 E6
Lindens. WN8 ... 16 B4
Lindens The. L31 ... 28 C7
Lindeth Ave. L44 ... 51 B3
Lindholme. WN8 ... 16 C3
Lindisfarne Dr. L12 ... 41 A3
Lindley Ave. WN5 ... 25 C5
Lindley Cl. 6 L7 ... 68 C8
Lindley St. L7 ... 68 C8
Lindrick Cl. L35 ... 57 A4
Lindsay Rd. L4 ... 53 D8
Lindsay St. WA9 ... 58 E3
Lindwall Cl. L43 ... 50 C1
Linear Pk. L46 ... 49 C1
Linear View. WA12 ... 46 C1
Lineside Cl. L25 ... 70 B5
Linford Gr. WA11 ... 44 C5
Ling St. L7 ... 53 B2
Lingdale Ave. L43 ... 65 F6
Lingdale Ct. L43 ... 65 F7
Lingdale Rd.
Birkenhead L41 & L43 ... 65 F7
Lingdale Rd. West Kirby L48 63 A3
Lingdales. L37 ... 10 B5
Lingfield Cl. L36 ... 55 D1
Lingfield Gr. L14 ... 54 D2
Lingfield Rd. Liverpool L14 ... 54 D2
Lingfield Rd. Runcorn WA7 ... 84 E1
Lingham Cl. L46 ... 49 D2
Lingham La.
Wallasey L46 & L47 ... 49 C3
Lingham La. Wallasey L46 ... 49 D1
Lingham Prim Sch. L46 ... 49 D1
Lingholme Rd. WA10 ... 43 E4
Lingley Green Ave. WA5 ... 74 D8
Lingley Rd. WA5 ... 74 D6
Lingmell Ave. WA11 ... 33 C1
Lingmell Rd. L11 & L12 ... 54 B8
Lingtree Rd. L32 ... 29 B3
Lingwell Ave. WA8 ... 72 D2
Lingwood Rd. WA5 ... 74 F6
Linhope Way. L17 ... 68 C3
Link Ave. Crosby L23 ... 27 A5
Link Ave. St Helens WA11 ... 44 E5
Link Rd. L36 ... 56 B1
Links Ave. PR9 ... 1 F3
Links Cl. Bebington L63 ... 88 B6
Links Cl. Wallasey L45 ... 50 F7
Links Hey Rd. L48 ... 75 E6
Links Rd. L32 ... 30 A1
Links View. Birkenhead L43 ... 65 E5
Links View. Wallasey L45 ... 50 F8
Links View Cl. L25 ... 69 F2
Linkside. L63 ... 78 D7
Linkside Ave. WA2 ... 61 B6
Linkside Ct. L23 ... 26 A5
Linkside Rd. L25 ... 70 C1
Linkstor Rd. L25 ... 69 F3
Linksview Tower. L25 ... 69 F2
Linksway. L45 ... 50 F7
Linkway. WA10 ... 43 B6
Linkway Ave. WN4 ... 35 E5
Linkway E. WA9 ... 44 B2
Linkway W. WA10 & WA9 ... 44 A2
Linner Rd. L24 ... 82 D3
Linnet Cl.
Newton-le-W WA12 ... 46 C3
Linnet Cl. Warrington WA2 ... 61 D3
Linnet House. L17 ... 68 B5
Linnet La. L17 ... 68 C4
Linnet Way. L33 ... 29 E7
Linnets Way. L60 ... 85 E8
Linosa Cl. L6 ... 53 C4
Linslade Cl. L33 ... 29 F4
Linslade Cres. L33 ... 29 F4
Linton Ave. WA3 ... 35 F2
Linton St. 1 L4 ... 38 F1
Linville Ave. L23 ... 26 B4
Linwood Rd. L42 ... 66 E3
Lionel St. WA9 ... 58 F7
Lions Cl. 2 L43 ... 65 F6
Lipton Cl. L20 ... 38 C2
Lisburn La. L13 ... 53 E7
Lisburn Rd. L17 ... 68 E2
Liscard Cres. L44 & L45 ... 51 B4
Liscard Gr. L44 & L45 ... 51 A4
Liscard House. 9 L44 ... 51 B4
Liscard Prim Sch. L44 & L45 51 C5
Liscard Rd. Liverpool L15 ... 68 D7
Liscard Rd. Wallasey L44 ... 51 C4
Liscard Village. L45 ... 51 B5
Liscard Way. L44 ... 51 B4
Lisieux RC Inf Sch. L11 ... 39 F2
Lisleholme Cl. L12 ... 54 C6
Lisleholme Cres. L12 ... 54 C6
Lisleholme Rd. L12 ... 54 C6
Lismore Ct. L23 ... 26 C4
Lismore Rd. L18 ... 69 A2
Lister Cres. L7 ... 53 C2
Lister Dr. L13 & L6 ... 53 E4
Lister Drive Cty Prim Sch.
L13 ... 53 E4
Lister Rd. L7 ... 53 C2
Liston St. L4 ... 38 F2
Litcham Cl. L49 ... 65 A7
Litherland Ave. L46 ... 49 D1
Litherland Cres. WA11 ... 44 C7
Litherland High Sch. L21 ... 27 D2
Litherland Moss Prim Sch.
L21 ... 27 D1
Litherland Pk. L21 ... 38 B8
Litherland Rd. L20 ... 38 C4
Litherland Rd. L20 ... 38 C5
Little Acre. L31 ... 28 E8
Little Barn Hey. L30 ... 27 D5
Little Brewery La. L37 ... 9 F6
Little Brook La. L32 ... 40 D8
Little Canning St. 1 L8 ... 67 F7
Little Catharine St. L8 ... 67 F7
Little Croft. L35 ... 56 D3
Little Crosby Rd. L23 ... 26 E6
Little Ct. L3 ... 52 C4
Little Delph. WA11 ... 45 C7
Little Digmoor Cty Sch.
WN8 ... 24 B6
Little Hardman St. 7 L1 ... 67 E8
Little Heath Rd. L24 ... 82 E3
Little Hey La. L37 ... 10 B4
Little Heyes St. L4 & L5 ... 53 A6
Little Howard St. L3 ... 52 B4
Little Huskisson St.
L7 & L8 ... 67 F7
Little La. Neston L64 ... 86 C1
Little La. Southport PR9 ... 2 B1
Little Moss Hey. L28 ... 55 C7
Little Parkfield Rd. L17 ... 68 B4
Little St. WA9 ... 44 E1
Little St Bride St. 12
L7 & L8 ... 67 F8
Little Storeton La. L63 ... 78 A6
Littlecote Cl. 16 WA9 ... 58 C4
Littledale Rd. Liverpool L14 ... 54 D3
Littledale Rd. Wallasey L44 ... 51 D3
Littledale Rd.
Warrington WA5 ... 74 F7
Littlemore Cl. L49 ... 64 D5
Littler Rd. WA11 ... 45 A5
Littlestone Cl. WA8 ... 73 A4
Littleton Cl. L43 ... 65 E4
Littondale Ave. L35 ... 57 D2
Liver Ind Est. L9 ... 39 C4
Liver St. L1 & L72 ... 67 C8
Livermore Ct. L8 ... 68 C6
Liverpool Airport. L24 ... 82 C2
Liverpool Ave. PR8 ... 7 D5
Liverpool Coll (Lower Sch).
L17 ... 68 F4
Liverpool Coll of F Ed. L1 ... 67 E7
Liverpool Coll (Upper Sch).
L18 ... 68 F4
Liverpool Hope Univ Coll.
L17 ... 68 B2
Liverpool Hope Univ Coll.
L16 ... 69 D6
Liverpool Institute Blackburn
House High Sch for Girls.
L1 ... 67 F8
Liverpool Inst for the Performing
Arts. L1 ... 67 E8
Liverpool Maternity Hospl.
L7 ... 67 F8
Liverpool Old Rd. PR8 ... 7 C1
Liverpool Pl. WA8 ... 72 C1
Liverpool Rd.
Ashton-in-M WN4 ... 35 A3
Liverpool Rd.
Bickerstaffe L39 ... 22 C5
Liverpool Rd.
Crosby L22 & L23 ... 26 E3
Liverpool Rd. Formby L37 ... 10 A1
Liverpool Rd.
Garswood WA11 & WN4 ... 34 D2
Liverpool Rd. Haydock WA11 45 B8
Liverpool Rd. Heswall L64 ... 86 F3
Liverpool Rd. Hightown L37 ... 18 A8
Liverpool Rd.
Huyton-w-R L14 & L36 & L34 55 D4
Liverpool Rd.
Huyton-w-R L34 ... 56 B6
Liverpool Rd. Maghull L31 ... 20 D4
Liverpool Rd. Maghull L39 ... 21 F4
Liverpool Rd.
Neston L64 & L63 ... 86 F1
Liverpool Rd. Ormskirk L39 ... 13 B2
Liverpool Rd.
Skelmersdale WN8 ... 23 C8
Liverpool Rd. Southport PR8 ... 4 A3
Liverpool Rd. Southport PR8 ... 7 E6
Liverpool Rd.
St Helens WA10 ... 43 F3
Liverpool Rd.
Warrington WA5 & WA8 ... 74 E6
Liverpool Rd N. L31 ... 20 C2
Liverpool Rd S. Maghull L31 20 C1
Liverpool Rd S. Maghull L31 28 C7
Liverpool Row. WA12 ... 60 D8
Liverpool St. WA10 ... 43 F3
Liverpool Womens Hospl.L8 68 A8
Liversidge Rd. L42 ... 66 D4
Livesley's La.
Great Altcar L37 ... 10 F2
Livesley's La. Haskayne L37 ... 11 A2
Livingston Ave. L17 ... 68 C4
Livingston Ct. L17 ... 68 C3
Livingston Dr. L17 ... 68 C3
Livingston Dr N. L17 ... 68 C3
Livingston Dr S. L17 ... 68 C3
Livingstone Gdns. L41 ... 66 C7
Livingstone Rd.
Birkenhead L42 ... 66 F3
Livingstone Rd.
Wallasey L46 ... 50 B4
Livingstone St. 2
Ashton-in-M WN4 ... 35 A5
Livingstone St.
Birkenhead L41 ... 66 C7
Llanrwst Cl. L8 ... 67 E5
Lloyd Ave. L41 ... 66 B7
Lloyd Cl. L6 ... 52 F4
Lloyd Cres. WA12 ... 45 F3
Lloyd Dr. L49 ... 64 D3
Lloyd Rd. L34 ... 56 E7
Lloyd St. WA11 ... 44 F6
Lobelia Ave. L9 ... 39 B4
Lochinvar St. L4 & L9 ... 38 F3
Lochmore Rd. L18 ... 69 B1
Lochryan Rd. L19 ... 81 B8
Lock Rd. L62 ... 89 A8
Lock St. WA9 ... 44 C5
Locke St. L19 ... 81 C4
Locker Ave. WA2 ... 61 B2
Locker La. WN4 ... 35 F4
Locker Pk. L49 ... 64 C4
Lockerbie Cl. WA2 ... 61 E4
Lockerby Rd. L7 ... 53 D2
Lockett Rd.
Ashton-in-M WN4 ... 35 C6
Lockett Rd. Widnes WA8 ... 73 B3
Lockton Rd. L34 ... 41 B5
Loddon Cl. L49 ... 65 B7
Lodge La. Bebington L62 ... 79 B6
Lodge La. Bickerstaffe WA11 23 D1
Lodge La. Liverpool L8 ... 68 B7
Lodge La.
Newton-le-W WA11 & WA12 &
WN4 ... 46 B8
Lodge La. Widnes WA8 ... 72 B4
Lodge Rd. Orrell WN5 ... 25 E4
Lodge Rd. Widnes WA8 ... 84 B8
Lodwick St. L20 ... 38 B1
Lofthouse Gate. WA8 ... 72 F4
Logan Rd. L41 ... 51 B1
Lognor Rd. L32 ... 29 C2
Lognor Wlk. L32 ... 29 C2
Logwood Rd. L36 ... 71 A8
Lombard Rd. L46 ... 49 F2
Lombardy Ave. L49 ... 64 B2
Lomond Gr. L46 ... 64 F8
Lomond Rd. L7 ... 53 E2
London Fields. WN5 ... 33 E5
London La. PR8 ... 8 D8
London Rd. Liverpool L3 ... 52 E2
London Rd. Liverpool L3 ... 52 F2
London Row. WA12 ... 60 D8
London Sq. PR8 ... 4 B7
London St. PR8 & PR9 ... 4 B7
Londonderry Rd. L13 ... 53 E7
Long Acres Rd. L64 ... 86 E2
Long Ave. L9 ... 39 B6
Long Hey. L35 ... 56 D2
Long Hey Rd. L48 ... 75 E7
Long Heys or Back La.
WN8 ... 16 F5
Long La. Bickerstaffe L39 ... 22 B7
Long La. Crosby L23 & L29 ... 27 A8
Long La. Formby L37 ... 9 E4
Long La. Liverpool L9 ... 39 C5
Long La. Liverpool L10 & L9 ... 39 E4
Long La. Liverpool L15 ... 68 F8
Long La. Liverpool L19 ... 81 C7
Long La. Maghull L29 ... 19 B1
Long La. Maghull L39 ... 21 F8
Long La. Skelmersdale WN8 24 E3
Long La. Warrington WA2 ... 61 B1
Long Lane Cty Prim Sch.
WA2 ... 61 B2
Long Meadow. Heswall L60 ... 85 F6
Long Meadow.
St Helens WA10 ... 43 B4
Long Meanygate. PR9 ... 5 F8
Long View Prim Sch. L36 ... 55 E6
Longacre. PR9 ... 1 F3
Longacre Cl. L45 ... 50 D5
Longborough Rd. L34 ... 41 C2
Longcliffe Dr. PR8 ... 7 C4
Longcroft Ave. L19 ... 81 E7
Longcroft Sq. L19 ... 81 E7
Longdale La. L29 ... 27 D8
Longden Rd. WN4 ... 35 A3
Longdown Rd. L10 ... 40 B6
Longfellow St. L20 ... 38 A5
Longfellow St. Liverpool L8 ... 68 C7
Longfield. L37 ... 10 B5
Longfield Ave. L23 ... 26 E6
Longfield Cl. L49 ... 64 D4
Longfield Rd. L21 ... 38 B6
Longfield Rd.
Warrington WA2 ... 61 C1
Longfield Wlk. L23 ... 26 E6
Longfold. L31 ... 20 E1
Longford Rd. PR8 ... 4 A2
Longford St. L8 ... 68 A3
Longhey. WN8 ... 16 C4
Longland Rd. L45 ... 51 B6
Longmead Ave. WN4 ... 35 C4
Longmeadow Rd. L34 ... 41 D4
Longmoor Cl. L10 ... 39 E7
Longmoor Gr. L9 ... 39 B6
Longmoor Inf Sch. L9 ... 39 B6
Longmoor La. L10 & L9 ... 39 D7
Longmoor Lane Jun Sch. L9 39 B6
Longmoor Sch. L10 ... 39 F8
Longreach Rd. L14 ... 54 F3
Longridge Ave.
Birkenhead L49 ... 64 E6
Longridge Ave.
St Helens WA11 ... 44 D5
Longridge Wlk. 10 L4 ... 52 E8
Longshaw Ave. WN5 ... 25 E1
Longshaw Cl. WN5 ... 25 E1
Longshaw Comm. WN5 ... 33 E8
Longshaw Lea. L27 ... 70 F4
Longshaw Old Rd. WN5 ... 25 E1
Longshaw St. WA5 ... 60 F1
Longstone Wlk. L7 ... 68 B8
Longton Ave. WA3 ... 47 C7
Longton Dr. L37 ... 10 A6
Longton La. L35 ... 57 B4
Longton Lane Comm Prim Sch.
L35 ... 57 B5
Longview Ave. Rainhill L35 ... 57 A4
Longview Ave. Wallasey L45 51 B5
Longview Cres. L36 ... 55 F3
Longview Dr. L36 ... 56 A3
Longview La. L36 ... 55 F4
Longview Rd.
Huyton-w-R L36 ... 55 F3
Longview Rd. Rainhill L35 ... 57 A4
Longville St. L8 ... 67 E5
Longwood Cl. WA11 ... 32 C1
Longworth Way. L25 ... 70 A3
Lonie Gr. WA10 ... 57 C8
Lonsboro Rd. L44 ... 51 C3
Lonsdale Ave. Ormskirk L39 13 F7
Lonsdale Ave.
St Helens WA10 ... 57 B7
Lonsdale Ave. Wallasey L45 51 A6
Lonsdale Cl. Litherland L21 ... 27 B2
Lonsdale Cl. 3 Widnes WA8 84 C8
Lonsdale Mews. L21 ... 27 B2
Lonsdale Rd. Formby L37 ... 9 F3
Lonsdale Rd. Litherland L21 ... 27 B2
Lonsdale Rd. Liverpool L26 ... 82 E6
Lonsdale Rd. Southport PR8 ... 4 D4
Lonsdale Villas. L45 ... 51 A6
Looe Cl. WA8 ... 72 E2
Looe Rd. L11 ... 40 D5
Looms The. L64 ... 86 B2
Loomsway. L61 ... 76 D6
Loraine St. L5 ... 52 F5
Lord Nelson St. L1 & L3 ... 52 E2
Lord Sefton Way. L37 ... 10 E2
Lord St. Ashton-in-M WN4 ... 35 D4
Lord St.
Birkenhead L41 & L72 ... 66 E7
Lord St. Liverpool L1 ... 52 C1
Lord St. Liverpool L19 ... 81 D4
Lord St. Newton-le-W WA12 46 A3
Lord St. Runcorn WA7 ... 84 F3
Lord St. Southport PR8 & PR9 4 B7
Lord St. St Helens WA10 ... 44 A5
Lord St W. PR8 ... 4 A6
Lordens Cl. L14 ... 55 A5
Lordens Rd. L14 ... 55 A5
Lords Ave. L43 ... 65 C8
Loreburn Rd. L15 ... 69 B6
Lorenzo Dr. Liverpool L11 ... 53 F8
Loretto Dr. L49 ... 65 A6
Loretto Rd. L44 ... 50 F4
Lorn St. L41 ... 66 E6
Lorne Ct. L43 ... 66 B4
Lorne Rd. Birkenhead L43 ... 66 A5
Lorne Rd. Crosby L22 ... 26 D1
Lorne St. L7 ... 53 E3
Lorton Ave. WA11 ... 44 A8
Lorton St. L8 ... 68 B7
Lostock Cl. WN5 ... 33 E5
Lothair Rd. L4 ... 53 A7
Lothian St. L8 ... 68 A5
Loudon Gr. L8 ... 68 A6
Lough Gn. L63 ... 79 A2
Loughrigg Ave. WA11 ... 33 B1
Louis Braille Cl. L30 ... 27 F4
Louis Pasteur Ave. L30 ... 27 F4
Lourdes Hospl. L18 ... 68 F5
Love La. Liverpool L3 ... 52 B4
Love La. Wallasey L44 ... 51 B3
Lovel Rd. L24 ... 82 D3
Lovel Terr. WA8 ... 84 B5
Lovel Way. L24 ... 82 D3
Lovelace Rd. L19 ... 81 B7
Lovett Dr. L35 ... 56 E5
Low Bank Rd. WN4 ... 34 F4
Low Hill. L6 & L7 ... 53 A3
Low Wood Gr. L61 ... 77 C4
Low Wood St. L6 ... 53 A2
Lowcroft. WN8 ... 16 C3
Lowden Ave. L21 ... 27 B1
Lowe House RC Prim Sch.
WA10 ... 43 F4
Lowe St. Golborne WA3 ... 47 A8
Lowe St. St Helens WA10 ... 43 F4
Lowe St S. WA10 ... 43 F3
Lowe's La. WN8 ... 15 F8
Lowell St. L4 ... 38 F1
Lower Alt Rd. L38 ... 17 F4
Lower Appleton Rd. WA8 ... 73 B1
Lower Bank View. L20 ... 38 B1
Lower Breck Rd. L6 ... 53 C5
Lower Carr La. L38 ... 19 B7
Lower Castle St. L2 ... 52 C1
Lower Cl. L26 ... 83 A8
Lower Farm Rd. L25 ... 70 A7
Lower Flaybrick Rd. L43 ... 65 E8
Lower Gn. L49 ... 65 A3
Lower Hey. L23 ... 27 B5
Lower House La.
Liverpool L11 ... 40 A3
Lower House La.
Widnes WA8 ... 84 F8
Lower La. L10 & L11 & L9 ... 39 F6
Lower Lee Sch. L25 ... 69 E4
Lower Mersey View. L20 ... 38 B1
Lower Milk St. 17 L3 ... 52 C2
Lower Prom. Southport PR8 ... 4 A7
Lower Prom. Southport PR8 ... 4 B8
Lower Rd. Bebington L62 ... 79 B6
Lower Rd.
Liverpool L26 & WA8 ... 83 C7
Lower Thingwall La. L61 ... 77 C5
Lowerson Cres. L11 ... 53 E8
Lowerson Rd. L11 & L13 ... 53 E8
Lowes Gn. L37 ... 10 B3
Loweswater Cl. WA2 ... 61 B3
Loweswater Cres. WA11 ... 45 A6

Loweswater Way. L33 ... 29 D4
Lowfield Ind Est. WA9 ... 57 F5
Lowfield La. WA9 ... 57 F5
Lowfield Rd. L14 ... 54 C3
Lowfields Ave. L62 ... 88 E3
Lowfields Cl. L62 ... 88 E3
Lowlands Rd. WA7 ... 84 F2
Lowndes Rd. L6 ... 53 D6
Lowry Bank. L44 ... 51 E3
Lowswood. L37 ... 9 E5
Lowther Ave. Litherland L10 28 D2
Lowther Ave. Maghull L31 ... 20 F2
Lowther Cres. WA10 ... 57 B8
Lowther Dr. L35 ... 57 C3
Lowther St. L7 & L8 ... 68 A7
Lowton Gdns. WA3 ... 47 B5
Lowton Rd. WA3 ... 36 C1
Lowton West Cty Prim Sch. WA3 ... 47 D8
Lowwood Gr. L41 ... 66 D5
Lowwood Rd. L41 ... 66 D5
Loxley Rd. PR8 ... 4 D4
Loyola Hey. L35 ... 72 E8
Lucan Rd. L17 ... 68 E2
Lucania St. L19 ... 81 C4
Lucerne Rd. L44 ... 51 D2
Lucerne St. L17 ... 68 C3
Lucius Cl. L9 ... 38 F7
Lucknow St. L17 ... 68 C4
Ludlow. WN8 ... 16 C4
Ludlow Ct. L48 ... 63 C1
Ludlow Dr. Ormskirk L39 ... 13 D7
Ludlow Dr. West Kirby L48 ... 63 B1
Ludlow Gr. L62 ... 79 D1
Ludlow St. L4 ... 38 F1
Ludwig Rd. 1 L4 ... 53 B6
Lugard Rd. L17 ... 68 E2
Lugsmore La. WA10 ... 43 D1
Luke St. Ashton-in-M WN4 ... 35 D5
Luke St. Liverpool L8 ... 67 F6
Luke St. Wallasey L44 ... 51 E2
Lulworth. WN8 ... 16 C4
Lulworth Ave. L22 ... 26 C1
Lulworth Rd. Liverpool L25 ... 70 C5
Lulworth Rd. Southport PR8 .. 3 F5
Lumber La. WA5 ... 59 F8
Lumby Ave. L36 ... 55 E3
Lumley Rd. L44 ... 51 D3
Lumley St. L19 ... 81 B7
Lumley Wlk. L24 ... 83 E1
Lunar Dr. L30 ... 27 F4
Lunar Rd. L9 ... 39 B6
Lune Ave. L31 ... 20 E2
Lune St. L23 ... 26 E4
Lune Way. WA8 ... 72 C1
Lunehurst. WA3 ... 47 E8
Lunesdale Ave. L9 ... 39 B7
Lunsford Rd. L14 ... 54 F4
Lunt Ave. Litherland L30 ... 28 A2
Lunt Ave. Prescot L35 ... 56 E3
Lunt La. L29 ... 27 D8
Lunt Rd. L20 ... 38 C5
Lunt Rd. Litherland L29 ... 27 D8
Lunt Rd. Maghull L29 ... 19 C1
Lunt's Heath Rd. WA8 ... 73 B5
Lunts Heath Cty Prim Sch. WA8 ... 73 B5
Lupin Dr. WA11 ... 45 F6
Lupton Dr. L23 ... 27 A4
Luscombe Cl. L26 ... 83 A8
Lusitania Rd. L4 ... 39 B2
Luther Gr. WA9 ... 45 B2
Luton Gr. L4 ... 52 F8
Luton St. L5 ... 52 C6
Lutyens Cl. 2 L4 ... 52 F7
Luxmore Rd. L4 ... 39 A1
Lycett Rd. Liverpool L4 ... 53 C7
Lycett Rd. Wallasey L45 ... 50 E5
Lyceum Pl. 5 L1 ... 52 D1
Lydbrook Cl. L42 ... 66 F3
Lydbury Cl. WA5 ... 60 D2
Lydbury Cres. L32 ... 40 F8
Lydd Cl. L24 ... 82 B4
Lydford Rd. L12 ... 54 B8
Lydia Ann St. L1 & L72 ... 67 D8
Lydia Wlk. L10 ... 40 B7
Lydiate Cty Prim Sch. L31 ... 20 C4
Lydiate La. Crosby L23 & L29 & L30 ... 27 C6
Lydiate La. Liverpool L25 & L26 ... 70 D2
Lydiate La. Raby L64 ... 87 E1
Lydiate Pk. L23 ... 27 B6
Lydiate Rd. L20 ... 38 C5
Lydiate Station Rd. L31 ... 19 E5
Lydiate The. L60 ... 85 F7
Lydieth Lea. L27 ... 70 E6
Lydney Rd. L36 ... 55 B4
Lydstep Ct. WA5 ... 60 E2
Lyelake Cl. L32 ... 29 F1
Lyelake La. L40 & L39 ... 14 F2
Lyelake Rd. L32 ... 29 F1
Lyle St. L5 ... 52 D5
Lyme Cl. L36 ... 56 A6
Lyme Comm Inf Sch. WA12 45 F4
Lyme Cross Rd. L36 ... 55 F6
Lyme Gr. L36 ... 55 F5
Lyme St. Haydock WA11 ... 45 E6
Lyme St. Newton-le-W WA12 45 F4
Lymecroft. L25 ... 69 F2
Lymington Rd. L44 ... 50 F4
Lymm Rd. L43 ... 65 C7
Lynas Gdns. L19 ... 81 B8
Lynas St. L41 ... 66 D8
Lyncot Rd. L9 ... 39 B8
Lyncroft Rd. L44 ... 51 C2
Lyndale. WN8 ... 16 B4
Lyndale Ave. Bebington L62 . 88 E4
Lyndale Ave. Warrington WA2 ... 61 F2
Lyndene Rd. L25 ... 70 A7
Lyndhurst. Maghull L31 ... 20 D1
Lyndhurst. Skelmersdale WN8 ... 16 B4
Lyndhurst Ave. Heswall L61 77 A3
Lyndhurst Ave. Liverpool L18 69 A3
Lyndhurst Cl. L61 ... 77 A5
Lyndhurst Rd. Crosby L23 ... 27 A4
Lyndhurst Rd. Hoylake L47 .. 48 E1
Lyndhurst Rd. Irby L61 ... 76 C6
Lyndhurst Rd. Liverpool L18 68 F3
Lyndhurst Rd. Southport PR8 4 B2
Lyndhurst Rd. Wallasey L45 50 F6
Lyndhurst Way. L36 ... 55 E2
Lyndon Dr. L18 ... 69 B4
Lyndor Cl. L25 ... 70 B1
Lyndor Rd. L25 ... 70 B1
Lyneham. L35 ... 56 F2
Lynholme Rd. L4 & L6 ... 53 B7
Lynmouth Rd. L17 ... 80 E8
Lynn Cl. WA10 ... 43 C4
Lynnbank. L43 ... 66 B4
Lynnbank Rd. L18 ... 69 D5
Lynscott Pl. L16 ... 69 D8
Lynsted Rd. L14 ... 54 F3
Lynton Cl. Heswall L60 ... 86 B6
Lynton Cl. Liverpool L19 ... 81 B8
Lynton Cl. Warrington WA5 . 74 E4
Lynton Cres. WA8 ... 72 E2
Lynton Ct. Crosby L23 ... 26 B4
Lynton Ct. Hoylake L47 ... 63 A6
Lynton Dr. Bebington L63 ... 79 A3
Lynton Dr. Southport PR8 ... 3 E1
Lynton Gn. L25 ... 69 F4
Lynton Gr. WA9 ... 58 C5
Lynton Rd. Huyton-w-R L36 .. 56 B3
Lynton Rd. Southport PR8 ... 3 E1
Lynton Rd. Wallasey L45 ... 50 E6
Lynton Way. WA10 ... 43 B6
Lynwood Ave. Golborne WA3 47 E6
Lynwood Ave. Ormskirk L39 13 C3
Lynwood Ave. Wallasey L44 51 A3
Lynwood Cl. WN8 ... 24 D7
Lynwood Dr. L61 ... 76 E6
Lynwood End. L39 ... 13 C3
Lynwood Gdns. L9 ... 39 F5
Lynwood Rd. L9 ... 39 A5
Lynxway The. L12 ... 54 D4
Lyon Cl. WA10 ... 43 F3
Lyon Rd. L4 ... 53 B6
Lyon St. Ashton-in-M WN4 ... 34 F7
Lyon St. Liverpool L19 ... 81 D4
Lyon St. St Helens WA10 ... 43 F3
Lyons Cl. L46 ... 49 E1
Lyons Rd. Southport PR8 ... 4 A5
Lyons Rd. Wallasey L46 ... 49 E1
Lyons Rd. Warrington WA5 .. 74 F4
Lyra Rd. L22 ... 26 D1
Lyster Rd. L20 ... 38 A3
Lytham Cl. L10 ... 28 F1
Lytham Ct. L32 ... 29 C3
Lytham Rd. Ashton-in-M WN4 ... 34 F5
Lytham Rd. Southport PR9 ... 2 A4
Lytham Rd. Widnes WA8 ... 73 C2
Lytham Way. L14 ... 54 E6
Lytles Cl. L37 ... 10 A2
Lyttelton Rd. L17 ... 68 E2
Lytton Ave. L42 ... 66 F1
Lytton Gr. L21 ... 38 A6
Lytton St. L6 ... 52 F3

Mab La. L12 & L14 ... 54 F7
Mab Lane Jun & Inf Sch. L12 ... 54 E7
Mabel Fletcher Centre Comm Coll. L15 ... 53 F1
Macalpine Cl. L49 ... 65 A6
Macbeth St. L20 ... 38 C1
Macdermott Rd. WA8 ... 84 F5
Macdona Dr. L48 ... 75 B8
Macdonald Ave. WA11 ... 44 E5
Macdonald Dr. L49 ... 64 D3
Macdonald Rd. L46 ... 64 C8
Macdonald St. L15 ... 68 E8
Mace Rd. L11 ... 40 C3
MacFarren St. 2 L13 ... 54 A3
Mack Gr. L30 ... 27 D2
Mackenzie Cl. 7 L6 ... 53 A4
Mackenzie Rd. L46 ... 50 B3
Mackenzie St. L6 ... 53 A5
Mackenzie Wlk. 6 L6 ... 53 A4
Macket's La. Liverpool L25 ... 82 C7
Mackets Cl. L25 ... 70 C1
MacQueen St. L13 ... 54 A2
Maddock Rd. L44 ... 51 D5
Maddock St. L41 ... 66 C8
Maddocks St. L13 ... 54 A2
Maddrell St. L3 ... 52 B4
Madelaine St. L8 ... 68 A6
Madeley Cl. L48 ... 63 B1
Madeley Dr. L48 ... 63 B1
Madeley St. L6 ... 53 C3
Madeline McKenna Ct. WA8 72 C3
Madryn Ave. L33 ... 30 A2
Madryn St. L8 ... 68 A5
Maelor Cl. L63 ... 88 C6
Mafeking Cl. 1 L15 ... 68 F8
Mafeking Pl. WN4 ... 35 C3
Magazine Ave. L45 ... 51 B7
Magazine Brow. L45 ... 51 C7
Magazine La. Bebington L63 & L62 ... 79 E4
Magazine La. Wallasey L45 .. 51 C7
Magazine Rd. L62 ... 79 D3
Magazines Prom. L45 ... 51 C7
Magdala St. L7 & L8 ... 68 C7
Magdalen Dr. WN4 ... 34 F4
Magdalene Sq. L30 ... 27 F4
Maggots Nook Rd. WA11 ... 24 A1
Maghull High Sch. L31 ... 28 C8
Maghull La. L31 ... 21 B1
Maghull Smallholdings Est. L31 ... 20 F3
Maghull St. L1 & L72 ... 67 C8
Maghull Sta. L31 ... 28 E7
Magnolia Cl. Liverpool L26 ... 70 D2
Magnolia Cl. St Helens WA11 ... 44 F5
Magnolia Wlk. L49 ... 64 C2
Magnum St. L5 ... 52 F5
Maguire Ave. L20 ... 38 E4
Mahan Ct. 7 L8 ... 67 F7
Maharishi School of the Age of Enlightenment. L40 ... 16 A5
Mahon Ave. L20 ... 38 D6
Maiden La. L13 ... 53 D7
Maidford Jun Mix & Inf Sch. L14 ... 54 F5
Maidford Rd. L14 ... 54 F4
Main Ave. L35 & WA10 ... 57 C7
Main Cl. WA11 ... 45 A6
Main Dr. L35 ... 56 E1
Main La. WA3 ... 47 F3
Main Rd. L62 ... 79 B4
Main St. WN5 ... 33 E5
Mains Ave. WN2 ... 35 F7
Mainside Rd. L32 ... 29 F1
Maintree Cres. L24 ... 83 A4
Mainwaring Rd. Bebington L62 ... 88 D8
Mainwaring Rd. Wallasey L44 ... 51 D3
Mairscough La. L39 ... 12 B1
Maitland Cl. L8 ... 68 B7
Maitland Rd. L45 ... 51 C8
Maitland St. 4 L8 ... 68 B7
Major Lester Jun Mix Inf Sch. L5 ... 52 F7
Major St. L5 ... 52 D6
Makepeace Wlk. 3 L8 ... 67 F6
Makin St. L4 ... 38 F2
Malcolm Ave. WA2 ... 61 D1
Malcolm Cres. L63 ... 88 C6
Malcolm Gr. L20 ... 38 D1
Malcolm Pl. L15 ... 53 F1
Malden Rd. L6 ... 53 C3
Maldon Cl. L26 ... 82 F6
Maldwyn Rd. L44 ... 51 B5
Maley Cl. L8 ... 68 A4
Malham Cl. PR8 ... 4 E3
Malhamdale Ave. L35 ... 57 D2
Malin Cl. L24 ... 83 D2
Mall The. L6 ... 53 A5
Mallaby St. L41 ... 66 A8
Mallard Cl. Liverpool L12 ... 40 F3
Mallard Cl. Liverpool L26 ... 70 E1
Mallard Cl. Ormskirk L39 ... 13 C2
Mallard Cl. Warrington WA2 61 D3
Mallard House. L31 ... 20 B4
Mallard Way. St Helens WA11 ... 44 B6
Mallard Way. Wallasey L46 .. 49 C1
Mallee Ave. PR9 ... 2 A3
Mallee Cres. PR9 ... 2 A3
Malleson Rd. L13 ... 53 E7
Mallins Cl. L8 ... 68 A4
Mallory Ave. L31 ... 20 B4
Mallory Gr. WA11 ... 44 D6
Mallory Rd. L42 ... 66 D2
Mallow Rd. L6 ... 53 C3
Mallow Way. L36 ... 70 F8
Mallowdale Cl. L62 ... 88 F5
Malmesbury Cl. 2 L49 ... 64 C4
Malmesbury Rd. L11 ... 39 E2
Malpas Ave. L43 ... 66 A2
Malpas Dr. L63 ... 78 E7
Malpas Gr. L45 ... 51 A6
Malpas Rd. Liverpool L11 ... 40 D5
Malpas Rd. Wallasey L45 ... 51 A6
Malt St. L7 ... 68 B8
Malta St. L8 ... 67 F5
Malta Wlk. 5 L8 ... 67 F5
Maltkiln La. L39 ... 21 E8
Malton Ave. WA3 ... 47 E7
Malton Cl. WA8 ... 72 C5
Malton Rd. L25 ... 70 C2
Malvern Ave. L14 ... 54 F2
Malvern Cl. Ashton-in-M WN4 ... 35 B4
Malvern Cl. L32 ... 29 C4
Malvern Cl. Warrington WA5 74 F8
Malvern Cres. L14 ... 54 F2
Malvern Cty Prim Sch. L14 . 54 F2
Malvern Gr. Birkenhead L42 . 66 D2
Malvern Gr. Litherland L10 ... 28 C2
Malvern Rd. L20 ... 38 C5
Malvern Rd. Haydock WA9 ... 45 A4
Malvern Rd. Liverpool L6 ... 53 C3
Malvern Rd. Wallasey L45 ... 50 D5
Malwood St. L8 ... 67 F4
Manchester Rd. Prescot L34 56 C5
Manchester Rd. Southport PR9 ... 4 C7
Manchester Row. WA12 ... 60 D8
Manchester St (Kingsway). L1 ... 52 D2
Mandela Ct. L8 ... 68 B5
Mandeville Rd. PR8 ... 7 B5
Mandeville St. L4 ... 38 F2
Manesty's La. L1 ... 52 D1
Manfield. WN8 ... 16 A3
Manfred St. 1 L6 & L7 ... 53 A2
Manica Cres. L10 ... 39 F6
Manion Ave. L31 ... 20 B5
Manion Cl. L31 ... 20 B5
Manley Ave. WA3 ... 35 F2
Manley Cl. L43 ... 65 F3
Manley Rd. Crosby L22 ... 26 D2
Manley Rd. Huyton-w-R L36 . 71 A8
Mann Island. L3 & L69 ... 52 B1
Mann St. L8 ... 67 E6
Mannering Rd. L17 ... 68 C4
Manners La. L60 ... 85 E6
Manning Rd. PR8 ... 4 E6
Manning St. WA10 ... 43 F3
Manningham Rd. L4 & L6 ... 53 C6
Manor Ave. Crosby L23 ... 26 D5
Manor Ave. Golborne WA3 ... 47 C8
Manor Ave. Newton-le-W WA12 ... 45 F4
Manor Ave. Rainhill L35 ... 57 C2
Manor CE Jun Sch The. WA12 ... 45 F4
Manor Cl. L20 ... 38 E2
Manor Cl. Garswood WN4 ... 34 C3
Manor Cl. Liverpool L11 ... 40 D3
Manor Cres. L25 ... 70 B1
Manor Ct. WA3 ... 47 C8
Manor Dr. Birkenhead L49 ... 65 A6
Manor Dr. Crosby L23 ... 26 D5
Manor Dr. Litherland L30 ... 28 B3
Manor Farm Rd. L36 ... 55 F1
Manor Gr. L32 ... 29 B2
Manor Gr. Skelmersdale WN8 ... 15 F1
Manor High Sch. L23 ... 26 C6
Manor Hill. L43 ... 66 A6
Manor House. Bebington L62 88 D8
Manor House Cl. Maghull L31 ... 20 C1
Manor House Cl. St Helens WA11 ... 33 B1
Manor House Dr. WN8 ... 24 E3
Manor La. Birkenhead L42 ... 67 A2
Manor La. Wallasey L44 & L45 ... 51 C5
Manor Lodge. L37 ... 9 E4
Manor Pl. Bebington L62 ... 79 D5
Manor Pl. Widnes WA8 ... 72 B1
Manor Prim Comm Sch. L43 65 C7
Manor Rd. Bebington L62 ... 88 E6
Manor Rd. Crosby L23 ... 26 C5
Manor Rd. Haydock WA11 ... 45 F7
Manor Rd. Hoylake L47 ... 63 C7
Manor Rd. Irby L61 ... 76 D6
Manor Rd. Liverpool L25 ... 70 B1
Manor Rd. Raby L63 ... 87 A7
Manor Rd. Southport PR9 ... 2 A2
Manor Rd. Wallasey L44 & L45 ... 51 C5
Manor Rd. Widnes WA8 ... 72 B1
Manor Rd Sta. L47 ... 63 C7
Manor St. Golborne WA3 ... 36 B1
Manor St. St Helens WA9 ... 44 C2
Manor View. L12 ... 40 F1
Manor Way. L25 ... 70 B1
Manorbier Cres. L9 ... 39 A3
Manorside Cl. L49 ... 64 F6
Manorwood Dr. L35 ... 56 F2
Mans Sq. 5 L20 ... 38 C3
Manse Gdns. WA12 ... 46 D4
Mansell Cl. WA8 ... 73 C5
Mansell Dr. L26 ... 82 E6
Mansell Rd. L6 ... 53 B3
Mansfield St. Golborne WA3 35 F1
Mansfield St. Liverpool L3 ... 52 E3
Manston Rd. WA5 ... 74 F3
Manton Rd. L6 ... 53 C3
Manvers Rd. L16 ... 54 E1
Manville Rd. L45 ... 51 B7
Manville St. WA9 ... 44 C1
Manx Jane's La. PR9 ... 2 A4
Maple Ave. Golborne WA3 ... 47 F7
Maple Ave. Haydock WA11 .. 45 B7
Maple Ave. Newton-le-W WA12 ... 46 D2
Maple Ave. Widnes WA8 ... 73 B1
Maple Cl. Billinge WN5 ... 33 D5
Maple Cl. L21 ... 38 A6
Maple Cl. Formby L37 ... 9 C1
Maple Cl. Liverpool L12 ... 40 D3
Maple Cl. Prescot L35 ... 56 E3
Maple Cres. Huyton-w-R L36 55 D2
Maple Cres. Warrington WA5 74 F3
Maple Dr. WN2 ... 36 B7
Maple Gr. Bebington L62 ... 88 C8
Maple Gr. Liverpool L8 ... 68 C6
Maple Gr. Prescot L35 ... 56 E5
Maple Gr. St Helens WA10 ... 43 C3
Maple Gr. WA2 ... 61 B6
Maple St. Ashton-in-M WN4 . 35 A6
Maple St. Birkenhead L41 ... 66 D5
Maple St. Southport PR8 ... 4 E6
Maple Towers. L33 ... 29 F3
Maple Tree Gr. L60 ... 77 C1
Mapledale Rd. L18 ... 69 B5
Maples Ct. L43 ... 66 A3
Mapleton Cl. L43 ... 65 E1
Maplewood. Skelmersdale WN8 ... 16 A4
Maplewood. Southport PR9 ... 1 F2
Maplewood Cl. L27 ... 70 E5
Maplewood Gr. L43 ... 65 E8
Marathon Cl. L6 ... 52 F4
Marble Cl. L20 ... 38 C2
Marble Pl. PR8 ... 4 B7
Marbury Rd. L32 ... 29 C2
Marc Ave. L31 & L32 ... 29 B4
March Rd. L6 ... 53 D5
Marcham Way. L11 ... 40 B1
Marchbank Rd. WN8 ... 15 D1
Marchfield Rd. L9 ... 38 F5
Marchwood Way. L25 ... 70 A7
Marcien Way. WA8 ... 72 F3
Marcot Rd. L6 ... 53 D4
Marcross Cl. WA5 ... 60 E1
Marcus St. L41 ... 66 D7
Mardale Ave. St Helens WA11 ... 44 B8
Mardale Ave. Warrington WA2 ... 61 C3
Mardale Cl. Liverpool L27 ... 71 A3
Mardale Cl. Southport PR8 ... 7 B4
Mardale Lawn. L27 ... 71 A3
Mardale Rd. Huyton-w-R L36 55 C5
Mardale Rd. Liverpool L27 ... 71 A3
Mardale Wlk. L36 ... 55 C5
Mareth Cl. L18 ... 69 A2
Marford Rd. L12 ... 54 B7
Marfords Ave. L63 ... 88 C7
Margaret Ave. L20 ... 38 C6
Margaret Ave. St Helens WA9 ... 58 C8
Margaret Beavan Sch. L12 .. 54 A7
Margaret Cl. L6 ... 53 A4
Margaret Ct. WA10 ... 43 D1
Margaret Rd. L4 ... 38 E2
Margaret Rd. Crosby L23 ... 26 A5
Margaret St. Liverpool L6 ... 53 A4
Margaret St. St Helens WA9 58 E3
Margery Rd. WA10 ... 43 C1

Maria Rd. L4 & L9 38 F3
Marian Ave. WA12 45 F3
Marian Cl. L35 57 C2
Marian Cl The. L30 27 E4
Marian Dr. Birkenhead L46 64 E8
Marian Dr. Rainhill L35 57 B2
Marian Rd. WA11 45 E7
Marian Sq The. L30 27 F3
Marian Way The. L30 27 E3
Marians Dr. L39 13 E7
Maricourt RC High Sch. Maghull L31 28 D8
Maricourt RC High Sch. Maghull L31 28 E8
Marie Curie Ave. L30 27 F3
Marina Ave. L21 38 B8
Marina Ave. St Helens WA9 58 C7
Marina Cres. Huyton-w-R L36 55 D1
Marina Cres. Litherland L30 28 A1
Marina Dr. WA2 61 C1
Marina Rd. L37 9 F1
Marine Cres. L22 37 D8
Marine Dr. Heswall L60 85 D6
Marine Dr. Southport PR8 & PR9 1 D4
Marine Dr. Southport PR8 3 E7
Marine Par. PR8 4 A8
Marine Park Mansions. L45 37 B1
Marine Pk. L48 63 B3
Marine Prom. L45 37 B1
Marine Rd. L47 63 A7
Marine Terr. Seaforth L22 37 D8
Marine Terr. Wallasey L45 51 C7
Mariners Rd. Crosby L23 26 B3
Mariners Rd. Wallasey L45 51 C7
Mariners Way. 3 L20 38 C3
Mariners Wharf. L3 67 D6
Marion Gr. L18 69 B2
Marion Pl. WN2 35 F8
Marion Rd. L20 38 D6
Marion St. L41 66 E6
Maritime Cl. WA12 46 C5
Maritime Ct. Birkenhead L49 65 B1
Maritime Ct. Litherland L30 27 F5
Maritime Ct. Liverpool L12 54 A8
Maritime Grange. 15 L44 51 E2
Maritime Lodge. L5 52 F6
Maritime Pk. 4 L41 66 C5
Maritime Pl. L3 52 E3
Maritime View. L42 66 D3
Maritime Way. 6 L1 & L72 67 D8
Marius Cl. L4 52 F8
Mark Rake. L62 79 D1
Mark Rd. L38 17 F4
Mark St. L5 52 E7
Market App. WN4 35 B3
Market Cross. L39 13 E5
Market Pl. Birkenhead L41 66 F6
Market Pl. Prescot L34 56 D6
Market Sq. 17 L1 52 D1
Market St. Birkenhead L41 & L72 66 E6
Market St. Hoylake L47 63 B7
Market St. Newton-le-W WA12 46 A3
Market St. Southport PR8 4 B7
Market St. 9 St Helens WA10 44 A3
Market Way. 16 Liverpool L1 52 D1
Market Way. Ormskirk L39 13 E5
Markfield Cres. Liverpool L25 70 C1
Markfield Cres. St Helens WA11 44 C5
Markfield Rd. L20 38 C5
Markham Dr. PR8 4 E2
Marksway. L61 77 A4
Marl Gr. WN5 25 D4
Marl Rd. L33 30 C3
Marl Rd. Litherland L30 28 B3
Marland. WN8 16 A4
Marlborough. WN8 16 A4
Marlborough Ave. Litherland L30 28 A2
Marlborough Ave. Maghull L31 20 D3
Marlborough Cres. WA8 73 A5
Marlborough Gr. L43 66 C4
Marlborough Pl. 5 L3 52 C3
Marlborough Rd. Crosby L23 26 D3
Marlborough Rd. Liverpool L13 53 E6
Marlborough Rd. Prescot L34 56 E7
Marlborough Rd. Seaforth L22 37 E8
Marlborough Rd. Southport PR9 4 C7
Marlborough Rd. Wallasey L45 51 C7
Marlborough St. 4 L3 52 C3
Marlbrook Rd. L25 70 B6
Marldon Ave. L23 26 E2
Marldon Rd. L11 & L12 54 B8
Marled Hey. L28 55 A8
Marley Cl. L35 57 E1
Marlfield La. L61 77 A4
Marlfield Rd. L12 54 B6
Marline Ave. L63 88 C6
Marling Pk. WA8 72 B1
Marlowe Cl. L19 81 C5
Marlowe Dr. L12 & L13 54 A6
Marlowe Rd. L44 51 A4
Marlsford St. L6 53 C3
Marlston Ave. L61 76 F6
Marlwood Ave. L45 50 E5
Marmaduke St. L7 53 B1
Marmion Ave. L20 38 E7
Marmion Cl. WA3 36 E1
Marmion Rd. Hoylake L47 63 B7
Marmion Rd. Liverpool L17 68 C4
Marmonde St. L4 52 E8
Marnwood Rd. L32 29 D1
Marnwood Wlk. 5 L32 29 C1
Marple Cl. L43 65 E3
Marquis House. L62 79 B8
Marquis St. Bebington L62 79 B7
Marquis St. Birkenhead L41 & L42 66 E4
Marquis St. 4 Liverpool L3 52 E2
Marron Ave. WA2 61 B2
Marsden Ave. WA10 43 D4
Marsden Cl. L44 51 D5
Marsden Rd. Liverpool L26 82 F6
Marsden Rd. Southport PR9 4 E7
Marsden St. 7 L6 53 A3
Marsden Way. 8 L6 53 A3
Marsh Ave. L20 38 E6
Marsh Brows. L37 9 E2
Marsh Hall Rd. WA8 73 B4
Marsh La. Bebington L63 78 C7
Marsh La. L20 38 C4
Marsh La. Hightown L38 18 E6
Marsh La. Warrington WA5 74 C2
Marsh St. L20 & L4 38 D1
Marsh St. St Helens WA9 44 C3
Marshall Ave. St Helens WA9 58 C8
Marshall Ave. Warrington WA5 60 F2
Marshall Cl. L33 29 F5
Marshall Pl. L3 52 C4
Marshall St. L41 66 C8
Marshall's Cl. L31 20 C4
Marshalls Cross Rd. WA9 58 B7
Marshallsay. L37 10 A2
Marsham Cl. L49 65 A7
Marsham Rd. L25 70 C5
Marshfield Cl. L36 55 F3
Marshfield Ct. L46 49 E3
Marshfield Rd. L11 40 B1
Marshgate. WA8 84 B6
Marshgate Rd. L11 & L12 40 C2
Marshlands Rd. 1 L45 50 E6
Marshside Prim Sch. PR9 2 A5
Marshside Rd. Southport PR9 1 F4
Marsland Gr. WA9 58 E8
Marston Cl. Bebington L62 88 E3
Marston Cl. Birkenhead L43 65 F3
Marston Cres. L38 18 A2
Marten Ave. L63 88 C7
Martensen St. L7 53 B1
Martin Ave. Newton-le-W WA12 46 C5
Martin Ave. St Helens WA10 43 F6
Martin Ave. Warrington WA2 61 E1
Martin Cl. Irby L61 76 C6
Martin Cl. Liverpool L18 69 A1
Martin Cl. Rainhill L35 57 A4
Martin Gr. L35 56 E5
Martin Rd. L18 69 A1
Martin's La. L44 51 C4
Martindale Rd. Bebington L63 & L62 79 E1
Martindale Rd. Liverpool L18 69 D5
Martindale Rd. St Helens WA11 33 C2
Martine Cl. L32 29 B4
Martinhall Rd. L9 39 F4
Martins La. WN8 24 D7
Martland Ave. Golborne WA3 47 E7
Martland Ave. Litherland L10 28 E2
Martland Rd. L25 70 C4
Martlesham Cres. L49 64 B3
Martlett Rd. L12 54 D5
Martock. L35 56 F2
Marton Cl. L24 82 D3
Marton Gn. L24 82 D2
Marton Rd. L36 55 E6
Marvin St. L6 53 A3
Mary Ave. PR8 7 E6
Mary Rd. L20 38 D6
Mary St. WA9 58 E3
Mary Stockton Ct. 5 L21 38 A6
Marybone. L3 52 D2
Maryfield. L23 26 E3
Maryland La. L46 49 D1
Maryland St. L1 67 E8
Marylebone Ave. WA9 57 F6
Marymount Convent Sch. L44 51 B3
Maryton Cl. L18 69 D2
Maryville Rd. L34 56 E6
Marywell Cl. WA9 58 D7
Masefield Ave. WA8 84 F8
Masefield Cres. L30 38 D8
Masefield Gr. Liverpool L16 69 F8
Masefield Gr. St Helens WA10 43 D5
Masefield House. L62 79 A7
Masefield Pl. L30 38 E8
Masefield Rd. L23 27 C6
Maskell Rd. L13 53 F3
Mason Ave. WA8 73 B4
Mason Cl. WN4 35 D4
Mason St. Abram WN2 36 B8
Mason St. Crosby L22 26 D1
Mason St. Liverpool L7 53 A1
Mason St. Liverpool L25 70 A2
Mason St. Wallasey L45 51 B8
Massam's La. L37 9 F6
Massey Ave. WA5 60 F2
Massey Pk. L45 51 A5
Massey St. WA9 58 C8
Massey St. L41 66 D8
Mather Ave. Golborne WA3 47 E6
Mather Ave. Liverpool L18 & L19 69 C2
Mather Ave. St Helens WA9 44 E3
Mather Rd. L43 66 B5
Mathew St. L2 52 C1
Mathieson Rd. WA8 84 E5
Matlock Ave. 7 Liverpool L9 39 A6
Matlock Ave. Southport PR8 4 B4
Matlock Cl. Southport PR8 4 B4
Matlock Cl. Warrington WA5 60 A1
Matlock Cres. PR8 4 B4
Matlock Rd. PR8 4 B4
Matthew Arnold Jun Mix & Inf Sch. L8 68 A3
Matthew St. L44 51 E2
Maud Roberts Ct. L21 38 A8
Maud St. L8 68 A6
Maunders Ct. L23 27 A5
Maureen Wlk. L10 40 B7
Mauretania Rd. L4 39 A2
Mavis Dr. L49 65 A3
Mawdsley Cl. L37 10 B3
Mawdsley St. L20 52 C7
Mawdsley Terr. L39 13 F7
Max Rd. L14 54 F6
Maxton Rd. L6 53 C3
Maxwell Cl. L49 65 A6
Maxwell Pl. L13 53 F6
Maxwell Rd. L13 53 F6
Maxwell St. WA10 43 E3
May Ave. Abram WN2 36 C7
May Ave. Wallasey L44 51 D2
May Cl. L21 38 B6
May Pl. L3 52 E1
May Rd. Heswall L60 86 A8
May St. L20 38 C5
May St. Golborne WA3 36 B2
May St. Liverpool L3 52 E1
Maybank Cl. PR9 2 A1
Maybank Gr. L17 68 F1
Maybank Rd. L42 66 D4
Maybury Way. L17 68 C2
Mayer Ave. L63 78 F4
Mayew Rd. L61 76 F6
Mayfair Ave. Crosby L23 26 E5
Mayfair Ave. Liverpool L14 54 F3
Mayfair Cl. Hightown L38 17 F2
Mayfair Cl. Liverpool L6 53 B4
Mayfair Cl. Warrington WA5 74 D7
Mayfair Gr. WA8 72 D1
Mayfayre Ave. L31 20 B5
Mayfield. L4 52 E8
Mayfield Ave. Formby L37 9 C1
Mayfield Ave. St Helens WA9 57 E8
Mayfield Ave. Widnes WA8 72 B1
Mayfield Cl. Liverpool L12 54 C6
Mayfield Cl. Liverpool L27 70 C6
Mayfield Ct. Formby L37 9 F5
Mayfield Ct. Widnes WA8 73 A2
Mayfield Dr. L62 89 B6
Mayfield Gdns. Liverpool L19 81 A7
Mayfield Gdns. Neston L64 86 E1
Mayfield Rd. Bebington L63 79 A3
Mayfield Rd. Liverpool L19 81 A7
Mayfield Rd. Orrell WN8 25 B7
Mayfield Rd. Wallasey L45 50 F5
Mayfield St. WN4 35 A3
Mayfields House. L62 79 B7
Mayfields N. L62 79 B7
Mayfields S. L62 79 B7
Mayflower Ind Est. L37 10 A1
Maynard St. L8 68 B7
Maypole Ct. L30 27 D5
Maypole Ind Est. WN2 36 C7
Maytree Wlk. WN8 16 B4
Mayville Rd. L18 69 B5
Mc Clellan Pl. WA8 73 B1
McBride St. L19 81 C6
McCormack Ave. WA9 44 E3
McCulloch St. WA9 44 C3
McFarlane Ave. WA10 43 C4
McGough Cl. WA9 58 A3
McGregor St. L5 52 F5
McKee Ave. WA2 61 B2
McKeown Cl. L5 52 D5
McMinnis Ave. WA9 45 B2
McVinnie Rd. L35 56 F6
Mead Ave. L21 38 C8
Meade Cl. L35 57 D1
Meade Rd. L13 53 E6
Meadfoot Rd. L46 49 D1
Meadow Ave. Southport PR8 4 C4
Meadow Ave. St Helens WA9 58 D3
Meadow Bank. Maghull L31 20 B2
Meadow Bank. Ormskirk L39 13 F5
Meadow Bank Sch. L10 39 F8
Meadow Brow. PR9 2 D5
Meadow Cl. Newton-le-W WA12 45 F3
Meadow Cl. Skelmersdale WN8 24 D7
Meadow Cl. Westhead L40 14 E4
Meadow Cl. Widnes WA8 72 D3
Meadow Clough. WN8 16 B4
Meadow Cres. L49 65 B2
Meadow Dr. Liverpool L36 70 F8
Meadow Dr. Ormskirk L39 13 C2
Meadow Hey. L20 38 A6
Meadow Hey Cl. L25 70 B3
Meadow La. Birkenhead L42 66 F2
Meadow La. Liverpool L11 & L12 54 B8
Meadow La. Maghull L31 20 F1
Meadow La. Raby L64 87 F1
Meadow La. Southport PR8 7 D3
Meadow La. St Helens WA9 44 F2
Meadow Oak Dr. L25 70 A4
Meadow Rd. L48 63 F3
Meadow St. L45 51 A8
Meadow The. L49 65 B3
Meadow View. Crosby L21 27 B3
Meadow View. Southport PR8 4 D4
Meadow Way. L11 40 B1
Meadow Wlk. L61 76 E3
Meadowbank Cl. L14 54 E5
Meadowbrook Rd. L46 64 D7
Meadowcroft. Ashton-in-M WN4 34 F6
Meadowcroft. Formby L37 9 F2
Meadowcroft. Heswall L60 77 C1
Meadowcroft. Skelmersdale WN8 16 B4
Meadowcroft. St Helens WA9 58 C6
Meadowcroft Pk. L12 & L14 54 D4
Meadowcroft Rd. L47 48 E1
Meadowfield Cl. L42 66 F2
Meadows The. L35 57 C3
Meadowside. L46 50 B4
Meadowside Ave. WN4 35 A8
Meadowside Rd. L62 88 D8
Meadowside Sch. L49 65 B2
Meadway. Bebington L62 79 C2
Meadway. Birkenhead L49 65 B6
Meadway. Golborne WA3 47 D8
Meadway. Heswall L60 85 F6
Meadway. Litherland L30 28 A2
Meadway. Liverpool L15 69 C8
Meadway. Maghull L31 28 B7
Meadway. Prescot L35 56 F4
Meadway. Wallasey L45 51 A5
Meadway. Widnes WA8 72 A1
Meander The. L12 40 E1
Measham Cl. WA11 44 C5
Measham Way. L12 40 E3
Medbourne Cres. L32 40 F8
Meddowcroft Rd. 5 L45 51 A6
Medea St. L5 52 E6
Medea Tower. L5 52 E6
Medlar Way. WN4 34 F5
Medlock Ct. L43 66 A5
Medlock St. L4 & L69 52 E7
Medway. 2 L20 38 C3
Medway Cl. Ashton-in-M WN4 34 F6
Medway Cl. Warrington WA2 61 E2
Medway Rd. L42 67 A2
Meeting La. WA5 74 E5
Melbourne St. St Helens WA9 57 E7
Melbourne St. Wallasey L45 51 A8
Melbreck. WN8 16 A4
Melbreck Rd. L18 & L19 69 B1
Melbury Rd. L14 & L36 55 C6
Melda Cl. 3 L6 52 F3
Meldon Cl. L11 40 C2
Meldreth Cl. L37 9 C1
Meldrum Rd. L15 69 B6
Melford Dr. Ashton-in-M WN4 35 A4
Melford Dr. Birkenhead L43 65 E1
Melford Dr. Orrell WN5 25 D3
Melford Gr. L6 53 D6
Meliden Gdns. Birkenhead L41 66 E4
Meliden Gdns. St Helens WA9 58 F7
Melksham Dr. L61 76 D7
Melling Ave. L9 39 B7
Melling Dr. L32 29 E3
Melling La. L31 28 F7
Melling Rd. L20 38 C5
Melling Rd. Liverpool L9 & L10 39 C8
Melling Rd. Southport PR9 4 E7
Melling Rd. Wallasey L45 51 C7
Melling Way. L32 29 E3
Mellings Ave. WN5 25 E1
Melloncroft Dr. L48 75 C7
Melloncroft Dr W. L48 75 C7
Mellor Cl. L35 71 A7
Mellor Rd. L42 66 C2
Mellowfield Sch. PR9 4 C7
Melly Rd. L17 68 B3
Melmerby Cl. WN4 34 F3
Melrose. L46 65 A8
Melrose Ave. Burtonwood WA5 59 F7
Melrose Ave. Crosby L23 26 E3
Melrose Ave. Hoylake L47 63 B7
Melrose Ave. Southport PR9 2 B5
Melrose Ave. St Helens WA10 43 B5
Melrose Cres. WN4 34 C3
Melrose Gdns. 5 Birkenhead L43 65 F1
Melrose Rd. L33 29 D6
Melrose Rd. Liverpool L4 & L5 52 D8
Melrose Rd. Seaforth L22 37 E8
Melton Cl. L49 64 E5
Melverley Rd. L32 29 B2
Melville Ave. L42 67 A1
Melville Cl. St Helens WA10 43 D4
Melville Cl. Widnes WA8 73 D1
Melville Pl. L7 68 A8
Melville Rd. Bebington L63 78 E5
Melville Rd. L20 38 C7
Melville St. L8 68 A5
Melwood Dr. L12 54 C7
Menai Mews. L34 56 E6
Menai Rd. L20 38 D6
Menai St. L41 & L43 66 C6
Mendell Cl. L62 88 E8
Mendell Prim Sch. L62 88 E8
Mendip Ave. WA2 61 B3
Mendip Cl. Birkenhead L42 66 C1
Mendip Cl. Liverpool L26 82 E7
Mendip Gr. WA9 44 F3
Mendip Rd. Birkenhead L42 66 C1
Mendip Rd. Liverpool L15 69 A6
Menivale Cl. PR9 2 B5
Menlo Ave. L61 76 F6
Menlo Cl. L43 65 F4
Menlove Ave. L18 & L25 69 D4
Menlove Ct. L18 69 C5
Menlove Gdns N. L18 69 C5
Menlove Gdns S. L18 69 B5
Menlove Gdns W. L16 & L18 69 B5
Menlove Mansions. L18 69 C6
Menstone Rd. L13 53 F4
Mentmore Cres. L11 40 B1
Mentmore Rd. L18 69 A2
Menzies St. L8 68 A4
Meols Cl. Formby L37 9 E2
Meols Cl. Hale L24 83 E2
Meols Cop Ctr The. PR9 5 A4
Meols Cop High Sch. PR8 4 F5
Meols Cop Sta. PR9 4 F7
Meols Dr. L47 & L48 63 A4
Meols Par. Hoylake L47 48 D1
Meols Sta. L47 63 E8
Mercer Ave. L32 29 C1

Mercer Ct. 8 L20 .... 38 C3
Mercer Ct. Liverpool L14 .... 54 E5
Mercer Dr. L4 .... 52 E8
Mercer Heights. L32 .... 29 C2
Mercer Rd. Birkenhead L43 .. 65 E8
Mercer Rd. Haydock WA11 ... 45 D6
Mercer St. Burtonwood WA5 .... 59 E6
Mercer St. Liverpool L19 .... 81 C5
Mercer St. Newton-le-W WA12 .... 46 D4
Mercer's La. L39 .... 22 B4
Merchant Taylors' Jun Sch. L23 .... 26 E3
Merchant Taylors' Sch. Crosby L23 .... 26 E3
Merchant Taylors' Sch. Crosby L23 .... 26 E4
Merchants Cres. WA3 .... 36 E1
Mere Ave. L63 .... 88 B6
Mere Bank. L17 .... 68 E4
Mere Cl. WN8 .... 15 F2
Mere Farm Gr. L43 .... 65 F4
Mere Farm Rd. L43 .... 65 F4
Mere Gn. L4 .... 39 A1
Mere Gr. WA11 .... 33 B1
Mere Hey. WA10 .... 43 A3
Mere La. Heswall L60 .... 76 E2
Mere La. Liverpool L5 .... 52 F6
Mere La. Wallasey L45 .... 50 E7
Mere Park Rd. L49 .... 64 C3
Mere Pk. L23 .... 26 D4
Mere Rd. Ashton-in-M WN4 .. 35 C4
Mere Rd. Formby L37 .... 9 D2
Mere Rd. Newton-le-W WA12 46 F4
Merebank. L43 .... 65 E4
Merebrook Gr. L33 .... 29 F5
Merecliff. L36 .... 55 B8
Merecroft Ave. L44 .... 51 C2
Meredale Rd. L18 .... 69 A4
Meredith St. L19 .... 81 E5
Merefield Sch. Southport PR9 2 B3
Merefield Sch. Southport PR8 7 B4
Mereheath. L46 .... 49 E3
Mereheath Gdns. L46 .... 49 E3
Mereland Cl. WN5 .... 25 E6
Merepark Dr. PR9 .... 2 B4
Mereview Cres. L12 .... 40 D3
Merewood. WN8 .... 16 A4
Meribel Cl. L23 .... 27 A5
Meriden Ave. L63 .... 79 A1
Meriden Cl. Southport PR8 .... 7 B5
Meriden Cl. St Helens WA11 .... 44 D6
Meriden Rd. L25 .... 70 B6
Merland Way. WA9 .... 44 F2
Merlewood Ave. PR9 .... 2 B3
Merlin Ave. L49 .... 64 D6
Merlin Cl. Birkenhead L49 .... 64 D6
Merlin Cl. St Helens WA11 ... 44 B6
Merlin Ct. L26 .... 70 D1
Merlin St. L8 .... 67 F6
Merrick Cl. WA2 .... 61 E3
Merriford Gn. L4 .... 39 B1
Merrills La. L49 .... 65 A5
Merrilocks Gn. L23 .... 26 A5
Merrilocks Rd. L23 .... 26 B5
Merrilox Ave. L31 .... 20 D3
Merrion Cl. L25 .... 69 F3
Merritt Ave. L41 .... 66 B8
Merrivale Rd. L25 .... 70 C2
Mersey Ave. Formby L37 .... 9 E6
Mersey Ave. Liverpool L19 ... 80 F8
Mersey Ave. Maghull L31 .... 20 F2
Mersey Cotts. L19 .... 81 D5
Mersey Ct. Crosby L23 .... 26 C3
Mersey Ct. 14 Wallasey L44 .... 51 E2
Mersey House. L20 .... 38 B4
Mersey La S. L42 .... 67 A2
Mersey Mount. L41 & L42 .... 66 E3
Mersey Park Prim Sch. L42 . 66 D3
Mersey Rd. Birkenhead L42 .... 67 A2
Mersey Rd. Birkenhead L42 . 67 A3
Mersey Rd. Crosby L23 .... 26 C3
Mersey Rd. Liverpool L17 & L19 .... 80 E8
Mersey Rd. Orrell WN5 .... 25 F7
Mersey St. St Helens WA9 ... 45 A3
Mersey St. 2 Wallasey L44 51 E2
Mersey View. Crosby L22 .... 26 C2
Mersey View. Liverpool L19 . 81 C6
Mersey View Rd. WA8 .... 84 B4
Mersey View Sch. L17 .... 68 E1
Merseybank House. L62 .... 79 B8
Merseybank Rd. L62 .... 79 B7
Merstone Cl. L26 .... 82 F7
Merthyr Gr. L16 .... 54 E1
Merton Bank Cty Prim Sch. WA9 .... 44 C4
Merton Bank Rd. WA11 & WA9 .... 44 C5
Merton Cl. L36 .... 55 B2
Merton Cres. L36 .... 55 B2
Merton Dr. Birkenhead L49 .. 65 A3
Merton Dr. Huyton-w-R L36 . 55 A2
Merton Gr. L20 .... 38 C3
Merton Gr. Crosby L22 & L23 26 C3
Merton Pl. L43 .... 66 C6
Merton Rd. Bebington L62 .... 89 B3
Merton Rd. L20 & L69 .... 38 C3
Merton Rd. Wallasey L45 .... 51 B5
Merton St. WA9 .... 44 C5
Merton Towers. L20 .... 38 D3
Mesham Cl. L49 .... 64 E5
Meteor Cres. WA2 .... 61 D2
Methuen St. Birkenhead L41 .... 66 A8
Methuen St. Liverpool L15 .... 68 E8
Mews The. Huyton-w-R L28 .. 55 C7
Mews The. Liverpool L17 & L19 .... 68 F1
Meyrick Rd. L11 .... 39 E2
Micawber Cl. L8 .... 67 F5
Michael Dragonette Ct. L3 .. 52 C4
Michael's La. L39 .... 8 C3
Michaels Cl. L37 .... 9 E3
Mickering La. L39 .... 21 C5
Micklefield Rd. L15 .... 68 F6
Mickleton Dr. PR8 .... 7 A5
Middle Moss La. Great Altcar L37 .... 10 F3
Middle Moss La. Haskayne L37 .... 11 A2
Middle Rd. Liverpool L24 .... 82 F4
Middle Rd. Liverpool L24 .... 82 F5
Middle Way. L11 .... 40 D5
Middle Withins La. L37 & L38 .... 19 A7
Middlefield Rd. L18 & L25 .... 69 E3
Middleham Cl. L32 .... 29 C1
Middlehey Rd. L34 .... 41 D4
Middlehurst Ave. WA10 .... 43 F4
Middlehurst Cl. L34 .... 57 A7
Middlemass Hey. L27 .... 70 E5
Middlesex Rd. L20 .... 38 D4
Middleton Rd. Crosby L22 .... 26 F2
Middleton Rd. Liverpool L7 .. 53 E3
Middlewood. Golborne WA3 47 E8
Middlewood. Skelmersdale WN8 .... 16 A4
Middlewood Cl. L39 .... 21 C7
Middlewood Dr. L39 .... 21 C7
Middlewood Rd. L39 .... 21 C7
Midghall St. L3 .... 52 C3
Midhurst Dr. PR8 .... 7 B4
Midhurst Rd. L12 .... 41 A3
Midland St. 7 Birkenhead L41 .... 66 C5
Midland St. Widnes WA8 .... 73 B1
Midland Terr. L22 .... 26 D1
Midlothian Dr. L23 .... 26 C3
Midway Rd. L36 .... 55 F4
Milbrook Cres. L32 .... 29 E3
Milbrook Dr. L32 .... 29 E3
Milbrook Wlk. L32 .... 29 E3
Mildenhall Rd. L25 .... 70 B7
Mildenhall Way. L25 .... 70 B7
Mildmay Rd. L20 .... 38 B5
Mildmay Rd. Liverpool L11 ... 39 E2
Mile End. L5 .... 52 D4
Miles Cl. L49 .... 64 C2
Miles La. L49 .... 64 C2
Miles St. L8 .... 68 A4
Milestone Hey. L28 .... 55 B8
Milford Cl. L37 .... 9 C1
Milford Dr. L12 .... 40 E3
Milford St. L5 .... 52 C6
Milk St. 5 WA10 .... 44 A3
Mill Ave. WA5 .... 74 E7
Mill Bank. L13 .... 53 F6
Mill Brow. Bebington L63 .... 78 D6
Mill Brow. St Helens WA10 ... 43 B4
Mill Brow. St Helens WA9 .... 58 D5
Mill Brow. Widnes WA8 .... 73 C1
Mill Brow Cl. WA9 .... 58 D5
Mill Cl. Crosby L23 .... 26 E6
Mill Cl. Warrington WA2 .... 61 E4
Mill Ct. L30 .... 27 D5
Mill Dam La. L40 .... 14 D8
Mill Farm Cl. WA2 .... 61 E3
Mill Green La. WA8 .... 73 E5
Mill Hey. L35 .... 57 E1
Mill Hey Rd. L48 .... 75 D6
Mill Hill. L43 .... 66 A3
Mill Hill Rd. L49 & L61 .... 76 C7
Mill House Sch. WA12 .... 46 F3
Mill House View. WN8 .... 25 C7
Mill La. Birkenhead L49 .... 64 C2
Mill La. Bold Heath WA8 .... 73 D6
Mill La. L20 .... 38 D3
Mill La. Cronton WA8 .... 72 D6
Mill La. Haskayne L39 .... 12 F1
Mill La. Heswall L60 .... 86 B8
Mill La. L32 .... 29 D4
Mill La. Knowsley L34 .... 41 D5
Mill La. Liverpool L3 .... 52 D2
Mill La. Liverpool L13 & L15 .. 54 A1
Mill La. Liverpool L12 & L13 .. 54 A6
Mill La. Newton-le-W WA12 . 46 E3
Mill La. Orrell WN8 .... 25 A8
Mill La. Raby L64 .... 87 F1
Mill La. Rainford WA11 .... 32 C4
Mill La. Rainhill L35 .... 57 D1
Mill La. Skelmersdale WN8 ... 15 F2
Mill La. Southport PR9 .... 2 A1
Mill La. St Helens WA9 .... 58 D5
Mill La. Wallasey L44 .... 51 A3
Mill La. Warrington WA2 .... 60 F4
Mill Lane Cres. PR9 .... 2 A1
Mill Park Dr. L62 .... 88 E3
Mill Park Inf & Jun Schs. L62 .... 88 E3
Mill Rd. Bebington L63 .... 78 D6
Mill Rd. Bebington L62 .... 79 D3
Mill Rd. Heswall L61 .... 77 A6
Mill Rd. Liverpool L6 .... 52 F4
Mill Rd. Liverpool L6 .... 53 A4
Mill Rd. Orrell WN5 .... 25 D5
Mill Rd. Southport PR8 .... 7 D5
Mill Sq. Litherland L10 .... 28 E2
Mill St. Ashton-in-M WN4 .... 35 C2
Mill St. Birkenhead L42 .... 66 D4
Mill St. Golborne WA3 .... 47 A8
Mill St. Liverpool L8 .... 67 E5
Mill St. Liverpool L25 .... 70 A2
Mill St. Ormskirk L39 .... 13 F5
Mill St. Prescot L34 .... 56 D6
Mill St. Southport PR8 .... 4 C6
Mill St. St Helens WA10 .... 43 F4
Mill View. 5 L8 .... 67 E5
Mill View Ct. L39 .... 22 E6
Mill View Dr. L63 .... 78 C6
Mill Wood Ave. WA10 .... 42 F3
Millachip Ct. L6 .... 53 B4
Millar's Pace. PR9 .... 2 B5
Millbank La. L31 & L39 .... 20 F3
Millbank Rd. L44 .... 51 A3
Millbeck Gr. WA11 .... 33 B2
Millbrook Bsns Ctr. WA11 .... 32 C3
Millbrook Cl. WN8 .... 15 E2
Millbrook La. WA10 .... 43 B4
Millbrook Prim Sch. L32 .... 29 D3
Millburn Hts. L5 .... 52 E5
Millbutt Cl. L63 .... 78 D6
Millcroft. L23 .... 27 A5
Millcroft Ave. WN5 .... 25 D5
Millcroft Pk. L49 .... 64 B3
Millcroft Rd. L25 .... 70 C1
Miller Ave. L23 .... 26 D5
Miller Cl. L8 .... 67 F4
Miller's Bridge. L20 .... 38 B2
Millers Cl. L46 .... 64 C7
Millers Ct. L39 .... 13 F5
Millers Fold. WA10 .... 43 B4
Millers Way. L46 .... 64 C8
Millerscroft. L32 .... 29 C4
Millersdale. 13 WA9 .... 58 C4
Millersdale Ave. L9 .... 39 B7
Millersdale Cl. L62 .... 88 F5
Millersdale Rd. L18 .... 69 A4
Millfield Cl. Bebington L63 ... 78 D5
Millfield Cl. Liverpool L13 .... 54 A6
Millfield La. WN4 .... 34 E1
Millfield Rd. WA8 .... 73 C2
Millfields. WA10 .... 43 B3
Millgreen Cl. L12 .... 40 E3
Millhouse Cl. L46 .... 49 B1
Millhouse La. L46 .... 49 B1
Millhouse Lodge. PR8 .... 7 D5
Millingford Ave. WA3 .... 35 F2
Millingford Gr. WN4 .... 35 B3
Millingford Ind Est. WA3 .... 47 A8
Millington Cl. L43 .... 65 E1
Millom Ave. L35 .... 57 B4
Millom Gr. Liverpool L12 .... 40 C1
Millom Gr. St Helens WA10 .. 57 C8
Millrose Cl. WN8 .... 15 F2
Millstead Hospital Sch. L15 69 B8
Millstead Rd. L15 .... 69 B8
Millstead Wlk. L15 .... 69 A8
Millthwaite Ct. L44 .... 50 F4
Millthwaite Rd. L44 .... 50 F4
Millvale St. L6 .... 53 C3
Millway Rd. L24 .... 83 A4
Millwood. L63 .... 78 D6
Millwood Cl. WN4 .... 35 A5
Millwood Ct. L24 .... 83 A4
Millwood Cty Prim Jun Mix Sch. L24 .... 83 A3
Millwood Gdns. L35 .... 56 F2
Millwood Rd. L24 .... 82 F3
Milman Cl. Birkenhead L49 .. 64 F4
Milman Cl. Ormskirk L39 .... 13 D3
Milman Ct. L25 .... 69 E3
Milman Rd. L4 .... 39 A1
Milne Rd. 5 L13 .... 53 E8
Milner Cop. L60 .... 86 A8
Milner Rd. Heswall L60 .... 86 A8
Milner Rd. Liverpool L17 .... 68 E1
Milner St. Birkenhead L41 .... 66 A8
Milner St. Liverpool L8 .... 68 B8
Milnthorpe Cl. 11 L4 .... 52 E8
Milnthorpe Rd. WA5 .... 59 E6
Milnthorpe St. L19 .... 81 C6
Milroy St. L7 .... 53 B1
Milton Ave. Liverpool L14 .... 54 F2
Milton Ave. Newton-le-W WA12 .... 46 B3
Milton Ave. Prescot L35 .... 56 F3
Milton Ave. Widnes WA8 .... 84 F8
Milton Cl. L35 .... 56 E3
Milton Cres. L60 .... 77 A1
Milton Dr. L39 .... 14 A4
Milton Gr. WN5 .... 25 F6
Milton Pavement. 7 L41 .... 66 D6
Milton Rd. Birkenhead L42 ... 66 C4
Milton Rd. L4 .... 38 E2
Milton Rd. Crosby L22 .... 26 E2
Milton Rd. Golborne WA3 .... 47 D7
Milton Rd. Liverpool L7 .... 53 E2
Milton Rd. Wallasey L44 .... 51 D2
Milton Rd. West Kirby L48 .... 63 A3
Milton Rd. Widnes WA8 .... 84 F8
Milton Rd E. L42 .... 66 D4
Milton St. L20 .... 38 B4
Milton St. Southport PR9 .... 5 A7
Milton St. St Helens WA9 .... 58 B2
Milton Way. L31 .... 20 B1
Milvain Dr. WA2 .... 61 C1
Milverton St. L6 .... 53 C4
Mimosa Rd. L15 .... 69 B7
Mindale Rd. L15 .... 68 F8
Mine Way. WA11 .... 45 F7
Mine's Ave. L34 .... 56 E6
Minehead Gr. WA9 .... 58 D5
Minehead Rd. L17 & L19 .... 80 E8
Miners Way. L24 .... 83 A3
Mines Ave. L17 & L19 .... 80 F8
Minshull St. L7 .... 53 A1
Minstead Ave. L33 .... 30 A2
Minster Ct. L8 .... 68 A8
Minto Cl. L7 .... 53 C2
Minto St. L7 .... 53 B2
Minton Way. WA8 .... 73 B5
Mintor Rd. L33 .... 30 A2
Minver Rd. L12 .... 54 D7
Miranda Ave. L63 .... 78 E7
Miranda Pl. L20 .... 38 D1
Miranda Rd. L20 .... 38 D1
Mirfield Cl. Golborne WA3 ... 47 D7
Mirfield Cl. Liverpool L26 .... 82 F6
Mirfield St. L6 .... 53 C3
Miriam Pl. 2 L41 .... 65 F8
Miriam Rd. L4 .... 53 A6
Miskelly St. L20 .... 52 C8
Mission Wlk. L6 .... 53 A3
Missouri Rd. L13 .... 53 D7
Mistlethrush Way. 2 L12 ... 40 F3
Miston St. L20 .... 52 C8
Misty Cl. WA8 .... 72 C2
Mitchell Ave. WA5 .... 59 E5
Mitchell Cres. L21 .... 38 B8
Mitchell Rd. Billinge WN5 .... 33 E5
Mitchell Rd. Prescot L34 .... 56 C6
Mitchell Rd. St Helens WA10 43 C1
Mitchell St. Ashton-in-M WN4 .... 35 C2
Mitchell St. Golborne WA3 ... 47 A8
Mithril Cl. WA8 .... 73 E3
Mitre Cl. L35 .... 56 D1
Mitten's La. L37 .... 10 B3
Mitylene St. L5 .... 52 E6
Mobberley Way. L63 .... 79 A3
Mockbeggar Dr. L45 .... 50 D8
Mockbeggar Wharf. L45 .... 50 E7
Mockets Prim Sch. L25 .... 70 D1
Modred St. L8 .... 67 F5
Moel Famau View. L17 .... 68 B2
Moels Cop Rd. PR8 .... 4 F4
Moffat Rd. L9 .... 39 C7
Moffatdale Rd. L4 .... 53 C8
Molesworth Gr. L16 .... 54 F1
Molineux Ave. L14 .... 54 D1
Molland Cl. L12 .... 54 D8
Mollington Ave. L11 .... 39 F2
Mollington Rd. L32 .... 29 C2
Mollington Rd. Wallasey L44 51 C3
Mollington St. L41 .... 66 E5
Molly's La. L33 .... 41 D7
Molton Rd. L15 & L16 .... 69 C8
Molyneux Cl. Birkenhead L49 .... 64 F5
Molyneux Cl. Huyton-w-R L36 .... 55 F2
Molyneux Cl. Prescot L35 .... 56 D4
Molyneux Ct. L14 .... 54 D1
Molyneux Ct. Liverpool L11 .. 40 B3
Molyneux Dr. Prescot L35 .... 56 D4
Molyneux Dr. Wallasey L45 . 51 C8
Molyneux Rd. Crosby L22 .... 26 E2
Molyneux Rd. Liverpool L6 ... 53 B3
Molyneux Rd. Liverpool L18 . 68 F4
Molyneux Rd. Maghull L31 ... 28 F7
Molyneux Rd. Ormskirk L39 . 21 C7
Molyneux Way. L10 .... 28 C3
Mona St. Birkenhead L41 .... 65 F7
Mona St. L20 .... 38 D6
Mona St. St Helens WA10 .... 43 D3
Monaghan Cl. L9 .... 39 A7
Monash Rd. L11 & L13 .... 53 F8
Monastery La. WA9 .... 58 E7
Monastery Rd. 4 Liverpool L6 .... 53 C6
Monastery Rd. St Helens WA9 .... 58 E7
Mond Rd. Liverpool L10 .... 40 A7
Mond Rd. 5 Widnes WA8 .... 73 A1
Monfa Rd. L20 .... 38 C6
Monfa Rd. L20 .... 38 D6
Monica Dr. WA8 .... 73 A5
Monica Rd. L25 .... 70 B1
Monica Terr. WN4 .... 35 B2
Monk Rd. L44 & L45 .... 51 B4
Monk St. Birkenhead L41 .... 66 F6
Monk St. Liverpool L5 .... 52 F6
Monk's Way. L48 .... 63 C2
Monkfield Way. L19 .... 81 D4
Monks Carr La. L38 .... 19 A6
Monks Cl. L37 .... 10 A1
Monks Dr. L37 .... 10 A1
Monks Ferry. L41 .... 66 F6
Monks Way. Bebington L63 .. 78 F4
Monks Way. Liverpool L25 ... 70 B2
Monksdown Jun & Inf Sch. L11 .... 40 A1
Monksdown Rd. L11 .... 40 A1
Monksferry Wlk. L19 .... 80 F7
Monkswell Dr. L15 .... 69 A8
Monkswell St. L8 .... 68 A3
Monkswood Cl. WA5 .... 60 E2
Monmouth Cres. WN4 .... 35 D2
Monmouth Dr. L10 .... 28 F1
Monmouth Gr. WA9 .... 44 D2
Monmouth Rd. L44 .... 50 F4
Monro Cl. L8 .... 67 F4
Monro St. L8 .... 67 F4
Montagu Rd. L37 .... 9 E5
Montague Rd. L13 .... 54 A2
Montclair Dr. L15 & L18 .... 69 B6
Monterey Rd. L13 .... 54 B2
Montfort Dr. L19 .... 81 A7
Montgomery Ave. PR9 .... 5 B6
Montgomery Cl. L35 .... 56 D2
Montgomery Hill. Birkenhead L48 .... 64 A1
Montgomery Hill. Irby L48 .. 76 A8
Montgomery House. 8 L21 37 F7
Montgomery Rd. Huyton-w-R L36 .... 55 E4
Montgomery Rd. Liverpool L9 .... 39 A7
Montgomery Rd. Widnes WA8 .... 84 D8
Montgomery Way. L6 .... 53 B4
Montpellier Cres. L45 .... 51 A8
Montreal St. WN7 .... 36 E4
Montrey Cres. WN4 .... 34 C3
Montrose Ave. L44 .... 51 E1
Montrose Cl. WA2 .... 61 F4
Montrose Ct. L12 .... 54 E7
Montrose Dr. PR9 .... 1 F1
Montrose Rd. L13 .... 53 E6
Montrose Way. L13 .... 53 F2
Montrovia Cres. L10 .... 39 F6
Monville Rd. L9 .... 39 C7
Moor Cl. Crosby L23 .... 26 F5
Moor Cl. Southport PR8 .... 7 D2
Moor Coppice. L23 .... 26 F5
Moor Ct. L10 .... 40 A7
Moor Dr. Crosby L23 .... 26 F4
Moor Dr. Skelmersdale WN8 24 D7
Moor House. 3 L23 .... 26 E5
Moor La. Crosby L23 .... 26 F5
Moor La. Heswall L60 .... 85 F8
Moor La. Ince Blundell L38 ... 18 E2
Moor La. Liverpool L4 .... 39 A2
Moor La. Liverpool L10 .... 40 A7
Moor La. Liverpool L10 & L32 40 B8
Moor La. Maghull L29 .... 19 D1
Moor La. Southport PR8 .... 7 C2

Moor La. Widnes WA8 84 F7
Moor La S. WA8 84 F7
Moor Pl. L3 52 E2
Moor Rd. WN5 25 E6
Moor St. Liverpool L2 52 C1
Moor St. Ormskirk L39 13 F5
Moorbridge Cl. L30 28 A5
Moorcroft Rd. Huyton-w-R L36 55 E5
Moorcroft Rd. Liverpool L18 69 D1
Moorcroft Rd. Wallasey L45 50 D5
Moore Ave. Birkenhead L42 66 E2
Moore Ave. St Helens WA9 45 B3
Moore Cl. WA8 73 D2
Moore Dr. WA11 45 F6
Moore St. L20 38 B5
Mooreway. L35 57 E1
Moorfield. L33 29 F6
Moorfield Ctr The. L33 29 F6
Moorfield Cty Prim Sch. WA8 73 D3
Moorfield Dr. L64 86 C1
Moorfield Rd. Crosby L23 27 A5
Moorfield Rd. St Helens WA10 43 D5
Moorfield Rd. Widnes WA8 73 D3
Moorfields. L2 52 C2
Moorfields Ave. L43 65 D4
Moorfields Sta. L2 52 C2
Moorfoot Rd. WA9 44 F3
Moorfoot Way. L33 29 D6
Moorgate. L39 13 E4
Moorgate Ave. L23 26 F4
Moorgate Rd. Kirkby L32 & L33 41 A7
Moorgate St. 8 L7 53 B1
Moorhey Rd. L31 28 D6
Moorhouses. L38 17 F3
Moorings Cl. L64 86 B1
Moorings The. Heswall L60 85 C8
Moorings The. Maghull L31 20 B4
Moorland Ave. L23 26 E5
Moorland Cl. L60 86 A7
Moorland Pk. L60 86 A7
Moorland Rd. Ashton-in-M WN4 35 E5
Moorland Rd. Birkenhead L42 66 E3
Moorland Rd. Maghull L31 28 D6
Moorlands Rd. L23 27 B6
Moorside Cl. L23 26 F4
Moorside Ct. WA8 84 F7
Moorside Prim Sch. WN8 24 E7
Moorside Rd. L23 26 F4
Moorway. L60 86 B8
Moorwood Cres. WA9 58 C4
Moray Cl. WA10 43 E5
Morcott La. L24 83 D2
Morden Ave. WN4 35 B3
Morden St. L6 53 C3
Morecambe St. L6 53 C5
Morecroft Rd. L42 67 A1
Morella Rd. L4 53 C8
Morello Dr. L63 79 B2
Moret Cl. L23 27 A5
Moreton Ave. 1 WA9 58 C4
Moreton Cl. WA3 35 F1
Moreton Gr. L45 50 E6
Moreton Rd. L49 64 F6
Moreton Sta. L46 49 E2
Morgan Ave. WA2 61 C2
Morgan Hts. L10 40 A8
Morgan Mews. L30 27 D3
Morgan St. WA9 44 D3
Morland Ave. L62 88 D6
Morley Ave. L41 66 B8
Morley Rd. Southport PR9 4 E8
Morley Rd. Wallasey L41 & L44 51 A3
Morley St. Liverpool L4 52 E7
Morley St. St Helens WA10 43 F5
Morley Way. 1 WA10 43 F4
Morningside. L23 26 F3
Morningside Pl. L11 39 F1
Morningside Rd. L11 & L13 53 F8
Morningside View. L11 53 F8
Morningside Way. L11 53 F8
Mornington Ave. L22 & L23 26 E2
Mornington Rd. Southport PR9 4 C7
Mornington Rd. Wallasey L45 51 B6
Mornington St. L8 67 E5
Morpeth Cl. L46 64 B8
Morpeth Rd. L47 63 A5
Morpeth St. L8 67 F7
Morpeth Wharf. L41 & L72 66 E8
Morris Cl. WA11 45 A5
Morris Ct. L43 65 F5
Morris Rd. WN8 25 A7
Morris St. WA9 44 E1
Morrison Jun Sch. L18 68 F5
Morrissey Cl. WA10 43 D4
Morston Ave. L32 40 E8
Morston Cres. L32 40 E8
Morston Wlk. L32 40 E8
Mortimer St. L41 & L72 66 F6
Mortlake Cl. WA8 72 C3
Morton St. L8 67 F5
Morval Cres. L4 38 E2
Morven Cl. WA2 61 E3
Morven Gr. PR8 & PR9 4 E7
Moscow Dr. Liverpool L13 53 F5
Moscow Dr. Liverpool L13 54 A5
Mosedale Ave. WA11 33 B1
Mosedale Rd. Bebington L62 79 E2
Mosedale Rd. Liverpool L9 39 A5
Moseley Ave. L44 & L45 51 A4
Moseley Rd. L63 79 A1
Moses St. L8 67 F4
Mosley St. PR8 4 B4
Moss Ave. WN5 25 D3
Moss Bank. L39 13 D2
Moss Bank Ct. L39 13 D2
Moss Bank Pk. L21 38 A8
Moss Bank Rd. St Helens WA11 33 B2
Moss Bank Rd. St Helens WA10 & WA11 43 F8
Moss Brow. WA11 31 E7
Moss Delph La. L39 13 C1
Moss End Way. L33 30 D3
Moss Gate Gr. L14 55 A3
Moss Gate Rd. L14 55 A3
Moss Gn. L37 10 B4
Moss Gr. Birkenhead L42 66 C2
Moss Gr. Liverpool L8 68 C6
Moss Green Way. WA9 45 A1
Moss La. Bickerstaffe L39 22 F2
Moss La. Bickerstaffe WN8 23 F6
Moss La. Birkenhead L42 66 B2
Moss La. L21 38 C8
Moss La. L9 & L20 38 F6
Moss La. Formby L37, L39 ,L38 & L23 10 D5
Moss La. Golborne WA3 47 B5
Moss La. Hightown L38 18 C2
Moss La. L33 29 F7
Moss La. L33 30 B3
Moss La. Knowsley WA11 42 F8
Moss La. Litherland L21 & L30 27 D1
Moss La. Maghull L31 20 D5
Moss La. Maghull L31 20 E2
Moss La. Rainford WA11 32 E5
Moss La. Southport PR9 5 B8
Moss La. St Helens WA11 43 B7
Moss La. St Helens WA9 45 A1
Moss Lane View. WN8 23 F6
Moss Nook. L39 13 C2
Moss Nook La. L31 29 B7
Moss Nook La. Rainford WA11 31 E6
Moss Nook La. Rainford WA11 31 F5
Moss Pits Cl. L10 39 F7
Moss Pits La. Liverpool L10 & L9 39 E7
Moss Pits La. Liverpool L15 69 B7
Moss Rd. Orrell WN5 25 D3
Moss Rd. Southport PR8 4 C2
Moss Side. Formby L37 10 B4
Moss Side. Huyton-w-R L14 55 A3
Moss St. Liverpool L3 & L6 & L7 52 F2
Moss St. Liverpool L19 81 C6
Moss St. Prescot L34 56 D7
Moss View. L21 38 C8
Moss View. Maghull L31 20 F1
Moss View. Southport PR8 7 E5
Moss Way. L11 40 C4
Mossborough Hall La. WA11 31 C2
Mossborough Rd. WA11 31 E4
Mossbrow Rd. L36 55 E4
Mosscraig. L36 55 C7
Mosscroft. L33 30 A5
Mosscroft Cl. L36 56 A4
Mosscroft Cty Prim Sch. L36 56 A3
Mossdale Dr. L35 57 D3
Mossdale Rd. Ashton-in-M WN4 35 A8
Mossdale Rd. L33 29 F5
Mossdene Rd. Wallasey L44 50 F4
Mossfield Rd. L9 38 F6
Mossgiel Ave. PR8 7 B5
Mosshill Cl. L31 20 C3
Mosslands. WA10 43 A4
Mosslands Dr. L44 & L45 50 E4
Mosslands Lower Sch. L44 50 F3
Mosslands Sch The. L45 50 E4
Mosslawn Rd. L32 30 A1
Mosslea Pk. L18 68 F4
Mossley Ave. Bebington L62 88 D8
Mossley Ave. Liverpool L18 68 F5
Mossley Hill Dr. L17 & L18 68 E4
Mossley Hill Hospl. L18 68 E3
Mossley Hill Rd. L18 & L19 68 F2
Mossley Hill Sta. L18 69 A3
Mossley Rd. L42 66 E3
Mossock Hall Golf Course. L39 21 D3
Mosspits Inf Sch. L15 69 B6
Mossville Cl. L18 69 A2
Mossville Rd. L18 69 B2
Mossy Bank Rd. L44 51 D4
Mostyn Ave. Heswall L60 85 C8
Mostyn Ave. Litherland L10 28 C2
Mostyn Ave. Liverpool L19 81 D8
Mostyn Ave. West Kirby L48 63 B1
Mostyn Cl. L4 52 E7
Mostyn Gdns. L64 86 B1
Mostyn House Sch. L64 86 C1
Mostyn St. L44 51 B2
Mother Teresa RC Prim Sch. L5 52 D4
Motherwell Cres. PR8 4 F3
Mottershead Rd. WA8 73 A1
Mottram Cl. L32 29 F2
Moughland La. WA7 84 F1
Mould St. L5 52 D5
Mounsey Rd. L41 & L42 66 D5
Mount Ave. Bebington L63 78 D7
Mount Ave. L20 38 D7
Mount Ave. Heswall L60 85 F8
Mount Carmel Prep Sch. L39 13 D2
Mount Cl. L32 29 C4
Mount Cres. L32 29 C4
Mount Cres. Orrell WN5 25 F6
Mount Ct. Heswall L60 85 F8
Mount Ct. 4 Wallasey L45 51 A8
Mount Dr. L63 78 D7
Mount Gr. L41 66 C5
Mount Grove Pl. 14 L41 66 C5
Mount Haven Cl. L49 65 A5
Mount House Cl. L37 10 B5
Mount House Rd. L37 10 B5
Mount Olive. L43 66 A3
Mount Park Ct. L25 70 A3
Mount Pk. Bebington L63 78 D7
Mount Pk. Liverpool L25 70 A3
Mount Pleasant. Birkenhead L43 66 B3
Mount Pleasant. Crosby L22 26 D1
Mount Pleasant. Liverpool L1 & L3 & L7 52 E1
Mount Pleasant. Liverpool L3 & L7 52 F1
Mount Pleasant. Widnes WA8 73 B2
Mount Pleasant Ave. WA9 45 B3
Mount Pleasant Rd. L45 51 B7
Mount Prim Sch. L45 51 A8
Mount Rd. Bebington L63 & L42 78 D5
Mount Rd. Birkenhead L49 65 A5
Mount Rd. Birkenhead L42 66 D1
Mount Rd. L31 & L32 29 B3
Mount Rd. Wallasey L45 51 A7
Mount Rd. West Kirby L48 63 C1
Mount St. Crosby L22 26 D1
Mount St. Liverpool L1 67 E8
Mount St. Liverpool L25 70 A2
Mount St. Southport PR9 4 D7
Mount St. Widnes WA8 73 B1
Mount The. Heswall L60 85 F8
Mount The. Skelmersdale WN8 24 B8
Mount The. Wallasey L44 51 C4
Mount Vernon. L7 53 A1
Mount Vernon Gn. 9 L7 53 A2
Mount Vernon St. 6 L7 53 A2
Mount Vernon View. 7 L7 53 A2
Mount Wood Rd. L42 78 C8
Mountfield Ct. WN5 25 F7
Mountway. L63 78 D7
Mountwood. WN8 16 A4
Mountwood Lodge. PR8 7 C5
Mowbray Ave. WA11 44 C5
Mowbray Ct. L20 38 C1
Mowbray Gr. L13 54 A1
Mowbray Grove. L13 54 A1
Mowcroft La. WA5 74 B3
Moxen Dale. L27 70 F4
Moxon St. WA10 43 D2
Moyles Cl. WA8 72 D2
Mozart Cl. L8 68 B6
Much Woolton RC Prim Sch. L25 70 B2
Muirfield Cl. L14 54 E6
Muirfield Dr. PR8 7 C4
Muirfield Rd. L36 55 C1
Muirhead Ave. L12 & L13 & L11 53 F7
Muirhead Ave E. Liverpool L11 & L12 40 B1
Mulberry Ave. Golborne WA3 47 F7
Mulberry Ave. St Helens WA10 43 C3
Mulberry Cl. L33 29 F6
Mulberry Gr. L44 51 D3
Mulberry Pl. L7 67 F8
Mulberry Rd. L42 66 F2
Mulberry St. L7 & L8 67 F8
Mulcrow Cl. WA9 44 D4
Mulgrave St. L8 68 A7
Mullberry St. L7 52 F1
Mullen Cl. WA5 60 F1
Mulliner St. L7 68 C7
Mullins Ave. WA12 46 C5
Mullion Cl. Liverpool L26 82 E8
Mullion Cl. Southport PR9 2 B5
Mullion Rd. L11 40 C5
Mullion Wlk. L11 40 C5
Mulveton Rd. L63 78 F3
Mumfords Gr. L47 48 E1
Mumfords La. L47 48 E1
Muncaster Cl. L62 79 D1
Muncaster Dr. WA11 32 B6
Municipal Golf Course. L47 63 B6
Munro Ave. WN5 25 E6
Munster Rd. L13 54 B3
Murat Gr. L22 26 D1
Murat St. L22 26 D1
Murcote Rd. L14 54 F5
Muriel Cl. WA5 74 D6
Muriel St. L4 53 A8
Murphy Gr. WA9 44 E4
Murray Gr. L48 63 A3
Murrayfield Dr. L46 49 F4
Murrayfield Hospl. L61 77 D5
Murrayfield Rd. L25 70 B6
Murrayfield Wlk. L25 70 B6
Musker Dr. L30 27 C3
Musker Gdns. L23 26 F3
Musker St. L23 26 F3
Muspratt Rd. L21 38 A6
Muttocks Rake. L30 27 D5
Myddleton La. WA2 61 C6
Myers Ct. L23 26 F2
Myers Rd E. L23 26 E3
Myers Rd W. L23 26 D3
Myerscough Ave. L20 38 E5
Mynsule Rd. L63 78 F3
Myrtle Ave. Ashton-in-M WN4 34 F6
Myrtle Ave. Haydock WA11 45 B7
Myrtle Ave. Newton-le-W WA12 46 C2
Myrtle Gr. Billinge WN5 33 D4
Myrtle Gr. Crosby L22 26 D2
Myrtle Gr. Southport PR9 4 E7
Myrtle Gr. Wallasey L44 51 E3
Myrtle Par. L7 67 F8
Myrtle St. L7 & L8 68 A8

Nairn Cl. L63 88 D4
Nansen Gr. 4 L4 39 A1
Nant Park Ct. L45 51 C8
Nantwich Cl. L49 65 A2
Napier Cl. WA10 43 E3
Napier Dr. L46 64 F8
Napier Rd. L62 79 B8
Napier St. L20 38 B1
Napier St. St Helens WA10 43 E3
Napier Terr. PR8 4 A5
Naples Rd. L44 51 D3
Napps Cl. L25 69 F7
Napps Way. Heswall L61 77 A2
Napps Way. Liverpool L25 69 F8
Napps Wlk. L25 69 F7
Nares Cl. WA5 60 C1
Narrow Croft Rd. L39 13 B1
Narrow La. L39 13 B1
Narrow Lane (Clieves Hills). L39 12 E6
Narrow Moss La. L39 & L40 13 E8
Naseby Cl. L43 65 C4
Naseby St. L4 38 F2
Natal Rd. L9 39 B6
Nathan Gr. L33 29 F4
Naughton Lea. WA8 72 D3
Navigation Cl. L30 28 A4
Naylor Ave. WA3 47 B8
Naylor Rd. Birkenhead L43 65 E8
Naylor Rd. Widnes WA8 73 D1
Naylor St. L3 52 D3
Naylor's Rd. Liverpool L25 & L27 70 D5
Naylor's Rd. Liverpool L27 70 D7
Naylorsfield Dr. L25 & L27 70 C6
Nazeby Ave. L23 27 A3
Neale Dr. L49 64 E3
Neasham Cl. L26 82 F8
Nedens Gr. L31 20 C3
Nedens La. L31 20 C3
Needham Cres. L43 65 D4
Needham Rd. L7 53 C2
Needwood Dr. L63 78 F3
Neil St. WA8 73 C2
Neills Rd. WA9 59 B6
Neilson Rd. L17 68 C3
Neilson St. L17 68 B3
Nell's La. L39 20 F5
Nelson Ave. L35 56 E2
Nelson Ct. L8 67 A1
Nelson Dr. L61 76 E3
Nelson Pl. L35 56 E2
Nelson Rd. Birkenhead L42 67 A1
Nelson Rd. L21 38 B7
Nelson Rd. Liverpool L7 53 B1
Nelson St. L20 38 B2
Nelson St. Liverpool L1 & L72 67 D7
Nelson St. Liverpool L1 67 E8
Nelson St. Liverpool L15 68 E8
Nelson St. Newton-le-W WA12 46 A3
Nelson St. Southport PR8 4 A6
Nelson St. Wallasey L45 51 C7
Nelson's Croft. L63 79 A3
Nelville Rd. L9 39 C7
Neptune St. L41 66 D8
Ness Gr. L32 29 C2
Neston Ave. WA9 58 B4
Neston Cty High Sch. L64 86 F1
Neston Gdns. L41 66 B8
Neston Parkgate Cty Prim Sch. L64 86 C1
Neston Rd. L63 86 F5
Neston St. L4 38 F1
Neston St Mary's CE Prim Sch. L64 86 F1
Netherby St. L8 67 F4
Netherfield. WA8 84 E8
Netherfield Cl. L43 65 C4
Netherfield Rd N. L4 & L5 52 E6
Netherfield Rd S. L5 & L6 52 F4
Netherley Rd. Liverpool L35 & L27 71 C3
Netherley Rd. Widnes WA8 72 A2
Netherton Gn. L30 27 F5
Netherton Grange. L30 28 B3
Netherton Ind Est. L30 38 F8
Netherton La. L30 27 E5
Netherton Moss Cty Prim Sch. L30 27 E3
Netherton Park Prim Sch. L30 27 F1
Netherton Park Rd. L21 & L30 38 D8
Netherton Rd. Birkenhead L46 64 E8
Netherton Rd. L20 38 D6
Netherton Rd. Liverpool L18 & L19 69 A1
Netherton Way. L20 & L21 & L30 38 E8
Netherwood Rd. L11 39 E2
Netley St. L4 52 E8
Nettlestead Rd. Liverpool L11 40 A1
Neva Ave. L46 64 D8
Neverstitch Cl. WN8 15 F2
Neverstitch Rd. WN8 15 D2
Nevill St. PR8 4 B7
Neville Ave. St Helens WA9 45 B2
Neville Ave. Warrington WA2 61 D1
Neville Cl. L43 65 C4
Neville Rd. Bebington L62 88 E8
Neville Rd. Crosby L22 26 E1
Neville Rd. Wallasey L44 51 A4
Neville St. WA12 46 A3
Nevin St. 6 L6 53 A3
Nevison St. 11 L7 53 B1
Nevitte Cl. L28 55 A8
New Acres Cl. L43 65 C8
New Bank Pl. WA8 72 B1
New Bank Rd. WA8 72 B1
New Barn Ave. WN4 35 C3
New Barnet. WA8 72 F4
New Bird St. L1 & L72 67 D7
New Brighton Prim Sch. L45 51 C8
New Brighton Sta. L45 51 A8
New Chester Rd. Bebington L62 & L42 79 C5

New Chester Rd. Bebington L62 & L66 ... 89 A2
New Chester Rd. Birkenhead L41 & L42 ... 66 F4
New Court Way. L39 ... 13 F5
New Cross St. Prescot L34 .. 56 D7
New Cross St. 1 St Helens WA10 ... 43 F3
New Cross St. 6 St Helens WA10 ... 43 F4
New Cswy. L37 & L38 ... 18 B7
New Cut Cl. PR8 ... 8 A8
New Cut La. Knowsley L34 ... 42 A8
New Cut La. Rainford L33 & WA11 ... 31 B1
New Cut La. Southport L39 & PR8 ... 8 D6
New Ferry By-Pass. L62 ... 79 B7
New Ferry Rd. L62 ... 79 B8
New Fold. WN5 ... 25 C4
New Fort Way. L20 ... 38 A6
New Foul La. PR8 ... 5 A4
New Glade Hill. WA11 ... 44 E6
New Hall La. L11 ... 39 E1
New Hedley Gr. L5 ... 52 C5
New Henderson St. L8 ... 67 E5
New Hey. L12 ... 54 B5
New Hey Rd. L49 ... 65 C3
New Heys Comm Comp Sch. L18 ... 69 D1
New Heys Comm Comp Sch. L19 ... 81 D8
New Hutte Jun Sch. L26 ... 82 E6
New Hutte La. L26 ... 82 F6
New Hutte Prim Sch. L26 ... 82 E6
New Islington. L3 ... 52 E2
New La. Haskayne L39 ... 11 E3
New La. Ormskirk L39 ... 13 E2
New La. Southport PR9 ... 2 E3
New Meadow La. L37 & L38 ... 18 F8
New Mill Stile. L25 ... 70 A3
New Park Ormskirk Golf Course. L40 ... 14 E6
New Quay. L3 ... 52 B2
New Rd. Formby L37 ... 10 A5
New Rd. Liverpool L13 ... 53 E5
New Rd. Prescot L34 ... 56 E7
New Road Ct. L13 ... 53 E5
New School La. L66 ... 89 B1
New St. Ashton-in-M WN4 ... 35 C4
New St. Haskayne L39 ... 12 B8
New St. St Helens WA9 ... 58 C7
New St. Wallasey L44 ... 51 E2
New Strand. L20 ... 38 C3
New Tower Ct. L45 ... 51 C8
New Town Gdns. L32 ... 29 E2
New Way. L39 ... 22 C2
New Way Bsns Ctr. L44 ... 51 D2
Newark Cl. Birkenhead L43 .. 65 C4
Newark Cl. Huyton-w-R L36 .. 55 D6
Newark Cl. Litherland L30 ... 28 B5
Newark St. L4 ... 38 F1
Newbold Cres. L48 ... 63 E3
Newbold Gr. L12 ... 40 F2
Newborough Ave. Crosby L23 ... 27 A4
Newborough Ave. 9 Liverpool L18 ... 68 F5
Newborough Cl. WA5 ... 60 E2
Newborough Prep Sch. L25 69 F3
Newbridge Cl. Birkenhead L49 ... 65 B3
Newbridge Cl. Garswood WN4 ... 34 D3
Newbridge Cl. Warrington WA5 ... 60 D2
Newburn. L43 ... 66 B5
Newburn St. 7 L4 ... 39 A2
Newburns La. L43 ... 66 B3
Newbury Cl. Huyton-w-R L36 ... 55 D1
Newbury Cl. Widnes WA8 ... 73 A3
Newbury Way. L14 ... 54 E5
Newby Ave. L35 ... 57 A4
Newby Cl. PR8 ... 7 B3
Newby Dr. L36 ... 55 C3
Newby Gr. L12 ... 40 C2
Newby Pl. WA11 ... 44 A8
Newby St. L4 ... 52 F8
Newcastle Rd. L15 ... 69 A6
Newcombe St. L6 ... 53 B5
Newcroft Rd. L25 ... 69 F4
Newdales Cl. L43 ... 65 C8
Newdown Rd. L11 ... 40 D5
Newdown Wlk. L11 ... 40 D5
Newell Rd. L44 & L45 ... 51 B5
Newenham Cres. L14 ... 54 E3
Newfield Cl. L23 ... 27 C6
Newfield Sch. L23 ... 27 B5
Newgate Rd. WN8 ... 24 F7
Newhall La. L47 ... 63 B6
Newhall St. L1 & L69 & L72 & L8 ... 67 E7
Newhaven Rd. Wallasey L45 51 C7
Newhaven Rd. Warrington WA2 ... 61 B4
Newholme Cl. L12 ... 40 E3
Newhope Rd. L41 ... 66 C7
Newhouse Rd. L15 ... 68 D7
Newick Rd. L32 ... 29 C1
Newington. L1 ... 52 E1
Newland Cl. WA8 ... 72 C3
Newland Ct. L17 ... 68 C3
Newland Dr. L44 & L45 ... 51 A4
Newlands Cl. 10 L6 ... 53 A4
Newlands Dr. WA3 ... 47 D8
Newlands Rd. Bebington L63 79 B4
Newlands Rd. St Helens WA11 ... 44 C7
Newlands St. L6 ... 53 A4
Newlands Wlk. 9 L6 ... 53 A4
Newling St. L41 ... 66 C7
Newlyn Ave. Litherland L21 . 27 B1
Newlyn Ave. Maghull L31 ... 20 E1
Newlyn Cl. L47 ... 48 E2
Newlyn Dr. Ashton-in-M WN4 ... 35 B1
Newlyn Dr. Skelmersdale WN8 ... 24 D7
Newlyn Gdns. WA5 ... 74 D3
Newlyn Gr. WA11 ... 44 D7
Newlyn Rd. Hoylake L47 ... 48 E2
Newlyn Rd. Liverpool L11 ... 40 D5
Newman St. L4 ... 52 D7
Newmorn Ct. L17 ... 68 C2
Newport Ave. L45 ... 50 D7
Newport Cl. Birkenhead L43 65 C4
Newport Ct. Liverpool L5 ... 52 C5
News La. WA11 ... 23 F2
Newsham Cl. WA8 ... 72 B4
Newsham Cty Prim Sch. L6 53 C4
Newsham Dr. L6 ... 53 D5
Newsham Rd. L36 ... 71 A8
Newsham St. L5 ... 52 D5
Newstead Ave. L23 ... 26 B3
Newstead Rd. L7 & L8 ... 68 C7
Newstet Rd. L33 ... 30 C2
Newton Bank Sch. WA12 ... 46 E4
Newton Cl. L12 ... 54 B8
Newton Comm Hospl.WA12 46 B2
Newton Cross La. L48 ... 63 E2
Newton Ct. L13 & L7 ... 53 E1
Newton Cty Prim Sch. WA12 ... 46 D3
Newton Dr. L48 ... 63 E2
Newton Gr. WA2 ... 61 F3
Newton La. WA12 ... 46 E6
Newton Park Dr. WA12 ... 46 F3
Newton Park Rd. L48 ... 63 E2
Newton Rd. Billinge WN5 & WA9 & WN4 33 F6
Newton Rd. Golborne WA12 & WA3 ... 47 D5
Newton Rd. Hoylake L47 ... 63 C7
Newton Rd. Liverpool L13 ... 53 E3
Newton Rd. St Helens WA9 . 45 A3
Newton Rd. Wallasey L44 ... 51 A4
Newton Rd. Warrington WA2 & WA12 ... 60 F8
Newton Rd. Winwick WA2 ... 61 A5
Newton St. Birkenhead L41 .. 66 C7
Newton St. Southport PR9 ... 5 A7
Newton Way. Birkenhead L49 ... 64 F5
Newton Way. Liverpool L3 ... 52 F1
Newton Wlk. L20 ... 38 B4
Newton-le-Willows Comm Sch. WA12 ... 46 D5
Newton-le-Willows Sta. WA12 ... 46 E3
Nicander Rd. L15 & L18 ... 68 F5
Nicholas Rd. Crosby L23 ... 26 B3
Nicholas Rd. Widnes WA8 ... 84 C8
Nicholas St. 3 L3 ... 52 D3
Nicholl Rd. WA10 ... 43 A5
Nicholls Dr. L61 ... 76 F4
Nicholson St. WA9 ... 44 E4
Nickleby Cl. L8 ... 67 F5
Nicol Mere Cty Prim Sch. WN4 ... 35 B5
Nicol Mere Dr. WN4 ... 35 A5
Nicol Rd. WN4 ... 35 B5
Nicola Ct. L45 ... 51 C6
Nidderdale Ave. L35 ... 57 D3
Nigel Rd. L60 ... 86 C8
Nightingale Cl. L27 ... 70 F5
Nightingale Rd. L12 ... 40 F3
Nimrod St. L4 ... 38 F1
Nine Tree Prim Sch. L28 ... 41 A1
Nipe La. WA11 & WN8 ... 24 B5
Nithsdale Rd. L15 ... 68 E6
Nixon St. L4 ... 38 F2
Nixon's La. PR8 ... 7 E7
Nixons La. WN8 ... 24 D7
Noctorum Ave. L43 & L49 ... 65 C4
Noctorum Dell. L43 ... 65 D4
Noctorum La. L43 ... 65 E5
Noctorum Rd. L43 ... 65 E5
Noctorum Way. L43 ... 65 D3
Noel Gate. L39 ... 13 B1
Noel St. L8 ... 68 C7
Nolan St. PR8 ... 4 C5
Nook La. Golborne WA3 ... 47 B8
Nook La. St Helens WA9 ... 44 F1
Nook Rise. L15 ... 69 B8
Nook The. Birkenhead L48 ... 64 B2
Nook The. Birkenhead L43 ... 66 B5
Nook The. Liverpool L25 ... 70 C3
Nook The. St Helens WA10 .. 43 B6
Noon Ct. WA12 ... 46 B1
Norbeck Ave. L14 ... 54 F2
Norbreck Ave. L14 ... 54 F2
Norburn Cres. L37 ... 9 F2
Norbury Ave. Bebington L63 78 E5
Norbury Ave. Billinge WN5 .. 33 D6
Norbury Ave. 8 Liverpool L18 ... 68 F5
Norbury Cl. Bebington L63 ... 78 F5
Norbury Cl. Southport PR9 ... 2 C5
Norbury Fold. L35 ... 57 E1
Norbury Gdns. L41 ... 66 E4
Norbury Rd. L32 ... 29 D2
Norbury Wlk. L32 ... 29 D2
Norcliffe Rd. L35 ... 57 B4
Norcott Dr. WA5 ... 59 F6
Norfield. L39 ... 13 F5
Norfolk Cl. Birkenhead L43 .. 65 C4
Norfolk Cl. L20 ... 38 D4
Norfolk Dr. Warrington WA5 74 E6
Norfolk Dr. West Kirby L48 .. 63 C1
Norfolk Gr. PR8 ... 3 F1
Norfolk Pl. L21 ... 38 A7
Norfolk Pl. Widnes WA8 ... 84 C8
Norfolk Rd. Maghull L31 ... 28 C7
Norfolk Rd. Orrell WN5 ... 25 E1
Norfolk Rd. Southport PR8 ... 3 F1
Norfolk Rd. St Helens WA10 43 D1
Norfolk St. L1 & L72 ... 67 D7
Norgate St. 16 L4 ... 52 F7
Norland St. WA8 ... 73 D1
Norland's La. Cronton L35 & WA8 ... 72 E8
Norland's La. Cronton L35 & WA8 ... 72 F7
Norlands Ct. L42 ... 66 E1
Norley Ave. L62 ... 88 E3
Norley Dr. WA10 ... 43 B3
Norley Pl. L26 ... 82 E6
Norma Rd. L22 ... 26 E1
Norman Ave. Haydock WA11 46 A7
Norman Ave. Newton-le-W WA12 ... 46 E3
Norman Pannell Prim Sch. L27 ... 70 E5
Norman Rd. L20 ... 38 C7
Norman Rd. Crosby L23 ... 26 D3
Norman Rd. Wallasey L44 ... 51 E2
Norman St. Birkenhead L41 & L43 ... 65 F8
Norman St. Liverpool L3 ... 52 F2
Normandale Rd. L4 ... 39 D1
Normandy Rd. L36 ... 55 D3
Normanhurst. L39 ... 14 A4
Normans Rd. WA9 ... 58 F7
Normanston Cl. L43 ... 66 B4
Normanston Rd. L43 ... 66 B4
Normanton Ave. L17 ... 68 C3
Normington Cl. L31 ... 20 C4
Norris Cl. L43 ... 65 C4
Norris Green Cres. Liverpool L11 ... 39 F1
Norris Green Rd. L12 ... 54 B6
Norris Green Way. 6 L11 ... 40 A1
Norris House Dr. L39 ... 21 C8
Norris Rd. L34 ... 56 C6
Norris Way. L37 ... 10 B3
Norseman Cl. L12 ... 54 B8
North Ave. Golborne WN7 ... 36 F4
North Ave. Litherland L10 ... 28 E2
North Ave. Liverpool L24 ... 82 A6
North Barcombe Rd. L16 ... 69 D7
North Breeze Hill. 8 L4 & L9 ... 38 F2
North Brooke Way. L49 ... 65 A3
North Cantril Ave. L12 ... 54 F8
North Cheshire Trad Est. L43 ... 77 E8
North Cl. L62 ... 79 C2
North Dingle. Liverpool L4 ... 52 D8
North Dingle. Liverpool L4 ... 52 E7
North Dr. Heswall L60 ... 86 A7
North Dr. Liverpool L12 & L13 ... 54 B6
North Dr. Liverpool L15 ... 69 A8
North Dr. Wallasey L45 ... 50 F8
North End La. Hightown L38 18 A6
North End La. Liverpool L26 . 70 E3
North Florida Rd. WA11 ... 45 E8
North Front. L35 ... 56 E1
North Gr. L18 ... 69 C1
North Hill St. Liverpool L8 ... 67 F5
North Hill St. Liverpool L8 ... 68 A6
North John St. Liverpool L2 . 52 C1
North John St. St Helens WA10 ... 43 F3
North Leach Dr. PR8 ... 7 A5
North Linkside Rd. L25 ... 70 C1
North Manor Way. L25 ... 70 C2
North Meade. L31 ... 20 C2
North Mersey Bsns Ctr. L33 30 D4
North Moor La. L39 ... 12 F8
North Moss La. L37 & L39 ... 10 D7
North Mossley Hill Rd. L17 & L18 ... 68 F3
North Mount Rd. L32 ... 29 C4
North Par. Hoylake L47 ... 63 B7
North Par. L32 ... 29 E2
North Par. Liverpool L24 ... 82 E3
North Par. Neston L64 ... 86 B2
North Park Brook Rd. WA5 . 60 E1
North Park Rd. L32 ... 29 C4
North Parkside Wlk. L12 ... 54 A8
North Perimeter Rd. L33 ... 30 D4
North Rd. Bebington L62,L65,L19 ... 89 E2
North Rd. Birkenhead L42 ... 66 D3
North Rd. Liverpool L13 & L14 ... 54 C2
North Rd. Liverpool L24 ... 82 E5
North Rd. Southport PR9 ... 2 C4
North Rd. St Helens WA10 ... 43 F5
North Rd. West Kirby L48 ... 63 A2
North St. Ashton-in-M WN4 .. 35 D5
North St. Haydock WA11 ... 45 E6
North St.Liverpool L1,L2,L3 .. 52 D2
North St. Newton-le-W WA12 45 F4
North St. Southport PR9 ... 4 F8
North Sudley Rd. L17 & L19 68 E2
North View. Huyton-w-R L36 56 A2
North View. Liverpool L7 ... 53 A1
North View. Warrington WA5 74 E7
North William St. 5 L44 ... 51 E2
Northam Cl. PR9 ... 2 A5
Northbrook Cl. L8 ... 68 A7
Northbrook Rd. L44 ... 51 D3
Northbrook St. L8 ... 68 A7
Northcote Cl. 1 L5 & L6 ... 52 F4
Northcote Prim Sch. L9 ... 39 A3
Northcote Rd. L9 ... 38 F3
Northcote Rd. Wallasey L45 50 D5
Northdale Rd. L15 ... 68 F8
Northdunes. L38 ... 17 F4
Northern La. WA8 ... 72 A3
Northern Perimeter Rd. Litherland L30 ... 28 B5
Northern Rd. L24 ... 82 E4
Northern Rd The. L23 ... 26 F4
Northfield. WN8 ... 16 B4
Northfield Cl. WA9 ... 58 D3
Northfield Ct. WN3 ... 36 C1
Northfield Rd. L20 & L9 ... 38 E6
Northgate Rd. L13 ... 54 A5
Northmead Rd. L19 ... 81 E7
Northolt Ct. WA2 ... 61 E1
Northop Rd. 8 L45 ... 51 A6
Northpark Ct. L44 ... 51 E3
Northridge Rd. L61 ... 77 A5
Northumberland Gr. L8 ... 67 D5
Northumberland St. L8 ... 67 E5
Northumberland Terr. L5 ... 52 E6
Northumberland Way. L30 . 27 C3
Northway. Heswall L60 ... 77 D1
Northway. Liverpool L15 ... 54 B1
Northway. Maghull L31 & L39 20 E4
Northway. Ormskirk L39 ... 13 A1
Northway. Skelmersdale WN8 ... 16 B2
Northway. Warrington WA2 . 61 B2
Northway. Widnes WA8 ... 72 D1
Northway Jun, Mix & Inf Sch. L15 ... 54 B1
Northway Prim Sch. L31 ... 20 E3
Northways. L62 ... 79 D3
Northwich Cl. L23 ... 27 B6
Northwood Ave. WA12 ... 46 F3
Northwood Rd. Birkenhead L43 ... 65 F1
Northwood Rd. Huyton-w-R L36 ... 55 F4
Norton Ave. WA5 ... 74 E5
Norton Dr. L61 ... 76 C7
Norton Gr. Maghull L31 ... 28 D6
Norton Gr. St Helens L35 ... 57 D7
Norton Rd. L48 ... 63 A3
Norton St. L20 ... 38 B5
Norton St. Liverpool L3 & L69 52 E2
Norville Rd. L14 ... 54 C2
Norwich Ave. Ashton-in-M WN4 ... 35 D3
Norwich Ave. Golborne WA3 47 D8
Norwich Dr. L49 ... 65 A7
Norwich Rd. L15 ... 69 A6
Norwich Way. L32 ... 29 E2
Norwood Ave. Ashton-in-M WN4 ... 34 F6
Norwood Ave. Golborne WA3 ... 47 F7
Norwood Ave. Litherland L21 27 B1
Norwood Ave. Southport PR9 4 E7
Norwood Cl. L6 ... 53 B4
Norwood Cres. PR9 ... 4 E7
Norwood Ct. L49 ... 64 D3
Norwood Gdns. PR9 ... 4 F7
Norwood Gr. Liverpool L6 ... 53 B4
Norwood Gr. Rainford WA11 32 A6
Norwood Prim Sch. PR9 ... 4 E7
Norwood Rd. Birkenhead L49 ... 64 D4
Norwood Rd. Southport PR8 & PR9 ... 4 F6
Norwood Rd. Wallasey L44 .. 51 B2
Norwood Way. L6 ... 53 B4
Norwyn Rd. L11 ... 39 E2
Nostell Rd. WN4 ... 35 A5
Notre Dame High Sch (Lower Sch). L4 ... 52 E7
Notre Dame High Sch (Upper Sch). L5 ... 52 F7
Nottingham Cl. L35 ... 57 C5
Nottingham Rd. L36 ... 55 C1
Nowshera Ave. L61 ... 76 F5
Nuffield Cl. L49 ... 64 F4
Nugent House Sch. WN5 ... 33 D4
Nun Cl. L43 ... 66 B3
Nunn St. WA9 ... 44 D3
Nunsford Cl. L21 ... 27 D2
Nunthorpe Rd. L34 ... 41 B5
Nurse Rd. L61 ... 77 B6
Nurseries The. L37 ... 10 A2
Nursery Ave. L39 ... 14 A6
Nursery Cl. Birkenhead L43 .. 66 C3
Nursery Cl. Liverpool L25 ... 82 C8
Nursery Cl. Widnes WA8 ... 73 D3
Nursery Dr. L37 ... 9 F2
Nursery La. L19 ... 81 C7
Nursery Rd. Maghull L31 ... 20 C4
Nursery Rd. St Helens L35 ... 57 D7
Nut St. L35 ... 57 D7
Nutgrove Ave. L35 ... 57 D7
Nutgrove Hall Dr. L35 & WA9 ... 57 D6
Nutgrove Methodist Prim Sch. L35 ... 57 D7
Nutgrove Rd. L35 ... 57 D7
Nuthall Rd. PR8 ... 4 F3
Nuttall St. L7 ... 53 C1
Nyland Rd. L36 ... 55 E5

O'Brien Gr. WA9 ... 44 E4
O'Connell Cl. WA11 ... 45 C6
O'Connell Rd. L3 ... 52 D4
O'Keeffe Rd. WA9 ... 44 C4
O'Neill St. L20 ... 38 B4
O'Reilly Ct. L3 ... 52 C4
O'Sullivan Cres. WA11 ... 44 E5
Oak Ave. Abram WN2 ... 36 C7
Oak Ave. Birkenhead L49 ... 64 D6
Oak Ave. Golborne WA3 ... 47 B8
Oak Ave. Haydock WA11 ... 45 E7
Oak Ave. Liverpool L9 ... 39 B6
Oak Ave. Newton-le-W WA12 46 D3
Oak Ave. Ormskirk L39 ... 13 D4
Oak Bank. L41 ... 66 C5
Oak Cl. Birkenhead L46 ... 64 D7
Oak Cl. Liverpool L12 ... 40 F1
Oak Cl. Prescot L35 ... 56 E3
Oak Cres. WN8 ... 15 D1
Oak Gn. L39 ... 13 F5
Oak La. L12 ... 40 C2
Oak La N. L11 & L12 ... 40 D2
Oak Leigh. L13 ... 53 E5
Oak Rd. Bebington L63 ... 78 F7
Oak Rd. Bebington L66 ... 88 E1
Oak Rd. Liverpool L36 ... 70 D8
Oak Rd. Prescot L35 ... 56 E3
Oak Rd. Warrington WA5 ... 74 F3
Oak St. L20 ... 38 C4
Oak St. Southport PR8 ... 4 E6
Oak St. St Helens WA9 ... 58 E8
Oak Terr. L7 ... 53 C2
Oak Tree Ct. WN8 ... 16 D3
Oak Vale. L13 ... 54 B2

Oak View. L24 ... 83 A3
Oakbank Rd. L18 ... 68 E5
Oakbank St. L44 ... 51 C3
Oakbourne Cl. L17 ... 68 C2
Oakdale Ave. L44 ... 51 D2
Oakdale Dr. L49 ... 64 C2
Oakdale Rd. Crosby L22 ... 26 D2
Oakdale Rd. Liverpool L18 ... 69 A5
Oakdale Rd. Wallasey L41 & L44 ... 51 D2
Oakdene Cl. L62 ... 88 D5
Oakdene Prim Sch. L35 ... 57 D2
Oakdene Rd. Birkenhead L42 66 C3
Oakdene Rd. Liverpool L4 ... 53 B7
Oakenden Cl. WN4 ... 35 A6
Oakenholt Rd. Birkenhead L46 ... 64 E8
Oakenholt Rd. 2 Wallasey L46 ... 49 E1
Oakes St. L3 ... 52 F2
Oakfield. L4 ... 53 B6
Oakfield Ave. Golborne WA3 35 F1
Oakfield Ave. Liverpool L25 . 70 A4
Oakfield Cl. L35 ... 57 D7
Oakfield Cty Inf Sch. WA8 .. 84 B8
Oakfield Cty Jun Sch. WA8 . 84 B8
Oakfield Dr. Formby L37 ... 9 D4
Oakfield Dr. Liverpool L36 ... 70 F8
Oakfield Dr. Widnes WA8 ... 84 A8
Oakfield Gr. L36 ... 70 F8
Oakfield Rd. Bebington L62 .. 88 C8
Oakfield Rd. Hightown L38 ... 17 F2
Oakfield Rd. Liverpool L4 & L6 ... 53 A6
Oakham Dr. Litherland L10 .. 28 F1
Oakham Dr. Wallasey L46 ... 49 B1
Oakham St. L8 ... 67 E6
Oakhill Cl. Liverpool L12 ... 40 D3
Oakhill Cl. Maghull L31 ... 20 D2
Oakhill Cottage La. L31 ... 20 D4
Oakhill Dr. L31 ... 20 D4
Oakhill Pk. L13 ... 54 B2
Oakhill Rd. Liverpool L13 ... 54 B3
Oakhill Rd. Maghull L31 ... 20 D3
Oakhurst Cl. L25 ... 70 B5
Oakland Cl. L21 ... 38 C6
Oakland Dr. L49 ... 65 A6
Oakland Rd. L19 ... 80 F8
Oakland Vale. L45 ... 51 C8
Oaklands. L35 ... 57 C3
Oaklands Ave. L23 ... 26 E5
Oaklands Ct. WA9 ... 58 C4
Oaklands Dr. Bebington L63 . 79 A6
Oaklands Dr. Heswall L60 & L61 ... 77 A1
Oaklands Rd. WA3 ... 47 F7
Oaklands Terr. L60 & L61 ... 77 A2
Oaklea Rd. L61 ... 76 F6
Oakleaf Mews. L43 ... 65 D5
Oaklee Gr. L33 ... 30 A4
Oakleigh. WN8 ... 24 D2
Oakleigh Gr. L63 ... 78 F6
Oakley Ave. WN5 ... 33 E6
Oakley Cl. L12 ... 40 E3
Oakmere Dr. L49 ... 64 C4
Oakmere Dr. WA5 ... 74 F3
Oakridge Cl. L62 ... 79 C2
Oakridge Rd. L62 ... 79 C2
Oaks Cl. WA9 ... 58 D3
Oaks La. L61 ... 77 A4
Oaks The. Bebington L62 ... 88 C8
Oaks The. Liverpool L12 ... 40 F3
Oaks The. St Helens WA9 ... 58 D4
Oaksmeade Cl. L12 ... 40 F2
Oakston Ave. L35 ... 57 D2
Oaksway. L60 ... 86 C6
Oaktree Pl. L42 ... 66 F3
Oaktree Rd. WA10 ... 43 A5
Oakwood. WN8 ... 16 D3
Oakwood Ave. Ashton-in-M WN4 ... 35 A2
Oakwood Ave. Southport PR8 7 D6
Oakwood Cl. Liverpool L25 ... 70 B5
Oakwood Cl. Liverpool L27 ... 70 E5
Oakwood Dr. Birkenhead L43 65 E8
Oakwood Dr. Huyton-w-R L36 ... 55 F1
Oakwood Dr. Southport PR8 .. 7 E5
Oakwood Rd. L26 ... 82 F7
Oakworth Cl. L33 ... 29 E4
Oakworth Dr. Bebington L62 79 C7
Oakworth Dr. Huyton-w-R L36 ... 71 A7
Oarside Dr. L45 ... 51 A6
Oatfield La. L21 ... 27 B2
Oatlands Rd. L32 ... 29 C2
Oatlands The. L48 ... 63 C1
Oban Dr. Garswood WN4 ... 34 C4
Oban Dr. Heswall L60 ... 86 A8
Oban Rd. L4 ... 53 B6
Oberon St. L20 ... 38 C1
Observatory Rd. L43 ... 65 E8
Ocean Rd. L21 ... 38 B7
Oceanic Rd. L13 ... 53 F2
Octavia Hill Rd. L21 ... 27 C1
Odsey St. L7 ... 53 C2
Off Botanic Rd. PR9 ... 2 A1
Ogden Cl. L12 ... 54 A8
Ogle Cl. L35 ... 56 E5
Oglet La. Liverpool L24 ... 82 C2
Oglet La. Liverpool L24 ... 82 D1
Oil St. L3 ... 52 B4
Okehampton Rd. L16 ... 69 D8
Okell Dr. Liverpool L26 ... 70 D1
Okell Dr. Liverpool L26 ... 70 F1
Old Acre. L38 ... 17 F3
Old Barn Rd. 2 Liverpool L4 & L6 ... 53 B6
Old Barn Rd. Wallasey L44 ... 51 A3
Old Bidston Rd. L41 ... 66 B8
Old Boston. WA11 ... 46 A7
Old Boston Trad Est. WA11 ... 46 B8
Old Boundary Way. L39 ... 13 F6
Old Chester Rd. Bebington L63 & L42 ... 78 F8
Old Chester Rd. Birkenhead L41 & L42 & L63 66 F2
Old Church Yd. L2 ... 52 B1
Old Colliery Rd. L35 ... 56 D3
Old Colliery Yd. WN4 ... 34 C3
Old Dover Rd. L36 ... 70 C8
Old Eccleston La. WA10 ... 43 C3
Old Engine La. WN8 ... 15 C2
Old Farm Rd. Crosby L23 ... 26 F4
Old Farm Rd. Kirkby L32 ... 40 F6
Old Gorsey La. L41 & L44 ... 51 C1
Old Hall. L35 ... 71 E8
Old Hall Cl. L31 ... 28 D7
Old Hall Dr. WN4 ... 35 A2
Old Hall Gdns. WA11 ... 32 A7
Old Hall La. L32 ... 29 D2
Old Hall Rd. Bebington L63 & L62 ... 79 F1
Old Hall Rd. Maghull L31 ... 28 D7
Old Hall St. L2 & L3 ... 52 C2
Old Haymarket. L1 ... 52 D2
Old Hey Wlk. WA12 ... 46 B1
Old Higher Rd. WA8 ... 83 D5
Old Hutte La. L24 & L26 ... 83 A6
Old La. Formby L37 ... 9 F6
Old La. Haskayne L39 ... 11 E3
Old La. Maghull L31 ... 20 E4
Old La. Prescot L34 & L35 ... 56 F6
Old La. Rainford WA11 ... 31 F7
Old La. Rainhill L35 ... 57 B3
Old Leeds St. L3 ... 52 B2
Old Links Cl. PR9 ... 5 B8
Old Maryland La. L46 ... 49 E1
Old Meadow. L34 ... 41 C4
Old Meadow Rd. L61 ... 76 E4
Old Mill Ave. WA9 ... 58 D5
Old Mill Cl. Heswall L60 ... 86 B7
Old Mill Cl. Liverpool L15 ... 69 A8
Old Mill Hill. L39 ... 13 D3
Old Mill La. Formby L37 ... 9 F4
Old Mill La. Knowsley L34 ... 41 E4
Old Mill La. Liverpool L15 ... 69 A8
Old Moss La. L39 ... 11 B5
Old Nook La. WA11 ... 44 E6
Old Orchard. L35 ... 56 E1
Old Park La. PR9 ... 5 A8
Old Post Office Pl. 3 L1 ... 52 D1
Old Prescot Cl. L31 ... 21 C2
Old Pump La. L49 ... 64 C3
Old Quarry The. L25 ... 70 A2
Old Racecourse Rd. L31 ... 28 B8
Old Rd. WN4 ... 35 A4
Old Rectory Gn. Holt Green L39 ... 21 A7
Old Rectory Gn. Litherland L29 ... 27 F7
Old Riding. L14 ... 54 F5
Old Roan Sta. L30 ... 28 B3
Old Ropery. L2 ... 52 C1
Old Rough La. L32 & L33 ... 29 F2
Old School House La. WA2 . 61 A7
Old School Pl. WN4 ... 35 A2
Old Thomas La. L14 ... 54 D1
Old Town La. L37 ... 9 E4
Old Upton La. WA8 ... 72 E4
Old Wargrave Rd. WA12 ... 46 C3
Old Whint Rd. WA11 ... 45 A6
Old Wood Rd. L61 ... 76 F3
Oldbridge Rd. L24 ... 82 F3
Oldershaw Sch The. L45 ... 51 A5
Oldfield. L35 ... 56 F4
Oldfield Cl. L60 ... 76 E2
Oldfield Cotts. L61 ... 76 C2
Oldfield Dr. L60 ... 76 D2
Oldfield Gdns. L60 ... 76 D1
Oldfield La. L48 ... 64 A5
Oldfield Rd. Heswall L60 & L61 ... 76 D1
Oldfield Rd. Liverpool L19 ... 81 A8
Oldfield Rd. Wallasey L45 ... 50 F6
Oldfield St. WA10 ... 43 F5
Oldfield Way. L60 ... 76 E1
Oldgate. WA8 ... 84 C7
Oldham Pl. L1 ... 52 E1
Oldham St. 2 L1 ... 67 E8
Oleander Dr. WA10 ... 43 C4
Olga Rd. WA9 ... 58 C7
Olinda St. L62 ... 79 B7
Olive Cres. L41 ... 66 E4
Olive Gr. Huyton-w-R L36 ... 55 D2
Olive Gr. Litherland L30 ... 28 A1
Olive Gr. Liverpool L15 ... 54 A1
Olive Gr. Skelmersdale WN8 15 E1
Olive Gr. Southport PR8 & PR9 4 E7
Olive La. L15 ... 69 A8
Olive Mount. L41 ... 66 E4
Olive Mount Hospl. L15 ... 69 B8
Olive Mount Hts. L15 ... 69 A8
Olive Mount Rd. L15 ... 69 A8
Olive Mount Wlk. L15 ... 69 B8
Olive Rd. L22 ... 37 E8
Olive Vale. L15 ... 68 F8
Olivedale Rd. L18 ... 68 F5
Oliver La. L41 ... 66 E6
Oliver Lyme Rd. L34 ... 56 E6
Oliver Rd. WA10 ... 57 C8
Oliver St. L41 ... 66 D6
Oliver St E. L41 ... 66 E6
Olivetree Rd. L15 ... 54 B1
Olivia Cl. L43 ... 65 C4
Olivia Mews. L43 ... 65 C4
Olivia St. L20 ... 38 D1
Ollerton Cl. L43 ... 65 C4
Ollery Gn. L30 ... 28 B4
Olney St. L4 ... 38 F2
Olton St. L15 ... 68 E8
Olympic Way. L30 & L9 ... 39 B8
Onslow Cres. PR8 ... 4 A2
Onslow Rd. Bebington L62 ... 79 B8
Onslow Rd. Liverpool L6 & L7 53 C3
Onslow Rd. 6 Wallasey L45 51 B8
Openfields Cl. L26 ... 70 E2
Oppenheim Ave. WA10 ... 57 C8
Oran Way. L36 ... 55 D3
Orange Gr. Liverpool L8 ... 68 C6
Orange Gr. Warrington WA2 61 E2
Orange Tree Cl. L28 ... 55 B8
Orb Cl. L11 ... 40 C3
Orb Wlk. 4 L11 ... 40 C4
Orchard Ave. L14 & L16 ... 54 D1
Orchard Cl. St Helens WA11 44 D7
Orchard Cl. St Helens L34 ... 57 A7
Orchard Ct. Birkenhead L41 . 66 F3
Orchard Ct. Maghull L31 ... 20 F1
Orchard Dale. L23 ... 26 F4
Orchard Dene. L35 ... 57 C3
Orchard Gdns. L35 ... 71 E8
Orchard Grange. L46 ... 64 C7
Orchard Hey. Litherland L30 28 B4
Orchard Hey. Maghull L31 ... 28 E8
Orchard Hey. St Helens WA10 ... 43 A3
Orchard La. PR8 ... 7 D4
Orchard Lodge. L39 ... 13 F6
Orchard Rd. L46 ... 49 E1
Orchard St. WN4 ... 35 C3
Orchard The. Huyton-w-R L36 ... 55 E2
Orchard The. Liverpool L17 ... 68 F1
Orchard The. Ormskirk L39 .. 13 D5
Orchard The. Wallasey L45 .. 51 A7
Orchard View. L39 ... 13 D1
Orchard Way. Bebington L63 78 D6
Orchard Way. Widnes WA8 . 72 A3
Orchid Gr. L8 ... 67 F3
Orford Cl. L24 ... 83 E2
Orford Gn. WA2 ... 61 D1
Orford St. L15 ... 68 F8
Oriel Cl. Litherland L10 ... 28 D3
Oriel Cl. Liverpool L2 ... 52 C1
Oriel Cres. L20 ... 38 C1
Oriel Dr. L10 ... 28 D3
Oriel Lodge. L20 ... 38 C2
Oriel Rd. Ashton-in-M WN4 .. 34 F4
Oriel Rd. Birkenhead L42 ... 66 E3
Oriel Rd. L20 ... 38 C1
Oriel Rd. L20 ... 38 C2
Oriel St. L3 ... 52 D3
Orient Dr. L25 ... 70 B3
Origen Rd. L16 ... 54 D1
Oriole Cl. WA10 ... 57 B7
Orith Ave. WA10 ... 42 F3
Orkney Cl. St Helens WA11 .. 44 D7
Orkney Cl. Widnes WA8 ... 73 E3
Orlando Cl. L43 ... 65 C4
Orlando St. L20 ... 38 C1
Orleans Rd. L13 ... 54 A3
Ormande St. WA9 ... 44 B1
Ormesby Gr. L63 ... 88 B6
Ormiston Rd. L45 ... 51 B7
Ormond Ave. L40 ... 14 E4
Ormond Cl. WA8 ... 72 C2
Ormond Mews. L43 ... 65 C4
Ormond St. Liverpool L3 ... 52 C2
Ormond St. Wallasey L45 ... 51 B5
Ormond Way. L43 ... 65 C4
Ormonde Ave. L31 ... 28 C7
Ormonde Cres. L33 ... 30 A2
Ormonde Dr. L31 ... 28 C8
Orms Way. L37 ... 9 E3
Ormsby St. L15 ... 68 E7
Ormside Gr. 7 WA9 ... 58 D7
Ormskirk Bsns Pk. L39 ... 13 F6
Ormskirk CE Prim Sch. L39 . 14 A6
Ormskirk & District General Hospl. L39 ... 14 A4
Ormskirk Gram Sch. L39 ... 13 F4
Ormskirk Old Rd. L39 ... 22 F7
Ormskirk Rd. Bickerstaffe L39 ... 22 E7
Ormskirk Rd. Bickerstaffe WA11 ... 23 D1
Ormskirk Rd. Knowsley L33 & L34 ... 41 D4
Ormskirk Rd. Litherland L10,L30,L68,L9 ... 28 B2
Ormskirk Rd. Orrell WN8 ... 25 A7
Ormskirk Rd. Rainford WA11 ... 31 E7
Ormskirk Rd. Skelmersdale WN8 ... 15 C1
Ormskirk Rd. Skelmersdale WN8 ... 24 D7
Ormskirk Rd. Skelmersdale WN8 ... 24 F7
Ormskirk St. WA10 ... 44 A3
Ormskirk Sta. L39 ... 13 F5
Ormskirk West End Cty Prim Sch. L39 ... 13 E7
Orphan Dr. Liverpool L6 & L7 53 D3
Orphan Dr. Liverpool L6 ... 53 D4
Orphan St. L7 ... 68 A8
Orrell Gdns. WN5 ... 25 F6
Orrell Hey. L20 ... 38 D7
Orrell Hill La. L38 ... 18 C4
Orrell Holgate Prim Sch. WN5 ... 25 E5
Orrell La. L20 & L9 ... 38 F7
Orrell Mount. L20 ... 38 C7
Orrell Park Sta. L9 ... 39 A6
Orrell Prim Sch. L20 ... 38 D5
Orrell Rd. L20 & L21 ... 38 C7
Orrell Rd. Orrell WN5 ... 25 E7
Orrell Rd. Wallasey L45 ... 51 C7
Orrell St. WA9 ... 44 C3
Orrell St James' Road Cty Jun & Inf Sch. WN5 ... 25 D4
Orrell Sta. WN5 ... 25 E4
Orrell Water Pk. WN5 ... 25 E4
Orret's Meadow Rd. L49 ... 65 B3
Orrets Meadow Sch. L46 ... 64 F8
Orry St. L5 ... 52 D5
Orrysdale Rd. L48 ... 63 A3
Orsett Rd. L32 ... 40 F8
Orston Cres. L63 ... 79 B2
Ortega Cl. L62 ... 79 C7
Orthes St. L3 ... 52 F1
Orton Rd. L16 ... 69 C8
Orton Way. WN4 ... 34 F3
Orville St. WA9 ... 58 F7
Orwell Cl. Formby L37 ... 9 D1
Orwell Cl. St Helens WA9 ... 58 A3
Orwell Rd. L4 & L5 ... 52 D8
Osbert Rd. L23 ... 26 B4
Osborne Ave. Wallasey L45 . 51 B7
Osborne Ave. Warrington WA2 ... 61 D1
Osborne Gr. L45 ... 51 B6
Osborne Rd. Ashton-in-M WN4 ... 35 A4
Osborne Rd. Birkenhead L43 66 B5
Osborne Rd. Formby L37 ... 9 E1
Osborne Rd. Golborne WA3 . 47 E7
Osborne Rd. Litherland L21 .. 27 C1
Osborne Rd. Liverpool L13 ... 53 E6
Osborne Rd. Southport PR8 ... 7 B6
Osborne Rd. St Helens WA10 43 A5
Osborne Rd. Wallasey L45 ... 51 C7
Osborne Vale. 8 L45 ... 51 B7
Osborne Wood. L17 ... 68 D1
Osmaston Rd. L42 ... 66 A1
Osprey Cl. Liverpool L27 ... 70 F5
Osprey Cl. Warrington WA2 . 61 E3
Ossett Cl. L43 ... 65 C4
Osterley Gdns. L9 ... 38 F6
Oteley Ave. L62 ... 88 D8
Othello Cl. L20 ... 38 C1
Otterburn Cl. L46 ... 64 B8
Otterspool Dr. L17 ... 80 D8
Otterspool Rd. L17 ... 68 D1
Otterton Rd. L11 ... 40 C5
Ottery Cl. PR9 ... 2 A5
Ottley St. L6 ... 53 C3
Otway St. L19 ... 81 C4
Oueenswood Ave. L63 ... 78 E7
Oulton Cl. Birkenhead L43 ... 65 E2
Oulton Cl. Maghull L31 ... 20 B4
Oulton La. L36 ... 70 D8
Oulton Rd. L16 ... 69 D6
Oulton Way. L43 ... 65 E3
Oundle Cl. L25 ... 82 B7
Oundle Dr. L10 ... 28 C3
Oundle Rd. L46 ... 49 E1
Our Lady Immaculate Prim Sch. L5 ... 52 E6
Our Lady Of Compassion RC Prim Sch. L37 ... 10 A3
Our Lady of Fatima Sch. L6 53 A4
Our Lady of Good Help RC Prim Sch. L15 ... 69 A8
Our Lady of Lourdes RC Prim Sch. Southport PR8 ... 4 A1
Our Lady of Lourdes RC Prim Sch. Wallasey L46 ... 50 B4
Our Lady of Mount Carmel RC Prim Sch. L8 ... 67 F5
Our Lady of Perpetual Succour Inf Sch. WA8 ... 72 C1
Our Lady of Perpetual Succour RC Inf Sch. WA8 ... 72 B1
Our Lady of Perpetual Succour RC Jun Sch. WA8 ... 84 A8
Our Lady of Pity RC Prim Sch. L49 ... 64 D2
Our Lady of Reconciliation Mix Inf Sch. L3 ... 52 C4
Our Lady of the Assumption RC Jun & Prim Schs. L25 ... 70 B6
Our Lady of Walsingham RC Jun (Aided) Sch. L30 ... 27 F2
Our Lady of Walsingham RC Prim Sch. L30 ... 27 F2
Our Lady Queen of Peace RC High Sch. WN8 ... 15 F4
Our Lady Queen of Peace RC Inf Sch. L21 ... 27 B2
Our Lady & St Edward's RC Prim Sch. L41 ... 66 B8
Our Lady & St Smithin RC Prim Sch. L11 ... 40 C5
Our Lady Star of the Sea RC Prim Sch. L21 ... 38 A6
Our Lady's Bishop Eton RC Prim Sch. L18 ... 69 C5
Our Lady's RC Prim Sch. Prescot L34 ... 56 D7
Our Lady's RC Prim Sch. St Helens WA9 ... 44 E2
Ouse St. L8 ... 68 A5
Out La. L25 ... 70 B3
Outer Central Rd. L24 ... 82 F5
Outer Forum. L11 ... 39 E2
Outlet La. L31 & L39 ... 21 F1
Oval Sports Ctr The. L63 ... 78 F7
Oval The. L45 ... 50 F6
Overbury St. L7 ... 68 B8
Overchurch Inf Sch. L49 ... 64 F6
Overchurch Jun Sch. L49 ... 64 F6
Overchurch Rd. L46 & L49 ... 64 E6
Overdale Ave. L61 ... 77 D5
Overdale Prim Sch. L33 ... 29 F4
Overdale Rd. L64 ... 88 A1
Overdene Wlk. L32 ... 29 F1
Overgreen Gr. L46 ... 49 D1
Overstrand. L48 ... 63 A2
Overton Ave. L21 ... 27 B1
Overton Cl. Birkenhead L43 . 65 F3
Overton Cl. L32 ... 29 D1
Overton Rd. L44 ... 51 B4
Overton St. L7 ... 53 B1
Overton Way. L43 ... 65 F3
Ovington Dr. PR8 ... 4 E3
Ovolo Rd. L13 ... 54 A4
Owen Ave. L39 ... 13 F6
Owen Cl. WA10 ... 43 D1
Owen Dr. L24 ... 82 B3
Owen Rd. Knowsley L33 ... 41 C7
Owen Rd. Liverpool L4 ... 52 D8
Owen Rd. Rainhill L35 ... 57 C2
Owen St. WA10 ... 43 D1
Owen's La. L39 ... 11 E2
Ox La. L35 ... 71 C6
Oxborough Cl. WA8 ... 72 F4
Oxbow Rd. L12 ... 54 E8
Oxendale Cl. L8 ... 68 B7
Oxenham Rd. WA2 ... 61 A3

Oxenholme Cres. L11 40 A1
Oxford Ave. L21 38 B8
Oxford Ave. L20 38 E3
Oxford Cl. L17 68 C2
Oxford Ct. PR8 3 F4
Oxford Dr. Crosby L22 26 C2
Oxford Dr. Heswall L63 86 F6
Oxford Dr. Liverpool L26 83 A8
Oxford Gdns. PR8 3 E4
Oxford House. L20 38 E3
Oxford Rd. L20 38 D3
Oxford Rd. Crosby L22 26 C1
Oxford Rd. Huyton-w-R L36 56 A3
Oxford Rd. Liverpool L9 39 B8
Oxford Rd. Orrell WN5 25 F8
Oxford Rd. Skelmersdale WN8 15 E1
Oxford Rd. Southport PR8 3 E4
Oxford Rd. Wallasey L44 51 C4
Oxford St. Liverpool L7 52 F1
Oxford St. Newton-le-W WA12 46 B3
Oxford St. 2 St Helens WA10 43 F4
Oxford St. St Helens WA10 43 F5
Oxford St E. L7 53 A1
Oxhouse Rd. WN5 25 D4
Oxley Ave. L46 50 B3
Oxley St. WA9 58 D7
Oxton Cl. Liverpool L32 40 B8
Oxton Cl. Liverpool L17 68 C2
Oxton Cl. Widnes WA8 72 C4
Oxton Ct. L43 66 B4
Oxton Rd. Birkenhead L41 66 C5
Oxton Rd. Wallasey L44 51 B3
Oxton St. L4 52 F8
Oxton St Saviour's CE (Aided) Prim Sch. L43 66 A3

Pacific Rd. Birkenhead L41 & L72 66 F7
Pacific Rd. L20 38 B4
Packenham Rd. L13 53 F6
Paddington. L7 53 A1
Paddock Cl. L23 26 B6
Paddock Dr. L64 86 D2
Paddock Gr. WA9 58 D3
Paddock Hey. L27 70 D6
Paddock Rd. WN8 24 C5
Paddock The. Ashton-in-M WN4 34 F6
Paddock The. Birkenhead L46 64 C7
Paddock The. Birkenhead L49 65 B5
Paddock The. Formby L37 10 A5
Paddock The. Heswall L60 86 C8
Paddock The. Kirkby L32 40 D7
Paddock The. Liverpool L25 70 B4
Paddock The. Ormskirk L39 13 C3
Paddock The. Prescot L34 56 F7
Paddock The. Southport PR8 7 C4
Padeswood Cl. WA9 58 C6
Padgate Cty High Sch. WA2 61 F2
Padstow Cl. Liverpool L26 70 E1
Padstow Cl. Southport PR9 2 A5
Padstow Cl. Warrington WA5 74 E3
Padstow Dr. WA10 43 B6
Padstow Rd. Birkenhead L49 64 C2
Padstow Rd. Liverpool L16 69 D8
Page Ct. L37 9 F3
Page La. WA8 73 C1
Page Moss Ave. L36 55 B4
Page Moss La. L14 & L36 55 A3
Page Moss Par. L36 55 B4
Page Moss Prim Sch. L36 55 A3
Page Wlk. L3 52 E3
Pagebank Rd. L14 & L36 55 A3
Pagefield Rd. L15 69 A6
Pagewood Cl. L43 65 D4
Paignton Cl. Billinge WN5 33 E8
Paignton Cl. Huyton-w-R L36 56 B3
Paignton Cl. Warrington WA5 74 E4
Paignton Rd. Liverpool L16 69 D8
Paignton Rd. Wallasey L45 50 F6
Paisley Ave. Bebington L62 88 E4
Paisley Ave. St Helens WA11 44 E7
Paisley St. L3 52 B3
Palace Arc. WN4 35 B3
Palace Rd. Liverpool L9 39 A6
Palace Rd. Southport PR8 3 E5
Palatine Arc. 8 WA10 44 A3
Palatine Rd. Bebington L62 79 C1
Palatine Rd. Southport PR8 3 F5
Palatine Rd. Wallasey L44 51 D2
Palatine The. 6 L20 38 C3
Palermo St. L44 51 D2
Paley Cl. L4 52 F7
Palin Dr. WA5 74 F6
Pall Mall. L2 & L3 52 C3
Palladio Rd. L13 54 B4
Palm Ave. WN4 34 D5
Palm Cl. L9 39 C3
Palm Ct. WN8 15 E2
Palm Gr. Birkenhead L43 66 B5
Palm Gr. Liverpool L25 70 B1
Palm Gr. Southport PR8 & PR9 4 E6
Palm Hill. L43 66 B4
Palmer Cl. 7 WA10 43 F4
Palmerston Ave. L21 38 A7
Palmerston Cl. L18 68 F3
Palmerston Dr. L21 38 B7
Palmerston Rd. Liverpool L18 68 F3
Palmerston Rd. Liverpool L19 81 C6
Palmerston Rd. Southport PR9 4 F6
Palmerston Rd. Wallasey L44 50 F4
Palmerston St. L42 66 F2
Palmwood Ave. L35 57 D2
Palmwood Cl. L43 65 E1
Paltridge Way. L61 76 F4
Pamela Cl. L10 40 B6
Pampas Gr. L9 39 B4
Pankhurst Rd. L21 27 C2
Pansy St. L5 52 D7
Parade. L3 67 B8
Parade Cres. L24 82 E2
Parade St. WA10 44 A4
Parade The. L64 86 B1
Paradise La. Formby L37 10 A6
Paradise La. Prescot L35 56 D2
Paradise St. Liverpool L1 52 D1
Paradise St. Liverpool L1 & L72 67 D8
Paragon Cl. WA8 73 B5
Parbold Ave. WA11 44 D6
Parbold Ct. WA8 84 D8
Parbrook Cl. L36 55 D6
Parbrook Rd. L36 55 D5
Parchments The. WA12 46 D4
Parish CE Prim Sch. WA10 44 B4
Park Ave. Crosby L23 26 E5
Park Ave. Formby L37 9 F1
Park Ave. Golborne WA3 35 F2
Park Ave. Haydock WA11 45 A6
Park Ave. Liverpool L9 39 D7
Park Ave. Liverpool L18 68 E3
Park Ave. Maghull L31 20 D3
Park Ave. Ormskirk L39 13 E5
Park Ave. Orrell WN5 25 E1
Park Ave. Rainhill L35 57 C4
Park Ave. Southport PR9 4 E8
Park Ave. St Helens L34 57 A7
Park Ave. Wallasey L44 51 D3
Park Ave. Widnes WA8 73 B1
Park Ave N. WA12 46 C2
Park Ave S. WA12 46 C2
Park Brow Cty Prim Sch. L32 41 A8
Park Brow Dr. L32 29 F1
Park Cl. Birkenhead L41 66 C6
Park Cl. Hightown L37 17 E8
Park Cl. L32 29 B3
Park Cres. Haskayne L39 11 F4
Park Cres. Southport PR9 1 D1
Park Ct. L22 26 E1
Park Dr. Birkenhead L41 66 A7
Park Dr. Birkenhead L41 & L43 66 C6
Park Dr. Crosby L23 26 A4
Park Dr. Crosby L23 27 A7
Park Gr. L41 66 D5
Park High Sch. Birkenhead L41 66 A7
Park High Sch. Birkenhead L43 66 B6
Park Hill Ct. 6 L8 67 F4
Park Hill Rd. L8 67 F4
Park Hospl. L6 53 D5
Park Ind Est. WN4 34 E3
Park La. L20 38 E7
Park La. Golborne WN2 & WN7 36 D6
Park La. Litherland L30 28 A1
Park La. Liverpool L30 & L9 39 A8
Park La. Liverpool L1 & L72 67 D8
Park La. Maghull L31 20 F3
Park La. Wallasey L47 49 A2
Park La W. L30 27 F2
Park Lane Dr. L31 21 B2
Park Lane Inf Sch. WN4 34 F7
Park Link. L39 13 B1
Park Pl. L20 38 C3
Park Pl. Liverpool L8 67 E6
Park Prim Sch. Skelmersdale WN8 15 E1
Park Prim Sch. Wallasey L44 51 B3
Park Rd. Bebington L62 79 B5
Park Rd. Bebington L62 88 F6
Park Rd. Birkenhead L42 66 E3
Park Rd. Crosby L22 26 E1
Park Rd. Formby L37 9 E1
Park Rd. Golborne WA12 47 A7
Park Rd. Heswall L60 86 B8
Park Rd. Hoylake L47 48 F1
Park Rd. L32 29 C3
Park Rd. Liverpool L8 67 F5
Park Rd. Ormskirk L39 13 E5
Park Rd. Orrell WN5 25 F1
Park Rd. Prescot L34 56 C7
Park Rd. Southport PR9 1 D1
Park Rd. Southport PR9 4 D8
Park Rd. St Helens WA9 44 D4
Park Rd. Wallasey L44 51 C3
Park Rd. Warrington WA2 61 D1
Park Rd. Warrington WA5 74 E6
Park Rd. West Kirby L48 63 A2
Park Rd. Widnes WA8 73 B1
Park Rd E. L41 & L43 66 C6
Park Rd N. Birkenhead L41 66 B7
Park Rd N. Newton-le-W WA12 46 E4
Park Rd S. Birkenhead L43 66 B6
Park Rd S. Newton-le-W WA12 46 D2
Park Rd W. Birkenhead L41 & L43 66 A7
Park Rd W. Southport PR9 1 C1
Park Road Prim Sch. WA5 74 E6
Park St. Birkenhead L41 66 D7
Park St. Birkenhead L41 66 E7
Park St. L20 38 D3
Park St. Haydock WA11 45 A6
Park St. Liverpool L8 67 E5
Park St. St Helens WA9 44 C4
Park St. Wallasey L44 51 C4
Park Terr. L22 37 E8
Park The. Huyton-w-R L36 55 E1
Park The. Warrington WA5 74 D3
Park Vale Rd. L9 39 A6
Park View. Abram WN2 36 B8
Park View. Ashton-in-M WN4 35 B2
Park View. Bebington L62 88 C8
Park View. Crosby L22 & L23 26 D2
Park View. Crosby L23 27 B7
Park View. Huyton-w-R L36 55 C4
Park View. Liverpool L6 53 D5
Park View. Newton-le-W WA12 46 E3
Park View Ct. L17 68 E5
Park View Flats. L21 38 A8
Park View Prim Sch. L36 55 C4
Park W. L60 85 E7
Park Wall Rd. L29 & L38 19 B2
Park Way. Formby L37 9 F1
Park Way. Hoylake L47 48 E1
Park Way. Huyton-w-R L34 & L36 55 D7
Park Way. Liverpool L8 67 F7
Park Way E. L32 29 B3
Park Way W. L32 29 B3
Parkbourn. L31 21 A2
Parkbourn Dr. L31 21 A2
Parkbourn N. L31 21 A2
Parkbourn Sq. L31 21 A2
Parkbridge Rd. L42 66 C3
Parkend Rd. L42 66 C3
Parker Ave. L21 37 F7
Parker Cres. L39 13 F7
Parker St. L1 52 D1
Parkfield Ave. Birkenhead L41 66 D6
Parkfield Ave. Litherland L30 28 A1
Parkfield Cl. L41 66 C7
Parkfield Dr. L44 51 B4
Parkfield Gr. L31 20 C1
Parkfield Pl. L41 66 D6
Parkfield Rd. Bebington L63 79 A3
Parkfield Rd. Crosby L22 26 F2
Parkfield Rd. Liverpool L17 68 B4
Parkfield Sch. L32 40 E8
Parkfields. WN2 36 C6
Parkfields La. WA2 61 F2
Parkgate La. L63 & L64 86 F5
Parkhill Prim Sch. L8 67 F4
Parkhill Rd. L42 66 C3
Parkholme. L22 26 E1
Parkhurst Rd. Birkenhead L42 66 C2
Parkhurst Rd. Liverpool L11 39 F1
Parkinson Rd. L9 39 A4
Parkland Ct. L43 65 C8
Parklands. Knowsley L34 41 E3
Parklands. Rainford WA11 31 F7
Parklands. Skelmersdale WN8 16 D2
Parklands. Southport PR9 4 E8
Parklands. Widnes WA8 72 C3
Parklands Dr. L60 86 C6
Parks The. WA12 35 B1
Parkside. L44 51 D3
Parkside Ave. Ashton-in-M WN4 34 F8
Parkside Ave. St Helens WA9 58 B3
Parkside Cl. Bebington L63 79 A5
Parkside Cl. Liverpool L27 70 E4
Parkside Cres. WN5 25 F6
Parkside Ct. WA8 73 A2
Parkside Dr. L11 & L12 54 B8
Parkside Rd. Bebington L63 79 A6
Parkside Rd. Birkenhead L42 66 E3
Parkside Rd. Golborne WA12 & WA3 47 B2
Parkside Sch. L39 13 E5
Parkside St. L6 52 F3
Parkstile La. L11 40 C4
Parkstone Rd. L42 66 C3
Parkvale Ave. L43 77 E8
Parkview Dr. L27 70 E4
Parkview Rd. L11 40 E5
Parkway. Crosby L23 26 F2
Parkway. Irby L49 76 F7
Parkway. Litherland L30 27 F5
Parkway. Wallasey L45 50 E7
Parkway Cl. L49 76 F7
Parkwood Cl. L62 88 E8
Parkwood Rd. Liverpool L25 70 A4
Parkwood Rd. Prescot L35 56 E2
Parlane St. WA9 44 C4
Parle Ct. 5 L6 53 B5
Parliament Cl. 6 L1 67 E7
Parliament Pl. L8 67 F7
Parliament St. Liverpool L1 ,L69 ,L72 ,L8 67 D7
Parliament St. Orrell WN8 25 C7
Parliament St. St Helens L35 & WA9 57 D7
Parlington Cl. WA8 84 C7
Parlow Rd. 4 L11 & L13 53 E8
Parnell Rd. L63 79 A2
Parr Comm High Sch. WA9 44 E3
Parr Flat Comm Jun Sch. WA9 45 A3
Parr Gr. Birkenhead L49 64 C4
Parr Gr. Haydock WA11 45 A6
Parr Ind Est. WA9 44 E2
Parr Mount St. WA9 44 C3
Parr St. L21 38 B8
Parr St. Litherland L21 27 B1
Parr St. Liverpool L1 & L69 & L72 67 D8
Parr St. St Helens WA10 & WA9 44 B3
Parr St. 1 Widnes WA8 73 C1
Parr Stocks Rd. WA9 44 D3
Parr's La. L39 13 D1
Parren Ave. L35 56 C1
Parrmount Ct. WA9 44 C3
Parrs Rd. L43 66 B3
Parry St. L44 51 D2
Parson's Brow. WA11 31 E6
Parsonage Brow. WN8 25 A8
Parsonage Gn. L24 83 E1
Part St. PR8 4 B6
Parthenon Dr. L11 39 E2
Partington Ave. L20 38 E4
Parton St. L6 & L7 53 C3
Partridge Rd. Crosby L23 26 B4
Partridge Rd. L32 29 B3
Pasture Ave. L46 49 E2
Pasture Cl. Garswood WN4 34 E6
Pasture Cl. Liverpool L25 70 B1
Pasture Cl. St Helens WA9 58 C4
Pasture Cres. L46 49 E2
Pasture La. WA11 32 A4
Pasture Rd. L46 49 D2
Pastures The. Southport PR9 2 D5
Pastures The. West Kirby L48 63 F2
Pateley Cl. L32 29 C1
Pateley Wlk. L24 82 F4
Paterson St. L41 66 C6
Paton Cl. L48 63 D3
Patricia Ave. L41 50 F1
Patricia Ct. 9 WA10 43 F4
Patricia Gr. L20 38 D6
Patrick Ave. L20 38 E7
Patten St. L41 66 B8
Patten's Cl. L30 27 D4
Patten's Wlk. L34 41 E5
Patterdale Ave. WA2 61 C2
Patterdale Cl. PR8 7 B3
Patterdale Cres. L31 20 E2
Patterdale Dr. WA10 57 B8
Patterdale Rd. Ashton-in-M WN4 35 A8
Patterdale Rd. Bebington L63 78 F3
Patterdale Rd. Liverpool L15 68 F6
Patterson St. WA12 46 B3
Paul Cl. WA5 74 D6
Paul McCartney Way. 5 L6 53 B3
Paul Orr Ct. L3 52 C4
Paul St. L3 52 D3
Paul's La. PR9 1 F3
Pauline Wlk. L10 40 B7
Paulsfield Dr. L46 & L49 64 E7
Paulton Cl. L8 67 F4
Paulton Vale. L44 51 A2
Paveley Bank. L27 70 D6
Pavilion Cl. L8 68 B7
Paxton Pl. WN8 24 C4
Paxton Rd. L36 55 E4
Paxton St. L5 52 E6
Peacehaven. WN8 15 E1
Peacehaven Cl. L16 69 F8
Peach Gr. Haydock WA11 45 E7
Peach Gr. L31 29 B4
Peach Tree Cl. L24 83 E2
Pear Gr. L6 53 B3
Pear Tree Cl. Hale L24 83 E1
Pear Tree Cl. Heswall L60 77 C1
Pear Tree Rd. L36 70 E8
Pearce Cl. L25 69 F6
Pearson Dr. L20 38 E7
Pearson Rd. L41 & L42 66 E5
Pearson St. L15 68 F8
Peartree Ave. L12 40 F1
Peasefield Rd. L14 55 A4
Peasley Cross La. WA9 44 C2
Peasley View. WA9 44 C2
Peatwood Ave. L32 40 F7
Peckers Hill Rd. WA9 58 E7
Peckmill Gn. L27 70 F4
Pecksniff Cl. 4 L8 67 F5
Peebles Ave. WA11 44 E6
Peebles Cl. Garswood WN4 34 C4
Peebles Cl. L33 29 D6
Peech St. L3 & L7 52 F1
Peel Ave. L41 66 F3
Peel Cl. L35 56 E3
Peel House La. WA8 73 B2
Peel Pl. Liverpool L8 67 F7
Peel Pl. St Helens WA10 44 A5
Peel Rd. L20 38 A5
Peel Rd. Skelmersdale WN8 24 E5
Peel St. Liverpool L8 68 A4
Peel St. Newton-le-W WA12 46 A3
Peel St. Runcorn WA7 84 F3
Peel St. Southport PR8 & PR9 4 F6
Peel Wlk. L31 20 B2
Peet Ave. Ormskirk L39 13 D4
Peet Ave. St Helens WA10 43 C3
Peet St. L7 53 B1
Peet's La. PR9 2 A1
Pelham Gr. L17 68 C4
Pelham Rd. L44 51 A3
Pemberton Rd. Birkenhead L49 65 B2
Pemberton Rd. Garswood WN3 & WN5 34 A8
Pemberton Rd. Liverpool L13 54 A3
Pemberton St. WA10 43 E3
Pembertons Ct. L34 56 E6
Pembrey Way. L25 82 D8
Pembroke Ave. L46 64 E7
Pembroke Ct. L41 66 E4
Pembroke Gdns. L3 52 F2
Pembroke Pl. L3 52 F2
Pembroke Rd. L20 38 C1
Pembroke Rd. L20 38 C2
Pembroke St. L3 52 F2
Pembury Cl. L12 40 E3
Penarth Cl. L7 68 B8
Penbroke St. L3 52 F1
Pencombe Rd. L36 55 C4
Pendennis Rd. L44 51 C3
Pendennis St. L6 53 B5
Pendine Cl. Liverpool L6 53 C4
Pendine Cl. Warrington WA5 60 C2
Pendle Ave. WA11 44 D5
Pendle Cl. L49 64 E6
Pendle Dr. Litherland L21 27 C4
Pendle Dr. Ormskirk L39 14 A6
Pendle Pl. WN8 24 D4
Pendle Rd. WA3 36 C1
Pendle View. L21 27 C4
Pendle Villas. L21 27 C3
Pendlebury St. WA9 58 C3
Pendleton Gn. L26 82 E7
Pendleton Rd. 8 L4 39 A2
Penfold. L31 20 E1
Penfold Cl. L18 69 D5
Pengallo Hey. L27 70 F5
Pengwern Gr. L15 68 D8
Pengwern St. L8 68 A5
Penhale Cl. L17 68 B2
Penketh Cty High Sch. WA5 74 F5

Penketh Cty Prim Sch. WA5 74 D4
Penketh Gn. L24 82 E4
Penketh Pl. WN8 24 C5
Penketh South Cty Prim Sch. WA5 74 E3
Penkett Ct. L45 51 C6
Penkett Gr. L45 51 C6
Penkett Rd. L45 51 C6
Penkford La. WA5 45 D2
Penkford Sch. WA12 45 E2
Penkford St. WA12 45 E3
Penlake Ind Est. WA9 58 E6
Penlake La. WA9 58 F7
Penley Cres. L32 29 B2
Penmann Cl. L26 82 F7
Penmann Cres. L26 82 F7
Penmark Cl. WA5 60 C2
Penmon Dr. L61 76 F3
Penn La. WA7 84 F1
Pennant Ave. L12 40 C1
Pennard Ave. L36 55 D5
Pennine Cl. WA9 44 E3
Pennine Dr. WA9 44 F3
Pennine La. WA3 36 C1
Pennine Pl. WN8 24 B6
Pennine Rd. Bebington L42 78 C8
Pennine Rd. Wallasey L44 50 F4
Pennine Rd. Warrington WA2 61 E2
Pennine Way. L32 29 C4
Pennington Ave. L20 38 E6
Pennington Ave. Ormskirk L39 13 E6
Pennington Flash Ctry Pk. WA3 36 F4
Pennington La. WA5 & WA9 45 D2
Pennington Rd. L21 38 C6
Pennington St. 2 L4 38 F2
Pennington's Pl. L36 55 E2
Pennsylvania Rd. L13 53 D7
Penny La. Burtonwood WA5 45 D1
Penny La. Cronton L35 & WA8 72 B6
Penny La. Haydock WA11 & WA12 46 A7
Penny La. Liverpool L17 & L18 & L15 68 F5
Penny Lane Neighbourhood Ctr. L15 69 A6
Pennystone Cl. L49 64 D6
Penpoll Ind Est. L20 38 C6
Penrhos Rd. L47 63 A6
Penrhyd Rd. L61 76 D5
Penrhyn Ave. L21 38 B7
Penrhyn Ave. Heswall L61 77 A6
Penrhyn Rd. L34 41 B6
Penrhyn St. L5 52 D5
Penrith Ave. Southport PR8 7 C3
Penrith Ave. Warrington WA2 61 C2
Penrith Cres. Ashton-in-M WN4 35 B4
Penrith Cres. Maghull L31 20 E2
Penrith Rd. WA10 57 B7
Penrith St. L41 66 C5
Penrose Ave E. L14 54 F2
Penrose Ave W. L14 54 E2
Penrose Pl. WN8 24 E4
Penrose St. L5 52 F6
Penryn Ave. WA11 44 D7
Penryn Cl. WA5 74 E3
Pensall Dr. L60 & L61 76 F2
Pensarn Gdns. WA5 60 D2
Pensarn Rd. L13 53 F2
Pensby Cl. L61 77 A5
Pensby Cty Inf Sch. L61 76 F3
Pensby Hall La. L60 & L61 76 F2
Pensby High Sch for Boys. L61 76 D4
Pensby High Sch for Girls. L61 76 E3
Pensby Jun Sch. L61 76 F3
Pensby Park Prim Sch. L61 76 E4
Pensby Rd. L60 & L61 77 A4
Pentire Ave. WA10 43 B6
Pentland Ave. 6 Liverpool L4 39 A1
Pentland Ave. St Helens WA9 44 F3
Pentland Ave. Warrington WA2 61 B3
Pentland Pl. WA2 61 B3
Pentland Rd. L33 30 A4
Penton Wlk. 12 L6 53 A3
Penuel Rd. 10 L4 38 F2
Peover St. L3 52 D3
Peploe Rd. L4 39 D2
Peplow Rd. L32 29 B2
Pepper St. L24 83 D1
Pera Cl. 11 L6 53 A3
Perch Pool La. PR9 5 F4
Percival Ct. PR8 4 A6
Percival La. WA7 84 E2
Percy Rd. L44 51 E2
Percy St. L20 38 B5
Percy St. Liverpool L8 67 F7
Percy St. St Helens WA9 58 F7
Percy Villas. L9 39 A4
Perimeter Rd. L33 30 E2
Perriam Rd. L19 81 D8
Perrin Rd. L45 50 E5
Perrins Rd. WA5 59 F6
Perry Brook Comm Prim Sch. WN4 35 A7
Perry St. L3 & L8 67 D6
Perrybrook Wlk. WN4 35 D4
Perryside. L44 51 E2
Pershore Gr. PR8 7 A4
Pershore House Sch. L42 66 B1
Pershore Rd. L32 40 E8
Perth Ave. WA9 57 E7
Perth Cl. L33 29 D6
Perth Cl. Warrington WA2 61 F3
Perth St. L6 53 A3
Peter Lloyd L Ctr. L13 53 F6
Peter Mahon Way. L20 38 B4
Peter Price's La. L63 78 E4
Peter Rd. L4 38 E1
Peter Rd. L4 38 F2
Peter St. Ashton-in-M WN4 35 C3
Peter St. Golborne WA3 47 A8
Peter St. Liverpool L1 52 D2
Peter St. St Helens WA10 43 F4
Peter St. 8 Wallasey L44 51 E2
Peter's La. L1 52 D1
Peterborough Dr. L30 27 F4
Peterborough Rd. L15 69 A6
Peterhouse Walk. WN4 34 F3
Peterlee Cl. WA9 57 F7
Peterlee Way. L30 28 A1
Petersfield Cl. L30 28 A1
Peterstone Cl. WA5 60 D2
Peterwood. L42 67 A1
Petherick Rd. L11 40 C5
Petton St. L5 52 F6
Petunia Cl. L14 55 A4
Petworth Ave. WA2 61 B3
Petworth Cl. L24 82 B4
Petworth Rd. PR8 7 B6
Peveril St. L4 & L9 38 F3
Pharmacy Rd. L24 82 C5
Pheasant Field. L24 83 C2
Pheasant Gr. L26 70 E1
Philbeach Rd. L11 & L4 39 D2
Philharmonic Ct. 5 L7 67 F8
Philip Dr. PR8 7 F6
Philip Gr. WA9 58 C7
Philip Rd. WA8 84 B8
Philips Dr. WA5 74 E6
Phillimore Rd. L6 & L7 53 C3
Phillip Gr. L14 54 F5
Phillip's Cl. L37 9 F2
Phillip's La. L37 9 F2
Phillips Cl. L23 27 B6
Phillips St. L3 52 C3
Phillips Way. L60 85 E8
Phipps' La. WA5 59 E7
Phoenix Ave. WA5 60 F2
Physics Rd. L24 82 C5
Phythian Cl. L6 53 B3
Phythian Cres. WA5 74 F4
Phythian St. Liverpool L6 53 A3
Phythian St. St Helens WA11 44 F6
Picadilly. WN5 33 E5
Pickerill Rd. L49 64 D3
Pickering Rake. L30 27 D5
Pickering Rd. Wallasey L45 51 B8
Pickering Rd. Widnes WA8 84 B5
Pickering St. L6 53 A5
Pickmere Dr. Bebington L62 88 F3
Pickmere Dr. Bebington L62 88 F4
Pickop St. 6 L3 52 C3
Pickwick St. L8 67 F6
Picow Farm Rd. WA7 84 E1
Picow St. 1 WA7 84 F1
Picton Cl. Bebington L62 88 E3
Picton Cl. Birkenhead L43 65 F4
Picton Cres. L15 68 E8
Picton Gr. L15 68 D8
Picton Rd. Crosby L22 26 D1
Picton Rd. Liverpool L15 68 E8
Piele Rd. WA11 45 E8
Piercefield Rd. L37 9 F5
Pierpoint St. WA12 47 A7
Pighue La. Liverpool L13 & L7 53 F1
Pighue La. Liverpool L13 54 A1
Pigot St. WA10 43 E3
Pigotts Rake. L30 27 D5
Pike House Rd. WA10 43 A5
Pike Pl. WA10 43 B4
Pikelaw Pl. WN8 24 C5
Pikes Hey Rd. L48 75 F7
Pilch La. L14 & L36 54 F3
Pilch La E. L36 55 A2
Pilchbank Rd. L14 54 E4
Pilgrim Cl. WA2 61 A6
Pilgrim St. Birkenhead L41 66 F6
Pilgrim St. Liverpool L1 67 E8
Pilkington Rd. PR8 4 D5
Pilkington St. WA11 31 F6
Pilling Cl. PR9 1 F5
Pilling La. L31 20 A5
Pilling Pl. WN8 24 C5
Pilot Gr. L15 68 D8
Pimblett Rd. WA11 45 E7
Pimblett St. WA3 47 A7
Pimbley Gr E. L31 28 C6
Pimbley Gr W. L31 28 C6
Pimbo La. Orrell WN8 25 A4
Pimbo La. Skelmersdale WN5 & WN8 24 F3
Pimbo Rd. Rainford WA11 & WN5 32 E7
Pimbo Rd. Skelmersdale WN8 24 C5
Pimhill Cl. L8 68 A6
Pincroft Way. L4 52 D7
Pine Ave. Bebington L63 78 F3
Pine Ave. Newton-le-W WA12 46 D2
Pine Ave. Ormskirk L39 13 F7
Pine Ave. St Helens WA10 43 F6
Pine Ave. Widnes WA8 73 B2
Pine Cl. Haydock WA11 45 C6
Pine Cl. Huyton-w-R L36 55 D4
Pine Cl. L32 29 C3
Pine Cl. Prescot L35 56 E3
Pine Cl. Skelmersdale WN8 15 F1
Pine Crest. L39 13 B2
Pine Ct. L41 66 D6
Pine Dale. WA11 31 E7
Pine Dr. L39 13 F6
Pine Gr. L20 38 D4
Pine Gr. Crosby L22 26 D2
Pine Gr. Golborne WA3 47 C8
Pine Gr. Ormskirk L39 13 F7
Pine Gr. Southport PR9 4 D7
Pine Mews. L1 67 E7
Pine Rd. L60 86 C8
Pine Tree Ave. L43 65 C4
Pine Tree Cl. L46 64 F8
Pine Tree Gr. L46 64 F8
Pine Tree Rd. L36 70 D8
Pine View Dr. L61 77 A3
Pine Walks. Bebington L42 78 B8
Pine Walks. Birkenhead L42 66 B1
Pine Way. L60 76 E2
Pinedale Cl. L43 65 D4
Pinehey. L64 86 D1
Pinehurst Ave. Crosby L22 26 C2
Pinehurst Ave. Liverpool L4 53 C7
Pinehurst Avenue Jun Sch. L4 53 C7
Pinehurst Rd. L4 53 C7
Pinehurst Road Inf Sch. L4 53 C7
Pinemore Rd. L18 69 A2
Pineridge Cl. L62 79 C2
Pines The. Bebington L63 79 B3
Pines The. Liverpool L12 40 F4
Pinetree Ct. L44 50 F5
Pinetree Dr. L48 63 D1
Pinewood. Ashton-in-M WN4 35 A2
Pinewood. Skelmersdale WN8 16 D3
Pinewood Ave. Formby L37 9 D1
Pinewood Ave. Liverpool L12 40 D3
Pinewood Cl. Abram WN2 36 C7
Pinewood Cl. Formby L37 9 D2
Pinewood Cl. Liverpool L27 70 E6
Pinewood Cres. WN5 25 E6
Pinewood Dr. L60 86 B8
Pinewood Gdns. L33 29 E5
Pinewood Rd. WA5 59 F7
Pinfold Cl. Litherland L30 27 E5
Pinfold Cl. Southport PR8 7 B3
Pinfold Cres. L32 41 A8
Pinfold Ct. 1 Crosby L23 26 D5
Pinfold Ct. West Kirby L47 63 A4
Pinfold Dr. WA10 43 A3
Pinfold La. Knowsley L34 41 C3
Pinfold La. Southport PR8 7 B3
Pinfold La. West Kirby L47 & L48 63 A4
Pinfold Pl. WN8 24 D4
Pinfold Rd. L25 82 C7
Pingot Rd. WN5 33 E5
Pingwood La. L33 30 A5
Pinnington Rd. L35 56 E3
Pintail Cl. WA11 44 B6
Piper's Cl. L60 85 D8
Piper's End. L60 85 D8
Piper's La. Heswall L60 & L61 76 C1
Piper's La. Heswall L60 85 D8
Pipers The. WA3 47 F8
Pipit Ave. WA12 46 C3
Pipit Cl. L26 70 E2
Pirrie Rd. L9 39 D3
Pit Hey Pl. WN8 24 C5
Pit La. WA8 73 A4
Pit Pl. L25 70 A2
Pitch Cl. L49 64 D4
Pitsmead Rd. L32 29 E1
Pitt St. Liverpool L1 & L72 67 D8
Pitt St. Southport PR9 4 F6
Pitt St. St Helens WA9 44 C3
Pitt St. St Helens WA9 44 C4
Pitts House La. PR9 5 B8
Pitville Ave. L18 69 A3
Pitville Cl. L18 69 A2
Pitville Gr. L18 69 A3
Pitville Rd. L18 69 A3
Plane Cl. L9 39 C3
Plane Tree Gr. WA11 46 A7
Plane Tree Rd. L63 78 E5
Planetree Rd. L12 54 F8
Plantation Prim Sch. L26 82 F8
Plantation Rd. L62 79 F2
Planters The. Birkenhead L49 64 C4
Planters The. Litherland L30 28 A4
Platt Gr. L42 79 A8
Platts St. WA11 45 A6
Plattsville Rd. L18 69 A5
Playfield Rd. L12 54 F7
Playfield Wlk. L12 54 E7
Pleasance Way. WA12 46 D4
Pleasant Hill St. L3 & L8 67 D6
Pleasant St. L20 38 B2
Pleasant St. 3 Liverpool L3 52 E1
Pleasant St. Wallasey L45 51 B7
Pleasant Street Prim Sch. L3 52 E1
Pleasant View. L20 38 B2
Pleasant View. Liverpool L7 53 E2
Pleasington Cl. L43 65 E4
Pleasington Dr. L43 65 E4
Pleasureland. PR8 3 F7
Plemont Rd. L13 54 A5
Plessington RC High Sch. L42 79 A7
Plex La. L39 12 C5
Plex Moss La. L39 & PR8 11 D8
Plimsoll St. 5 L7 53 B1
Plough La. L40 & WN8 15 A4
Plover Cl. WA12 46 C3
Pluckington Rd. L36 56 B3
Plum Tree Cl. Huyton-w-R L28 55 B8
Plum Tree Cl. St Helens L35 57 A6
Plumbers Way. L36 55 F2
Plumer St. Birkenhead L41 66 A8
Plumer St. Liverpool L15 68 E8
Plumpton La. L39 8 E2
Plumpton St. L6 52 F4
Plymyard Ave. L62 88 D5
Plymyard Cl. L62 88 D5
Pocket Nook St. WA9 44 C4
Pocklington Ct. WA2 61 F1
Podium Rd. L13 54 A4
Poets Cnr. L62 79 B5
Poets Gn. L35 56 F3
Poleacre Dr. WA8 72 D2
Poll Hill Rd. L60 76 F1
Poll Moll Ctr. L3 52 C3
Pollard Rd. L15 54 A1
Pollitt Cres. WA9 58 C3
Pollitt Sq. L62 79 C8
Polperro Cl. WA5 74 E3
Pomfret St. L8 68 A6
Pomona St. L3 52 E1
Pond Green Way. WA9 44 F1
Pond View Cl. L60 86 C8
Pond Wlk. WA9 45 A1
Ponsonby Rd. L45 50 E5
Ponsonby St. L8 68 A6
Pontville Sch. L39 13 D3
Pool Bank. L62 79 B6
Pool End. WA9 44 F2
Pool Hey. L28 55 B8
Pool Hey La. PR8 & PR9 5 B3
Pool La. Bebington L62 79 D5
Pool La. Birkenhead L49 65 A2
Pool St. Birkenhead L41 66 D7
Pool St. Southport PR9 2 D5
Poolbank Rd. L62 79 B7
Poole Ave. WA2 61 B2
Poole Cres. WA2 61 B2
Poole Rd. L44 51 D5
Poole Wlk. 5 L8 68 A4
Poolside Wlk. PR9 2 C4
Poolwood Rd. L49 65 B3
Pope John Paul High Sch. L24 82 F3
Pope St. L20 38 B5
Poplar Ave. Birkenhead L49 64 F5
Poplar Ave. Crosby L23 26 F5
Poplar Ave. Garswood WN4 34 D5
Poplar Ave. Newton-le-W WA12 46 D3
Poplar Ave. St Helens WA10 43 A4
Poplar Ave. Warrington WA5 74 E3
Poplar Bank. Huyton-w-R L36 55 E2
Poplar Bank. Southport PR9 1 D1
Poplar Dr. Bebington L63 79 A4
Poplar Dr. L32 29 D3
Poplar Dr. Liverpool L5 & L6 53 A5
Poplar Dr. Skelmersdale WN8 15 F1
Poplar Farm Cl. L46 64 C6
Poplar Gr. Haydock WA11 45 C6
Poplar Gr. Prescot L35 56 E5
Poplar Gr. Seaforth L21 37 F6
Poplar Gr. St Helens WA10 43 C3
Poplar Rd. Birkenhead L43 66 B4
Poplar Rd. Haydock WA11 45 C6
Poplar Rd. Liverpool L25 70 A3
Poplar St. Golborne WA3 36 B1
Poplar St. Southport PR8 4 E6
Poplar Way. L4 52 D8
Poplars Ave. Warrington WA2 61 A4
Poplars Ave. Warrington WA2 61 C3
Poplars Pl. WA2 61 D2
Poplars The. WA3 36 B1
Poppleford Cl. L25 & L27 70 D5
Poppy La. L39 14 B1
Porchester Rd. L11 39 F1
Porkbury Ct. L43 66 A3
Porlock Ave. Liverpool L16 69 E5
Porlock Ave. St Helens WA9 58 C5
Porlock Cl. Heswall L60 86 B6
Porlock Cl. Warrington WA5 74 E4
Port Cswy. L62 79 D4
Port of Liverpool Euro Rail Terminal. L21 37 E7
Port Sunlight Sta. L62 79 B5
Portal Mews. L61 76 F3
Portal Rd. L61 76 F3
Portbury Cl. L62 79 C6
Portbury Way. L62 79 C6
Portbury Wlk. L62 79 C6
Portelet Rd. L13 53 F4
Porter Ave. WA12 46 C5
Porter Cl. L35 57 E1
Porter St. L3 52 B4
Porthcawl Cl. WA8 72 C3
Portia Ave. L63 78 E7
Portia Gdns. L42 78 E7
Portia St. L20 38 C1
Portico Ave. L35 57 A6
Portico Ct. L35 57 A6
Portico La. L35 57 A6
Portland Ave. L22 26 C2
Portland Cl. WN2 36 A8
Portland Gdns. L3 52 C4
Portland Pl. L5 52 E4
Portland Prim Sch. L41 66 A8
Portland St. Birkenhead L41 66 A8
Portland St. Liverpool L3 52 C4
Portland St. Newton-le-W WA12 45 F4
Portland St. Runcorn WA7 84 F3
Portland St. Southport PR8 4 B5
Portland St. Wallasey L45 37 A1
Portland Way. WA9 44 F1
Portlemouth Rd. L11 40 C5
Portloe Ave. L26 70 F1
Portman Rd. L15 68 D7
Porto Hey Rd. L61 76 D5
Porton Rd. L32 29 C1
Portreath Way. WA10 43 B6
Portree Ave. L63 88 D5
Portree Cl. L9 39 A5
Portrush St. L13 53 E6
Portwood Cl. L8 68 B8
Post Office Ave. PR9 4 B7
Potter Pl. WN8 24 D5
Potters La. WA8 83 F5
Pottery Cl. L35 56 C3
Pottery Fields. L34 56 E6
Pottery La. 3 Liverpool L8 67 F4
Pottery La. Prescot L35 & L36 56 C3
Poulsom Dr. L30 27 D3
Poulter Rd. L9 39 B7
Poulton Bridge Rd. L41 & L44 51 A3
Poulton Cl. L26 82 E6
Poulton Dr. 7 Ashton-in-M WN4 34 F5
Poulton Dr. Widnes WA8 84 D8

Poulton Green Cl. L63 78 F1
Poulton Hall Rd. Bebington L63 88 A7
Poulton Hall Rd. Wallasey L44 51 A3
Poulton Lancelyn Prim Sch. L63 79 A2
Poulton Rd. Bebington L63 79 A2
Poulton Rd. Southport PR9 4 F7
Poulton Rd. Wallasey L44 51 C3
Poulton Royd Dr. L63 78 F2
Poverty La. L31 28 F8
Povey Rd. WA2 61 D1
Powderworks La. L31 21 C3
Powell Dr. WN5 33 D3
Powell St. Birkenhead L43 65 F8
Powell St. St Helens WA9 58 E7
Power Rd. Bebington L42 79 A8
Power Rd. Bebington L62 79 F1
Powis St. L8 68 A5
Pownall Sq. 19 L3 52 C2
Pownall St. L1 & L72 67 D8
Poynter St. WA9 57 E6
Pratt Rd. L34 56 C6
Precinct. L63 79 A3
Precinct The. L62 79 D1
Precincts The. L23 26 E4
Preesall Cl. PR9 1 F4
Preesall Way. L11 40 C5
Premier St. Liverpool L5 52 F5
Premier St. 2 Liverpool L5 53 A5
Prentice Rd. L42 66 E1
Prenton Ave. WA9 58 C4
Prenton Cty Inf Sch. L43 66 A1
Prenton Cty Jun Sch. L43 66 A1
Prenton Dell Ave. L43 78 A8
Prenton Dell Rd. L43 77 F8
Prenton Farm Rd. L43 78 A8
Prenton Gn. L24 82 E3
Prenton Golf Course. L43 77 F8
Prenton Hall Rd. Bebington L43 78 A8
Prenton Hall Rd. Birkenhead L43 & L42 65 F1
Prenton High Sch. L42 66 D1
Prenton La. L42 66 B1
Prenton Prep Sch. L43 66 B3
Prenton Rd E. L42 66 D3
Prenton Rd W. L42 66 C2
Prenton Village Rd. Bebington L43 78 A8
Prenton Village Rd. Birkenhead L43 65 F1
Prenton Way. Birkenhead L43 & L49 65 D1
Prenton Way. Heswall L43 & L49 77 E8
Prentonpark Rd. L42 66 C2
Prentonwood Ct. L42 66 C1
Prescot Coll of F Ed. L34 56 E6
Prescot Cty Prim & Jun Sch. L34 56 E6
Prescot Dr. L6 & L7 53 E3
Prescot Gn. L39 13 D3
Prescot Rd. L31 & L32 29 C6
Prescot Rd. Liverpool L13 & L7 53 E3
Prescot Rd. Maghull L31 & L39 21 D6
Prescot Rd. St Helens WA10 43 D2
Prescot Rd. Tarbock Green L35 71 F5
Prescot Rd. Widnes WA8 72 D2
Prescot St. Liverpool L3 & L7 52 F2
Prescot St. Wallasey L45 51 A8
Prescot Sta. L35 56 E5
Prescott Ave. WA3 35 F2
Prescott Rd. WN8 24 F4
Prescott St. WA3 36 A1
Preseland Rd. L23 26 E3
Pressfield Sch. PR9 2 A3
Prestbury Ave. Birkenhead L43 65 E2
Prestbury Ave. Southport PR8 7 B5
Prestbury Cl. L43 65 E2
Prestbury Rd. L11 39 F4
Preston Ave. L34 56 C5
Preston Gr. L6 53 C5
Preston New Rd. PR9 2 B4
Preston Rd. PR9 4 E8
Preston St. Liverpool L1 52 D2
Preston St. St Helens WA9 58 A2
Preston Way. L23 27 A4
Prestwick Dr. L23 26 C6
Prestwood Cres. L14 54 F4
Prestwood Pl. WN8 24 F4
Prestwood Rd. L14 54 F4
Pretoria Rd. Ashton-in-M WN4 35 B4
Pretoria Rd. Liverpool L9 39 B6
Price Gr. WA9 45 A2
Price St. Birkenhead L41 & L72 66 D7
Price St. 2 Liverpool L1 67 D8
Price's La. L43 66 B4
Priesthouse Cl. L37 10 A3
Priesthouse La. L37 10 A3
Primrose Cl. Formby L37 10 B5
Primrose Cl. Southport PR9 2 C6
Primrose Cl. Warrington WA2 61 D2
Primrose Cl. Widnes WA8 72 E1
Primrose Dr. L36 55 E5
Primrose Gr. Haydock WA11 45 E7
Primrose Gr. 6 Wallasey L44 51 E2
Primrose Hill. Bebington L62 79 B6
Primrose Hill. Liverpool L3 52 D2
Primrose Rd. Birkenhead L41 65 F7
Primrose Rd. Liverpool L18 69 C5
Primrose St. L4 & L5 52 D7
Primrose View. WN4 35 C2
Primula Dr. L9 39 B4
Prince Albert Mews. 1 L1 67 E7
Prince Alfred Rd. L15 69 A6
Prince Andrew's Gr. WA10 43 C6
Prince Charles Gdns. PR8 3 F4
Prince Edward St. L41 66 C7
Prince Edwin St. L3 & L5 52 E4
Prince St. Ashton-in-M WN4 35 A5
Prince St. Seaforth L22 37 E8
Prince William St. L8 67 E6
Princes Ave. Bebington L62 88 E6
Princes Ave. Crosby L23 26 D4
Princes Ave. Liverpool L8 68 A6
Princes Ave. West Kirby L48 63 B2
Princes Bvd. L63 78 E8
Princes Ct. L8 68 B6
Princes Gate E. 1 L8 68 B6
Princes Gate House. 3 L8 68 B6
Princes Gate W. 2 L8 68 B6
Princes Gdns. L3 52 C3
Princes Par. L3 52 B2
Princes Park Mansions. L8 68 B5
Princes Pl. WA8 72 E1
Princes Rd. Liverpool L8 68 A6
Princes Rd. St Helens WA10 43 C1
Princes Sch. L8 68 A7
Princes St. L20 38 B1
Princes St. Liverpool L2 52 C2
Princes St. Newton-le-W WA12 46 B3
Princes St. Southport PR8 4 A6
Princes Way. WA11 44 A8
Princess Ave. Ashton-in-M WN4 35 C3
Princess Ave. Haydock WA11 46 A7
Princess Ave. St Helens WA10 43 E6
Princess Ave. Warrington WA5 74 E7
Princess Dr. Huyton-w-R L14 & L36 & L12 55 A5
Princess Dr. Liverpool L14 54 F6
Princess Pavement. 14 L41 66 E6
Princess Rd. Ashton-in-M WN4 35 C3
Princess Rd. Wallasey L45 51 B7
Princess St. L2 52 C1
Princess Terr. L43 66 C5
Princess Way. L21 38 A7
Princesway. L45 51 A6
Prior Farm Cl. L19 81 A7
Prior St. L20 38 B6
Priors Cl. L25 70 B2
Priorsfield. L46 64 E8
Priorsfield Rd. L25 70 C2
Priorswood Pl. WN8 24 F4
Priory CE Prim Sch The. L41 66 C7
Priory Cl. Bebington L63 79 A3
Priory Cl. Formby L37 10 B2
Priory Cl. Liverpool L17 68 B2
Priory Cl. Prescot L35 56 C1
Priory Ct. L25 70 B2
Priory Day Hospl. L43 65 D6
Priory Gdns. Southport PR8 3 F4
Priory Gdns. St Helens WA10 43 F7
Priory Gr. L39 13 D4
Priory Grange. PR8 4 A4
Priory Mews. PR8 3 F6
Priory Nook. WN8 25 C7
Priory Rd. Ashton-in-M WN4 34 F5
Priory Rd. Liverpool L4 & L6 53 B7
Priory Rd. Orrell WN8 25 C7
Priory Rd. Wallasey L44 51 E3
Priory Rd. West Kirby L48 63 C2
Priory St. Birkenhead L41 66 F6
Priory St. Liverpool L19 81 D4
Priory The. Neston L64 86 E1
Priory The. Winwick WA2 61 A7
Priory Wharf. L41 66 F6
Pritchard Ave. L21 37 F7
Pritt St. L3 52 E3
Private Dr. L61 77 D5
Prizett Rd. L19 81 B7
Probyn Rd. L45 50 E5
Procter Ct. L30 27 D4
Procter Rd. Birkenhead L42 67 A1
Proctor Rd. Formby L37 9 C4
Proctor Rd. Hoylake L47 63 C6
Proctors Cl. WA8 73 D2
Progress Pl. 11 L2 52 C2
Promenade. Southport PR8 1 B1
Promenade. Southport PR8 4 B8
Promenade. Southport PR8 6 F6
Promenade Gdns. Liverpool L17 & L8 68 A3
Promenade Hospl. PR8 4 B8
Prophet Wlk. L8 67 F5
Prospect Ct. L6 53 D3
Prospect Pl. WN8 24 F5
Prospect Rd. Birkenhead L42 66 B1
Prospect Rd. St Helens WA9 44 D4
Prospect St. 2 L7 53 A2
Prospect Vale. Liverpool L6 & L7 53 D3
Prospect Vale. Wallasey L45 50 F5
Prospect Way. L30 28 B3
Providence Cres. L8 67 E6
Provident St. WA9 45 A3
Province Rd. L20 38 D6
Prussia St. 3 L3 52 C2
Pudsey St. L3 52 E2
Pugin St. L4 52 F7
Pulford Ave. L43 66 A2
Pulford Rd. L63 78 F5
Pulford St. 9 L4 52 F7
Pullman Cl. L60 86 D8
Pump La. L48 & L49 64 B4
Pump Rd. L41 66 F8
Punnell's La. L31 19 F5
Purbeck Dr. L61 76 D7
Purdy Cl. WA5 60 D1
Purley Gr. L18 69 A2
Purley Rd. L22 26 C2
Purser Gr. L15 68 D8
Pye Cl. WA11 46 B8
Pye Rd. L60 86 A8
Pye St. L15 69 A7
Pye's Cotts. L39 20 E7
Pyecroft Cl. WA5 74 D6
Pyecroft Rd. WA5 74 D6
Pyes Gdns. WA11 44 B7
Pyes La. L28 & L36 55 C7
Pygon's Hill La. L31 20 D6
Pym St. L4 38 F2
Pyramids The. L41 66 D6
Qakfield Rd. L4 53 B6
Quadrangle The. L18 69 B4
Quadrant The. L47 63 B6
Quail Cl. WA2 61 D3
Quaker La. L60 76 E1
Quakers Meadow. L34 41 D4
Quarry Ave. L63 79 A4
Quarry Bank. Birkenhead L41 66 D5
Quarry Bank. L33 29 F3
Quarry Cl. Heswall L60 76 F2
Quarry Cl. L33 29 F3
Quarry Cl. Liverpool L13 54 A5
Quarry Ct. WA8 72 C1
Quarry Dale. L33 29 F3
Quarry Dr. Ormskirk L39 13 C1
Quarry Gn. L33 29 F3
Quarry Hey. L33 29 F3
Quarry La. Heswall L61 77 A6
Quarry La. Raby L64 87 B1
Quarry Rd. L20 38 E2
Quarry Rd. Crosby L23 27 A6
Quarry Rd. Liverpool L13 54 A5
Quarry Rd. Raby L64 87 C1
Quarry Rd E. Bebington L63 79 A4
Quarry Rd E. Heswall L60 76 F2
Quarry Rd W. L60 76 E1
Quarry St. L25 69 F3
Quarry St S. L25 70 A2
Quarrybank St. 5 L41 66 C5
Quarrybank Workshops. L41 66 C5
Quarryside Dr. L33 30 A3
Quebec St. WN2 & WN7 36 E5
Queen Anne St. Liverpool L3 52 E3
Queen Anne St. Southport PR8 4 B7
Queen Ave. L2 52 C1
Queen Elizabeth Ct. L21 38 A8
Queen Mary Sch The. L9 39 D4
Queen Mary's Dr. L62 79 B6
Queen Sq. L1 52 D2
Queen St. Birkenhead L41 66 E4
Queen St. Golborne WA3 47 B8
Queen St. Liverpool L19 81 C5
Queen St. Newton-le-W WA12 46 B3
Queen St. Ormskirk L39 13 E4
Queen St. Seaforth L22 37 D8
Queen St. St Helens WA10 44 A5
Queen St. Wallasey L44 & L45 51 B5
Queen's Ave. Ashton-in-M WN4 35 B3
Queen's Ave. Hoylake L47 63 D8
Queen's Ave. Widnes WA8 84 B8
Queen's Cl. Liverpool L19 81 C6
Queen's Cl. Runcorn WA7 84 F1
Queen's Rd. Ashton-in-M WN4 35 B4
Queen's Rd. L20 38 C2
Queen's Rd. Formby L37 9 D2
Queen's Rd. Hoylake L47 63 B7
Queen's Rd. Liverpool L6 53 A4
Queen's Rd. Runcorn WA7 84 F1
Queen's Rd. Wallasey L44 51 E4
Queens Ave. L37 9 E5
Queens Croft. L37 9 D2
Queens Ct. Liverpool L6 53 A5
Queens Ct. Liverpool L16 54 C1
Queens Dr. Birkenhead L43 66 A1
Queens Dr. Golborne WA3 47 C8
Queens Dr. Heswall L60 85 E8
Queens Dr. Liverpool L12 & L13 54 B4
Queens Dr. Newton-le-W WA12 46 C5
Queens Dr. St Helens WA10 43 C6
Queens Drive Mossley Hill. Liverpool L15 & L18 69 B5
Queens Drive Stoneycroft. L13 & L14 54 B3
Queens Drive Walton. Liverpool L4 & LN9 39 B2
Queens Drive Wavertree. L15 & L13 69 C7
Queens Drive West Derby. Liverpool L13 53 F7
Queens Gn. L39 11 F5
Queens Mews. 11 L6 53 A5
Queens Park Recn Ctr. WA10 43 E4
Queens Rd. Birkenhead L42 67 A1
Queens Rd. Crosby L23 26 E4
Queens Rd. Haydock WA11 46 A7
Queens Rd. Orrell WN5 25 C5
Queens Rd. Prescot L34 56 E6
Queens Rd. Southport PR9 4 C8
Queens Rd. St Helens WA10 43 C1
Queens Wharf. L1 & L3 & L72 67 C7
Queensberry St. L8 67 F5
Queensbury. L48 63 D3
Queensbury Ave. L62 79 E1
Queensbury Way. WA8 72 E3
Queenscourt Rd. L12 54 C5
Queensdale Rd. L18 69 A5
Queensland Ave. WA9 57 E7
Queensland Pl. WA9 57 E7
Queensland St. L7 68 B8
Queensway. Crosby L22 & L23 26 F2
Queensway. Heswall L60 86 C6
Queensway. Rainford WA11 32 A5
Queensway. Runcorn WA7 84 F3
Queensway. St Helens WA11 44 A8
Queensway. Wallasey L45 51 A6
Queensway. Widnes WA8 84 F6
Queensway (Mersey Tunnel). L41 66 F7
Quernmore Rd. L33 30 A3
Quernmore Wlk. L33 30 A3
Quickswood Cl. L25 69 F5
Quickswood Dr. L25 69 F5
Quickswood Gn. L25 69 F5
Quickthorn Cres. L28 55 B7
Quigley Ave. L30 28 A1
Quigley St. L41 66 E4
Quinesway. L49 65 A5
Quintbridge Cl. L26 82 E8
Quinton Cl. PR8 7 A4
Quorn St. L7 53 B2
Raby Ave. L63 88 B6
Raby Cl. Bebington L63 88 A7
Raby Cl. Heswall L60 85 F7
Raby Cl. Widnes WA8 73 E2
Raby Dr. Bebington L63 88 A6
Raby Dr. Birkenhead L46 64 D7
Raby Gr. L42 78 D8
Raby Hall Rd. L63 88 A6
Raby Mere Rd. L63 87 D5
Raby Park Rd. L64 86 F1
Raby Rd. L63 & L64 87 B5
Rachel St. L5 52 D4
Radburn Cl. L23 27 B5
Radburn Rd. L23 27 B5
Radford Ave. L63 79 B2
Radford Cl. WA8 84 C7
Radlett Cl. WA5 74 E3
Radley Dr. Heswall L63 86 F6
Radley Dr. Litherland L10 28 C3
Radley La. WA2 61 E4
Radley Rd. L44 50 F5
Radley St. WA9 57 E7
Radley's Ct. 4 L8 67 F6
Radmore Rd. L14 54 D3
Radnor Ave. L60 76 F1
Radnor Cl. L26 82 E6
Radnor Dr. L20 38 E4
Radnor Dr. Southport PR9 1 F3
Radnor Dr. Wallasey L45 51 C6
Radnor Dr. Widnes WA8 72 D2
Radnor Pl. Birkenhead L43 66 C6
Radnor Pl. Liverpool L6 53 D5
Radstock Gr. WA9 58 D5
Radstock Rd. Liverpool L6 53 C3
Radstock Rd. Wallasey L45 50 E5
Radway Rd. L36 55 F5
Raeburn Ave. Bebington L62 88 E6
Raeburn Ave. West Kirby L48 63 C3
Raeburn Prim Sch. L62 88 D6
Raffles Rd. L41 & L42 66 D5
Raffles St. L1 67 E7
Rafter Ave. L20 38 E6
Raglan St. L19 81 C5
Raglan Wlk. L19 81 C5
Rail Cl. WA11 23 F2
Railside Ct. L5 52 C5
Railton Ave. L35 57 D2
Railton Cl. L35 57 D2
Railton Rd. L11 39 E2
Railway App. L39 13 F5
Railway Ave. PR9 2 F5
Railway Bldgs. L47 63 B6
Railway Path. L39 13 E4
Railway Rd. Birkenhead L42 67 A1
Railway Rd. Golborne WA3 36 B1
Railway Rd. Ormskirk L39 13 F5
Railway Rd. Skelmersdale WN8 23 E8
Railway St. Liverpool L19 81 C5
Railway St. Newton-le-W WA12 46 B3
Railway St. Southport PR8 4 B5
Railway St. St Helens WA9 44 B4
Railway Terr. PR8 4 A5
Railway View. WA5 45 D1
Rainbow Cl. WA8 72 C3
Rainbow Dr. L31 & L32 29 B4
Rainbow Dr. Liverpool L26 82 E8
Raines Cl. L49 64 E4
Rainford Ave. L20 38 E5
Rainford Brook Lodge Cty Prim Sch. WA11 32 A8
Rainford By-Pass. Rainford WA11 31 E6
Rainford By-Pass. Rainford WA11 32 B3
Rainford CE Prim Sch. WA11 32 A6
Rainford Gdns. 25 L1 52 D1
Rainford High Sch. WA11 32 A8
Rainford Ind Est. WA11 32 C4
Rainford Junction. WA11 23 F2
Rainford Rd. Bickerstaffe L39 & WA11 WN8 23 C4
Rainford Rd. Billinge WA11 & WN5 33 C5
Rainford Rd. St Helens WA10 & WA11 43 C6
Rainham Cl. L19 81 C8
Rainhill High Sch. L35 57 E2
Rainhill Hospl (Annexe). L35 57 C5
Rainhill Neuro-Psychiatric Unit. L35 57 B6
Rainhill Park Prim Sch. L35 57 D3
Rainhill Rd. L35 57 C5
Rainhill St Ann's CE Prim Sch. L35 57 C3
Rainhill Sta. L35 57 C3
Rake Cl. L49 65 A4
Rake Hey. L46 64 B8
Rake Hey Cl. L46 64 C8
Rake La. Birkenhead L49 65 A4
Rake La. Wallasey L45 51 B6
Rake The. L62 79 D1
Rakersfield Ct. L45 51 C8
Rakersfield Rd. L45 51 C8
Raleigh Ave. L35 56 D2
Raleigh Cl. WA5 60 D1

Raleigh Rd. Neston L64 ... 86 F1
Raleigh Rd. Wallasey L46 ... 50 B4
Raleigh St. L20 ... 38 B1
Ralph's Wife's La. PR9 ... 2 E6
Rame Cl. L10 ... 40 B6
Ramford St. WA9 ... 44 D2
Ramilies Rd. L15 & L18 ... 68 F5
Ramleh Cl. L23 ... 26 B3
Rampit Cl. WA11 ... 45 F7
Ramsbrook Cl. L24 ... 82 C4
Ramsbrook La. L24 ... 83 C3
Ramsbrook Rd. L24 ... 82 C4
Ramsey Cl. Ashton-in-M WN4 ... 35 B2
Ramsey Cl. Liverpool L19 ... 81 D8
Ramsey Cl. Prescot L35 ... 56 E3
Ramsey Cl. Widnes WA8 ... 73 E3
Ramsey Ct. L48 ... 63 B1
Ramsey Rd. L19 ... 81 D7
Ramsfield Rd. L24 ... 83 A4
Ramsons Cl. L26 ... 70 E1
Randall Dr. L30 ... 27 C3
Randle Ave. WA11 ... 31 E8
Randle Cl. L63 ... 79 A2
Randle Hts. L11 ... 40 E5
Randles Rd. L34 ... 41 A5
Randolph St. 12 L4 ... 52 F7
Randon Gr. 5 WA10 ... 43 F4
Ranelagh Ave. L21 ... 38 A8
Ranelagh Dr. PR8 ... 7 F7
Ranelagh Dr N. L19 ... 81 A8
Ranelagh Dr S. L19 ... 81 A8
Ranelagh Pl. L3 ... 52 E1
Ranelagh St. L1 ... 52 D1
Ranfurly Rd. L19 ... 81 B7
Rangemore Rd. L18 ... 69 A1
Rankin St. Liverpool L8 ... 67 F4
Rankin St. Wallasey L44 ... 51 A2
Ranleigh Dr. WN8 ... 16 A8
Ranmore Ave. WN4 ... 34 D4
Ranworth Cl. L11 ... 39 E3
Ranworth Pl. L11 ... 39 F3
Ranworth Rd. WA5 ... 74 E6
Ranworth Sq. L11 ... 39 F3
Ranworth Square Jun & Mix Inf Sch. L11 ... 39 F3
Ranworth Way. L11 ... 39 F3
Rappart Rd. L44 ... 51 D3
Ratcliff Pl. L35 ... 57 B4
Rathbone Hosp. L13 ... 54 A2
Rathbone Prim Sch. L7 ... 53 A2
Rathbone Rd. Hightown L38 ... 17 F4
Rathbone Rd. Liverpool L15 & L13 ... 68 F8
Rathlin Cl. WA8 ... 73 E3
Rathmore Ave. L18 ... 69 A3
Rathmore Cl. L43 ... 66 A3
Rathmore Cres. PR9 ... 2 B3
Rathmore Dr. L43 ... 66 A4
Rathmore Rd. L43 ... 66 A4
Raven Cl. 10 L6 ... 53 A3
Raven Meols La. L37 ... 9 F2
Ravendale Cl. L43 ... 65 D4
Ravenfield Cl. L26 ... 82 E8
Ravenfield Dr. WA8 ... 72 C3
Ravenglass Ave. L31 ... 20 D2
Ravenhead Ave. L32 ... 40 E7
Ravenhead Dr. WN8 ... 25 A7
Ravenhead Rd. WA10 ... 43 E1
Ravenhead Way. WN8 ... 24 F6
Ravenhill Cres. L46 ... 49 F4
Ravenhurst Way. L35 ... 56 D1
Ravenna Rd. L19 ... 81 D8
Ravenscroft. L37 ... 9 F2
Ravenscroft Ave. L39 ... 13 E4
Ravenscroft Cty Prim Sch. L33 ... 29 E5
Ravenscroft Rd. 1 L43 ... 66 C5
Ravenside Ind Pk. L19 ... 81 F5
Ravensthorpe Gn. L11 ... 39 F3
Ravenstone Dr. WA9 ... 58 D7
Ravenstone Rd. L19 ... 81 B8
Ravenswood Ave. L42 ... 78 F8
Ravenswood Rd. Heswall L60 & L61 ... 77 A2
Ravenswood Rd. 7 Liverpool L13 ... 54 A3
Rawcliffe Cl. WA8 ... 72 F4
Rawcliffe Rd. 3 Birkenhead L41 & L42 ... 66 D5
Rawcliffe Rd. Liverpool L9 ... 39 A4
Rawlins St. L7 ... 53 D3
Rawlinson Cres. L26 ... 83 B8
Rawlinson Ct. PR9 ... 4 D8
Rawlinson Gr. PR9 ... 1 F1
Rawlinson Rd. Liverpool L13 ... 54 A2
Rawlinson Rd. Southport PR9 ... 1 E1
Rawson Cl. L21 ... 37 F7
Rawson Rd. L21 ... 37 F7
Rawson Road Prim Sch. L21 ... 37 F6
Raydale Cl. Golborne WA3 ... 36 E1
Raydale Cl. Liverpool L9 ... 39 A3
Raymond Ave. L30 ... 28 A1
Raymond Pl. L5 ... 52 D4
Raymond Rd. L44 ... 51 C3
Raynham Rd. L13 ... 53 F2
Reade Cl. L63 ... 79 A1
Reading Cl. L5 ... 52 D7
Reading St. L5 ... 52 D7
Reads Ct. L9 ... 38 F6
Reapers Way. L30 ... 28 A4
Reay St. WA8 ... 73 C2
Rebecca Gdns. WA9 ... 58 C7
Recreation Ave. WN4 ... 35 D4
Recreation Dr. WN5 ... 33 E5
Recreation St. WA9 ... 44 D4
Rector Rd. L4 & L6 ... 53 C7
Rectory Ave. WA3 ... 47 C8
Rectory CE Prim Sch. WN4 ... 34 D5
Rectory Cl. Birkenhead L41 & L42 ... 66 D4
Rectory Cl. Heswall L60 ... 85 F7
Rectory Cl. Winwick WA2 ... 61 A6
Rectory Dr. Liverpool L26 ... 71 A1
Rectory La. Heswall L60 ... 85 E7
Rectory La. Winwick WA2 ... 61 A6
Rectory Rd. Garswood WN4 ... 34 D5
Rectory Rd. Southport PR9 ... 2 A1
Rectory Rd. West Kirby L48 ... 63 B1
Red Bank Ave. WA12 ... 46 F1
Red Banks. L48 ... 75 D6
Red Barn Rd. WN5 ... 33 C6
Red Barnes. L37 ... 9 F5
Red Cat La. WA11 ... 32 F5
Red Cross St. L1 ... 52 C1
Red Cut La. L33 ... 41 F8
Red Delph La. WA11 ... 23 E1
Red Fold. L39 ... 13 C2
Red Hill Rd. L63 ... 78 B5
Red Lion Cl. L31 ... 20 C1
Red Lomes. L30 ... 27 D5
Red Rock Cl. L6 ... 53 B4
Red Rock St. L6 ... 53 B4
Red Rum Cl. L9 ... 39 D8
Red Sands. L39 ... 13 D3
Redbourn Ave. L26 ... 82 F6
Redbourn St. L6 ... 53 C6
Redbourne Ave. L24 & L26 ... 82 F6
Redbourne Dr. WA8 ... 72 B4
Redbrook Cl. L62 ... 88 D6
Redbrook St. L6 ... 53 C6
Redbrow Way. L33 ... 29 E4
Redburn Cl. 1 L8 ... 68 A4
Redcar Cl. PR8 ... 4 F3
Redcar Dr. L62 ... 88 D5
Redcar Mews. L6 ... 53 C6
Redcar Rd. L45 ... 50 D6
Redcar St. L6 ... 53 C6
Redcliffe Gdns. L39 ... 13 E3
Redcote Ct. L48 ... 63 A1
Redcroft. 2 L49 ... 64 C3
Redditch Cl. L49 ... 64 C4
Redesdale Cl. WA2 ... 61 E2
Redfern St. L20 ... 52 C8
Redfield Cl. L44 ... 51 D4
Redford Cl. L49 ... 64 C4
Redford St. L6 ... 53 C6
Redgate. Formby L37 ... 10 A2
Redgate. Ormskirk L39 ... 13 D5
Redgate Ave. L23 ... 27 A4
Redgate Dr. Formby L37 ... 10 B2
Redgate Dr. St Helens WA9 ... 44 D3
Redgate Prim Sch. L37 ... 10 A2
Redgate Rd. WN4 ... 35 B6
Redgrave St. 4 L7 ... 53 C2
Redhill Ave. L32 ... 41 A8
Redhills Dr. PR8 ... 4 F3
Redhouse Bank. L48 ... 63 A3
Redhouse La. L48 ... 63 A3
Redington Rd. L19 ... 81 E8
Redland Ct. WN2 ... 35 E7
Redland Rd. L9 ... 39 B8
Redmain Gr. WA3 ... 47 E8
Redmain Way. L12 ... 40 F2
Redmayne Cl. WA12 ... 46 B4
Redmere Dr. L60 ... 86 D8
Redmires Cl. L7 ... 68 B8
Redmond St. L41 ... 66 E4
Redmoor Cres. L33 ... 29 E5
Redpoll Gr. L26 ... 70 E2
Redruth Ave. WA11 ... 44 D7
Redruth Rd. L11 ... 40 D5
Redshank Cl. WA12 ... 46 C4
Redstone Cl. L47 ... 63 D8
Redstone Dr. L60 ... 76 C1
Redstone Pk. 3 L45 ... 51 A8
Redstone Rise. L43 ... 65 D6
Redvers Ave. L66 ... 89 A2
Redvers Dr. L9 ... 38 F6
Redwing La. L25 ... 70 A4
Redwing Way. L26 ... 70 D2
Redwood Ave. L31 ... 20 C3
Redwood Cl. L25 ... 70 B5
Redwood Dr. Ormskirk L39 ... 13 D4
Redwood Dr. St Helens WA11 ... 44 F5
Redwood Gr. L20 ... 38 C4
Redwood Rd. L25 ... 70 B5
Redwood Way. L33 ... 29 F6
Reed's La. WA11 ... 32 A3
Reedale Cl. L18 ... 69 A4
Reedale Rd. L18 ... 69 A4
Reeds Ave E. L46 ... 50 A3
Reeds Ave W. L46 ... 49 F3
Reeds Brow. WA11 ... 32 B8
Reeds La. Wallasey L46 ... 49 F3
Reeds Rd. L36 ... 55 E4
Reeds The. L39 ... 13 D6
Reedville. L43 ... 66 B5
Reedville Gr. L46 ... 49 F2
Reedville Rd. L63 ... 78 F5
Reeves Ave. L20 ... 38 E5
Reeves St. WA9 ... 44 E3
Regal Cres. WA8 ... 84 B8
Regal Dr. WA10 ... 43 C5
Regal Rd. L11 ... 40 C3
Regal Tower. L11 ... 40 C3
Regal Wlk. L4 ... 52 F7
Regent Ave. Ashton-in-M WN4 ... 34 F5
Regent Ave. Haydock WA11 ... 45 B7
Regent Ave. Litherland L30 ... 27 F3
Regent Ave. Liverpool L14 ... 54 E2
Regent Cl. PR8 ... 3 F4
Regent Ct. PR9 ... 4 C8
Regent Rd. L20 & L5 ... 38 A3
Regent Rd. Crosby L23 ... 26 D4
Regent Rd. Liverpool L5 ... 52 B6
Regent Rd. Southport PR8 ... 3 F4
Regent Rd. Wallasey L45 ... 50 D6
Regent Rd. Widnes WA8 ... 73 B1
Regent St. Liverpool L3 ... 52 B4
Regent St. Newton-le-W WA12 ... 46 A3
Regents Cl. L61 ... 77 B6
Regents Rd. WA10 ... 43 C1
Regents Way. L63 ... 78 D8
Regina Ave. L22 ... 26 C2
Regina Rd. L9 ... 39 A6
Reginald Rd. WA9 ... 58 E6
Reginald Rd Ind Pk. WA9 ... 58 E6
Reigate Cl. L25 ... 70 C3
Renacres La. L39 ... 8 F6
Rendal Cl. L5 & L6 ... 53 A5
Rendcombe Gn. L11 ... 39 F3
Rendel Cl. WA12 ... 46 D2
Rendel St. L41 ... 66 D7
Rendelsham Cl. L49 ... 64 E5
Renfrew Ave. Bebington L62 ... 88 E5
Renfrew Ave. St Helens WA11 ... 44 E7
Renfrew St. L7 ... 53 A2
Renfrey Cl. L39 ... 13 E8
Rennell Rd. L14 ... 54 C3
Rennie Ave. WA10 ... 43 C4
Renshaw St. L1 ... 52 E1
Renville Rd. L14 ... 54 C2
Renwick Ave. L35 ... 57 A4
Renwick Rd. L9 ... 39 B
Renwick Sq. WN4 ... 34 F3
Repton Gr. L10 ... 28 C2
Repton Rd. L16 ... 69 D8
Reservoir Rd. Birkenhead L42 ... 66 B1
Reservoir Rd. Liverpool L25 ... 69 F3
Reservoir Rd N. L42 ... 66 B1
Reservoir St. Liverpool L6 ... 53 A4
Reservoir St. St Helens L35 ... 57 C7
Rest Hill Rd. L63 ... 78 C5
Retford Rd. L33 ... 30 A2
Retford Wlk. 5 L33 ... 29 F2
Reva Rd. L14 ... 54 F3
Revesby Cl. WA8 ... 72 D2
Rex Cohen Ct. L17 ... 68 E5
Rexmore Rd. L18 ... 69 A2
Rexmore Way. L15 ... 68 E7
Reynolds Ave. WA9 ... 45 B2
Reynolds Cl. L6 ... 53 A4
Reynolds Way. L25 ... 70 A3
Rhiwlas St. L8 ... 68 A5
Rhodesia Rd. L9 ... 39 C6
Rhodesway. L60 ... 86 B7
Rhona Cl. L63 ... 88 C4
Rhona Dr. WA5 ... 74 E6
Rhosesmor Cl. L32 ... 40 F6
Rhosesmor Rd. L32 ... 40 F6
Rhyl St. Liverpool L8 ... 67 F5
Rhyl St. Widnes WA8 ... 84 F7
Ribble Ave. Maghull L31 ... 20 E2
Ribble Ave. Rainhill L35 ... 57 C3
Ribble Ave. Southport PR9 ... 2 C4
Ribble Cl. WA8 ... 73 F3
Ribble Cres. WN5 ... 33 C3
Ribble House. L25 ... 70 C3
Ribble Rd. L25 ... 70 C3
Ribble St. L41 ... 50 F1
Ribbledale Rd. L18 ... 69 A4
Ribbler's La. Kirkby L32 ... 40 E7
Ribbler's La. Kirkby L34 ... 40 F6
Ribblesdale Ave. L9 ... 39 B7
Ribblesdale Cl. L62 ... 88 F5
Ribchester Way. L35 ... 71 A7
Rice Hey Rd. L44 ... 51 C4
Rice La. L4 & L9 ... 38 F3
Rice La. Liverpool L9 ... 39 A4
Rice La. Wallasey L44 ... 51 D4
Rice Lane Jun & Inf Sch. L9 ... 39 A5
Rice Lane Sta. L9 ... 39 A5
Rice St. L1 ... 67 E8
Rich View. L43 ... 66 B3
Richard Allen Way. 9 L5 ... 52 F4
Richard Chubb Dr. L44 & L45 ... 51 D6
Richard Evans Comm Sch. WA11 ... 45 A6
Richard Evans Jun Sch. WA11 ... 44 F6
Richard Gr. L14 ... 54 F5
Richard Hesketh Dr. L32 ... 29 C2
Richard Kelly Cl. L4 ... 53 D8
Richard Kelly Dr. L4 & L13 ... 39 D2
Richard Kelly Pl. L13 ... 53 D8
Richard Martin Rd. L21 ... 27 C1
Richard Rd. L23 ... 26 A5
Richards Gr. WA9 ... 44 E4
Richardson Rd. L42 ... 78 E8
Richardson St. L15 & L7 ... 68 C7
Richland Rd. L13 ... 53 F5
Richmond Ave. L21 ... 38 A8
Richmond Ave. Haydock WA11 ... 45 B7
Richmond Cl. Bebington L63 ... 79 A6
Richmond Cl. Hightown L38 ... 17 F2
Richmond Cl. St Helens WA10 ... 42 F4
Richmond Cres. L30 ... 27 F3
Richmond Ct. L21 ... 38 B7
Richmond Gdns. WA12 ... 46 C2
Richmond Gr. L31 ... 20 E3
Richmond Pk. L6 ... 53 C5
Richmond Rd. Ashton-in-M WN4 ... 34 F5
Richmond Rd. Bebington L63 ... 78 F6
Richmond Rd. Crosby L23 ... 26 E5
Richmond Rd. Southport PR8 ... 3 F2
Richmond Row. L3 ... 52 E3
Richmond St. Liverpool L1 ... 52 D1
Richmond St. Wallasey L45 ... 37 B1
Richmond St. Widnes WA8 ... 73 C1
Richmond Terr. L6 ... 53 B5
Richmond Way. Heswall L60 & L61 ... 76 F2
Richmond Way. Heswall L61 ... 77 A6
Richmond Way. Huyton-w-R L35 & L36 ... 71 A7
Rickaby Cl. L63 ... 88 C8
Rickman St. L4 ... 52 D7
Rickman Way. L36 ... 70 F8
Riddock Rd. L21 ... 38 B6
Ridge Cl. PR9 ... 2 C5
Ridge The. L60 ... 76 D2
Ridgeborne Cl. WA5 ... 60 D2
Ridgefield Rd. L61 ... 76 F5
Ridgemere Rd. L61 ... 76 F5
Ridgetor Rd. L25 ... 70 A3
Ridgeview Rd. L43 ... 65 D5
Ridgeway. WA3 ... 47 E7
Ridgeway Dr. L31 ... 20 E3
Ridgeway High Sch. L43 ... 65 D4
Ridgeway The. Bebington L63 ... 78 D8
Ridgeway The. Cronton WA8 ... 72 C6
Ridgeway The. Heswall L60 ... 86 B7
Ridgeway The. Hoylake L47 ... 63 E7
Ridgeway The. Liverpool L25 ... 70 A3
Ridgewell Ave. WA3 ... 47 D8
Ridgewood Dr. Heswall L61 ... 76 F5
Ridgewood Dr. St Helens WA9 ... 58 D6
Ridgmont Ave. L11 ... 39 F2
Riding Cl. WA9 ... 58 C4
Riding Fold. L26 ... 70 D2
Riding Hill Rd. L34 ... 41 D2
Riding La. Ashton-in-M WN4 ... 35 F5
Riding La. Haskayne L39 ... 11 E4
Riding St. Liverpool L3 ... 52 F2
Riding St. Southport PR8 ... 4 B6
Ridings Hey. L43 ... 65 D4
Ridings The. Birkenhead L43 ... 65 D5
Ridings The. Southport PR9 ... 2 A3
Ridley Gr. L48 ... 63 A3
Ridley La. L31 ... 20 D1
Ridley Rd. L6 ... 53 C3
Ridley St. L41 & L43 ... 66 C5
Ridsdale. 2 WA8 ... 84 C8
Ridsdale Lawn. L27 ... 71 A3
Rigby Dr. L49 ... 64 D2
Rigby Rd. L31 ... 20 B3
Rigby St. Ashton-in-M WN4 ... 35 A3
Rigby St. Golborne WA3 ... 47 A8
Rigby St. Liverpool L3 ... 52 C2
Rigby St. St Helens WA10 ... 43 F3
Rigby St. St Helens WA10 ... 43 F4
Riley Ave. L20 ... 38 D5
Rimington Ave. WA3 ... 36 C1
Rimmer Ave. L14 & L16 ... 55 A1
Rimmer Cl. L21 ... 38 B7
Rimmer Gn. PR8 ... 5 D1
Rimmer Gr. WA9 ... 44 E3
Rimmer St. L3 ... 52 E2
Rimmer's Ave. Formby L37 ... 9 E6
Rimmer's Ave. Southport PR8 ... 4 B6
Rimmerbrook Rd. L25 ... 70 B7
Rimmers Ct. L41 ... 65 F7
Rimmington Rd. L17 ... 68 E2
Rimrose Rd. L20 ... 38 A4
Rimrose Valley Rd. L23 ... 27 B4
Ringcroft Rd. L13 ... 54 B2
Ringley Ave. WA3 ... 35 F1
Ringo Starr Dr. 6 L6 ... 53 B3
Ringsfield Rd. L24 ... 83 A2
Ringway. L64 ... 86 F2
Ringway Rd. L25 ... 70 C4
Ringways. L62 ... 79 D3
Ringwood. L43 ... 66 A3
Ringwood Ave. L14 ... 54 F2
Ripley Ave. L21 ... 27 B1
Ripley Cl. L31 ... 20 E1
Ripon Ave. WA3 ... 47 D8
Ripon Cl. Huyton-w-R L36 ... 56 B3
Ripon Cl. Litherland L30 ... 27 F1
Ripon Cl. Newton-le-W WA12 ... 46 C5
Ripon Cl. Southport PR8 ... 4 F3
Ripon Dr. WN4 ... 35 D2
Ripon Rd. L45 ... 50 F6
Ripon St. Birkenhead L42 ... 66 E4
Ripon St. L4 ... 38 F1
Risbury Cl. L11 ... 39 F2
Rishton Cl. 10 L5 ... 53 A5
Rishton St. 8 L5 ... 53 A5
Ritchie Ave. L9 ... 39 C6
Ritherup La. L35 ... 57 C4
Ritson St. L8 ... 68 B6
Rivacre Rd. L62 & L65 & L66 ... 89 C2
River Avon St. 3 Liverpool L8 ... 68 B7
River Avon St. 1 Liverpool L8 ... 68 C7
River Cl. L37 ... 10 B1
River Gr. L62 ... 79 B8
River St. L41 ... 66 D6
River View. Bebington L62 ... 79 C8
River View. Crosby L22 ... 26 C2
Riverbank Cl. L60 ... 85 F6
Riverbank Rd. Heswall L60 ... 85 E6
Riverbank Rd. Liverpool L19 ... 81 A7
Rivermeade. PR8 ... 4 D4
Rivers St. WN5 ... 25 E6
Riversdale Ct. L19 ... 80 F8
Riversdale Mews. L19 ... 80 F8
Riversdale Rd. Liverpool L19 ... 80 F7
Riversdale Rd. 3 Seaforth L21 ... 37 F7
Riversdale Rd. Wallasey L44 ... 51 D4
Riversdale Rd. West Kirby L48 ... 63 A2
Riverside. Bebington L62 ... 79 B5
Riverside. Hightown L38 ... 17 F4
Riverside. Liverpool L12 ... 40 E1
Riverside. West Kirby L48 ... 75 B8
Riverside Cl. L20 ... 38 A5
Riverside Ct. L47 ... 63 A3
Riverside Dr. L17 & L3 & L8 ... 68 B2
Riverside Gr. WA9 ... 58 D7
Riverside Prim Sch. L44 ... 51 E3
Riverslea Rd. L23 ... 26 B2
Riverview Heights. L19 ... 80 F7
Riverview Rd. L44 ... 51 E3
Riverview Wlk. 4 L8 ... 67 F4
Riviera Dr. L42 ... 66 D1
Rivington Ave. Birkenhead L43 ... 65 E4
Rivington Ave. Golborne WA3 ... 36 C1
Rivington Ave. St Helens WA10 ... 43 F6
Rivington Cl. PR8 ... 4 A3
Rivington Dr. Bickershaw WN2 ... 36 F8
Rivington Dr. Orrell WN8 ... 25 C7
Rivington Prim Sch. WA10 ... 43 E5

Rivington Rd. St Helens WA10 ... 43 D4
Rivington Rd. Wallasey L44 . 51 D3
Rivington St. WA10 ... 43 D3
RL Hughes Prim Sch. WN4 . 35 A3
Road N. L6 ... 53 D6
Roadside Ct. WA3 ... 47 C8
Rob La. WA12 ... 46 E5
Robarts Rd. L4 ... 53 B6
Robbin's Bridge. L31 ... 20 E5
Robeck Rd. L13 ... 54 B1
Robert Dr. L49 ... 64 E3
Robert Gr. L14 ... 54 E5
Robert St. Birkenhead L41 ... 66 D7
Robert St. Widnes WA8 ... 73 B1
Roberts Ave. WA11 ... 45 A5
Roberts Dr. L20 ... 38 E7
Roberts Prim Sch. L20 ... 38 E7
Roberts St. L3 ... 52 B3
Robertson St. L8 ... 67 E5
Robin Way. L49 ... 65 B2
Robin's La. WA11 ... 33 A8
Robina Rd. WA9 ... 58 D8
Robins La. WA9 ... 58 D8
Robins Lane Comm Prim Sch. WA9 ... 58 C8
Robinson Pl. WA9 ... 44 D3
Robinson Rd. L21 ... 27 C1
Robsart St. L5 ... 52 E5
Robson Pl. WN2 ... 36 B8
Robson St. Liverpool L4 & L5 52 F6
Robson St. Liverpool L13 ... 54 A1
Roby Cl. L35 ... 57 C4
Roby Mount Ave. L36 ... 55 D2
Roby Rd. Huyton-w-R L36 ... 55 C2
Roby Rd. Liverpool L14 & L36 54 F1
Roby St. L20 ... 38 C4
Roby St. Liverpool L15 ... 68 E7
Roby St. St Helens WA10 ... 43 D1
Roby Sta. L36 ... 55 C2
Roby Well Way. WN5 ... 33 D5
Rochester Ave. L30 ... 27 F1
Rochester Cl. WA3 ... 47 A8
Rochester Gdns. WA10 ... 43 D1
Rochester Rd. L42 ... 67 A1
Rock Ave. L60 ... 76 F1
Rock Cl. L42 ... 66 F2
Rock Ct. L13 ... 54 A3
Rock Ferry By-Pass. Birkenhead L42 ... 67 A2
Rock Ferry High Sch. L42 ... 78 F8
Rock Ferry Prim Sch. L42 ... 66 F2
Rock Ferry Sta. L42 ... 66 F2
Rock Gr. L13 ... 54 A3
Rock La. Litherland L31 ... 28 F5
Rock La. Widnes WA8 ... 72 E3
Rock La. Widnes WA8 ... 72 F4
Rock La E. L42 ... 67 A2
Rock La W. L42 ... 66 F1
Rock Mount Cl. L25 ... 69 F3
Rock Mount Pk. L25 ... 69 F3
Rock Park Rd. L42 ... 67 B1
Rock St. Golborne WA3 ... 36 A2
Rock St. Liverpool L13 ... 54 A3
Rock St. St Helens WA9 ... 57 C8
Rock View. L31 ... 29 A4
Rock View. Liverpool L5 ... 52 E6
Rockbank Rd. L13 ... 53 F5
Rockbourne Ave. L25 ... 69 F5
Rockbourne Gn. L25 ... 69 F5
Rockbourne Way. L25 ... 69 F5
Rockfield Cl. WA8 ... 72 D2
Rockfield Gdns. L31 ... 20 C2
Rockfield Rd. L4 ... 53 A7
Rockford Ave. L32 ... 40 E7
Rockford Cl. L32 ... 40 E7
Rockford Wlk. L32 ... 40 E7
Rockhill Rd. L25 ... 70 B2
Rockhouse St. L6 ... 53 C5
Rockingham Ct. L33 ... 29 F4
Rockingham St. L5 ... 52 D6
Rockland Rd. Crosby L22 ... 26 E2
Rockland Rd. Wallasey L45 .. 50 F7
Rocklands Ave. L63 ... 79 A7
Rocklands La. L63 ... 87 C8
Rockley St. 8 L4 ... 52 E8
Rockmount Rd. L17 & L19 ... 68 F1
Rockpoint Ave. L45 ... 51 C7
Rockside Rd. L18 ... 69 A1
Rockville Rd. L13 & L14 ... 54 C1
Rockville St. L42 ... 66 F2
Rockwell Cl. L12 ... 54 D8
Rockwell Rd. L12 ... 54 E8
Rocky La. Heswall L60 ... 85 F8
Rocky La. Liverpool L6 ... 53 C5
Rocky La. Liverpool L15 & L16 ... 69 D8
Rocky La S. L60 ... 86 A8
Rockybank Rd. L42 ... 66 D3
Roderick Rd. 1 L4 ... 39 A2
Roderick St. 3 L3 ... 52 E3
Rodick St. L25 ... 69 F2
Rodmell Rd. L9 ... 39 B6
Rodney St. Birkenhead L41 .. 66 E5
Rodney St. Liverpool L1 & L3 ... 67 E8
Rodney St. St Helens WA10 . 43 E4
Roe Alley. L1 ... 52 D1
Roe La. PR9 ... 4 E8
Roe St. L1 ... 52 D2
Roeburn Way. WA5 ... 74 D3
Roedean Cl. Liverpool L25 ... 82 B8
Roedean Cl. Maghull L31 ... 20 D2
Roehampton Dr. L23 ... 26 C6
Roemarsh Cl. L11 ... 40 B2
Roften Ind Est. L66 ... 88 D1
Rogers Ave. L20 ... 38 E5
Rogerson's Gn. L26 ... 70 E2
Rokeby Ave. WA3 ... 36 D1
Rokeby Cl. L3 ... 52 E3
Rokeby St. L3 ... 52 E3
Rokeden. WA12 ... 46 D4
Roker Ave. L44 ... 51 A3
Rokesmith Ave. L7 ... 68 C8
Roland Ave. Bebington L63 .. 78 E6
Roland Ave. Runcorn WA7 ... 84 F1
Roland Ave. St Helens WA11 44 C7
Roleton Cl. L30 ... 28 B4
Rolleston Dr. Bebington L63 79 A4
Rolleston Dr. Wallasey L45 .. 50 F6
Rolling Mill La. WA9 ... 58 F8
Rollo St. L4 ... 52 E7
Roman Cl. WA12 ... 46 C2
Roman Rd. Ashton-in-M WN4 ... 35 A5
Roman Rd. Bebington L43 ... 78 A8
Roman Rd. Hoylake L47 ... 48 D1
Rome Cl. L36 ... 55 D3
Romer Rd. L6 & L7 ... 53 C3
Romford Way. L26 ... 82 F6
Romiley Dr. WN8 ... 15 F2
Romilly St. L6 ... 53 B3
Romley St. L4 ... 38 F1
Romney Cl. WA8 ... 73 E2
Romsey Ave. L37 ... 10 B2
Romulus St. L7 ... 53 D2
Ronald Cl. L22 ... 26 F1
Ronald House Sch. L23 ... 26 E5
Ronald Rd. L22 ... 26 F1
Ronald Ross Ave. L30 ... 27 F3
Ronald St. L13 ... 53 F3
Ronaldshay. WA8 ... 73 E2
Ronaldsway. Birkenhead L49 64 F6
Ronaldsway. Crosby L23 ... 27 A6
Ronaldsway. Heswall L60 ... 85 F6
Ronaldsway. Liverpool L10 ... 40 A7
Ronaldsway. Liverpool L26 ... 83 A8
Ronan Cl. L20 ... 38 A4
Ronan Rd. WA8 ... 84 E5
Rone Cl. L46 ... 64 D8
Rookery Ave. WN4 ... 35 B2
Rookery Dr. WA11 ... 32 A5
Rookery La. WA11 ... 32 B5
Rookery Rd. PR9 ... 1 F1
Rookery The. WA12 ... 46 D4
Rooks Way. L60 ... 85 E8
Rooley The. L36 ... 55 D1
Roosevelt Dr. L9 ... 39 B8
Roper St. Liverpool L8 ... 67 F5
Roper St. St Helens WA9 ... 44 C4
Ropers Bridge Cl. L35 ... 56 D2
Ropewalk The. L64 ... 86 C1
Rosalind Ave. L63 ... 78 E7
Rosalind Way. L20 ... 38 D1
Rosclare Dr. L45 ... 50 F6
Roscoe Ave. WA12 ... 46 E3
Roscoe Cl. L35 ... 71 A7
Roscoe Cty Prim Sch. L13 ... 53 E7
Roscoe La. L1 ... 67 E8
Roscoe Pl. 1 L1 ... 67 E8
Roscoe St. Liverpool L1 & L3 67 E8
Roscoe St. St Helens WA10 . 43 D3
Roscommon St. L5 ... 52 E4
Roscote Cl. L60 ... 85 F7
Roscote The. L60 ... 85 F7
Rose Ave. Abram WN2 ... 36 B7
Rose Ave. L20 ... 38 C7
Rose Ave. Haydock WA11 ... 45 E6
Rose Ave. St Helens WA9 ... 58 C7
Rose Bank Rd. L16 ... 69 D7
Rose Brae. L18 ... 69 B4
Rose Brow. L25 ... 70 A4
Rose Cres. Skelmersdale WN8 ... 15 E1
Rose Cres. Southport PR8 ... 7 C2
Rose Cres. Widnes WA8 ... 84 F7
Rose Ct. L15 ... 68 E7
Rose Dr. WA11 ... 32 A5
Rose Hill. Liverpool L3 ... 52 D3
Rose Hill. Southport PR8 & PR9 ... 4 D6
Rose Hill View. WN4 ... 34 F7
Rose La. L18 ... 69 A3
Rose Lea Cl. WA8 ... 73 A4
Rose Mount. L43 ... 66 B4
Rose Mount Cl. L43 ... 66 A3
Rose Mount Dr. L45 ... 51 A6
Rose Mount Pk. L43 ... 66 A3
Rose Pl. Birkenhead L42 ... 66 D4
Rose Pl. Birkenhead L41 ... 66 F3
Rose Pl. Liverpool L3 ... 52 D3
Rose Pl. Liverpool L3 ... 52 E3
Rose Pl. Ormskirk L39 ... 13 D2
Rose St. Liverpool L1 ... 52 D2
Rose St. Liverpool L25 ... 69 F2
Rose St. Widnes WA8 ... 84 F7
Rose Vale. L5 ... 52 E5
Rose View Ave. WA8 ... 73 A2
Rose Villas. L15 ... 69 A7
Roseacre. L48 ... 63 A3
Rosebank Rd. L36 ... 55 C5
Rosebank Way. L36 ... 55 C5
Rosebay Cl. L37 ... 10 A3
Roseberry Rd. WN4 ... 35 A5
Roseberry St. L8 ... 68 A7
Rosebery Ave. Crosby L22 ... 26 C2
Rosebery Ave. Wallasey L44 ... 51 C4
Rosebery Gr. L42 ... 66 B2
Rosebery Rd. WA10 ... 43 D5
Rosebery St. PR9 ... 5 A6
Rosebourne Cl. L17 ... 68 C2
Rosecroft. L62 ... 88 C6
Rosecroft Cl. L39 ... 13 E6
Rosecroft Ct. L47 ... 63 A6
Rosedale Ave. Crosby L23 ... 26 F4
Rosedale Ave. Golborne WA3 ... 47 C7
Rosedale Cl. L9 ... 39 B4
Rosedale Rd. Birkenhead L42 66 E3
Rosedale Rd. Liverpool L18 .. 69 B5
Rosefield Ave. L63 ... 78 E7
Rosefield Rd. L25 ... 70 C1
Roseheath Dr. L26 ... 83 A6
Roseheath Prim Sch. L26 ... 82 F7
Rosehill Ave. WA9 ... 59 B5
Rosehill Ct. L25 ... 70 A4
Rosehill Dr. L39 ... 13 C2
Rosehill Sch. WN4 ... 34 F7
Roseland Cl. L31 ... 20 B4
Roselands Ct. L42 ... 66 E1
Roselea Dr. PR9 ... 2 C4
Rosemary Cl. Birkenhead L43 ... 65 E8
Rosemary Cl. Liverpool L7 ... 68 A8
Rosemary Dr. WA12 ... 46 F3
Rosemary La. Formby L37 ... 9 F3
Rosemary La. Haskayne L39 12 B4
Rosemead Ave. L61 ... 77 A4
Rosemont Rd. L17 ... 68 F2
Rosemoor Dr. L23 ... 27 A5
Rosewarne Cl. L17 ... 68 B2
Rosewell Ct. L28 ... 55 B6
Rosewood Cl. Abram WN2 ... 36 B7
Rosewood Cl. Huyton-w-R L28 ... 55 B7
Rosewood Cl. Liverpool L27 . 70 E5
Rosewood Dr. L46 ... 64 B8
Rosewood Gdns. L11 ... 40 B1
Rosina Cl. WN4 ... 34 F6
Roskell Rd. L25 ... 82 C7
Roslin Ct. L43 ... 66 B4
Roslin Rd. Birkenhead L43 ... 66 B4
Roslin Rd. Irby L61 ... 76 D6
Roslyn St. L41 ... 66 F3
Ross Ave. L46 ... 50 C4
Ross Cl. Billinge WN5 ... 33 E6
Ross Cl. Knowsley L34 ... 41 D3
Ross St. St Helens WA9 ... 44 C4
Ross St. Widnes WA8 ... 73 B1
Ross Tower Ct. L45 ... 51 C8
Rossall Ave. L10 ... 28 D3
Rossall Cl. L24 ... 83 E2
Rossall Rd. Liverpool L13 ... 54 B2
Rossall Rd. Wallasey L46 ... 49 F1
Rossall Rd. Widnes WA8 ... 73 D2
Rossendale Cl. L43 ... 65 D4
Rossett Ave. L15 & L17 ... 68 E6
Rossett Cl. WA5 ... 60 E2
Rossett Rd. L23 ... 26 C3
Rossett St. L6 ... 53 C5
Rossini St. L21 ... 38 A6
Rosslyn Ave. L31 ... 28 B8
Rosslyn Cres. L46 ... 64 E8
Rosslyn Dr. L46 ... 64 E8
Rosslyn Pk. 1 L46 ... 64 E7
Rosslyn St. L17 ... 68 B3
Rossmore Gdns. L4 ... 53 C8
Rostherne Ave. Golborne WA3 ... 47 D8
Rostherne Ave. Wallasey L44 ... 51 A3
Rostherne Cres. WA8 ... 72 D2
Rosthwaite Gr. WA11 ... 33 B1
Rosthwaite Rd. L12 ... 54 C6
Rostron Cres. L37 ... 9 E1
Rothay Dr. WA5 ... 74 D3
Rothbury Cl. L46 ... 64 C8
Rothbury Ct. WA9 ... 58 B2
Rothbury Rd. L14 ... 54 F6
Rotherwood Cl. L63 ... 78 D6
Rothesay Ct. L63 ... 78 F4
Rothesay Dr. Bebington L62 . 88 E4
Rothesay Dr. Crosby L23 ... 26 F3
Rothesay Gdns. 3 L43 ... 65 F1
Rothley Ave. PR8 ... 7 A4
Rothsay Cl. WA11 ... 44 E6
Rothwell Cl. L39 ... 13 D5
Rothwell Dr. Ormskirk L39 ... 13 B2
Rothwell Dr. Southport PR8 ... 7 A4
Rothwell Rd. WA3 ... 36 C1
Rothwell St. 15 L6 ... 53 A4
Rothwells La. L23 ... 27 B7
Rotten Row. PR8 ... 3 F6
Rotunda St. L5 ... 52 D5
Roughdale Ave. Kirkby L32 .. 40 F7
Roughdale Ave. St Helens WA9 ... 58 B4
Roughdale Cl. L32 ... 40 F7
Roughhedge House. L28 ... 55 B8
Roughwood Dr. L33 ... 29 F3
Round Hey. L28 ... 55 A8
Round Meade The. L31 ... 20 C2
Roundabout The. WA8 ... 72 D6
Roundway The. L38 ... 17 F3
Roundwood Dr. WA9 ... 44 B1
Routledge St. WA8 ... 73 B1
Rowan Ave. Golborne WA3 .. 47 F7
Rowan Ave. Liverpool L12 ... 40 F1
Rowan Cl. St Helens WA11 .. 44 D7
Rowan Cl. St Helens WA11 .. 44 F5
Rowan Cl. Warrington WA5 . 74 F6
Rowan Ct. Birkenhead L49 ... 64 C2
Rowan Ct. Liverpool L17 ... 68 E2
Rowan Dr. L32 ... 29 D3
Rowan Gr. Bebington L63 ... 78 E4
Rowan Gr. Liverpool L36 ... 70 D8
Rowan La. WN8 ... 16 B4
Rowan Park Sch. L23 ... 26 D4
Rowan Park Upper Sch. L20 38 D7
Rowan Tree Cl. L49 ... 64 B3
Rowans The. L39 ... 21 A7
Rowena Cl. L23 ... 26 F4
Rowsley Gr. L9 ... 39 B7
Rowson Ct. L45 ... 51 B8
Rowson St. Prescot L34 ... 56 D7
Rowson St. Wallasey L45 ... 51 B7
Rowthorn Cl. WA8 ... 84 E8
Rowton Cl. L43 ... 65 F3
Roxborough Cl. WA5 ... 60 A6
Roxborough Wlk. L25 ... 70 C3
Roxburgh Ave. Birkenhead L42 ... 66 D2
Roxburgh Ave. Liverpool L17 68 C3
Roxburgh St. L20 & L4 ... 38 E1
Royal Ave. WA8 ... 72 A1
Royal Birkdale Golf Links. PR8 ... 3 D3
Royal Cl. L37 ... 10 A1
Royal Cres. L37 ... 10 A1
Royal Croft. L12 ... 54 B4
Royal Gr. WA10 ... 43 D1
Royal Infmy. L3 ... 52 F2
Royal Liverpool Children's Hospl The. L7 ... 67 F8
Royal Liverpool Univ Hospl. L3 & L7 ... 52 F2
Royal Mail St. L3 ... 52 E1
Royal Pl. WA8 ... 84 B8
Royal School for the Blind The. L15 ... 69 A7
Royal St. L4 ... 52 E7
Royal Terr. PR8 ... 4 A7
Royal The. L47 ... 62 F6
Royden Ave. L44 ... 51 D5
Royden Cres. WN5 ... 33 E5
Royden Pk. L48 ... 76 A8
Royden Rd. Billinge WN5 ... 33 E5
Royden Rd. Birkenhead L49 . 64 E6
Royden St. L8 ... 67 F4
Royden Way. L3 ... 67 E3
Royhsay Cl. L5 ... 52 F4
Royston Ave. L44 ... 51 D4
Royston Cl. WA3 ... 47 E8
Royston St. L7 ... 53 B1
Royton Rd. L22 ... 26 F2
Rubbing Stone. L48 ... 75 D6
Ruby St. Liverpool L8 ... 68 A3
Rudd Ave. WA9 ... 45 B2
Rudd St. L47 ... 63 B7
Ruddington Rd. PR8 ... 4 E2
Rudgate. L35 ... 56 E2
Rudgrave Cl. L43 ... 65 D4
Rudgrave Mews. L44 ... 51 D5
Rudgrave Pl. L44 ... 51 D5
Rudgrave Sq. L44 ... 51 D5
Rudley Wlk. L24 ... 82 F2
Rudloe Ct. WA2 ... 61 F1
Rudston Inf & Jun Sch. L16 69 D8
Rudston Rd. L16 ... 69 D7
Rudyard Cl. L14 ... 54 C3
Rudyard Rd. L14 ... 54 D3
Ruff La. L39 & L40 ... 14 B4
Rufford Ave. L31 ... 20 E3
Rufford Cl. Liverpool L10 ... 39 F8
Rufford Cl. Prescot L35 ... 56 F5
Rufford Dr. PR9 ... 2 F5
Rufford Rd. L20 ... 38 C5
Rufford Rd. Liverpool L6 & L7 ... 53 D3
Rufford Rd. Rainford WA11 .. 31 F8
Rufford Rd. Southport PR9 ... 2 C4
Rufford Rd. Wallasey L44 ... 51 C3
Rufford St. 4 WN4 ... 34 F5
Rufford Wlk. WA11 ... 44 E6
Rugby Dr. Litherland L10 ... 28 F1
Rugby Dr. Orrell WN5 ... 25 F8
Rugby Rd. Liverpool L9 ... 39 B8
Rugby Rd. Wallasey L44 ... 50 F4
Ruislip Cl. L25 ... 70 C2
Ruislip Ct. WA2 ... 61 F1
Rullerton Rd. L44 & L45 ... 51 A4
Rumford Pl. 4 L2 & L3 ... 52 C2
Rumford St. L2 ... 52 C1
Rumney Pl. L4 ... 52 E8
Rumney Rd. L4 ... 52 E8
Rumney Rd W. L4 ... 52 D8
Runcorn Docks Rd. WA7 ... 84 E2
Runcorn Sta. WA7 ... 84 F2
Rundle Rd. L17 ... 68 E1
Rundle St. L41 ... 66 A8
Runic St. L13 ... 53 F2
Runnell The. L64 ... 86 D4
Runnell's La. L23 ... 27 C5
Runnymede. L36 ... 55 D4
Runnymede Cl. L25 ... 70 A4
Runnymede Ct. 2 WA8 ... 73 C1
Runnymede Dr. WA11 ... 45 A6
Runnymede Gdns. 5 WA8 . 73 C1
Runnymede Wlk. WA8 ... 73 C2
Runton Rd. L25 ... 70 C5
Rupert Rd. L36 ... 55 D3
Ruscar Cl. L26 ... 70 E2
Ruscolm Cl. WA5 ... 74 D7
Ruscombe Rd. L14 ... 55 A6
Rushden Rd. L32 ... 30 A1
Rushey Hey Rd. L32 ... 29 F1
Rushlake Dr. L27 ... 70 D5
Rushmere Rd. L11 ... 39 F2
Rushmoor Ave. WN4 ... 35 E4
Rusholme Cl. L26 ... 83 A6
Rushton Ave. WA12 ... 46 B4
Rushton Cl. WA8 ... 72 F3
Rushton Pl. L25 ... 70 A2
Rushton's Wlk. L30 ... 27 D4
Ruskin Ave. Birkenhead L42 . 66 F1
Ruskin Ave. Newton-le-W WA12 ... 46 C4
Ruskin Ave. Wallasey L44 ... 51 A3
Ruskin Ave. Warrington WA2 61 C2
Ruskin Dr. WA10 ... 43 D5
Ruskin St. L4 ... 38 E1
Ruskin Way. L36 ... 55 D1
Rusland Ave. L61 ... 76 F4
Rusland Rd. L32 ... 40 F8
Russel Ct. WA8 ... 73 B4
Russell Ave. PR9 ... 5 A7
Russell Ct. PR9 ... 2 B4
Russell Pl. 5 L3 ... 52 E1
Russell Rd. Birkenhead L42 .. 67 A2
Russell Rd. Huyton-w-R L36 . 56 B2
Russell Rd. Liverpool L15 & L18 ... 68 F5
Russell Rd. Liverpool L19 ... 81 C6
Russell Rd. Runcorn WA7 ... 84 E1
Russell Rd. Southport PR9 ... 5 A6
Russell Rd. Wallasey L45 ... 50 E5
Russell St. Birkenhead L41 & L72 ... 66 E7
Russell St. Liverpool L3 ... 52 E1
Russet Cl. Liverpool L27 ... 70 E5
Russet Cl. St Helens WA10 ... 43 F5
Russian Ave. L13 ... 53 F5
Russian Dr. L13 ... 53 F5
Ruth Evans Ct. L35 ... 57 A4
Rutherford Cl. L7 ... 53 E1
Rutherford Rd. Liverpool L15 & L18 ... 69 B6
Rutherford Rd. Maghull L31 . 28 E7
Rutherford Rd. St Helens WA10 ... 43 C6
Rutherglen Ave. L23 ... 26 F2

Ruthin Cl. WA5 .... 60 E3
Ruthven Rd. L21 .... 38 A7
Ruthven Rd. Liverpool L13 ... 54 B1
Rutland Ave.
Golborne WA3 .... 47 D7
Rutland Ave.
Liverpool L15 & L17 .... 68 D6
Rutland Ave. Liverpool L26 .. 83 A8
Rutland Cl. 4 L5 .... 53 A5
Rutland Cres. L39 .... 13 E7
Rutland Dr. WN4 .... 35 C4
Rutland House. L23 .... 26 B3
Rutland Rd. PR8 .... 4 D5
Rutland St. L20 .... 38 D4
Rutland St. Runcorn WA7 .... 84 F2
Rutland St. St Helens WA10 43 F5
Rutland Way. L36 .... 56 B3
Rutter Ave. WA5 .... 60 F2
Rutter St. L8 .... 67 E5
Ryburn Rd. L39 .... 13 E4
Rycot Rd. L24 .... 82 C4
Rycroft Rd. Hoylake L47 .... 63 E8
Rycroft Rd. Liverpool L10 ..... 39 E7
Rycroft Rd. Wallasey L44 ..... 51 C2
Rydal Ave. Birkenhead L43 .... 65 C5
Rydal Ave. Crosby L23 .... 26 F2
Rydal Ave. Formby L37 .... 9 D3
Rydal Ave. Orrell WN5 .... 25 F7
Rydal Ave. Prescot L34 .... 56 F6
Rydal Bank. Bebington L63 .... 79 A7
Rydal Bank. Wallasey L44 .... 51 C4
Rydal Cl. Ashton-in-M WN4 .. 35 C4
Rydal Cl. Heswall L61 .... 76 F4
Rydal Cl. L33 .... 29 D4
Rydal Cl. Litherland L10 .... 28 F2
Rydal Gr. WA11 .... 44 A7
Rydal Pl. WN2 .... 36 B8
Rydal Rd. L36 .... 55 E1
Rydal St. Liverpool L5 & L6 ... 53 A5
Rydal St. Newton-le-W WA12 46 C3
Rydal Way. WA8 .... 72 C1
Rydecroft. L25 .... 69 F2
Ryder Cl. Ormskirk L39 .... 13 C2
Ryder Cl. Rainhill L35 .... 57 A4
Ryder Cres. Ormskirk L39 .... 13 C1
Ryder Cres. Southport PR8 ..... 7 E7
Ryder Rd. WA8 .... 73 B4
Rydinge The. L37 .... 10 A6
Rye Cl. WA9 .... 58 D4
Rye Croft. L21 .... 27 B3
Rye Gr. L14 .... 54 E6
Rye Hey Rd. L32 .... 29 F2
Rye Moss La. L37 & L38 .... 19 B8
Ryecote. L32 .... 40 E7
Ryecroft Ave. WA3 .... 36 E1
Ryecroft Rd. L60 .... 86 C7
Ryedale Cl. L8 .... 68 B7
Ryefield La. L21 .... 27 B3
Ryegate Rd. L19 .... 81 B8
Ryeground La. L37 .... 10 A5
Ryland Pk. L61 .... 77 A5
Rylands Hey. L49 .... 64 D4
Ryleys Gdns. 9 L2 .... 52 C2
Rymer Gr. 2 L4 .... 39 A1
Rymers Gn. L37 .... 9 E4

Sackville Rd. WA10 .... 43 C6
Sacred Heart Prim Sch. L7 . 53 A2
Sacred Heart RC High Sch.
L23 .... 26 E3
Sacred Heart RC Prim Sch.
L33 .... 29 F2
Sacred Heart RC Prim Sch.
Wallasey L46 .... 49 F1
Sacred Heart Schs. WA10 ... 43 F3
Sadler St. WA8 .... 73 C1
Sadler's La. WA11 .... 42 E7
Saffron Mews. L23 .... 27 B6
Sagar Fold. L39 .... 21 D8
Sainsbury's Ctr. L25 .... 70 B2
SS Peter & Paul RC High Sch.
Widnes WA8 .... 72 F2
SS Peter & Paul RC High Sch.
Widnes WA8 .... 84 E8
SS Peter & Paul RC Prim Sch.
L33 .... 29 F6
SS Peter & Paul RC Prim Sch.
Wallasey L45 .... 51 B8
St Aelred's RC High Sch.
WA12 .... 46 D4
St Agnes RC Prim Sch. L36 . 55 F1
St Agnes Rd.
Huyton-w-R L36 .... 55 F2
St Agnes Rd. Liverpool L4 .... 52 D8
St Aidan's CE Comm Sch.
WA9 .... 58 E3
St Aidan's Cl. WN5 .... 33 E6
St Aidan's Ct. L43 .... 65 F6
St Aidan's RC Prim Sch. L36 55 F3
St Aidan's Terr. 1
Birkenhead L43 .... 65 F6
St Aidan's Terr. Liverpool L5 52 D6
St Aidan's Way. L30 .... 27 E3
St Alaysius RC Jun & Inf Schs.
L36 .... 55 C4
St Alban Rd. WA5 .... 74 E5
St Alban's RC Prim Sch. L44 51 B4
St Alban's Rd.
Birkenhead L41 & L43 .... 66 A6
St Alban's Rd. L20 & L69 ...... 38 C3
St Alban's Rd. Wallasey L44 51 B4
St Alban's Sq. L20 & L69 ...... 38 C2
St Albans. L6 .... 53 B5
St Albans Cl. WA11 .... 46 A7
St Albans Ct. L5 .... 52 C5
St Alberts RC Prim Sch. L28 55 A8
St Ambrose Barlow RC High Sch.
L30 .... 28 A5
St Ambrose Croft. L30 .... 27 E4
St Ambrose Gr. L4 & L6 .... 53 B6
St Ambrose RC Jun Mix & Inf
Sch. L24 .... 83 A2
St Ambrose Rd. WA8 .... 73 C1
St Ambrose Way. 10 L3 .... 52 F4
St Andrew Rd. L4 & L6 .... 53 B6
St Andrew St. L3 .... 52 F1
St Andrew's CE Prim Sch.
Bebington L63 .... 78 F6
St Andrew's CE Prim Sch.
Warrington WA2 .... 61 C3
St Andrew's Dr. L23 .... 26 C6
St Andrew's Gr. L30 .... 27 C3
St Andrew's Pl. PR8 .... 4 B6
St Andrew's RC Prim Sch.
L25 .... 82 D7
St Andrew's Rd.
Birkenhead L43 .... 66 B6
St Andrew's Rd. Crosby L23 26 B6
St Andrew's View. L33 .... 29 E5
St Andrews Ave. L12 & L14 . 54 E6
St Andrews Ct. Seaforth L22 37 E8
St Andrews Ct. 10
St Helens WA10 .... 43 F3
St Andrews Gdns. 5 L3 .... 52 E2
St Andrews Gr. WA11 .... 44 B6
St Andrews Maghull CE Prim Sch.
L31 .... 20 D1
St Andrews Pl. L17 .... 68 C3
St Andrews Rd.
Bebington L63 .... 79 A4
St Andrews Rd. L20 .... 38 C6
St Ann Pl. L35 .... 57 C4
St Anne St. Birkenhead L41 . 66 C8
St Anne St. Birkenhead L41 .. 66 D7
St Anne St. Liverpool L3 .... 52 E3
St Anne Terr. L41 .... 66 C7
St Anne's Cl. Birkenhead L41 66 D7
St Anne's Cl. Formby L37 .... 9 F6
St Anne's Cotts. L14 .... 54 C3
St Anne's Path. L37 .... 9 F6
St Anne's Pl. L41 .... 66 C8
St Anne's RC Prim Sch.
Liverpool L7 .... 68 B8
St Anne's RC Prim Sch.
Ormskirk L39 .... 13 E4
St Anne's RC Prim Sch.
St Helens WA9 .... 58 D7
St Anne's Rd. Formby L37 ...... 9 F6
St Anne's Rd.Huyton-w-R L36 55 F1
St Anne's Rd. Liverpool L17 . 68 F1
St Anne's Rd. Ormskirk L39 . 13 D4
St Anne's Rd. Widnes WA8 .. 73 B2
St Anne's (Stanley) CE Prim Sch.
L13 .... 54 A3
St Annes Ct. L17 .... 68 E1
St Annes Gdns. L17 .... 68 F1
St Annes Gr. L17 .... 68 F1
St Annes RC Prim Sch. L36 . 55 D1
St Annes Rd. PR9 .... 1 F4
St Anns Rd. WA10 .... 43 C3
St Anselm's Coll. L43 .... 66 A6
St Anselm's Coll Prep Sch.
L43 .... 66 A5
St Anthony of Padua RC Jun &
Inf Sch. L18 .... 68 F4
St Anthony's Gr. L30 .... 27 D3
St Anthony's Rd. L23 .... 26 B4
St Anthony's Sh Ctr. L5 .... 52 D5
St Asaph Dr. WA5 .... 60 E3
St Asaph Gr. L30 .... 27 F1
St Augustine of Canterbury RC
High Sch. WA11 .... 44 E5
St Augustine St. L5 .... 52 D5
St Augustine's Way. L30 .... 27 E4
St Austel Cl. WA5 .... 74 E3
St Austell Cl. L46 .... 49 B1
St Austells Rd. L4 .... 38 E2
St Austin's RC Prim Sch.
Liverpool L19 .... 81 A7
St Austin's RC Prim Sch.
St Helens L35 .... 57 D7
St Bartholomew's RC Prim Sch.
L35 .... 57 E1
St Bartholomews Ct. 8
WA10 .... 43 F3
St Bartholomews Day Hospl.
L36 .... 55 C2
St Basil RC Prim Sch. WA8 . 72 A2
St Bede's RC High Sch. L39 13 D4
St Bede's RC Inf & Jun Sch.
WA8 .... 73 A1
St Bedes Cl. L39 .... 13 D3
St Benedict's RC High Sch.
L49 .... 65 B4
St Benet's RC Jun Aided Sch.
L30 .... 27 F4
St Benet's RC Prim Sch.
L30 .... 28 A4
St Benet's Way. L30 .... 27 E3
St Bernard's Cl. L30 .... 27 D3
St Bernard's Dr. L30 .... 27 D3
St Bernard's RC Prim Sch.
L8 .... 68 B7
St Bride St. 10 L8 .... 67 F8
St Bride's Rd. L44 .... 51 D5
St Brides Cl. WA5 .... 74 E3
St Bridget's CE Prim Sch.
L48 .... 63 B1
St Bridget's Gr. L30 .... 27 D3
St Bridget's La. L48 .... 63 B1
St Bridget's RC Prim Sch.
WA2 .... 61 E3
St Bridgets Cl. WA2 .... 61 F3
St Brigid's Cres. L5 .... 52 C5
St Brigid's RC Prim Sch. L28 55 A7
St Catherine's Hospl. L42 ... 66 D3
St Catherine's RC Prim Sch.
WA3 .... 47 E7
St Catherine's Rd. L20 .... 38 C3
St Catherines Cl. L36 .... 55 E1
St Catherines Gdns. L42 .... 66 D4
St Cecilia's RC Prim Schs.
L13 .... 53 E5
St Chad's Dr. L32 .... 29 E2
St Chad's Par. L32 .... 29 E2
St Christopher's Ave. L30 ... 27 D4
St Christopher's RC Inf Sch.
L24 .... 82 D3
St Christopher's RC Jun Sch.
L24 .... 82 D4
St Chrysostoms Way. 17
L6 .... 53 A4
St Clair Dr. PR9 .... 2 A1
St Clares RC Prim Sch. L15 68 E6
St Cleopas' CE Prim Sch. L8 67 F4
St Columba's Cl. L44 .... 51 D5
St Columba's RC Prim Sch.
L36 .... 55 E5
St Cuthbert's Cl. 3
Liverpool L12 .... 40 E3
St Cuthbert's Cl.
Southport PR9 .... 2 A2
St Cuthbert's RC Comm Sch.
WA9 .... 44 F1
St Cuthbert's RC Prim Sch.
L13 .... 53 F3
St Cuthbert's Rd. PR9 .... 2 A2
St Cyrils Cl. L27 .... 70 C6
St Damian's Croft. L30 .... 27 E3
St David Rd. Bebington L62 . 89 A6
St David Rd.
Birkenhead L43 .... 66 A6
St David's Rd. 4 L4 & L6 .... 53 B6
St Davids Cl. L35 .... 57 C4
St Davids Dr. WA5 .... 60 E2
St Davids Gr. L30 .... 27 D2
St Davids La. L43 .... 65 D5
St Davids Rd. L14 & L36 .... 55 B5
St Domingo Gr. L4 & L5 .... 53 A6
St Domingo Rd. L5 .... 52 E6
St Domingo Vale. L4 & L5 ... 53 A6
St Dominic's RC Jun & Inf Sch.
L14 .... 55 B6
St Dunstan's Gr. L30 .... 27 D3
St Edmond's Rd. L20 .... 38 C2
St Edmund Arrowsmith RC High
Sch. WN4 .... 35 A2
St Edmund of Canterbury RC
Comp Sch. L14 .... 55 B6
St Edmund's RC Prim Sch.
Crosby L22 .... 26 D1
St Edmund's RC Prim Sch.
Skelmersdale WN8 .... 15 F1
St Edmunds Rd. L63 .... 78 F5
St Edward's Coll. L12 .... 54 B5
St Edwards Cl. L41 .... 66 B8
St Elizabeth's RC Inf Sch.
L21 .... 38 C6
St Elizabeth's RC Jun Sch.
L21 .... 38 C6
St Elmo Rd. L44 .... 51 D5
St Finbar's RC Prim Sch.
L8 .... 68 A3
St Francis de Sales RC Inf Sch.
L4 .... 38 E2
St Francis de Sales RC Jun Sch.
L4 .... 38 E1
St Francis Xavier Coll.
Liverpool L15 .... 69 C8
St Francis Xavier Coll.
Liverpool L25 .... 69 F4
St Gabriel's Ave. L36 .... 56 A2
St Gabriel's CE Prim Sch.
L36 .... 56 A2
St George of England High Sch.
L20 .... 38 D6
St George's Ave. WA10 .... 43 C5
St George's CE Prim Sch. L5 52 F5
St George's Ct. WA8 .... 84 D8
St George's Hill. L5 .... 52 F5
St George's Hts. L5 .... 52 F5
St George's Mount. L45 ...... 51 B8
St George's Pk. L45 .... 51 B8
St George's Pl. Liverpool L1 . 52 D2
St George's Pl.
Southport PR8 & PR9 .... 4 B7
St George's Prim Sch. L45 .. 50 F5
St George's RC Prim Sch.
Maghull L31 .... 28 D7
St George's RC Prim Sch.
Maghull L31 .... 28 D8
St George's Rd. Formby L37 .. 9 E4
St George's Rd.
Hightown L38 .... 17 F5
St George's Rd.
Huyton-w-R L36 .... 55 E5
St George's Rd.
Wallasey L45 .... 50 E6
St George's Way. 19
Liverpool L1 .... 52 D1
St George's Way. Raby L63 . 87 A7
St Georges Ave. L42 .... 66 D2
St Georges Gr.
Birkenhead L46 .... 64 D8
St Georges Gr.
Litherland L30 .... 27 D2
St Georges Rd. WA10 .... 43 D2
St Gerard's RC Jun Mix Sch.
L5 .... 52 D6
St Gregory's Croft. L30 .... 27 E4
St Gregory's RC Inf Sch.
L31 .... 20 C4
St Gregory's RC Jun Mix & Inf
Sch. L27 .... 70 E5
St Gregory's RC Jun Sch.
L31 .... 20 C4
St Helen's Cl. L43 .... 66 B6
St Helen's Coll Newton Campus.
WA12 .... 46 B4
St Helens Central Sta. WA9 44 B3
St Helens Comm Coll.
WA10 .... 43 F3
St Helens Hospl.
St Helens WA9 .... 44 C1
St Helens Hospl.
St Helens WA9 .... 58 C8
St Helens Junction Sta.
WA9 .... 58 F7
St Helens Linkway.
Rainhill L35 & WA9 .... 57 F4
St Helens Linkway.
St Helens WA9 .... 58 A8
St Helens Rd.
Ormskirk L39 .... 14 A2
St Helens Rd.
Prescot L34 & WA10 .... 56 E7
St Helens Rd.
Rainford WA11 .... 32 B1
St Helens Ret Pk. WA9 .... 44 B3
St Helens Tech Campus.
WA9 .... 44 B4
St Hilary Brow. L44 .... 50 F4
St Hilary Dr. L44 .... 50 F5
St Hilda St. 9 L4 .... 52 E8
St Hilda's CE High Sch. L17 68 D5
St Hildas Ct. L8 .... 68 D6
St Hugh's Cl. L43 .... 66 B6
St Hugh's RC Jun & Inf Sch.
L15 .... 68 D8
St Ives Ct. L41 .... 66 A7
St Ives Gr. L13 .... 53 F3
St Ives Rd. L43 .... 66 A6
St Ives Way. L26 .... 70 F1
St James CE Prim Sch.
WA11 .... 45 E6
St James' Cl. Liverpool L12 .. 54 A6
St James Cl.
Ormskirk L40 .... 14 C3
St James Cres. WN2 .... 36 F8
St James Ct. 12 WA10 .... 43 F3
St James Dr. L20 .... 38 B4
St James Mount. L35 .... 57 C2
St James Pl. L69 & L8 .... 67 E6
St James' RC Prim Sch. L20 38 B4
St James' RC Prim Sch.
Orrell WN5 .... 25 D4
St James RC Prim Sch.
Skelmersdale WN8 .... 16 B4
St James Rd.
Birkenhead L41 & L43 .... 65 F8
St James' Rd.
Huyton-w-R L36 .... 55 E1
St James Rd.
Liverpool L1 & L8 .... 67 E7
St James' Rd. Orrell WN5 .... 25 D4
St James' Rd. Prescot L34 ... 56 E6
St James Rd. Rainhill L35 .... 57 C2
St James Rd. Wallasey L45 . 51 B8
St James St.
Liverpool L1 & L69 & L72 ..... 67 D7
St James St. Southport PR8 ... 4 B6
St James Way. L30 .... 27 D4
St Jerome's RC Prim Sch.
L37 .... 9 C3
St Jerome's Way. L30 .... 27 E4
St Joan of Arc RC Prim Sch.
L20 .... 38 A5
St John Almond High Sch.
L19 .... 81 D6
St John Bosco High Sch.
L11 .... 40 B3
St John Bosco RC Prim Sch.
L31 .... 20 B2
St John Fisher RC Prim Sch.
Knowsley L34 .... 41 D4
St John Fisher RC Prim Sch.
Widnes WA8 .... 73 D1
St John Southworth RC Prim Sch.
WN4 .... 35 D4
St John St. Birkenhead L41 .. 66 D6
St John St.
Newton-le-W WA12 .... 46 A3
St John St. St Helens WA10 . 43 D1
St John Stone RC Prim Sch.
PR8 .... 7 D2
St John Vianney RC Prim Sch.
WA9 .... 57 E6
St John's Ave. L9 .... 39 A5
St John's CE (Aided) Prim Sch.
L22 .... 26 D1
St John's CE Prim Sch. L22 26 D1
St John's Cl. L47 .... 63 D8
St John's Ct. L22 .... 26 D1
St John's Ctr & Mkt. L1 .... 52 D1
St John's La. L1 .... 52 D2
St John's Pavement. 6 L41 66 D6
St John's Pl. L22 .... 26 D1
St John's RC Inf Sch. L63 .... 78 F7
St John's RC Jun Sch. L63 .. 78 F7
St John's RC Prim Sch. L4 .. 52 E7
St John's Rd. Bebington L62 89 A5
St John's Rd. L20 .... 38 C1
St John's Rd. Crosby L22 ..... 26 D1
St John's Rd.
Huyton-w-R L36 .... 55 F1
St John's Rd. Liverpool L36 . 70 E8
St John's Rd. Southport PR8 .. 3 F1
St John's Rd. Wallasey L45 . 50 E5
St John's Sq.
Birkenhead L41 .... 66 D6
St John's Sq. 18
Liverpool L1 .... 52 D1
St John's St. WN2 .... 36 B8
St John's Terr. L20 .... 38 B1
St John's Way. 13 L1 .... 52 D1
St Johns Ct. 9 WA10 .... 43 F3
St Johns RC Prim Sch. WN8 16 C1
St Joseph's Cl. WA5 .... 74 E5
St Joseph's RC Jun & Inf Sch.
L32 .... 29 E1
St Joseph's RC Prim Sch.
Birkenhead L49 .... 65 A5
St Joseph's RC Prim Sch.
Huyton-w-R L36 .... 55 F3
St Joseph's RC Prim Sch.
Wallasey L44 .... 51 D2
St Joseph's RC Prim Sch.
Warrington WA5 .... 74 E5
St Josephs Cres. L3 .... 52 E3
St Judes Ct. 7 WA10 .... 43 F3
St Julie RC Prim Sch. WA10 43 A4
St Julie's High Sch. L25 ...... 70 A1
St Kilda's Rd. L46 .... 64 D7
St Laurence Gr. L32 .... 40 F8
St Laurence's RC Prim Sch.
Birkenhead L41 .... 66 D7
St Laurence's RC Prim Sch.
L32 .... 29 F1
St Lawrence Cl. 2 L8 .... 68 A4
St Lawrence's CE Prim Sch.
L4 .... 38 E1
St Leo's RC Prim Sch. L35 .. 56 E2

St Leonard's Cl. L30 ... 27 D4
St Lucia Rd. L44 ... 51 D5
St Luke's Ave. WA3 ... 47 D8
St Luke's CE Prim Sch. Formby L37 ... 9 D1
St Luke's CE Prim Sch. Golborne WA3 ... 47 E7
St Luke's CE Prim Sch. St Helens WA10 ... 43 D3
St Luke's Church Rd. L37 & L38 ... 17 C8
St Luke's Cres. WA8 ... 73 B4
St Luke's Ct. L4 ... 39 A2
St Luke's Dr. Formby L37 ... 9 C2
St Luke's Dr. Orrell WN5 ... 25 E4
St Luke's Gr. Litherland L30 . 27 D4
St Luke's Gr. Southport PR9 ... 4 E7
St Luke's Halsall CE Prim Sch. L23 ... 26 D5
St Luke's Pl. 8 L1 ... 67 E8
St Luke's RC Prim Sch. Prescot L35 ... 56 F4
St Luke's RC Prim Sch. Skelmersdale WN8 ... 24 E6
St Luke's Rd. Crosby L23 ... 26 E4
St Luke's Rd. Southport PR9 .. 4 D7
St Luke's Rd. St Helens WA10 ... 43 D4
St Lukes Cl. L14 ... 54 F6
St Lukes Ct. 11 WA10 ... 43 F3
St Malachy's RC Jun Mix & Inf Sch. L8 ... 67 E5
St Margaret Mary's Sec Sch. L14 ... 54 F3
St Margaret's (Anfield) CE Sch. L6 ... 53 C5
St Margaret's Ave. WA2 ... 61 D1
St Margaret's CE Jun Sch. WA2 ... 61 C1
St Margaret's Gr. L30 ... 27 C3
St Margaret's Jun Mix & Inf Sch. L8 ... 67 F7
St Margaret's Rd. L47 ... 63 A6
St Margarets CE High Sch. L17 ... 68 E1
St Margarets CE Inf Sch. WA2 ... 61 C2
St Marie's RC Jun Mix & Inf Sch. L33 ... 30 A3
St Marie's RC Prim Sch. PR8 4 B8
St Mark's Gr. L30 ... 27 C4
St Mark's RC Prim Sch. L26 83 A8
St Mark's Rd. L36 ... 55 F1
St Mark's St. WA11 ... 45 A6
St Marks RC Prim Sch. WN8 24 E8
St Martin's Mews. 1 L5 ... 52 E4
St Martins Gr. L32 ... 40 F7
St Mary & St Thomas's Prim Sch. WA10 ... 43 F4
St Mary's Arc. 11 WA10 ... 44 A3
St Mary's Ave. Billinge WN5 33 C4
St Mary's Ave. 4 Liverpool L4 ... 39 A2
St Mary's Ave. Wallasey L44 51 B4
St Mary's CE Prim Sch. L62 89 A5
St Mary's CE (VA) Prim Sch. L20 ... 38 B3
St Mary's Cl. Hale L24 ... 83 E2
St Mary's Cl. Liverpool L13 ... 53 F1
St Mary's Coll. Crosby L23 ... 26 E4
St Mary's Coll. Wallasey L45 50 C5
St Mary's Coll. Wallasey L45 50 E6
St Mary's Coll Prep Sch. L23 ... 26 B3
St Mary's Ct. L49 ... 65 A4
St Mary's Dr. L30 ... 27 C2
St Mary's Gate. L41 ... 66 F6
St Mary's Gdns. PR8 ... 7 F7
St Mary's Gr. 5 L4 ... 39 A2
St Mary's High Sch. L8 ... 68 B5
St Mary's La. L4 ... 39 A2
St Mary's Mkt. WA10 ... 44 A3
St Mary's Pl. 6 Liverpool L4 39 A2
St Mary's Pl. Liverpool L25 ... 70 A2
St Mary's RC Inf Sch. WA12 46 C4
St Mary's RC Jun Sch.WA12 46 B3
St Mary's RC Prim Sch. L23 26 D8
St Mary's Rd. Crosby L22 ... 26 F1
St Mary's Rd. Huyton-w-R L36 ... 55 F2
St Mary's Rd. Liverpool L19 . 81 B7
St Mary's Rd. Warrington WA5 ... 74 F5
St Mary's St. L44 ... 51 B4
St Mary's & St Paul's CE Sch. L35 ... 56 D4
St Marys Ct. L25 ... 70 A2
St Marys Gdns. 7 L8 ... 67 E7
St Marys High Sch. L17 ... 68 D5
St Marys West Derby CE Sch. L12 ... 54 B7
St Mathew's RC Prim Sch. WN8 ... 24 D7
St Mathews Ave. L21 ... 38 D8
St Mathews Cl. L4 ... 39 D2
St Matthew's RC Prim Sch. L4 ... 53 E8
St Matthews CE Prim Sch. L35 ... 57 D7
St Matthews Ct. 6 WA10 ... 43 F3
St Matthews Gr. WA10 ... 57 C8
St Mawes Cl. WA8 ... 72 E2
St Mawes Way. WA10 ... 43 B6
St Mawgan Ct. WA2 ... 61 F2
St Michael & All Angels RC Prim Sch. L49 ... 65 D2
St Michael Jubilee Golf Course. WA8 ... 84 E7
St Michael Rd. L39 ... 20 F7
St Michael's Church Rd. L17 68 C2
St Michael's Cl. Liverpool L17 ... 68 C2
St Michael's Cl. Southport PR9 1 F3
St Michael's Cl. Widnes WA8 84 C7
St Michael's Gr. Litherland L30 ... 27 C3
St Michael's Gr. Liverpool L6 53 B4
St Michael's in the Hamlet Inf Sch. L17 ... 68 B3
St Michael's Ind Est. WA8 .. 84 C6
St Michael's RC Prim Sch. Liverpool L6 ... 53 B4
St Michael's RC Prim Sch. Widnes WA8 ... 84 C7
St Michael's Rd. Crosby L23 26 C6
St Michael's Rd. . Liverpool L17 ... 68 B3
St Michael's Rd. Widnes WA8 ... 84 C7
St Michael's Sta. L17 ... 68 B2
St Michaels Ct. L36 ... 55 E3
St Michaels Gr. L46 ... 64 D8
St Michaels Pk. L39 ... 21 A7
St Michaels Rd. WA9 ... 58 A3
St Monica's Dr. L30 ... 27 D4
St Monica's Prim Sch. L20 .. 38 E5
St Nicholas CE Prim Sch. L23 ... 26 B3
St Nicholas CE Sch. L22 ... 26 C2
St Nicholas' Dr. L30 ... 27 D4
St Nicholas Gr. 1 WA9 ... 58 D7
St Nicholas Pl. L3 ... 52 B1
St Nicholas RC Jun Mix & Inf Sch. L3 ... 52 F1
St Nicholas Rd. Prescot L35 56 D1
St Nicholas' Rd. Wallasey L45 ... 50 D5
St Oswald House. 6 L13 ... 54 A3
St Oswald's Ave. L43 ... 50 C1
St Oswald's CE (VA) Prim Sch. L30 ... 27 F3
St Oswald's La. L30 ... 27 F3
St Oswald's Mews. L43 ... 50 C1
St Oswald's RC Jun Mix Sch. L13 ... 54 A2
St Oswald's RC Prim Sch. WN4 ... 35 B3
St Oswald's St. L13 ... 54 A2
St Oswalds Cl. Litherland L30 27 F3
St Oswalds Cl. Winwick WA2 61 B6
St Oswalds Rd. WN4 ... 35 A2
St Paschal Baylon RC Prim Sch. L16 ... 69 E7
St Patrick's Cl. L33 ... 29 E5
St Patrick's Dr. L30 ... 27 D4
St Patrick's RC Jun Sch. L8 67 F6
St Patrick's RC Prim Sch. PR9 ... 2 A2
St Paul. L42 ... 66 F3
St Paul of the Cross RC Prim Sch. WA5 ... 59 E6
St Paul St. WA10 ... 43 E3
St Paul's Ave. 10 L44 ... 51 E2
St Paul's Cl. L42 ... 66 E2
St Paul's Pas. PR8 ... 4 A6
St Paul's Pl. L20 ... 38 D2
St Paul's RC Jun Sch. L12 ... 54 C6
St Paul's RC Prim Sch. Birkenhead L43 ... 65 C7
St Paul's RC Prim Sch. Liverpool L12 ... 54 B6
St Paul's Rd. Birkenhead L42 66 F3
St Paul's Rd. Wallasey L44 ... 51 E2
St Paul's Sq. 2 Liverpool L3 52 C2
St Paul's Sq. Southport PR8 ... 4 A6
St Paul's St. PR8 ... 4 A6
St Paul's & St Timothy's Inf Sch. L12 ... 54 C6
St Paul's Villas. L42 ... 66 F2
St Pauls Cl. L33 ... 29 D5
St Peter & Paul RC Prim Sch. WA11 ... 44 B7
St Peter's Ave. L37 ... 9 D4
St Peter's CE Prim Sch. L37 10 A5
St Peter's CE Prim Sch. Garswood WN4 ... 34 F6
St Peter's CE Prim Sch. Heswall L60 ... 85 F8
St Peter's CE Prim Sch. Newton-le-W WA12 ... 46 E4
St Peter's Cl. Formby L37 ... 9 D4
St Peter's Cl. Heswall L60 ... 85 F7
St Peter's Mews. L42 ... 67 B1
St Peter's RC High Sch.WN5 25 F7
St Peter's RC Prim Sch. L43 65 C3
St Peter's Rd. Birkenhead L42 ... 67 A1
St Peter's Rd. Liverpool L9 ... 39 C6
St Peter's Rd. Southport PR8 . 4 A3
St Peter's Row. L31 ... 28 D6
St Peter's Way. L43 ... 65 C4
St Peters Cl. L33 ... 29 D5
St Peters Ct. Liverpool L17 ... 68 B4
St Peters Ct. 13 St Helens WA10 ... 43 F3
St Philip's Ave. L21 ... 38 C7
St Philip's CE Prim Sch. L21 38 C8
St Philip's Prim Sch. PR8 ... 4 C5
St Philips Church & Comm Sch. WA5 ... 60 B1
St Philips Ct. 5 WA10 ... 43 F3
St Philomena's RC Jun Sch. L9 ... 39 F4
St Raymond's RC Prim Sch. L30 ... 27 E4
St Richards RC Prim Sch. WN8 ... 15 D1
St Robert Bellarmine RC Prim Sch. L20 ... 38 D7
St Sebastian's Prim Sch. L7 53 D2
St Seiriol Gr. L43 ... 66 A6
St Silas CE Prim Sch. L8 ... 68 A5
St Simons Ct. 4 WA10 ... 43 F3
St Stephen Rd. WA5 ... 74 F5
St Stephen's Ave. WA2 ... 61 B3
St Stephen's Gr. L30 ... 27 D3
St Stephen's RC Prim Sch. WA2 ... 61 B2
St Stephen's Rd. Birkenhead L42 ... 66 B1
St Stephen's Rd. Hightown L38 ... 17 F4
St Stephens Cl. Heswall L60 86 C6
St Stephens Cl. Liverpool L25 ... 70 C5
St Stephens Ct. L42 ... 66 B1
St Stephens Pl. 4 L3 ... 52 D3
St Teresa's Prim Sch. WA10 43 D4
St Teresa's RC Inf Sch. PR8 . 4 A4
St Teresa's RC Jun Mix Inf Schs. L11 ... 39 F2
St Teresa's Rd. WA10 ... 43 D4
St Theresa's RC Prim Sch. WA9 ... 58 C3
St Thomas Becket RC Comp Comm Sch. L36 ... 56 A3
St Thomas CE Prim Sch. Ashton-in-M WN4 ... 35 C3
St Thomas CE Prim Sch. Maghull L31 ... 20 D4
St Thomas Ct. WA8 ... 72 E1
St Thomas the Martyr CE Prim Sch. WN8 ... 25 B7
St Thomas's Ct. WN8 ... 25 C7
St Thomas's Dr. L30 ... 27 D3
St Vincent de Paul RC Sch. L1 ... 67 D8
St Vincent Rd. Birkenhead L43 ... 66 A6
St Vincent Rd. Wallasey L44 51 D5
St Vincent Rd. Warrington WA5 ... 74 F5
St Vincent St. L3 ... 52 E2
St Vincent Way. L3 ... 52 E2
St Vincent's Cl. L12 & L14 ... 54 E6
St Vincent's RC Comm Sch. WA9 ... 45 A3
St Vincent's RC Prim Sch. WA5 ... 74 F3
St Vincent's Sch. L14 ... 54 E6
St Vincent's Way. Southport PR8 ... 4 A4
St Werburgh's RC Prim Sch. L41 ... 66 D5
St Werburgh's Sq. 13 L41 ... 66 E6
St Wilfrid's RC High Sch. L21 ... 38 C7
St William of York RC Prim Sch. L23 ... 27 B5
St William Rd. L23 ... 27 B5
St William Way. L23 ... 27 B5
St Winefride's RC Inf Sch. L20 ... 38 C2
St Winefride's RC Jun Sch. L20 ... 38 C3
St Winifred Rd. Rainhill L35 . 57 B5
St Winifred Rd. Wallasey L45 ... 51 B7
Saker St. 17 L4 ... 52 F7
Salacre Cl. L49 ... 65 A4
Salacre Cres. L49 ... 65 A4
Salacre La. L49 ... 65 A4
Salacre Terr. L49 ... 65 A5
Salcombe Dr. Liverpool L25 . 82 B7
Salcombe Dr. Southport PR9 . 2 A5
Salem View. L43 ... 66 B3
Salerno Dr. L36 ... 55 D3
Saleswood Ave. WA10 ... 43 A3
Salford Rd. PR8 ... 7 C5
Salisbury Ave. Litherland L30 28 A1
Salisbury Ave. West Kirby L48 ... 63 A2
Salisbury Dr. L62 ... 79 B7
Salisbury House. L20 ... 38 B4
Salisbury Pk. L16 ... 69 D5
Salisbury Rd. 1 Ashton-in-M WN4 ... 35 A5
Salisbury Rd. L20 ... 38 B5
Salisbury Rd. Haydock WA11 45 E8
Salisbury Rd. Liverpool L9 ... 39 A3
Salisbury Rd. Liverpool L5 ... 52 F6
Salisbury Rd. Liverpool L4 & L5 ... 53 A6
Salisbury Rd. Liverpool L15 .. 68 D8
Salisbury Rd. Liverpool L19 .. 81 A6
Salisbury Rd. Wallasey L45 .. 51 A8
Salisbury St. Birkenhead L41 66 D5
Salisbury St. Golborne WA3 . 47 A8
Salisbury St. Liverpool L3 ... 52 F3
Salisbury St. 3 Prescot L34 56 D6
Salisbury St. Southport PR9 ... 5 A6
Salisbury Terr. L15 ... 68 F8
Salkeld Ave. WN4 ... 34 F3
Sallowfields. WN5 ... 25 D5
Sally's La. PR9 ... 2 B2
Salop St. L4 ... 52 F8
Saltash Cl. L26 ... 82 E8
Saltburn Rd. L45 ... 50 D5
Salthouse Quay. L1 & L3 & L72 ... 67 C8
Saltney St. L3 ... 52 B4
Saltpit La. L31 ... 20 E1
Salwick Cl. PR9 ... 1 F5
Samaria Ave. L62 ... 79 C7
Sambourn Fold. PR8 ... 7 A5
Samuel St. L35 ... 57 D7
Sanbec Gdns. WA8 ... 72 D5
Sandalwood Dr. L43 ... 65 D4
Sandalwood Gdns. WA9 ... 58 C7
Sandbeck St. L8 ... 67 F3
Sandbourne. L46 ... 65 A8
Sandbrook Ct. L46 ... 64 E8
Sandbrook Gdns. WN5 ... 25 D5
Sandbrook La. L46 ... 64 F8
Sandbrook Prim Sch. L46 ... 65 A8
Sandbrook Rd. Liverpool L25 70 A7
Sandbrook Rd. Orrell WN5 .. 25 C5
Sandbrook Rd. Southport PR8 7 D4
Sandbrook Way. PR8 ... 7 C3
Sandcliffe Rd. L45 ... 50 E7
Sandeman Rd. L4 ... 53 D8
Sanderling Rd. L33 ... 30 A3
Sanderson Cl. WA5 ... 74 D6
Sandfield. L36 ... 55 D2
Sandfield Ave. L47 ... 48 D1
Sandfield Cl. Bebington L63 . 78 D6
Sandfield Cl. Golborne WA3 47 F8
Sandfield Cl. Liverpool L12 .. 54 C5
Sandfield Cotts. L39 ... 13 D2
Sandfield Cres. WA10 ... 43 F3
Sandfield Park Sch. L12 ... 54 B5
Sandfield Pk. L60 ... 85 D8
Sandfield Pk E. L12 ... 54 C6
Sandfield Pl. L20 ... 38 B4
Sandfield Rd. Bebington L63 78 D6
Sandfield Rd. Birkenhead L49 ... 65 B2
Sandfield Rd. L20 ... 38 D3
Sandfield Rd. Liverpool L25 . 70 B4
Sandfield Rd. St Helens WA10 ... 43 A5
Sandfield Rd. Wallasey L45 . 51 B7
Sandfield Wlk. L12 & L13 ... 54 B4
Sandford Dr. L31 ... 20 D2
Sandford Rd. WN5 ... 25 C5
Sandford St. L41 & L72 ... 66 E7
Sandforth Cl. L12 ... 54 A6
Sandforth Rd. L12 & L13 ... 54 B6
Sandgate Cl. L24 ... 82 B4
Sandham Gr. L60 ... 86 D7
Sandham Rd. L24 ... 83 A4
Sandhead St. L15 & L7 ... 68 D8
Sandhey Rd. L47 ... 63 C8
Sandheys. L64 ... 86 C1
Sandheys Ave. L22 ... 26 C1
Sandheys Cl. L4 ... 52 E7
Sandheys Dr. PR9 ... 1 F1
Sandheys Gr. L22 ... 26 C2
Sandheys Rd. L45 ... 51 B7
Sandheys Terr. L22 ... 26 C1
Sandhills. L38 ... 17 F3
Sandhills Ind Ctr. L5 ... 52 C6
Sandhills La. L20 & L5 ... 52 C7
Sandhills Sta. L5 ... 52 C7
Sandhills The. L46 ... 49 E3
Sandhills View. L45 ... 50 D5
Sandhurst. 2 L23 ... 26 C4
Sandhurst Cl. Formby L37 ... 9 C1
Sandhurst Cl. Seaforth L21 .. 37 F7
Sandhurst Dr. L10 ... 28 E2
Sandhurst Rd. Liverpool L26 83 A6
Sandhurst Rd. Rainhill L35 ... 57 B4
Sandhurst St. L17 ... 68 B3
Sandhurst Way. L31 ... 20 B5
Sandicroft Rd. L12 ... 40 F2
Sandilands Gr. L38 ... 17 F3
Sandino St. L8 ... 67 E6
Sandirngham Dr. L17 ... 68 B4
Sandiway. Bebington L63 ... 88 C6
Sandiway. Hoylake L47 ... 48 D1
Sandiway. Huyton-w-R L36 ... 55 F1
Sandiway. Prescot L35 ... 56 D2
Sandiway Ave. WA8 ... 72 A1
Sandiway Ct. PR9 ... 4 E8
Sandiways. L31 ... 20 E1
Sandiways Ave. L30 ... 28 A2
Sandiways Rd. L45 ... 50 E6
Sandlea Pk. L48 ... 63 A2
Sandlewood Gr. L33 ... 29 F4
Sandon Cl. L35 ... 57 B4
Sandon Gr. WA11 ... 32 A6
Sandon Lodge. 8 L21 ... 38 A6
Sandon Pl. WA8 ... 73 D1
Sandon Prom. L44 ... 51 E4
Sandon Rd. Southport PR8 ... 3 F1
Sandon Rd. Wallasey L44 ... 51 E4
Sandon St. Crosby L22 ... 26 D1
Sandon St. 15 Liverpool L7 & L8 ... 67 F8
Sandon Way. L5 ... 52 B6
Sandown Ct. 4 Liverpool L15 ... 68 F8
Sandown Ct. Southport PR9 ... 4 C8
Sandown La. L15 ... 68 F8
Sandown Park Rd. L10 ... 28 E3
Sandown Rd. Liverpool L15 .. 53 F1
Sandown Rd. Seaforth L21 .. 37 F7
Sandpiper Cl. Birkenhead L49 ... 64 D6
Sandpiper Cl. Newton-le-W WA12 ... 46 C4
Sandpiper Gr. L26 ... 70 E1
Sandpiper Pl. 17 L6 ... 53 A3
Sandra Dr. WA12 ... 46 E3
Sandridge Rd. Heswall L61 ... 76 F5
Sandridge Rd. Wallasey L45 ... 51 B7
Sandringham Ave. Hoylake L47 ... 63 C7
Sandringham Ave. 2 Seaforth L22 ... 37 E8
Sandringham Cl. Bebington L62 ... 79 A7
Sandringham Cl. Hoylake L47 ... 63 C7
Sandringham Cl. L33 ... 29 E5
Sandringham Ct. PR8 ... 4 B8
Sandringham Dr. St Helens WA9 ... 58 C7
Sandringham Dr. Wallasey L45 ... 51 A8
Sandringham Rd. Formby L37 9 E1
Sandringham Rd. Liverpool L13 ... 53 E6
Sandringham Rd. Maghull L31 ... 28 C8
Sandringham Rd. Seaforth L21 & L22 ... 37 E8
Sandringham Rd. Southport PR8 ... 3 E3
Sandringham Rd. Southport PR8 ... 7 C5
Sandringham Rd. Widnes WA8 ... 73 A4
Sandrock Rd. L45 ... 51 B7
Sands Rd. L18 ... 68 F4
Sandstone Dr. Rainhill L35 ... 57 A5
Sandstone Dr. West Kirby L48 ... 63 E2
Sandstone La. 2 L8 ... 67 F4
Sandstone Rd E. L13 ... 54 A4
Sandstone Rd W. L13 ... 53 F4

Sandstone Wlk. L60 86 A7
Sandwash Cl. WA11 32 B4
Sandway Cres. L11 40 A2
Sandy Brow La. Golborne WA3 47 E2
Sandy Brow La. Knowsley L33 41 E8
Sandy Gn. L9 39 C6
Sandy Gr. L13 53 F6
Sandy House. 5 L21 37 F7
Sandy Knowe. L15 69 A8
Sandy La. L21 38 A7
Sandy La. Cronton WA8 72 E5
Sandy La. Golborne WA12 & WA3 46 F8
Sandy La. Heswall L60 77 A1
Sandy La. Hightown L38 18 A3
Sandy La. Irby L61 76 C7
Sandy La. L31 29 A6
Sandy La. Liverpool L9 39 C6
Sandy La. Liverpool L13 53 F6
Sandy La. Maghull L31 20 C5
Sandy La. Maghull L39 21 B6
Sandy La. Ormskirk L40 14 D7
Sandy La. Orrell WN5 25 D4
Sandy La. Skelmersdale WN8 15 D1
Sandy La. St Helens WA11 43 F8
Sandy La. Wallasey L45 50 E6
Sandy La. Warrington WA2 61 C2
Sandy La. Warrington WA8 74 B6
Sandy La. West Kirby L48 63 B1
Sandy La Ctr. WN8 15 D1
Sandy La N. L61 76 C8
Sandy La W. WA2 61 B3
Sandy Rd. L21 38 A7
Sandy Rd. Seaforth L21 37 F7
Sandy Way. L43 66 A5
Sandymount Dr. Bebington L63 78 F4
Sandymount Dr. Wallasey L45 51 A7
Sandyville Gr. 2 L4 53 E8
Sandyville Rd. L11 & L4 53 E8
Sanfield Cl. L39 13 E6
Sangness Dr. PR8 4 E3
Sankey Rd. Maghull L31 28 D7
Sankey Rd. St Helens WA11 44 F5
Sankey St. Golborne WA3 47 A8
Sankey St. Liverpool L1 67 E8
Sankey St. Newton-le-W WA12 46 A3
Sankey St. St Helens WA9 44 D2
Sankey Sta. WA5 74 F6
Sankey Valley Ind Est. WA12 46 A2
Sankey Valley Park. WA5 60 D6
Sankey Valley Pk. Haydock WA11 & WA12 45 D3
Sankey Valley Pk. St Helens WA11 44 E7
Santon Ave. L13 53 E5
Santon Dr. WA3 47 E8
Sanvino Ave. PR8 7 D5
Sapphire Dr. L33 29 E5
Sapphire St. L13 53 F1
Sarah's Croft. L30 27 E3
Sark Rd. L13 53 F4
Sarsfield Ave. WA3 47 D8
Sartfield Cl. L16 69 E8
Sarum Rd. L25 70 B7
Satinwood Rd. WN4 34 F2
Saughall Massie La. L49 64 F5
Saughall Massie Rd. Birkenhead L46 & L49 64 D6
Saughall Massie Rd. West Kirby L48 63 E4
Saughall Rd. L46 64 C7
Saunby St. L19 81 C4
Saunders Ave. L35 56 D4
Saunders St. PR8 & PR9 1 C1
Saundersfoot Cl. WA5 60 E2
Savia RC High Sch. L30 38 E8
Saville Rd. Liverpool L13 54 B2
Saville Rd. Maghull L31 20 C3
Savon Hook. L37 10 B1
Savoylands Cl. L17 68 C2
Sawdon Ave. PR8 4 E3
Sawley Ave. WA3 36 D1
Sawpit La. L36 55 F2
Saxby Rd. L14 55 A6
Saxenholme. PR8 3 F5
Saxon Cl. L6 53 B5
Saxon Ct. WA10 43 E4
Saxon Rd. Crosby L23 26 D3
Saxon Rd. Hoylake L47 63 C8
Saxon Rd. Southport PR8 3 F5
Saxon Rd. Wallasey L46 49 F1
Saxon Terr. WA8 73 B1
Saxon Way. L33 29 E6
Saxonia Rd. L4 39 B2
Saxony Rd. L7 53 A2
Sayce St. WA8 73 B1
Scafell Ave. WA2 61 C3
Scafell Cl. Bebington L63 & L62 88 D3
Scafell Cl. Liverpool L27 71 A3
Scafell Lawn. L27 71 A3
Scafell Rd. WA11 44 A7
Scafell Wlk. L27 71 A4
Scaffold La. L38 18 D4
Scape La. L23 26 E5
Scargreen Ave. L11 39 F3
Scarisbrick Ave. L21 38 B7
Scarisbrick Ave. Southport PR8 4 A7
Scarisbrick Cl. L31 20 E3
Scarisbrick Cres. L11 39 D3
Scarisbrick Ct. PR8 4 C6
Scarisbrick Dr. L11 39 D2
Scarisbrick New Rd. Southport PR8 4 D5
Scarisbrick Pl. L11 39 D2
Scarisbrick Rd. Liverpool L11 39 D2
Scarisbrick Rd. Rainford WA11 31 F7
Scarisbrick St. Ormskirk L39 13 E6
Scarisbrick St. Southport PR9 4 B7
Scarsdale Rd. L11 39 F1
Scarth Hill La. Ormskirk L39 14 A2
Scarth Hill La. Ormskirk L39 & L40 14 B2
Sceptre Cl. WA12 46 A3
Sceptre Rd. L11 40 C3
Sceptre Tower. L11 40 C3
Sceptre Wlk. L11 40 C3
Scholar St. L7 68 C7
Scholes La. L34 & L35 & WA10 57 C7
Scholes Pk. WA10 57 B7
Schomberg St. L6 53 B3
School Ave. L37 9 F3
School Brow. WN5 33 E5
School Cl. Liverpool L27 70 C7
School Cl. Ormskirk L39 13 C1
School Cl. Wallasey L46 49 F1
School Dr. WN5 33 E5
School Hill. L60 85 F7
School House Gn. L39 13 F5
School La. Bebington L63 78 D5
School La. Bebington L62 79 B7
School La. Bebington L66 88 F1
School La. Bold Heath WA8 73 E7
School La. L21 38 A7
School La. L21 38 B8
School La. Formby L37 9 F3
School La. Garswood WN4 34 C3
School La. Haskayne L39 11 F4
School La. Hoylake L47 48 D1
School La. Hoylake L47 63 B7
School La. Huyton-w-R L36 56 A2
School La. Irby L61 76 B6
School La. L31 29 A5
School La. Knowsley L34 41 B5
School La. Litherland L10 28 E1
School La. Liverpool L1 52 D1
School La. Liverpool L25 82 B8
School La. Maghull L31 21 A1
School La. Neston L64 86 B1
School La. Orrell WN5 & WN8 25 C7
School La. Raby L64 87 B2
School La. Rainhill L35 57 F1
School La. Skelmersdale WN8 15 E1
School La. Wallasey L43 50 C1
School La. Wallasey L44 50 E5
School La. Westhead L40 14 E3
School Rd. Hightown L38 17 F4
School Rd. Warrington WA2 61 C1
School St. Ashton-in-M WN4 35 D5
School St. Golborne WA3 47 A8
School St. Newton-le-W WA12 46 B3
School St. St Helens WA11 44 F6
School Terr. WA3 47 A8
School Way. Liverpool L24 82 B4
School Way. Widnes WA8 73 D3
Schoolfield Cl. L49 65 B2
Schoolfield Rd. L49 65 B2
Science Rd. L24 82 C4
Scone Cl. L11 40 C3
Score La. L16 69 D8
Score The. St Helens WA9 58 A7
Score The. St Helens WA9 58 C8
Scorecross. WA9 58 B8
Scoresby Rd. L46 50 B3
Scorton St. L6 53 C5
Scotchbarn La. L34 & L35 56 F6
Scoter Rd. L33 29 F2
Scotia Ave. L62 79 C7
Scotia Rd. L13 54 A4
Scotia Wlk. WA3 47 F8
Scotland Pl. L3 52 D3
Scotland Rd. L3 & L5 52 D4
Scots Pl. L41 65 F7
Scott Ave. Huyton-w-R L36 71 A8
Scott Ave. Prescot L35 56 F3
Scott Ave. Widnes WA8 84 F8
Scott Cl. Liverpool L4 52 F7
Scott Cl. Maghull L31 20 D1
Scott Dr. L39 13 F7
Scott Rd. WA3 36 D2
Scott St. L20 38 B5
Scott St. Southport PR9 5 A7
Scott St. Wallasey L45 51 B5
Scott Wlk. WA12 46 B1
Scotts Ave. WA9 58 A3
Scotts Quay. L44 51 F1
Scythes The. Birkenhead L49 64 D4
Scythes The. Litherland L30 28 B4
Scythia Cl. L62 79 C7
Sea Rd. L45 50 F7
Sea View. L47 63 B7
Sea View La. L61 76 D6
Sea View Rd. L20 38 B4
Seabank Ave. L44 51 C5
Seabank Cott. L47 48 E2
Seabank Rd. Heswall L60 85 E6
Seabank Rd. Southport PR8 & PR9 4 B8
Seabank Rd. Wallasey L44 & L45 51 C6
Seacombe Prom. L44 51 E3
Seacombe Tower. L5 52 E6
Seacombe View. L44 51 E2
Seacroft Cl. L14 55 A6
Seacroft Cres. PR9 2 B5
Seacroft Rd. L14 55 A6
Seafield. L37 10 A2
Seafield Ave. Crosby L23 26 F4
Seafield Ave. Heswall L60 85 E6
Seafield Dr. L45 51 A7
Seafield Rd. Bebington L62 79 B8
Seafield Rd. L20 38 B4
Seafield Rd. L9 38 F5
Seafield Rd. Southport PR8 7 C6
Seaford Pl. WA2 61 A4
Seafore Cl. L31 20 B4
Seaforth Dr. L46 64 E7
Seaforth & Litherland Sta. L21 38 A7
Seaforth Rd. L21 38 A6
Seaforth Vale N. L21 38 A6
Seaforth Vale W. L21 38 A6
Seagram Cl. L9 39 C8
Sealand Ave. L37 9 E2
Sealand Cl. Formby L37 9 D2
Sealand Cl. Warrington WA2 61 E1
Sealy Cl. L63 79 A1
Seaman Rd. L15 68 E7
Seascale Ave. WA10 57 B8
Seath Ave. WA9 44 E4
Seathwaite Cl. L23 26 B3
Seathwaite Cres. L33 29 D4
Seaton Cl. L12 41 A3
Seaton Gr. L35 57 D6
Seaton Pl. WN8 15 E3
Seaton Rd. Birkenhead L42 66 C4
Seaton Rd. 1 Wallasey L45 51 A6
Seaton Way. PR9 2 A5
Seaview Ave. Bebington L62 89 B6
Seaview Ave. Irby L61 76 D6
Seaview Ave. Wallasey L45 51 B5
Seaview Rd. L44 & L45 51 A5
Seaview Terr. L22 26 C1
Seawood Gr. L46 64 D7
Second Ave. Birkenhead L43 65 C6
Second Ave. Crosby L23 26 D4
Second Ave. Liverpool L9 39 D7
Second Ave. Rainhill L35 57 B4
Sedbergh Ave. L10 28 C3
Sedbergh Rd. L44 & L45 50 F5
Sedburgh Gr. L36 55 C3
Sedburn Rd. L32 41 A7
Seddon Cl. WA10 42 F3
Seddon Pl. WN8 15 E3
Seddon Rd. Liverpool L19 81 C6
Seddon Rd. St Helens WA10 57 B8
Seddon St. 5 Liverpool L1 & L72 67 D8
Seddon St. St Helens WA10 43 F7
Seddons Ct. 1 L34 56 D6
Sedgefield Rd. L46 65 A8
Sedgemoor Rd. L11 39 F3
Sedgewick Cres. WA5 59 E6
Sedgley Wlk. L36 55 F5
Sedley St. L6 53 B5
Seeds La. L9 39 C8
Seel Rd. L36 56 A2
Seel St. L1 & L68 & L72 & L75 67 D8
Seeley Ave. L41 66 A7
Sefton Ave. L21 38 B7
Sefton Ave. Orrell WN5 25 D5
Sefton Ave. Widnes WA8 73 A3
Sefton Cl. L32 29 C3
Sefton Cl. Orrell WN5 25 D5
Sefton Dr. Crosby L23 27 A7
Sefton Dr. L32 29 C3
Sefton Dr. Litherland L10 28 E2
Sefton Dr. Liverpool L17 & L8 68 C5
Sefton Dr. Maghull L31 28 B8
Sefton Fold Dr. WN5 33 D5
Sefton Fold Gdns. WN5 33 D5
Sefton Gdns. L39 21 D7
Sefton General Hospl. L15 68 D6
Sefton Gr. L17 68 C4
Sefton House. L9 39 B7
Sefton La. L31 28 B8
Sefton Lane Ind Est. L29 & L31 28 A8
Sefton Mill Ct. L29 27 F7
Sefton Mill La. L29 27 F7
Sefton Moss La. L30 27 D2
Sefton Moss Villas. L21 38 B8
Sefton Park Rd. L17 & L8 68 B5
Sefton Rd. Bebington L62 79 A8
Sefton Rd. Birkenhead L42 67 A1
Sefton Rd. L21 38 B8
Sefton Rd. L20 38 D5
Sefton Rd. Formby L37 9 E2
Sefton Rd. Garswood WN4 34 F6
Sefton Rd. Liverpool L9 39 A4
Sefton Rd. Orrell WN5 25 D5
Sefton Rd. Wallasey L45 51 B7
Sefton Ret Pk. L30 28 A3
Sefton St. L21 38 B7
Sefton St. Liverpool L3 & L8 67 D5
Sefton St. Newton-le-W WA12 45 F3
Sefton St. Southport PR8 4 C5
Sefton View. L21 38 B8
Sefton View. Crosby L23 27 A4
Sefton View. Orrell WN5 25 D5
Segar's La. PR8 & L39 7 E4
Selborne. L35 56 F2
Selborne Cl. 1 L8 68 A7
Selborne St. Liverpool L8 68 A7
Selbourne Cl. L49 65 C3
Selby Cl. WA10 43 D2
Selby Dr. L37 10 B2
Selby Gr. L36 56 B3
Selby Pl. WN8 15 D2
Selby Rd. L9 39 A6
Selby St. L45 51 B5
Seldon St. L7 53 B2
Selina Rd. L4 38 F2
Selkirk Ave. Bebington L62 88 E4
Selkirk Ave. Garswood WN4 34 D4
Selkirk Dr. WA10 43 B5
Selkirk Rd. L13 53 F2
Sellar St. L4 52 E7
Selont House. 3 L8 67 F5
Selsdon Rd. L22 26 C2
Selsey Cl. L7 68 B8
Selside Lawn. L27 71 A4
Selside Rd. L27 71 A4
Selside Wlk. L27 70 F4
Selston Cl. L63 79 A2
Selworthy Gn. L16 69 D6
Selworthy Rd. Southport PR8 3 D3
Selworthy Rd. Southport PR8 3 E3
Selwyn Cl. WA8 73 E3
Selwyn St. L4 38 E1
Sennen Rd. L32 40 F8
Sephton Dr. L39 13 F7
September Rd. L6 53 D6
Serenade Rd. L33 29 F6
Sergrim Rd. L36 55 D3
Serin Cl. WA12 46 C3
Serpentine N The. L23 26 A5
Serpentine Rd. L44 51 C4
Serpentine S The. L23 26 B4
Serpentine The. Crosby L23 26 A4
Serpentine The. Liverpool L19 81 A8
Serpentine The. Ormskirk L39 21 D8
Servia Rd. L21 38 B7
Serville House. L17 68 B4
Servite Cl. L22 26 C2
Servite Ct. L25 70 C1
Sessions Rd. L4 52 E7
Seth Powell Way. L36 55 D5
Settrington Rd. L11 39 F1
Seven Acre Rd. L23 27 B5
Seven Acres La. L61 77 A5
Sevenoaks Ave. PR8 7 B5
Seventh Ave. L9 39 D7
Severn Cl. Billinge WN5 33 D3
Severn Cl. St Helens WA9 58 C6
Severn Cl. Warrington WA2 61 E2
Severn Cl. Widnes WA8 73 F3
Severn Rd. Ashton-in-M WN4 35 E5
Severn Rd. L33 29 F6
Severn Rd. Rainhill L35 57 B3
Severn St. Birkenhead L41 51 A1
Severn St. Liverpool L5 52 F6
Severs St. L6 53 B4
Sewell St. L34 56 D6
Sexton Ave. WA9 45 B2
Sexton Way. L14 54 E2
Seymoor Ct. L14 54 D1
Seymour Ct. L42 66 E4
Seymour Dr. L31 20 E3
Seymour Pl W. 4 L45 51 B8
Seymour Rd. L21 38 B7
Seymour Rd. Liverpool L14 54 D2
Seymour St. Birkenhead L41 & L42 66 E4
Seymour St. L20 38 B2
Seymour St. Liverpool L3 52 E2
Seymour St. Wallasey L45 51 B8
Shacklady Rd. L33 30 A4
Shackleton Cl. WA5 60 C1
Shackleton Rd. L46 50 B4
Shadwell Cl. L5 52 B5
Shadwell St. L5 52 B5
Shaftesbury Ave. Southport PR8 8 A8
Shaftesbury Ave. Warrington WA5 74 E2
Shaftesbury Gr. PR8 4 A1
Shaftesbury Rd. Crosby L23 26 D4
Shaftesbury Rd. Southport PR8 4 A1
Shaftesbury St. L8 67 E6
Shaftesbury Terr. L13 54 A3
Shaftesbury Way. WA5 59 F7
Shaftsbury Ave. L33 29 E5
Shaftway Cl. WA11 45 F7
Shakespeare Ave. L42 66 F1
Shakespeare Gr. WA2 61 C2
Shakespeare Rd. Liverpool L6 53 A4
Shakespeare Rd. Neston L64 86 E1
Shakespeare Rd. St Helens WA9 58 A3
Shakespeare Rd. Wallasey L44 51 D2
Shakespeare Rd. Widnes WA8 73 A1
Shakespeare St. L20 38 A5
Shakespeare St. Liverpool L19 81 C4
Shakespeare St. Liverpool L19 81 C5
Shakespeare St. Southport PR8 4 B5
Shakspeare Cl. L6 53 A4
Shaldon Cl. 3 L32 41 A8
Shaldon Gr. 2 L32 41 A8
Shaldon Rd. L32 41 A8
Shaldon Wlk. 5 L32 41 A8
Shalem Ct. L63 78 C5
Shalford Gr. L48 63 D2
Shallcross Ct. L6 53 A4
Shallcross Pl. 12 L6 53 A4
Shallmarsh Cl. L63 78 D5
Shallmarsh Rd. L63 78 D5
Shalom Ct. L17 & L18 68 E5
Shamrock Rd. L43 65 F7
Shanklin Cl. WA5 74 C6
Shanklin Rd. L15 53 F1
Shannon St. L41 50 F1
Shard Cl. L11 40 B5
Shard St. WA9 58 E7
Sharon Sq. WN2 35 F8
Sharpeville Cl. L4 52 D7
Sharples Cres. L23 27 A3
Sharrock St. PR8 4 B7
Shavington Ave. L43 65 F3
Shaw Cl. L39 8 F6
Shaw Cres. L37 10 B3
Shaw Entry. L35 & WA8 72 A7
Shaw Hill St. L1 52 D2
Shaw La. Birkenhead L49 64 C2
Shaw La. Haskayne L39 11 E6
Shaw La. Prescot L35 56 E4
Shaw Rd. L24 82 D5
Shaw St. Ashton-in-M WN4 35 B5
Shaw St. Birkenhead L41 66 D5
Shaw St. Haydock WA11 45 E6
Shaw St. Hoylake L47 63 B7
Shaw St. Liverpool L3 & L6 52 F3
Shaw St. Runcorn WA7 84 F2
Shaw St. St Helens WA10 & WA9 44 B4
Shaw's Ave. PR8 4 A1
Shaw's Rd. PR8 4 A1
Shawbury Ave. L63 78 D7

Shawell Ct. WA8 .... 73 E2
Shaws Alley. L1 & L72 .... 67 C8
Shaws Dr. L47 .... 63 D8
Shaws Garth. L39 .... 8 F6
Shawton Rd. L16 .... 69 D8
Shearman Cl. L61 .... 77 A4
Shearman Rd. L61 .... 77 A4
Shearwater Cl. L27 .... 70 F4
Sheen Rd. L45 .... 51 C7
Sheffield Row. WA12 .... 60 D8
Sheil Pl. L6 & L7 .... 53 C3
Sheil Rd. L6 .... 53 C3
Sheila Wlk. L10 .... 40 B6
Sheilings The. WA3 .... 47 F8
Shelagh Ave. WA8 .... 73 A1
Sheldon Cl. L63 .... 79 A1
Sheldon Rd. L12 .... 54 D8
Shelley Cl. L36 .... 56 A1
Shelley Dr. L39 .... 13 D6
Shelley Gr. PR8 & PR9 .... 4 F6
Shelley House. L62 .... 79 A7
Shelley Pl. L35 .... 56 F3
Shelley Rd. WA8 .... 73 A1
Shelley St. L20 .... 38 B4
Shelley St. St Helens WA9 .... 58 B2
Shelley Way. L48 .... 75 B8
Shellfield Rd. PR9 .... 2 A4
Shellingford Rd. L14 .... 55 A4
Shelly Gr. L19 .... 81 C5
Shelton Cl. WA8 .... 73 F3
Shelton Dr. PR8 .... 7 A4
Shelton Rd. L45 .... 51 A6
Shenley Cl. L63 .... 78 F6
Shenley Rd. L15 .... 69 C8
Shenley Way. PR9 .... 2 D5
Shenstone St. L7 .... 53 B1
Shenton Ave. WA11 .... 44 D6
Shepherd Cl. L49 .... 64 C4
Shepherd St. L7 .... 52 F2
Shepherd's La. L39 .... 12 E5
Sheppard Ave. L16 & L36 .... 70 A8
Shepston Ave. 7 L4 .... 39 A1
Shepton Rd. L36 .... 55 D6
Sherborne Ave. Litherland L30 .... 27 E4
Sherborne Ave.Liverpool L25 82 D8
Sherborne Rd. L45 .... 50 F5
Sherborne Sq. L36 .... 55 E2
Sherbourne Way. WA5 .... 59 F6
Sherburn Cl. L9 .... 39 D8
Sherdley Cty Prim Sch. WA9 .... 58 C6
Sherdley Park Dr. WA9 .... 58 B7
Sherdley Rd. St Helens WA9 44 B1
Sherdley Rd. St Helens WA9 57 F7
Sherdley Rd. St Helens WA9 58 A8
Sheri Dr. WA12 .... 46 E2
Sheridan Ave. WA3 .... 47 D7
Sheriff Cl. 3 L5 .... 52 E4
Sheringham Cl. Birkenhead L49 .... 65 A7
Sheringham Cl. St Helens WA9 .... 44 D3
Sheringham Rd. WA5 .... 74 E6
Sherlock Ave. WA11 .... 45 E7
Sherlock La. L44 .... 51 A2
Sherman Dr. L35 .... 57 D1
Sherrat St. WN8 .... 15 D1
Sherringham Rd. PR8 .... 3 E2
Sherry Ct. L17 .... 68 E5
Sherry La. L49 .... 65 A2
Sherwell Cl. L15 .... 54 A1
Sherwood Ave. Ashton-in-M WN4 .... 35 C4
Sherwood Ave. Crosby L23 .. 26 D5
Sherwood Ave. Irby L61 .... 76 C7
Sherwood Ave. Ormskirk L39 .... 13 C2
Sherwood Cl. Rainhill L35 .... 57 C5
Sherwood Cl. Widnes WA8 .. 72 C1
Sherwood Cres. WA5 .... 59 E6
Sherwood Ct. Huyton-w-R L36 .... 55 F2
Sherwood Ct. Liverpool L12 . 40 F3
Sherwood Dr. Bebington L63 78 E7
Sherwood Dr. Skelmersdale WN8 .... 16 D3
Sherwood Gr. L47 .... 63 F7
Sherwood House. PR8 .... 7 C5
Sherwood Rd. Crosby L23 .... 26 C5
Sherwood Rd. Hoylake L47 .. 63 F8
Sherwood Rd. Wallasey L44 51 C3
Sherwood St. L3 .... 52 B4
Sherwood's La. L10 .... 39 F8
Sherwyn Rd. L4 .... 53 C8
Shetland Cl. Warrington WA2 .... 61 E4
Shetland Cl. Widnes WA8 .... 73 E3
Shetland Dr. L62 .... 88 E8
Shevington Cl. St Helens WA9 .... 58 C7
Shevington Cl. Widnes WA8 73 E3
Shevington's La. L33 .... 29 E6
Shewell Cl. L42 .... 66 D4
Shiel Rd. L45 .... 51 B7
Shimmin St. L7 .... 53 A1
Shipley Wlk. L24 .... 82 D4
Shipton Cl. Birkenhead L43 .. 65 E1
Shipton Cl. Widnes WA8 .... 72 D3
Shirdley Ave. L32 .... 40 F7
Shirdley Cres. PR8 .... 7 C3
Shirdley Wlk. L32 .... 40 F7
Shire Gn. 6 WA9 .... 58 C6
Shirebourne Ave. WA11 .... 44 B7
Shireburn Rd. L37 .... 9 D5
Shires The. WA10 .... 43 F2
Shirley Rd. L19 .... 81 C8
Shirley St. L44 .... 51 E3
Shirwell Gr. WA9 .... 58 C4
Shobdon Cl. L12 .... 40 F4
Shop La. L31 .... 20 C1
Shop Rd. L34 .... 41 C4
Shore Bank. L62 .... 79 C8
Shore Dr. L62 .... 79 C6
Shore Rd. Birkenhead L41 & L72 .... 66 F7
Shore Rd. Seaforth L20 & L21 37 F5
Shore Rd. Southport PR8 .... 7 B6
Shore Rd. West Kirby L48 .... 75 C7
Shorefields. L62 .... 79 C7
Shorefields Comm Comp Sch. L8 .... 68 A3
Shorefields Comp Sch. L8 .. 68 B4
Shorefields House. L62 .... 79 C7
Shorefields Village. L8 .... 67 F3
Shoreside Cty Prim Sch. PR8 7 B4
Short Cl. WA12 .... 45 E3
Short Croft La. L37 .... 10 D1
Short St. Golborne WA3 .... 36 B1
Short St. Haydock WA11 .... 45 E6
Short St. Newton-le-W WA12 45 E3
Shortfield Rd. L49 .... 65 A4
Shortfield Way. L49 .... 65 A4
Shortwood Rd. L14 .... 54 F3
Shorwell Cl. WA5 .... 74 C7
Shottesbrook Gn. L11 .... 39 F3
Shrewsbury Ave. Crosby L22 26 D3
Shrewsbury Ave. Litherland L10 .... 28 D2
Shrewsbury Cl. 3 L43 .... 65 F6
Shrewsbury Dr. L49 .... 65 A6
Shrewsbury Pl. L19 .... 81 C6
Shrewsbury Rd. Birkenhead L43 & L41 & L44 & L45 .... 66 A5
Shrewsbury Rd. Heswall L60 77 A1
Shrewsbury Rd. Liverpool L19 .... 81 C6
Shrewsbury Rd. West Kirby L48 .... 63 A1
Shrewton Rd. L25 .... 70 B7
Shropshire Cl. L30 .... 28 A4
Shuttle Hillock Rd. WN2 .... 36 F7
Shuttleworth Cl. L49 .... 64 E6
Sibford Rd. L12 .... 54 D5
Sibley Ave. WN4 .... 35 D4
Siddall St. WA10 .... 43 F7
Siddeley Dr. WA12 .... 45 F4
Siddeley St. L17 .... 68 C3
Sidewell St. L19 .... 81 C5
Sidgreave St. WA10 .... 43 E3
Siding La. Bickerstaffe WA11 23 C1
Siding La. L33 .... 30 C7
Sidings The. L42 .... 66 F2
Sidlaw Ave. WA9 .... 44 F3
Sidmouth Cl. WA5 .... 74 E4
Sidney Ave. L45 .... 51 A8
Sidney Gdns. L41 .... 66 E4
Sidney Pl. L7 .... 68 A8
Sidney Powell Ave. L32 .... 29 C2
Sidney Rd. Birkenhead L41 .. 66 E4
Sidney Rd. L20 .... 38 D2
Sidney Rd. Neston L64 .... 86 F1
Sidney Rd. Southport PR9 .... 4 F8
Sidney St. Birkenhead L41 & L72 .... 66 E7
Sidney St. St Helens WA10 .. 43 D4
Signal Works Rd. L9 .... 39 E8
Silcock St. WA3 .... 36 A1
Silcroft Rd. L32 .... 40 E8
Silkstone Cl. Liverpool L7 .... 68 B8
Silkstone Cl. St Helens WA10 .... 43 D3
Silkstone St. WA10 .... 43 D3
Silver Ave. WA11 .... 45 A5
Silver Birch Gr. WN4 .... 35 A5
Silver Birch Way. L31 .... 20 B5
Silver Leigh. L17 .... 68 D1
Silverbeech Ave. L18 .... 69 B4
Silverbeech Rd. L44 .... 51 C3
Silverbirch Gdns. L45 .... 50 E5
Silverburn Ave. L46 .... 49 F1
Silverdale. PR8 .... 3 E4
Silverdale Ave. L13 .... 53 E5
Silverdale Cl. L36 .... 70 E8
Silverdale Dr. L21 & L30 .... 38 D8
Silverdale Gr. WA11 .... 44 A8
Silverdale Rd. Bebington L63 78 F7
Silverdale Rd. Birkenhead L43 .... 66 A4
Silverdale Rd. Newton-le-W WA12 .... 46 B4
Silverlea Ave. L45 .... 51 B5
Silverlime Gdns. L35 .... 57 C7
Silverstone Dr. L36 .... 70 D8
Silverstone Gr. L31 .... 20 B4
Silverthorne Dr. PR9 .... 1 F1
Silverton Rd. L17 .... 80 E8
Silverwell Rd. L11 .... 40 D5
Silvester St. L5 .... 52 D5
Sim St. L3 .... 52 E3
Simm's Rd. L6 .... 53 D6
Simms Ave. WA9 .... 44 E3
Simon Ct. L48 .... 63 A2
Simon's Croft. L30 .... 27 C3
Simons Cl. L35 .... 71 D8
Simonsbridge. L48 .... 75 D6
Simonside. WA8 .... 72 C2
Simonstone Gr. 5 WA9 .... 58 D7
Simonswood Ind Pk. L33 .... 30 B6
Simonswood La. Bickerstaffe L39 .... 22 A2
Simonswood La. L32 & L33 . 30 A2
Simonswood La. Maghull L39 .... 21 F3
Simonswood Prim Sch. L33 30 A2
Simonswood Wlk. L33 .... 30 A2
Simpkin St. WN2 .... 36 C8
Simpson St. Birkenhead L41 66 D6
Simpson St. Liverpool L1 & L72 .... 67 D7
Sinclair Ave. Prescot L35 .... 56 F5
Sinclair Ave. Warrington WA2 .... 61 B2
Sinclair Ave. Widnes WA8 ... 84 F8
Sinclair Cl. L35 .... 56 F6
Sinclair Dr. L15 & L18 .... 69 B6
Sinclair St. L19 .... 81 C4
Sineacre La. L33 & L39 .... 30 E8
Singleton Ave. Birkenhead L42 .... 66 C3
Singleton Ave. St Helens WA11 .... 44 D5
Singleton Dr. L34 .... 41 D3
Sir Alfred Jones Meml Hospl. L19 .... 81 C6
Sir Howard St. 13 L7 .... 67 F8
Sir Howard Way. 14 L8 .... 67 F8
Sir Thomas St. L1 .... 52 D2
Sirdar Cl. L7 .... 68 B8
Siskin Cl. WA12 .... 46 C3
Siskin Gn. L25 .... 70 A4
Sisters Way. L41 .... 66 D6
Sixpenny La. PR8 .... 7 D1
Sixth Ave. L9 .... 39 D7
Skeffington. L35 .... 56 E2
Skelhorne St. L1 & L3 .... 52 E1
Skellington Fold. L27 .... 70 E5
Skelmersdale Coll. WN8 .... 16 B1
Skelmersdale Coll. WN8 .... 16 B4
Skelmersdale Coll (Westbrook Ctr). WN8 .... 24 B8
Skelmersdale Rd. L39 & WN8 .... 23 B7
Skelmersdale Sports Ctr. WN8 .... 24 C7
Skelton Cl. WA11 .... 44 A7
Skelton St. WN4 .... 34 F6
Skerries Rd. L4 .... 53 A7
Skiddaw Rd. L62 .... 79 E2
Skipton Ave. PR9 .... 2 C6
Skipton Rd. Huyton-w-R L36 56 B3
Skipton Rd. Liverpool L4 .... 53 B7
Skirving Pl. L5 .... 52 D6
Skirving St. L5 .... 52 E6
Skye Cl. WA8 .... 73 E3
Slack House Cotts. L39 .... 14 A3
Slag La. Golborne WA3 .... 36 F2
Slag La. Golborne WA3 .... 47 D8
Slag La. Haydock WA11 .... 45 B7
Slaidburn Cres. Golborne WA3 .... 35 F2
Slaidburn Cres. Southport PR9 .... 2 B5
Slate La. WN8 .... 15 C2
Slater Pl. L1 & L69 & L72 .... 67 D8
Slater St. L1 & L68 & L69 & L72 & L75 67 D8
Slatey Rd. L43 .... 66 B5
Sleaford Rd. L14 .... 55 B6
Sleepers Hill. L4 .... 52 F7
Slessor Ave. L48 .... 63 D3
Slim Rd. L36 .... 55 E3
Slingsby Dr. L49 .... 65 A4
Small Ave. WA2 .... 61 C2
Small Cres. WA2 .... 61 C2
Small La. Ormskirk L39 .... 13 A3
Small La. Ormskirk L39 .... 13 F4
Small La S. L39 .... 12 D6
Smallshaw Cl. WN4 .... 35 A2
Smallwoods Mews. L60 .... 76 E1
Smeaton St. L4 .... 38 E1
Smethurst Hall Pk. WN5 .... 25 C2
Smethurst Rd. WN5 .... 25 C2
Smilie Ave. L46 .... 49 C1
Smith Ave. L41 .... 66 B8
Smith Dr. L20 .... 38 E5
Smith Pl. L5 .... 52 D6
Smith Rd. WA8 .... 86 A7
Smith St. Liverpool L4 & L5 .. 52 E6
Smith St. Prescot L34 .... 56 E6
Smith St. Skelmersdale WN8 15 D1
Smith St. St Helens WA9 .... 58 E7
Smithdown Gr. L7 .... 68 B8
Smithdown La. Liverpool L7 53 A1
Smithdown La. Liverpool L7 & L8 .... 68 B8
Smithdown Pl. 5 L15 & L18 69 A5
Smithdown Rd. L15 & L7 & L8 & L18 .... 68 D7
Smithfield St. 16 Liverpool L2 & L3 .... 52 C2
Smithfield St. St Helens WA9 .... 44 D2
Smithy Brow. WA3 .... 61 F8
Smithy Cl. Cronton WA8 .... 72 C5
Smithy Cl. Formby L37 .... 10 B4
Smithy Gn. L37 .... 10 B4
Smithy Hey. L48 .... 63 C2
Smithy Hill. L63 .... 87 A6
Smithy La. Cronton WA8 .... 72 C5
Smithy La. Haskayne L39 .... 12 A6
Smithy La. Holt Green L39 ... 21 A6
Smock La. WN4 .... 34 C4
Smollett St. L20 .... 38 B6
Smollett St. Liverpool L7 .... 53 B2
Smyth Rd. WA8 .... 73 D2
Snaefell Ave. L13 .... 53 E5
Snaefell Gr. L13 .... 53 E5
Snape Gn. PR8 .... 5 E1
Snave Cl. L21 .... 38 B5
Snottesbrook Gn. L11 .... 39 F3
Snowberry Cl. WA8 .... 73 E4
Snowberry Rd. L14 .... 55 A7
Snowden Rd. L46 .... 64 C8
Snowdon Cl. WA5 .... 74 E6
Snowdon Gr. WA9 .... 58 C7
Snowdon La. L5 .... 52 C5
Snowdon Rd. L42 .... 66 D2
Snowdrop Ave. L41 .... 65 F7
Snowdrop St. L5 .... 52 D7
Soho Pl. L3 .... 52 E3
Soho St. L3 .... 52 E3
Solar Rd. L9 .... 39 B6
Solly Ave. L42 .... 66 E2
Solomon St. L7 .... 53 B2
Solva Cl. L6 .... 52 F4
Solway Cl. Ashton-in-M WN4 35 A4
Solway Cl. Warrington WA2 . 61 F4
Solway St. Birkenhead L41 ... 51 A1
Solway St. Liverpool L8 .... 68 B7
Soma Ave. L21 .... 38 C8
Somerford Rd. L14 .... 55 A4
Somerford Wlk. WA8 .... 73 E3
Somerset Dr. PR8 .... 7 C3
Somerset Pl. L6 .... 53 D5
Somerset Rd. L20 .... 38 D4
Somerset Rd. Crosby L22 & L23 .... 26 C2
Somerset Rd. Heswall L61 ... 76 E4
Somerset Rd. Wallasey L45 . 50 E5
Somerset Rd. West Kirby L48 .... 63 C3
Somerset St. WA9 .... 44 D2
Somerton St. L15 .... 68 E8
Somerville. L44 .... 51 C3
Somerville Cl. L63 .... 88 B6
Somerville Gr. L22 .... 26 D2
Somerville Prim Sch. L44 .... 51 D3
Somerville Rd. Crosby L22 ... 26 D2
Somerville Rd. Widnes WA8 .... 84 D8
Sommer Ave. L12 .... 54 A7
Sonning Ave. L21 .... 27 B1
Sonning Rd. L4 .... 39 D2
Sorany Cl. L23 .... 27 B6
Sorogold St. WA9 .... 44 C3
Sorrel Cl. L43 .... 65 D5
Sougher's La. WN4 .... 34 F7
South Albert Rd. L17 .... 68 C4
South Ave. Golborne WN7 ... 36 F4
South Ave. Prescot L34 .... 56 C5
South Bank. L43 .... 66 B3
South Bank Rd. Liverpool L7 53 D2
South Bank Rd. Liverpool L19 .... 81 B7
South Bank Terr. WA7 .... 84 F3
South Barcombe Rd. L16 .... 69 E7
South Boundary Rd. L32 & L33 .... 41 C8
South Cantril Ave. L12 & L14 54 F7
South Chester St. L8 .... 67 F6
South Cloughton Rd. L41 & L43 .... 66 D6
South Dale. WA5 .... 74 F5
South Dr. Birkenhead L49 .... 65 A6
South Dr. Heswall L60 .... 86 A7
South Dr. Irby L61 .... 76 C5
South Dr. Liverpool L12 .... 54 C5
South Dr. Liverpool L15 .... 69 A8
South Ferry Quay. L3 & L69 67 D5
South Front. L35 .... 56 E1
South Gr. Liverpool L8 .... 68 A4
South Gr. Liverpool L18 .... 69 C1
South Hey Rd. L61 .... 76 D5
South Highville Rd. L16 .... 69 D6
South Hill Gr. 8 L8 .... 68 A4
South Hill Rd. Birkenhead L43 .... 66 C4
South Hill Rd. Liverpool L8 .. 68 A4
South Hunter St. 1 L1 & L69 .... 67 F8
South John St. Liverpool L1 . 52 C1
South John St. St Helens WA9 .... 44 C3
South La. Warrington WA5 & WA8 .... 74 B4
South La. Widnes WA8 .... 73 F4
South Lancashire Ind Est. WN4 .... 35 B6
South Lane Entry. WA8 .... 73 F5
South Manor Way. L25 .... 70 C1
South Meade. L31 .... 20 B1
South Mossley Hill Rd. L19 & L18 .... 81 B8
South Par. L32 .... 29 E2
South Par. Liverpool L24 .... 82 E2
South Par. West Kirby L48 ... 63 A1
South Park Ct. L32 .... 29 C3
South Park Rd. L32 .... 29 C3
South Park Way. L20 .... 38 D2
South Parkside Dr. L12 .... 54 C6
South Parkside Wlk. L12 .... 54 B2
South Quay. L3 .... 67 D7
South Rd. Birkenhead L42 .... 66 D3
South Rd. Crosby L22 .... 26 E1
South Rd. Liverpool L14 .... 54 D2
South Rd. Liverpool L19 .... 80 F6
South Rd. Liverpool L24 .... 82 F4
South Rd. West Kirby L48 .... 63 B1
South Sefton Bsns Ctr. L20 . 38 B2
South St. Liverpool L8 .... 68 A5
South St. St Helens L35 & WA9 .... 57 D7
South Station Rd. L25 .... 70 B4
South Sudley Rd. L19 .... 81 A8
South Terr. L39 .... 13 E4
South View. Bebington L62 .. 79 D5
South View. Huyton-w-R L36 56 B2
South View. Seaforth L22 .... 37 E8
South Villas. 5 L45 .... 51 B7
South Way. L15 .... 69 B8
South Wirral High Sch. L62 88 D4
South Wirral Ret Pk. L62 .... 79 D3
Southbank Rd. PR8 .... 4 C5
Southbourne Rd. L45 .... 50 D5
Southbrook Rd. L27 .... 70 C7
Southbrook Way. L25 & L27 70 C6
Southcroft. L33 .... 29 F4
Southcroft Rd. L45 .... 50 D5
Southdale Rd. Birkenhead L42 .... 66 E2
Southdale Rd. Liverpool L15 68 F8
Southdean Rd. L14 .... 55 B6
Southern Cres. L8 .... 67 E5
Southern Rd. Liverpool L24 .. 82 E2
Southern Rd. Southport PR8 .. 4 A6
Southern's La. WA11 .... 32 A6
Southey Gr. L31 .... 28 D6
Southey Rd. WA10 .... 57 C8
Southey St. L20 .... 38 B4
Southey St. Liverpool L15 .... 68 E7
Southfield Rd. L9 .... 38 F6
Southfields Ave. WA5 .... 74 F6
Southfront. L35 .... 71 E8
Southgate Cl. L12 .... 40 E3
Southgate Rd. L13 .... 54 B3
Southlands Ave. WA5 .... 74 F3
Southlands Ct. 7 WA7 .... 84 F1
Southlands Mews. 6 WA7 . 84 F1
Southmead Gdns. L19 .... 81 E7
Southmead Prim Sch. L35 .. 56 F2

Southmead Rd. L19 ... 81 E7
Southpark Ct. L44 ... 51 E3
Southport & Ainsdale Golf Links. PR8 ... 7 D7
Southport Coll. PR9 ... 4 C7
Southport General Hospl. PR8 ... 4 D5
Southport Holiday Village. PR8 ... 6 F6
Southport New Rd. PR9 ... 2 F5
Southport Old Links (Golf Course). PR9 ... 5 B8
Southport Old Rd. L37 & PR8 ... 10 B7
Southport Rd. L20 ... 38 E4
Southport Rd. Crosby L23 ... 27 A7
Southport Rd. Formby L37 ... 10 A5
Southport Rd. Haskayne L39 12 A6
Southport Rd. Maghull L31 & L39 ... 20 B5
Southport Rd. Ormskirk L39 & L40 ... 13 D8
Southport Rd. Southport PR8 5 B2
Southport St. WA9 ... 45 A3
Southport Zoo. PR8 ... 3 F7
Southridge Rd. L61 ... 77 A5
Southward Rd. WA11 ... 46 A7
Southwark Gr. L30 ... 27 F1
Southway. Skelmersdale WN8 ... 16 B1
Southway. Widnes WA8 ... 84 D8
Southwell Cl. WA3 ... 47 C8
Southwell Pl. 4 L8 ... 67 E5
Southwell St. L8 ... 67 E5
Southwick Rd. L42 ... 66 E3
Southwood Rd. L17 ... 68 B3
Southworth La. WA2 & WA3 61 E7
Southworth Rd. WA12 ... 46 F4
Sovereign Hey. 1 L11 ... 40 C3
Sovereign Rd. L11 ... 40 C3
Sovereign Way. L11 ... 40 C3
Spa La. L40 & WN8 ... 15 C4
Sparks La. L61 ... 77 B6
Sparling St. L1 & L72 ... 67 D7
Sparrow Hall Cl. L9 ... 39 F4
Sparrow Hall Rd. L11 & L9 ... 39 F4
Sparrowhawk Cl. L26 ... 70 E1
Spawell Cl. WA3 ... 47 E8
Speakman Ave. WA12 ... 46 C5
Speakman Rd. WA10 ... 43 D5
Speakman St. WA7 ... 84 F3
Speedwell Cl. L60 ... 86 C8
Speedwell Dr. L60 ... 86 C8
Speedwell Rd. L41 & L43 ... 65 F7
Speke Bvd. Liverpool L24 ... 82 C4
Speke Bvd. Liverpool L24 & WA8 ... 82 D4
Speke Church Rd. L24 ... 82 B3
Speke Hall Ave. L24 ... 82 B3
Speke Hall Rd. L24 & L25 ... 82 B6
Speke Rd. Liverpool L25 ... 70 A2
Speke Rd. Liverpool L19 ... 81 D5
Speke Rd. Liverpool L19 & L24 ... 81 E5
Speke Rd. Liverpool L25 & L24 ... 82 C8
Speke Rd. Widnes WA8 ... 84 C6
Speke Sch. L24 ... 82 D3
Speke Town La. L24 ... 82 C4
Spekeland Rd. L7 ... 68 C8
Spellow La. L4 ... 52 F8
Spence Ave. L20 ... 38 D5
Spencer Ave. L46 ... 50 A1
Spencer Cl. L36 ... 70 F8
Spencer Gdns. WA9 ... 58 D8
Spencer Pl. L20 ... 38 D7
Spencer St. L20 ... 38 B4
Spencer St. Liverpool L6 ... 52 F4
Spencer's La. Litherland L10 & L31 ... 28 F3
Spencer's La. Orrell WN5 ... 25 D7
Spencer's La. Southport L39 .. 8 B3
Spencers La. WN8 ... 24 B7
Spenser Ave. L42 ... 66 F1
Spenser Rd. L64 ... 86 E1
Spice St. L9 ... 39 B5
Spicer Gr. L32 ... 29 E2
Spindle Hillock. WN4 ... 34 D4
Spindus Rd. L24 ... 82 B3
Spinney Ave. WA8 ... 72 A1
Spinney Cl. L39 ... 13 D3
Spinney Cl. Kirkby L33 ... 41 C8
Spinney Cl. St Helens WA9 .. 58 C4
Spinney Cres. L23 ... 26 B6
Spinney Gn. WA10 ... 43 A2
Spinney Rd. L33 ... 41 D8
Spinney The. Bebington L63 79 B3
Spinney The. Formby L37 ... 10 A5
Spinney The. Heswall L60 ... 86 C5
Spinney The. Huyton-w-R L28 ... 55 A7
Spinney The. Neston L64 ... 86 D1
Spinney The. Prescot L34 ... 56 C7
Spinney The. Rainford WA11 31 F6
Spinney The. West Kirby L48 63 E2
Spinney View. L33 ... 41 D8
Spion Kop. WN4 ... 35 A3
Spital Heyes. L63 ... 79 B3
Spital Rd. L63 & L62 ... 79 C3
Spital Sta. L63 ... 79 B3
Spofforth Rd. L15 & L7 ... 68 D8
Spooner Ave. L21 ... 38 C8
Sprainger St. L3 ... 52 B4
Sprakeling Pl. L20 ... 38 E7
Spray St. WA10 ... 43 E4
Spreyton Cl. L11 ... 40 C2
Sprig Cl. L9 ... 39 D8
Spring Bank Rd. 2 L4 & L6 . 53 B5
Spring Cl. PR8 ... 4 A5
Spring Field. WA11 ... 23 E2
Spring Gdns. L31 ... 28 E8
Spring Gr. L12 ... 54 C6
Spring Rd. WN5 ... 25 F8
Spring St. L41 ... 66 F3
Spring Vale. L45 ... 50 E7
Springbourne Rd. L17 ... 68 B2
Springbrook Cl. WA10 ... 43 A4
Springcroft. L64 ... 86 C1
Springdale Cl. L12 ... 54 D7
Springfield. L3 ... 52 E3
Springfield Ave. L21 ... 38 C8
Springfield Ave. Golborne WA3 ... 46 F8
Springfield Ave. West Kirby L48 ... 63 F2
Springfield Cl. Birkenhead L49 ... 65 C2
Springfield Cl. Formby L37 ... 9 C2
Springfield Cl. St Helens WA10 ... 57 C8
Springfield La. WA10 ... 43 A4
Springfield Pk. WA11 ... 45 C7
Springfield Rd. Maghull L39 20 F6
Springfield Rd. St Helens WA10 & WA9 ... 57 C8
Springfield Rd. Widnes WA8 84 A8
Springfield Sch. L32 ... 40 E7
Springfield Sq. L4 ... 52 F8
Springfield Way. L12 ... 54 E8
Springhill Ave. L62 ... 88 D6
Springmeadow Rd. L25 ... 70 A5
Springmount. WA3 ... 47 E7
Springpool. WA9 ... 58 D7
Springville Rd. L9 ... 39 C7
Springwell Rd. L20 ... 38 D6
Springwell Rd. L20 ... 38 D7
Springwood Ave. L19 & L25 81 E7
Springwood Gr. L32 ... 40 F7
Springwood Prim Sch. L19 . 81 D8
Springwood Way. L62 ... 79 A8
Spruce Cl. WA3 ... 47 F7
Spruce Gr. L28 ... 55 B7
Spruce Way. L37 ... 9 C3
Spur Cl. L11 ... 40 C3
Spur The. L23 ... 26 D3
Spurgeon Cl. L5 ... 52 F5
Spurling Rd. WA5 ... 59 F6
Spurrier's La. L31 ... 29 D8
Spurstow Cl. L43 ... 65 F3
Spymers Croft. L37 ... 10 A6
Square The. L64 ... 86 B1
Squire St. Liverpool L7 ... 53 A1
Squire St. Liverpool L7 ... 68 A8
Squires Ave. 3 WA8 ... 73 A1
Squirrel Gn. L37 ... 9 C5
Stable Cl. L49 ... 64 D4
Stables Ct. WA9 ... 44 C2
Stackfield The. L48 ... 63 F3
Stadium Rd. L62 ... 79 E2
Stafford Cl. L36 ... 56 A4
Stafford Moreton Way. L31 20 D1
Stafford Rd. Southport PR8 ... 4 A1
Stafford Rd. St Helens WA10 43 D1
Stafford St. Liverpool L3 ... 52 E2
Stafford St. Skelmersdale WN8 ... 15 D1
Stainburn Ave. L11 ... 39 F3
Stainer Cl. L14 ... 54 F5
Stainton Cl. Liverpool L26 ... 82 E8
Stainton Cl. St Helens WA11 44 B8
Stairhaven Rd. Liverpool L19 69 B1
Stairhaven Rd. Liverpool L19 81 B8
Stakes The. L46 ... 49 E3
Stalbridge Ave. L18 ... 68 F5
Staley Ave. L23 ... 26 F3
Staley St. L20 ... 38 D6
Stalisfield Ave. L11 ... 40 A1
Stalisfield Gr. L11 ... 40 A2
Stalisfield Pl. L11 ... 40 A2
Stalmine Rd. L9 ... 39 A4
Stamford Rd. Skelmersdale WN8 ... 15 D2
Stamford Rd. Southport PR8 . 4 B2
Stamford St. L7 ... 53 C2
Stamfordham Dr. L19 ... 81 D7
Stamfordham Gr. L19 ... 81 D7
Stamfordham Pl. L19 ... 81 D7
Stanbury Ave. L63 ... 79 A6
Stand Farm Rd. L12 ... 40 F3
Stand Park Ave. L30 ... 27 F2
Stand Park Cl. L30 ... 27 F2
Stand Park Rd. L16 ... 69 D6
Stand Parkway. L30 ... 27 E3
Standale Rd. L15 ... 68 F8
Standard Pl. L42 ... 66 F3
Standard Rd. L11 ... 40 C4
Standen Cl. WA10 ... 43 E4
Standhouse La. L39 ... 13 C2
Standish Ave. WN5 ... 33 E5
Standish Ct. WA8 ... 84 D8
Standish Dr. WA11 ... 32 A7
Standish St. Liverpool L3 ... 52 D2
Standish St. St Helens WA10 & WA9 ... 44 B4
Standring Garden. WA10 ... 57 B8
Stanfield Ave. L5 ... 52 F5
Stanfield Dr. L63 ... 78 F3
Stanford Ave. 2 L45 ... 51 B7
Stanford Cres. L25 ... 82 D8
Stangate. L31 ... 20 B2
Stanhope Dr. Bebington L62 79 D1
Stanhope Dr. Huyton-w-R L36 ... 55 C3
Stanhope St. Liverpool L3 & L8 ... 67 E6
Stanhope St. St Helens WA10 ... 43 F5
Stanier Way. L7 ... 53 C1
Staniforth Pl. L16 ... 54 D1
Stanlawe Rd. L37 ... 9 E6
Stanley Ave. Bebington L42 . 78 C8
Stanley Ave. Rainford WA11 31 F7
Stanley Ave. Southport PR8 ... 3 F3
Stanley Ave. Wallasey L45 ... 50 D6
Stanley Ave. Warrington WA5 ... 74 D7
Stanley Bank Rd. WA11 ... 45 A7
Stanley Bglws. L34 ... 41 C3
Stanley Cl. Liverpool L4 ... 52 D7
Stanley Cl. Wallasey L44 ... 51 E2
Stanley Cl. Widnes WA8 ... 73 C2
Stanley Cres. L34 ... 56 C6
Stanley Ct. L41 & L42 ... 66 F3
Stanley Gdns. L9 ... 38 F5
Stanley High Sch. PR9 ... 1 F4
Stanley House. L20 ... 38 B4
Stanley La. L62 ... 88 F4
Stanley Park Ave N. L4 ... 39 B2
Stanley Park Ave S. L4 ... 53 B8
Stanley Pk. L21 ... 27 B1
Stanley Rd. Bebington L62 ... 79 A8
Stanley Rd. L20 & L69 & L5 .. 38 C3
Stanley Rd. Formby L37 ... 9 E6
Stanley Rd. Hoylake L47 ... 62 F6
Stanley Rd. Huyton-w-R L36 . 55 E3
Stanley Rd. Liverpool L5 ... 52 D5
Stanley Rd. Maghull L31 ... 28 C6
Stanley Rd. Orrell WN8 ... 25 B7
Stanley Rd. Seaforth L22 ... 37 E8
Stanley Rd. Wallasey L41 ... 50 F1
Stanley Sch. L61 ... 77 A6
Stanley St. Liverpool L1 & L2 52 C1
Stanley St. Liverpool L7 ... 53 E3
Stanley St. Liverpool L19 ... 81 C4
Stanley St. Newton-le-W WA12 ... 46 A3
Stanley St. Ormskirk L39 ... 13 F5
Stanley St. Southport PR8 & PR9 ... 4 B8
Stanley St. Wallasey L44 ... 51 E2
Stanley Terr. Liverpool L18 .. 69 A3
Stanley Terr. 7 Wallasey L45 ... 51 B7
Stanley Villas. 5 WA7 ... 84 F1
Stanley Way. WN8 ... 15 E3
Stanlowe View. L19 ... 80 F6
Stanmore Pk. L49 ... 64 B3
Stanmore Rd. L15 & L18 ... 69 B6
Stannanought Rd. Skelmersdale WN8 ... 16 E2
Stanner Cl. WA5 ... 60 D2
Stanney Cl. L62 ... 88 E3
Stanny Field Dr. L23 ... 27 B6
Stannyfield Cl. L23 ... 27 B6
Stansfield Ave. L31 ... 20 F1
Stanstead Ave. 1 WA5 ... 74 F3
Stanton Ave. L21 ... 27 A1
Stanton Cl. Haydock WA11 .. 45 C6
Stanton Cl. Litherland L30 ... 27 D5
Stanton Cres. L32 ... 29 C2
Stanton Rd. Bebington L63 .. 78 F3
Stanton Rd. 6 Liverpool L18 68 F5
Stanton Rd Prim Sch. L63 ... 79 A3
Stanwood Cl. WA10 ... 42 F3
Stapehill Cl. L13 ... 54 B2
Stapeley Hospl. L18 ... 68 F4
Staplands Rd. L14 ... 54 D2
Stapleford Rd. L25 ... 70 D6
Staplehurst Cl. L12 ... 40 E3
Stapleton Ave. Birkenhead L49 ... 64 D4
Stapleton Ave. Liverpool L24 82 D3
Stapleton Ave. Rainhill L35 .. 57 C4
Stapleton Cl. L35 ... 57 C4
Stapleton Rd. Formby L37 ... 9 D1
Stapleton Rd. Rainhill L35 ... 57 C5
Stapleton Way. WA8 ... 84 B5
Stapley Cl. WA7 ... 84 F1
Star Inn Cotts. WA11 ... 32 A5
Star St. L8 ... 67 E6
Starling Gr. L12 ... 40 F1
Startham Ave. WN5 ... 33 D3
Starworth Dr. L62 ... 79 C7
Statham Ave. WA2 ... 61 C2
Statham Rd. Birkenhead L43 65 C8
Statham Rd. Skelmersdale WN8 ... 15 E3
Statham Way. L39 ... 13 E4
Station App. Hoylake L47 ... 63 E8
Station App. Ormskirk L39 ... 13 F5
Station App. Wallasey L46 ... 49 E2
Station Ave. WN5 ... 25 D5
Station Mews. L32 ... 29 C3
Station Rd. Banks PR9 ... 2 F5
Station Rd. Garswood WN4 . 34 C3
Station Rd. Haskayne L39 ... 11 E7
Station Rd. Haydock WA11 .. 45 C6
Station Rd. Heswall L61 ... 77 E5
Station Rd. Heswall L60 ... 85 F6
Station Rd. Hoylake L47 ... 63 B6
Station Rd. Huyton-w-R L36 . 55 C2
Station Rd. L31 ... 29 B3
Station Rd. Liverpool L25 ... 70 B5
Station Rd. Maghull L31 ... 20 A6
Station Rd. Maghull L31 ... 28 E8
Station Rd. Ormskirk L39 ... 13 F6
Station Rd. Prescot L34 & L35 ... 56 D5
Station Rd. Rainhill L35 ... 57 C3
Station Rd. Runcorn WA7 ... 84 F2
Station Rd. Southport PR8 ... 7 C5
Station Rd. St Helens WA9 .. 58 E7
Station Rd. Wallasey L41 ... 50 F1
Station Rd. Wallasey L44 ... 51 A4
Station Rd. Warrington WA5 74 E3
Station Rd. Warrington WA5 74 F6
Station Rd. West Kirby L61 .. 75 F4
Station St. L35 ... 57 C3
Statton Rd. L13 ... 54 B1
Staveley Rd. Liverpool L19 ... 81 B8
Staveley Rd. Skelmersdale WN8 ... 15 E3
Staveley Rd. Southport PR8 ... 7 D4
Stavert Cl. L11 ... 40 B3
Staverton Rd. L32 ... 29 C1
Stavordale Rd. L46 ... 65 A8
Steble St. L8 ... 67 F5
Steel Ave. L45 ... 51 C6
Steel Ct. L5 ... 52 C6
Steeple The. L48 ... 75 D6
Steeple View. L33 ... 29 E5
Steeplechase Cl. L9 ... 39 C8
Steers Croft. L28 ... 55 A8
Stein Ave. WA3 ... 47 E8
Steinberg Ct. L3 ... 52 C4
Stella Prec. L21 ... 38 A6
Stephen Way. L35 ... 57 B5
Stephens La. 10 L2 ... 52 C2
Stephenson Ct. 11 L7 ... 53 C1
Stephenson Rd. Liverpool L13 ... 54 A2
Stephenson Rd. Newton-le-W WA12 ... 46 D2
Stephenson St. WN2 ... 36 B8
Stephenson Way. Formby L37 ... 10 C3
Stephenson Way. Liverpool L15 ... 53 E1
Stepney Gr. 1 L4 ... 39 A1
Sterling Way. L5 ... 52 D6
Sterrix Ave. L21 & L30 ... 27 C2
Sterrix Gn. L21 ... 27 C2
Sterrix La. L21 & L30 ... 27 C2
Steve Biko Cl. 2 L8 ... 68 B7
Stevenage Cl. WA9 ... 57 F7
Stevens Rd. L60 ... 86 C7
Stevens St. L35 & WA9 ... 57 D8
Stevenson Cres. WA10 ... 43 D4
Stevenson Dr. L63 ... 78 F3
Stevenson St. L15 ... 68 F8
Steward Ct. L35 ... 56 F5
Steward's Ave. WA8 ... 84 F8
Stewart Ave. L20 ... 38 E4
Stewart Cl. L61 ... 76 F3
Stewerton Cl. WA3 ... 35 E2
Stile Hey. L23 ... 27 B5
Stiles Rd. L33 ... 29 F6
Stiles The. L39 ... 13 E5
Stirling Ave. L23 ... 26 E3
Stirling Cres. WA9 ... 58 C6
Stirling Ct. PR9 ... 2 A2
Stirling Dr. WN4 ... 34 D4
Stirling Rd. L24 ... 82 B3
Stirling St. L44 ... 51 B2
Stockbridge La. L28 & L36 ... 55 C5
Stockbridge Pl. 6 L5 ... 53 A5
Stockbridge Prim Sch. L14 . 55 C6
Stockbridge St. L5 ... 53 A5
Stockdale Cl. 2 L3 ... 52 C3
Stockley Cres. L39 ... 22 E6
Stockmoor Rd. L11 ... 39 F3
Stockpit Rd. L33 ... 30 D2
Stocks Ave. WA9 ... 44 E3
Stocks La. WA5 ... 74 D5
Stockswell Rd. L35 & WA8 ... 71 F4
Stockton Gr. L35 ... 57 D6
Stockton Wood Inf Sch. L24 82 C3
Stockton Wood Jun Sch. L24 ... 82 C3
Stockton Wood Rd. L24 ... 82 C3
Stockville Rd. L18 & L25 ... 69 E4
Stoddart Rd. 2 L4 ... 39 A2
Stoke Cl. L62 ... 88 E3
Stoke St. L41 ... 66 C8
Stokesay. L43 ... 65 D6
Stokesley Ave. L32 ... 29 C2
Stone Cross La. WA3 ... 47 C7
Stone Hall La. WN8 ... 16 F4
Stone Hay. L35 ... 56 D1
Stone Pit Cl. WA3 ... 36 F1
Stone Pit La. WA3 ... 47 F2
Stone Sq. L20 ... 38 E6
Stone St. L3 ... 52 B4
Stonebarn Dr. L31 ... 20 C3
Stonebridge La. L10 & L11 .. 40 B6
Stoneby Dr. L45 ... 51 A7
Stonechat Cl. L27 ... 70 E4
Stonecrop. L18 ... 69 E5
Stonecross Dr. L35 ... 57 D1
Stonedale Cres. L11 ... 40 B4
Stonefield Rd. L14 ... 55 A4
Stonehaven Cl. L16 ... 69 F8
Stonehey Dr. L48 ... 75 C8
Stonehey Rd. L32 ... 40 E8
Stonehey Wlk. L32 ... 40 E8
Stonehill Ave. Bebington L63 79 A6
Stonehill Ave. 3 Liverpool L4 ... 53 B6
Stonehill St. L4 ... 53 B6
Stonehouse Mews. L18 ... 69 D3
Stonehouse Rd. L45 ... 50 E5
Stoneleigh Cl. PR8 ... 7 C4
Stoneleigh Gr. L42 ... 78 F8
Stoneridge Ct. L43 ... 65 C8
Stoneville Rd. L13 ... 54 A4
Stoney Hey Rd. L45 ... 51 A7
Stoney La. L35 ... 57 A3
Stoney View. L35 ... 57 B3
Stoneycroft. L12 & L13 ... 54 B4
Stoneycroft Cl. L13 ... 54 A5
Stoneycroft Cres. L13 ... 54 A5
Stoneyhurst Ave. L10 ... 28 C3
Stonham Cl. L49 ... 64 E5
Stonyfield. L30 ... 27 E5
Stonyhurst Cl. WA11 ... 44 B7
Stonyhurst Rd. L25 ... 70 B1
Stopford St. L8 ... 67 F4
Stopgate La. L33 ... 30 C7
Stopgate La. Liverpool L11 & L68 & L9 ... 39 D3
Store St. L20 ... 38 D1
Storeton Cl. L43 ... 66 B3
Storeton La. L61 ... 77 C4
Storeton Rd. L42 & L43 ... 66 B2
Stormont Rd. L19 ... 81 B6
Storrington Ave. L11 ... 40 B3
Storrington Heys. L11 ... 40 B3
Storrsdale Rd. L18 ... 69 B3
Stour Ave. L35 ... 57 C3
Stourcliffe Rd. L44 ... 51 A4
Stourport Cl. 1 L49 ... 64 C4
Stourton Rd. Kirkby L32 ... 40 F8
Stourton Rd. Southport PR8 .. 7 C4
Stourton St. L44 ... 51 C2
Stourvale Rd. L26 ... 82 F7
Stowe Ave. L10 ... 28 E2
Stowe Cl. L25 ... 82 B7
Stowell St. L7 ... 67 F8
Stowford Cl. L11 ... 40 C2
Strada Way. L3 ... 52 F3
Strafford Dr. L20 ... 38 E4
Straight Up La. PR9 ... 5 D8

Strand Ave. WN4 35 B4
Strand House. 7 L20 38 C3
Strand Rd. L20 38 B3
Strand Rd. L20 38 C4
Strand Rd. Hoylake L47 63 B7
Strand St. L1 & L3 52 C1
Strand The. Ashton-in-M WN4 35 B4
Strand The. Liverpool L2 & L3 52 C1
Strange Rd. WN4 34 D3
Stratford Cl. PR8 7 A6
Stratford Rd. L19 80 F8
Strathallan Cl. L60 76 E2
Strathcona Rd. Liverpool L15 68 E8
Strathcona Rd. Wallasey L45 51 C6
Strathcona St. L15 68 E7
Strathearn Rd. L60 85 F7
Strathmore Ave. WN4 35 A5
Strathmore Dr. L23 26 E3
Strathmore Gr. WA9 58 C6
Strathmore Rd. L6 53 C4
Stratton Cl. L25 69 E3
Stratton Rd. L32 29 C1
Stratton Wlk. 2 L32 29 C1
Strauss Cl. L8 68 B6
Strawberry Rd. L11 39 E2
Streatham Ave. L18 68 F5
Streatham House Sch. L23 26 D4
Street Hey La. L64 88 B1
Stretton Ave. Billinge WN5 33 E5
Stretton Ave. Golborne WA3 47 E7
Stretton Ave. St Helens WA9 44 F3
Stretton Ave. Wallasey L44 51 A4
Stretton Cl. Bebington L62 88 E3
Stretton Cl. Birkenhead L43 65 E3
Stretton Cl. Liverpool L12 41 A3
Stretton Dr. PR9 4 F8
Stretton Way. L35 & L36 71 C8
Strickland St. WA10 & WA9 44 B4
Stringhey Rd. L44 & L45 51 C5
Stroma Rd. L18 69 B1
Stroud Cl. L49 64 C3
Stuart Ave. Liverpool L25 82 C7
Stuart Ave. Wallasey L46 49 F1
Stuart Cl. L46 65 A8
Stuart Cres. WN5 33 E5
Stuart Dr. L14 54 E3
Stuart Gr. L20 38 D1
Stuart Rd. Birkenhead L42 66 D3
Stuart Rd. L20 & L4 38 E3
Stuart Rd. Crosby L22 & L23 26 F2
Stuart Rd. L31 29 B3
Stuart Rd. St Helens WA10 43 C6
Stubshaw Cross CE Prim Sch. WN4 35 E5
Studholme St. L20 52 C7
Studland Rd. L9 39 E4
Studley Rd. L45 50 F6
Sturdee Rd. L13 & L15 54 B1
Sturgess Cl. L39 13 F7
Sturgess St. WA12 45 F3
Suburban Rd. 6 L6 53 C6
Sudbrook Cl. WA3 47 E8
Sudbury Cl. L25 70 D2
Sudbury Rd. L22 26 B2
Sudbury Way. L24 82 B4
Sudell Ave. L31 20 F2
Sudell La. L31 & L39 20 E6
Sudley (Art Gal, Liby & Mus). L18 68 F2
Sudley Grange. L17 68 F1
Sudley Inf Sch. L17 68 E2
Sudley Jun Sch. L17 68 E1
Sudworth Rd. L45 51 A7
Suez St. WA12 46 B3
Suffield Rd. L4 52 D8
Suffolk Pl. WA8 84 C7
Suffolk Rd. PR8 8 A8
Suffolk St. L20 38 D4
Suffolk St. Liverpool L1 & L69 & L72 67 D8
Suffolk St. Runcorn WA7 84 F3
Suffton Pk. L32 29 C1
Sugar La. L34 41 D3
Sugar St. L9 39 B5
Sugnall St. 8 L7 67 F8
Sulby Ave. L13 53 E5
Sulby Cl. PR8 3 F3
Sulgrave Cl. L16 54 C1
Sullivan Ave. L49 64 F4
Sumley Cl. WA11 44 D5
Summer Cl. L5 52 C5
Summer Seat. L3 52 D4
Summer St. WN8 16 A4
Summerfield. L62 79 D2
Summerfield Ave. St Helens WA10 42 F3
Summerfield Ave. Warrington WA5 60 F2
Summerhill Dr. L31 28 F7
Summerhill Prim Sch. L31 28 F8
Summers Ave. L20 38 E4
Summers Rd. L3 67 D4
Summerseat. L20 38 A3
Summertrees Ave. L49 64 D4
Summertrees Cl. L49 64 D4
Summerwood. L61 76 D7
Summerwood La. L39 12 D8
Summit The. L44 51 C5
Summit Way. L25 69 F3
Sumner Ave. L39 11 F4
Sumner Cl. L35 57 D1
Sumner Gr. L33 29 F5
Sumner Rd. Birkenhead L41 & L43 65 F8
Sumner Rd. Formby L37 9 F3
Sumner St. WA11 45 A6
Sunbeam Rd. L13 54 B3
Sunbeam St. WA12 46 C3
Sunbourne Rd. L17 68 B2
Sunbury Dr. PR8 7 B4
Sunbury Rd. Liverpool L4 53 B7
Sunbury Rd. Wallasey L44 51 C3
Sunbury St. WA10 57 C8
Suncroft Rd. L60 86 C7
Sundale Ave. L35 56 F6
Sundew Cl. L9 38 F7
Sundridge St. 10 L8 68 A4
Sunfield Rd. L46 49 F2
Sunlight St. L6 53 C5
Sunloch Cl. L9 39 D8
Sunningdale. L46 65 A8
Sunningdale Ave. WA8 72 B1
Sunningdale Cl. Burtonwood WA5 59 F6
Sunningdale Cl. Huyton-w-R L36 55 C1
Sunningdale Dr. Bebington L63 88 B6
Sunningdale Dr. Crosby L23 26 C6
Sunningdale Dr. Heswall L61 77 A5
Sunningdale Rd. Liverpool L15 68 F8
Sunningdale Rd. Wallasey L45 50 F8
Sunny Bank. Bebington L63 78 D6
Sunny Bank. Birkenhead L49 64 F6
Sunny Bank Cotts. WA8 74 A4
Sunny Bank Rd. L16 69 D7
Sunny Dr. WN5 25 F6
Sunny Rd. PR9 2 A2
Sunnybank Ave. L43 65 D4
Sunnybank Cl. WA12 46 C4
Sunnyfields. L39 14 A5
Sunnygate Rd. L19 81 B8
Sunnymede Dr. L31 20 D3
Sunnymede Sch. PR8 3 F6
Sunnyside. Liverpool L8 68 B5
Sunnyside. Ormskirk L39 21 C7
Sunnyside. Southport PR8 3 F3
Sunnyside. Wallasey L46 49 D2
Sunnyside. Warrington WA5 74 E6
Sunnyside Rd. Ashton-in-M WN4 34 F7
Sunnyside Rd. Crosby L22, L23 26 D3
Sunsdale Rd. 6 L18 69 A5
Surby Cl. L16 69 E8
Surrey Ave. L49 64 E5
Surrey Cl. PR9 2 C5
Surrey Dr. L48 75 C8
Surrey St. L20 38 D4
Surrey St. St Helens WA9 44 D3
Surrey St. Wallasey L44 51 A3
Susan Dr. WA5 74 D5
Susan Gr. L46 64 D8
Susan St. WA8 73 C2
Sussex Cl. L20 38 D4
Sussex Cl. Heswall L61 76 E4
Sussex Gr. WA9 44 C2
Sussex Rd. Maghull L31 28 D7
Sussex Rd. Southport PR8 & PR9 4 D6
Sussex Rd. West Kirby L48 63 C3
Sussex St. L20 38 D4
Sussex St. Crosby L22 26 C2
Sussex St. Widnes WA8 73 D1
Sutcliffe St. L6 53 B3
Sutherland Dr. L62 88 D4
Sutherland Rd. L34 & L35 56 E6
Sutton Cl. L62 88 E3
Sutton Comm High Sch. WA9 58 B6
Sutton Comm L Ctr. WA9 58 B6
Sutton Heath Rd. St Helens WA9 57 F7
Sutton Heath Rd. St Helens WA9 57 F8
Sutton Manor Comm Sch. WA9 58 A2
Sutton Moss Rd. St Helens WA9 58 F8
Sutton Oak CE Prim Sch. WA9 58 E8
Sutton Oak Dr. WA9 44 D1
Sutton Park Dr. WA9 58 C7
Sutton Rd. Formby L37 9 E1
Sutton Rd. St Helens WA9 44 D1
Sutton Rd. Wallasey L45 51 B7
Sutton St. L13 53 E5
Sutton Wood Rd. L24 82 C3
Sutton's La. L37 10 E3
Swainson Rd. L10 39 F7
Swale Ave. L35 57 C3
Swaledale Ave. L35 57 D3
Swaledale Cl. Bebington L62 88 E5
Swaledale Cl. Warrington WA5 74 F7
Swalegate. L31 20 C2
Swallow Cl. L33 29 E7
Swallow Cl. Liverpool L12 40 F3
Swallow Cl. Liverpool L27 70 F5
Swallow Fields. L9 39 F4
Swallowhurst Cres. L11 40 A2
Swan Alley. L39 13 E5
Swan Ave. WA9 45 A2
Swan Cres. L15 69 B8
Swan Ct. L43 65 F2
Swan Delph. L39 13 C2
Swan Hey. L31 28 E7
Swan La. L39 20 F6
Swan Rd. WA12 45 E4
Swan St. L13 53 F3
Swan Wlk. L31 28 E7
Swanpool La. L39 13 C2
Swanside Ave. L14 54 E3
Swanside Rd. L14 54 E3
Swanston Ave. 8 L4 39 A1
Sweden Gr. L22 26 D1
Sweeting St. L2 52 C1
Swift Cl. WA2 61 E3
Swift Gr. L12 40 F4
Swift St. WA10 44 A5
Swift's Cl. L30 27 D4
Swift's La. Litherland L30 27 D4
Swifts La. Litherland L30 27 E3
Swinbrook Gn. L11 39 F3
Swinburn Gr. WN5 25 D1
Swinburne Cl. L16 69 F8
Swinburne Rd. WA10 43 D5
Swindale Ave. WA2 61 B3
Swindale Cl. L8 68 B7
Swindon Cl. Birkenhead L49 64 C4
Swindon Cl. Liverpool L5 52 D7
Swindon St. Liverpool L5 52 D7
Swindon St. Liverpool L8 67 F7
Swinford Ave. WA8 73 E2
Swiss Rd. L6 53 C3
Swisspine Gdns. L35 57 C7
Sword Cl. 4 L11 40 C3
Sword Wlk. L11 40 C3
Swynnerton Way. WA8 73 B5
Sybil Rd. L4 53 A7
Sycamore Ave. Birkenhead L49 64 D6
Sycamore Ave. Crosby L23 26 F6
Sycamore Ave. Golborne WA3 36 A1
Sycamore Ave. Haydock WA11 45 A5
Sycamore Ave. Liverpool L26 82 F6
Sycamore Ave. Newton-le-W WA12 46 C3
Sycamore Ave. Widnes WA8 73 B2
Sycamore Cl. Birkenhead L49 64 D7
Sycamore Cl. Liverpool L9 39 C3
Sycamore Cl. St Helens WA10 43 B4
Sycamore Dr. WN8 15 E2
Sycamore Gdns. WA10 43 E6
Sycamore Gr. L37 9 C1
Sycamore Pk. L18 69 D2
Sycamore Rd. Birkenhead L42 66 D4
Sycamore Rd. Crosby L22 26 E2
Sycamore Rd. Liverpool L36 70 E8
Sycamore Rise. L49 64 C2
Sydenham Ave. L17 & L8 68 C6
Sydenham House. L17 68 C5
Syders Gr. L34 41 C3
Sydney St. L9 39 A6
Sylvan Ct. L25 70 B1
Sylvandale Gr. L62 79 D2
Sylvania Rd. L4 39 A2
Sylvester Prim Sch The. L36 55 F1
Sylvia Cl. L10 40 B6
Sylvia Cres. WA2 61 D1
Syren St. L20 52 C8
Syston Ave. WA11 44 C6
Tabby's Nook. WN8 16 A8
Tabley Ave. WA8 72 D2
Tabley Cl. L43 65 F2
Tabley Rd. L15 68 D7
Tabley St. L1 & L72 67 D8
Tadlow Cl. L37 9 C1
Taggart Ave. L16 69 D6
Tagus Cl. L8 68 B6
Tagus St. L8 68 B7
Tailor's La. L31 28 E8
Talaton Cl. PR9 2 A5
Talbot Ave. L63 78 A1
Talbot Cl. WA10 43 F4
Talbot Ct. Birkenhead L43 66 A4
Talbot Ct. Huyton-w-R L36 55 E1
Talbot Dr. PR8 4 B6
Talbot Rd. L43 66 A4
Talbot St. Ashton-in-M WN4 35 D4
Talbot St. Golborne WA3 47 A8
Talbot St. Southport PR8 4 A6
Talbotville Rd. L13 54 C1
Talgarth Way. L25 70 A7
Taliesin St. L5 52 D5
Talisman Way. L20 38 A4
Talland Cl. L26 70 E1
Tallarn Rd. L32 29 B2
Talton Rd. L15 68 D7
Tamar Rd. WA11 45 C6
Tamarisk Gdns. L35 57 C7
Tamneys The. WN8 15 F1
Tamworth St. Liverpool L8 67 E5
Tamworth St. Newton-le-W WA12 46 A3
Tamworth St. St Helens WA10 43 E4
Tan House La. WA5 60 A5
Tanar Cl. L62 79 B3
Tanat Dr. L18 69 B4
Tancred Rd. Liverpool L4 53 A7
Tancred Rd. Wallasey L45 51 A5
Tanfields. WN8 15 F1
Tanhouse Rd. Crosby L23 27 B5
Tanhouse Rd. Skelmersdale WN8 16 D1
Tanhouse Rd. Skelmersdale WN8 24 C8
Tanhouse Rd. Skelmersdale WN8 24 E7
Tanner's La. WA3 47 B8
Tannery La. WA5 74 D3
Tansley Cl. L48 63 E2
Tanworth Gr. L46 49 B1
Tapley Pl. L13 53 F2
Taplow St. 5 L6 53 B6
Tarbock Rd. Huyton-w-R L36 55 E1
Tarbock Rd. Liverpool L36 70 F8
Tarbock Rd. Liverpool L24 82 D4
Tarbot Hey. L46 64 C8
Tarbrock Ct. L30 27 D5
Target Rd. L60 85 C8
Tariff St. L5 52 D5
Tarleswood. WN8 15 F1
Tarleton Cl. L26 82 E8
Tarleton Rd. PR9 5 A8
Tarleton St. L1 52 D1
Tarlton Cl. L35 57 B5
Tarn Brow. L39 13 C3
Tarn Cl. Ashton-in-M WN4 35 B5
Tarn Cl. Liverpool L25 & L27 70 D6
Tarn Gr. WA11 44 B8
Tarn Rd. L37 9 D3
Tarncliff. L28 55 C8
Tarnside Rd. WN5 25 E6
Tarnway. WA3 47 F7
Tarporley Cl. L43 65 F3
Tarran Dr. L46 49 D2
Tarran Rd. L46 49 D2
Tarran Way E. L46 49 D2
Tarran Way N. L46 49 D3
Tarran Way S. L46 49 D2
Tarran Way W. L46 49 D2
Tarves Wlk. 4 L33 29 F2
Tarvin Cl. Golborne WA3 47 E7
Tarvin Cl. Southport PR9 2 D5
Tarvin Cl. St Helens WA9 58 B3
Tarvin Rd. L62 88 F3
Tasker Terr. L35 57 C4
Tasman Gr. WA9 57 E7
Tate Cl. WA8 72 D2
Tate Gallery. L3 67 B8
Tate St. L4 52 F8
Tatlock Cl. WN5 33 E5
Tatlock St. L5 52 C4
Tattersall Rd. L21 38 B7
Tatton Dr. WN4 34 F4
Tatton Rd. Birkenhead L41 & L42 66 D5
Tatton Rd. Liverpool L9 39 A6
Taunton Ave. WA9 58 D5
Taunton Dr. L10 28 F2
Taunton Rd. Huyton-w-R L36 56 B2
Taunton Rd. Wallasey L45 50 E6
Taunton St. L15 68 E8
Taurus Rd. L14 55 A4
Tavener Cl. L63 88 C5
Tavistock Dr. PR8 7 B6
Tavistock Rd. Wallasey L45 50 E6
Tavistock Rd. Warrington WA5 74 E4
Tavistock Wlk. L8 67 F4
Tavlin Ave. WA5 60 F1
Tawd Rd. WN8 24 C8
Tawd St. L4 52 E8
Taylor Ave. L39 14 A5
Taylor Cl. WA9 58 E8
Taylor Rd. WA11 45 F7
Taylor St. B,head L41,L72 66 E7
Taylor St. Golborne WN3 36 C1
Taylor St. Liverpool L5 52 D5
Taylor St. Skelmersdale WN8 15 C1
Taylor St. St Helens WA9 58 E8
Taylor St. Widnes WA8 73 C1
Taylor Street Ind Est. L5 52 D5
Taylor's La. Widnes WA5 74 A2
Taylors Cl. L4 38 E3
Taylors La. L4 & L9 38 F3
Teal Cl. Ormskirk L39 13 C2
Teal Cl. St Helens WA11 44 B6
Teal Cl. Warrington WA2 61 E3
Teal Gr. L26 70 E1
Teals Way. L60 85 E8
Tears La. WN8 15 F8
Teasville Rd. L18 69 E4
Tebay Cl. L31 20 F2
Tebay Rd. L62 88 E8
Technical & Nautical Catering Coll. L8 67 E8
Teck St. L7 53 A2
Tedburn Cl. L25 & L27 70 C4
Tedbury Cl. L32 40 E8
Tedbury Wlk. L32 40 E8
Tedder Ave. PR9 5 A7
Tedder Sq. WA8 84 D8
Teehey Cl. L63 78 D6
Teehey Gdns. L63 78 D6
Teehey La. L63 78 D6
Tees Cl. L4 38 D1
Tees Pl. L4 38 D1
Tees St. L4 38 E1
Tees St. Wallasey L41 50 F1
Teesdale Cl. WA5 74 F7
Teesdale Rd. Bebington L63 78 E4
Teesdale Rd. Haydock WA11 45 C7
Teilo St. L8 68 A5
Telegraph Rd. Heswall L60 86 A7
Telegraph Rd. Irby L48, L60,L61 76 C4
Telegraph Rd. West Kirby L48 75 F7
Telegraph Way. L32 29 E2
Telford Cl. Birkenhead L43 66 B4
Telford Cl. Widnes WA8 72 D4
Tempest Hey. 8 L2 52 C2
Temple Ct. L2 52 C1
Temple La. L2 52 C1
Temple Rd. L42 66 C2
Temple St. L2 52 C2
Templemartin. WN8 15 F2
Templemore Ave. L18 69 A3
Templemore Rd. L43 66 A4
Tenbury Dr. WN4 35 A4
Tenby. WN8 15 E2
Tenby Ave. L21 27 A1
Tenby Cl. WA5 60 F2
Tenby Dr. L46 64 F8
Tenby St. 4 L5 53 A6
Tennis St. WA10 43 E5
Tennis St N. WA10 43 E5
Tennyson Ave. 3 L42 66 F1
Tennyson Dr. Ormskirk L39 13 D6
Tennyson Dr. Orrell WN5 25 D1
Tennyson Dr. Warrington WA2 61 C2
Tennyson House. L62 79 A7
Tennyson Rd. Huyton-w-R L36 71 A8
Tennyson Rd. Widnes WA8 73 A1
Tennyson St. L20 38 B5
Tennyson St. St Helens WA9 58 B2
Tennyson Wlk. 1 L8 67 F6
Tensing Rd. L31 20 D1
Tenterden St. L5 52 D4
Terence Rd. L16 69 D6
Terminus Rd. Bebington L62 79 D3

Terminus Rd. Huyton-w-R L36 55 C5
Tern Cl. L33 29 E7
Tern Cl. Widnes WA8 73 B4
Tern Way. St Helens L34 & WA10 57 A7
Tern Way. Wallasey L46 49 B1
Ternhall Rd. L10 & L9 39 F4
Ternhall Way. L11 & L9 39 F4
Terret Croft. L28 55 B7
Tetbury St. L41 66 C5
Tetlow St. L4 52 F8
Tetlow Way. L4 52 F8
Teulon Cl. 1 L4 52 F7
Teversham. WN8 15 F2
Tevlot. WN8 15 E2
Tewit Hall Cl. L24 82 C3
Tewit Hall Rd. L24 82 C3
Tewkesbury. WN8 15 E2
Tewkesbury Cl. Liverpool L12 40 F4
Tewkesbury Cl. Liverpool L25 70 D2
Tewkesbury Rd. WA3 47 B8
Teynham Ave. L34 41 D4
Teynham Cres. L11 39 F2
Thackeray Gdns. L30 38 D8
Thackeray Pl. 2 L8 67 F6
Thackeray Sq. L8 67 F6
Thackeray St. L8 67 F6
Thackray Rd. WA10 57 D8
Thames Cl. WA2 61 D2
Thames Dr. WN5 25 F7
Thames Rd. WA9 58 C6
Thames St. L8 68 B6
Thanet. WN8 15 F2
Thatto Heath Comm Prim Sch. WA9 57 E8
Thatto Heath Rd. WA10 & WA9 57 D8
Thatto Heath Sta. WA9 57 D8
Thealby Cl. WN8 15 E2
Thermal Rd. L62 79 E4
Thetford Rd. WA5 74 E6
Thickwood Moss La. WA11 32 A5
Thingwall Ave. L14 54 D3
Thingwall Dr. L49 & L61 77 A6
Thingwall Hall Dr. L14 54 D2
Thingwall La. L14 54 E3
Thingwall Prim Sch. L61 77 A6
Thingwall Rd. Heswall L61 76 E6
Thingwall Rd. Liverpool L15 69 B8
Thingwall Rd E. L61 77 B7
Third Ave. Birkenhead L43 65 B6
Third Ave. Crosby L23 26 D4
Third Ave. Liverpool L9 39 D7
Thirlmere Ave. Abram WN2 36 B8
Thirlmere Ave. Ashton-in-M WN4 35 C4
Thirlmere Ave. Birkenhead L43 65 C5
Thirlmere Ave. L21 38 D8
Thirlmere Ave. Formby L37 10 A2
Thirlmere Ave. Orrell WN8 25 B7
Thirlmere Ave. Orrell WN5 25 F7
Thirlmere Ave. St Helens WA11 44 B8
Thirlmere Ave. Warrington WA2 61 C3
Thirlmere Cl. L31 20 E2
Thirlmere Dr. L21 38 D8
Thirlmere Dr. Southport PR8 7 B3
Thirlmere Dr. Wallasey L45 51 B5
Thirlmere Gn. L5 53 A5
Thirlmere Rd. Golborne WA3 36 C1
Thirlmere Rd. Hightown L38 18 A4
Thirlmere Rd. Liverpool L4 & L5 53 A5
Thirlmere Way. WA8 84 C8
Thirlmere Wlk. L33 29 D4
Thirlstane St. L17 68 B3
Thirsk. WN8 15 E2
Thistledown Cl. 3 L8 68 A3
Thistleton Ave. L41 & L43 65 F8
Thistlewood Rd. L7 53 E2
Thistley Hey Rd. L32 29 F2
Thomas Dr. Liverpool L13 & L14 54 C2
Thomas Dr. Prescot L35 56 C4
Thomas Gray Inf Sch. L20 38 B4
Thomas Gray Jun Sch. L20 38 B5
Thomas La. L14 54 D2
Thomas St. Birkenhead L41 66 E5
Thomas St. 7 Birkenhead L41 66 E6
Thomas St. Golborne WA3 47 A8
Thomas Winder Ct. L5 52 D6
Thomaston St. L5 52 E6
Thompson Ave. L39 14 B5
Thompson Cl. WA12 46 B1
Thompson St. Ashton-in-M WN4 35 D4
Thompson St. Birkenhead L41 & L42 66 E4
Thompson St. St Helens WA10 43 D1
Thomson Rd. L21 38 A7
Thomson St. L6 53 B4
Thorburn Cl. L62 79 B8
Thorburn Cres. L62 79 B8
Thorburn Ct. L8 67 C1
Thorburn Lodge. L8 67 C1
Thorburn Rd. L62 79 B8
Thorburn St. L7 53 B1
Thorley Cl. L15 54 A1
Thorn Cl. WA5 74 F3
Thorn Rd. WA10 43 C3
Thorn Tree Cl. L24 83 E2
Thornaby Gr. L35 57 D6
Thornbeck Ave. L38 17 F3
Thornbeck Ct. 3 L12 40 F3
Thornber. WN8 15 F2
Thornbridge Ave. L21 38 D8
Thornbury. WN8 15 F2
Thornbury Ave. WA3 47 E7
Thornbury Rd. L4 53 C7
Thornbush Cl. WA3 36 E1
Thornby. WN8 15 F2
Thorncliffe Rd. L44 51 A3
Thorncroft Dr. L61 77 B4
Thorndale. WN8 15 F2
Thorndale Rd. L22 26 D2
Thorndyke Cl. L35 57 E1
Thornes Rd. 11 L6 & L7 53 B3
Thorness Cl. L49 64 C2
Thorneycroft St. L41 66 A8
Thornfield Cl. WA3 47 C8
Thornfield Hey. L63 79 A2
Thornfield Rd. L9 38 F5
Thornfield Rd. Crosby L23 27 A6
Thornham Ave. WA9 58 C8
Thornham Cl. L49 65 A7
Thornhead La. L12 54 D6
Thornhill. L39 21 B8
Thornhill Cl. L39 21 B8
Thornhill Rd. Garswood WN4 34 C4
Thornhill Rd. Liverpool L15 69 A7
Thornholme Cres. L11 40 A1
Thornhurst. L32 40 E7
Thornleigh Ave. L62 88 F3
Thornley Rd. L46 64 C7
Thorns Dr. L49 64 C2
Thorns The. L31 20 B2
Thornside Wlk. L25 70 B4
Thornton. Skelmersdale WN8 15 F2
Thornton. Widnes WA8 84 E8
Thornton Ave. Bebington L63 78 D8
Thornton Ave. L20 38 D7
Thornton Cl. WN4 34 F4
Thornton Common Rd. L63 87 D7
Thornton Cres. L60 86 B6
Thornton Gr. L63 78 D8
Thornton Hough Prim Sch. L63 87 B7
Thornton House. L63 87 B6
Thornton Pl. L8 67 F4
Thornton Prim Sch. L23 27 B6
Thornton Rd. Bebington L42 78 D8
Thornton Rd. L20 38 C5
Thornton Rd. Liverpool L16 54 F1
Thornton Rd. Southport PR9 4 F7
Thornton Rd. 4 Wallasey L45 51 A6
Thornton St. Birkenhead L41 66 A8
Thornton St. L21 38 B6
Thorntree Cl. L8 68 A3
Thornvale. WN2 36 C7
Thornwood. WN8 15 F2
Thornycroft Rd. L15 68 D7
Thorpe. WN8 15 F2
Thorpe Bank. L63 78 F8
Thorridge. L46 65 A8
Thorstone Dr. L61 76 C7
Thorsway. Birkenhead L42 66 F2
Thorsway. West Kirby L48 75 D8
Three But La. L12 & L13 54 A7
Three Lanes End. L48 64 B5
Three Pools. PR9 2 C3
Three Sisters Rd. WN4 35 B7
Three Sisters Recn Area. WN4 35 C7
Three Tuns La. L37 9 F3
Threlfall St. L8 68 A4
Threlfall's La. PR9 1 F2
Threlfalls Cl. PR9 1 F3
Thresher Ave. 4 L49 64 C4
Threshers The. L30 28 A4
Throne Rd. L11 40 C3
Throne Wlk. 3 L11 40 C4
Thurcroft Dr. WN8 15 E2
Thurlby Cl. WN4 35 D4
Thurlow. WA3 47 E7
Thurne Way. L25 70 A6
Thurnham St. L6 53 C5
Thursby Cl. 2 Kirkby L32 40 F8
Thursby Cl. Southport PR8 7 B3
Thursby Cres. 1 L32 40 F8
Thursby Rd. L62 79 E2
Thursby Wlk. 3 L32 40 F8
Thurstaston Rd. Heswall L60 85 F8
Thurstaston Rd. Irby L61 76 C6
Thurston. WN8 15 E2
Thurston Rd. L4 53 B6
Tibbs Cross La. WA8 73 D8
Tiber Street CP Jun Sch. L8 68 B6
Tichbourne Way. 2 L6 52 F3
Tickle Ave. WA9 44 E3
Tide Way. L45 50 E8
Tilbrook Dr. WA9 58 D6
Tilcroft. WN8 15 E2
Tillotson Cl. L8 67 E5
Tilney St. L9 39 A6
Tilstock Ave. L62 79 B8
Tilstock Cres. L43 65 F2
Tilston Cl. L9 39 D3
Tilston Rd. L32 29 C2
Tilston Rd. Liverpool L9 39 D4
Tilston Rd. 6 Wallasey L45 51 A6
Timmis Cres. WA8 73 A1
Timms Cl. L37 9 F5
Timms La. L37 9 F5
Timon Ave. L20 38 E5
Timor Ave. WA9 57 E8
Timpron St. L7 68 C8
Timway Dr. L12 54 E8
Tinas Way. L49 65 A5
Tinkersley Way. L7 53 B1
Tinsley Ave. PR8 4 E3
Tinsley St. 4 L4 53 A7
Tinsley's La. PR8 5 A1
Tintagel. WN8 15 E2
Tintagel Rd. L11 40 D5
Tintern Ave. WN4 35 D3
Tintern Cl. WA5 60 E2
Tintern Dr. Birkenhead L46 64 E8
Tintern Dr. Formby L37 10 B2
Tiptree Cl. L12 40 F4
Titchfield St. L3 & L5 52 D4
Tithe Barn La. L32 29 D1
Tithe Barn Rd. WN4 34 C2
Tithebarn Cl. L60 85 F7
Tithebarn Dr. L64 86 B2
Tithebarn Gr. L15 69 A7
Tithebarn La. L31 29 A5
Tithebarn Rd. Crosby L23 26 F4
Tithebarn Rd. Garswood WN4 34 D2
Tithebarn Rd. Knowsley L34 41 D4
Tithebarn Rd. Southport PR8 & PR9 4 E6
Tithebarn St. Liverpool L2 & L3 52 C2
Tithebarn St. Orrell WN8 25 B7
Tiverton Ave. Skelmersdale WN8 15 E2
Tiverton Ave. Wallasey L44 51 B4
Tiverton Cl. Huyton-w-R L36 56 B3
Tiverton Cl. Widnes WA8 72 C3
Tiverton Rd. L26 82 E6
Tiverton Sq. WA5 74 E4
Tiverton St. L15 68 E8
Tivoli Villa's. L45 37 C1
Tobermory Cl. WA11 45 A5
Tobin Cl. L3 52 C4
Tobin St. L44 51 D4
Tobruk Rd. L36 55 D4
Todd Rd. WA9 44 B3
Toft St. L7 53 C2
Toftwood Ave. L35 57 D1
Toftwood Gdns. L35 57 D1
Toleman Ave. L42 79 A5
Toll Bar Cnr. L62 79 B7
Toll Bar Rd. WA2 61 A3
Tollemache Rd. L41 & L43 65 E7
Tollemache St. L45 37 C1
Tollerton Rd. L12 54 A7
Tolpuddle Rd. L25 69 F2
Tolpuddle Way. L4 52 D8
Tolver St. WA10 44 A4
Tom Mann Cl. L3 52 D3
Tonbridge Cl. L24 82 B4
Tonbridge Dr. L10 28 D3
Tongbarn. WN8 15 E2
Tontine. WN5 25 C5
Tontine Mkt. WA10 44 A3
Tontine Rd. WN5 & WN8 25 C6
Toothill Cl. WN4 35 B5
Topcliffe Gr. L12 41 A3
Topgate Cl. L60 86 B8
Topham Dr. L9 28 B1
Topsham Cl. L25 & L27 70 C4
Tor View Rd. L15 69 A6
Torcross Cl. PR9 2 A5
Torcross Way. Liverpool L25 & L27 70 C4
Torcross Way. Liverpool L26 70 F1
Toronto Cl. L36 55 D7
Toronto St. L44 51 E3
Torquay Dr. WN5 33 E8
Torr St. L5 52 E6
Torrington Dr. Heswall L61 77 B7
Torrington Dr. Liverpool L26 82 E6
Torrington Gdns. L61 77 B7
Torrington Rd. Liverpool L19 81 B7
Torrington Rd. Wallasey L44 & L45 51 A4
Torrisholme Rd. L11 & L9 39 D3
Torus Rd. L13 54 A4
Torwood. L43 65 D6
Tothale Turn. L26 & L27 70 F4
Totland Cl. WA5 74 C7
Totnes Ave. L26 70 F1
Totnes Dr. PR9 2 A5
Totnes Rd. L11 40 C5
Tourney Gn. WA5 60 A2
Towcester St. L21 38 B6
Tower Coll. L35 57 D1
Tower End. L37 9 C5
Tower Gdns. L2 52 C1
Tower Hill. Birkenhead L42 66 D3
Tower Hill. Ormskirk L39 14 A5
Tower Hill Rd. WN8 25 B6
Tower Nook. WN8 25 A5
Tower Prom. L45 37 C1
Tower Quays. L41 66 E8
Tower Rd. Birkenhead L42 66 B1
Tower Rd. Birkenhead L42 66 D3
Tower Rd. Birkenhead L41 66 E8
Tower Rd N. L60 76 F2
Tower Rd S. L60 76 F1
Tower St. L3 67 E4
Tower Way. L25 70 A3
Tower Wharf. L41 66 E8
Towerlands St. L7 53 B1
Towers Ave. L31 20 C2
Towers Rd. L16 69 C6
Towers The. L42 66 D2
Town Fields. 2 L45 50 E6
Town Green & Aughton Sta. L39 21 C8
Town Green Ct. L39 21 C8
Town Green La. L39 21 C8
Town La. Bebington L63 78 E7
Town La. Hale L24 & WA8 83 E2
Town La. Southport PR8 4 E3
Town Lane Inf Sch. L63 78 E6
Town Lane (Kew). PR8 4 E3
Town Meadow La. L46 49 C1
Town Rd. L42 66 E3
Town Row. L12 54 B6
Towneley Ct. WA8 73 A1
Townfield Ave. WN4 35 B2
Townfield Cl. L43 65 E3
Townfield Gdns. L63 78 F7
Townfield Inf Sch. L43 65 E3
Townfield Jun Sch. L43 65 E3
Townfield La. Bebington L63 78 F7
Townfield La. Birkenhead L43 65 F3
Townfield Rd. L48 63 B2
Townfields. WN4 35 A3
Townsend Ave. L11 & L13 39 E2
Townsend La. L13 & L6 53 C6
Townsend St. Liverpool L5 52 C6
Townsend St. Wallasey L41 50 F1
Townsend View. Litherland L21 27 B2
Townsend View. Liverpool L11 39 E3
Townshend Ave. L61 76 D4
Towson St. L5 52 F6
Toxteth Gr. L8 68 A4
Toxteth St. L8 67 F5
Tracks La. WN5 25 D3
Tracy Dr. WA12 46 E3
Trafalgar Ave. L44 51 D5
Trafalgar Dr. L63 79 A4
Trafalgar Rd. Southport PR8 3 E3
Trafalgar Rd. Wallasey L44 51 C5
Trafalgar St. WA10 43 E4
Trafalgar Way. 4 Liverpool L6 52 F3
Trafalgar Way. 20 Liverpool L6 53 A3
Tragan Dr. WA5 74 D3
Tramway Rd. L17 68 C3
Transport Mus. WA10 44 A4
Trap Hill. L37 9 C2
Trapwood Cl. WA10 43 B3
Travers' Entry. WA9 59 A7
Traverse St. WA9 44 C3
Travis Dr. L33 29 F5
Trawden Way. L21 27 C4
Treborth St. L8 68 A5
Trecastle Rd. L33 30 A4
Treen Cl. PR9 2 B6
Treesdale Cl. PR8 3 F4
Treetops Dr. L41 50 D1
Treforris Rd. L45 50 F7
Trefula Pk. L12 54 A6
Tremore Cl. L11 40 C1
Trendeal Rd. L11 40 D5
Trent Ave. Liverpool L14 54 F2
Trent Ave. Maghull L31 20 F2
Trent Cl. Liverpool L12 40 D3
Trent Cl. Rainhill L35 57 B3
Trent Cl. St Helens WA9 58 C5
Trent Cl. Widnes WA8 73 B4
Trent Pl. L35 57 B3
Trent Rd. Ashton-in-M WN4 35 E5
Trent Rd. Billinge WN5 33 D3
Trent Rd. Rainhill L35 57 B3
Trent St. Liverpool L5 52 C6
Trent St. Wallasey L41 50 F1
Trent Way. L60 86 C6
Trentham Ave. L18 68 F5
Trentham Cl. WA8 73 B4
Trentham Rd. L32 29 C1
Trentham Rd. Wallasey L44 51 C3
Trentham St. WA7 84 F3
Trentham Wlk. 1 L32 29 C1
Tressel Dr. WA9 58 A3
Tressell St. L9 38 F3
Trevelyan Dr. WN5 25 D1
Trevelyan St. L4 38 F3
Treviot Cl. L33 29 D6
Trevor Dr. L23 26 F4
Trevor Rd. Liverpool L9 39 A6
Trevor Rd. Southport PR8 7 C4
Trimley Cl. L49 64 E5
Tring Cl. L49 65 A7
Trinity Ct. L47 63 B7
Trinity Gdns. PR8 4 A6
Trinity Gr. L22 & L23 26 B2
Trinity La. L41 & L72 66 E7
Trinity Mews. PR9 4 C7
Trinity Pl. L20 38 D3
Trinity Prim Sch. WN8 15 F1
Trinity Rd. L20 & L69 38 C2
Trinity Rd. Hoylake L47 63 B7
Trinity Rd. Wallasey L44 51 C5
Trinity St. Birkenhead L41 66 C7
Trinity St. St Helens WA9 44 C3
Trinity Wlk. 4 L3 52 E3
Trispen Cl. L26 82 E8
Trispen Rd. L11 40 D4
Trispen Wlk. L11 40 D4
Tristram's Croft. L30 27 D3
Troon Cl. Bebington L63 88 C5
Troon Cl. Haydock WA11 45 A5
Troon Cl. Liverpool L14 54 F6
Trossach Cl. WA2 61 E2
Trotwood Cl. L9 39 D8
Troutbeck Ave. Maghull L31 20 E2
Troutbeck Ave. Newton-le-W WA12 45 E4
Troutbeck Cl. L49 65 A2
Troutbeck Gr. WA11 33 B2
Troutbeck Rd. Ashton-in-M WN4 35 C5
Troutbeck Rd. Liverpool L18 69 D5
Trouville Rd. L4 53 C7
Trowbridge St. L3 52 E1
Trueman Cl. L43 65 C8
Trueman St. L1 & L2 & L3 52 D2
Truro Ave. Litherland L30 27 F4
Truro Ave. Southport PR9 2 B5
Truro Cl. WA11 44 D7
Truro Rd. L15 69 A6
Tudor Ave. Bebington L63 79 A3
Tudor Ave. Wallasey L44 51 E2
Tudor Cl. Liverpool L7 52 F1
Tudor Ct. Ormskirk L39 13 F6
Tudor Grange. L49 64 D3
Tudor Mansions. PR8 3 F6
Tudor Rd. Birkenhead L42 66 E3
Tudor Rd. Crosby L23 26 D3
Tudor Rd. Liverpool L25 82 C7
Tudor Rd. Southport PR8 7 B6
Tudor St. L6 53 B3
Tudor View. L33 29 E5
Tudorville Rd. L63 78 F5
Tudorway. L60 86 B8
Tue La. WA8 72 B6
Tuffins Cnr. L27 70 D5
Tulip Ave. L41 65 F7
Tulip Rd. Haydock WA11 45 F6
Tulip Rd. Liverpool L15 69 B7

Tulketh St. PR8 4 B7
Tullimore Rd. L18 69 A1
Tullis St. WA10 43 E2
Tulloch St. L6 53 B3
Tully Ave. WA12 45 F3
Tumilty Ave. L20 38 E4
Tunnel Rd. Birkenhead L41 66 F5
Tunnel Rd. Liverpool L7 & L8 68 B8
Tunstall Cl. L49 64 E5
Tunstall St. L15 & L7 68 C7
Tunstall's Way. WA9 58 D4
Tupman St. 2 L8 67 F5
Turmar Ave. L61 77 B6
Turnacre. Formby L37 10 B6
Turnacre. Liverpool L14 54 E3
Turnall Rd. WA8 84 B7
Turnberry. WN8 15 D2
Turnberry Cl. Huyton-w-R L36 55 C1
Turnberry Cl. Liverpool L14 54 F6
Turnberry Cl. Wallasey L46 49 B1
Turnberry Way. PR9 2 D5
Turnbridge Rd. L31 20 C3
Turner Ave. L20 38 E7
Turner Cl. Liverpool L8 68 A3
Turner Cl. Widnes WA8 72 D3
Turner St. 13 L41 66 C5
Turney Rd. L44 51 A4
Turning La. PR8 5 A1
Turnpike Rd. L39 13 A2
Turnstone Ave. WA12 46 C4
Turnstone Cl. L12 40 E3
Turnstone Dr. L26 70 E1
Turret Hall Dr. WA3 47 E8
Turret Rd. L45 51 A6
Turriff Dr. L63 88 C4
Turriff Rd. L14 55 A4
Turton Cl. L24 83 E1
Turton St. Golborne WA3 47 A8
Turton St. Liverpool L5 52 D6
Tuscan Cl. WA8 73 B5
Tuson Dr. WA8 72 F4
Tweed Cl. L6 53 C4
Tweed St. L41 51 A1
Twickenham Dr. Huyton-w-R L36 55 D1
Twickenham Dr. Wallasey L46 50 A3
Twickenham St. 6 L6 53 B6
Twig La. Huyton-w-R L36 55 C4
Twig La. Maghull L31 20 E1
Twiss St. L8 68 A5
Twist Ave. WA3 47 C8
Twistfield Cl. PR8 3 F5
Two Butt La. L35 57 A5
Twomey Cl. L5 52 C4
Twyford Ave. L21 27 B1
Twyford Cl. Maghull L31 20 E1
Twyford Cl. Widnes WA8 73 B5
Twyford La. WA8 73 D6
Twyford Pl. WA9 44 C3
Twyford St. L6 53 B6
Tyberton Pl. L25 82 C6
Tyburn Cl. L63 78 F2
Tyburn Rd. L63 78 F2
Tyler Wlk. WA3 47 F8
Tyndall Ave. L22 37 F8
Tyne Cl. Liverpool L4 52 E8
Tyne Cl. St Helens WA9 57 D6
Tyne Cl. Warrington WA2 61 E2
Tyne St. L41 50 F1
Tynemouth Cl. 9 L5 & L6 53 A5
Tynron Gr. L43 65 D5
Tynville Rd. L9 39 C7
Tynwald Cl. L13 53 F4
Tynwald Cres. WA8 72 F5
Tynwald Hill. L13 53 F4
Tynwald Pl. L13 53 F4
Tynwald Rd. L48 63 A2
Tyrer Rd. Newton-le-W WA12 46 C1
Tyrer Rd. Ormskirk L39 13 F7
Tyrer St. 11 Liverpool L1 52 D1
Tyrer St. Wallasey L41 50 F1
Tyrer's Ave. L31 20 B5
Tyrers Cl. L37 9 F2

Uldale Cl. Liverpool L11 40 A2
Uldale Cl. Southport PR8 7 B3
Uldale Way. L11 40 A2
Ullet Rd. L15 & L17 & L8 68 C5
Ullet Wlk. L17 68 D5
Ullswater Ave. Ashton-in-M WN4 35 B5
Ullswater Ave.B,head L43 65 D6
Ullswater Ave. Orrell WN5 25 F7
Ullswater Ave. St Helens WA11 44 B8
Ullswater Ave. Warrington WA2 61 D3
Ullswater Cl. L33 29 D4
Ullswater Rd. WA3 36 C1
Ullswater St. L5 & L6 53 A5
Ulster Rd. L13 54 B3
Ultonia St. L19 81 C4
Ulverscroft. L43 65 F4
Ulverston Ave. WA2 61 B4
Ulverston Cl. Haydock WA11 45 A6
Ulverston Cl. Maghull L31 20 E2
Ulverston Lawn. L27 70 F4
Umbria St. L19 81 C4
Undercliffe Rd. L13 54 A4
Underhill Rd. WA10 43 D2
Underlea Open Air Sch. L14 54 D3
Underley St. L7 68 C7
Underley Terr. L62 79 B7
Unicorn Rd. L11 40 C4
Union Bank La. WA8 58 C1
Union Ct. L2 52 C1
Union St. Birkenhead L41 66 F3
Union St. Liverpool L3 52 B2
Union St. Southport PR9 4 C8
Union St. St Helens WA10 44 A4
Union St. Wallasey L44 51 D4
Union Terr. L45 37 B1
Unit Rd. PR8 7 D5
Unity Gr. L34 41 A5
Univ of Liverpool. L3 & L7 52 F1
University Rd. L20 38 D2
Unsworth Ave. WA3 36 E1
Unsworth Ct. WA2 61 F1
Up Holland High Sch. WN5 25 C4
Upavon Ave. L49 64 B3
Upholland Rd. WN5 25 D2
Upholland Sta. WN8 24 F4
Upland Dr. WN4 35 D4
Upland Rd. Birkenhead L49 65 A6
Upland Rd. St Helens WA10 57 C8
Uplands Cl. WA10 57 B8
Uplands Rd. L62 79 C2
Upper Aughton Rd. PR8 4 B4
Upper Baker St. L6 53 A3
Upper Beau St. 9 L3 & L5 52 E4
Upper Beckwith St. L41 66 B8
Upper Brassey St. L41 66 A8
Upper Bute St. 5 L3 52 E4
Upper Duke St. L1 67 E8
Upper Essex St. L8 67 F5
Upper Flaybrick Rd. L43 65 E7
Upper Frederick St. L1 & L72 67 E7
Upper Hampton St. L8 67 F7
Upper Harrington St. L8 67 E6
Upper Hill St. Liverpool L8 67 E6
Upper Hill St. Liverpool L8 67 F6
Upper Hill St. 12 Liverpool L8 67 F7
Upper Hope Pl. 4 L7 67 F8
Upper Huskisson St. L7 & L8 68 A7
Upper Mann St. Liverpool L8 67 E5
Upper Mann St. Liverpool L8 67 E6
Upper Mason St. L7 53 A1
Upper Milk St. L3 52 C2
Upper Newington. L1 52 E1
Upper Park St. L8 67 F5
Upper Parliament St. L8 ,L69 68 A7
Upper Pitt St. Liverpool L1 & L72 67 D8
Upper Pitt St. Liverpool L1 & L72 67 E7
Upper Pownall St. L1 & L72 67 D8
Upper Raby Rd. L64 87 A2
Upper Rice La. L44 51 C5
Upper Stanhope St. Liverpool L8 67 E7
Upper Stanhope St. Liverpool L8 67 F7
Upper Warwick St. L8 67 F6
Upper William St. L3 52 B4
Uppingham. WN8 15 D1
Uppingham Ave. L10 28 E2
Uppingham Rd. Liverpool L13 53 F5
Uppingham Rd. Wallasey L44 50 F5
Upton Ave. PR8 7 B6
Upton Barn. L31 20 C2
Upton Bridle Path. WA8 72 F4
Upton Cl. Birkenhead L49 64 F5
Upton Cl. Golborne WA3 47 D8
Upton Cl. Liverpool L24 82 E3
Upton Ct. L49 65 A6
Upton Cty Inf Sch. WA8 72 B3
Upton Dr. WA5 74 F5
Upton Gn. L24 82 E3
Upton Grange. WA8 72 D4
Upton Hall Convent Sch. L49 64 F5
Upton La. WA8 72 F4
Upton Park Dr. L49 65 A6
Upton Rd. Birkenhead L46 & L49 64 E8
Upton Rd. Birkenhead L41 & L43 65 D6
Upton Sta. L43 65 C5
Upwood Rd. WA3 47 D7
Urmson Rd. L45 51 B5
Urmston Ave. WA12 46 B5
Ursula St. L20 38 D1
Ursuline RC Prim Sch. L23 26 B3
Utkinton Cl. L43 65 F3
Utting Ave. Liverpool L4 53 B8
Utting Ave E. L11 39 F2
Uxbridge St. 6 Liverpool L7 53 B1
Uxbridge St. Liverpool L7 68 B8

Vale Cl. L25 69 F2
Vale Cres. PR8 7 C2
Vale Ct. 4 L21 38 A6
Vale Dr. L45 51 C7
Vale La. L40 15 F5
Vale Lodge. L9 39 A4
Vale Owen Rd. WA2 61 D1
Vale Rd. Crosby L23 26 D4
Vale Rd. Liverpool L25 69 F2
Valencia Gr. L34 56 F7
Valencia Rd. L15 69 A8
Valentia Rd. L47 63 B7
Valentine Gr. L10 28 E1
Valentine Rd. WA12 45 F3
Valentines Way. L9 28 C1
Valerian Rd. L41 65 F7
Valerie Cl. L10 40 B6
Valescourt Rd. L12 54 C5
Valeview Towers. L25 69 F2
Valewood Prim Sch. L23 26 D5
Valiant Cl. WA2 61 F2
Valkyrie Rd. L45 51 A5
Vallance Rd. L4 & L6 53 C7
Valley Cl. Crosby L23 27 B4
Valley Cl. Litherland L10 28 F1
Valley Ct. WA2 61 F1
Valley Rd. Bebington L62 88 D8
Valley Rd. L32 29 D1
Valley Rd. Liverpool L10 & L32 40 B8
Valley Rd. Liverpool L4 53 B6
Valley Rd. Wallasey L41 50 E1
Valley View. WA12 46 B1
Valley Views. L25 70 A6
Valleybrook Gr. L63 79 B2
Vanbrugh Cres. L4 53 C7
Vanbrugh Rd. L4 & L6 53 D7
Vanderbilt Ave. L9 39 B8
Vanderbyl Ave. L62 79 C2
Vandries St. L3 52 B4
Vandyke St. L8 68 C7
Vanguard St. L5 52 F6
Vardon St. L41 66 D8
Varley Rd. Liverpool L19 69 A1
Varley Rd. St Helens WA9 44 C4
Varlian Cl. L40 14 C3
Varthen St. 6 L4 & L5 53 A7
Vaughan Cl. L37 9 D4
Vaughan Rd. Southport PR8 4 B4
Vaughan Rd. Wallasey L45 51 C8
Vaughan St. L41 65 F8
Vaux Cres. L20 38 D5
Vaux Pl. L20 38 D5
Vauxhall Cl. WA5 74 F4
Vauxhall Rd. L3 & L5 52 C4
Venables Cl. L63 79 B1
Venables Dr. L63 79 A1
Venice St. L4 & L5 52 F6
Venmore St. L4 & L5 53 A6
Ventnor Cl. WA5 74 D7
Ventnor Rd. L15 68 F8
Venture Ct. L41 66 F5
Verda St. WN2 36 B8
Verdala Pk. L18 69 C2
Verdi Ave. L21 38 A6
Verdi St. L21 37 F6
Vere St. L8 67 E5
Vermont Ave. L23 26 D4
Vermont Rd. L23 26 D4
Vermont Way. L20 38 C4
Verney Cres. L19 81 C8
Verney Cres S. L19 81 C8
Vernon Ave. Bebington L66 89 A2
Vernon Ave. Wallasey L44 51 D2
Vernon Ct. PR8 4 D5
Vernon Rd. PR9 5 A8
Vernon St. Liverpool L1 & L2 52 C2
Vernon St. St Helens WA9 44 C4
Verona St. L5 52 F6
Verulam Cl. L8 68 A7
Verulam Rd. PR9 2 B3
Verwood Cl. L61 76 D7
Verwood Dr. L12 41 A3
Veryan Cl. L26 70 F1
Vescock St. L5 52 D4
Vesuvius Pl. L5 52 D6
Vesuvius St. L5 52 D6
Vetch Hey. L27 70 E5
Viaduct St. WA12 46 A3
Vicar Rd. L4 & L6 53 C7
Vicarage Cl. Birkenhead L42 66 B1
Vicarage Cl. Formby L37 9 D4
Vicarage Cl. Hale L24 83 E1
Vicarage Cl. Liverpool L18 69 B2
Vicarage Cl. Ormskirk L39 & L40 14 B3
Vicarage Dr. WA11 45 B7
Vicarage Gr. L44 51 C5
Vicarage La. Ormskirk L39 & L40 14 C3
Vicarage La. Southport PR9 2 F7
Vicarage Lawn. L25 70 C5
Vicarage Pl. L34 56 C6
Vicarage Rd. Ashton-in-M WN4 35 B2
Vicarage Rd. Formby L37 9 D4
Vicarage Rd. Golborne WN2 36 B1
Vicarage Rd. Haydock WA11 45 A7
Vicarage Rd. Orrell WN5 25 D4
Vicarage Wlk. L39 13 E5
Viceroy Ct. PR8 4 A6
Viceroy St. L5 52 F6
Vickers Rd. WA8 84 F4
Victor St. L15 68 D8
Victoria Ave. Crosby L23 26 C4
Victoria Ave. Heswall L60 86 A6
Victoria Ave. Liverpool L14 54 D2
Victoria Ave. 3 Liverpool L15 68 F8
Victoria Ave. St Helens WA11 44 A8
Victoria Ave. Warrington WA5 74 D6
Victoria Ave. Widnes WA8 73 A3
Victoria Bridge Rd. PR8 4 C6
Victoria Central Comm Hospl. L44 51 B4
Victoria Cl. L17 68 E3
Victoria Ct. Liverpool L17 68 B4
Victoria Ct. Liverpool L15 69 A8
Victoria Dr. Birkenhead L42 67 A1
Victoria Dr. L9 38 F6
Victoria Dr. West Kirby L48 63 A2
Victoria Gdns. L43 66 B4
Victoria Gr. WA8 73 A3
Victoria House. L34 56 D6
Victoria La. L43 66 B4
Victoria Mount. L43 66 B4
Victoria Par. L45 37 C1
Victoria Park Rd. L42 66 D2
Victoria Pk. WN8 15 C1
Victoria Pl. Liverpool L13 54 A3
Victoria Pl. Rainhill L35 57 C3
Victoria Pl. Wallasey L44 51 F2
Victoria Rd. Bebington L63 78 D6
Victoria Rd. Birkenhead L42 66 D4
Victoria Rd. Crosby L23 26 D4
Victoria Rd. Formby L37 9 D5
Victoria Rd. Garswood WN4 34 D4
Victoria Rd. Huyton-w-R L36 55 F2
Victoria Rd. Ince Blundell L38 18 E3
Victoria Rd. Liverpool L13 53 E6
Victoria Rd. Liverpool L17 & L18 68 E3
Victoria Rd. Newton-le-W WA12 46 C3
Victoria Rd. Ormskirk L39 13 C2
Victoria Rd. Seaforth L22 37 E8
Victoria Rd. Wallasey L45 37 C1
Victoria Rd. Wallasey L45 51 B8
Victoria Rd. Warrington WA5 74 D4
Victoria Rd. West Kirby L48 63 B1
Victoria Sq. 2 WA10 44 A3
Victoria St. Bebington L62 79 B5
Victoria St. Liverpool L1 & L2 52 D2
Victoria St. Rainford WA11 31 F7
Victoria St. Rainhill L35 57 C3
Victoria St. Southport PR8 4 B8
Victoria St. St Helens WA10 44 A5
Victoria Terr. Bickershaw WN2 36 F8
Victoria Terr. Liverpool L15 69 A6
Victoria Terr. Rainhill L35 57 C3
Victoria Way. Formby L37 9 D5
Victoria Way. Southport PR8 3 F7
Victory Ave. PR9 5 A7
Victory Cl. L30 38 E8
Vienna St. Liverpool L5 52 F6
View Rd. L35 57 C2
Viking Cl. L21 38 A7
Village Cl. L45 50 E6
Village Courts. L30 27 F5
Village Ct. Birkenhead L43 66 A4
Village Ct. Irby L61 76 D6
Village Ct. Liverpool L17 68 C2
Village Green Ct. L43 65 C8
Village Nook. L10 28 E2
Village Rd. Bebington L63 78 D6
Village Rd. Birkenhead L43 66 A4
Village Rd. Heswall L60 85 F7
Village Rd. West Kirby L48 63 C1
Village St. L6 52 F4
Village The. Bebington L63 79 A5
Village The. Birkenhead L49 65 A5
Village Way. Hightown L38 17 F4
Village Way. Wallasey L45 50 E6
Villas Rd. L31 21 B2
Villiers Cres. WA10 42 F4
Villiers Rd. L34 41 C6
Vincent Ct. L1 & L72 67 D8
Vincent Naughton Ct. L41 66 F5
Vincent Rd. Litherland L21 27 C1
Vincent Rd. Rainhill L35 57 C4
Vincent St. 4 Birkenhead L41 66 D6
Vincent St. Liverpool L13 54 A1
Vincent St. St Helens WA10 44 A4
Vine Cres. WA5 74 F6
Vine House. L21 38 A6
Vine St. L7 68 A8
Vineries The. L25 69 E3
Vineside Rd. L12 54 D6
Vineyard St. L19 81 E5
Vining Rd. L35 56 F6
Vining St. L8 67 F6
Viola St. L20 38 C1
Violet Rd. Birkenhead L41 65 F7
Violet Rd. L21 38 B6
Violet St. WN4 35 B2
Virgil St. Liverpool L5 52 E4
Virgil St. St Helens WA10 43 E4
Virgin's La. L23 27 A6
Virginia Ave. L31 20 D3
Virginia Gr. L31 20 C3
Virginia Rd. L45 37 B1
Virginia St. Liverpool L3 52 B2
Virginia St. Southport PR8 4 C6
Vista Ave. WA12 46 A4
Vista Rd. WA11 & WA12 46 A6
Vittoria Cl. L41 66 D7
Vittoria St. L41 66 D7
Vivian Ave. 12 L44 51 E2
Vivian Dr. PR8 4 A2
Voelas St. L8 68 A6
Vogan Ave. L23 27 A3
Volunteer St. 3 WA10 43 F4
Vronhill Cl. L8 68 A6
Vulcan Cl. Birkenhead L43 65 F8
Vulcan Cl. Newton-le-W WA12 46 C1
Vulcan Cl. Warrington WA2 61 F2
Vulcan Ind Est. WA12 46 D1
Vulcan St. 3 Birkenhead L41 65 F8
Vulcan St. L20 38 B4
Vulcan St. Liverpool L3 52 B4
Vulcan St. Liverpool L19 81 C4
Vulcan St. Southport PR9 4 C7
Vyner Cl. L43 65 E6
Vyner Prim Sch. L43 50 D1
Vyner Rd. L45 50 F5
Vyner Rd N. Birkenhead L43 65 D7
Vyner Rd N. Liverpool L25 70 A5
Vyner Rd S. Birkenhead L43 65 D6
Vyner Rd S. Liverpool L25 70 B5
Vyrnwy St. 1 L5 53 A6

Waddicar La. L31 29 B4
Waddington Cl. Golborne WA3 47 F8
Waddington Cl. Warrington WA2 61 F1
Wade Deacon High Sch. WA8 73 A2
Wadebridge Rd. L10 40 B6
Wadeson Rd. L4 39 D2
Wadham Rd. L20 38 C2
Wagon La. WA11 45 B6
Waine St. St Helens WA9 44 D4
Waine St. St Helens WA11 44 F6
Wainwright Cl. 2 L7 68 C8
Wainwright Gr. L19 81 B6
Wakefield Dr. L46 49 F4
Wakefield Rd. L30 28 A2
Wakefield St. Golborne WA3 47 A7
Wakefield St. Liverpool L3 52 E3
Walby Cl. L49 65 C2
Walden Rd. L14 54 C3
Waldgrave Pl. L15 54 B1
Waldgrave Rd. L15 54 B1
Waldron. WN9 23 D8

Waldron Cl. 3 L3 .... 52 C3
Walford Cl. L63 .... 78 F2
Walford Rd. WN4 .... 35 C3
Walk The. Liverpool L24 .... 82 A2
Walk The. Southport PR8 .... 4 A5
Walker Ave. WA9 .... 58 B3
Walker Cl. L37 .... 9 F2
Walker Dr. L20 .... 38 C7
Walker Mews. L42 .... 66 D3
Walker Pl. L42 .... 66 D3
Walker Rd. L21 .... 38 A7
Walker St. Bebington L62 .... 79 B6
Walker St. Birkenhead L42 ... 66 D3
Walker St. Hoylake L47 .... 63 B7
Walker St. Liverpool L6 .... 53 A3
Walker Way. L9 .... 38 F6
Walker's Croft. L45 .... 50 F5
Walkers La. St Helens WA9 .. 58 A3
Walkers La. Warrington WA5 74 E3
Wallace Ave. L36 .... 56 A4
Wallace Dr. L36 .... 56 A4
Wallace St. L9 .... 39 A6
Wallacre Rd. L44 .... 50 F4
Wallasey Bridge Rd. L41 ..... 50 F2
Wallasey Rd. L44 & L45 .... 51 A4
Wallasey Sch. L46 .... 50 A3
Wallasey Sta. L45 .... 50 E6
Wallasey Village. L44 & L45 50 E6
Wallasey Village Sta. L45 .... 50 E5
Wallbrook Ave. WN5 .... 25 D1
Wallcroft St. WN8 .... 23 E8
Waller Cl. L4 .... 52 E7
Waller St. L20 .... 38 B6
Wallgate Rd. L25 .... 69 F6
Wallgate Way. L25 .... 69 F6
Wallingford Rd. L49 .... 64 F4
Wallrake. L60 .... 85 F7
Walmer Ct. PR8 .... 3 F4
Walmer Rd. Seaforth L22 ..... 37 E8
Walmer Rd. Southport PR8 .... 4 A3
Walmesley Dr. WA11 .... 32 A5
Walmesley Rd. WA10 .... 43 A5
Walmsley St. Liverpool L5 .... 52 C5
Walmsley St.
Newton-le-W WA12 .... 46 D4
Walmsley St. Wallasey L44 .. 51 C5
Walney Rd. L12 .... 54 A8
Walnut Ave. L9 .... 39 C3
Walnut St. PR8 .... 4 C4
Walpole Ave. L35 .... 56 F3
Walpole Gr. WA2 .... 61 C2
Walro Mews. PR9 .... 2 A3
Walsh Cl. Liverpool L3 .... 52 C4
Walsh Cl.
Newton-le-W WA12 .... 46 C5
Walsh Rd. L14 .... 54 C2
Walsingham Ct. L44 .... 51 D3
Walsingham Rd.
Liverpool L16 .... 69 E8
Walsingham Rd.
Wallasey L44 .... 51 D3
Walsingham Rd.
Warrington WA5 .... 74 F5
Walter Beilin Ct. L17 .... 68 E5
Walter Gr. WA9 .... 58 F7
Walter St. Ashton-in-M WN4 35 D4
Walter St. Liverpool L5 .... 52 B5
Walter St. Widnes WA8 .... 73 D1
Waltham Rd. L6 .... 53 C6
Waltho Ave. L31 .... 20 E1
Walton Ave. WA5 .... 74 E5
Walton Breck Rd.
Liverpool L4 & L5 .... 52 F7
Walton Hall Ave. L11 & L4 ... 39 C2
Walton Hospl. L9 .... 38 F3
Walton Junction Sta. L9 ...... 38 F4
Walton La. L4 .... 52 F8
Walton Park Gdns. L4 .... 39 A2
Walton Pk. L9 .... 39 A4
Walton Rd. Liverpool L4 & L5 52 E7
Walton Rd. St Helens WA10 43 D6
Walton St. 16
Birkenhead L41 .... 66 E6
Walton St. Southport PR9 ...... 4 C8
Walton St Mary CE Prim Sch.
L4 .... 38 F2
Walton Vale. L9 .... 39 A6
Walton Village. L4 .... 39 A2
Wambo La. L25 .... 70 C5
Wandsworth Rd. L11 .... 39 F1
Wango La. L10 .... 28 F1
Wanishar La. L39 .... 12 A5
Wansfell Pl. WA2 .... 61 A3
Wantage View. L36 .... 70 C8
Wapping. Liverpool L1 & L72 67 C8
Wapshare Rd. L11 .... 53 E8
Warbler Cl. L26 .... 70 D2
Warbreck Ave. L9 .... 39 A6
Warbreck Moor. L9 .... 39 B7
Warbreck Rd. L9 .... 39 A6
Warburton Hey. L35 .... 57 C4
Ward Ave. L37 .... 9 D2
Ward Cl. WA5 .... 60 B1
Ward Gr. L42 .... 78 F8
Ward rake. L30 .... 27 D4
Ward Rd. L23 .... 26 A5
Ward St. Liverpool L3 .... 52 E2
Ward St. Prescot L34 .... 56 D7
Ward St. St Helens WA10 ..... 44 A4
Warden St. 6 L4 .... 52 E8
Wardgate Ave. L12 .... 40 E3
Wareing Rd. L9 .... 39 C6
Waresley Cres. L11 & L9 ..... 39 E4
Wargrave CE Prim Sch.
WA12 .... 46 C1
Wargrave House Sch. WA12 46 D1
Wargrave Mews. WA12 .... 46 C1
Wargrave Rd. WA12 .... 46 C2
Warham Rd. L4 .... 53 C7
Waring Ave. Birkenhead L42 66 D2
Waring Ave. St Helens WA9 . 45 B2
Warkworth Cl.
Huyton-w-R L36 .... 71 A8
Warkworth Cl. Widnes WA8 72 C3
Warmington Rd. L14 .... 54 C3
Warner Dr. L4 .... 53 C8
Warnerville Rd. L13 .... 54 B1
Warnley Cl. WA8 .... 72 D3
Warren Ct. PR8 .... 3 E5
Warren Dr. Birkenhead L43 .. 65 C6
Warren Dr.
Newton-le-W WA12 .... 46 F4
Warren Dr. Wallasey L45 ..... 50 F8
Warren Gn. L37 .... 9 D3
Warren Hey. L63 .... 79 A1
Warren House Rd. L22 .... 26 B2
Warren Hurst. 2 L45 .... 51 A8
Warren Rd. Crosby L23 .... 26 B4
Warren Rd. Hoylake L47 ...... 63 A7
Warren Rd. Southport PR9 ..... 5 A8
Warren Rd. Warrington WA2 61 D1
Warren St. 6 L3 .... 52 E1
Warren The. L49 .... 65 B5
Warren Way. L60 .... 76 D1
Warrenhouse Rd. L33 .... 30 B4
Warrington Bsns Pk. WA2 ... 61 C1
Warrington Collegiate Inst.
WA2 .... 61 B1
Warrington New Rd. WA9 ... 44 B3
Warrington Old Rd.
St Helens WA9 .... 44 B2
Warrington Old Rd.
St Helens WA9 .... 44 B3
Warrington Rd.
Abram WA3 & WN2 .... 36 B7
Warrington Rd.
Ashton-in-M WN4 .... 35 B2
Warrington Rd.
Bold Heath L35 & WA8 .... 73 D7
Warrington Rd. Cronton L35 72 F8
Warrington Rd.
Golborne WA12 .... 47 A6
Warrington Rd.
Prescot L34 & L35 .... 56 E5
Warrington Rd. Rainhill L35 . 57 A4
Warrington Rd.
Warrington WA5 .... 74 F4
Warrington Rd.
Widnes WA8 .... 73 D1
Warrington Rd Cty Prim Sch.
WA8 .... 73 D1
Warrington St. L42 .... 66 E4
Warton Cl. L25 .... 70 C2
Warton St. L20 .... 38 B6
Warton Terr. L21 .... 38 B6
Warwick Ave.
Ashton-in-M WN4 .... 35 D2
Warwick Ave. Crosby L23 ..... 26 D3
Warwick Ave.
Newton-le-W WA12 .... 46 E2
Warwick Ave.
Warrington WA5 .... 74 D7
Warwick Cl. Birkenhead L43 66 C5
Warwick Cl. Huyton-w-R L36 56 A3
Warwick Cl. Southport PR8 .... 4 B4
Warwick Ct. 3 L8 .... 68 A6
Warwick Dr. Wallasey L45 ... 51 C6
Warwick Dr. West Kirby L48 75 C8
Warwick Rd. Birkenhead L49 64 F6
Warwick Rd. L20 .... 38 D4
Warwick Rd. Huyton-w-R L36 56 A3
Warwick St. Liverpool L8 ...... 67 E6
Warwick St. Southport PR8 .... 4 B4
Warwick St. St Helens WA10 43 D3
Wasdale Ave. Maghull L31 ... 20 F2
Wasdale Ave.
St Helens WA11 .... 44 B8
Wasdale Rd.
Ashton-in-M WN4 .... 35 A8
Wasdale Rd. Liverpool L9 ..... 39 A5
Washbrook Ave. L43 .... 65 C8
Washbrook Way. L39 .... 13 E4
Washington Par. L20 .... 38 C3
Washway La. WA10 & WA11 44 A7
Wasley Cl. WA2 .... 61 F3
Wastdale Ct. L46 .... 49 C1
Wastdale Dr. L46 .... 49 C1
Wastdale Mews. L46 .... 49 C1
Wastle Bridge Rd. L36 .... 55 E5
Watchyard La. L37 .... 10 A4
Water La. Southport PR9 .... 2 D5
Water La.
Tarbock Green L35 .... 71 D5
Water St. Bebington L62 .... 79 C5
Water St. Birkenhead L41 .... 66 F6
Water St. Crosby L23 .... 27 B6
Water St. Liverpool L2 .... 52 C1
Water St.
Newton-le-W WA12 .... 46 C4
Water St. 1 Seaforth L22 ... 37 E8
Water St. St Helens WA10 ... 43 F3
Water St. Wallasey L44 .... 51 D4
Water Tower Rd. L64 .... 86 E1
Waterdale Cres. WA9 .... 58 D7
Waterdale Pl. WA9 .... 58 D7
Waterfield Cl. L63 .... 78 D5
Waterfoot Ave. PR8 .... 7 B3
Waterford Rd. L43 .... 65 F5
Watergate La. L25 .... 70 B2
Watergate Sch The. L25 ...... 70 B2
Watergate Way. L25 .... 70 B2
Waterhouse St. L5 .... 52 F4
Waterland La. WA9 .... 44 F2
Waterloo Cl. L22 .... 37 D8
Waterloo Ct. L42 .... 79 A6
Waterloo EMI Day Hospl.
L22 .... 26 E1
Waterloo Pl. L41 .... 66 E5
Waterloo Rd.
Liverpool L3 & L5 .... 52 B4
Waterloo Rd. Runcorn WA7 . 84 F2
Waterloo Rd. Runcorn WA7 . 84 F3
Waterloo Rd. Seaforth L22 .. 37 E8
Waterloo Rd. Southport PR8 .. 3 E2
Waterloo Rd. Wallasey L45 . 37 B1
Waterloo St. Liverpool L15 ... 69 A7
Waterloo St. 3
St Helens WA10 .... 44 A3
Waterloo Sta. L22 .... 26 E1
Watermede. WN5 .... 25 E3
Waterpark Cl. L43 .... 65 F1
Waterpark Dr. L28 & L12 ..... 55 A7
Waterpark Rd. L42 & L43 ..... 66 A2
Waters Edge Apartments.
L45 .... 37 C1
Waterside. Litherland L30 .... 27 E5
Waterside. St Helens WA9 ... 44 B4
Waterside Ct. WA9 .... 44 B4
Waterside La. WA8 .... 84 C5
Waterway Ave. L30 .... 28 B3
Waterworks La.
Bebington L66 .... 88 E1
Waterworks La.
Winwick WA2 .... 61 B7
Waterworks Rd. L39 .... 14 A6
Waterworks St. L20 .... 38 D3
Watery La. St Helens WA9 ... 44 E1
Watery La. Warrington WA2 60 E6
Watford Rd. L4 .... 53 B7
Watkins Ave. WA12 .... 45 F3
Watkinson St. L1 & L72 .... 67 D7
Watkinson Way. L35 & WA8 73 C5
Watling Ave. L21 .... 27 B1
Watling Way. L35 .... 57 A6
Watmough St. 6 L3 .... 52 E4
Watson Ave.
Ashton-in-M WN4 .... 35 C3
Watson Ave. Golborne WA3 . 35 F1
Watson St. L41 .... 66 D7
Watton Beck Cl. L31 .... 20 F2
Watton Cl. L12 .... 41 A2
Watts Cl. L33 .... 30 A4
Watts La. L20 .... 38 E6
Wauchope St. L15 .... 68 E8
Wavell Ave. Southport PR9 .... 5 B7
Wavell Ave. Widnes WA8 ..... 84 D8
Wavell Cl. PR9 .... 5 B7
Wavell Rd. L36 .... 55 E4
Waverley.
Skelmersdale WN8 .... 15 D1
Waverley Gr. L42 .... 66 C2
Waverley Rd. Crosby L23 ..... 26 C3
Waverley Rd. Golborne WA3 36 D1
Waverley Rd. Hoylake L47 ... 63 C7
Waverley Rd. Liverpool L17 . 68 C4
Waverley St. L20 .... 38 B3
Waverley St. Southport PR8 .. 4 A7
Waverton Ave. L43 .... 65 E2
Wavertree Ave.
Liverpool L13 & L15 & L7 .... 53 F1
Wavertree Ave. Widnes WA8 84 F8
Wavertree Bvd. L7 .... 53 D1
Wavertree Bvd S. L7 .... 53 E1
Wavertree CE Prim Sch.
L15 .... 69 A7
Wavertree Gdns. L15 .... 68 F7
Wavertree Gn. L15 .... 69 A7
Wavertree House. L13 .... 54 A1
Wavertree Nook Rd.
Liverpool L15 .... 69 C8
Wavertree Prim Sch. L15 .... 68 D7
Wavertree Rd. L15 & L7 .... 53 B1
Wavertree Retail Pk. L7 ...... 53 C1
Wavertree Technology Pk.
L7 .... 53 E1
Wavertree Trad Est. L15 ..... 68 E7
Wavertree Vale. L15 .... 68 D8
Wayfarers Arc. PR8 .... 4 B7
Wayfarers Dr. WA12 .... 46 E2
Waylands Dr. L25 .... 82 B7
Wayville Cl. L18 .... 69 B2
Waywell Cl. WA2 .... 61 F3
Weardale Rd. L15 .... 68 E6
Wearhead Cl. WA3 .... 46 F7
Weasdale Cl. WA9 .... 58 D7
Weates Cl. WA8 .... 73 F3
Weatherby. L49 .... 65 B4
Weatherhead High Sch. L45 51 A7
Weatherhead Lower Sch.
L45 .... 51 B7
Weaver Ave. L33 .... 29 F6
Weaver Ave. Rainhill L35 ..... 57 C3
Weaver Ct. L25 .... 70 C3
Weaver Gr. WA9 .... 45 A3
Weaver House. L25 .... 70 C3
Weaver Ind Est. L19 .... 81 C4
Weaver St. L4 .... 38 F3
Weavers La. L31 .... 28 F6
Webb Cl. 8 L7 .... 53 C1
Webb Dr. WA5 .... 59 F6
Webb St. Liverpool L7 .... 68 C7
Webb St. St Helens WA9 ...... 44 D1
Webber Rd. L33 .... 30 C1
Webster Ave. L20 .... 38 E4
Webster Ave. Wallasey L44 . 51 D6
Webster Dr. L32 .... 29 E2
Webster Rd. L15 & L7 .... 68 D7
Webster St. L21 .... 38 C6
Webster St. Liverpool L3 ...... 52 D2
Websters Holt. L49 .... 64 F6
Wedge Ave. WA11 .... 45 A5
Wedgewood St. L7 .... 53 B2
Wedgwood Dr. WA8 .... 73 B4
Wednesbury Dr. WA5 .... 74 F6
Weedon Ave. WA12 .... 46 B5
Weightman Gr. 4 L9 .... 39 A6
Weirside. WA9 .... 58 D6
Welbeck Ave. Liverpool L18 . 68 F5
Welbeck Ave.
Newton-le-W WA12 .... 46 D2
Welbeck Ct. L22 .... 26 D1
Welbeck Rd.
Ashton-in-M WN4 .... 35 C4
Welbeck Rd. Southport PR8 ... 4 A4
Welbeck Terr. PR8 .... 4 A4
Welbourne. WN8 .... 15 D1
Welbourne Rd. L16 .... 54 C1
Weld Blundell Ave. L31 .... 20 B5
Weld Dr. L37 .... 9 D4
Weld Par. PR8 .... 3 F4
Weld Rd. Crosby L23 .... 26 C3
Weld Rd. Southport PR8 .... 3 F5
Weldon Dr. L39 .... 13 F4
Weldon St. L4 .... 38 F2
Welfield Pl. L8 .... 68 A4
Welford Ave. Birkenhead L43 65 F2
Welford Ave. Golborne WA3 47 C7
Well Brow Rd. L4 .... 39 A1
Well La. Bebington L63 .... 78 D6
Well La. Birkenhead L49 ...... 64 C3
Well La. Birkenhead L42 ...... 66 E2
Well La. L20 .... 38 D3
Well La. Haskayne L39 .... 11 E6
Well La. Heswall L60 .... 86 B6
Well La. Liverpool L16 & L25 69 F7
Well La. Warrington WA5 ..... 74 F3
Well Lane Prim Sch. L42 ...... 66 E3
Welland Cl. L26 .... 82 E6
Welland Rd.
Ashton-in-M WN4 .... 35 E5
Welland Rd. Bebington L63 .. 78 D5
Wellbeck Rd. WN4 .... 35 C5
Wellbrae Cl. L49 .... 64 D5
Wellbrook Cl. L24 .... 82 D4
Wellbrook Gn. L24 .... 82 D3
Wellcroft Rd. L36 .... 55 F4
Wellcross Rd. WN8 .... 25 B6
Weller St. L8 .... 67 F5
Weller Way. L8 .... 68 A4
Wellesbourne Jun & Inf Sch.
L11 .... 39 F2
Wellesbourne Pl. L11 .... 40 A2
Wellesbourne Rd. L11 .... 40 A3
Wellesley Rd. Liverpool L8 ... 68 A4
Wellesley Rd. Wallasey L44 . 51 B4
Wellfield. Rainford WA11 ..... 32 A4
Wellfield. Widnes WA8 .... 73 A3
Wellfield Ave. L32 .... 29 F1
Wellfield La. L40 .... 14 C3
Wellfield Rd. L9 .... 39 A4
Wellgreen Rd. L25 .... 70 A7
Wellgreen Wlk. L25 .... 70 A7
Wellington Ave. L15 .... 68 E7
Wellington Cl.
Bebington L42 .... 79 A6
Wellington Cl.
Litherland L10 .... 28 C3
Wellington Cl.
Newton-le-W WA12 .... 46 A3
Wellington Fields. L15 .... 68 D6
Wellington Gate. L24 .... 83 E2
Wellington Gdns. WA12 .... 46 A3
Wellington Gr. L15 .... 68 F8
Wellington Rd.
Bebington L63 .... 79 A6
Wellington Rd.
Birkenhead L43 .... 66 A4
Wellington Rd. L21 .... 38 A7
Wellington Rd. Liverpool L8 67 F4
Wellington Rd. Liverpool L15 68 E7
Wellington Rd.
Wallasey L45 & L43 .... 37 A1
Wellington Sch. L63 .... 79 A6
Wellington St. Crosby L22 ... 26 D1
Wellington St. 2
Liverpool L3 .... 52 D3
Wellington St. Liverpool L19 81 C6
Wellington St.
Newton-le-W WA12 .... 46 A3
Wellington St. Southport PR8 4 A6
Wellington Terr.
Birkenhead L41 .... 66 D5
Wellington Terr.
Liverpool L8 .... 68 A5
Wellington Terr.
St Helens WA10 .... 44 A5
Wells Ave. WN5 .... 33 D6
Wells St. L15 .... 68 F8
Wellstead Cl. L15 .... 69 A8
Wellstead Rd. L15 .... 69 A8
Wellstead Wlk. L15 .... 69 A8
Welsby Cl. WA2 .... 61 F3
Welsh Rd. L66 .... 89 A1
Welshpool Cl. WA5 .... 60 D2
Welton Ave. L49 .... 64 F5
Welton Cl. L24 .... 82 D3
Welton Gn. L24 .... 82 D3
Welton Rd. L62 .... 79 E3
Welwyn Ave. PR8 .... 7 E6
Welwyn Cl. WA9 .... 57 F6
Wembley Gdns. L9 .... 38 F6
Wembley Rd. Crosby L23 ..... 26 F3
Wembley Rd. Liverpool L18 . 69 B5
Wendell St. L7 & L8 .... 68 C7
Wendover Ave. L17 .... 68 C3
Wendover Cl.
Birkenhead L43 .... 65 D4
Wendover Cl.
Haydock WA11 .... 45 D7
Wendron Rd. L11 .... 40 D5
Wenger Rd. WA8 .... 73 B5
Wenlock Dr. L26 .... 82 E7
Wenlock Rd. L4 .... 53 B7
Wenning Ave. L31 .... 20 E2
Wennington Rd.
Southport PR9 .... 4 F7
Wensley Ave. L26 .... 82 F7
Wensley Rd. Golborne WA3 . 47 E7
Wensley Rd. Liverpool L9 ..... 39 A7
Wensleydale. L9 .... 39 A7
Wensleydale Ave.
Bebington L62 .... 88 E5
Wensleydale Ave.
Rainhill L35 .... 57 D3
Wensleydale Cl. Maghull L31 20 B2
Wensleydale Cl.
Warrington WA5 .... 74 F8
Wentworth Ave. L45 .... 51 B7
Wentworth Cl.
Birkenhead L43 .... 65 D4
Wentworth Cl. Southport PR8 7 C4
Wentworth Cl. Widnes WA8 73 A5
Wentworth Dr.
Bebington L63 .... 88 C5
Wentworth Dr. Liverpool L5 . 52 F4
Wentworth Gr. L36 .... 55 B2
Wernbrook Cl. L43 .... 65 D4
Wernbrook Rd. L4 .... 53 C7
Wervin Cl. L43 .... 65 E2
Wervin Rd. Birkenhead L43 .. 65 E2
Wervin Rd. L32 .... 29 D1
Wervin Way. L32 .... 29 D1

Wescoe Cl. WN5 25 E5
Wesley Ave. Haydock WA11 45 F7
Wesley Ave. Wallasey L44 51 C5
Wesley Gr. L44 51 E3
Wesley Pl. L15 68 F8
Wesley St. Seaforth L22 37 D8
Wesley St. Southport PR8 4 B7
West Albert Rd. L17 68 B4
West Allerton Sta. L18 69 B1
West Ave. WA3 36 B1
West Bank Dock Est. WA8 84 E5
West Bank Rd. L7 53 E2
West Cl. Birkenhead L43 65 D5
West Cl. St Helens L34 57 A7
West Derby Comp Sch (Bankfield Wing). L13 53 F6
West Derby Golf Course. L14 54 E6
West Derby Rd. Liverpool L6 53 B4
West Derby Rd. Liverpool L13 & L6 53 E5
West Derby Sch. L12 54 A5
West Derby St. L7 & L3 53 A2
West Derby Village. L12 54 B7
West Dr. Birkenhead L49 65 A5
West Dr. Heswall L60 86 A7
West End Gr. WA11 45 A6
West End Rd. WA11 44 F6
West Gillibrands Ind Est. WN9 23 E8
West Gr. L60 85 F8
West Kirby Gram Sch for Girls. L47 63 A3
West Kirby Prim Sch. L47 63 A3
West Kirby Rd. L46 & L48 64 C6
West Kirby Residential Sch. L47 63 A3
West Kirby Sta. L48 63 A2
West La. L37 9 F6
West Mains. L24 83 A3
West Meade. L31 20 B2
West Mount. WN5 25 F6
West Oakhill Pk. L13 54 A2
West Orchard La. L9 39 D7
West Park Rd. WA10 43 D2
West Pk Gdns. L43 65 C8
West Quay Rd. WA2 60 F3
West Rd. Birkenhead L43 65 D5
West Rd. L9 38 F3
West Rd. Liverpool L14 54 C2
West Rd. Liverpool L24 82 D5
West Side. WA9 44 C2
West Side Ave. WA11 45 A6
West St. Prescot L34 56 C6
West St. Southport PR8 4 A7
West St. St Helens WA10 43 D1
West St. Wallasey L45 51 B5
West View. Birkenhead L41 66 F4
West View. Huyton-w-R L36 56 B2
West View. Warrington WA2 61 F1
West View Ave. L36 56 B2
West Way. L46 49 E1
West Way Sq. L46 49 E1
Westbank Ave. L45 51 C7
Westbank Rd. L42 66 C3
Westbourne Ave. Crosby L23 27 B6
Westbourne Ave. West Kirby L48 63 B2
Westbourne Gdns. PR8 3 D4
Westbourne Gr. L48 63 B2
Westbourne Rd. Birkenhead L43 66 C5
Westbourne Rd. Southport PR8 3 D4
Westbourne Rd. Wallasey L44 50 F4
Westbourne Rd. West Kirby L48 63 B2
Westbrook Ave. L34 56 B6
Westbrook Cres. WA5 60 B2
Westbrook Ctr. WA5 60 C1
Westbrook Rd. Birkenhead L46 64 C7
Westbrook Rd. Liverpool L25 70 C5
Westbrook Way. WA5 60 B1
Westbury Cl. L17 68 C1
Westbury St. L41 66 E4
Westcliffe Rd. Liverpool L12 54 A7
Westcliffe Rd. Southport PR8 3 F5
Westcombe Rd. L4 53 C7
Westcott Rd. L4 & L6 53 B6
Westcott Way. L43 65 D3
Westdale Rd. Birkenhead L42 66 E2
Westdale Rd. Liverpool L15 68 F8
Westdale View. L15 68 F8
Western Ave. Bebington L62 79 D3
Western Ave. Huyton-w-R L14 & L36 55 B3
Western Ave. Liverpool L24 82 C3
Western Dr. L19 81 A7
Westerton Rd. L12 54 E6
Westfield Ave. Ashton-in-M WN4 35 A4
Westfield Ave. Liverpool L14 54 E2
Westfield Cres. WA7 84 E1
Westfield Cty Prim Sch. WA7 84 E1
Westfield Dr. L12 40 E3
Westfield Mews. WA7 84 F1
Westfield Rd. L20 & L9 38 E6
Westfield Rd. Runcorn WA7 84 E1
Westfield Rd. Wallasey L44 51 D1
Westfield St. WA10 43 F3
Westfield Wlk. L32 29 B2
Westgate. Skelmersdale WN8 23 D8
Westgate. Widnes WA8 84 B7
Westgate Dr. WN5 25 D5
Westgate Rd. Bebington L62 79 B4
Westgate Rd. 3 Liverpool L15 69 A5
Westhaven Cres. L39 13 C1
Westhead Ave. Golborne WA3 36 E1
Westhead Ave. L32 & L33 29 F2
Westhead Cl. L32 & L33 30 A1
Westhead Wlk. L32 & L33 29 F2
Westhead Wlk. L32 & L33 30 A1
Westhouse Cl. L63 88 C5
Westlands Cl. L64 86 F1
Westleigh Pl. WA9 58 C5
Westminster Ave. L30 27 F4
Westminster Cl. L4 38 E1
Westminster Cl. Widnes WA8 84 B8
Westminster Ct. L43 65 F5
Westminster Dr. Bebington L62 88 D7
Westminster Dr. Haydock WA11 45 F7
Westminster Dr. Southport PR8 7 A4
Westminster Rd. L20 & L4 38 D1
Westminster Rd. Liverpool L4 52 E8
Westminster Rd. Wallasey L44 51 B4
Westmoreland Pl. L5 52 D5
Westmoreland Rd. Southport PR8 4 D5
Westmoreland Rd. Wallasey L45 51 C7
Westmoreland St. L3 52 C3
Westmorland Ave. Litherland L30 27 C3
Westmorland Ave. Widnes WA8 73 B1
Westmorland Rd. L36 55 E2
Weston Ct. L23 26 B3
Weston Gr. L31 28 D6
Weston Point Expressway. WA7 84 E2
Weston Rd. WA7 84 F1
Westover Cl. L31 20 C1
Westover Rd. L31 20 C1
Westvale Prim Sch. L32 29 B2
Westview Cl. L43 65 D4
Westward Ho. L48 75 D6
Westward View. L22 26 B2
Westway. Birkenhead L49 64 E4
Westway. Birkenhead L43 65 D4
Westway. Heswall L60 85 F6
Westway. Hightown L38 17 F4
Westway. Liverpool L15 69 B8
Westway. Maghull L31 20 C2
Westwick Pl. L36 55 B3
Westwood Cl. PR8 4 E3
Westwood Ct. Birkenhead L43 65 F5
Westwood Ct. Neston L64 86 E2
Westwood Gr. L44 51 A4
Westwood Rd. Birkenhead L43 65 C6
Westwood Rd. Liverpool L18 81 C8
Westwood View. L8 68 A3
Wetherby Ave. L45 50 E5
Wetherby Cl. WA12 46 C5
Wetherby Ct. L36 55 C5
Wethersfield Rd. L43 65 E4
Wetstone La. L48 63 C1
Wexford Ave. L24 83 D2
Wexford Cl. L43 65 E4
Wexford Rd. L43 65 F4
Weybourne Cl. L49 65 A7
Weyman Ave. L35 56 E3
Weymoor Cl. L63 78 F2
Weymouth Ave. WA9 44 F1
Weymouth Cl. L16 69 F8
Weymouth Rd. WA5 59 F6
Whaley La. L49 & L61 76 F6
Whalley Ave. Rainford WA11 31 F6
Whalley Ave. St Helens WA10 43 E7
Whalley Ct. L30 27 D4
Whalley Dr. Formby L37 10 A2
Whalley Dr. Ormskirk L39 21 D8
Whalley Gr. WA8 73 D3
Whalley Rd. 2 L41 & L42 66 D5
Whalley St. L8 67 F4
Whalleys Rd. WN8 16 B5
Wharf Rd. WA12 45 E2
Wharf St. L62 79 C5
Wharfdale Cl. 1 WA5 74 F7
Wharfedale Ave. L42 66 B2
Wharfedale Dr. Bebington L62 88 F5
Wharfedale Dr. Rainhill L35 57 D3
Wharfedale Rd. L45 50 F6
Wharfedale St. L19 81 E5
Wharmby Rd. WA11 45 E6
Wharncliffe Rd. L13 54 A3
Wharton Cl. L49 64 D6
Wheat Hill Rd. L27 & L36 70 E8
Wheatacre. WN8 23 E8
Wheatcroft Rd. L18 69 D2
Wheatear Cl. L27 70 E4
Wheatfield Cl. Birkenhead L46 64 F7
Wheatfield Cl. Litherland L30 28 B3
Wheatfield Rd. WA8 72 C5
Wheatfield View. L21 27 B2
Wheathill Sch. L27 70 D7
Wheathills Ind Est. L27 70 E6
Wheatland Bsns Ctr. L44 51 D2
Wheatland Cl. WA9 58 C4
Wheatland La. L44 51 D2
Wheatland Rd. L60 86 C7
Wheatlands Cl. L27 70 D7
Wheatley Ave. L20 38 E5
Wheatley Ave. Newton-le-W WA12 46 C5
Wheatsheaf Ave. WA9 58 D6
Wheatsheaf Wlk. L39 13 E5
Wheeler Dr. L31 29 B4
Whernside. WA8 72 C3
Whetstone Ct. 4 L41 66 D5
Whetstone La. L41 & L42 66 D5
Whimbrel Ave. WA12 46 C3
Whimbrel Pk. L26 70 E1
Whinbury Ct. 15 WA9 58 C4
Whinchat Ave. WA12 46 C4
Whincraig. L36 55 C7
Whinfell Rd. L12 54 C5
Whinfield Rd. L9 38 F6
Whinfield Rd. Crosby L23 27 B6
Whinhowe Rd. L11 40 B2
Whinmoor Cl. L43 65 D6
Whinmoor Rd. Liverpool L10 40 A7
Whinmoor Rd. Liverpool L12 54 C5
Whinney Gr E. L31 28 C6
Whinney Gr W. L31 28 C6
Whiston Hosp. L35 56 F4
Whiston La. L36 56 B4
Whiston Willis Prim Sch. L35 56 E3
Whitburn. WN8 15 D1
Whitburn Cl. WN4 34 D4
Whitburn Rd. L33 30 A4
Whitby Ave. Southport PR9 2 D6
Whitby Ave. Wallasey L45 50 E5
Whitby Ave.Warrington WA2 61 D2
Whitby St. L6 53 D6
Whitcroft Rd. L6 53 D3
White House Cl. WA11 45 B6
White Lodge Ave. L36 55 D3
White Lodge Cl. L62 88 D5
White Lodge Dr. WN4 35 D4
White Meadow Dr. L23 27 A6
White Moss Rd. WN8 23 C7
White Moss Rd S. WN8 23 D7
White Rock Ct. L6 53 B4
White Rock St. L6 53 B4
White St. L1 & L72 67 D8
White Thorn Assessment Sch. L10 39 F8
Whitebeam Cl. L33 29 F6
Whitebeam Dr. L12 40 D3
Whitebeam Gdns. L35 57 C6
Whitebeam Wlk. L49 64 B2
Whitechapel. L1 52 D1
Whitecroft Ave. WA3 36 E1
Whiteeside Cl. L49 65 A4
Whitefield Ave. Liverpool L4 52 E8
Whitefield Ave. Newton-le-W WA12 46 E2
Whitefield Cl. Golborne WA3 47 A8
Whitefield Cl. Hightown L38 17 F2
Whitefield Dr. L32 29 C1
Whitefield Jun Mix & Inf Sch. L6 53 A4
Whitefield La. L35 71 A6
Whitefield Rd. Liverpool L9 39 A5
Whitefield Rd. Liverpool L6 53 B5
Whitefield Rd. St Helens WA10 43 D5
Whitefield Way. 11 L6 53 A4
Whitegate Cl. L34 41 D4
Whitegates Cl. L64 87 E1
Whitegates Cres. L64 87 E1
Whitehall Cl. L4 38 E1
Whitehart Cl. L4 39 B1
Whitehaven Cl. PR8 7 B3
Whiteheath Way. L46 49 F3
Whitehedge Rd. L19 81 B7
Whitehey. WN9 23 E8
Whitehey Rd. WN8 23 E8
Whitehorn Dr. L28 55 B8
Whitehouse Ave. L37 10 A3
Whitehouse La. Formby L37 10 A3
Whitehouse La. Heswall L60 77 D1
Whitehouse Rd. L13 54 B2
Whitelands Meadow. L49 64 E5
Whiteledge Rd. WN8 24 B6
Whiteleys La. L40 14 D2
Whiterails Dr. L39 13 D6
Whiterails Mews. L39 13 D6
Whiteside Ave. WA11 44 E5
Whiteside Cl. L5 52 D5
Whiteside Rd. WA11 45 B6
Whitestock. WN8 23 E8
Whitestone Cl. L34 41 C2
Whitethorn Ave. WA5 74 F5
Whitewell Dr. L49 64 F7
Whitewood Cl. WN4 35 A6
Whitfield Ct. L42 66 D4
Whitfield Gr. WA11 45 A6
Whitfield La. L60 77 A1
Whitfield St. L42 66 D4
Whitford Rd. L42 66 D4
Whitham Ave. L23 26 F3
Whithorn St. L15 & L7 68 D8
Whitland Rd. L6 53 D3
Whitledge Gn. WN4 35 A5
Whitledge Rd. WN4 35 A5
Whitley Cres. WN1 36 B7
Whitley Dr. 1 L44 & L45 51 C5
Whitley St. L3 52 B4
Whitlow Ave. WA3 35 F1
Whitman St. L15 68 E7
Whitmoor Cl. L35 57 E1
Whitney Pl. L25 70 C2
Whitney Rd. L25 70 C2
Whitstone Cl. L25 69 E2
Whitstone Dr. WN8 24 D7
Whittaker Ave. WA2 61 D2
Whittaker Cl. L13 53 F1
Whittaker St. WA9 44 D1
Whittier St. L7 & L8 68 C7
Whittle Ave. Haydock WA11 45 A5
Whittle Ave. Warrington WA5 74 F8
Whittle Cl. L5 52 E6
Whittle Dr. L39 13 E7
Whittle Hall La. WA5 74 F6
Whittle St. Liverpool L4 & L5 52 E6
Whittle St. St Helens WA10 43 D1
Whittlewood Ct. L33 29 F4
Whitwell Cl. WA5 74 D7
Wicket Cl. L11 40 D5
Wickham Cl. L44 51 E2
Wicks Cres. L37 9 C4
Wicks Gdns. L37 9 D3
Wicks Gn. L37 9 C3
Wicks Green Cl. L37 9 C3
Wicks La. L37 9 D3
Widdale Ave. L35 57 D3
Widgeons Covert. L63 86 F5
Widmore Rd. L25 70 C4
Widnes Coll. WA8 72 E5
Widnes Rd. Warrington WA5 74 C3
Widnes Rd. Widnes WA5 & WA8 73 F2
Wiend The. Bebington L63 79 A5
Wiend The. Birkenhead L42 66 D1
Wigan Rd. Ashton-in-M WN4 35 A5
Wigan Rd. Billinge WN5 33 F7
Wigan Rd. Golborne WA3 36 B3
Wigan Rd. Ormskirk L39 & L40 14 A5
Wigan Rd. Skelmersdale WN8 23 F8
Wigan Rd. Westhead L40 14 E4
Wightman Ave. WA12 46 C5
Wightman St. L6 53 B3
Wignalls Meadow. L38 17 F3
Wigston Cl. PR8 7 B4
Wilberforce Rd. L4 39 B2
Wilbraham Pl. L5 52 D5
Wilbraham St. Liverpool L5 52 D5
Wilbraham St. St Helens WA9 58 E3
Wilbur St. WA9 58 E7
Wilburn St. L4 38 F1
Wilcock Rd. WA11 46 B8
Wilcove. WN8 15 F1
Wild Pl. L20 38 E7
Wildbrook Dr. L41 50 D1
Wildcherry Gdns. L35 57 C7
Wildcote Cl. WA8 73 C4
Wilde St. L3 52 E2
Wilfer Cl. L7 68 C8
Wilkes Ave. L46 50 B3
Wilkie St. L15 68 E7
Wilkin St. L4 52 E7
Wilkinson St. 6 L41 66 C5
Willan St. L43 66 B4
Willard Ave. WN5 25 D3
Willard St. L20 38 D6
Willaston Rd. Liverpool L4 39 B1
Willaston Rd. Raby L63 & L64 87 D4
Willaston Rd. Wallasey L46 49 D1
Willedstan Ave. L23 26 E3
William Beamont Cty High Sch. WA2 61 C1
William Brown St. L1 & L3 52 D2
William Gladstone CE Sch The. L21 38 A7
William Harvey Cl. L30 27 F3
William Henry St. L20 38 B2
William Henry St. Liverpool L3 & L6 52 E3
William Morris Ave. L20 38 E5
William Moult St. L5 52 D5
William Penn Cl. WA5 74 E5
William Rd. WA11 44 F6
William Roberts Ave. L32 29 C2
William St. Birkenhead L41 66 E6
William St. St Helens WA10 44 A4
William St. Wallasey L44 51 E2
William St. Widnes WA8 73 C1
William Wall Rd. L21 27 B2
Williams Ave. L20 38 E5
Williams Ave. Newton-le-W WA12 46 C5
Williams St. L34 56 D6
Williamson Ct. L25 70 C1
Williamson Sq. 23 L1 52 D1
Williamson St. 24 Liverpool L1 52 D1
Williamson St. St Helens WA9 44 C4
Willingdon Rd. L14 & L16 54 E1
Willington Ave. L62 88 E3
Willink Rd. WA11 44 C7
Willis Cl. L35 56 D2
Willis La. L35 56 D2
Williton Rd. L16 69 E5
Willmer Rd. Birkenhead L41 & L42 66 D5
Willmer Rd. Liverpool L4 53 B7
Willoughby Cl. WA5 60 C1
Willoughby Dr. St Helens WA10 57 B8
Willoughby Rd. Crosby L22 26 E1
Willoughby Rd. Liverpool L14 54 F2
Willoughby Rd. Wallasey L44 51 A4
Willow Ave. L32 29 C3
Willow Ave. Liverpool L36 70 E8
Willow Ave. Newton-le-W WA12 46 E4
Willow Ave. Prescot L35 56 E3
Willow Ave. Widnes WA8 73 B2
Willow Bank Est. WA12 46 F4
Willow Cl. L14 54 E2
Willow Ct. WA9 58 D4
Willow Dene. L11 40 D6
Willow Dr. WN8 15 E1
Willow Gn. Liverpool L25 69 F4
Willow Gn. Ormskirk L39 13 F5
Willow Gr. Ashton-in-M WN4 35 E5
Willow Gr. Birkenhead L46 64 D7
Willow Gr. Formby L37 9 F4
Willow Gr. Golborne WA3 36 A1
Willow Gr. Liverpool L15 69 A8
Willow Gr. Prescot L35 56 E5
Willow Gr. Southport PR9 4 E7
Willow Hey. Maghull L31 28 E7
Willow Hey. Skelmersdale WN8 15 F1
Willow House. 7 L21 38 A6
Willow House. Liverpool L11 40 D6
Willow La. L63 87 D3
Willow Lea. L43 66 A4
Willow Pk. L49 64 C4
Willow Rd. Haydock WA11 45 E7

Willow Rd. Liverpool L15 68 E8
Willow Rd. Newton-le-W WA12 46 E4
Willow Rd. St Helens WA10 43 C3
Willow Tree Ave. WA9 58 D4
Willow Tree Prim Sch. WA9 58 D4
Willow Way. Crosby L23 26 E5
Willow Way. Liverpool L11 40 D6
Willow Wlk. WN8 16 B4
Willowbank Cl. L36 55 C5
Willowbank Rd. Bebington L62 79 B6
Willowbank Rd. Birkenhead L42 66 D3
Willowbrow Rd. L63 & L64 87 D3
Willowcroft Rd. L44 51 C2
Willowdale. WA12 46 E3
Willowdale Rd. Liverpool L9 39 A4
Willowdale Rd. Liverpool L18 68 F5
Willowfield Gr. WN4 35 A2
Willowhey. PR9 1 F4
Willowmeade. L11 40 B3
Willows The. Liverpool L6 53 B5
Willows The. Southport PR8 3 F6
Willows The. 3 St Helens WA9 58 C4
Willows The. Wallasey L45 50 E7
Wills Ave. L31 20 C2
Wilmcote Gr. PR8 7 B4
Wilmere La. L35 & WA8 73 A6
Wilmot Ave. WA5 74 F6
Wilmot Dr. WA3 46 F7
Wilne Rd. 3 L45 51 A6
Wilsden Rd. WA8 72 B1
Wilsford Cl. WA3 36 B1
Wilson Ave. L44 51 E4
Wilson Cl. St Helens WA10 43 F3
Wilson Cl. Widnes WA8 73 D1
Wilson Gr. L19 81 C6
Wilson Rd. Huyton-w-R L36 56 A1
Wilson Rd. Prescot L35 56 D4
Wilson Rd. Wallasey L44 51 E4
Wilson St. 9 L8 68 A4
Wilsons La. L21 38 B8
Wilstan Ave. L63 78 D5
Wilton Gr. L13 54 A2
Wilton Grange. L47 63 A4
Wilton Rd. Birkenhead L42 67 A1
Wilton Rd. Huyton-w-R L36 55 D1
Wilton St. Ashton-in-M WN4 35 A6
Wilton St. Liverpool L3 52 E2
Wilton St. Wallasey L44 51 B4
Wiltons Dr. L34 41 D3
Wimbledon St. Liverpool L15 68 E7
Wimbledon St. Wallasey L44 & L45 51 B5
Wimborne Cl. L14 55 B6
Wimborne Pl. L14 55 B5
Wimborne Rd. L14 55 B5
Wimborne Way. L61 76 D7
Wimbourne Ave. L61 77 A5
Wimbrick Cl. L46 64 F8
Wimbrick Cres. L39 13 D3
Wimbrick Hey. L46 65 A8
Wimpole St. L7 53 B2
Winchester Ave. Ashton-in-M WN4 35 A3
Winchester Ave. Crosby L22 26 D3
Winchester Ave. Litherland L10 28 D3
Winchester Cl. Liverpool L25 82 B7
Winchester Cl. Orrell WN5 25 F7
Winchester Dr. L44 & L45 51 A5
Winchester Pl. WA8 84 C8
Winchester Rd. Garswood WA11 34 E1
Winchester Rd. Liverpool L6 53 C6
Winchester Rd. Orrell WN5 25 D2
Winchfield Rd. L15 68 F6
Windbourne Rd. L17 68 C2
Windermere Ave. St Helens WA11 44 B8
Windermere Ave. Warrington WA2 61 D3
Windermere Ave. Widnes WA8 73 B4
Windermere Cres. PR8 7 C3
Windermere Dr. L33 29 D4
Windermere Dr. Liverpool L12 40 C1
Windermere Dr. Maghull L31 20 E2
Windermere Dr. Rainford WA11 23 F2
Windermere House. L17 68 D2
Windermere Rd. Abram WN2 36 B8
Windermere Rd. Birkenhead L43 & L49 65 C5
Windermere Rd. Haydock WA11 45 B6
Windermere Rd. Hightown L38 18 A4
Windermere Rd. Orrell WN5 25 F8
Windermere St. Liverpool L5 & L6 53 B5
Windermere St. Widnes WA8 73 B4
Windermere Terr. L17 & L8 68 B5
Windfield Gn. L19 81 D3
Windfield Rd. L19 & L24 81 D4
Windgate. WN8 15 F1
Windle Ash. L31 20 C2
Windle Ave. L23 27 A3
Windle City. WA10 43 F6
Windle Ct. L64 86 E2
Windle Gr. WA10 43 C6
Windle Hall Dr. WA10 43 E7
Windle Smithers. WA10 43 C7
Windle St. WA10 43 F5
Windle Vale. WA10 43 E5
Windlebrook Cres. WA10 43 B6
Windlehurst Ave. WA10 43 E6
Windlehurst Prim Sch. WA10 43 E6
Windleshaw RC Prim Sch. WA10 43 D5
Windleshaw Rd. WA10 43 E5
Windmill Ave. Crosby L23 26 F5
Windmill Ave. Ormskirk L39 13 F5
Windmill Cl. L33 29 E5
Windmill Gdns. L43 65 C8
Windmill Hts. WN8 25 A8
Windmill La. WA5 74 E5
Windmill Rd. WN8 24 F7
Window La. L19 81 C4
Windrows. WN8 15 F1
Windsor Ave. L21 38 A8
Windsor Ave. Newton-le-W WA12 46 D2
Windsor Cl. Bebington L62 79 A7
Windsor Cl. Birkenhead L49 64 D3
Windsor Cl. Litherland L30 27 F5
Windsor Ct. 5 Liverpool L8 67 F6
Windsor Ct. Southport PR8 3 E4
Windsor Day Hospl. L8 67 F7
Windsor Dr. WA11 46 A7
Windsor Mews. L62 79 A7
Windsor Park Rd. L10 28 E3
Windsor Prim Sch. L8 67 F6
Windsor Rd. Ashton-in-M WN4 35 C1
Windsor Rd. Billinge WN5 33 F5
Windsor Rd. L20 38 E5
Windsor Rd. Crosby L23 26 D5
Windsor Rd. Formby L37 9 F1
Windsor Rd. Golborne WA3 47 C8
Windsor Rd. Huyton-w-R L36 55 B3
Windsor Rd. 5 Liverpool L9 39 A6
Windsor Rd. Liverpool L13 53 D6
Windsor Rd. Maghull L31 28 C8
Windsor Rd. Orrell WN8 25 A8
Windsor Rd. Prescot L35 56 F4
Windsor Rd. Southport PR9 4 D7
Windsor Rd. St Helens WA10 43 D4
Windsor Rd. Widnes WA8 73 A4
Windsor St. Liverpool L69 & L8 67 F6
Windsor St. Wallasey L45 37 B1
Windsor View. L8 68 B7
Windus St. WA10 43 E3
Windy Arbor Brow. L35 71 C8
Windy Arbor Cl. L35 56 D1
Windy Arbor Rd. L35 56 D1
Windy Bank. L62 79 B6
Windy Bank Ave. WA3 47 E8
Windy Harbour Rd. PR8 7 E7
Wineva Gdns. L23 26 F3
Winford St. L44 51 D3
Winfrith Cl. L63 78 F2
Winfrith Dr. L63 78 F2
Winfrith Rd. L25 & L27 70 C4
Wingate Ave. L35 & WA9 57 D6
Wingate Cl. L43 65 E4
Wingate Rd. Bebington L62 88 E5
Wingate Rd. L33 29 F3
Wingate Rd. Liverpool L17 68 E2
Wingate Towers. L36 55 D4
Wingate Wlk. L33 30 A3
Wingfield Cl. L29 27 D8
Wingrave Way. L11 & L12 40 B1
Winhill. L25 70 A4
Winifred La. L39 21 B8
Winifred Rd. L10 40 B7
Winifred St. L7 53 B1
Winkle St. 1 L8 67 F5
Winnard St. WA3 36 B2
Winnington Rd. L47 & L48 63 A4
Winsford Cl. WA11 45 F7
Winsford Dr. WA5 59 E7
Winsford Rd. L13 53 F6
Winsham Cl. L32 40 F8
Winsham Rd. L32 40 F8
Winskill Rd. L11 40 A1
Winslade Rd. L4 39 B2
Winslow St. L4 52 F8
Winsor St. L41 66 C5
Winstanley Coll. WN5 25 F3
Winstanley House. L62 79 B7
Winstanley Ind Est. WA2 61 B1
Winstanley Rd. Ashton-in-M WN2 35 F8
Winstanley Rd. Bebington L62 79 B7
Winstanley Rd. Crosby L22 26 E2
Winstanley Rd. Garswood WN5 34 A8
Winstanley Rd. Garswood WN4 &WN5 34 B6
Winstanley Rd. Orrell WN5 25 F3
Winstanley Rd. Skelmersdale WN8 23 F8
Winster Dr. L27 & L35 71 A3
Winsters The. WN8 15 F1
Winston Ave. Newton-le-W WA12 46 C3
Winston Ave. St Helens WA9 45 B2
Winston Cres. PR8 4 E2
Winston Dr. L43 65 C5
Winston Gr. L46 64 E8
Winstone Rd. L14 55 A4
Winter Gr. WA9 45 B3
Winter St. 19 L6 53 A3
Winterburn Cres. L12 54 D7
Winterburn Heights. L12 54 D7
Winterhey Ave. L44 51 B3
Winthrop Pk. L43 65 E5
Winton Cl. L45 51 A8
Winton Rd. WA3 47 E6
Winwick CE Prim Sch. WA2 61 A6
Winwick La. WA3 47 E3
Winwick Link Rd. WA12 & WA2 61 C6
Winwick Psychiatric Hospl. WA2 61 A6
Winwick Rd. Newton-le-W WA12 46 F1
Winwick Rd. Warrington WA2 61 A2
Winwick View. WA5 45 D1
Winwood Hall. L25 70 A1
Wirral Bsns Pk The. L49 64 F3
Wirral Cl. L63 78 F3
Wirral Ctry Pk. L60 86 A4
Wirral Cty Gram Sch for Boys. L63 78 F4
Wirral Cty Gram Sch for Girls. L63 78 F5
Wirral Ed Ctr. L62 88 D8
Wirral Gdns. L63 78 F3
Wirral Ladies' Golf Course The. L43 65 E5
Wirral Leisure Pk. L62 79 E3
Wirral Metropolitan Coll. L45 51 C6
Wirral Metropolitan Coll. L42 66 C3
Wirral Metropolitan Coll. L62 89 A7
Wirral Mount. Wallasey L45 50 F5
Wirral Mount. West Kirby L48 63 D3
Wirral View. L19 80 F6
Wirral Villas. L45 50 E6
Wirral Way. L43 65 C5
Witham Cl. L30 28 A4
Witham Rd. WN8 15 D1
Withburn Cl. L49 64 E5
Withen's La. L44 & L45 51 C5
Withens Rd. L31 20 D3
Withens The. L28 55 B8
Withensfield. L45 51 B6
Withert Ave. L63 78 D8
Within Way. L24 83 E1
Withington Rd. Liverpool L24 82 F3
Withington Rd. Wallasey L44 51 D3
Withins Field. L38 17 F3
Withins La. L38 19 A7
Withins Rd. WA11 45 F8
Withnell Cl. L13 54 B2
Withnell Rd. L13 54 B2
Withycombe Rd. WA5 74 E4
Witley Ave. L46 49 E1
Witley Cl. L46 49 E1
Witney Cl. L49 64 C3
Wittenham Cl. L49 64 F4
Wittering La. L60 85 D7
Witterings The. L64 86 E1
Wittom Rd. L13 53 E6
Witton Way. WA11 32 A7
Woburn Ave. WA12 46 D2
Woburn Cl. Haydock WA11 45 F7
Woburn Cl. Liverpool L13 53 F4
Woburn Dr. WA8 72 D6
Woburn Hill. L13 53 F4
Woburn Pl. L42 66 F2
Woburn Rd. Wallasey L45 51 B6
Woburn Rd. Warrington WA2 61 A4
Wokefield Way. WA10 43 C5
Wokingham Gr. L36 70 E8
Wolfe St. 1 L8 67 E5
Wolfenden Ave. L20 38 E5
Wolferton Cl. L49 65 B7
Wolfrick Dr. L63 79 B1
Wolfson Sq. WN4 34 F4
Wollaton Dr. PR8 4 F3
Wolmer St. WN4 35 A4
Wolseley Rd. WA10 43 F4
Wolsey Cl. WN4 35 A5
Wolsey St. L20 38 C1
Wolstenholme Sq. 1 L1 & L72 67 D8
Wolverton. WN8 23 F8
Wolverton St. L6 53 C5
Women's Hospl The. L7 67 F8
Wood Ave. L20 38 F5
Wood Cl. Birkenhead L41 & L72 66 D7
Wood Cl. L32 29 D2
Wood End Ct. WA8 73 D2
Wood Gn. Birkenhead L43 65 C8
Wood Gn. Prescot L34 56 C6
Wood Gr. L13 53 F2
Wood La. Birkenhead L49 64 D4
Wood La. Haskayne L37 & L39 11 D1
Wood La. Huyton-w-R L36 56 B2
Wood La. Liverpool L27 70 F4
Wood La. Neston L64 86 D2
Wood La. Prescot L34 56 C6
Wood La. Wallasey L45 50 E6
Wood Lea. L12 40 E3
Wood Rd. L26 82 F7
Wood St. Bebington L62 79 B5
Wood St. Birkenhead L41 & L72 66 E7
Wood St. L21 38 B6
Wood St. Golborne WA3 47 B8
Wood St. Hoylake L47 63 B7
Wood St. Liverpool L1 52 D1
Wood St. Liverpool L19 81 C6
Wood St. Prescot L34 56 D6
Wood St. St Helens WA9 44 C4
Wood St. Widnes WA8 73 C1
Wood View Rd. L25 69 F4
Wood's La. WN4 35 C5
Woodbank Cl. L16 69 F8
Woodbank Pk. L43 65 F4
Woodberry Cl. L43 65 D4
Woodbine St. L5 52 D7
Woodbourne Rd. L14 54 D4
Woodbridge Ave. L26 70 D2
Woodbrook Ave. L9 38 F7
Woodburn Bvd. L63 78 E8
Woodburn Dr. L60 85 F6
Woodchurch CE Prim Sch. L49 65 B2
Woodchurch Ct. L42 66 C3
Woodchurch High Sch. L49 65 C3
Woodchurch La. L42 66 C2
Woodchurch Rd. Birkenhead L43 65 D1
Woodchurch Rd. Birkenhead L41 & L42 & L43 66 C3
Woodchurch Rd. Liverpool L13 54 A4
Woodchurch Road Prim Schs. L42 66 C3
Woodclose. L66 89 A1
Woodcot La. L60 76 E1
Woodcote Bank. L63 79 A7
Woodcote Cl. WA2 61 D1
Woodcotes The. L62 88 D6
Woodcroft. WN8 23 F8
Woodcroft Dr. L60 & L61 76 F2
Woodcroft La. L63 78 E8
Woodcroft Rd. L15 68 D7
Woodcroft Way. 4 WA9 58 C4
Woodedge. WN4 35 A3
Woodend. Heswall L61 76 F5
Woodend. Prescot L35 71 E8
Woodend Ave. Crosby L23 26 E6
Woodend Ave. Liverpool L24 & L25 82 C5
Woodend Ave. Maghull L31 28 C7
Woodend Cty Prim Sch. L31 28 C7
Woodend La. L24 82 C4
Woodene Cl. 1 L32 41 A7
Woodfarm Hey. L28 55 A8
Woodfield Ave. L63 78 E8
Woodfield Cres. WN4 35 A2
Woodfield Rd. Bebington L63 79 A3
Woodfield Rd. L9 38 F5
Woodfield Rd. Heswall L61 76 E4
Woodfield Rd. Huyton-w-R L36 55 C2
Woodfield Rd. Ormskirk L39 13 D3
Woodford Ave. WA3 47 D7
Woodford Rd. Bebington L62 79 B8
Woodford Rd. Liverpool L14 54 E4
Woodford Rd. St Helens WA10 43 C6
Woodgate. L25 & L27 70 C6
Woodger St. L19 81 C5
Woodgreen Rd. L13 54 A4
Woodhall Ave. L44 51 D4
Woodhall Rd. L13 54 A3
Woodhead Rd. L62 79 C6
Woodhead St. L62 79 B7
Woodhey Ct. L63 78 F7
Woodhey Gr. L63 78 F7
Woodhey Rd. Bebington L63 78 F7
Woodhey Rd. Liverpool L19 81 A8
Woodhill. L49 65 B4
Woodhouse Cl. L4 52 E7
Woodin Rd. L42 79 A8
Woodkind Hey. L63 79 A2
Woodland Ave. Hoylake L47 48 D1
Woodland Ave. Newton-le-W WA12 46 F3
Woodland Ave. Widnes WA8 72 F1
Woodland Dr. Ashton-in-M WN4 35 B5
Woodland Dr. Birkenhead L49 65 A3
Woodland Dr.Wallasey L45 51 C7
Woodland Gr. L63 & L42 78 F8
Woodland Rd. Bebington L63 & L42 78 F8
Woodland Rd. Birkenhead L43 & L49 65 A3
Woodland Rd. L31 29 A4
Woodland Rd. Liverpool L4 53 D8
Woodland Rd. Liverpool L26 82 E7
Woodland Rd. Seaforth L21 37 F7
Woodland Rd. West Kirby L48 63 E2
Woodland View. L23 27 A7
Woodlands Cl. Formby L37 9 D2
Woodlands Cl. Ormskirk L39 14 A4
Woodlands Dr. L61 77 C4
Woodlands Ind Est. WA12 46 C6
Woodlands Pk. L12 54 A5
Woodlands Prim Sch. Birkenhead L41 66 D5
Woodlands Prim Sch. Formby L37 9 D3
Woodlands Rd. Formby L37 9 D3
Woodlands Rd. Huyton-w-R L36 55 C2
Woodlands Rd. Irby L61 76 D5
Woodlands Rd. Liverpool L17 68 E2
Woodlands Rd. St Helens WA11 44 C7
Woodlands Sq. Liverpool L27 71 A4
Woodlands The. Birkenhead L49 64 F6
Woodlands The. 1 Birkenhead L41 66 D5
Woodlands The. Prescot L34 56 F7
Woodlands The. Southport PR8 7 C5
Woodlea Cl. Bebington L62 88 D5
Woodlea Cl. Southport PR9 2 D5
Woodlee Rd. L25 70 C4
Woodleigh Cl. L31 20 B5
Woodley Fold. WA5 74 F4
Woodley Park Rd. WN8 16 B4
Woodley Rd. L31 28 D6
Woodmoss La. PR8 5 E2
Woodpecker Cl. Birkenhead L49 64 D5
Woodpecker Cl. Liverpool L12 40 F1
Woodpecker Dr. L26 70 E2
Woodrock Rd. L25 70 B1
Woodrow. WN8 23 E8
Woodruff St. L8 67 F4
Woods Cl. L39 12 A4
Woods Ct. WA12 46 A3
Woods-Lee Cotts. L62 79 D2
Woodside Ave. Ashton-in-M WN4 35 A8
Woodside Ave. Birkenhead L46 64 D7
Woodside Ave. Southport PR8 7 B3

Woodside Ave.
  St Helens WA11 .... 43 F8
Woodside Bsns Pk. L41 ..... 66 F7
Woodside Cl. Liverpool L12 . 54 B8
Woodside Cl. Orrell WN8 ..... 25 C8
Woodside Rd.
  Haydock WA11 .... 45 E7
Woodside Rd. Heswall L61 .. 76 E6
Woodside Rd.
  Warrington WA5 .... 74 F6
Woodside St. 9 L7 .... 53 B1
Woodslee Prim Sch. L62 ..... 79 D2
Woodsorrel Rd.
  Birkenhead L41 .... 65 F7
Woodsorrel Rd.
  Liverpool L15 .... 69 B7
Woodstock Ave. WA12 .... 46 D2
Woodstock Dr. PR8 .... 7 F8
Woodstock Gr. WA8 .... 72 D2
Woodstock Rd. L44 .... 51 A3
Woodstock St. L5 .... 52 D5
Woodvale Airfield. PR8 .... 7 A2
Woodvale Cl.
  Birkenhead L43 .... 65 C8
Woodvale Cl.
  Warrington WA2 .... 61 E1
Woodvale Dr. WA3 .... 36 E1
Woodvale Prim Sch. PR8 ...... 7 D3
Woodvale Rd. Liverpool L12 40 F3
Woodvale Rd. Liverpool L25 70 B2
Woodvale Rd. Southport PR8   7 E2
Woodview. L34 .... 41 D3
Woodview Ave. L44 .... 51 E2
Woodview Cres. WA8 .... 84 A8
Woodview Rd. WA8 .... 84 A8
Woodville Ave. L22 & L23 ... 26 D3
Woodville Pl. WA8 .... 72 D1
Woodville Rd. L42 & L43 ..... 66 C4
Woodville St. WA10 & WA9 . 44 B4
Woodville Terr. L6 .... 53 B3
Woodward Rd.
  Bebington L42 & L62 .... 79 A8
Woodward Rd. L33 .... 30 D4
Woodway. L49 .... 64 D4
Woodyear Rd. L62 .... 88 E7
Woolacombe Ave. WA9 ...... 58 C5
Woolacombe Rd. L16 .... 69 E6
Wooler Cl. L46 .... 64 C8
Woolfall Cl. L36 .... 55 B4
Woolfall Cres. L36 .... 55 B4
Woolfall Heath Ave. L36 ..... 55 D5
Woolfall Hts. L36 .... 55 C5
Woolfall Terr. 2 L21 .... 38 A6
Woolhope Rd. L4 .... 39 B2
Woolton Bvd. L25 .... 70 B1

Woolton Cl. WN4 .... 34 F5
Woolton Cty Jun Sch. L25 .. 70 B3
Woolton Golf Course. L25 .. 82 B8
Woolton Hill Rd. L18 & L25 . 69 F4
Woolton Little St. L7 .... 53 A1
Woolton Mount. L25 .... 70 A3
Woolton Park Cl. L25 .... 70 A3
Woolton Pk. L25 .... 70 A3
Woolton Rd.
  Liverpool L19 & L25 .... 81 E7
Woolton St. L25 .... 70 B2
Woolton Views. L25 .... 82 D8
Worcester Ave. 3
  Golborne WA3 .... 47 B8
Worcester Ave.
  Liverpool L13 .... 53 D7
Worcester Ct. L20 .... 38 B3
Worcester Dr. L13 .... 53 D7
Worcester Dr N. L13 .... 53 D7
Worcester Rd.
  Birkenhead L43 .... 65 D8
Worcester Rd. L20 .... 38 D3
Worcester Rd. L42 .... 66 F1
Wordsworth Ave.
  Birkenhead L42 .... 66 F1
Wordsworth Ave.
  Orrell WN5 .... 25 D1
Wordsworth Ave.
  Orrell WN5 .... 25 F6
Wordsworth Ave.
  St Helens WA9 .... 58 A3
Wordsworth Ave.
  Widnes WA8 .... 84 A8
Wordsworth Cl. L39 .... 13 D6
Wordsworth House. L62 ..... 79 F7
Wordsworth St. L20 .... 38 A5
Wordsworth St. Liverpool L8 68 C7
Wordsworth Way. L36 .... 55 F1
Wordsworth Wlk. L48 .... 75 B8
Worrow Cl. L11 .... 40 B3
Worrow Rd. L11 .... 40 B3
Worsley Brow. WA9 .... 58 E8
Worsley St. Golborne WA3 . 47 A8
Worsley St. St Helens WA11 44 F6
Worthing Cl. PR8 .... 3 F3
Worthing St. L22 .... 26 C2
Worthington St. L8 .... 67 D6
Wortley Rd. L10 .... 39 E7
Wotton Dr. WN4 .... 35 D4
Wray Ave. WN4 .... 58 D4
Wrayburn Cl. L7 .... 68 C8
Wrekin Cl. L25 .... 70 B1

Wrekin Dr. L10 .... 28 E2
Wren Gr. L26 .... 70 E1
Wrenbury Cl. L43 .... 65 F2
Wrenbury St. 3 L7 .... 53 C2
Wrenfield Gr. L17 .... 68 C2
Wrexham Cl. WA5 .... 60 E1
Wright St. Abram WN2 ...... 36 B7
Wright St. Ashton-in-M WN4 35 A6
Wright St. Liverpool L5 ...... 52 D5
Wright St. Southport PR9 ..... 4 C7
Wright St. Wallasey L44 ..... 51 D4
Wright's La.
  Burtonwood WA5 .... 59 F3
Wrights La. Widnes WA5 .... 73 F2
Wrights Terr. Liverpool L15 . 69 A7
Wrights Terr. Southport PR8 . 4 B3
Wrigley Rd. WA11 .... 45 E6
Wrigleys Cl. L37 .... 9 F5
Wrigleys La. L37 .... 9 F5
Wroxham Cl. L49 .... 65 A4
Wroxham Dr. L49 .... 65 A4
Wroxham Rd. WA5 .... 74 E6
Wroxham Way. L49 .... 65 A5
Wryneck Cl. WA10 .... 57 B7
Wrynose Rd. L62 .... 88 E8
Wulstan St. L4 & L5 .... 52 D7
Wycherley Rd. L42 .... 66 D3
Wycherley St. 2 L34 .... 56 D6
Wycliffe Rd. Haydock WA11 45 E7
Wycliffe Rd.
  Liverpool L4 & L6 .... 53 C7
Wycliffe St. L42 .... 66 F2
Wye Cl. L42 .... 66 F3
Wye St. L5 .... 52 F6
Wyedale Rd. WA11 .... 45 C6
Wyke Cop Rd. PR8 & PR9 ... 5 D2
Wyke La. PR8 & PR9 .... 5 D8
Wyke Rd. L35 .... 56 E5
Wyke Wood La. PR9 .... 5 F7
Wykeham St. L4 .... 52 D7
Wykeham Way. L4 .... 52 D7
Wyken Gr. WA11 .... 44 C5
Wyllin Rd. L33 .... 30 A2
Wylva Ave. L23 .... 27 A3
Wylva Rd. L4 .... 53 A7
Wyncroft Rd. WA8 .... 84 C7
Wyncroft St. L8 .... 68 A4
Wyndale Cl. L18 .... 69 B3
Wyndcote Rd. L18 .... 69 B5
Wyndham Ave. L14 .... 55 A2
Wyndham Rd. L45 .... 50 D5
Wyndham St. 3 L4 .... 38 B3
Wynne Rd. WA10 .... 43 E5
Wynnstay Ave. L31 .... 20 D3

Wynnstay St. L8 .... 68 A6
Wynstay Rd. L47 .... 63 C8
Wynwood Pk. L36 .... 55 C1
Wyre Rd. 5 L5 .... 52 F7
Wyrescourt Rd. L12 .... 54 D5
Wyresdale Ave.
  Southport PR8 .... 4 D4
Wyresdale Ave.
  St Helens WA10 .... 43 E7
Wyresdale Rd. L9 .... 39 B7
Wyrevale Gr. WN4 .... 35 C3
Wysall Cl. WA11 .... 44 D5
Wyswall Cl. L26 .... 70 E2
Wythburn Cres. WA11 ..... 44 C8
Wyvern Rd. L46 .... 64 E8

Yanwath St. L7 & L8 .... 68 B7
Yarcombe Cl. L26 .... 70 F1
Yardley Ctr. L33 .... 30 C1
Yardley Dr. L63 .... 79 A1
Yardley Rd. L33 .... 30 C1
Yarmouth Rd. WA5 .... 74 E6
Yarrow Ave. L31 .... 20 F2
Yates' Ct. L34 .... 56 D5
Yates St. L8 .... 67 E5
Yeadon. WN8 .... 16 B1
Yeadon Wlk. L24 .... 82 C3
Yellow House La. PR8 .... 4 B6
Yelverton Cl. L26 .... 70 F1
Yelverton Rd.
  Birkenhead L42 .... 66 E3
Yelverton Rd.
  Liverpool L4 & L6 .... 53 C7
Yeoman's Cotts. L47 .... 63 C6
Yew Bank Rd. L16 .... 69 D7
Yew Tree Ave.
  Newton-le-W WA12 ...... 46 A4
Yew Tree Ave.
  St Helens WA9 .... 58 C6
Yew Tree Cl. Birkenhead L49 65 A2
Yew Tree Cl.
  Liverpool L12 & L14 ...... 54 F6
Yew Tree Farm Trad Est.
  WA11 .... 46 A8
Yew Tree Gn. L31 .... 29 B4
Yew Tree La. L12 & L14 .... 54 E6
Yew Tree Rd. Bebington L63 78 E4
Yew Tree Rd. Liverpool L9 .. 39 A4
Yew Tree Rd. Liverpool L25 . 82 C8
Yew Tree Rd. Liverpool L36 . 70 E8
Yew Tree Rd. Ormskirk L39 . 13 E7
Yew Tree Rd. Wallasey L46 . 49 F1
Yew Way. L46 .... 49 F1
Yewdale. WN8 .... 16 A1
Yewdale Ave. WA11 .... 33 B1

Yewdale Pk. L43 .... 66 B4
Yewdale Rd.
  Ashton-in-M WN4 .... 35 A7
Yewdale Rd. Liverpool L9 .. 39 B4
Yewtree La. L48 .... 63 B2
Yewtree Rd. L18 .... 69 D3
York Ave. Crosby L23 ...... 26 D4
York Ave.
  Liverpool L15 & L17 .... 68 D6
York Ave. Southport PR8 .... 4 A5
York Ave. Wallasey L44 .... 51 D3
York Ave. Warrington WA5 . 74 E7
York Ave. West Kirby L48 .. 75 B8
York Cl. Formby L37 .... 9 F6
York Cl. Litherland L30 ..... 27 F5
York Cl. St Helens WA10 ... 43 F4
York Cotts. L25 .... 70 B4
York Gdns. PR8 .... 4 A5
York Rd. Ashton-in-M WN4 . 35 B3
York Rd. Crosby L23 .... 26 E4
York Rd. Formby L37 .... 10 A3
York Rd. Huyton-w-R L36 .. 56 A3
York Rd. Maghull L31 ...... 28 D7
York Rd. Southport PR8 ..... 3 F4
York Rd. Wallasey L44 ..... 51 D3
York Rd. Widnes WA8 ...... 84 C8
York Rd. S. WN4 .... 35 C2
York St. Bebington L62 .... 79 D5
York St. L9 .... 38 F3
York St. Golborne WA3 ..... 36 A1
York St. Liverpool L1 & L72 . 67 D8
York St. Liverpool L19 ..... 81 C4
York St. Seaforth L22 ...... 37 D8
York Terr. Liverpool L5 .... 52 E6
York Terr. Southport PR9 .... 4 C8
York Villas. 8 L5 .... 52 F7
York Way. Huyton-w-R L36 . 56 B3
York Way. Liverpool L19 ... 81 D3
Yorkaster Rd. L18 .... 69 C1
Youatt Ave. L35 .... 56 E4
Youens Way. L14 .... 54 E4
Yvonne Cl. WN4 .... 35 D5

Zander Gr. L12 .... 40 F3
Zetland Rd. Birkenhead L41 . 66 D5
Zetland Rd. 5 Liverpool L18 68 F5
Zetland Rd. Wallasey L45 ... 50 F7
Zetland St. PR9 .... 4 D7
Zig Zag Rd. Liverpool L12 .. 54 D5
Zig Zag Rd. Wallasey L45 .. 51 B6

Ordnance Survey

STREET ATLASES

**The Ordnance Survey Street Atlases provide unique
and definitive mapping of entire counties**

Street Atlases available

- Berkshire
- Bristol and Avon
- Buckinghamshire
- Cardiff, Swansea and Glamorgan
- Cheshire
- Derbyshire
- Durham
- Edinburgh

- East Essex
- West Essex
- Glasgow
- Greater Manchester
- North Hampshire
- South Hampshire
- Hertfordshire
- East Kent
- West Kent
- Lancashire

- Merseyside
- Nottinghamshire
- Oxfordshire
- Staffordshire
- Surrey
- East Sussex
- West Sussex
- Tyne and Wear
- Warwickshire
- South Yorkshire
- West Yorkshire

The Street Atlases are revised and updated on a regular basis and new titles are added to the series. Each title is available in three formats and as from 1996 the atlases are being produced in colour. All the atlases contain Ordnance Survey mapping.

The series is available from all good bookshops or by mail order direct from the publisher. However, the order form on the following pages may not reflect the complete range of titles available so it is advisable to check by telephone before placing your order.

Payment can be made in the following ways:

By phone *Phone your order through on our special Credit Card Hotline on 01733 371999 (Fax: 01733 370585). Speak to our customer service team during office hours (9am to 5pm) or leave a message on the answering machine, quoting your full credit card number plus expiry date and your full name and address.*

By post *Simply fill out the order form (you may photocopy it) and send it to: Reed Books Direct, 43 Stapledon Road, Orton Southgate, Peterborough PE2 6TD.*

STREET ATLASES ORDER FORM

NEW COLOUR EDITIONS

	HARDBACK	SPIRAL	POCKET	£ Total
	Quantity @ £10.99 each	Quantity @ £8.99 each	Quantity @ £4.99 each	
BERKSHIRE	☐ 0 540 06170 0	☐ 0 540 06172 7	☐ 0 540 06173 5	➤
	Quantity @ £10.99 each	Quantity @ £8.99 each	Quantity @ £3.99 each	£ Total
MERSEYSIDE	☐ 0 540 06480 7	☐ 0 540 06481 5	☐ 0 540 06482 3	➤
	Quantity @ £12.99 each	Quantity @ £8.99 each	Quantity @ £4.99 each	£ Total
SURREY	☐ 0 540 06435 1	☐ 0 540 06436 X	☐ 0 540 06438 6	➤
	Quantity @ £12.99 each	Quantity @ £9.99 each	Quantity @ £4.99 each	£ Total
DURHAM	☐ 0 540 06365 7	☐ 0 540 06366 5	☐ 0 540 06367 3	➤
GREATER MANCHESTER	☐ 0 540 06485 8	☐ 0 540 06486 6	☐ 0 540 06487 4	➤
HERTFORDSHIRE	☐ 0 540 06174 3	☐ 0 540 06175 1	☐ 0 540 06176 X	➤
TYNE AND WEAR	☐ 0 540 06370 3	☐ 0 540 06371 1	☐ 0 540 06372 X	➤
SOUTH YORKSHIRE	☐ 0 540 06330 4	☐ 0 540 06331 2	☐ 0 540 06332 0	➤
WEST YORKSHIRE	☐ 0 540 06329 0	☐ 0 540 06327 4	☐ 0 540 06328 2	➤
	Quantity @ £14.99 each	Quantity @ £9.99 each	Quantity @ £4.99 each	£ Total
LANCASHIRE	☐ 0 540 06440 8	☐ 0 540 06441 6	☐ 0 540 06443 2	➤

BLACK AND WHITE EDITIONS

	HARDBACK	SOFTBACK	POCKET	£ Total
	Quantity @ £12.99 each	Quantity @ £9.99 each	Quantity @ £4.99 each	
BRISTOL AND AVON	☐ 0 540 06140 9	☐ 0 540 06141 7	☐ 0 540 06142 5	➤
CARDIFF	☐ 0 540 06186 7	☐ 0 540 06187 5	☐ 0 540 06207 3	➤
CHESHIRE	☐ 0 540 06143 3	☐ 0 540 06144 1	☐ 0 540 06145 X	➤
DERBYSHIRE	☐ 0 540 06137 9	☐ 0 540 06138 7	☐ 0 540 06139 5	➤
EDINBURGH	☐ 0 540 06180 8	☐ 0 540 06181 6	☐ 0 540 06182 4	➤
GLASGOW	☐ 0 540 06183 2	☐ 0 540 06184 0	☐ 0 540 06185 9	➤
STAFFORDSHIRE	☐ 0 540 06134 4	☐ 0 540 06135 2	☐ 0 540 06136 0	➤

See more titles overleaf

Ordnance Survey **STREET ATLASES ORDER FORM**

BLACK AND WHITE EDITIONS

	HARDBACK Quantity @ £12.99 each	SOFTBACK Quantity @ £8.99 each	POCKET Quantity @ £4.99 each	£ Total
EAST ESSEX	0 540 05848 3	0 540 05866 1	0 540 05850 5	➤
WEST ESSEX	0 540 05849 1	0 540 05867 X	0 540 05851 3	➤
NORTH HAMPSHIRE	0 540 05852 1	0 540 05853 X	0 540 05854 8	➤
SOUTH HAMPSHIRE	0 540 05855 6	0 540 05856 4	0 540 05857 2	➤
EAST KENT	0 540 06026 7	0 540 06027 5	0 540 06028 3	➤
NOTTINGHAMSHIRE	0 540 05858 0	0 540 05859 9	0 540 05860 2	➤
OXFORDSHIRE	0 540 05986 2	0 540 05987 0	0 540 05988 9	➤
EAST SUSSEX	0 540 05875 0	0 540 05874 2	0 540 05873 4	➤
	Quantity @ £12.99 each	Quantity @ £9.99 each	Quantity @ £4.99 each	£ Total
BUCKINGHAMSHIRE	0 540 05989 7	0 540 05990 0	0 540 05991 9	➤
WEST KENT	0 540 06029 1	0 540 06031 3	0 540 06030 5	➤
WEST SUSSEX	0 540 05876 9	0 540 05877 7	0 540 05878 5	➤

BLACK AND WHITE EDITIONS

	HARDBACK Quantity @ £10.99 each	SOFTBACK Quantity @ £8.99 each	POCKET Quantity @ £4.99 each	£ Total
WARWICKSHIRE	0 540 05642 1	—	—	➤

Name...

Address...

....

....Postcode

◆ Free postage and packing

◆ All available titles will normally be dispatched within 5 working days of receipt of order but please allow up to 28 days for delivery

☐ Please tick this box if you do not wish your name to be used by other carefully selected organisations that may wish to send you information about other products and services

Registered Office: Michelin House, 81 Fulham Road, London SW3 6RB.
Registered in England number: 1974080

I enclose a cheque / postal order, for a **total** of [ ]
made payable to *Reed Book Services*, or please debit my

☐ Access ☐ American Express ☐ Visa

account by [ ]

Account no ☐☐☐☐ ☐☐☐☐ ☐☐☐☐ ☐☐☐☐
Expiry date ☐☐ ☐☐

Signature..

Post to:
Reed Books Direct, 43 Stapledon Road, Orton Southgate, Peterborough PE2 6TD